Learning Biblical Hebrew Interactively

*To Lorie,
for your ceaseless encouragement
and tireless support*

Learning Biblical Hebrew Interactively

Volume 1
Units 0-6

Student Edition, Revised

Paul Overland

SHEFFIELD PHOENIX PRESS
2016

Copyright © 2016 Sheffield Phoenix Press

Published by Sheffield Phoenix Press
Department of Biblical Studies, University of Sheffield
45 Victoria Street, Sheffield S3 7QB

www.sheffieldphoenix.com

All rights reserved.
No part of this publication may be reproduced or transmitted in any form or by any means, electronic or mechanical, including photocopying, recording or any information storage or retrieval system, without the publisher's permission in writing.

A CIP catalogue record for this book
is available from the British Library

Typeset by Paul Overland
Printed by Lightning Source

ISBN 978-1-910928-12-7 (hbk)
ISBN 978-1-910928-13-4 (pbk)

Table of Contents

Volume I

Preliminary Materials

Preface to revised edition xii	Illustrations xxi
To the instructor xiii	Acknowledgments xxii
To the student xviii	Abbreviations and symbols xxiii
Cultural references xx	

Unit 0 — א...ב... *Learning the alphabet* 1
consonants, vowels, and syllables

0.1 א to ד, vowels, syllables (pt. 1) 2	0.5 שׁ to ת, vowels, syllables (pt. 5) 54
0.2 ה to י, vowels, syllables (pt. 2) 21	**You can read the Bible** 64
0.3 כ to ס, vowels, syllables (pt. 3) 28	**How to write Hebrew letters** 65
0.4 ע to ר, vowels, syllables (pt. 4) 37	**Practice writing sheet** 70

Unit 1 — הֲשָׁלוֹם לָךְ? *Getting acquainted* 71
verbless questions, predicative participles

1.1 Greetings and introductions 72	1.3 Searching for something 94
(*verbless questions,* יֵשׁ *and* אֵין)	(*predicative participles*)
1.1 David Story 76	1.3 Jonah Episode 95
1.2 Saying goodbye 91	**You can read the Bible** 101
(*a wish [sample jussive]*)	

| UNIT 2 | מַה־בַּכְּלִי הַגָּדוֹל?
Describing what you see
nouns, adjectives, prepositions, and the inquiry, "מִזֶּה?" | ....105 |

2.1	Specifying a particular object .... 106 (*definite article, construct chains [sing.]*) 2.1 Jonah Episode 107		2.3	Jonah Episode 129
2.2	Responding to a greeting .... 122 (*verbless sentences*) 2.2 Jonah Episode 122		2.4	Explaining where to find something .... 147 (*prepositional phrases, relative pronoun אֲשֶׁר*) 2.4 Jonah Episode 149
2.3	Describing a person or object .... 126 (*adjectives*)		2.5	Sending someone on a trip .... 160 (*prepositional phrases, cont.*)
			You can read the Bible 167

| UNIT 3 | מָה־אַתָּה עֹשֶׂה?
Talking about the here-and-now
pronouns, participles, and infinitives | ....173 |

3.1	Designating an object and who owns it .... 174 (*independent and demonstrative pronouns, comparative, infinitives construct*) 3.1 Jonah Episode 177		3.3	Describing what people are doing...... 216 (*participles and pronouns, cont., construct chains [pl]*) 3.3 Jonah Episode 218
3.2	Discussing job descriptions................ 197 (*participles and pronouns, cont.*) 3.2 Jonah Episode 200		3.4	Designating a recipient .... 231 (*pronouns [cont.], prepositions and nouns with suffixes*)
			You can read the Bible 241

| CONTENTS | בַּסֵּפֶר הַזֶּה... | vii |

UNIT 4

מַה־יַּעֲשׂוּ מָחָר?
Talking about what they will do tomorrow
יִקְטֹל conjugation (part 1) 251

- **4.1** Describing what a group (men or men and women) is about to do 253
  (*qal* בִּנְיָן, יִקְטֹל 3mpl)
  4.1 Jonah Episode 254

- **4.2** Describing what an object is for 267
  (*purpose statements, inf. construct*)
  4.2 Jonah Episode 268

- **4.3** Describing what a man will do 278
  (יִקְטֹל 3ms)

- 4.3 Jonah Episode 280

- **4.4** Describing what a group of women will do 289
  (יִקְטֹל 3fpl)
  4.4 Jonah Episode 290

- **4.5** Describing what a woman will do 301
  (יִקְטֹל 3fs)
  4.5 Jonah Episode 301

- **You can read the Bible** 307

UNIT 5

מַה־תַּעֲשֶׂה בָּרִאשֹׁנָה?
Talking about what you will do first
יִקְטֹל conjugation (part 2), ordinal numbers 313

- **5.1** Describing what your group is about to do 315
  (*qal* בִּנְיָן, יִקְטֹל 1cpl, 2 mpl / fpl)
  5.1 Jonah Episode 317

- **5.2** Describing what you yourself are about to do 332
  (יִקְטֹל 1cs)
  5.2 Jonah Episode 333

- **5.3** Discussing plans with a friend 340
  (יִקְטֹל 2ms / fs)
  5.3 Jonah Episode 341

- **5.4** Nuancing messages with ability, possibility, or obligation 352
  (*modal* יִקְטֹל *meanings, geminate and stative* יִקְטֹל)

- **You can read the Bible** 365

| UNIT 6 | מָה עָשִׂיתָ אֶתְמוֹל:
Sharing memories of yesterday
קָטַל *conjugation* | ....371 |ವ

6.1 Explaining what you did, in contrast to what a friend did .... 373 (*qal* בִּנְיָן, קָטַל 1cs *and* 3ms, ‑ה locative)

6.1 Jonah Episode 375

6.2 Describing what was done by a woman, or by a group of people .... 393 (קָטַל 3fs *and* 3cpl)

6.2 Jonah Episode 395

6.3 Getting clarification from a friend concerning what he or she has been doing .... 405 (קָטַל 2ms *and* 2mpl)

6.3 Jonah Episode 406

6.4 Interviewing a group to learn what they have been involved in, and why .... 420 (יִקְטֹל 1cpl *and* 2fpl)

6.4 Jonah Episode 421

6.5 Adding story layers in reporting, and sapiential expressions .... 432 (קָטַל *meanings such as gnomic present, future, irreal usages; also geminate and stative* קָטֵל)

You can read the Bible 437

VOLUME I REFERENCE MATERIALS 447

Appendix for units 0–6 449
Pronominal (object) suffixes 481
Verbs (Qal בִּנְיָן) 501

Glossaries 517
Maps 563

VOLUME II

PRELIMINARY MATERIALS

| To the instructor .... xii | To the student .... xii |

UNIT 7 — הֲיָדַעְתָּ אֵת אֲשֶׁר־נַעֲשָׂה לָאָרוֹן: Telling a story
vav-conversive and nifal בִּנְיָן 1

- 7.1 Telling a simple story 2
  (*vav-conversive* וַיִּקְטֹל *[pt. 1]*, explanatory asides, pluperfect with קָטַל)
  7.1 Jonah Episode 5
- 7.2 Telling an intermediate story 21
  (*vav-conversive* וַיִּקְטֹל *[pt. 2]*, fronting an element)
- 7.3 Telling a more complex story 29
  (*nifal* בִּנְיָן *[pt. 1]*, vav-conversive וְקָטַל as apodosis)
- 7.3 Jonah Episode 31
- 7.4 Reporting multiple related events 58
  (*nifal* בִּנְיָן *[pt. 2]*, additional uses of וְקָטַל, oaths)
  7.4 Jonah Episode 60
- 7.5 Ranking objects in order of appearance 86
  (*ordinal numbers*)
  7.5 Jonah Episode 87
- **You can read the Bible** 98

UNIT 8 — הֲלוֹא תַגִּיד לִי אֶת־הַדָּבָר: Exchanging diplomatic messages
בִּנְיָן *hifil* 113

- 8.1 Introducing yourself and conveying a formal message 114
  (*hifil* בִּנְיָן: קָטַל *conjugation*)
  8.1 Jonah Episode 119
- 8.2 Developing a strategy for disaster-recovery 143
  (*hifil* בִּנְיָן: יִקְטֹל *conjugation*, יִקְטֹל with object suffixes)
  8.2 Jonah Episode 145
- **You can read the Bible** 160

| UNIT 9 | זֹאת עֲשׂוּ: **Issuing requests and commands** *command forms* | ....169 |

9.1	Issuing directives to an assistant........ 170 *(qal imperatives [ms, fs])*
	9.1 Jonah Episode..................... 171
9.2	Issuing directives to a group of people (men or mixed) .... 181 *(qal, nifal, and hifil imperatives [ms, mpl])*
	9.2 Jonah Episode..................... 182
9.3	Issuing directives to a group of women .... 189 *(qal, nifal, and hifil imperatives [fpl])*
	Jonah Episode............................. 190
9.4	Expressing a hope for an absent person, and calling a group to action................................... 196 *(jussive, cohortative)*
	9.4 Jonah Episode..................... 197
9.5	Instructing someone to refrain from an activity................................... 212 *(prohibitions with לֹא and אַל)*
	9.5 Jonah Episode..................... 213

You can read the Bible 220

| UNIT 10 | בַּמָּה אֲשַׁלֶּם לָךְ: **Conveying an apology** *piel בִּנְיָן and poetry* | ....229 |

10.1	Expressing an apology, and experimenting with poetry .... 230 *(piel בִּנְיָן: קָטַל conjugation, parallelism and chiasm)*
	10.1 Jonah Episode..................... 232
10.2	Using sophisticated poetic devices in a reconciliation statement .... 254 *(piel בִּנְיָן: יִקְטֹל conjugation and participles, palistrophe)*
	10.2 Jonah Episode..................... 256
10.3	Influencing behavior by appealing to character traits............................. 284 *(piel בִּנְיָן: infinitives and command forms, alphabetic acrostics)*
	10.3 Jonah Episode..................... 285

You can read the Bible 295

UNIT 11

בַּסֵּפֶר הַזֶּה...

לָמָּה לֹא שָׁלְחוּ אֶת־הָעָם: Describing what has happened to someone else 303

pual, hofal, and hitpael בִּנְיָנִים*, and true qal passive*

11.1 Reporting a calamity and its probable cause 304
(*pual* בִּנְיָן*, qal passive participles, true qal passive forms*)

11.1 Jonah Episode 306

11.2 Describing the effect of someone else's action, conveying respect 323
(*hofal* בִּנְיָן*, also* הִשְׁתַּחֲוָה)

11.2 Jonah Episode 324

11.3 Designing a vacation 339
(*hitpael* בִּנְיָן*, reflexive expressions*)

11.3 Jonah Episode 340

You can read the Bible 367

VOLUME II REFERENCE MATERIALS 375

Appendix for units 7–11 377
Syntax summary 395
Masoretic accents 410
Indices 417
Resources 433

Pronominal (object) suffixes 437
Verbs 457
Glossaries 507
Maps 553

Preface to Revised Edition

With heartfelt thanks to the following colleagues for their corrections and suggestions, it is a privilege to offer this revised edition: Steve Cook, Paul Ferris, Benjamin Noonan, Jennifer Noonan, and Bob Stallman. Many of these have created and contributed new teacher resources as well. These are freely available to instructors using the textbook (contact the author at poverlan@ashland.edu, or through www.LearningBiblicalHebrewInteractively.com).

It remains a distinct honor to work with David Clines, Ailsa Parkin, and the team at Sheffield Phoenix Press. Without their vision for this resource, combined with efficient assistance in its publication, it would not have been possible to offer it for use by instructors and learners of Biblical Hebrew.

Paul Overland
975 Thomas Drive
Ashland, Ohio 44805, USA
poverlan@ashland.edu
www.LearningBiblicalHebrewInteractively.com

To the instructor

A growing number of Biblical Hebrew professionals are requesting resources to help them take advantage of **Second Language Acquisition (SLA)** benefits for their own classrooms.[*] Since both teachers and students of Classical Greek and Latin are benefitting from SLA methods, should not Hebrew courses enjoy these advantages, as well? *Learning Biblical Hebrew Interactively* responds to this request, providing an SLA-oriented introductory textbook for Biblical Hebrew.

To enable a classically trained Hebrew instructor to employ SLA techniques, the Instructor Edition offers pedagogy tips at the outset of each lesson (see sample, next page). The Student Edition synchronizes with the Instructor Edition in layout and pagination, only without instructor notes.

A "both-and" Second Language Acquisition Biblical Hebrew textbook

Both **traditional elements** and the **new SLA pedagogy** combine in this textbook. Old and new are seamlessly combined in what is known as a "functional syllabus"—a curriculum that orients grammar presentation so that it empowers the learner to read, hear, and express meaningful communication.[1]

Traditional elements retained	New components integrated for **Second Language Acquisition**
♦ **Vocabulary** (over 500 words, primarily high-frequency) ♦ **Grammar and syntax** (cf. Grammatical index and Syntax summary) ♦ **Paradigms** ♦ **Bible readings** (more than 225 excerpted readings and two extended readings) ♦ Introduction to **poetry** ♦ Introduction to **Masoretic cantillation**	♦ Comprehensible[2] and meaningful[3] L2 **input** ♦ Meaningful L2 **output activities**[4] (in which students maintain control over the communication they produce) ♦ **Multi-experiential** L2 input (also output), including aural,[5] kinesthetic, and visual (over 230 illustrations and photos)[6] ♦ Connections to the L2 **cultural context** (more than 40 concise articles)[7] ♦ Narrative context for grammar and vocabulary through a **comprehensive serialized story**[8] ♦ **Immersion opportunities** through L2 class-navigation expressions[9]

Why concern ourselves with Second Language Acquisition?

According to a study reported in *When Dead Tongues Speak: Teaching Beginning Greek and Latin*, 90% of post-secondary students enrolled in a classical language course will **learn more effectively** in an SLA format.[10] This is due, in part, to the following:

♦ An SLA approach accesses **multiple learning styles**.

---

[*] Professor Frederick Greenspahn, past president of National Association of Professors of Hebrew, called for such a textbook in his *SBL Forum* essay, "Why Hebrew textbooks are different from those for other languages" (*SBL Forum*, July 2005, n.p., cited 15 November 2010, online: http://sbl-site.org/Article.aspx?ArticleID=420). He concluded: "Learning how to teach languages from those who have devoted their professional lives to that project can only increase our success at bringing students closer to the text that is the center of our concern."

- An SLA approach **lowers the affective filter**, leading to greater receptivity for learning.[11]
- An SLA approach expands **automaticity**.[12]
- An SLA approach expands **reading fluency** in target language (L2).[13]
- An SLA approach leads to increased **higher-level processing** of the L2 text.[14]

"Can I effectively teach this course without prior training in SLA?" and other important questions.

*Can I effectively teach this course, even though **I have not been trained in SLA**?* Yes, you can. These materials were specifically designed for and field-tested by instructors who had no training in SLA pedagogy. The **Instructor Edition** displays concise **pedagogy tips** at the start of every segment, both to specify the focal grammatical structure and to provide suggestions for conducting this part of the class session, as seen in the example from Unit 2, Module 1, Segment 1.

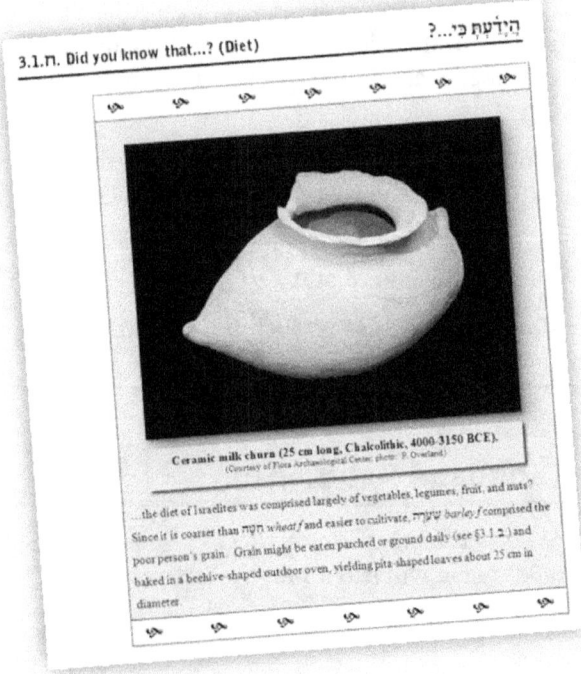

*How can I introduce elements of **culture**?* Teaching culture can be as simple as assigning students to read segments bearing the heading "Did you know…?" If you wish, you may expand an element of culture with readings from a resource such as King and Stager's *Life in Biblical Israel*.[15]

*Will I be able to teach this course, even if **I do not speak Biblical Hebrew** (or Modern Hebrew) conversationally?* Yes. This material was intentionally field-tested by instructors **without BH or MH conversational ability**. The expressions you will need are fully scripted in this textbook.

*Can I lead this course with minimal **lesson preparation**?* Again, the answer is "yes." Each segment is ready-to-use, whether it presents a grammar lesson or an SLA activity. Simply pre-read the lesson as you would for any course.

*Is this curriculum suitable for an L1 environment **other than English**?* Yes. The first six units have been translated and field-tested in a Portuguese L1 classroom (São Leopoldo, Brazil). Since SLA pedagogy employs less of L1 than traditional language instruction (English or otherwise), the benefits of SLA pedagogy accrue more easily to learners from any L1, not only English L1. In addition, the specific *LBHI* materials by design have sought to remain as western-culture-neutral as possible.

*Can this curriculum be adapted for **independent study**?* While intended for group learning and conversation, this textbook would be sufficient for independent students—especially if they take advantage of the segment-by-segment instructional videos. In addition, they should secure the help of a skilled tutor who will be able to review homework.

Integrated multimedia resources

The following integrated multimedia resources are freely available to help you teach this course (visit www.LearningBiblicalHebrewInteractively.com).

- A full complement of **instructional videos**. Oriented for students, you may use them to conduct your course as a "flipped classroom." Or you may assign them for selective viewing, such as when a student misses a live lecture or would benefit from additional reinforcement (see website).

- **PowerPoint presentations** (with audio) for each Jonah Episode. For use in-class, out-of-class, or both (see sample on left, available from website).

- **MP3 vocabulary files**. If they wish, students can review vocabulary on their mobile devices (audio, see website).

- Communicatively-styled **assessments**. Another tool to let you concentrate on teaching, rather than course-development (contact author).

- The website also enables instructors to **develop and exchange** new activities and visual aids developed when teaching with this textbook.

Origins in the "Cohelet Project"

Learning Biblical Hebrew Interactively began to take shape under the direction of SLA consultant, Dr. Diana Pulido, and Language Learning Technology consultant, Dr. Jörg Waltje, during the <u>Co</u>mmunicative <u>He</u>brew <u>L</u>earning and <u>T</u>eaching Project ("Cohelet Project"). This undertaking was made possible through generous funding from the Wabash Center for Teaching and Learning in Religion and Theology.

The first six units were written and field-tested over a three-year period during the course of the Cohelet Project. For more information concerning the Cohelet Project, please refer to "Can Communicative Principles Enhance Classical Language Acquisition?"[16] or visit https://sites.google.com/a/ashland.edu/cohelet/home.

---

[1] Concerning the importance of a **functional syllabus**, Elizabeth Tarone and George Yule observe: "In recent years, there has been a major shift in perspective within the language teaching profession concerning the nature of what is to be taught. In relatively simple terms, there has been a change of emphasis from presenting the language as a set of *forms* (grammatical, phonological, lexical) that have to be learned and practiced, to presenting language as a *functional system* that is used to fulfill a range of communicative purposes" (*Focus on the Language Learner: Approaches to Identifying and Meeting the Needs of Second Language Learners* [Oxford: Oxford University Press, 1989], 17). While grammatical competence (a primary aim of the Grammar-Translation Method) remains integral to communicative competence, current language pedagogy is not content to leave learners at this level.

[2] L2 messages expressed at a level that the learner can understand comprise **comprehensible input** (Stephen D. Krashen, *The Input Hypothesis: Issues and Implications* [New York: Longman, 1985], 2).

³ Concerning **meaningful input**, Krashen (1985) observes: "The goal is to focus the student entirely on the message; this requires the use of topics and activities in which real, not just realistic, communication takes place" (56). Elsewhere he writes, "[t]he best input is so interesting and relevant that the acquirer may even 'forget' that the message is encoded in a foreign language" (S. Krashen, *Principles and Practice in Second Language Acquisition* [New York: Pergamon, 1982], 66).

In contrast, sentences that are grammatically accurate but which lack connection to the learner's world do not qualify as meaningful. These are known as "display sentences." Sandra Savignon goes so far as to observe that "[t]he importance of meaningful language use at all stages in the acquisition of communicative skills has come to be recognized by language teachers around the world" (*Communicative Competence: Theory and Classroom Practice* [New York: McGraw-Hill, 1997], xi).

⁴ To qualify as **meaningful output**, the learner must have control over whatever response is evoked and may provide new information during the exchange (James F. Lee and Bill VanPatten, *Making Communicative Language Teaching Happen* [2d ed.; Boston: McGraw-Hill, 2003], 54 and 121). As Krashen comments, "[o]utput aids learning because it provides a domain for error correction" (Krashen [1982], 61). Swain goes so far as to state that "[c]omprehensible output…is a necessary mechanism of acquisition" (Merrill Swain, "Communicative competence: Some roles of comprehensible input and comprehensible output in its development," in *Input in Second Language Acquisition* [ed. Susan Gass and Carolyn Madden: Rowely, Mass.: Newbury House, 1985], 252).

⁵ Regarding **aural input**, see Lee and VanPatten, "Listening Comprehension," in *Making Communicative Language Teaching Happen*, 195–216. Paul Sulzberger observes: "Our ability to learn new words is directly related to how often we have been exposed to the particular combinations of the sounds that make up the words. Neural tissue required to learn and understand a new language will develop automatically from simple exposure to the language" ("Exposure to Sound Patterns Aids Language Learning," *Language Educator* [April 2009]: 9). Regarding the vital contribution of **aural output** skills (silently generating the sound of what we are reading) for the development of skilled readers, see Michael Pressley, *Reading Instruction that Really Works* (3d ed.; New York: Guilford Press, 2006), 51.

⁶ I.S. Paul Nation observes that learning an L2 word is enhanced when accompanied by a picture (**visual input**), since the picture leads to "mental elaboration that deepens or enriches the level of processing" of the target lexeme (*Learning Vocabulary in Another Language* [Cambridge: Cambridge University Press, 2001], 69). The more than 230 illustrations and photos integrated in this textbook, together with frequent suggestions for visual aids, help visual learners acquire the meaning of L2 words with reduced recourse to an L1 equivalent (known as "binding"). In addition, several of the output activities involve object manipulation, facilitating kinesthetic learning.

⁷ Regarding the place of **culture** in language learning, classicist John Gruber-Miller cautions, "Without a coherent and consistent cultural context, students of the ancient world cannot succeed in the task of reading, understanding, and interpreting Greek and Latin texts" (*When Dead Tongues Speak* [ed. John Gruber-Miller; Oxford: Oxford University Press, 2006], 14). See American Classical League, *Standards for Classical Language Learning* (Oxford, Ohio: American Classical League, Miami University, 1997; cited 8 April 2014). Online: http://www.aclclassics.org/uploads/assets/files/Standards_Classical_Learning.pdf. *Life in Biblical Israel* by Philip J. King and Lawrence E. Stager may be the finest resource currently available for cultural information (Louisville: Westminster John Knox, 2001). This volume has been beautifully produced, and would serve as an excellent companion volume for this course, while Ephraim Stern's *Archaeology of the Land of the Bible* (vol. 2, *The Assyrian, Babylonian, and Persian Periods*) can supply additional information for particular artifacts or excavation sites (series ed. David Noel Freedman; New Haven: Yale University Press, 2001).

⁸ Regarding **serialized story**, see Bonnie Adair-Hauk, Richard Donato, and Philomena Cuomo-Johansen, "Using a story-based approach to teach grammar," *Teacher's Handbook: Contextualized Language Instruction* (ed. J. L. Shrum and E. W. Glisan; Boston: Thomson Higher Education, 2005), 198–213.

⁹ The advantages of an **immersion environment** for language acquisition are axiomatic. This textbook supplies both instructor and student with several strategic and frequently recurring class navigation expressions (e.g., "I wish to ask a question," "Please repeat," and "I don't understand")—termed by Krashen, "tools for conversational management" (Krashen [1982], 139). In this way, class participants are able to take significant steps toward an immersion environment. Participants may add to these expressions as the course progresses.

[10] A. Deagon, "Cognitive style and learning strategies in Latin instruction," in J. Gruber-Miller, ed., *When Dead Tongues Speak: Teaching Beginning Greek and Latin* (Oxford: Oxford University Press, 2006), 27–49.

[11] The **affective filter** may consist of a learner's sense of anxiety, lack of self-confidence, lack of motivation, or fear of failure (Krashen [1985], 3–4).

[12] To achieve effective L2 reading, "we need to get to the level of automatized vocabulary rather than focusing on decoding in context" (A.H. Urquhart and C. J. Weir, *Reading in a Second Language: Process, Product, and Practice* [New York: Longman, 1998], 191; cf. Pressley, 205).

[13] This is due, in part, to the fact an SLA approach increases the likelihood that learners will develop three skills that brain imagery research has proven foundational for reading fluency: (a) the ability to phonologically analyze words (sounding out words), (b) the ability to recognize words by sight, and (c) the ability to recognize spoken words (cf. Pressley, 200–3).

[14] Pressley, 68.

[15] Philip J. King and Lawrence E. Stager, *Life in Biblical Israel* (Louisville: Westminster John Knox, 2001).

[16] For a report on the project and its findings, see Paul Overland, Lee Fields, and Jennifer Noonan, "Can Communicative Principles Enhance Classical Language Acquisition?", *Foreign Language Annals* 44:3 (Fall 2011), 583–93.

To the student

To get the most out of your textbook, why not take a moment to learn how it works? Visit www.Learning BiblicalHebrewInteractively.com for integrated multimedia resources. Learn expressions as you hear them pronounced for you.

A secret to language learning. To learn a language, look for ways to actually **communicate** with it, whether to express your opinion, to accomplish tasks, or to ask others to do something. Your textbook has been designed to provide a hands-on, interactive learning experience. Don't be afraid of making mistakes. We all do. As you use the language to communicate even simple messages, you will **internalize** it and thereby will become a much better **reader** of Hebrew—our ultimate goal.

How it is organized (units, modules, segments). The book is divided into "units." Each unit is broken up into "modules." And modules are subdivided into "segments." Thus the shorthand "§1.1.א." would refer to Unit 1, Module 1, and Segment א (*alef*, the first letter of the Hebrew alphabet).

JONAH STORY.
Successive episodes of a tale (inspired by the biblical account of Jonah) will show how target vocabulary and expressions may combine to tell a story. Let the story with its illustrations help you learn what words mean and how to use them. Before reading each new episode, you first will want (a) to learn its vocabulary, (b) to study the explanations, and (c) engage the activities that support that episode. Then return to read the story.

Words for responding   מִלִּים לַעֲנוֹת

New vocabulary appears at the front of each Jonah episode, clustered in two groups. Learn the first group—"Words for responding"—so well that you can speak or write them at will. As for the second group ("Words for hearing") learn them thoroughly enough that you can recognize these words when you hear them spoken or see them in writing.

TO THE STUDENT   לַתַּלְמִיד   xix

Explanations and activities.

Principles of grammar unfold under the heading "Explanation." These in turn lead to "Activities" where, with the help of a new language skill, you will express yourself, obtain something from someone else, or ask someone to do perform a task—all in Hebrew! Activities let you **communicate** in Hebrew.

> **5.1.ג. Activity:** "What will you (*mpl*) do today?"   מַה־תַּעֲשׂוּ הַיּוֹם?
>
> INTERACTIVE SKILL: Being able to respond when someone asks what your group plans to do
>
> Form groups of two. Your pair should consist of two males or a male and a female, due to the *mpl* form used for this activity. Drawing on verbs learned up to this point, select one activity you **both** may do later today (actual or outlandishly fictitious). Add detail by supplying an object or prepositional phrase.

Did you know that...?   הֲיָדַעְתָּ כִּי...?

Under the heading "Did you know that…," you will find brief articles highlighting some aspect of **culture** in the Ancient Near East. Often accompanied by illustrations, these articles range from customs of birth or death to topics such as pottery, travel, architecture, or warfare.

You can read the Bible.   אַתָּה תִקְרָא אֶת־הַתַּנַ"ךְ:

You will end each unit by reading from a collection of excerpts taken from the Hebrew Bible. Each selection is keyed to the module or segment that prepares you to read it. In addition to isolated excerpts (called "Selected readings") you will find longer "Connected readings" that extend over several units (Genesis 22 and Psalm 23).

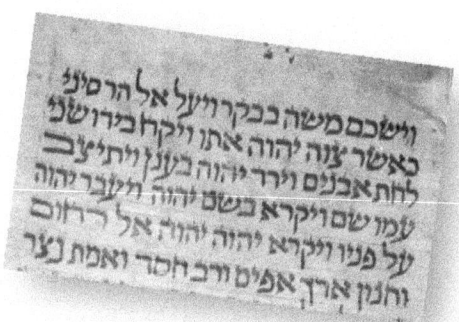

Cultural References

1. Square script (§0.1.ה.) I-9
2. Pillared house (§0.1.ל.) I-19
3. City walls (§0.3.ח.) I-36
4. Tanak (§0.5.ט.) I-61
5. Meaning of names (§1.1.ח.) I-87
6. Disclosing one's name (§1.2.ב.) I-92
7. The divine name (§1.2.ג.) I-92
8. Land travel (§1.3.ד.) I-100
9. Incised seals (§2.1.ח.) I-120
10. Leather goods (§2.3.ח.) I-146
11. Weights (§2.4.ה.) I-158
12. Obligation (§2.5.ה.) I-164
13. Greeting (§2.5.ז.) I-165
14. לֶחֶם food, bread (§3.1.ב.) I-184
15. Perfumes and spices (§3.1.ד.) I-190
16. Yes (§3.1.ו.) I-192
17. Diet (§3.1.ח.) I-194
18. Theophoric names (§3.2.ג.) I-212
19. Burial customs and afterlife (§3.2.ה.) I-214
20. Sea travel (§3.3.ז.) I-229
21. יָד hand (§4.1.ד.) I-261
22. Attention (the Shema, §4.1.ו.) I-262
23. Pottery (§4.1.ז.) I-263
24. Amphora and sea transport (§4.1.ח.) I-265
25. אַף nose, anger (§4.2.א.) I-270
26. נֶפֶשׁ soul, person (§4.2.ה.) I-276
27. Units of measure (§4.2.ו.) I-276
28. Calling for help (§4.3.ה.) I-288
29. ש.מ.ע בְּקוֹל obey (§4.4.ה.) I-297
30. Olive industry (§4.4.ז.) I-299
31. Body language (§5.1.ח.) I-328
32. Musical instruments (§5.1.ט.) I-328
33. Domesticated animals (§5.1.י.) I-330
34. Protocol idiom (§5.2.א.) I-335
35. תְּהוֹם watery depths (§6.1.ז.) I-388
36. Village settlement (§6.1.ט.) I-389
37. Birth (§6.1.י.) I-391
38. Marriage (§6.1.כ.) I-392
39. The voyage of Wenamun (§6.2.א.) I-397
40. Metallurgy (§6.3.ח.) I-418
41. Beverages (§7.1.ז.) II-19
42. Marketplace economics (§7.3.ט.) II-57
43. Oaths (§7.4.ה.) II-71
44. Siege warfare (§7.4.י.) II-82
45. Clothing (§7.5.ה.) II-95
46. עִבְרִי Hebrew, gentilics (§8.1.ג.) II-126
47. Casemate walls (§8.1.ח.) II-138
48. מַשָּׂא prophetic oracle (§8.1.ט.) II-139
49. Ketiv-qere כְּתִיב קְרֵי scribal tradition (§8.1.כ.) II-141
50. Hygiene and health (§8.2.ה.) II-157
51. Monumental architecture (§9.1.ה.) II-178
52. Monarch as paterfamilias (§9.4.ז.) II-210
53. Phonetic alphabet, literacy (§10.1.ה.) II-243
54. Furniture (§10.1.ו.) II-245
55. Palistrophic composition (§10.2.ט.) II-279
56. Warfare (§10.2.כ.) II-281
57. Acrostic composition (§10.3.ג.) II-293
58. Vehicles (§11.1.ו.) II-320
59. Water sources (§11.1.ז.) II-321
60. Sacred figurines (§11.2.ז.) II-335
61. Sacred spaces (§11.2.ח.) II-337

Illustrations

1. Torah scroll (§0.1.ה.) I-10
2. Pillared house diagram (§0.1.ל.) I-19
3. Hezekiah's "Broad Wall" (§0.3.ח.) I-36
4. 'Ōniyāhû seal (§2.1.ח.) I-121
5. Hematite weights, Ur (§2.4.ה.) I-158
6. Stone weights, Lachish (§2.4.ה.) I-159
7. Duck weights, Mesopotamian (§2.4.ה.) I-159
8. Saddle-quern and polisher stone (§3.1.ב.) I-185
9. Ceramic juglets, cosmetic palette (§3.1.ד.) I-190
10. Four-handled jug (§3.1.ה.) I-195
11. Ceramic milk churn (§3.1.ה.) I-196
12. Ossuary (§3.2.ה.) I-215
13. Lamps and juglet (§4.1.ז.) I-263
14. Canaanite jar, dipping pitcher (§4.1.ח.) I-263
15. Legio X Fretensius pavement brick (§4.1.ז.) .. I-264
16. Amphora, marine-encrusted pitcher (§4.1.ח.) . I-266
17. Assyrian pack animals (§4.2.ג.) I-277
18. Roller olive press (§4.4.ז.) I-299
19. Gethsemane olive grove (§4.4.ז.) I-300
20. Lever-beam press (base, receptacle, §4.4.ז.) ... I-300
21. Egyptian harp (§5.1.ט.) I-329
22. Finger cymbals (§5.1.ט.) I-329
23. Horse-drawn chariot, King Astartu (§5.1.י.) ... I-330
24. Tribute camels for Shalmaneser III (§5.1.י.) ... I-330
25. Ashurbanipal on horseback (§5.1.י.) ... I-331
26. Village of Deir el-Medina (§6.1.ט.) I-390
27. Necklace, earrings (§6.1.כ.) I-392
28. Copper axe blades (§6.3.ה.) I-418
29. Gold foil jewelry (§6.3.ה.) I-418
30. Jewelry from Tell el-'Ajjul (§6.3.ה.) I-419
31. Map of Ancient Near East .... I-564 and II-554
32. Map of Israel .... I-565 and II-555
33. Ceramic pitcher, jug, strainer, cup, and pilgrim flask (§7.1.ז.) II-20
34. Silver coil (§7.3.ט.) II-57
35. Grain silo, Megiddo (§7.4.י.) II-83
36. Sling stones, Lachish (§7.4.י.) II-84
37. Assyrian battering ram, Lachish (§7.4.י.) II-85
38. Loom weights and toggle pins (§7.5.ה.) II-95
39. Hebrew tribute-bearer (Black Obelisk, §7.5.ה.) II-96
40. Judean captives leaving Lachish (Black Obelisk, §7.5.ה.) II-96
41. Casemate gateway, Megiddo (§8.1.ה.) II-138
42. Mirror and combs (§8.2.ה.) II-158
43. Phoenician ivory, Nimrud (§9.1.ה.) ... II-179
44. Sargon II's lamassu bull (§9.1.ה.) II-179
45. Pillars in Great Hypostyle Hall of Seti I, Karnak (§9.1.ה.) II-180
46. Stela of King Hammurabi (§9.4.ז.) II-210
47. Seated Egyptian scribe (§10.1.ה.) II-243
48. Throne of Sennacherib (§10.1.ג.) II-245
49. Spear point and knife blade (§10.2.ב.) II-282
50. Assyrian archers, Tel Tayinat orthostats (§10.2.ב.) II-282
51. Eight-spoke Judean chariot, Lachish (§11.1.ג.) II-320
52. Horse-drawn chariot of Sargon II (§11.1.ג.) .. II-320
53. Megiddo water shaft (§11.1.ז.) II-321
54. Hezekiah's tunnel (§11.1.ז.) II-321
55. Silver bull from Alaca Hüyük (§11.2.ז.) II-335
56. Cast bronze figurine (§11.2.ז.) II-335
57. Asherah terracotta pillar figurine (§11.2.ז.) .. II-336
58. Small horned altar, Megiddo (§11.2.ה.) II-337
59. Large altar mound, Megiddo (§11.2.ה.) II-338

ACKNOWLEDGMENTS

These volumes owe a primary debt of gratitude to the Wabash Center for Teaching and Learning in Theology and Religion. Funding from the Wabash Center made it possible to undertake an initial three-year exploration into Second Language Acquisition for Biblical Hebrew (known as "The Communicative Hebrew Learning and Teaching Project," or "the Cohelet Project"). The administration and staff of Ashland Theological Seminary also affirmed this vision, serving as host institution during the Cohelet Project phase.

Without the dedicated and perceptive oversight of Second Language Acquisition Consultant Diana Pulido, we in the Cohelet Project would have been left merely to infer from SLA literature how best to proceed. Instead, we received personal coaching from a trained expert as she shepherded the process to a successful conclusion. Jörg Waltje served far beyond his official capacity at Language Learning Technology Consultant. His technological expertise combined with pedagogical insight to greatly multiply our effectiveness. Each of the instructors, whether serving as part of the Design Team or the Field Test Team, contributed invaluable skill, cordiality in collaboration, and dedication to the project. The Design Team members included: Randall Buth, Dwayne Howell, Marie Krahn, Jennifer Noonan (assistant), and myself (project director). Hélène Dallaire, Lee Fields, Bob Stallman, and Peter Vogt served on the Field Test Team. Marie Krahn additionally tested materials for usability outside an English context (after first translating the manual into Portuguese for her students in São Leopoldo, Brazil). Louise Waller patiently and engagingly brought the serialized story to life through her singular artistic skill. It has been my high privilege to work with these remarkable individuals.

I am deeply indebted to Professor Marc Brettler, Bronson Brown-deVost, and Lenin Prado for their careful review of all materials during the final stages of editing. Credit for fidelity to Biblical Hebrew expression belongs to them, while responsibility for any errors that escaped our notice rests with me.

To Kenneth Walther and Beth Hoffman go my thanks for the hours they gave to help photograph and to research background information concerning cultural artifacts in the Flora Archaeological Collection. Illustrations that list no photographer were supplied by the author.

It has been a distinct privilege to work with Professor David Clines and the staff of Sheffield Phoenix Press through the publication process. Their prompt and precise advice has been as helpful as their reputation for exceptional publications in Hebrew Bible is legendary.

Finally, my greatest thanks is due to my wife, Lorie. Absent her patient, cheerful encouragement, together with the countless ways she safeguarded time for writing—this seemingly endless undertaking may have remained just that.

Inquiries concerning supplemental textbook materials and training opportunities in SLA and Biblical Hebrew, together with suggestions for revisions, may be directed to:

Paul Overland
975 Thomas Drive
Ashland, Ohio 44805, USA
poverlan@ashland.edu
www.LearningBiblicalHebrewInteractively.com

ABBREVIATIONS AND SYMBOLS

Abbreviations

BDB   Brown, Francis, S. R. Driver, and Charles A. Briggs. *A Hebrew and English Lexicon of the Old Testament.* Clarendon Press: Oxford, 1907.

BH   Biblical Hebrew

BHS   *Biblia Hebraica Stuttgartensia.* Edited by A. Alt, O. Eissfeldt, and P. Kahle. Stuttgart: Deutche Bibelgesellschaft, 1977.

CHP   Wilfred G. E. Watson's *Classical Hebrew Poetry: A Guide to its Techniques* (Journal for the Study of the Old Testament: Supplement Series 26, Sheffield: University of Sheffield, 1984 and 1986.

ET   English translation

GKC   *Gesenius' Hebrew Grammar.* Edited by E. Kautzsch. Translated by A. E. Cowley. 2nd ed. Clarendon Press: Oxford, 1010.

HALOT   Koehler, Ludwig, Walter Baumgartner, and Johan J. Stamm. *The Hebrew and Aramaic Lexicon of the Old Testament.* Translated and edited by M. E. J. Richardson. 4 vols. Leiden: Brill, 1994-1999.

HB   Hebrew Bible

IBH   Lambdin, Thomas O. *Introduction to Biblical Hebrew.* New York: Charles Scribner's Sons, 1971.

IBHS   Waltke, Bruce K., and Michael O'Connor. *An Introduction to Biblical Hebrew Syntax.* Winona Lake, Indiana: 1990.

Joüon   Joüon, Paul, and Takamitsu Muraoka. *A Grammar of Biblical Hebrew.* 2nd ed. Rome: Gregorian and Biblical Press, 2009.

LBI   King, Philip J., and Lawrence E. Stager. *Life in Biblical Israel.* Louisville, Kentucky: Westminster John Knox, 2001.

MT   Masoretic Text

Symbols

◌́   the accented syllable in a Hebrew word (for words not displaying full Masoretic cantillation)

‡   a hypothetical form (as in אֱיְרֹד‡), a form that proper language usage would not employ, although it may display some of the rules for word formation

UNIT 0

א...ב...

Learning the alphabet

consonants, vowels, and syllables

By the conclusion of this unit, you will be able to pronounce any word in the Hebrew Bible. To help you build confidence in pronunciation, we will begin by learning the consonants, vowels, and the sounds they represent when combined into syllables.

This introductory unit helps you learn correct pronunciation by accompanying each Hebrew word with a representation of its sound, written in Latin letters. Representing the sounds of one script by means of a second script is called transliterating.

In this unit you will learn:

- the names of Hebrew consonants and vowels
- how to divide longer words into syllables
- how to pronounce words written in Hebrew
- how to read aloud two well-known verses from the Hebrew Bible

MODULE 0.1 א to ד, vowels, syllables (part 1)

0.1.א. (0.1.A.) Explanation: Direction of reading

Hebrew script follows a right-to-left flow pattern. In this exercise you will learn to transliterate the Hebrew name תָּמָר, writing it in Latin letters.[1] Use the "Letter code" (immediately below). It will supply you with the three consonants and one vowel used in תָּמָר.

Letter code

Beneath each Hebrew consonant you will find its Latin equivalent. The T-shaped symbol below the dotted ring (ׇ) is the vowel called "qameṣ" (pronounced *kah-mayts*). The sound this vowel produces is *ah*. When transliterating to Latin letters, we represent the qameṣ by "ā."

In the representation "ׇ", only the T-shaped symbol comprises the vowel. The dotted circle above it marks the space where a consonant would normally appear (as in תָ or מָ).

ר	מ	ת	**Consonants**
r	m	t	
ā (pronounced *ah*)			**Vowel**

---

[1] English letter shapes are known as "Latin" since they descended from that language at one stage of development.

Rely on the numbers in the following picture to learn in what **order** the letters should be sequenced. Remember to begin by reading the right-most consonant. Then look under that consonant to find the ensuing vowel.

Now you are ready to transliterate the Hebrew name תָּמָר. Write it in the boxes below, using Latin letters in the standard Latin direction (left-to-right). Hebrew does not distinguish between upper case and lower case letters. To follow the convention of many Latin-based languages, you will want to capitalize the first letter of תָּמָר since it is a name.

1	2	3	4	5
T				

Compare your answer with the note below.[2] You may want to refer back to this sample word to help you remember the reading sequence for letters in a Hebrew word.

Now we are ready to learn the alphabet. We will learn a few vowels and a few consonants at a time, until you have mastered the entire collection.

---

[2] The name תָּמָר is transliterated *Tāmār* (pronounced *Tah-mahr*), an important woman in Judah's family (see Genesis 38). If you guessed *Rāmāt*, remember that Hebrew is written right-to-left, so that ת *t* must be the first letter.

0.1.ב. (0.1.B.) Explanation: Vowels, part 1 (A-Class vowels)

Hebrew vowels belong to one of three classes: "A-Class vowels," "I/E-Class vowels," or "U/O-Class vowels." First we will learn the A-Class group of vowels. They earn the title "A-Class" because they produce the sound *ah*.

A-Class vowels

Four vowels are considered A-Class vowels. It is important to learn each vowel name (such as qameṣ) as well as the sound each produces (the vowel called "qameṣ" produces an *ah* sound).

Note: to encourage you to grow accustomed to read in Hebrew fashion (right-to-left), most tables in this book are formatted so that the right column is the initial column.

final qameṣ-hē[4]	ḥaṭef-pataḥ	pataḥ[3]	qameṣ	**Vowel name**
הָ	ֲ	ַ	ָ	**Vowel**
a as in *mark*	*a* as in *mark*	*a* as in *mark*	*a* as in *mark*	**Vowel sound**
â	ă	a	ā	**Transliteration**[5]

Since vowels in Hebrew regularly **follow** a consonant, next let's show the position of these vowels when they follow a consonant such as מ (called mēm, producing the *m* sound).[6] It is likely that in ancient times these various A-Class vowels yielded different sounds. However, we will follow Modern Hebrew pronunciation conventions, and so will pronounce each of these syllables the same: *mah*.

---

[3] We spell the words "ḥaṭef" and "pataḥ" using the diacritical symbol "ḥ" since English does not offer a corresponding combination of letters. This symbol represents the rough expulsion of air that occurs as you position the tongue against the roof of the mouth for the letter *k*, then open the passageway to let a small amount of air continuously escape (rather than emitting an explosion of air all at once, as with an actual "k"). Some imitate the hissing of a cat in this way. At the outset, you may substitute with a simple *k* sound if *ḥ* is difficult to produce.

[4] When the consonant ה hē follows a qameṣ vowel to conclude a word, the ה is an extension of the qameṣ vowel, indicating that it is a long vowel. Long and short vowels will be treated more fully below (see §0.4.ו.).

[5] The transliteration scheme employed here follows closely the "Academic Transliteration" found in *The SBL Handbook of Style*, Patrick H. Alexander, et al., eds. (Peabody, Massachusetts: Hendrickson, 1999), 26–28, with a few exceptions for the sake of clarity (e.g., spirant פ will be rendered "f" rather than "p" or "p̄").

[6] Two exceptions will be treated later (furtive pataḥ in §0.5.ב. and initial šureq in §0.4.ה.).

final qameṣ-hē	ḥatef-pataḥ	pataḥ	qameṣ	Vowel name
מָה	מֲ	מַ	מָ	**Vowel written with consonant מ**
mah	mah	mah	mah	**Syllable sound**
mâ	mă	ma	mā	**Transliteration**

Take a moment to practice reading the various A-Class vowels combined with the letter מ. Use the row labeled "Vowel written with consonant מ." Also take time to learn the names of the various vowels above (see row labeled "Vowel name" in previous table).

At this point in your study, the instructor may begin to give some simple instructions, in Hebrew. Here are two you may hear:

- **"What is this?"** Your instructor may invite you to tell him or her the **name** of a vowel by pointing to that vowel asking, "*Mah zeh?*" (*What is this?*). Answer by giving the appropriate vowel **name**, such as "qameṣ," "pataḥ," or "ḥatef-pataḥ."

- **"Read!"** Alternatively, if your instructor asks you to **pronounce** a particular syllable or word, you may hear this instruction: *Q'ra!* (*Read!* [addressed to a male]), or *Qir'i!* (*Read!* [addressed to a female]). Respond by sounding out the syllable or word that your instructor selects.

0.1.ג. Explanation: Consonants, part 1 (א, ב, ג, and ד)

The first four letters of the Hebrew alphabet are א ('alef), ב (bēt),[7] ג (gîmel), and ד (dalet). Over the next few pages you will learn the entire alphabet, shown below. For now, focus on these initial four letters.

In the "Name" column, letter names such as "bēt" include the vowel "ē." As you will learn in §0.2.א., "ē" represents the *ay* sound, as in the English word "bay." Thus, the letter ב produces the sound *b* and goes by the letter name "bēt"—pronounced *bayt* (or *bait*). The letter ר produces the sound *r* and goes by the letter name "rēš"—pronounced *raysh*.

The vowel "î" (appearing in letter names such as "gîmel") is pronounced *ee*. Thus the letter names "gîmel" and "šîn" are pronounced *geemel* and *sheen*, respectively. It is not uncommon to find letters such as these transliterated more casually (without diacritical marks): "*he*" (for "hē"), "*resh*" (for "rēš"), "*gimel*" (for "gîmel"), and "*shin*" (for "šîn").

Toward the end of this unit you will find a section titled "How to write Hebrew letters." Please study the tips provided there, and practice writing the letters as each new group of consonants is introduced. Use the "Practice writing sheet" located after "How to write Hebrew letters." It would be wise to make several copies of the blank "Practice writing sheet" in order to develop your skill in writing Hebrew.

---

[7] As you will learn in the next segment, בּ (with the "dagesh" dot) is the technical representation for the letter name "bēt" (pronounced "bait"), while the letter name of ב (without the dagesh) is "vēt" (rhymes with "bait"). It is conventional, however, when referring to the second letter of the alphabet (apart from its use in a specific word) to write it without the dagesh (ב), and to refer to it as "bēt."

Letter	Final form	Name	Sound	Trans-literation
א		ʾalef	(glottal stop)	ʾ
בּ		bēt	b	b
(ב)		(vēt)	(v)	(b̠)
ג		gîmel	g	g
ד		dalet	d	d
ה		hē	h	h
ו		vav	v	v
ז		zayin	z	z
ח		ḥēt	ḫ[8]	ḥ
ט		ṭēt	t	ṭ
י		yod	y	y
כ		kaf	k	k
(ך)	(ך)	(khaf)	(kh)	(k̠)

Letter	Final form	Name	Sound	Trans-literation
ל		lamed	l	l
מ	ם	mēm	m	m
נ	ן	nun	n	n
ס		samekh	s	s
ע		ʿayin	(voiced guttural)	ʿ
פ		pē	p	p
(פ)	(ף)	(fē)	(f)	(f)
צ	ץ	ṣadē	ts	ṣ
ק		qof	q[9]	q
ר		rēš	r	r
שׁ		šîn	sh	š
שׂ		śîn	s	ś
ת		tav	t	t

Although א actually is a consonant (called the glottal stop), it does not correspond to a single Latin letter. Instead, you will produce the glottal stop automatically if you simply pronounce whatever vowel immediately follows the letter א: אָ ʾā (pronounced *ah*), אָב ʾāb̠ (*ahv*), בָּאָ bāʾa (*bah-ah*).[10]

---

[8] As noted for the words "ḥaṭef" and "pataḥ," the symbol "ḫ" is pronounced *kh*, similar to the back-of-throat hissing sound emitted by an angry cat. The sound produced by ṭ we will not distinguish from *t*, although historically ṭ would likely have been produced as a velar (deep-throat) *t*, a sound still present in Modern Arabic.

[9] The letter ק represents a *k* sound produced deeper in the throat than the sound for כ.

[10] א represents a brief closing of the upper throat before expressing a vowel. In English it can be detected at the start of a word that begins with a vowel. Sense how your throat closes as you begin to say *at* (while it does **not** close when saying *hat*). It closes for *it* and *ought* (but not for *hit* or *hot*).

0.1.ד. Explanation: Dagesh (dot) in so-called Beged-Kefet letters

Six consonants are routinely written with a dagesh (the dot in the center of the letter) when they appear first in a phrase or when they follow a closed syllable.[11] Three of those six appear in this first cluster of letters: ב, ג, and ד. The entire group of six is called the Beged-Kefet group (note the accent on first syllables: *BEHged-KEHfet*). The letters ב, ג, and ד supply the sounds for the first part of the name ("Beged").[12]

Of the initial three Beged-Kefet letters (ב, ג, and ד), only in the case of ב does the dagesh alter pronunciation. When the **dagesh is present**, the flow of air is stopped (i.e., for ב, the lips must close to produce a *b* sound). The letter ב is named "bēt."

When the **dagesh is omitted** there is no "stop" of air flow (lips are not closed), resulting in the *v* sound. In Hebrew this *v* sound is written "ב" (note omission of dagesh). The letter ב is named "vēt" and is transliterated as *b̲*.[13]

When will a Beged-Kefet letter take the dagesh? It must have a dagesh (a) when it appears as the first letter of a word that begins a phrase or (b) when it follows a closed syllable.[14] To begin with, simply make it a habit to include a dagesh when the letter begins a word (e.g., בָּא *ba*ʾ).

---

[11] "Dagesh lene" (weak dagesh) is the complete name of this dagesh, contrasting the "dagesh forte" (explained in §0.4.א).

[12] The remaining three Beged-Kefet letters are כ, פ, and ת.

[13] Linguists call ב the spirantized or fricative form, while ב is the unaspirated or plosive form. Since the form ב (without the dagesh) is considered secondary, it has been enclosed in parentheses in the table above.

[14] For more explanation regarding the dagesh (lene and forte) see §0.4.א., also "Syllable division," §0.4.ח. Cf. R. Buth, *Living Biblical Hebrew* (Jerusalem: Biblical Language Center, 1999), 1:121.

0.1.ה. Do you know how to read? (Square script) הֲיָדַעְתָּ לִקְרֹא?[15]

The symbols representing the consonants of the Hebrew alphabet have changed their shape several times over the centuries. The particular script you are learning originated as the Jewish form of an Aramaic script that the exiled Israelites would have used in Babylonia. Subsequent to their return from captivity, scribes copied the Hebrew Bible into this script. Due to its largely rectangular pattern, it became known as "square script."[16]

To get a picture of how Hebrew letters appeared before the "square script" was adopted, compare the ʾŌniyāhû seal inscription (cf. §2.1.ח.). Inscribed stone weights also preserve a style of writing that predates the square script (cf. §2.4.ה.).

Hebrew refers to the process of writing with terms like כְּתוּב *kĕtûb* "script" (Esth. 1:22), and אוֹת *ʾôt* "distinguishing mark" (also "omen"). אוֹת is the term for the mark placed on Cain (Gen. 4:15).

---

[15] The heading "הֲיָדַעְתָּ לִקְרֹא" is transliterated: "*hăyādaʿtā liqrō*" (the sheva in לִקְרֹא is silent).

[16] *IBHS* §1.5.2.

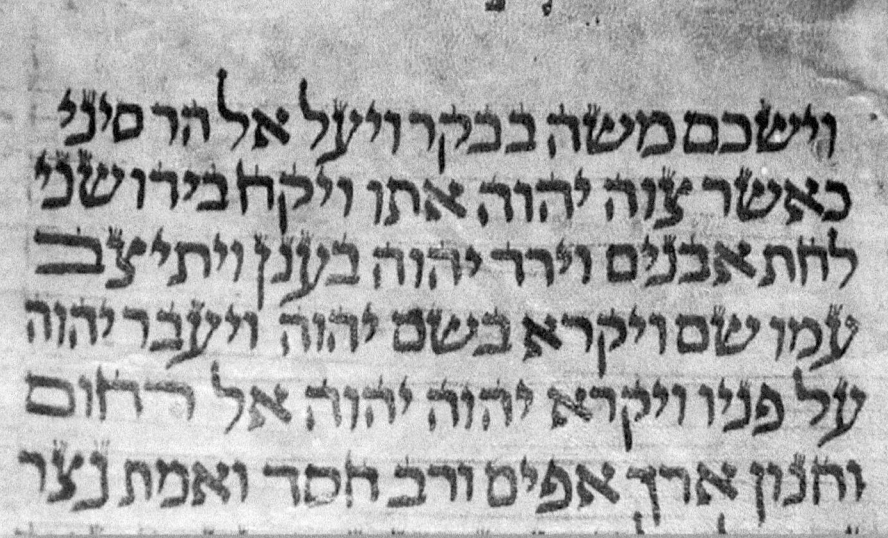

This Torah scroll presents unvocalized square script in a very clear hand, with decorative three-limbed "crowns" (*tagin*) at the top of letters such as נ, ע, צ, and ש. Written on leather, it may have originated in Turkey of the 15th cent. CE. Horizontal scoring supplied guidelines for the scribe. This excerpt begins at Exod. 34:4b (וַיַּשְׁכֵּם *and he got up early*). The double divine name in the fifth row (יהוה יהוה) corresponds to Exod. 34:6, a pivotal passage in the revelation of divine character.

(Courtesy of Doug and Jean Sherman Manuscript Library, Ashland Theological Seminary)

0.1.ו. Do you know how to speak Hebrew? (Accented syllables)

הֲיָדַ֫עְתָּ לְדַבֵּר יְהוּדִית?[17]

In Hebrew, the accent generally falls on the **final** syllable. Thus the word אָבַד is pronounced *ah-VAD*.[18]

When the accent falls on a syllable **other** than the final syllable, this textbook will generally mark it with a raised angular symbol called a chevron, as above the בֶּ in בֶּ֫גֶד *BEH-ged*.[19] (The vowel ֶ is called a "segol," sometimes spelled "seghol," and produces an *eh* sound.)

When you see **bold** font within a Hebrew word, it calls attention to particular letters. Bold font does *not* signify the accented syllable, although they may at times coincide.

0.1.ז. Explanation: Closing א

When an א closes a syllable, the א is silent.[20] Thus the word בָּא is simply pronounced *bah* (transliterated *bāʾ*), rather than *bah-ah*. You can recognize when an א is silent, because **no vowel will appear following the א**. In contrast, in the word בָּאָה the א is followed by a vowel, and so begins a new syllable. The word בָּאָה is pronounced *bah-ah* (transliterated *bāʾâ*). "ה" at the close of this word is the letter *hē*, to be introduced with the next group of letters.

---

[17] The heading "הֲיָדַ֫עְתָּ לְדַבֵּר יְהוּדִית?" is transliterated: "*hăyādaʿtā lĕdabbēr yĕhûdît?*"

[18] The accented syllable is known as the "tone" syllable. In most Hebrew words, the tone syllable will be the final syllable of a word. The final syllable of a word is known as the *ultima*, whether it is accented or not.

[19] When the vowels of a noun consist of two segols (as in בֶּ֫גֶד), the accent routinely falls on the **first syllable** rather than the last. These are called "segolate" (or "segholate") nouns because they contain two segols.

[20] Termed by linguists a "quiescent א."

0.1.ח. May I offer you advice? (Transliterating)   הַאִיעָצְךָ עֵצָה?[21]

> Converting material from one script into another is called "transliterating." Transliterating Hebrew into your native script may be helpful during the first few days of learning the language.
>
> However, if you allow yourself to transliterate for too long a period, it will seriously stunt your ability to learn Hebrew. Thus, after **the first week** it will be important to force yourself **not** to transliterate any longer. Instead, invest the time required to learn and review the script thoroughly. At this early stage of your study, the determination to **refrain from transliterating** will constitute **the single most important decision** helping you reach your goal of learning to read Hebrew.

0.1.ט. Practice: Pronouncing syllables

Practice reading aloud the syllables found in the next table. In the "Sounds like…" column you will find the formal transliteration of the syllable (in italics) followed by a simplified transliteration (italics in parentheses). The simplified transliteration will make it easier to remember the sounds represented by the formal transliterations.

Some of the syllables in the column labeled "Syllables" are only that: not genuine Hebrew words, but only syllables designed to help you practice new letters. Occasionally a genuine word will appear in the "Syllables" column. When a genuine word appears, you may also find its translation in the "Sounds

---

[21] The heading "הַאִיעָצְךָ עֵצָה" is transliterated *haʾîʿāṣĕkā ʿēṣâ*.

like…" column. These translations (or "glosses") will appear in regular font (not italics). For example, the first word in the left group is אָב. It is a genuine word, meaning "father." Don't worry about remembering the meanings. That will come later. For now, concentrate on pronouncing the syllables.

Cover the column entitled, "Sounds like…." Reveal it line-by-line *after* you have attempted to sound out the Hebrew word on your own.

Sounds like…	Syllables	Sounds like…	Syllables
ʾāḇ (*ahv*), father	אָב	ʾā (*ah*)	אָ
dāg (*dog*), fish	דָּג	ʾāg (*ahg*)	אָג
bāʾ (*bah*), he came	בָּא	bā (*bah*)	בָּ
gāʾ (*gah*)	גָּא	gā (*gah*)	גָּ
dāʾ (*dah*)	דָּא	dā (*dah*)	דָּ

For the next table, match Hebrew syllables from the "Syllables" column with the correct pronunciation found in the "Sounds like…" column. Write the appropriate alpha-numeral in the "Answer" column. One has been completed for you.

Sounds like…	Answer	Syllables	Alpha-numeral
bāg (*bog*)	ב.	אָבַד	א.
ʾāḇad (*ah-vahd*) he perished		בַּג	ב.
dāḇ (*dahv*)		בֶּגֶד	ג.
gāḏ (*gahd*) [a tribe's name]		גָּבַד	ד.
ʾăḏad (*ah-dahd*) [a man's name]		גַּד	ה.
gāḇad (*gah-vahd*)		דָּב	ו.
bāgaḏ (*bah-gahd*) he was deceitful		אָדָד	ז.

Letters of the alphabet have long been employed to signify both **alphabetic sequence** (analogous to "a, b, c") and **enumeration** (analogous to "1, 2, 3"). This textbook will use Hebrew letters as part of the **sequence** designation found in segment headings. Thus a designation "§1.3.א." would be analogous to

"§1.3.A." (referring to the first subdivision within §1.3), while "§1.3.ב." will be analogous to "§1.3.K" (since the letters "כ" and "K" both occupy the same position in their respective alphabets—position #11).

When **enumerating** an array of words or phrases (as in matching exercise above), Hebrew letters will stand for numbers. When letters-for-numbers represent numbers above the numeral 10, a convention of "tens and units" comes into play. Thus the numeral 11 is formed by י (representing "10") plus א (representing "1"): יא (read right-to-left).[22] The numeral 22 is formed by כ (representing "20") plus ב (for "2"): כב. Can you guess what number is expressed by the alpha-numerals לד? (Hint: ל = 30.)

To help you grow comfortable with letter names, try this exercise: select any Hebrew syllable or word in this unit, and "spell" it aloud. The syllable "דָּ" would be "spelled aloud" as "dalet, qameṣ." Similarly גָּד would be spelled as "gîmel, qameṣ, dalet." Can you spell aloud the remaining Hebrew words in the matching exercise above?

0.1.י. Practice: Illustrated words beginning with א or ב

The sketch below contains several persons or objects that—in Hebrew—begin with either א or ב. The words identifying these objects appear in the table located below the sketch (see col. 2). Admittedly, most of the words in this collection employ several letters that you have not yet learned. **You are expected to recognize only the initial letters (א or ב).** Be patient with the process and take advantage of

---

[22] To avoid employing numerals resembling the divine name, the letter-pair טו serves as 15, while טז serves as 16.

the transliterations to see how the remainder of each word is pronounced. As you gradually master more letters, you will feel rewarded since you will recognize not only initial letters, but also many—and eventually all—of the consonants and vowels!

Again—for the time being take note of only the **initial letter** of each word (a letter that you have learned), then pronounce the words with the help of the transliteration provided (see col. 3). To help you grow accustomed to pronunciation, simplified phonetic equivalents appear in parentheses. Meanings are provided simply for your enjoyment, not for memorization (col. 4). Occasionally a footnote will provide additional information that may interest you.

4. Meaning	3. Transliteration	2. Word	1. Initial letter
father	ʾāḇ (ahv)	אָב [23]	א
stone	ʾeḇen (EH-ven)	אֶבֶן [24]	
mother	ʾēm (aim)	אֵם	
house	bayit (BYE-it)	בַּיִת	ב
son	bēn (bane)	בֵּן [25]	
daughter	bat (bought)	בַּת [26]	

[23] The name אַבְרָהָם (Abraham ʾaḇrāhām, "father of a multitude") begins with אַב (with a pataḥ vowel).

[24] The name Ebenezer ("stone [reminding] of help") begins with the word אֶבֶן.

[25] "Benjamin" ("son of my right hand") begins with בֶּן (with a segol vowel).

[26] Can you recognize בַּת in the name "Bathsheba" (meaning "daughter of Sheba")?

To help you learn the alphabet, please do the following:

1. Locate a part of the sketch that corresponds to the first word.
2. As you focus on the Hebrew word (not its transliteration), pronounce the name of the first letter of that word. Repeat the letter name out loud two or three times.
3. Then write the initial letter of the word near the corresponding part of the sketch.
4. Repeat steps #1-3 with each word.

For example, find someone in the sketch who might qualify as an אָב (*āb* [pronounced *ahv*], meaning "father"). Say aloud, two or three times the letter's name: "א ("*'alef*"), א, א". Then, since אָב begins with the letter א, write the letter א on the sketch near the figure that may represent a father. Some learners will benefit by drawing the letter in the air, using broad strokes.

0.1.ב. Practice: Illustrated words beginning with ג or ד

Use the next sketch in the same manner. This time focus on words beginning with ג or ד. Practice pronouncing both the whole words as well as the names of individual letters that comprise those words.

4. Meaning	3. Transliteration	2. Word	1. Initial letter
large	gādôl (gah-dol)	גָּדוֹל	ג
camel	gāmāl (gah-mahl)	גָּמָל	
fish	dāg (dog)	דָּג	ד
door	delet (DEH-leht)	דֶּלֶת	
road	dere<u>k</u> (DEH-rekh)	דֶּרֶךְ	

0.1.ל. Did you know that...? (Pillared house) הֲיָדַ֫עְתָּ כִּי...?[27]

...a typical house in the Levant during the Iron Age (1200-587 BCE) consisted of four rooms on a rectangular floor plan? A storage room at the back wall stretched the width of the house. Perpendicular to this transverse room were three parallel rooms: two long, narrow rooms along the outer walls and one long, "broadroom" running down the middle, measuring 2.5–4 meters wide. The front door opened into one end of the broadroom. A row of stone pillars separated each side room from the broad, central room, hence the designation, "pillared house." The two side rooms served as stalls for livestock, with feeding troughs between pillars.

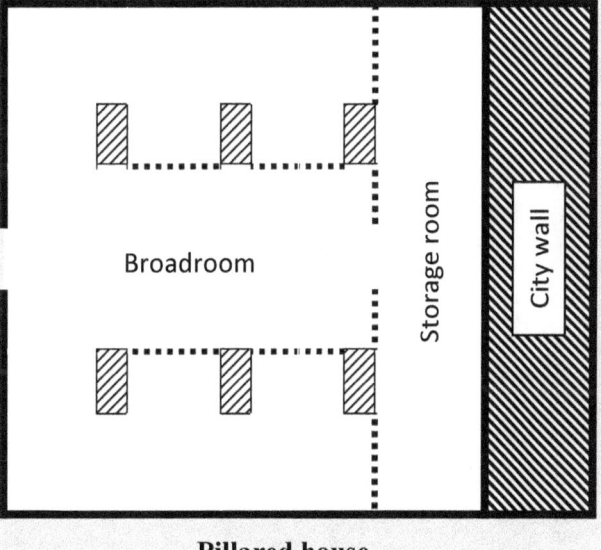

Pillared house

Walls consisted of sun-dried mud bricks with a plastered surface, raised on two or three courses of fieldstone. Ashlars (large, cuboid stones dressed on six sides) tended to be reserved for monumental projects. Cedar, acacia, juniper, oak, pine, or tamarisk tim-

---

[27] The heading "הֲיָדַ֫עְתָּ כִּי..." is transliterated: *hăyādaʿtā kî...*. A group of prophets asked a question of Elisha, beginning with this phrase (2 Kings 2:3).

ber served for joists, doors, and lintels. Narrow windows pierced the walls, allowing smoke to escape. In some houses, an inner stairway gave access to a second story. A flat roof offered additional living space in the warm climate.[28]

Homes belonging to extended families might cluster together in one sector of a town. By orienting their houses side-by-side, the continuous back wall would form a quasi community-wall, grouping their neighborhood within the town. At times the back wall of a house would be built into the city wall.

Would you like to know some Hebrew terms pertaining to this topic? Here are two:  בַּיִת *bayît* means "house," and עַמּוּד *'ammûd* is one of the words for "pillar."

---

[28] *LBI*, 21–35.

MODULE 0.2 ה to י, vowels, syllables (part 2)

0.2.א. Explanation: Vowels, part 2 (I/E-Class vowels)

The following six vowels are considered I/E-Class vowels. They produce either the *ee* sound or the sounds associated with an "e" vowel (whether "*ey*" as in "*whey*" or "*e*" as in "*pet*").

Once again, the vowel alone will appear beneath the respective vowel name. The syllable "מ-plus-vowel" is also shown.

ḥaṭef-segol	segol	ṣērê-yod	ṣērê[29]	ḥireq-yod	ḥireq	Vowel name
ֱ	ֶ	ֵי	ֵ	ִי	ִ	Vowel
e as in *pet*	*e* as in *pet*	*e* as in *whey*	*e* as in *whey*	*i* as in *machine*	*i* as in *machine*	Vowel sound
ĕ	e	ê	ē	î	i	Transliteration
מֱ	מֶ	מֵי	מֵ	מִי	מִ	Vowel written with consonant מ
mĕ	me	mê	mē	mî	mi	Transliteration

---

[29] Diacritical marks are provided for the vowel name "ṣērê" to help you learn its proper pronunciation: *tsayray*.

0.2.ב. Explanation: Consonants, part 2 (ה, ו, ז, ח, ט, and י)

The next group of six consonants includes ה, ו, ז, ח, ט, and י.

Trans-literation	Sound	Name	Final form	Letter
l	l	lamed		ל
m	m	mēm	ם	מ
n	n	nun	ן	נ
s	s	samekh		ס
ʿ	(voiced guttural)	ʿayin		ע
p (f)	p (f)	pē (fē)	(ף)	פ (פ)
ṣ	ts	ṣadē	ץ	צ
q	q	qof		ק
r	r	rēš		ר
š	sh	šîn		שׁ
ś	s	śîn		שׂ
t	t	tav		ת

Trans-literation	Sound	Name	Final form	Letter
ʾ	(glottal stop)	ʾalef		א
b (ḇ)	b (v)	bēt (vēt)		ב (ב)
g	g	gîmel		ג
d	d	dalet		ד
h	h	hē		ה
v	v	vav		ו
z	z	zayin		ז
ḥ	ḥ	ḥēt		ח
ṭ	t	ṭēt		ט
y	y	yod		י
k (ḵ)	k (kh)	kaf (khaf)	(ך)	כ (כ)

Concerning the letter ח, recall that the transliteration *ḥ* represents the sound *kh*. It resembles the noise made when trying to dislodge a particle from the base of your tongue.

The letter ט produces a *t* sound. Its throaty ("velar") texture has been lost in Hebrew.

0.2.ג. Explanation: Closing ה and י

Similar to the letter א, when ה closes a syllable it is silent. Thus the word זֶה is simply pronounced *zeh* (also transliterated *zeh*).[30]

When the letter י closes a syllable containing an **I/E-Class vowel**, it lengthens that vowel without changing how it is pronounced. Thus מִי is "longer" than מִ, but both are pronounced *mee*. Similarly, מֵי is "longer" than מֵ, but both are pronounced *mey*.

When the letter י closes a syllable containing an **A-Class vowel**, it produces a gliding vowel (diphthong). The diphthong will begin with an *ah* sound, gliding to an *ee* sound (as in the vowel sounds audible in the English words "lie" and "pie"). Thus אֵלַי is pronounced *ey-lah-ee*, not simply *ey-lah*. The proper transliteration of אֵלַי is *ʾēlay* (ל is the letter *lamed*, introduced in the next group).

0.2.ד. Do you know how to read? (Vowel letters)   הֲיָדַעְתָּ לִקְרֹא?

The earliest Hebrew inscriptions consisted only of consonants. Vowel symbols were later added to the text in two stages: (a) vowel letters and (b) vowel points.

First, scribes began identifying certain consonants that could also serve as "vowel letters." In the pre-exilic period (until 587 BCE), they began to employ three vowel letters at the **ends** of words to specify a long vowel. The vowel letters they employed were ו (for *û*), י (for *î*), and ה (for any other final vowel, often *ā*). In the post-exilic period, scribes began to employ ו and י **within** a word as well, with a wider range of vowel values. Vowel letters are known as *matres lectionis* ("mothers of reading").

A more complete system of vowel markings was developed by Masoretic scribes several centuries later, called *nequdot* or "vowel points." Most printed editions of

---

[30] As shown in the A-Class vowel table above (§0.1.ב.), when a syllable ends הָ... the ה represents a lengthening of the qameṣ vowel, so is not transliterated "*āh*" but "*â*." Thus מָה is rendered *mâ*, not *māh*.

> Hebrew Bibles in use today combine both stages, presenting *matres lectionis* together with *nequdot*. Lacking these (i.e., when presented without vowel points), a biblical text is known as the "consonantal text." For additional information concerning *matres lectionis* and *nequdot*, "*scriptio plene*" and "*scriptio defective*," please refer to the portion of the appendix corresponding to this segment. Although terms distinguishing consonants and vowels do not appear in the Hebrew Bible, the word later adopted for "vowel points" does appear: נְקֻדּוֹת *nĕquddôt* describes the "speckled" coloration of certain goats (Gen. 30:35).
>
>

0.2.ה. Practice: Pronouncing syllables

Here are several more syllables to practice reading aloud. Review them until you can pronounce them quickly with accuracy. The "Sounds like…" column offers transliteration followed by a simplified phonetic representation.

Cover the "Sounds like…" column. Reveal it line-by-line *after* you have attempted to pronounce the Hebrew word in the "Syllables" column.

Sounds like…	Syllables	Sounds like…	Syllables
ḥi (khee)	חִ	hā (hah)	הָ
ṭi (tee)	טִ	vā (vah)	וָ
yi (yee)	יִ	zā (zah)	זָ
hî (hee)	הִי	ḥā (khah)	חָ
vî (vee)	וִי	ṭā (tah)	טָ
zî (zee)	זִי	yā (yah)	יָ
ḥî (khee)	חִי	hi (hee)	הִ
ṭî (tee)	טִי	vi (vee)	וִ
hē (hey)	הֵ	zi (zee)	זִ

Using the alpha-numeral symbol, match Hebrew syllables from the "Syllables" column with the correct pronunciation given in the "Sounds like…" column. Item "א" has been completed for you.

Sounds like…	Answer	Syllables	Alpha-numeral
ḥê (khey)		וֵי	א.
ʾāḇî (ah-vee) my father		חֵי	ב.
ye (yeh)		טֶ	ג.
vê (vey)	א.	יְ	ד.
ṭe (teh)		הֵז	ה.
hĕz (hez)		וֱ	ו.
vĕ (veh)		דּוִד	ז.
dāvid (dah-veed) [a man's name]		חֵטִי	ח.
ḥēṭê (khey-tey)		אָבִי	ט.

Here is another group. See how many you can match correctly.

Sounds like…	Answer	Syllables	Alpha-numeral
hêṭîḇ (hey-teev) he treated well		בְּדָג	א.
bĕdāg (beh-dahg)	א.	הֵיטִיב	ב.
ṭeḇāʾ (TEH-vah)		וָו	ג.
ḥāgag (khah-gahg) he celebrated a feast		זָהָב	ד.
yāḇî (yah-vee)		חָגַג	ה.
beged (BEH-gehd) garment		טָבָא	ו.
zāhāḇ (zah-hav) gold		יֶאֱחָז	ז.
vāv (vahv)		בֶּגֶד	ח.
yeʾĕḥāz (yeh-eh-khahz)		יָבִי	ט.

0.2.1. Practice: Illustrated words beginning with ה, ו, or ז

Focus on words beginning with ה, ו, or ז. Pronounce the name of the initial letter as you locate the corresponding person object, or situation within the sketch. Then write that letter near the object.

4. Meaning	3. Transliteration	2. Word	1. Initial letter
splendor	hôd (hode)	הוֹד	ה
a woman who is walking	hôleket (hoe-LEH-khet)	הוֹלֶכֶת	
hush	has (hahss)	הַס	
mountain	har	הַר	
peg, nail	vāv (vahv)	וָו	ו
Vashti (Persian queen)	vaštî (vahsh-tee)	וַשְׁתִּי	
gold	zāhāb (zah-hahv)	זָהָב	ז
old	zāqēn (zah-kane)	זָקֵן	

0.2.1. Practice: Illustrated words beginning with ח, ט, or י

For this illustration, focus on words beginning with ח, ט, or י, labeling the objects with their respective initial letter. Say aloud the name of the initial letter as you label each object.

4. Meaning	3. Transliteration	2. Word	1. Initial letter
outside	ḥûṣ (khoots)	חוּץ	ח
strong	ḥāzāq (khah-zak)	חָזָק	
five	ḥāmēš (khah-maysh)	חָמֵשׁ	
good	ṭôḇ (tove)	טוֹב	ט
hand	yād (yahd)	יָד	י
child	yeled (YEH-led)	יֶלֶד	
sea	yām (yahm)	יָם	
moon	yārēaḥ (yah-RAY-akh)	יָרֵחַ	

MODULE 0.3   כ to ס, vowels, syllables (part 3)

0.3.א. Explanation: Vowels, part 3 (U/O-Class vowels)

Six vowels belong to the U/O-Class.

qameṣ-ḥaṭuf	ḥaṭef-qameṣ	šureq	qibbuṣ	ḥolem-vav	ḥolem	Vowel name
ָ	ֳ	וּ	ֻ	וֹ	ֹ	Vowel
o as in *remote*	*o* as in *remote*	*u* as in *lute*	*u* as in *lute*	*o* as in *mole*	*o* as in *mole*	Vowel sound
o	ŏ	û	u	ô	ō	Transliteration
מָ	מֳ	מוּ	מֻ	מוֹ	מֹ	Vowel written with consonant מ
mo	mŏ	mû	mu	mô	mō	Transliteration

Two of these vowels incorporate the symbol ו, yet they do not produce any *v* sound. They are the vowel ḥolem-vav (וֹ, pronounced *ô* as in *mole*) and the vowel šureq (וּ, pronounced *û* as in *lute*).[31]

The qameṣ-ḥaṭuf (ָ) is written the same as a standard qameṣ (ָ) but is pronounced *o*. This is a rare case where one symbol may have two pronunciations. Most often the qameṣ symbol represents an *ah* sound (not *o*).[32] Two features will help us recognize most of the circumstances when it should be pronounced as *o*.

1. When ָ appears in a syllable that is both **closed and unaccented**, it is a qameṣ-ḥaṭuf and so should be pronounced *o*.[33]

---

[31] For help in distinguishing וֹ as ḥolem-vav from וֹ as vav-plus-ḥolem, see below in §0.5.ג. The difference between וּ as šureq and וּ as vav-plus-dagesh is treated in §0.5.ד.

[32] The qameṣ that produces the *ah* sound is known simply as qameṣ, or more specifically as either qameṣ-gadol ("large qameṣ") or qameṣ-rahav ("broad qameṣ"), to distinguish it from the qameṣ pronounced *o*, known as qameṣ-ḥaṭuf (hurried / snatched qameṣ) or as qameṣ-qaṭan ("small qameṣ").

[33] To recognize closed syllables, see "Syllable division" in §0.4.ח.

2. When either a ◌ֳ (ḥatef-qameṣ) or another **qameṣ-ḥatuf follows** a ◌ָ, then that ◌ָ is a qameṣ-ḥatuf and so should be pronounced *o*.[34]

You will find that a handful of common words use the qameṣ-ḥatuf.[35] The following strategy may prove helpful: (a) memorize the frequently-occurring qameṣ-ḥatuf words as you encounter them, and (b) when in doubt, pronounce qameṣ vowels as *ah*. To help you develop good pronunciation habits more easily, qameṣ-ḥatuf vowels that appear in this textbook will regularly be highlighted by a note.

---

[34] E.g., the woman's name נָעֳמִי *noŏmî*. For a more complete discussion of the qameṣ-ḥatuf (or qameṣ-qaṭan, as some term it), see W. Weinberg, The *Qamāṣ Qāṭān* Structures," *Journal of Biblical Literature* 87 (1968), 151–65.

[35] By far the most common word employing a qameṣ-ḥatuf is כָּל־ *kol*, meaning *all* (as in כָּל־הַיּוֹם *kol-hayyôm* "all day long"). Can you distinguish which qameṣ is a qameṣ-ḥatuf in the following words: וַיָּ֫קָם *vayyaqom* "and he got up," וַיָּ֫מָת *vayyāmot* "and he died," וַיִּכְתָּב־שָׁ֫ם *vayyiktob-šām* "and he wrote there," and וַיִּשְׁמָרְךָ֫ *vayyišmorkā* "and he protected you"? Accents are displayed to show that the qameṣ-ḥatuf occurs in an unaccented syllable.

0.3.ב. Explanation: Consonants, part 3 (כ, ל, מ, נ, and ס)

Now let's focus on the consonants from כ to ס.

Trans-literation	Sound	Name	Final form	Letter
l	l	lamed		ל
m	m	mēm	ם	מ
n	n	nun	ן	נ
s	s	samekh		ס
ʿ	(voiced guttural)	ʿayin		ע
p	p	pē		פ
(f)	(f)	(fē)	(ף)	(פ)
ṣ	ts	ṣadē	ץ	צ
q	q	qof		ק
r	r	rēš		ר
š	sh	šîn		שׁ
ś	s	śîn		שׂ
t	t	tav		ת

Trans-literation	Sound	Name	Final form	Letter
ʾ	(glottal stop)	ʾalef		א
b	b	bēt		בּ
(b̲)	(v)	(vēt)		(ב)
g	g	gîmel		ג
d	d	dalet		ד
h	h	hē		ה
v	v	vav		ו
z	z	zayin		ז
ḥ	ḥ	ḥēt		ח
ṭ	t	ṭēt		ט
y	y	yod		י
k	k	kaf		כּ
(k̲)	(kh)	(khaf)	(ך)	(כ)

In this group of consonants we encounter another of the Beged-Kefet cluster: the letter כּ (or כ). When written with the dagesh, כּ is pronounced *k*. Lacking the dagesh, כ is pronounced with the roughness of *kh* (imitate the throaty sound of a cat hissing, or of a person clearing a particle from the mid-section of the tongue). As mentioned above under the letter ב, Beged-Kefet letters must have a dagesh when they begin a phrase or follow a closed syllable. When referred to apart from the context of a specific word, כ is spelled without the dagesh and is referred to by the letter name "kaf."[36]

---

[36] Concerning closed syllables, see "Syllable division," §0.4.ח., below.

0.3.ג. Explanation: Final forms (ך, ם, ן, ף, and ץ)

Perhaps you noticed that the letter כ may also be written ך. The form ך is called a "final form" since it is used whenever it appears as the last letter in a word. Final forms are simply an artistic variation of regular forms. They do not change the pronunciation or meaning of a word.

Here are all five letters having final forms, followed by a sample word showing their use. Notice that when writing final forms, the "tail" must extend **below** the line of writing (excepting ם).

Meaning of word	Word with final form	Final form	Initial form
to you	אֵלֶיךָ	ך	כּ (כ)
bread	לֶחֶם	ם	מ
he perceived	בִּין	ן	נ
silver	כֶּסֶף	ף	פּ (פ)
scoffer	לֵץ	ץ	צ

In the absence of any other ensuing vowel, a final ך is routinely followed by a silent sheva: ךְ....

0.3.ד. May I offer you advice? (Pronouncing names)   הַאִיעָצְךָ עֵצָה?

Several of the sample "syllables" you will encounter in the remainder of this unit are authentic Hebrew names. Your grasp of the sounds of Hebrew will advance significantly as you practice pronouncing these names with accuracy.

For example, when you encounter אָדָם, rather than pronouncing in English fashion, "Adam," read it with Hebrew vowel sounds and accentuation, *Ah-DAHM*. Remember: you are not reading English names written with Hebrew letters. Rather, you are reading Hebrew names *in Hebrew*.

0.3.ה. Practice: Pronouncing syllables

Here is another group of syllables for pronunciation practice. Read them repeatedly until you can pronounce them readily and with accuracy.

As before, cover the "Sounds like…" column, only revealing it after you have attempted to sound out the Hebrew word on your own. Note that כָּל־ in the second list is a closed, unaccented syllable.

Sounds like…	Syllables	Sounds like…	Syllables
nu (*nou*)	נֻ	*koh* (*coe*) thus	כֹּה
ŏ (*oh*)	עֳ	*lô* (*low*) to him	לוֹ
ḥŏ (*khoe*)	חֳ	*mō* (*moe*)	מֹ
nō (*no*)	נֹ	*nô* (*no*)	נוֹ
kol (*coal*) all [of]	כָּל־	*sô* (*so*)	סוֹ
ûḇênekā (*ou-vey-NEH-kha*) and among you	וּבֵינֶךָ	*ku* (*coo*)	כֻּ
bām (*bahm*) in them	בָּם	*sûs* (*sous*) horse	סוּס
yām (*yahm*) sea	יָם	*lu* (*lou*)	לֻ
sammîm (*sahmeem*) spices	סַמִּים	*mû* (*moo*)	מוּ

Several words in the next two exercises contain the vowel known as "sheva." As will be explained more fully in §0.4.ה., the sheva either has a very weak value (like the *a* in the English word *about*), or it will be silent. In the first exercise, the last entry (יְהוּדָה) employs a sheva in the first syllable, as do זְבֻלוּן and לְבָנוֹן in the the second exercise.

Match Hebrew "words" with entries in the "Sounds like…" column. In the answer column, write the letter corresponding to the appropriate Hebrew word. Item "א" again has been completed for you.

Sounds like…	Answer	Words	Alpha-numeral
ʾĕlōhîm (eh-low-heem) God or gods		בִּין	.א
bîn (bean) he perceived	.א	לָנוּ	.ב
lānû (LAH-nou) to us		אֱלֹהִים	.ג
kālēḇ (kah-leyv) [a man's name]		הֶבֶל	.ד
ʾahărōn [a man's name]		אָדָם	.ה
yĕhûdâ (yeh-hou-dah) [a tribe's name]		כָּלֵב	.ו
heḇel (HEH-vehl) [a man's name]		אַהֲרֹן	.ז
dān (dahn) [a tribe's name]		דָּן	.ח
ʾādām (ah-dahm) human [also a man's name]		יְהוּדָה	.ט

Here is another group for matching. You may recognize some of these names.

Sounds like…	Answer	Syllables	Alpha-numeral
lēvî (ley-vee) [a tribe's name]		לוֹט	.א
ʾăḇîgayil (ah-vee-GAH-yeel) [a woman's name]		לֵוִי	.ב
bāḇel (bah-vehl) [a city name]		זְבֻלוּן	.ג
zĕḇulûn (zeh-voo-loon) [a city name]		בָּבֶל	.ד
lôṭ (lote) [a man's name]	.א	אֲבִיגַיִל	.ה
sînay (see-nah-ee) [name of a mountain]		לְבָנוֹן	.ו
yônâ (yoh-nah) [a man's name]		סִינַי	.ז
lĕḇānôn (l'vah-known) [name of a country]		אִיזֶבֶל	.ח
ʾîzeḇel (ee-ZEH-vehl) [a woman's name]		יוֹנָה	.ט

0.3.1. Practice: Illustrated words beginning with כ or ל

Here are more illustrated words. These begin with either כ or ל. As before, practice pronouncing the initial letter as you write it alongside the corresponding part of the picture.

4. Meaning	3. Transliteration	2. Word	1. Initial letter
cup	*kôs* (*kohss*)	כּוֹס	כ
container	*kĕlî* (*k'lee*)	כְּלִי	
chair	*kissēʾ* (*kee-say*)	כִּסֵּא	
no, not	*lōʾ* (*low*)	לֹא	ל
bread, food	*leḥem* (*LEH-khem*)	לֶחֶם	
before, in front of	*lifnê* (*leaf-nay*)	לִפְנֵי	

0.3.ז. Practice: Illustrated words beginning with מ, נ, or ס

Watch for מ, נ, and ס—the initial letters featured in this group of illustrated words. Strengthen your grasp of the alphabet by labeling parts of the picture as you did with earlier illustrations.

4. Meaning	3. Transliteration	2. Word	1. Initial letter
water	*mayim* (MAH-yeem)	מַיִם	מ
king	*melek̲* (MEH-lekh)	מֶלֶךְ	
bitter	*mar*	מַר	
prophet	*nāb̲îʾ* (nah-vee)	נָבִיא	נ
river	*nāhār* (nah-har)	נָהָר	
Nineveh	*nînĕvēh* (nee-ne-vay)	נִינְוֵה	
hut, shelter	*sukâ* (soo-kah)	סֻכָּה	ס
book, scroll	*sēfer* (SAY-fehr)	סֵפֶר	

0.3.ח. Did you know that...? (City walls)   הֲיָדַעְתָּ כִּי...?

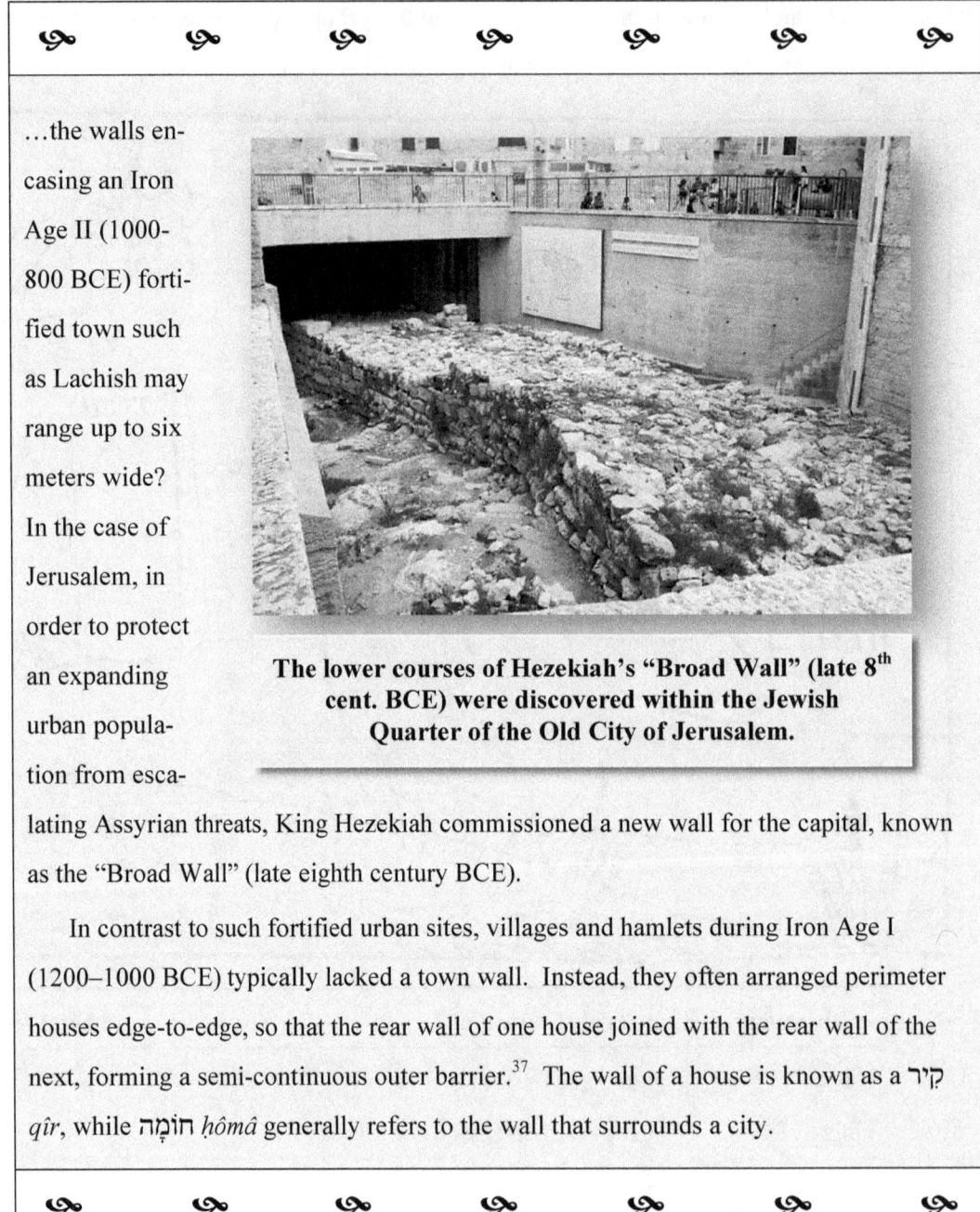

The lower courses of Hezekiah's "Broad Wall" (late 8th cent. BCE) were discovered within the Jewish Quarter of the Old City of Jerusalem.

...the walls encasing an Iron Age II (1000-800 BCE) fortified town such as Lachish may range up to six meters wide? In the case of Jerusalem, in order to protect an expanding urban population from escalating Assyrian threats, King Hezekiah commissioned a new wall for the capital, known as the "Broad Wall" (late eighth century BCE).

In contrast to such fortified urban sites, villages and hamlets during Iron Age I (1200–1000 BCE) typically lacked a town wall. Instead, they often arranged perimeter houses edge-to-edge, so that the rear wall of one house joined with the rear wall of the next, forming a semi-continuous outer barrier.[37] The wall of a house is known as a קִיר qîr, while חוֹמָה ḥômâ generally refers to the wall that surrounds a city.

---

[37] *LBI*, 219 and 231; cf. §0.1.ל.

MODULE 0.4 ע to ר, vowels, syllables (part 4)

0.4.א. Explanation: Dots within consonants, and consonants that resist them

There are three types of dots that commonly appear, centered within certain consonants: (a) the weak dagesh, (b) the strong dagesh, and (c) the mappiq.

- **A. First,** consider the **weak dagesh**. You have already encountered the weak dagesh, associated with **Beged-Kefet** letters, whenever they begin the first word of a new phrase or whenever they follow a closed syllable.[38] For example, the name of an Israelite spy in the Joshua account was כָּלֵב (note the dagesh), not כָלֵב. In addition, the most famous king of Israel was named דָּוִד, not דָוִד. This sort of dagesh is known as a **weak dagesh** or a "dagesh lene" (pronounced "dagesh leh-neh")

- **B.** The **second** type of dagesh may appear in nearly any consonant. It is not restricted to Beged-Kefet letters. Known as a **strong dagesh** (or "dagesh forte," pronounced "dagesh for-teh"), this second type serves as shorthand for **doubling** (or lengthening) of the consonant in which it appears. The doubling may be seen in transliteration (e.g., doubled middle ל in הִלֵּל *hil-lēl* and doubled מ in לִמֵּד *lim-mēd*). Today, few speakers of Hebrew attempt to articulate the doubled (or lengthened) letter when reading Hebrew aloud. Notice in the transliterations that no vowel is supplied between the doubled consonants, whether in the doubled *l* of *hil-lēl* or the doubled *m* of *lim-mēd*.[39]

    We say that the strong dagesh can appear in "nearly any consonant," since there is a handful of consonants that **resist** the strong dagesh: א, ה, ח, and ע. These consonants are known as

---

[38] See "Syllable division" in §0.4.ח., below.

[39] The dot in the נ of לְכָה־נָּא *please come* and in the ל of יְצַוֶּה־לָּךְ *he will command concerning you* is a third sort of dagesh. This dagesh is known as the **euphonic dagesh**. Often the euphonic dagesh will occur when a word **ending** in an unaccented syllable ◌ָה... or ◌ֶה... leads directly to a word that **begins** with an accented syllable. This particular type of euphonic dagesh is known as a "conjunctive dagesh." Like a strong dagesh, the euphonic dagesh is not restricted to Beged-Kefet letters (for more information, see GKC §20c-k and Joüon §18h). You will not be expected to know when to insert a euphonic dagesh; simply be aware that they do occur in the Hebrew Bible.

gutturals since they are produced in the back portion of the throat. The letter ר often behaves like a guttural, sharing with them the trait of resisting the strong dagesh. Consequently you will often find ר grouped with gutturals in an explanation of spellings.

Since the strong dagesh indicates that a consonant has **doubled**, and since it is physically difficult to pronounce a doubling (or lengthening) of gutturals, it comes as no surprise that these letters (with ר) would resist the dagesh.[40] Incidentally, gutturals also share another trait: they resist the sheva vowel, preferring an A-Class vowel instead.

C. The **third** type of dot appearing within certain consonants is known as a mappiq. In the Masoretic Text the mappiq appears only in the letter ה at the end of a word (hence the designation "mappiq-ה"). A mappiq in the letter ה serves to mark that ה as a genuine consonant that was originally part of that word or expression. In other words, when you discover a mappiq-ה you may be sure that this ה was not a vowel letter added later as a pronunciation aid (as in הֹ... endings). The mappiq preserves meaning. That is why a mappiq-ה will be retained as "h" when transliterated (notice "h" reflecting the mappiq-ה at the close of 'arṣāh [her land] and malkāh [her king], below)

In each of the following pairs of words, notice that the first word in a pair ends with a "**mappiq-ה**" (ה), while a related word below it does not. Although the mappiq does not affect the pronunciation, it is an important part of the spelling, for without it the meaning would change. A dagesh, on the other hand might change the pronunciation (compare פּ *p* with פ *f*), but will not change the meaning of a word.

Each mappiq-ה below has been marked with bold font to aid recognition. Bold font appearing within Hebrew words in this textbook does *not* signify the accented syllable.

her land	'ar-ṣāh	אַרְצָהּ	**With** mappiq-ה
toward (the) land	'ar-ṣâ	אַ֫רְצָה	**Without** mappiq-ה
her king	mal-kāh	מַלְכָּהּ	**With** mappiq-ה
a queen	mal-kâ	מַלְכָּה	**Without** mappiq-ה

---

[40] In lieu of doubling, gutturals and ר can effect either "compensatory lengthening" or "virtual doubling / gemination." On these, please see §2.1.א. in the appendix.

0.4.ב. Explanation: Consonants, Part 4 (ע, פ, צ, ק, and ר)

The next consonants are ע, פ, צ, ק, and ר.

Trans-literation	Sound	Name	Final form	Letter
l	l	lamed		ל
m	m	mēm	ם	מ
n	n	nun	ן	נ
s	s	samekh		ס
ʿ	(voiced guttural)	ʿayin		ע
p (f)	p (f)	pē (fē)	(ף)	פ (פ)
ṣ	ts	ṣadē	ץ	צ
q	q	qof		ק
r	r	rēš		ר
š	sh	šîn		שׁ
ś	s	śîn		שׂ
t	t	tav		ת

Trans-literation	Sound	Name	Final form	Letter
ʾ	(glottal stop)	ʾalef		א
b (b)	b (v)	bēt (vēt)		ב (ב)
g	g	gîmel		ג
d	d	dalet		ד
h	h	hē		ה
v	v	vav		ו
z	z	zayin		ז
ḥ	ḥ	ḥēt		ח
ṭ	t	ṭēt		ט
y	y	yod		י
k (k)	k (kh)	kaf (khaf)	(ך)	כ (כ)

The sound produced by the consonant ע issues from a place fairly deep within the throat. Imagine producing the *a* of *awkward* (or the *g* of *golf*) nearly at the point of swallowing.[41] When transliterating ע take care to use a **right**-facing single-quotation mark (ʿ), while reserving the **left**-facing single-quotation mark for the consonant א (ʾ).

The letter פ is the last of the Beged-Kefet letters. Like ב and כ, when written with a dagesh (פּ) it will stop the flow of air, producing the *p* sound. This form is referred to by the letter name "pē." Lacking a dagesh (פ) it produces the spirant *f* sound, and is referred to as the letter "fē." Having said that, it is

---

[41] C. Huart colorfully compares ע to "the guttural noise made by a camel being loaded with its pack saddle" (*Littérature Arabe* [Paris, 1902], 139, quoted in Joüon §5.l).

conventional when designating this letter apart from a specific word to write it simply, without the dagesh (פ), and to refer to this letter as "pē."

The letter צ resembles the sound *ts* at the end of *bats* or *boots*. While English does not generally begin a word with the sound *ts*, perhaps you have heard this sound in a European pronunciation of the Russian title "tsar" (when not pronounced simply as *zar*).

Similar to ע, the letter ק represents a *k* that is generated deep in the throat. Draw the base of the tongue back as you initiate the ק by briefly stopping the flow of air. If this is too difficult, you may begin by substituting the *k* sound.

When pronounced accurately, the letter ר will resemble a sustained ח, combined with a vibration of the vocal chords.[42] This may explain why ר shares certain principles together with guttural letters (א, ה, ח, and ע)—principles such as avoiding use of the dagesh.[43]

If the authentic pronunciation of ר is too difficult, you may substitute a short Spanish *r* (a single rolling of the *r* produced by touching the roof of the mouth behind upper teeth with the tip of the tongue). This sound will resemble the letter *d*, except that a ר will allow more air to pass when the tongue touches the roof of the mouth.

Notice that when writing the final forms ף and ץ, their tails must trail below the line of writing. The final forms are only calligraphic; they do not cause any change in pronunciation.

0.4.ג. Do you know how to read? ("ע" sometimes transliterated as "g")

הֲיָדַעְתָּ לִקְרֹא?

In casual transliteration, the consonant ע will normally be represented only by the vowel associated with it. Thus the primeval garden begins with עֵ and is transliterated "Eden" (notice the initial vowel "e," representing עֵ). Similarly, the king of Bashan (whom Joshua battled) was named עוֹג—transliterated "Og" (notice the initial vowel "o").

---

[42] This will resemble the French "*r*" of *rouge* or *rien*.

[43] Other traits of gutturals include preference for A-Class vowels and aversion to the sheva.

> Why, then, does the coastal city עַזָּה begin with a "g" ("Gaza") and not the vowel "a" ("Azah")? Words like "Gaza" reveal that the Phoenician alphabet (from which the Hebrew script was borrowed) was not able to represent all the distinct sounds audible in Israel and its neighboring countries.
>
> Hebrew possessed a regular ע sound similar to that found in Phoenician. In addition to this sound, Hebrew also had a sound resembling a rough "r." That is the sound found at the beginning of the word "Gaza." Arabic dedicates a distinct consonant to this rough *r*, calling it "*ghayn*." In the Hebrew script, however, the symbol ע was employed to represent both *ghayn* and *ʽayin*.
>
> In an effort to distinguish between the two, it has become conventional to transliterate historic *ghayn* words with "g." For another such example, look up the Hebrew spelling of the place that has been transliterated as "Gomorrah" (cf. Isa. 1:10).

0.4.ד. Explanation: Simple and compound shevas

Four vowels are known as "half vowels": the sheva alone (ְ, known as the "simple sheva") and three more that combine the sheva with another vowel ("compound shevas").[44] The compound shevas you have learned already. They correspond to each of the three vowel classes (A-Class ֲ ḥatef-pataḥ, I/E-Class ֱ ḥatef-segol, and U/O-Class ֳ ḥatef-qameṣ). Compound shevas serve as reduced vowels, providing for each class of vowels a shorter version of vowel within that class. Thus a shorter version of ַ would be ֲ.[45]

---

[44] "Sheva" is pronounced *sheh-VAH*.

[45] See the corresponding appendix segment regarding circumstances when a syllable may shift from a full vowel to a reduced vowel in the same class ("vowel reduction"), especially propretonic and pretonic reduction.

Technically, the sound produced by a compound sheva should be shorter than that of its corresponding full vowel. This pronunciation distinction is no longer maintained. Here are several words employing compound shevas.[46]

U/O-Class ◌ ḥaṭef-qameṣ	I/E-Class ◌ ḥaṭef-segol	A-Class ◌ ḥaṭef-pataḥ
אֳנִיָּה	יֶאֱרֹב	[47]לַחֲטוֹף
ʾŏ-niy-yâ	ye-ʾĕ-rōḇ	la-ḥă-ṭôf
a ship	he will lie in ambush	to seize

0.4.ה. Explanation: The simple sheva (part 1)

The sheva (◌) is the last vowel to be studied. A sheva produces either little sound (**vocal sheva**) or none at all (**silent sheva**), depending on the sort of syllable in which it appears.

When it is **vocal**, a sheva produces a very short and indeterminate sound, such as the sound produced by the letter *e* in the word *current*, by the letter *a* in *above*, or the *o* in *cannon*. As to vowel-class, it serves as a short vowel for all three classes. Although sharing with ◌ the transliteration symbol ĕ, it would be wise to develop a habit of pronouncing a vocal ◌ with a sound that is even more colorless than ◌, as the second vowels in *current*, *above*, and *cannon* would suggest.[48]

This segment presents **two principles** to help you recognize when the sheva makes a small sound (the **vocal** sheva).[49] A third vocal sheva principle will follow later.

---

[46] Technically a vocal sheva (simple or compound) does not merit a syllable of its own, but rather is joined to the next. To foster proper pronunciation, this textbook treats vocal shevas as separate syllables (cf. GKC §26m).

[47] A *ḥaṭef* vowel is a "seized" or restrained vowel.

[48] It may be helpful to associate ◌ with the phonetic value represented by ə (shewa).

[49] "Mobile sheva" is another term for the vocal sheva.

1. **First in a word.** When a sheva follows the initial consonant of a word it is **vocal**. Otherwise, that initial consonant would be inaudible. Here are several words featuring a sheva after the first consonant.

דְּבָרִים	יְהוּדָה	מְלָכִים	לְמוּאֵל	גְּבוּל
dĕ-bâ-rîm	yĕ-hû-dâ	mĕ-lā-kîm	lĕ-mû-ʾēl	gĕ-bûl
words	(tribe name)	kings	(man's name)	border

Words in this segment are transliterated with hyphens to indicate syllable divisions (syllabification). How syllabification simplifies reading will be explained more fully in §0.4.ח.

2. **Second in a pair.** When a pair of sheva vowels appears adjacent to each other, the first is silent while **the second is vocal**.

יִמְצְאוּ	יִסְפְּרוּ	יִזְכְּרוּ	יִמְלְכוּ	לַחְמְךָ
yim-ṣĕ-ʾû	yis-pĕ-rû	yiz-kĕ-rû	yim-lĕ-kû	laḥ-mĕ-kā
they will find	they will count	they will remember	they will rule	your bread

Silent sheva vowels are not transliterated. The sheva following מ in יִמְצְאוּ is silent. Thus the first syllable of יִמְצְאוּ is rendered *yim*, not *yimĕ*.[50]

There is another circumstance related to dagesh pairs: a sheva that follows a consonant containing a **doubling** dagesh (*dagesh forte*). A symbol such as זּ stands for זְזְ—two identical consonants with a pair of adjacent sheva vowels. Since the **second** of two **adjacent** sheva vowels is **vocalized**, the complete sound produced by זּ will be *zĕ*.[51] For dagesh-plus-sheva examples, please refer to the next table. Note especially the extra row (labeled "Pronunciation") to learn how these words should be vocalized.

---

[50] A silent sheva is also known as a "quiescent sheva."

[51] There are a handful of Hebrew speakers who helpfully articulate doubled letters with such precision that you can detect a slight lengthening or doubling of the consonant. But this is quite rare.

מְסַפְּרִים	סִפְּרוּ	דִּבְּרוּ	יְדֻבְּרוּ	יְחַזְּקוּ	Word
mĕ-sa-pĕ-rîm	si-pĕ-rû	di-bĕ-rû	yĕ-du-bĕ-rû	yĕ-ha-zĕ-qû	Pronunciation
mĕ-sap-pĕ-rîm	sip-pĕ-rû	dib-bĕ-rû	yĕ-dub-bĕ-rû	yĕ-haz-zĕ-qû	Transliteration
ones who recount	they recounted	they spoke	they will be spoken	they will strengthen	Meaning

Occasionally a double sheva appears at the **end** of a word. In such cases, **both** shevas are **silent**, as evident from the transliterations in the following examples.[52] These examples include two consonants not yet introduced: שׁ š [sh] and ת t.

נָפַלְתְּ	אָהַבְתְּ	וַיֵּשְׁתְּ	נֵרְדְּ[53]	וַיֵּבְךְּ
nā-falt	'ā-ha<u>b</u>t	vay-yēšt	nērd	vay-yē<u>b</u>k
you fell	you loved	and he drank	nard	and he wept

As noted earlier, a sheva symbol always appears in a final כ (ךְ) when no other vowel is present. This sheva is silent and is not transliterated (e.g., אֵילֵךְ 'ê-lē<u>k</u>).

The next segment will explain how to distinguish between long and short vowels. This skill, in turn, will further enable us to distinguish vocal from silent shevas.

0.4.1. Explanation: Long and short vowels

Vowels of all classes fall into three groups according to length. They may be long, short, or half vowels. First, consider long vowels. We have met them already, class-by-class. Now we will distinguish them according to length.

---

[52] The collision of consonants at the end of these words creates a rare violation of the rule discouraging adjacent consonants without intervening vowels.

[53] You may have heard of this perfume, prized in the ancient world, also known as "spikenard."

Long Vowels[54]

O-Class	U-Class	E-Class	I-Class	A-Class
ֹ and וֹ	וּ	ֵ and ֵי	ִי	[55] ָ and ָה

Short vowels comprise the next group.

Short Vowels

O-Class	U-Class	E-Class	I-Class	A-Class
[56] ָ	ֻ	ֶ	ִ	ַ

Both long and short vowels are known as "full vowels." The remaining vowels are half vowels, consisting of the sheva alone ("simple sheva") and various compound shevas. Half vowels are even shorter than so-called short vowels.

Half Vowels

General	U/O-Class	I/E-Class	A-Class
ְ	ֳ	ֱ	ֲ

To simplify learning, concentrate only on the first group—those known as long vowels. Recognizing long vowels will help us identify vocal shevas. This, in turn, helps to determine where syllables will divide. Syllabification can be a great aid when reading aloud.

0.4.ז. Explanation: The simple sheva (part 2)

In Part 1 of the sheva explanation (§0.4.ה.) we discovered these two rules for the vocal sheva:

---

[54] Of the "long vowels," the following are not subject to vowel reduction, and so are called "unchangeably long": ִי, ֵי, וּ, וֹ, and sometimes ֹ. "Changeably long" include ֵ, ָ, and ֹ. On occasion ִ, and ֶ may be long.

[55] Regular qameṣ (qameṣ-gadol).

[56] Qameṣ-ḥaṭuf (pronounced *o*).

1. **First in a word.** An initial sheva is **vocal**. Thus the name לְמוּאֵל is rendered *lĕ-mû-ʾēl*, not *lmû-ʾēl* (King Lemuel of Prov. 31:1).

2. **Second in a pair.** The second of two adjacent sheva vowels is **vocal**, while the first is silent. Thus יִפְדְיָה is rendered *yif-dĕ-yâ*, not *yi-fĕd-yâ* or *yi-fĕ-dĕ-yâ* (Iphdeiah of the tribe of Benjamin, 1 Chron. 8:25).

Now we will add a third vocal sheva rule.

3. **Following a long vowel.** A third principle involves syllables containing a long vowel (◌ָ, ◌ָה, ◌ֹ, ◌ִי, ◌ֵי, ◌ֹ, וֹ, or וּ) when followed by a sheva. When a syllable with a long vowel is followed by a consonant with sheva, the sheva is **vocal**.

Consider the word הוֹלְכִים, where a long vowel (וֹ) leads to a sheva. The long vowel in the syllable הוֹ (*hô*) dictates that the sheva of לְ will be vocal (*lĕ*): הוֹ-לְ-כִים *hô-lĕ-kîm*.

Here are more examples including long vowels from the various vowel classes. Begin by locating the sheva (there may be more than one). Then notice whether the preceding vowel is a long vowel. If long, the ensuing sheva will be vocal. Syllabification will aid in this process (see rows with hyphens).

Vocal sheva after long vowel				
U-Class	O-Class	I-Class	E-Class	A-Class
וּ	◌ֹ and וֹ	◌ִי	◌ֵ and ◌ֵי	[57] ◌ָ
בְּשׁוּבְכֶם	יוֹרְדִים	בַּהֲרִימְכֶם	יֵלְכוּ	יָדְךָ
בְּ-שׁוּ-בְ-כֶם	יוֹ-רְ-דִים	בַּ-הֲ-רִי-מְ-כֶם	יֵ-לְ-כוּ	יָ-דְ-ךָ
bĕ-šû-bĕ-kem	*yô-rĕ-dîm*	*ba-hă-rî-mĕ-kem*	*yē-lĕ-kû*	*yā-dĕ-kā*
when you return	ones who descend	when you raise up	they will go	your hand

To illustrate the opposite of "**vocal** sheva after **long** vowel," notice what happens when a sheva follows a **short** vowel. The sheva is **silent**.

---

[57] Regular qameṣ.

Silent sheva after short vowel		
U/O-Class	I/E-Class	A-Class
Sheva after ָֹ[58]	Sheva after ִ	Sheva after ַ
אָזְנְךָ	מִגְדָּל	כְּאַרְיֵה
אָזְ־נְךָ	מִגְ־דָּל	כְּ־אַרְיֵה
'oz-nĕ-kā	mig-dāl	kĕ-'ar-yē
your ear	a tower	like a lion

To summarize, the three rules for the **vocal** sheva may be expressed as: "**first in a word, second in a pair, following a long vowel.**"

0.4.ח. Explanation: Syllable division

After becoming comfortable with the Hebrew script, the single skill most helpful for smooth vocalization is the ability to segment longer words into syllables. Two basic principles govern syllable formation in Hebrew: how syllables **begin** and how they **end**.

1. All syllables must **begin with a consonant** (C), followed immediately by a vowel (v).[59] Syllables may **end** in one of two ways: either **closed** or **open**.

2. **Closed** syllables not only begin with a consonant, but also end with a consonant. The closed syllable, גַּד, for example, begins with the consonant ג, follows with the vowel ַ, and ends with the consonant ד. A closed syllable may be represented as CvC.

Often the second consonant in a closed syllable will be followed by a silent sheva, sometimes called a "syllable divider."[60] In the case of the "double sheva words" listed earlier, the first sheva

---

[58] Qameṣ-ḥaṭuf is a short O/U-Class vowel, pronounced o (see §0.3.א.).

[59] One spelling of the conjunction "and" consists only of the vowel וּ. This may be prefixed to a word, and comprises the sole exception to the rule requiring that syllables begin with a consonant.

[60] GKC §10.

in each case was a silent sheva, operating as a syllable marker (§0.4.ה., #2). Here are those words, again. By referring to the transliterations beneath each word you may see the syllabification.

לַחְמְךָ	יִמְלְכוּ	יִזְכְּרוּ	יִסְפְּרוּ	יִמְצְאוּ
laḥ-mĕ-ḵā	yim-lĕ-ḵû	yiz-kĕ-rû	yis-pĕ-rû	yim-ṣĕ-'û
your food	they will rule	they will remember	they will count	they will find

A lone silent sheva may likewise act as a syllable marker, as in these next examples (see also examples in the table above, "Silent sheva after short vowel," §0.4.ז.).

מַלְכִּי	כַּסְפָּם	חַרְבִּי	עַבְדְּךָ	רַגְלֶךָ
mal-kî	kas-pām	ḥar-bî	'ab-de-ḵā	rag-le-ḵā[61]
my king	their silver	my sword	your servant	your foot

3. In contrast, **open** syllables end with no additional consonant. They consist only of consonant-plus-vowel (Cv). For example, לִי begins with the consonant ל and ends with the vowel ִי. Since there is no additional closing consonant, לִי forms an open syllable (Cv).[62]

4. Note: As a rule, **long vowels** require either **an open** syllable or a **closed-and-accented** syllable. As a reminder, the following are long vowels: ָ, ָה, ֵ, ֵי, ִי, ֹ, ו, and וּ.

   Short vowels, on the other hand, appear in **closed-and-unaccented** syllables. They may also appear in open syllables (though less often than would long vowels).[63]

The next table offers some examples of words that have been divided into syllables. They contain both open and closed syllables. To help you distinguish closed from open, the **open** syllables have been marked by **bold type** in the transliteration (without regard to accented syllables).

---

[61] Are you remembering to stress the accented syllable as indicated by the chevron symbol, even when not reflected in the transliteration (*rag-LE-ḵā* and *'av-DE-ḵā*)?

[62] See appendix for examples and further explanation of open syllables.

[63] For a fuller treatment of syllable formation and vowel length, see GKC §26, also Joüon §28.

Word	גָּד	לִי	דָּן	בָּנָה	נָבָל	אֲבִיגַיִל
Syllabification	גָּד	לִי	דָּן	בָּ־נָה	נָ־בָל	אֲ־בִי־גַיִל
Transliteration	gād	lî	dān	bā-nâ	nā-<u>b</u>āl	'ă-<u>b</u>î-ga-yil
Translation	(*tribe name*)	to me	(*tribe name*)	he built	foolish	(*woman's name*)

And here are several more.

Word	דָּנִיֵּאל	אִיזֶבֶל	הִלֵּל	לִמֵּד
Syllabification	דָּ־נִי־אֵל	אִי־זֶ־בֶל	הִלּ־לֵל	לִמּ־מֵד
Transliteration	dā-nî-'ēl	'î-ze-<u>b</u>el	hil-lēl	lim-mēd
Translation	(*man's name*)	(*woman's name*)	he praised	he taught

After studying these examples, review them by covering all but the top row. Use vertical lines to divide each word into syllables. Draw a circle around open syllables. For more practice, turn to the word tables in the earlier segments concerning the sheva vowel (§§0.4.ז. and 0.4.ה.). Cover all but the top row and see if you can correctly divide the words into syllables.

0.4.ט. Practice: Pronouncing syllables

Here are some syllables to help you learn the new group of letters. For rapid recognition, the approximate sound is provided alongside strict transliteration in the "Sounds like" column. The list on the right is limited to single-syllables. The group on the left is polysyllabic.

To help you read with greater ease, practice dividing words in the polysyllabic group into syllables, beginning with עִירוֹ. Cover the far-left column labeled "Syllabification." After dividing a word into syllables, check your answer against the far-left column.

Syllabifi-cation	Sounds like…	Syllables	Sounds like…	Syllables
עִי־רוֹ	'îrô (eeroh) his city	עִירוֹ	'a (ah)	עַ
פְּ־דוּ־יִם	pĕdûyim (peh-dou-yeem) ransom	פְּדוּיִם	pā (pah)	פָּ
נִפְ־לְ־גָה	niflĕgâ (neef-leh-gah) it was separated	נִפְלְגָה	fă (fah)	פֳ
צֶ־לֶם	ṣelem (TSEH-lehm) statue, idol	צֶלֶם	ṣi (tsee)	צִ
קָרְ־בָּן	qorbān (kor-bahn) offering, gift	קָרְבָּן[64]	qe (keh)	קֶ
רָ־צוֹן	rāṣôn (rah-tsone) favor, pleasure	רָצוֹן	ra (rah)	רָ

Practice sounding-out the collection of names found in the next table. As noted earlier, Hebrew script does not distinguish between upper and lower case. With the "Syllabification" column covered, practice dividing into syllables the words found in the "Names" columns. Some of the names refer to people, others refer to places.

Syllabifi-cation	Sounds like…	Names	Syllabifi-cation	Sounds like…	Names
לְ־בָ־נוֹן	lĕbānôn (levah-known)	לְבָנוֹן	יִצְ־חַק	yiṣ-ḥaq (yeets-khaq)	יִצְחָק
בִּלְ־עָם	bil'am (beel-ahm)	בִּלְעָם	יַ־עֲ־קֹב	ya'ăqōb (yah-ah-kove)	יַעֲקֹב
יְ־רִ־חוֹ	yĕriḥô (yeh-ree-kho)	יְרִחוֹ	רָ־חֵל	rāḥēl (rah-kheyl)	רָחֵל
רִבְ־קָה	ribqâ (reev-kah)	רִבְקָה	דְּ־בֹ־רָה	dĕbōrâ (de-vo-rah)	דְּבֹרָה
אֶפְ־רַ־יִם	'efrayim (ef-RAH-yeem)	אֶפְרַיִם	עֵ־דֶן	'ēden (ey-dehn)	עֵדֶן
בֹּ־עַז	bō'az (boh-ahz)	בֹּעַז	קַ־יִן	qāyin (KAH-yeen)	קַיִן
חַ־בַקְ־קוּק	ḥabaqqûq (khah-vah-kook)	חֲבַקּוּק	כְּ־נַ־עַן	kĕna'an (keh-NAH-ahn)	כְּנַעַן

Once again, sharpen your grasp of Hebrew script by matching Hebrew names on the right with pronunciations given on the left. Push yourself to pronounce each word first by covering the "Sounds like" column. Then write in the answer column the letter corresponding to the appropriate Hebrew name.

---

[64] Note that the *first* ָ is a qameṣ-ḥatuf since it occurs in a closed, unaccented syllable.

UNIT 0   א...ב...   51

Sounds like…	Answer	Names	Alpha-numeral
karmel [name of a mountain]		גִּדְעוֹן	א.
malkî-ṣedeq (mahlki-TSEH-dehk)		יוֹסֵף	ב.
miṣrayim (meets-RAH-yim) Egypt		כַּרְמֶל	ג.
yôsēf (yo-safe)		מַלְכִּי־צֶדֶק	ד.
gid ʿôn (geed-ohn)	א.	מִצְרַיִם	ה.
pĕlā ʾyâ (peh-lah-yah)		עָמוֹס	ו.
rĕ ʾûḇēn (reh-oo-veyn)		פְּלָאיָה	ז.
ʿamôs (ah-mohss)		צִיּוֹן	ח.
ṣiyyôn (tsee-yown) [name of a mountain and a city]		רְאוּבֵן	ט.

Now take those same names and practice dividing them into syllables. Cover the columns so that only the first word is visible (יוֹסֵף). Using vertical stroke(s), divide it into syllables (יוֹ|סֵף). Check your answer by revealing the next word, together with the answer to the יוֹסֵף question.

	עָמוֹס	מַלְכִּי־צֶדֶק	כַּרְמֶל	יוֹסֵף
עָ־מוֹס		מַל־כִּי־צֶ־דֶק	כַּר־מֶל	יוֹ־סֵף

	גִּדְעוֹן	רְאוּבֵן	צִיּוֹן	פְּלָאיָה
גִּדְ־עוֹן		רְ־אוּ־בֵן	צִי־יוֹן	פְּ־לָא־יָה

As noted earlier, any consonant-plus-vocal-sheva (whether simple or compound) technically should be portrayed as joining with the next syllable (rather than comprising an independent syllable). Thus פְּלָאיָה would more strictly be syllabified as פְּלָא־יָה. In this textbook, a vocal sheva is given its own syllable as an aid to vocalization.

0.4.י. Practice: Illustrated words beginning with ע or פ

In the next sketch, look for items beginning either with ע or פ. Once again, practice learning these letters by labeling parts of the picture with the initial letter of objects found in the list below.

4. Meaning	3. Transliteration	2. Word	1. Initial letter
servant	ʿe̱bed (EH-vehd)	עֶבֶד	ע
city	ʿîr (ear)	עִיר	
people	ʿām (ahm)	עָם	
tree	ʿēṣ (eyts)	עֵץ	
mouth	peh	פֶּה	פ
fruit	pĕrî (p'ree)	פְּרִי	

0.4.ב. Practice: Illustrated words beginning with צ, ק, or ר

Words beginning with צ, ק, and ר are featured in the next sketch. As you pronounce the letter names when labeling parts of the picture, your mind will internalize the alphabet more deeply.

4. Meaning	3. Transliteration	2. Word	1. Initial letter
head	rōʾš (rohsh)	רֹאשׁ	ר
foot	regel (REH-gehl)	רֶגֶל	
pursuer	rôdēf (roe-deyf)	רוֹדֵף	
shepherd	rôʿeh (roe-eh)	רוֹעֶה	
soft	ra<u>k</u> (rakh)	רַךְ	
hungry	raʿē<u>b</u> (rah-eyv)	רָעֵב	

4. Meaning	3. Transliteration	2. Word	1. Initial letter
flock	ṣōʾn (tsown)	צֹאן	צ
distress	ṣar (tsar)	צַר	
voice, sound	qôl (coal)	קוֹל	ק
small	qāṭôn (kah-tone)	קָטוֹן	
hard	qāšeh (kah-sheh)	קָשֶׁה	

MODULE 0.5   שׂ to ת, vowels, syllables (part 5)

0.5.א. Explanation: Consonants, part 5 (שׁ, שׂ, and ת)

The last consonants are שׁ, שׂ, and ת.

Trans-literation	Sound	Name	Final form	Letter
l	l	lamed		ל
m	m	mēm	ם	מ
n	n	nun	ן	נ
s	s	samekh		ס
ʿ	(voiced guttural)	ʿayin		ע
p	p	pē		פ
(f)	(f)	(fē)	(ף)	(פ)
ṣ	ts	ṣadē	ץ	צ
q	q	qof		ק
r	r	rēš		ר
š	sh	šîn		שׁ
ś	s	śîn		שׂ
t	t	tav		ת

Trans-literation	Sound	Name	Final form	Letter
ʾ	(glottal stop)	ʾalef		א
b	b	bēt		ב
(b)	(v)	(vēt)		(ב)
g	g	gîmel		ג
d	d	dalet		ד
h	h	hē		ה
v	v	vav		ו
z	z	zayin		ז
ḥ	ḥ	ḥēt		ח
ṭ	t	ṭēt		ט
y	y	yod		י
k	k	kaf		כ
(k)	(kh)	(khaf)	(ך)	(כ)

Two pairs of consonants share equivalent sounds. The sound produced by שׂ (transliterated as *ś*) is the same as that produced by ס (transliterated as *s*). Some Hebrew words are attested with both spellings (e.g., כַּעַס and כַּעַשׂ both mean *irritation*).

Similarly, ת (*t*) will sound the same as ט (*t*). In Arabic, the letter corresponding to ט will display a more throaty texture. Perhaps it did in Hebrew as well, in ancient times (cf. Joüon §51i and m).

0.5.ב. Explanation: ח and ע, with a ◌ֲ vowel

Whenever a pataḥ follows the letters ח or ע as the last consonant of a word, a special rule affects pronunciation. The vowel is pronounced *before* the consonant rather than after it.[65] Thus in the word רוּחַ *rûaḥ* (spirit), the pataḥ is pronounced after וּ but before the ח (*rûaḥ* rather than *rûḥa*[‡66]). Similarly the name of the Genesis flood hero, נֹחַ, is pronounced *nō-aḥ*, not *nō-ḥa*.[‡]

Examples with the letter ע include רֵעַ (pronounced *rēaʿ*, not *rēʿa*[‡]) and מַדּוּעַ (rendered *maddûaʿ*, not *maddûʿa*[‡]). To remind us of this unusual pronunciation rule, Masoretes wrote the pataḥ symbol slightly to the right of the ח or ע, rather than directly under it.

0.5.ג. Explanation: Distinguishing forms of וֹ

The ḥolem-vav **vowel** may be confused with situations where the ו **consonant** is followed by a ḥolem vowel. Both may appear as וֹ.[67]

There is a simple way to distinguish these symbols. When you encounter וֹ, examine the consonant immediately preceding the וֹ. Does it already have a vowel? If it already has a vowel, then that preceding consonant is not depending on the ensuing וֹ to serve as its vowel. Hebrew syllables do not place two vowels next to each other. Therefore, when **וֹ is preceded by a vowel**, the symbol וֹ must represent the **consonant ו** plus a ḥolem vowel.

Consider the word עָוֹן *ʿāvôn*. Preceding וֹ is a vowel—a qameṣ. Since Hebrew does not allow syllables with adjacent vowels [CvvC] such as a qameṣ followed by a ḥolem-vav, therefore the וֹ in עָוֹן must

---

[65] This is known as a furtive pataḥ.

[66] The double-dagger symbol ‡ indicates that the word in question is strictly hypothetical, and would not appear in Biblical Hebrew.

[67] Some fonts print vav-consonant-plus-ḥolem showing the ḥolem on the left tip of the vav (וֹ *vō*), while the ḥolem-vav vowel places the ḥolem centered above the vav (וֹ *ô*).

comprise the consonant ו plus ḥolem vowel. Thus עָוֺן is a two-syllable word (עָ־וֺן), pronounced 'ā-vôn (not 'ā-ôn‡).

Ḥolem-vav (strictly the vowel וֹ)		Consonant vav plus ḥolem (ו consonant plus ◌ֹ vowel)	
gid'ôn (a man's name)	גִּדְעוֹן	'āvōn, iniquity	עָוֺן
yôšēḇ, one who dwells	יוֹשֵׁב	'ăvōnô, his iniquity	עֲוֺנוֹ

0.5.ד. Explanation: Distinguishing forms of וּ

Just as וֹ may refer to either of two phonetic values, so also when we encounter וּ we need to determine which of two phonetic values it represents. Is וּ representing the consonant ו-plus-strong-dagesh (vv)? Or does it represent the šureq vowel (û)? Consider the examples below.

The same strategy used earlier to distinguish between the two values of וֹ will now help us differentiate between וּ as consonant-plus-dagesh versus וּ as šureq. Examine the consonant immediately preceding the וּ. Does it already have a vowel? If so (as with pataḥ accompanying ע in עַוָּה), then וּ must serve as the next consonant (vv in 'avvâ). If not (note lack of any vowel other than וּ after א in רְאוּבֵן), then וּ must serve that consonant as its vowel (û in rĕ'ûḇēn).

Šureq (strictly the vowel וּ)		Consonant vav plus dagesh (ו consonant plus ◌ּ dagesh)	
rĕ'ûḇēn (not rĕ'-vv-ḇēn‡) [a man's name]	רְאוּבֵן	'avvâ (not 'aûâ‡) ruin	עַוָּה
kātĕḇû (not kātēḇ-vv‡) they wrote	כָּתְבוּ	'ivvāda' (not 'iûāda‡) I will become known	אִוָּדַע
ûḇĕyāḏ (not vv-ḇĕyāḏ‡) and in a hand	וּבְיָד	yivvālēḏ (not yiûālēḏ‡) he will be born	יִוָּלֵד

0.5.ה. Do you know how to read? (שׁ and ס) הֲיָדַעְתָּ לִקְרֹא?

The ability to distinguish a שׁ from ס was, in one instance, a life-preserving skill! Gileadite warriors had captured a river crossing on the Jordan and set up a checkpoint to intercept and kill any fleeing Ephraimite soldiers. However, what if a river-crosser—when challenged—claimed to be a non-Ephraimite? How could you tell whether he was telling the truth?

A simple test was administered: they would require the river-crosser to pronounce the word שִׁבֹּלֶת. If he could only say סִבֹּלֶת, he was exposed as an imposter and would be put to death, for Ephraimites could not form the שׁ sound. You may read the full account in Judg. 12:1-7.[68]

A question to ponder: how would you translate this story if the language you were translating into was a language that, like Ephraimite speech, could not distinguish "s" from "sh"? Greek is one such language. When translators of the Septuagint encountered this dilemma long ago, they solved it creatively by substituting for שִׁבֹּלֶת a Greek term meaning "password."

---

[68] The fact that this account spells the alternate pronunciation with the letter ס (in סִבֹּלֶת), rather than using a שׁ symbol (which would have resulted in שִׂבֹּלֶת) may indicate that at the time when this story was written down, the system of raised points for distinguishing two sounds associated with the glyph שׁ had not yet been devised. To transmit the story clearly the writer needed to use an unmistakable symbol, so used the consonant with an unmistakable value. Only ס could communicate the difference clearly. By the way, the word שִׁבֹּלֶת refers to a flowing stream or a torrent of water. Perhaps the interrogator pointed to the stream at the ford and asked, מַה־זֶּה? *What is this?*

0.5.1. Explanation: When a ◌ֹ vowel is adjacent to שׁ

Compare the two spellings: מֹשֶׁה and מֹשֶׁה. Both are pronounced *mōše* ("Moses"). In the second, however, the ḥolem (◌ֹ) after מ has joined with the raised dot of the *following* שׁ in a single dot.

Similarly, compare שֹׂנֵא and שֹׂנֵא. Both are pronounced *śōnē'* ("one who hates"). Once again, a ḥolem (◌ֹ) has joined with a dot above a שׂ—this time a *preceding* שׂ. These writing conventions are a sort of shorthand; they involve no change in meaning. Don't be surprised if you encounter them in a dictionaries (called "lexica," such as Brown-Driver-Briggs) or concordances (such as Even-Shoshan).

0.5.2. Practice: Pronouncing syllables

Here again are syllables and words using the new letters. The group on the right is monosyllabic. After covering the two columns on the left, see whether you can divide the polysyllabic words according to syllables, beginning with שָׁמָּה.

Syllabification	Sounds like…	Syllables	Sounds like…	Syllables
שָׁמְ־מָה	*šāmmâ* (SHAHM-mah) there, thence	שָׁמָּה	*šâ* (shah)	שָׁה
שִׂים	*śîm* (seem) put	שִׂים	*śa* (sah)	שַׂ
תָּ־עָה	*tā'â* (tah-ah) he wandered	תָּעָה	*tō* (toe)	תֹּ
הִתְ־פַּלְ־לֵל	*hitpallēl* (hit-pah-leyl) he intervened	הִתְפַּלֵּל	*tî* (tee)	תִּי

How many of the names in this next group can you recognize? Continue to aim for accurate Hebrew pronunciation, rather than relying on familiar patterns of your native language (thus pronounce יִתְרוֹ as *yitrô*, not "Jethro").

Syllabification	Sounds like…	Names	Syllabification	Sounds like…	Names
יִתְ־רוֹ	yitrô (yeet-row)	יִתְרוֹ	בֵּית לֶ־חֶם	bêt leḥem (beyt-LEH-khem)	בֵּית לֶחֶם
שָׂ־רָה	śārâ (sah-rah)	שָׂרָה	אַבְ־שָׁ־לֹם	ʾab̲šālōm[69] (av-sha-loam)	אַבְשָׁלֹם
אֶסְ־תֵּר	ʾestēr (es-tayr)	אֶסְתֵּר	יְ־הוֹ־שׁוּ־עַ	yĕhôšûaʿ (yeh-ho-shu-ah)	יְהוֹשׁוּעַ
שִׁמְ־שׁוֹן	šimšôn (sheem-shone)	שִׁמְשׁוֹן	שְׁ־לֹ־מֹה	šĕlōmōh (sheh-low-mow)	שְׁלֹמֹה

In the next table, see how accurately you can match Hebrew names with corresponding transliterations on the left.

Sounds like…	Answer	Names	Alpha-numeral
golyat (goal-yacht)		אָשֵׁר	א.
šĕmûʾēl (shʾmoo-ale)		גָּלְיַת	ב.
mošeh (mow-sheh)		יִשְׂרָאֵל	ג.
ʿēśāv (ay-sahv)		מְנַשֶּׁה	ד.
yiśrāʾēl (yees-rah-ale)		מֹשֶׁה	ה.
mĕnāšeh (mʾnah-sheh)		עֵשָׂו	ו.
ʾāšēr (ah-shayr)	א.	שְׁמוּאֵל	ז.

---

[69] The sheva in אַבְשָׁלֹם closes the first syllable אַבְ... and so is silent. The same is true with the shevas in יִתְרוֹ, אֶסְתֵּר, and שִׁמְשׁוֹן. Silent shevas do not need to be shown in transliteration.

0.5.ח. Practice: Illustrated words beginning with שׁ, שׂ, or ת

The final alphabet sketch focuses on words beginning with שׁ, שׂ, and ת. Since you now know all the consonants and vowels, see whether you can fill in the transliteration! Label picture parts, as usual.

4. Meaning	3. Transliter-ation	2. Word	1. Initial letter	4. Meaning	3. Transliter-ation	2. Word	1. Initial letter
field		שָׂדֶה	שׂ	peace		שָׁלוֹם	שׁ
sheep, lamb		שֶׂה		table		שֻׁלְחָן	
lip, edge		שָׂפָה		sun		שֶׁמֶשׁ	
prince		שַׂר		two		שְׁנַיִם	
under		תַּחַת	ת	teeth		שִׁנַּיִם	
palm tree		תָּמָר		sleep		שֵׁנָה	
Tarshish		תַּרְשִׁישׁ					

0.5.ט. Did you know that...? (Tanak)   הֲיָדַעְתָּ כִּי...?

...the books making up the Hebrew Bible contain expressions referring to parts of the literary collection? Among them are the following terms:

סֵפֶר מֹשֶׁה	*the book of Moses* (cf. Aramaic סְפַר מֹשֶׁה in Ezra 6:18)
סֵפֶר תּוֹרַת מֹשֶׁה	*the book of the law of Moses* (Neh. 8:1)
סֵפֶר הַתּוֹרָה	*the book of the Law* (2 Kings 22:8)
הַסֵּפֶר	*the book* (Neh. 8:5)
תּוֹרַת יהוה	*the law of the LORD* (cf. Pss. 1:2, 19:8 [ET v. 7])

Subsequent tradition introduced the designation תַּנַ״ךְ *Tanak* to encompass the entire Hebrew Bible. תַּנַ״ךְ is an acrostic comprised of the first letters of these three words:

תּוֹרָה	*Law*
נְבִיאִים	*Prophets*
כְּתוּבִים	*Writings*

Do you know why these three were chosen for the acrostic?

0.5.׳. Snapshot of vowels

The following table presents principle information concerning vowels.

						Vowel name	
	sheva	final qameṣ-hē	ḥatef-pataḥ	pataḥ	qameṣ		A-Class
	ׂ	הָ	ֲ	ַ	ָ	Vowel	
	a as in above	a as in mark	a as in mark	a as in mark	a as in mark	Vowel sound	
	ĕ	â	ă	a	ā	Transliteration	
sheva	ḥatef-segol	segol	ṣērê-yod	ṣērê	ḥireq-yod	ḥireq	Vowel name	
ְ	ֱ	ֶ	ֵי	ֵ	ִי	ִ	Vowel	I/E-Class
e as in current	e as in pet	e as in pet	e as in whey	e as in whey	i as in machine	i as in machine	Vowel sound	
ĕ	ĕ	e	ê	ē	î	i	Transliteration	
sheva	qameṣ-ḥaṭuf	ḥatef-qameṣ	šureq	qibbuṣ	ḥolem-vav	ḥolem	Vowel name	
ְ	ָ	ֳ	וּ	ֻ	וֹ	ֹ	Vowel	U/O-Class
o as in cannon	o as in remote	o as in remote	u as in lute	u as in lute	o as in mole	o as in mole	Vowel sound	
ĕ	o	ŏ	û	u	ô	ō	Transliteration	

0.5.ב. Snapshot of consonants

The following table collects principle information presented earlier concerning consonants, without explanatory footnotes.

Trans-literation	Sound	Name	Final form	Letter
l	l	lamed		ל
m	m	mēm	ם	מ
n	n	nun	ן	נ
s	s	samekh		ס
ʿ	(voiced guttural)	ʿayin		ע
p (f)	p (f)	pē (fē)	(ף)	פ (פ)
ṣ	ts	ṣadē	ץ	צ
q	q	qof		ק
r	r	rēš		ר
š	sh	šîn		שׁ
ś	s	śîn		שׂ
t	t	tav		ת

Trans-literation	Sound	Name	Final form	Letter
ʾ	(glottal stop)	ʾalef		א
b	b	bēt		ב
(ḇ)	(v)	(vēt)		(ב)
g	g	gîmel		ג
d	d	dalet		ד
h	h	hē		ה
v	v	vav		ו
z	z	zayin		ז
ḥ	ḥ	ḥēt		ח
ṭ	t	ṭēt		ט
y	y	yod		י
k	k	kaf		כ
(ḵ)	(kh)	(khaf)	(ך)	(כ)

You can read the Bible. אַתָּה תִּקְרָא אֶת־הַתָּנַ"ךְ׃

Selected readings

Using the information you have gained to this point, you now are ready to read aloud two famous Bible verses in Hebrew. Refer to the transliteration below each word to check your pronunciation. The designation "0.5.׀." in the upper right indicates that after completing §0.5.׀. you will be ready to read the corresponding Bible selection.

The Hebrew Bible opens with these words (Gen. 1:1). The following notes may help you: 0.5.׀.

(a) Remember to read right-to-left.

(b) In this sentence, the verb ("created") precedes its subject ("God").

(c) The symbol resembling a colon (׃) at the close of the line is called a *sof pasuq*. Masoretes used this symbol to mark the end of a verse.

בְּרֵאשִׁית	בָּרָא	אֱלֹהִים	אֵת הַשָּׁמַיִם	וְאֵת הָאָרֶץ׃	.1
bĕrēšît	bārā'	'ĕlōhîm	'ēt haššāmayim	vĕ'ēt hā'āreṣ	
in the beginning	created	God	the heavens	and the earth	

Isaiah overheard celestial attendants worship God with this exclamation (Isa. 6:3b). 0.5.׀.

קָדוֹשׁ קָדוֹשׁ קָדוֹשׁ	יהוה	צְבָאוֹת	מְלֹא	כָּל־	הָאָרֶץ	.2
qādôš, qādôš, qādôš	'ădōnāy[70]	ṣĕbā'ôt	mĕlō'	kol	hā'āreṣ	
holy, holy, holy	LORD of	hosts	full (is)	all	the earth	

כְּבוֹדוֹ׃

kĕbôdô

(with) his glory

---

[70] The Masoretic tradition reads אֲדֹנָי ('ădōnāy, meaning "my Lord" [also "my lords"]) for the divine name יהוה.

How to write Hebrew letters

By following these guidelines, you soon will develop a clear Hebrew handwriting style. Note especially any features circled in the column labeled "N.B." On the pages that follow, practice writing one line filled with the same letter. Begin by forming large letters, 8 or 10 letters per line.

Note: unless otherwise indicated below, all letters begin at upper border of writing line and extend to (but do not cross) lower line.

Practice Area	N.B.	Stroke Sequence (Begin in upper left)			Hand-written	
		א	א	א	א	א
Make one long diagonal stroke, followed by two offset strokes (not an "X"). The tags at ends of offset strokes are not necessary.							
	ב	ב	ב	ב	ב	ב
Base line must extend to the right, **past** vertical line (else mistaken for the letter כ).							
	ג	ג	ג	ג	ג	
ג is a narrow letter, half the width of ב or א. The base must form a fork.							
	ד	ד	ד	ד	ד	
Top line must extend beyond vertical line (else mistaken for the letter ר).							

					ה
	ה	ה ה	ה ה	ה	ה

Note the obvious gap preserved between left vertical stroke and cross bar (else mistaken for letter ח).

	ו		ו ו	ו	ו

ו is very narrow. The horizontal stroke curves immediately downward (to distinguish from ז).

	ז		ז	ז	ז

ז is also very narrow. The top bar is angled, fully crossing the vertical stroke (to distinguish from ו).

	ח		ח ח	ח	ח

Both vertical strokes must join with cross bar. An opening at upper left would be mistaken for ה.

	ט	ט	ט	ט	ט

Tags at top of "U" shape should tip inward at an angle, without touching each other (to distinguish from ס). Base line may be flat or curved.

	י			י	י

י is both narrow and short. It rides very high, just below the upper border of writing.

	כ		כ	כ	כ

Form a smooth curve, without protrusions at corners.					
		ד	→	ד	ד
The vertical stroke must extend below border of writing (to distinguish from ד and ר).					
		ל	↳	ל	ל
The top stroke must extend above the border of writing (to distinguish from ק, ד, and ר).					
		מ	מ	מ	מ
מ resembles a slightly rounded triangle, with a flat base and a tag on upper left slope.					
			ס	ר	ס
Maintain distinct corners in this letter to form a square, not a circle (to distinguish from ס).					
		נ	נ	נ	נ
נ is another narrow letter. The lower horizontal bar should extend farther to the left than the upper bar.					
				ו	ו
The tail of this final form must extend below border of writing (to distinguish from ו).					
		ס		ס	ס

Form a flat top, with slight left extension of the top bar.					
	ע	ע	ע	ע	ע
Horizontal tags at top of right and left arms are not essential.					
			פ	פ	פ
	ף			ף	ף
The tail of final form (ף) must extend below border of writing.					
	צ	צ	צ	צ	צ
The right arm must join long diagonal at its midpoint, not at the base (to distinguish from ע). Tags at tops of arms are helpful.					
	ץ	ץ	ץ	ץ	ץ
The tail must extend below line of writing; tags at tops of arms are helpful.					
	ק	ק	ק	ק	ק
Tail must extend below line of writing. The vertical stroke does not connect at top or side.					

	ר		ר	ר	ר

Slightly round the corner (to distinguish from the letter ד).

	שׁ	שׁ	שׁ	שׁ	שׁ

The middle arm is slightly diagonal. Horizontal tags at tops of arms are not essential. Avoid forming as the letter "w." The dot above right arm distinguishes šîn from the next consonant (śîn).

				שׂ	שׂ

Same as שׁ above, only locate the dot on left arm (not right arm) for śîn consonant.

	ת		ת	ת	ת

Top bar must extend to left beyond the left vertical stroke. The left vertical must touch top bar. The bottom of the left vertical will angle upward like check mark.

Practice writing sheet

UNIT 1

הֲשָׁלוֹם לָךְ?[1]

Getting acquainted

verbless questions, predicative participles

This unit will enable you to do the following:

- exchange greetings with a neighbor
- learn each other's name
- inquire: "What is this?"
- ask whether someone has an object
- indicate whether you do (or do not) have a particular object

---

[1] *How are you?* Use this expression when addressing one person, whether male or female (cf. 2 Kings 4:26). The first line of each unit's title gives a sample of the primary interactive skill presented in that unit. The second line of the heading identifies the primary interactive skill, while the third line indicates the principal grammatical features covered in the unit.

MODULE 1.1　　　　　　　　　　Greetings and introductions

1.1.א. Activity: "Hello!"　　　　　　　　　　שָׁלוֹם

INTERACTIVE SKILL: Exchanging a simple greeting with a friend

Observe and imitate how your instructor exchanges a simple Hebrew greeting.

Words for responding　　　　　　　　　　מִלִּים לַעֲנוֹת

The heading "Words for **responding**" will introduce vocabulary intended for **deep memory**. Learn these words so thoroughly that you will be able to recall them for use in a conversational **response** (as well as being able to recognize them in print or when spoken aloud). "Words for **responding**" will contrast "Words for **listening**," a vocabulary heading found in §1.1.ו.

| שָׁלוֹם | Hello *m* (*lit.*, peace, wholeness) |

The italicized letter "*m*" after "Hello" indicates that שָׁלוֹם is a masculine noun. Nouns in Hebrew are either masculine or feminine.

1.1.ב. Do you (*ms*) know the meaning of a word? (שָׁלוֹם)

הֲיָדַעְתָּ פֵּשֶׁר דָּבָר?

> Although שָׁלוֹם often is rendered *peace*, this concept involves much more than the absence of hostilities. שָׁלוֹם describes an expansive condition of intactness, both individually and corporately. One scholar describes שָׁלוֹם as "a state of being unimpaired and unthreatened, of ease and security, of felicity and wholeness in the broadest sense."[2]

---

[2] J. Hempel, *Die israelitischen Anshauungen von Segen und Fluch im Lichte altorientalischer Parallel*, BZAW 81 (1961), 58–59, quoted by F. J. Stendebach in "שָׁלוֹם," 13–49 in *Theological Dictionary of the Old Testament*, vol. 15, English translation (Grand Rapids: Eerdmans, 2006), cf. esp. p. 19.

1.1.ג. Activity: "Do you (*ms*) have a stone?"   הֲיֵשׁ לְךָ אֶבֶן?[3]

INTERACTIVE SKILL: Indicating that you do (or do not) possess an object; asking whether someone possesses a particular object.

Here are some useful expressions:

Words for responding   מִלִּים לַעֲנוֹת

When addressing a **woman**	When addressing a **man**	
(same)	...יֵשׁ לִי	I have…
(same)	...אֵין לִי	I do not have…
...יֵשׁ לָךְ	...יֵשׁ לְךָ	You (*s*) have…
...אֵין לָךְ	...אֵין לְךָ	You (*s*) do not have…
הֲיֵשׁ לָךְ אֶבֶן?	הֲיֵשׁ לְךָ אֶבֶן?	Do you (*s*) have a stone (אֶבֶן *f*)?
הֲיֵשׁ לָךְ לֶחֶם?	הֲיֵשׁ לְךָ לֶחֶם?	Do you (*s*) have (some) bread (לֶחֶם *m*)?
הֲיֵשׁ לָךְ כּוֹס?	הֲיֵשׁ לְךָ כּוֹס?	Do you (*s*) have a cup (כּוֹס *f*)?

Gender of nouns. As noted earlier, an italicized "*m*" indicates that a word is **masculine** in gender. An "*f*" indicates that a word is **feminine**. All Hebrew nouns are either masculine or feminine. It is important to learn the gender of a noun when learning its meaning.

Initially we will concentrate on singular nouns. Plural nouns will be explained in §2.3.א. "Singular" will be abbreviated "*s*," while "plural" will be abbreviated "*pl*."

---

[3] Unlike writing systems employed by languages such as English, Biblical Hebrew does not employ a question mark to signal the presence of a question. Generally you will recognize a question by noticing an interrogative particle such as הֲ... (that invites a yes / no answer) or מִי (that inquires, "Who...?"). To help you begin to recognize questions, initial portions of this textbook will employ the question mark.

Pronunciation of certain words at phrase-end. When a word having two segol vowels (such as אֶבֶן) appears at the end of a major phrase or at the end of a sentence, the first segol generally will be replaced by an A-class vowel, such as qameṣ. That is why אֶבֶן and לֶחֶם are pronounced אָבֶן and לָחֶם, respectively, when occurring at the end of a phrase.[4] Forms with phrase-end changes are called "pausal."

Suggestions for using the illustrated stories

Here are some ways to let the stories in this textbook deliver maximum benefit.

- Let the visual cues in the illustrations help you understand the written storyline.
- Practice pronunciation by using the PowerPoint with audio (go to LearningBiblicalHebrew Interactively.com).
- Read each story segment several times, until you can follow the content easily.
- Experiment by covering the caption for a given cell, and then see how many Hebrew words and phrases you can recall, pertaining to that cell.
- Retell a given story in simplified fashion, using your own (Hebrew) words.
- Finally, return to each story after a week or two has gone by. You will be encouraged by how much you have learned!

---

[4] The A-class vowel in these words is the original vowel. Familiarity with this vowel shift (i.e., a segol reverts to an A-class vowel) will be helpful when we add suffixes to these nouns (see suffixes with לֶחֶם in §3.4.ג.).

1.1 David Story: I have a stone.

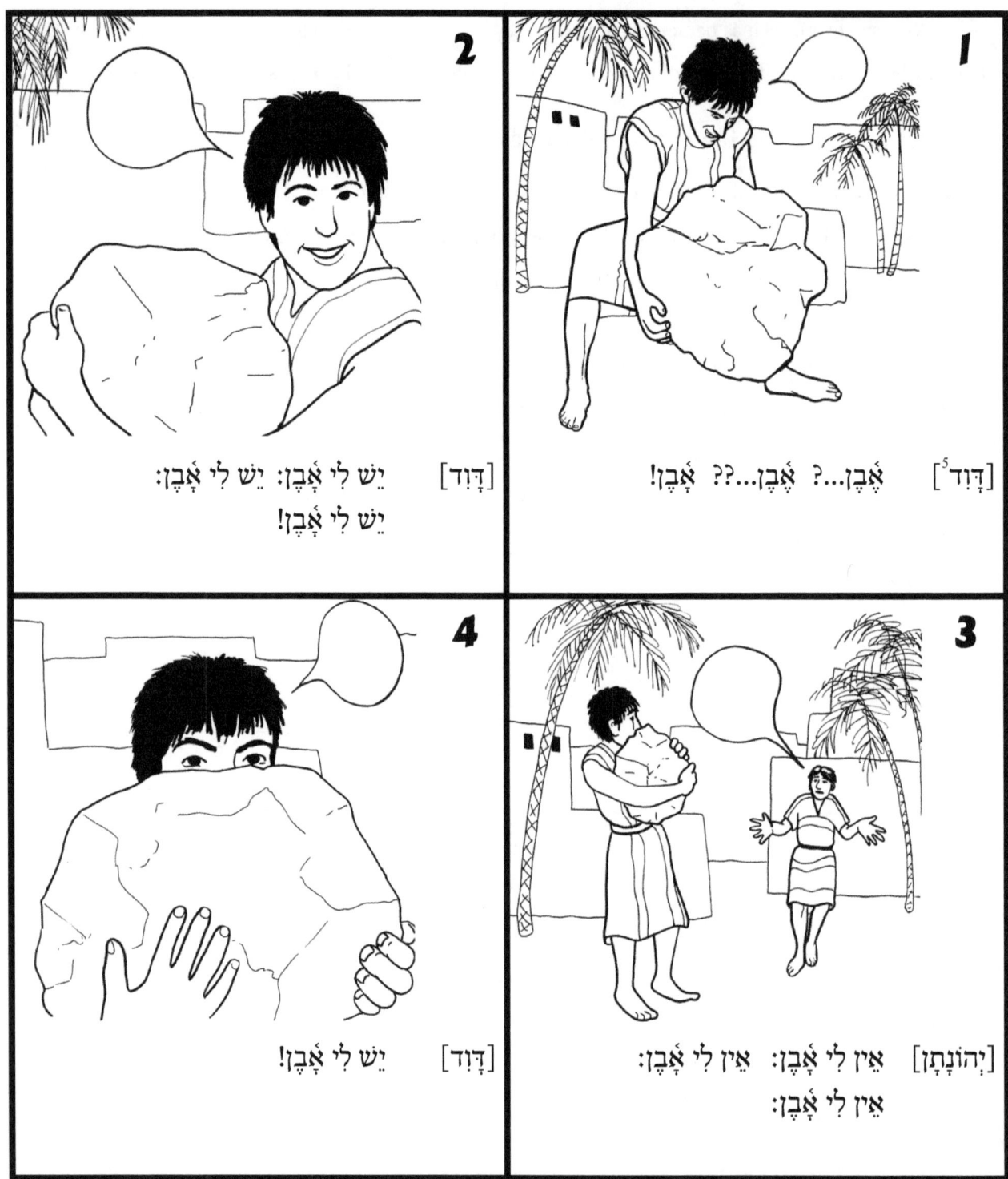

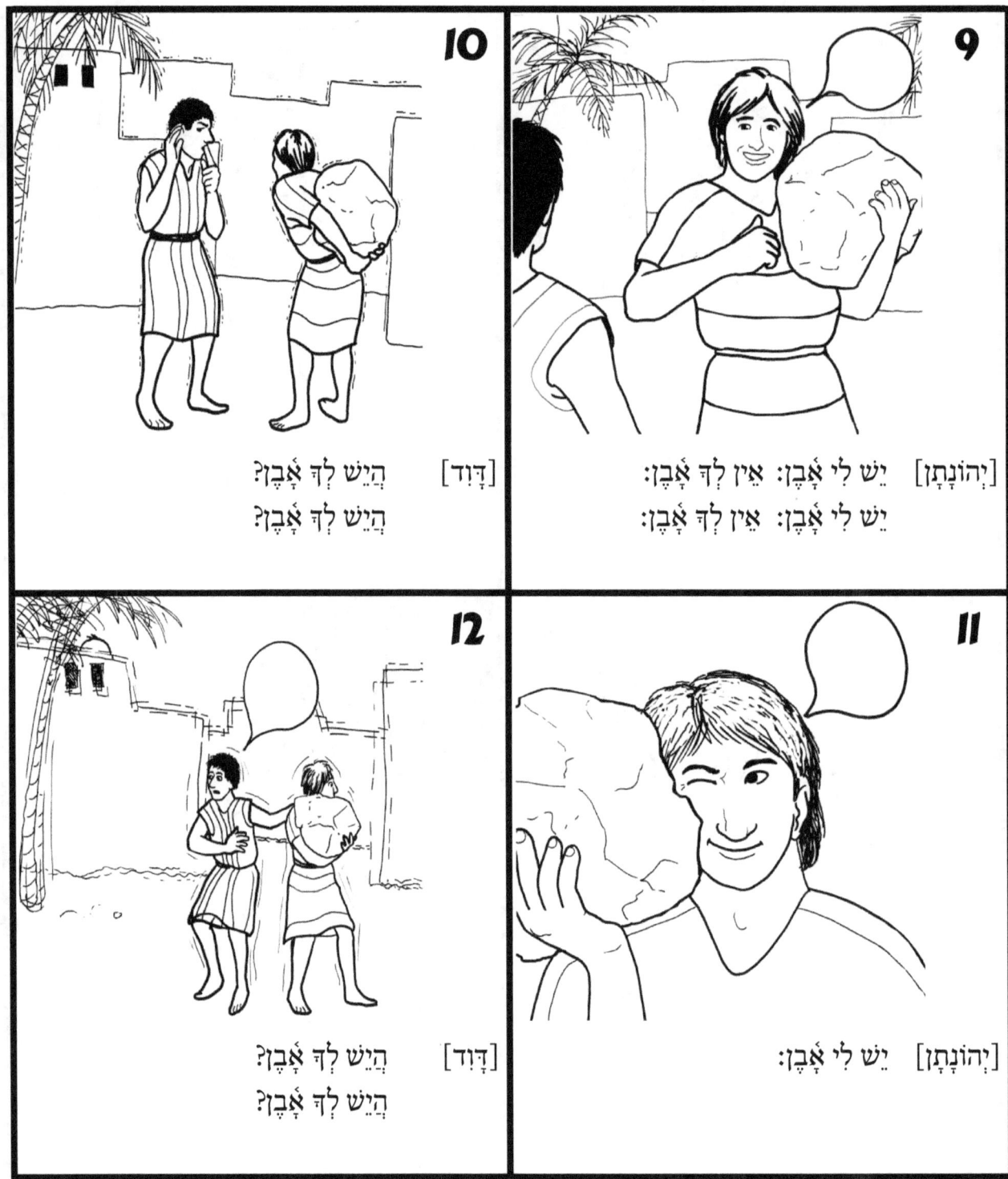

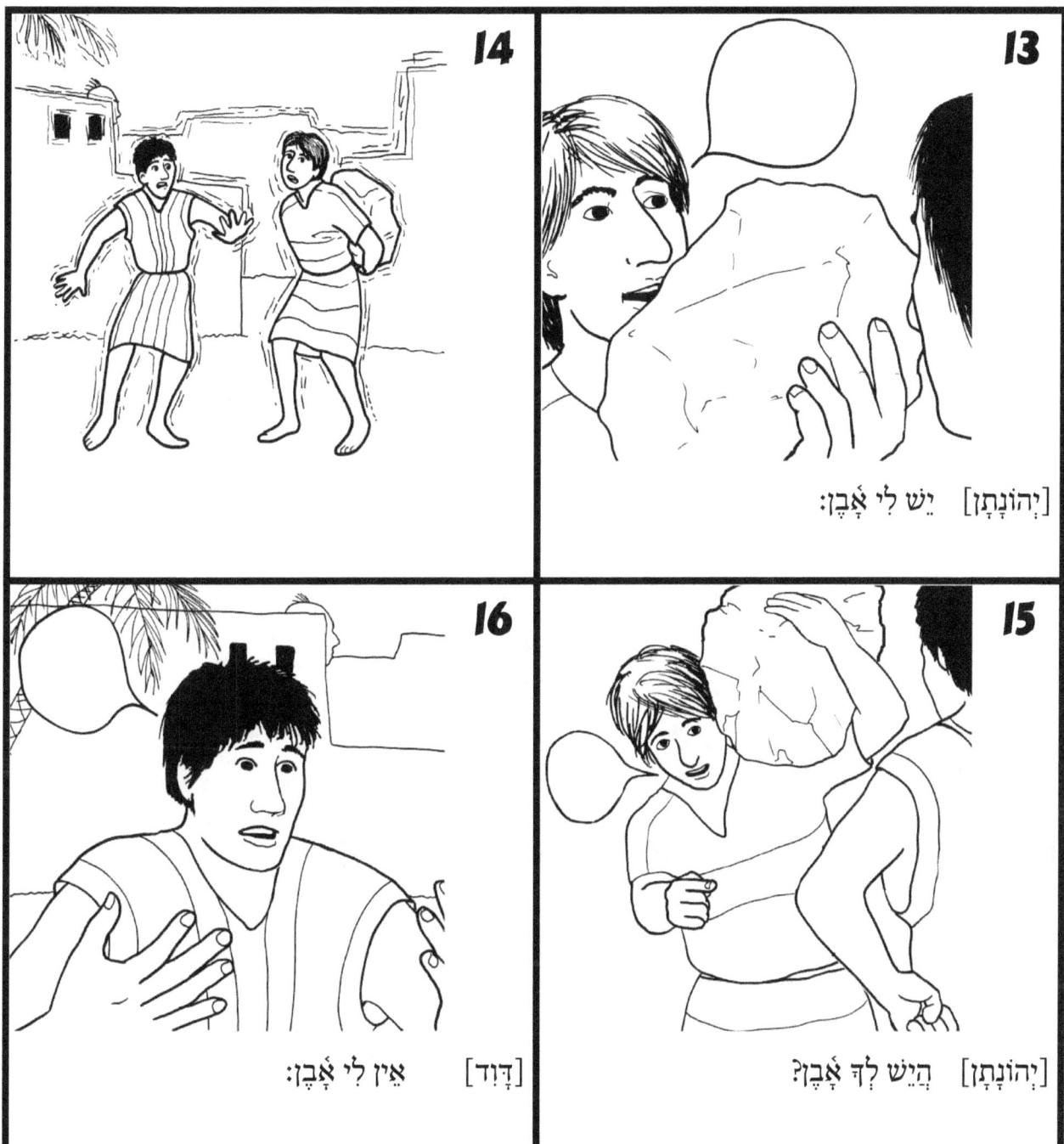

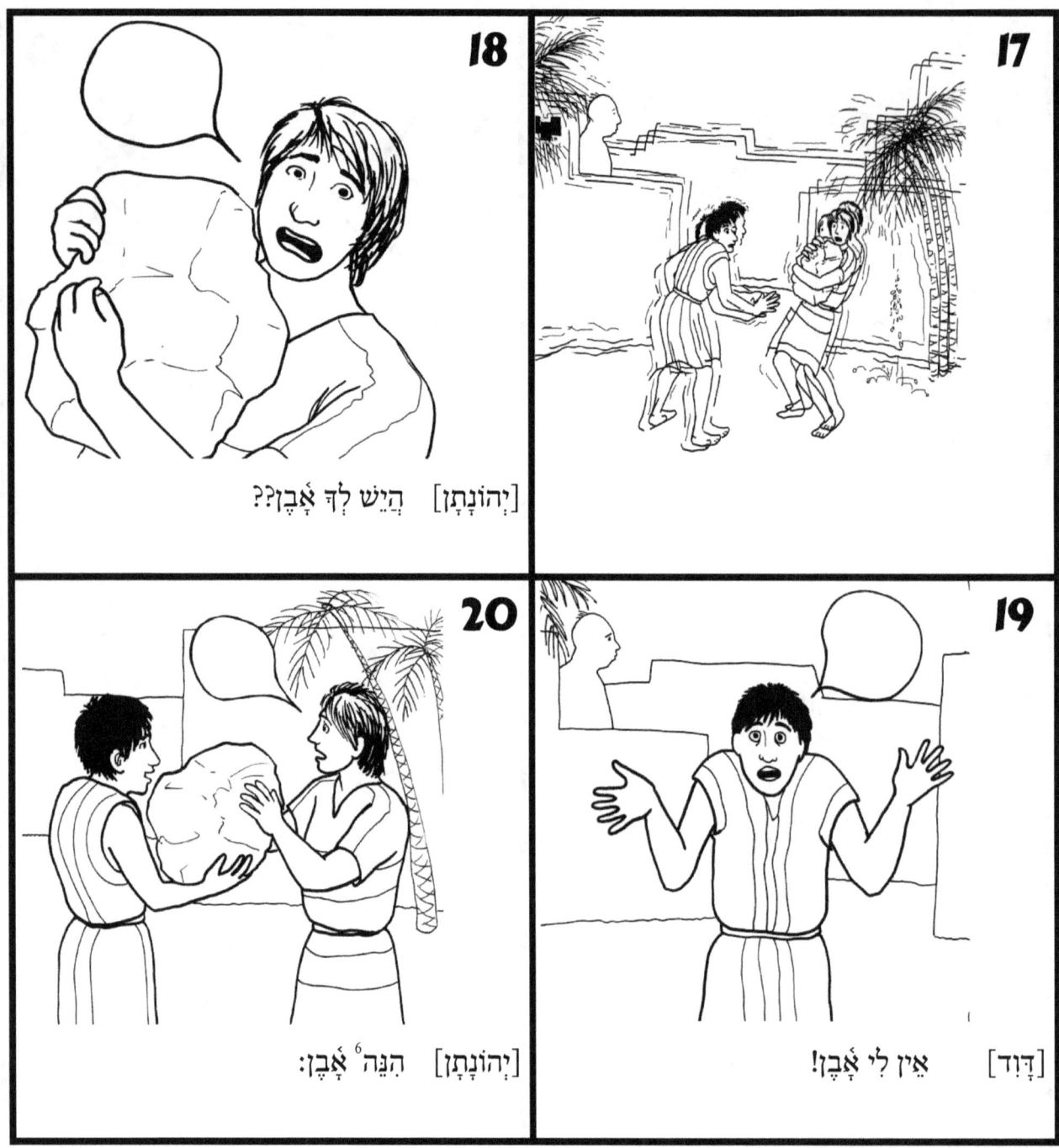

[6] הִנֵּה means *here is*.

[7] Did you notice that there are no vowels accompanying the word יהוה? This signifies the divine name, sometimes represented as YHWH (see Exod. 3:13-15). We will follow the Masoretic practice of pronouncing יהוה as אֲדֹנָי (meaning "Lord;" see further under §1.2.ג.). The phrase יְבָרֶכְךָ יהוה is a way of expressing appreciation for a kindness received. It means, "May the LORD bless you." If addressing a woman you would say, יְבָרֵכֵךְ יהוה.

1.1.ד. Do you (*ms*) know how to read? (Accent marks)   הֲיָדַ֫עְתָּ לִקְרֹא?

The Masoretes instituted a number of helpful symbols to indicate which syllable receives the accent. Called טְעָמִים or cantillation marks, they serve to guide vocal intonation as the Hebrew Bible is read in synagogues throughout the world today.

We will take advantage of a few of these marks in the "Selected Readings," beginning with Unit 6. The marks will be employed in full form within "Selected Readings" beginning with Unit 9.

Since use of the whole Masoretic cantillation system would be too daunting for early learners, we will employ a simpler code to signal the accented syllable. Watch for the symbol ◌֫ appearing above a letter, as in הֲיָדַ֫עְתָּ from the title of this segment. This indicates that the syllable דַ֫ע should be pronounced louder than any other syllable in that word. Similarly, in the word אֶ֫בֶן *stone* you will want to accent the syllable אֶ֫.

When we eventually encounter fully-cantillated words (Unit 9 and following), we will find that the symbol ◌֫ is part of a two-symbol accent known as *'ole veyorēd*. Until

> then, simply use the symbol ◌ֺ to detect the accented syllable in a word. For a more complete explanation of the cantillation system, please refer to the section entitled "Masoretic Accents" (vol. 2, pp. 410–15).

1.1.ה. Activity: Do you (*ms*) have…?   הֲיֵשׁ לְךָ...?

INTERACTIVE SKILL: Asking concerning a hidden or missing object

See if you can fool your classmates in the course of this fast-moving guessing game. As a bag containing several small stones is passed to you, you may choose either to **take** a stone (hiding it in your closed fist), **or** only to **pretend to take** a stone.

The "longer" and "shorter" alternatives below have the same basic meaning. The word אָֽיִן in the shorter negative reply is simply the word אֵין when it occurs at the end of a phrase.

Model

	Shorter	Longer	
Do you (*ms, fs*) have a stone?	הַאֶבֶן לְךָ?	הֲיֵשׁ לְךָ / לָךְ אֶבֶן?	Your neighbor will ask you
I have a stone.	אֶבֶן לִי׃	יֵשׁ לִי אֶבֶן׃	Your reply, if affirmative
I do not [have a stone].	אָֽיִן׃	אֵין [לִי אֶבֶן]׃	Your reply, if negative

You (*ms, fs*) have a stone.	יֵשׁ לְךָ / לָךְ אֶבֶן:	אֶבֶן לָךְ:	Your neighbor's assessment, if affirmative
You (*ms, fs*) do not [have a stone].	אֵין [לְךָ / לָךְ אֶבֶן]:	אֵין:	Your neighbor's assessment, if negative

1.1.1. Activity: "How are you (*ms / fs*)?"   הֲשָׁלוֹם לָךְ?

INTERACTIVE SKILL: How to ask how your friend is doing

After we grasp the question, הֲיֵשׁ לְךָ אֶבֶן?, it takes only a few steps to learn the greeting, "How are you?" הֲשָׁלוֹם לָךְ? (lit., *Do you have peace, wholeness?*). Notice the following:

- Since it is not customary to use the longer expression הֲיֵשׁ לְךָ שָׁלוֹם?, the word שָׁלוֹם will appear directly after the interrogative particle הֲ: הֲשָׁלוֹם...? (see column labeled "Shorter" in previous segment).
- לְךָ now is spelled לָךְ (because it appears at the end of a phrase).[8]

מִלִּים לַעֲנוֹת / Words for responding

צַר	distress, anxiety (*adjective as noun*) m

מִלִּים לִשְׁמֹעַ / Words for hearing

The heading "Words for hearing" will introduce vocabulary that you should learn well enough to recognize by sight or sound.

מְאֹד	much, greatly (*adverb*)

Drawing from expressions in the model below, ask several of your classmates how they are doing.

Model

How are you (*ms / fs*)?	הֲשָׁלוֹם לָךְ?	Inquiry
I am fine.	שָׁלוֹם לִי *or* שָׁלוֹם:	Reply #1, if you are fine
I am not in distress.	אֵין לִי צַר:	Reply #2, if you are so-so
I am not fine.	אֵין לִי שָׁלוֹם:	Reply #3, if you are not fine
I am in distress.	צַר לִי:	Reply #4, also if you are not fine
I am greatly distressed.	צַר לִי מְאֹד:	Reply #5, if you are doing badly

---

[8] Normally we would use ...לְךָ (lit. *to you, ms*) when addressing a man, and ...לָךְ (lit. *to you, fs*) when addressing a woman. However, at some point it became customary to pronounce לְךָ like the feminine form לָךְ, but only in this situation: *when* לָךְ *appears at the end of a sentence or major phrase*, due to the brief pause that would occur there. When a word alters its normal vocalization or accentuation due being located in a phrase-end pause, it is said to be "in pause," or is termed a "pausal form." The shift from אֶבֶן to אָבֶן is another instance of pausal spelling. For more information, see note concerning the retracted accent אָנֹכִי in the 3.1 Jonah Episode.

1.1.ז. Activity: Give (*ms*) (to) me...! תֶּן לִי...!

INTERACTIVE SKILL: Seeking and requesting a concealed object

For this game, see whether you can guess what your friend has hidden in his / her sack. If you guess correctly, you may ask your friend to give you the object.

Some or all of the following objects may appear in this game.

סֵפֶר	לֶחֶם	כֶּסֶף	כּוֹס	אֶבֶן
scroll, book *m*	food, bread *m*	(piece of) silver *m*	cup *f*	stone *f*

The following expressions will be helpful. Some of them are translated for you. See whether you can recall the meaning of expressions introduced earlier.

UNIT 1   הֲשָׁלוֹם לָךְ?   87

Words for responding   מִלִּים לַעֲנוֹת

הֲיֵשׁ לְךָ / לָךְ...?	
יֵשׁ לִי ...	
אֵין לִי ...	I don't have ....
תֵּן / תְּנִי לִי...!	Give to me...! *imv ms, fs* [a]

[a] "*Imv*" refers to *imperative*, the form of a verb used to issue commands. The abbreviations *ms* and *fs* refer to *masculine singular* and *feminine singular*, respectively.

1.1.ח. Did you (*ms*) know that...? (Meaning of names)   הֲיָדַעְתָּ כִּי...?

...unlike some modern names, most personal names in Hebrew bore a meaning that was easily discernable? Here are several samples:			
יְהוֹשָׁפָט	The LORD has Judged	אֱלִימֶלֶךְ	My God is King
מִיכָאֵל	Who is Like God?	בִּנְיָמִין	Son of Right Hand
נָעֳמִי	Pleasant	בָּרוּךְ	Blessed
רְאוּבֵן	See! A Son!	דָּן	Judge
שָׁאוּל	Asked-for-One	חַנָּה	The LORD is Gracious
שְׁאַלְתִּיאֵל	I Asked God	יְהוֹנָתָן	The LORD has Given

1.1.ט. Activity: "What is your (*ms*) name?" מַה־שְּׁמֶךָ?

INTERACTIVE SKILL: How to learn a friend's name

Words for responding

Abbreviations for words like "your" and "their": Words such as שְׁמִי, שְׁמְךָ, and שְׁמֶךָ located below include a possessive pronoun (such as "my" or "your") suffixed to a noun. Because the pronouns "your" and "their" are more gender-specific and number-specific in Hebrew than in English, when translating these suffixes we will need to add abbreviations to convey the full Hebrew meaning. When you see "*your ms*" it means that the person referred to by "*your*" is a single male. "*Your fpl*" would indicate several women are being addressed as owning something.

UNIT 1 — הֲשָׁלוֹם לְךָ?

שֵׁם	name *m*		אִישׁ	man, person *m*
שְׁמִי	my name		אִשָּׁה	woman *f*
שִׁמְךָ	your *ms* name		מַה, מַה־ᵃ, מָה	What?
שְׁמֵךְ	your *fs* name		מַה־זֶּה?	What is this?

ᵃ The interrogative מה has several spellings, the most common of which are listed above. Often מַה is joined to the following word with a maqqef (־), as in מַה־שִּׁמְךָ? *What is your name?* In those situations, the following word will begin with a dagesh, if possible.

Words for hearing — מִלִּים לִשְׁמֹעַ

מַה־שְּׁמֶךָᵃ?	What is your *ms* name?
מַה־שְּׁמֵךְ?	What is your *fs* name?

ᵃ שִׁמְךָ is pronounced שְׁמֶךָ when it stands alone or at the end of a sentence (called a "pausal form").

Refer to these expressions as you inquire your neighbor's name and as you tell your own name.

Model

What is your name *ms*?	מַה־שְּׁמֶךָ?		Inquiry
What is your name *fs*?	מַה־שְּׁמֵךְ?		
My name is Abraham.	שְׁמִי אַבְרָהָם:		Reply
My name is Sarah.	שְׁמִי שָׂרָה:		

1.1.י. Do you (*ms*) know the meaning of a word? (Manna)

הֲיָדַ֫עְתָּ פֵּ֫שֶׁר דָּבָר?

When the Israelites discovered the food that God miraculously provided in the wilderness, they asked each other: מָן הוּא? *What is it?* (מָן is an alternate form of מַה, meaning "What?") This question gave rise to naming the food מָן *man[na]* (cf. Exod. 16:15).

UNIT 1   הֲשָׁלוֹם לָךְ?

MODULE 1.2   Saying goodbye

1.2.א. Activity: "Goodbye (*ms*)!"   : יִשְׁמָרְךָ יהוה

INTERACTIVE SKILL: Conclude a brief conversation with leave-taking

Words for hearing   מִלִּים לִשְׁמֹעַ

יהוה	the LORD (*pronounced* אֲדֹנָי, *see* §1.2.ג.)
יִשְׁמָרְךָ / יִשְׁמְרֵךְ [a]	May he protect you! *ms, fs*
לֵךְ לְשָׁלוֹם / לְכִי לְשָׁלוֹם	Go in peace! *ms, fs*

[a] The first qameṣ in יִשְׁמָרְךָ is a qameṣ-ḥaṭuf, pronounced *o*. For an example of this form, see Ps. 121:7 (v. 6 in non-Hebrew versions). Note: occasionally the verse numbers in Hebrew do not match verse numbers in versions (most commonly in the Psalms). When they differ in the Psalms, you generally will find the corresponding material in the versions one or two verse numbers lower than in the Hebrew Bible. This is because versions do not include superscriptions in the verse numbering, while the Hebrew Bible does.

Partner with a friend to craft a brief conversation. Begin with the greeting "שָׁלוֹם" and end with one of two farewells ("leave-takings"): either יִשְׁמָרְךָ / יִשְׁמְרֵךְ יהוה *May the LORD protect you*, or לֵךְ / לְכִי לְשָׁלוֹם *Go in peace*. Between those outer parts of your conversation, choose two or three additional bits of conversation to exchange. Here are some ideas (leave-takings are included toward the end of this list and in the "Words for hearing" list above). Remember to use gender-appropriate forms.

מַה־שְּׁמֵךְ? What's your name *fs*?		הֲיֵשׁ לְךָ / לָךְ...? Do you have...?		תְּנִי לִי...: Give me *fs*....		תֵּן לִי...: Give me *ms*....
	אֵין לִי...: I don't have....		יֵשׁ לִי...: I have....		שְׁמִי...: My name is....	
לֵךְ / לְכִי לְשָׁלוֹם: Go in peace.		יִשְׁמָרְךָ / יִשְׁמְרֵךְ יהוה: May the LORD protect you.		מַה־שְּׁמֶךָ? What's your name *ms*?		מַה־זֶּה? What is this?

1.2.ב. Did you (*ms*) know that...? (Disclosing one's name) הֲיָדַעְתָּ כִּי...?

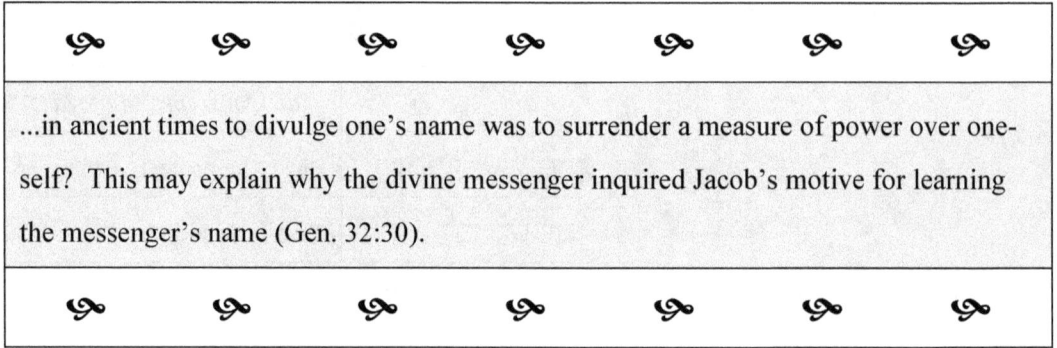

...in ancient times to divulge one's name was to surrender a measure of power over oneself? This may explain why the divine messenger inquired Jacob's motive for learning the messenger's name (Gen. 32:30).

1.2.ג. Did you (*ms*) know that...? (The divine name) הֲיָדַעְתָּ כִּי...?

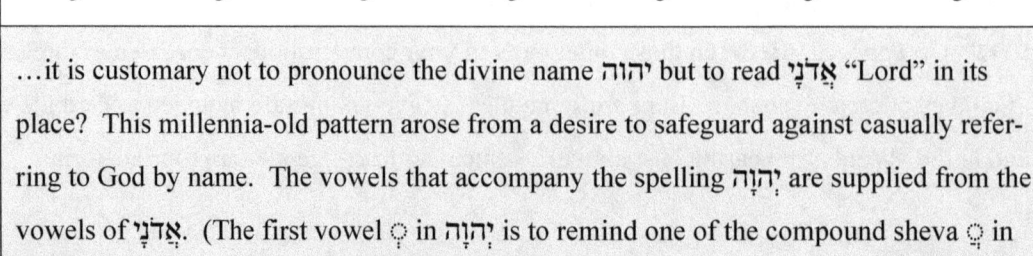

...it is customary not to pronounce the divine name יהוה but to read אֲדֹנָי "Lord" in its place? This millennia-old pattern arose from a desire to safeguard against casually referring to God by name. The vowels that accompany the spelling יְהוָה are supplied from the vowels of אֲדֹנָי. (The first vowel ְ in יְהוָה is to remind one of the compound sheva ֲ in the first syllable of אֲדֹנָי.)

    Many follow the custom of translating the word "יהוה" as "Lord" (note the use of small capitals). In this way the reader can know that the underlying Hebrew word is the divine name יהוה, rather than a word referring to a human, such as אָדוֹן (*lord* or *master*), אֲדֹנִי (*my lord* or *master*), or אֲדֹנַי (*my lords* or *masters*).

MODULE 1.3 — Searching for something

Unit 1 JONAH STORY: God is looking for a prophet

Have you ever been assigned a task you preferred not to do? If so, how hard did you work to avoid doing that task? In this module you will begin reading a story about someone who tried to avoid an assignment. You may recognize the story as vaguely resembling the Bible book with the same name: Jonah.

Successive episodes of the Jonah story—often diverging quite fancifully from the biblical account—will unfold from unit to unit through the remainder of the textbook. But before reading the first episode, please (a) become familiar with the vocabulary located below and (b) work through the activities found after the story episode. Then return to enjoy the story. The first activity begins in §1.3.א.

Words for responding — מִלִּים לַעֲנוֹת

לֶחֶם	bread,* food *m*	אֶבֶן	stone,* rock *f*
נָבִיא	prophet *m*	אֲנִי	I
עָלֶיךָ ל... / עָלַיִךְ ל...	you must... *ms, fs* (*or* be sure [to...])	אֲנִי מְבַקֵּשׁ... / אֲנִי מְבַקֶּשֶׁת...	I am looking for... *ms, fs*
שְׁנֵה־נָא / שְׁנִי־נָא	Repeat, please! *imv ms, fs*	אַתְּ	you *fs*
		אַתָּה	you *ms*
		כּוֹס	cup* *f*
		לֹא	no

* A word that has appeared in a previous vocabulary list will be marked with an asterisk (*).

Words for hearing / מִלִּים לִשְׁמֹעַ

נִינְוֵה	Nineveh	אֵינֶנִּי חָפֵץ... / אֵינֶנִּי חֲפֵצָה...	I don't want, desire... *m, f*
קוּם / קוּמִי	Get up! *imv ms, fs*	לֹא אָבִין	I don't understand
שֵׁב / שְׁבִי	Sit! *imv ms, fs*	לֵךְ אֶל-... / לְכִי אֶל-...	Go to...! *imv ms, fs*
תַּרְשִׁישׁ	Tarshish	לָלֶכֶת [אֶל-]	to go [to]

1.3 Jonah Episode: God is looking for a prophet.

א׳ = אֱלֹהִים, נ׳ = יוֹנָה הַנָּבִיא

As noted earlier, although the Hebrew Bible does not use ellipses, exclamation marks, or question marks for punctuation, you will find them helpful as you get started.

[9] *Repeat, please.* At times during this course you will need to ask someone to repeat what he or she has said. Whenever that happens, simply say, שְׁנֵה־נָא (if addressing a male) or שְׁנִי־נָא (when addressing a female), and watch what happens!

UNIT 1   הֲשָׁלוֹם לְךָ?

1.3.א. Activity: "I am looking for..."   ...אֲנִי מְבַקֵּשׁ:

INTERACTIVE SKILL: Inquiring what someone is looking for

Using the model below, find out what your neighbor is looking for. Your neighbor will respond by picking one of the persons / objects listed below, several of which you have already encountered.

Note: This question is primarily interested in the **object** ("**What** are you looking for?"), as opposed to asking about the **subject** ("What are **you** looking for?"). Consequently the reply will **begin** with the particular **object** that is sought.[10] This is one of the ways Hebrew displays versatility: bringing focus to part of a sentence by moving that part to the **front** of the sentence.

Objects or persons you might be looking for

אֶבֶן	אִישׁ	אִשָּׁה	לֶחֶם	נָבִיא	שָׁלוֹם	שֵׁם
	man		bread	prophet		

---

[10] If, on the other hand, the speaker did not wish to draw attention to any particular part of a verbless sentence, such a non-emphatic sentence (called "unmarked") would follow this word-order (or "syntax"): **subject**-first, **predicate**-second (provided by a participle in the current examples), followed by an **object** (whether noun, pronoun, or prepositional phrase), as in אֲנִי מְבַקֵּשׁ נָבִיא. "Verbless" describes a clause or sentence lacking a finite verb.

Review of words you will need

מַה, מַה־֯, מָה	אַתְּ	אַתָּה	אֲנִי
What?	you *fs*	you *ms*	I

Model

What are you looking for?	מָה[11] אַתָּה מְבַקֵּשׁ? מָה אַתְּ מְבַקֶּשֶׁת?	Inquiry ("you" *ms*, *fs*)
I'm looking for a stone.	אֶבֶן אֲנִי מְבַקֵּשׁ: אֶבֶן אֲנִי מְבַקֶּשֶׁת:	Reply ("I" *ms*, *fs*)

1.3.ב. Activity: "Go (*ms*) to Tarshish!"   לֵךְ אֶל־תַּרְשִׁישׁ!

INTERACTIVE SKILL: Telling someone where you would like him / her to go

Watch as your instructor models the response to certain instructions. Next, you can respond as well.

---

[11] As noted earlier, מָה is spelled with a qameṣ (not pataḥ) due to the ...אַ that opens the following word (אַתָּה).

UNIT 1   הֲשָׁלוֹם לְךָ?

Sample commands:

	קוּם... לֵךְ אֶל־נִינְוֵה:	Sending someone (*ms*, *fs*) to Nineveh
	קוּמִי... לְכִי אֶל־נִינְוֵה:	
	קוּם... לֵךְ אֶל־תַּרְשִׁישׁ:	Sending someone (*ms*, *fs*) to Tarshish
	קוּמִי... לְכִי אֶל־תַּרְשִׁישׁ:	
	קוּם... לֵךְ אֶל־נִינְוֵה וְלֵךְ אֶל־תַּרְשִׁישׁ:	Sending someone (*ms*, *fs*) to Nineveh and Tarshish
	קוּמִי... לְכִי אֶל־נִינְוֵה וּלְכִי אֶל־תַּרְשִׁישׁ:	
	שֵׁב / שְׁבִי:	Having someone (*ms*, *fs*) sit down

1.3.ג. May I offer you (*ms*) advice? (לֹא אָבִין)   הַאִיעָצְךָ עֵצָה?

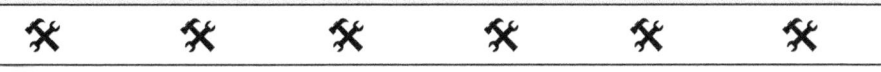

Whenever something happens in class that you don't quite grasp, you—like the Jonah character in the above episode—may ask for help **while remaining in the Hebrew language**. Simply call out: לֹא אָבִין *I don't understand*. Try it!

Remember that it is not necessary to grasp everything you hear or read on the first exposure. In fact, by employing an expression such as לֹא אָבִין to request an explanation, you will **deepen your learning** through practical use of the language.

In case you are wondering why we are using לֹא (not אֵין...) to negate אָבִין, it is because אָבִין *I understand* is a finite verb. Phrases with finite verbs employ לֹא for negation, while unmarked verbless phrases (such as [יֵשׁ] לִי אֶבֶן *I have a stone*) are negated with אֵין... (pronounced אַיִן when standing alone).

1.3.ד. Did you (*ms*) know that…? (Land travel)   הֲיָדַ֫עְתָּ כִּי...?

…it would require approximately two months for someone to travel to Nineveh on foot. In 701 BCE the Assyrian army averaged 32 km per day, marching from נִינְוֵה *Nineveh f* to Lachish, near Jerusalem.[12] If traveling by חֲמוֹר *donkey m*—a common means of transport—one might have averaged 40-48 km per day. סוּסִים *horses mpl* were used for pulling chariots in יִשְׂרָאֵל *Israel m*, but tended not to be used for riding, perhaps because mules and donkeys are more sure-footed in uneven terrain. Apart from main streets of towns, דְּרָכִים *roads mpl* were not paved in the Iron Age. For journeys over long distances, it was advisable to travel in groups. Bandits and wild animals made transit hazardous.

North-south travel in Palestine would have used one of two routes. To the west was דֶּ֫רֶךְ הַיָּם *the Way of the Sea* (*Via Maris*). From its origin in the Nile Delta, it paralleled the Mediterranean coastline northward through cities such as Gaza and Ashdod until reaching the Carmel range. There it turned east, going through Megiddo on its way to the Jezreel plain. It reached Damascus after passing along the northwest shore of יָם־כִּנֶּ֫רֶת *the Sea of Chinnereth* (Sea of Galilee, Num. 34:11; cf. Isa. 8:23 [ET 9:1]), eventually arriving in אֲרַם נַהֲרַ֫יִם *Mesopotamia* (Gen. 24:10). You may wish to add דֶּ֫רֶךְ הַיָּם to the map of Israel at the back of this book—simply by drawing a line connecting these various locations (see p. 564).

To the east lay דֶּ֫רֶךְ הַמֶּ֫לֶךְ *the King's Highway*. This route connected the Gulf of Aqaba port of Ezion-geber (on the northeastern arm of the Red Sea) with Damascus, by traversing the eastern plateau of the Jordan Valley (cf. Num. 20:17).[13]

---

[12] *LBI*, 186.

[13] *LBI*, 176–78.

You (ms) can read the Bible.　　אַתָּה תִּקְרָא אֶת־הַתַּנַ״ךְ:

You will discover two types of Bible readings at the close of each unit. The first is called "Selected Readings." These will illustrate the material found in particular modules of this unit. The second is called "A Connected Reading." A longer selection appears under this second heading, spread in serial fashion over multiple units.

Selected readings

Under the heading, "Selected Readings," you will find Bible verses that correlate to vocabulary or expressions within particular modules. A designation such as "1.1" at the upper right indicates that as soon as you are acquainted with the vocabulary and grammar of §1.1, you will be ready to read any Bible selection bearing the designation "1.1." It is not necessary to wait until you have mastered the entire unit before beginning to enjoy these Bible readings.

Some verses are followed by a second Hebrew phrase or sentence appearing in smaller font. This portion preserves some or all of the verse in its original form, together with cantillation (accent) marks. From time to time, your instructor may wish to point out elements from these notes. Cantillation marks will be explained later (see Selected Readings at the close of Unit 6, also the explanation of Masoretic accents found in vol. 2, pp. 410–15).

During a lonely night of wrestling, God's messenger asked Jacob the question found in the first line of this verse. (שְׁמֶךָ is the way שִׁמְךָ is spelled when it appears at the end of a phrase; there is no change in meaning.) The second line gives his reply.　　1.1

As noted above, the Hebrew in smaller font at the bottom of this entry preserves the entire verse. You do not need to translate the material in smaller font.

1.　מַה־שְּׁמֶךָ?

...יַעֲקֹב: (Gen. 32:28)

וַיֹּאמֶר אֵלָיו מַה־שְּׁמֶךָ וַיֹּאמֶר יַעֲקֹב:

Despite the marvel of speaking with God at a burning bush, Moses already began to think 1.1
ahead, wondering how the Israelite elders may respond to his announcement of rescue. So
he probed, "If they ask me, '[*insert question below*]' what shall I say?"

.2   ...מַה־שְּׁמוֹ ?ᵃ (Exod. 3:13)

ᵃ שְׁמוֹ שֵׁם (*with 3ms pronominal suffix* his)

...וְאָמְרוּ־לִי מַה־שְּׁמוֹ מָה אֹמַר אֲלֵהֶם:

Samuel was not particularly pleased to have been contacted after his death. King Saul 1.1
explained that he was in dire straits since the Philistines were attacking and God was not
responding. As a result Saul complained:

.3   ...צַר לִי מְאֹדᵃ:... (1 Sam. 28:15)

ᵃ מְאֹד very much, greatly

...וַיֹּאמֶר שָׁאוּל צַר־לִי מְאֹד:...

When he saw a woman approaching his house with determination, Elisha instructed his 1.1
servant Gehazi to ask her three questions. These appear in the first three lines below. The
fourth line gives the woman's reply.

.4   "הֲשָׁלוֹם לָךְ?"
"הֲשָׁלוֹם לְאִישֵׁךְ?ᵃ"
"הֲשָׁלוֹם לַיֶּלֶד?ᵇ"

"שָׁלוֹם": (2 Kings 4:26b)

ᵃ לְאִישֵׁךְ לְ + "your *fs* husband *m*"   ᵇ לַיֶּלֶד לְ + "the child"

עַתָּה רוּץ־נָא לִקְרָאתָהּ וֶאֱמָר־לָהּ הֲשָׁלוֹם לָךְ הֲשָׁלוֹם לְאִישֵׁךְ הֲשָׁלוֹם לַיֶּלֶד וַתֹּאמֶר שָׁלוֹם:

UNIT 1   הֲשָׁלוֹם לָךְ?

When traveling homeward after being healed, the Syrian general Naaman noticed Elisha's servant Gehazi running after his chariot. Naaman called back to him (see first line below). Gehazi's response appears in the second line.   1.1

"הֲשָׁלוֹם?"...

"...שָׁלוֹם"   (2 Kings 5:21b-22a)

...וַיֹּאמֶר הֲשָׁלוֹם: וַיֹּאמֶר׀ שָׁלוֹם...

The sage Agur exposes the limits of human knowledge with these questions: "Who has ascended to heaven and come down? [*Insert his additional questions, below.*] Surely you know!" (In the second line, שֵׁם is spelled שֶׁם־ because it is followed by a dash, called a maqqef: ־שֶׁם. As you soon will learn, this spelling is translated *name of*....)   1.1

מַה־שְּׁמוֹ?[a]   .6

...מַה־שֶּׁם־בְּנוֹ[b]?   (Prov. 30:4b)

[a] שֵׁם   (with 3ms pronominal suffix)   [b] בְּנוֹ *his son m*

מִי עָלָה־שָׁמַיִם׀ וַיֵּרַד מִי אָסַף־רוּחַ׀ בְּחָפְנָיו מִי צָרַר־מַיִם׀ בַּשִּׂמְלָה מִי הֵקִים כָּל־אַפְסֵי־אָרֶץ מַה־שְּׁמוֹ וּמַה־שֶּׁם־בְּנוֹ כִּי תֵדָע:

Jacob sent his son Joseph to Shechem to search for Joseph's brothers. A stranger found him wandering in the fields and asked what he was looking for. Joseph responded with this answer: 1.3

...אֶת־אַחַי[a] אָנֹכִי[b] מְבַקֵּשׁ:   (Gen. 37:16a)   .7

[a] אֶת־אַחַי *my brothers*   [b] אָנֹכִי אֲנִי

וַיֹּאמֶר אֶת־אַחַי אָנֹכִי מְבַקֵּשׁ:...

With these words the priests were instructed to pronounce a blessing on the people of Israel. 1.3
This is the first line of what came to be known as "the priestly blessing" or "the Aaronic
blessing." You will read the remainder in Unit 10 (Selected Reading #13).

8. יְבָרֶכְךָ יהוה וְיִשְׁמְרֶֽךָ[a] : (Num. 6:24)

[a] *pausal spelling of* יִשְׁמָרְךָ יִשְׁמְרֶךָ

A connected reading: The binding of Isaac (Gen. 22:1)   עֲקֵדַת יִצְחָק

In contrast to "Selected Readings" found above, under the heading "A Connected Reading" you will find successive parts of a continuous portion taken from the Hebrew Bible. The first connected reading goes by the title, "The Binding of Isaac" or עֲקֵדַת יִצְחָק (or simply עֲקֵדָה). It is found in Genesis 22.

See how much of the selection you can understand with the help of glosses. Here at the outset of your study, many words and phrases will be glossed in the footnotes. Consult an English translation if you get stuck. Note that when a gloss pertains to more than one word, the **end** of the phrase will be flagged with a superscript letter in the verse itself, while the **beginning** of the phrase will be flagged with a superscript in the footnote.

1. וַיְהִי[a] אַחַר[b] הַדְּבָרִים הָאֵלֶּה[c]
וְהָאֱלֹהִים[d] נִסָּה[e] אֶת[f]־אַבְרָהָם
וַיֹּאמֶר[g] אֵלָיו[h]
אַבְרָהָם
וַיֹּאמֶר
הִנֵּֽנִי[i] :

[a] וַיְהִי now it happened   [b] אַחַר after   [c] הַדְּבָרִים …these things (*or* events)   [d] וְהָאֱלֹהִים and [*or* that] God
[e] נִסָּה he [God] tested   [f] אֶת־ (*untranslatable particle*)   [g] וַיֹּאמֶר and he said   [h] אֵלָיו to him   [i] הִנֵּֽנִי Here I am

UNIT 2

מַה־בַּכְּלִי הַגָּדוֹל?[1]

Describing what you see

nouns, adjectives, prepositions, and the inquiry, "מָזֶה?"

This unit will enable you to describe objects, in particular specifying which of two similar objects you are talking about:

- the *big* money bag, in contrast to the *small* money bag
- the *wicked* king, in contrast to the *good* king

You will be able to describe objects by locating them with reference to other objects:

- The money is *in the water*.
- a man on the large rock

You will be able to explain what belongs to whom:

- The *ship's* baggage is dry.
- the prophet *of God*

You will be able to determine whether someone is talking about something general...

- *a* sturdy ship

...or something specific

- *the* sturdy ship

---

[1] *What is in the large container?*

MODULE 2.1 — Specifying a particular object

Unit 2 JONAH STORY: Jonah books passage to Tarshish

When was the last time you took a trip? Was it a business trip or a holiday? Did it involve making travel arrangements in foreign country? If so, did you encounter any difficulties because you did not understand another language? After reading Jonah's experience below, ask a classmate whether he or she has encountered a similar language challenge when traveling.

Words for responding — מִלִּים לַעֲנוֹת

הוּא	he, it *m*	אַיֵּה...?[a]	Where is...?
הִיא	she, it *f*	אֵיךְ יֹאמְרוּ בִּיהוּדִית "X"?[b]	How would one say in Judean… "X"?
הִנֵּה	behold, here is		
מַיִם	water *mpl*	אֶת־ (*or* אֵת)	(*particle preceding a definite direct object*)
מֶלֶךְ	king *m*		
		הַ...	the

[a] Hebrew offers various interrogatives to inquire "Where is?" These include אֵי־זֶה (in poetry often used rhetorically, as in Deut. 32:37, or with indirect clauses, as in Judg. 13:6 and 1 Sam. 9:18) and also אֵיפֹה (an expression that may also mean, "Of what sort?" or "In what place [is something occurring]?", as in Gen. 37:16 and Job 4:7). The interrogative introduced here is the adverb employed most frequently to inquire, "Where is [a person or object] located?", namely, אַיֵּה.

[b] The language spoken in Israel at the time of King Hezekiah was known as "Judean" (2 Kings 18:26, Neh. 13:24). Alternatively it was referred to as שְׂפַת־כְּנַעַן *the language* (lit., *lip*) *of Canaan* (Isa. 19:18). While a person from

this region would be known as עִבְרִי *a Hebrew* [*person*], we have no record showing that the term "Hebrew" was used to designate their language.

לָשׁוֹן	tongue / language, tongue / language of *m*	אֳנִיָּה	ship *f*

2.1 Jonah Episode: I'm looking for a ship.

ר׳ = רַב הַחֹבֵל, ע׳ס = עֲבָדִים, א׳ = אֱלֹהִים

[נ] שָׁלוֹם: אֲנִי מְבַקֵּשׁ אֳנִיָּה: אַיֵּה אֳנִיָּה?

[ע] הִנֵּה אֳנִיָּה:

In cell 3, because the subject אֳנִיָּה *ship* is feminine singular, the pronoun that refers to "ship" must also be feminine singular: "It (הִיא) is of / from Tarshish." The second sentence of cell 6 is similar. To explore the construct phrase in cell 3, see the discussion of ownership in §2.5.ג.

In the first sentence of cell 6, the pronoun הוא sets off the second half of the sentence, as if to say, "As for the ship's name, it (הוא) [is] 'The Water King.'"[2] Can you locate the masculine singular noun to which הוא refers?

2.1.א. Explanation: "The king"   הַמֶּלֶךְ

INTERACTIVE SKILL: How to mark an object as special, distinct from the rest

Hebrew has various ways to call attention or specify a noun. One way is to prefix that noun with the definite article "the." The definite article will attach to the front of a noun: הַ⊙..., as in הַמֶּלֶךְ. There is no change in the article, whether the noun is masculine or feminine, singular or plural.

The symbol ⊙ represents a dagesh in the first consonant of the word specified by the article. Thus, we may refer generally to מֶלֶךְ *a king*, or we may refer to הַמֶּלֶךְ *the king* if we wish to be more specific. If you do not want to specify a particular object, simply omit the article.[3]

הַשֵּׁם	שֵׁם	הַנָּבִיא	נָבִיא	הַמֶּלֶךְ	מֶלֶךְ
the name	**a** name	**the** prophet	**a** prophet	**the** king	**a** king

Sometimes the definite article is spelled with the following variations:

    ...הַ (with no dagesh in the ensuing word)

    ...הָ (omitting the dagesh and substituting a qameṣ for the pataḥ)

---

[2] This use of the pronoun is known as "copulative" since it infers the verb "to be" (...*it* [*is*]...).

[3] There is no indefinite article (*a, an*) in Hebrew. Sometimes we find the numeral "one" used where English would use *a / an*, as in the opening phrase of 1 Samuel: וַיְהִי אִישׁ אֶחָד *Now there was a* [lit., *one*] *man*... (1 Sam. 1:1).

...הֶ (omitting the dagesh and substituting a segol)

These variations are determined by the first letter of the word to which the article is attached. Please refer to the appendix entry for this segment (Appendix §2.1.א.) for more information concerning these alternative spellings of the definite article.

Some words are considered definite even though they have no definite article. Such is the case with names (proper nouns). Thus, because תַּרְשִׁישׁ is a name it is automatically definite. This will be developed further, below.

2.1.ב. Activity: Matching

INTERACTIVE SKILL: How to mark an object as special, distinct from the rest

Match the following Hebrew and English words by noting the number associated with an English word and writing that number to the right of the Hebrew word with the same meaning.

מַה־בַּכְּלִי הַגָּדוֹל?

1.	a king	אֶבֶן
2.	a name	אֳנִיָּה
3.	a ship	הָאֶבֶן
4.	a stone	הָאֳנִיָּה
5.	peace (wellbeing)	הַמַּיִם
6.	water	הַמֶּלֶךְ
7.	the king	הַשָּׁלוֹם
8.	the name	הַשֵּׁם
9.	the peace	מַיִם
10.	the water	מֶלֶךְ
11.	the ship	שָׁלוֹם
12.	the stone	שֵׁם

2.1.ג. Activity: "Where is…?"   אַיֵּה...?

INTERACTIVE SKILL: Locating missing objects or persons

Discover who has the objects listed in the preceding activity. Use the model below to discover whether your classmate has the particular object that you are wondering about. Remember to **include the definite article** throughout (whether asking or responding), since you are focusing on that **particular** object.

In the affirmative answer below, the word הִנֵּה indicates that something exists (like יֵשׁ *there is*), but adds a tone of immediacy: *Here is*….[4]

Model

Abraham, where is the stone?	אַבְרָהָם אַיֵּה הָאָבֶן?	Inquiry
Here is the stone!	הִנֵּה הָאָבֶן!	Affirmative reply
I don't know.	לֹא אֵדַע׃	Negative reply #1
Who knows?	מִי יוֹדֵעַ?	Negative reply #2
I don't have the stone.	אֵין לִי הָאָבֶן׃	Negative reply #3

---

[4] At times הִנֵּה will open a longer message consisting of multiple clauses or sentences. In such cases it may announce a circumstance in the first clause, distinguishing that clause from a consequential action in the second clause (e.g., Gen. 42:2 and 2 Sam. 8:5; cf. *IBH* §135).

2.1.ד. May I offer you (*ms*) advice? (How does one say...?)

הַאִיעָצְךָ עֵצָה?

> On occasion, everyone needs to ask the meaning of a foreign word. Here is an expression for that occasion—an expression you may use at any time in this course. It will be very helpful when you either encounter a new word or encounter a word whose meaning you have forgotten.
>
> **Model**
>
> | How would one say in English: "אֶבֶן"? | אֵיךְ יֹאמְרוּ בְּאַנְגְּלִית "אֶבֶן"? |
> |---|---|
>
> אֵיךְ means *how*; בְּאַנְגְּלִית means *in English* (בְּ + אַנְגְּלִית).[5]
>
> Try out this question with a classmate! See whether he or she can tell you the English meaning for any of the following eight words or expressions:
>
> שְׁמִי... קוּם... נָבִיא... מַה־זֶּה?... לֹא... הִנֵּה... אַיֵּה... מֶלֶךְ.
>
> Conversely, at times we will need to ask for the Hebrew equivalent of a word in our native language.
>
> **Model**
>
> | How would one say in Judean: "rock"? | אֵיךְ יֹאמְרוּ בִּיהוּדִית "rock"? |
> |---|---|
>
> Turn to a classmate and experiment with this question, too. Here are some nouns or expressions for which he or she may recall the corresponding Hebrew word:

---

[5] Admittedly, "English" is not a Biblical Hebrew word. If you wish, you may substitute בִּלְשׁוֹן אִיֵּי הַיָּם *in the language of faraway lands* (cf. Isa. 11:11).

> peace... name... stone... king... water... Nineveh
>
> **From this point forward**, whenever you encounter an unfamiliar word (whether new or forgotten), be sure to use the ...אֵיךְ יֹאמְרוּ question. As you do, you will deepen your grasp of Hebrew simply by remaining in the language.

※ ※ ※ ※ ※ ※

2.1.ה. Explanation: "Whose ...?"   ?לְמִי...

INTERACTIVE SKILL: Ownership—explaining "what belongs to whom"

Words for responding

In the nouns listed below, the first Hebrew word of each pair shows the basic form—a form that can stand alone (known as the "**absolute**" or "unbound" form).

The second Hebrew noun of each pair (the word to the left of the comma) is the form used when that word is closely associated with (or "bound to") an ensuing word. This second form is known as the "**construct**" or "bound" form. Often the construct form conveys possession (similar to an "apostrophe-S" following an English possessive noun, such as "ship's").

Frequently the Hebrew Bible indicates that a form is a construct form by binding it to the next word with a raised hyphen (called a "maqqef").[6] When collected in a vocabulary list, construct forms in this textbook will display a maqqef. Alternate construct spellings without the maqqef occasionally may be introduced as well (e.g., שֶׁם־ and שֵׁם, both construct). Early episodes of the Jonah story similarly will signal construct forms by following them with a maqqef. Later episodes will at times omit use of the maqqef, to help you grow accustomed to recognizing construct forms even without the maqqef.

---

[6] The maqqef is used to join other words as well. Already you have seen it used after אֶל־ *to* and אֶת־ (the particle which precedes a direct object that is definite, cf. §2.1.ז., below).

לָשׁוֹן, לְשׁוֹן־	tongue *or* language,* tongue *or* language of *m*	אֳנִיָּה, אֳנִית־	ship,* ship of *f*
שֻׁלְחָן, שֻׁלְחַן־	table, table of *m*	כִּסֵּא, כִּסֵּא־	chair, chair of *m* (*no change*)
שֵׁם, שֶׁם־ (*or* שֵׁם־)	name, name of *m*	לֶחֶם, לֶחֶם־	bread,* bread of *m* (*no change*)

To indicate that something belongs to someone (or something), simply state the owner **after** the entity that is owned. Thus כִּסֵּא־מֶלֶךְ means *a chair **of a king***. The phrase consisting of a construct form and the ensuing word or words to which it is bound is called a "construct chain;" a construct form is said to be in the "construct state."

If you wish to refer to a **particular king's** chair, make the **king** definite by adding the article to מֶלֶךְ. So you would say כִּסֵּא־הַמֶּלֶךְ ***the*** chair of ***the*** king (or ***the*** king's chair) instead of simply כִּסֵּא־מֶלֶךְ *a chair of a king*. Incidentally, *a* (or *the*) *king's chair* is the way to say *throne* in Hebrew.

כִּסֵּא־הַמֶּלֶךְ	כִּסֵּא־מֶלֶךְ	כִּסֵּא
the chair of the king	a chair of a king	chair
לֶחֶם־הַנָּבִיא	לֶחֶם־נָבִיא⁷	לֶחֶם
the bread of the prophet	bread of a prophet	bread

Note: Some nouns change their spelling slightly in the construct form. For example, nouns like אֳנִיָּה *ship* will often replace the ◌ָה... ending by a ◌ַת... ending. Thus אֳנִיָּה *ship* becomes אֳנִית *ship of* when expressed together with its owner.

אֳנִית־הַמֶּלֶךְ	אֳנִית־מֶלֶךְ	אֳנִיָּה
the ship of the king (*or* the king's ship)	a ship of a king (*or* a king's ship)	a ship

---

* As noted already, a word that has appeared in an earlier vocabulary list (whether the identical word or the root form) will be marked with an asterisk (*). Words without an asterisk are either new or introduce a new pattern relating to an already-familiar root.

⁷ The small vertical stroke to the left of the segol in לֶ is called a "meteg." Here it marks the syllable with a secondary stress (accent) among words joined by a maqqef. The primary stress remains on the last syllable of נָבִיא.

The **long** A-class vowel qameṣ in the last syllable of שֻׁלְחָן will **reduce to a short vowel** of the same class (a pataḥ): שֻׁלְחַן־. Otherwise, the qameṣ must become a qameṣ-ḥaṭuf because it now would stand in a closed, unaccented syllable (since an entire construct chain has only one accented syllable).

שֻׁלְחַן־הָאִשָּׁה	שֻׁלְחַן־אִשָּׁה	שֻׁלְחָן
the table of the woman (*or* the woman's table)	a table of a woman (*or* a woman's table)	a table

As with other languages, it is possible in Hebrew to string together **multiple** layers of owners: שֵׁם־אֳנִיַּת־הַמֶּלֶךְ *the name of the ship of the king.* Notice that **in English each member** of the construct chain takes on the article *the*, even though **in Hebrew only the final member** of the chain bears the article. Conversely, simply by omitting that final article, the entire chain would become indefinite: שֵׁם־אֳנִיַּת־מֶלֶךְ *a name of a ship of a king.*[8]

Finally, notice the following three examples. You will discover that they have been translated as if definite ("**the** chair," "**the** king," and "**the** language"). But can you find any definite articles in the final word of any of these phrases?

לְשׁוֹן־תַּרְשִׁישׁ	מֶלֶךְ־יִשְׂרָאֵל	כִּסֵּא־יוֹנָה
the language of Tarshish	**the** king of Israel (*or simply* Israel's king)	**the** chair of Jonah (*or simply* Jonah's chair)

Each of these construct chains ends with a **name**. Since names require no article to be definite, these chains are definite even though they contain no article.[9]

When a conjunction links together multiple nouns associated with a construct expression, the conjunction will appear in translation just as it appears in Hebrew. Thus if the **first** member of the construct

---

[8] Occasionally the context of a biblical passage will indicate that, despite a definite noun at the close of a construct chain, still the first member of the chain remains *indefinite* (e.g., אִישׁ הָאֲדָמָה "[Noah], **a** man of **the** land" in Gen. 9:20), and חֶלְקַת הַשָּׂדֶה "**a** plot of **the** field" in 2 Sam. 23:11). This is the exception, not the rule.

[9] At times Hebrew will use an article with a toponym (place name), although this will not occur with a person's name. So, although you will not find Jonah referred to with the article as הַיּוֹנָה, a toponym such as the Jordan River may be referred to either without an article simply as יַרְדֵּן, or alternatively with an article as הַיַּרְדֵּן. Both means of referring to the river are definite.

chain consists of multiple nouns, the resulting phrase would appear thus: "(A **and** B) of C," rather than the customary "A of B of C" (see "Compound first-member" example, below).

Conversely, if the **last** member of the construct chain consists of multiple nouns, the resulting phrase would appear thus: "A of (B **and** of C)" (see "Compound last-member" example, below). Alternatively, biblical writers could simply repeat the first word ("A of B and A of C"), rather than creating compound noun clusters.[10]

Compound last-member	Compound first-member
שֻׁלְחַן הַמֶּלֶךְ וְהַנָּבִיא	כִּסֵּא וְשֻׁלְחַן יוֹנָה
the table of the king **and** [of] the prophet	the chair **and** the table of Jonah

2.1.1. Activity: Matching

INTERACTIVE SKILL: Ownership—explaining "what belongs to whom"

Words for responding — מִלִּים לַעֲנוֹת

The following words will be useful in this matching exercise.

אֲבָנִים[a]	stones *fpl*
כֶּסֶף, כֶּסֶף־	silver, money (*but not* coin *or* currency) *m*
עִיר, עִיר־	city *f*

[a] The construct of plural nouns will be introduced later (§3.3.ה.).

---

[10] So we read of Pharaoh Neco's tribute imposed on Israel, consisting of מֵאָה כִכַּר־כֶּסֶף וְכִכַּר זָהָב *one hundred* **disks** *of silver and* **disks** *of gold* (rather than *disks of silver and gold*, 2 Kings 23:33).

To become familiar with expressing ownership, match the following phrases by writing the number of the correct translation in the blank next to the appropriate Hebrew phrase.

1.	a city of stones	אֳנִיַּת־מֶלֶךְ
2.	a king of silver	כֶּסֶף־הָאִישׁ
3.	a king's ship	לֶחֶם־הָאֳנִיָּה
4.	a name of a city	מֵי[11]־שָׁלוֹם
5.	the man's silver	מֶלֶךְ־כֶּסֶף
6.	the peace of the LORD	עִיר־אֲבָנִים
7.	the ship's bread	שְׁלוֹם־יהוה
8.	water(s) of peace (i.e., tranquil waters)	שֵׁם־עִיר

2.1.ז. Explanation and activity: "I am looking for..." אֲנִי מְבַקֵּשׁ...

INTERACTIVE SKILL: Inquire what someone is looking for

Before engaging this activity, please notice the word אֶת־ in the following question:

אֵיךְ יֹאמְרוּ בִּיהוּדִית אֶת־שֵׁם־הָאֳנִיָּה?

How does one say, in Judean, the ship's name?

The particle אֶת־ will precede a direct object, when that object is **definite**. While it is untranslatable in English, at times אֶת־ helps the reader / hearer to distinguish between a subject and an object.[12]

---

[11] *Water(s) of.*

[12] You will also find אֶת־ spelled as אֵת, when it is not followed by a maqqef.

Also notice אֶת־ in this statement by Jonah: לֹא אָבִין אֶת־לְשׁוֹן־תַּרְשִׁישׁ *I do not understand the language of Tarshish*. Although there is no definite article, yet לְשׁוֹן **is definite** because it is in construct with a proper noun (Tarshish). Thus the definite direct object marker אֶת־ is appropriate here.

Now we are ready for the activity. To discover what your neighbor needs or is looking for, please ask using the model below. He or she will pick something from the list of construct expressions in §2.1.ג., or may invent something else (please be sure that it follows the construct pattern of "I'm looking for **X, that belongs to Y**," not simply "I'm looking for X").

Model

What are you looking for?	מָה אַתָּה מְבַקֵּשׁ?	Inquiry (you *ms*)
	מָה אַתְּ מְבַקֶּשֶׁת?	Inquiry (you *fs*)
David's bread is what I am looking for. (*Or* I'm looking for **David's bread**.)	אֶת־לֶחֶם־דָּוִד אֲנִי מְבַקֵּשׁ / מְבַקֶּשֶׁת:	Reply (*ms* / *fs*)

Did you notice that in the above reply, the phrase אֶת־לֶחֶם־דָּוִד *David's bread* appears **at the front** of the sentence? As noted in the previous unit, it is appropriate to place at the front of a reply the particular information sought by the question (see §1.3.א.).

In contrast, if you do **not** need to draw attention to **what** you are looking for—then you would respond with a **neutral**, unmarked sequence: אֲנִי מְבַקֵּשׁ אֶת־לֶחֶם־דָּוִד: *I am looking for David's bread*. The unmarked sequence is: subject (whether noun or pronoun), then participle, followed by additional information (direct object or prepositional phrase, for example).

Note: In a sentence formed around a participle (such as מְבַקֵּשׁ / מְבַקֶּשֶׁת), any expression placed **ahead of the subject** is said to be "marked," drawing the focus of attention.[13]

---

[13] Randall Buth, "Word Order in the Verbless Clause: A Generative-Functional Approach," in *The Verbless Clause in Biblical Hebrew: Linguistic Approaches*, ed. Cynthia L. Miller (Winona Lake, Indiana: Eisenbrauns, 1999), 87–94, 101, and 107; *pace* Joüon §154f.a.1, who yet allows that "the predicate preceding a pronominal subject often does receive some prominence"). A generative approach indicates that a predicate preceding its subject (pronominal or otherwise) regularly receives prominence.

2.1.ח. Did you (*ms*) know that...? (Incised seals)   הֲיָדַ֫עְתָּ כִּי...?

...incised seals that served to mark ownership often were intricately crafted of gemstone? Together with the owner's name (written in reverse), they may feature a heraldic emblem.

One particular oval seal of jasper with its top pierced for a cord was found bearing the inscription לְאׇנִיָּ֫הוּ בֶּן מֵירָב (vowels not present in the original) *Belonging to ʾŌniyāhû, Son of Mêrav.* Since אוֹן means strength, the name *ʾŌniyāhû* would mean "The LORD is my strength." ל means [*belonging*] *to*; בֶּן is a construct form meaning *son of*. If not in construct, it would be spelled בֵּן *son, m.*

Likely dating to the seventh or eighth century BCE, this seal portrays a merchantman vessel as heraldic emblem. Single-masted, square-sailed, with rounded bow and stern, a side rudder, but without oars—this may be the only Israelite indication of the sort of vessel Solomon may have used in his fleet. Incidentally, did you notice the correlation between the emblem and a word you have learned—a word that sounds like the owner's name?[14]

---

[14] Nahman Avigad, "A Hebrew Seal Depicting a Sailing Ship," *Bulletin of the American Schools of Oriental Research*, 246 (Spring 1982): 59–62. For a photo of the seal, see "Highlights from the Michael Steinhardt Judaica Collection," n.p. Online: http://steinhardtjudaica.com/highlights.php?p=4. The script corresponds closely to that of other seals and inscribed gems dating from the ninth to the fifth centuries BCE (GKC, "Table of Alphabets," xvi.a). The reading מירב rather than מזרב is clearer in the seal (right oval) than in its impression (left oval). Although the spelling מירב does not appear in the Hebrew Bible as a name, it is reminiscent of מֵרַב, one of Saul's daughters (1 Sam. 18:17).

UNIT 2   מַה־בַּכְּלִי הַגָּדוֹל?   121

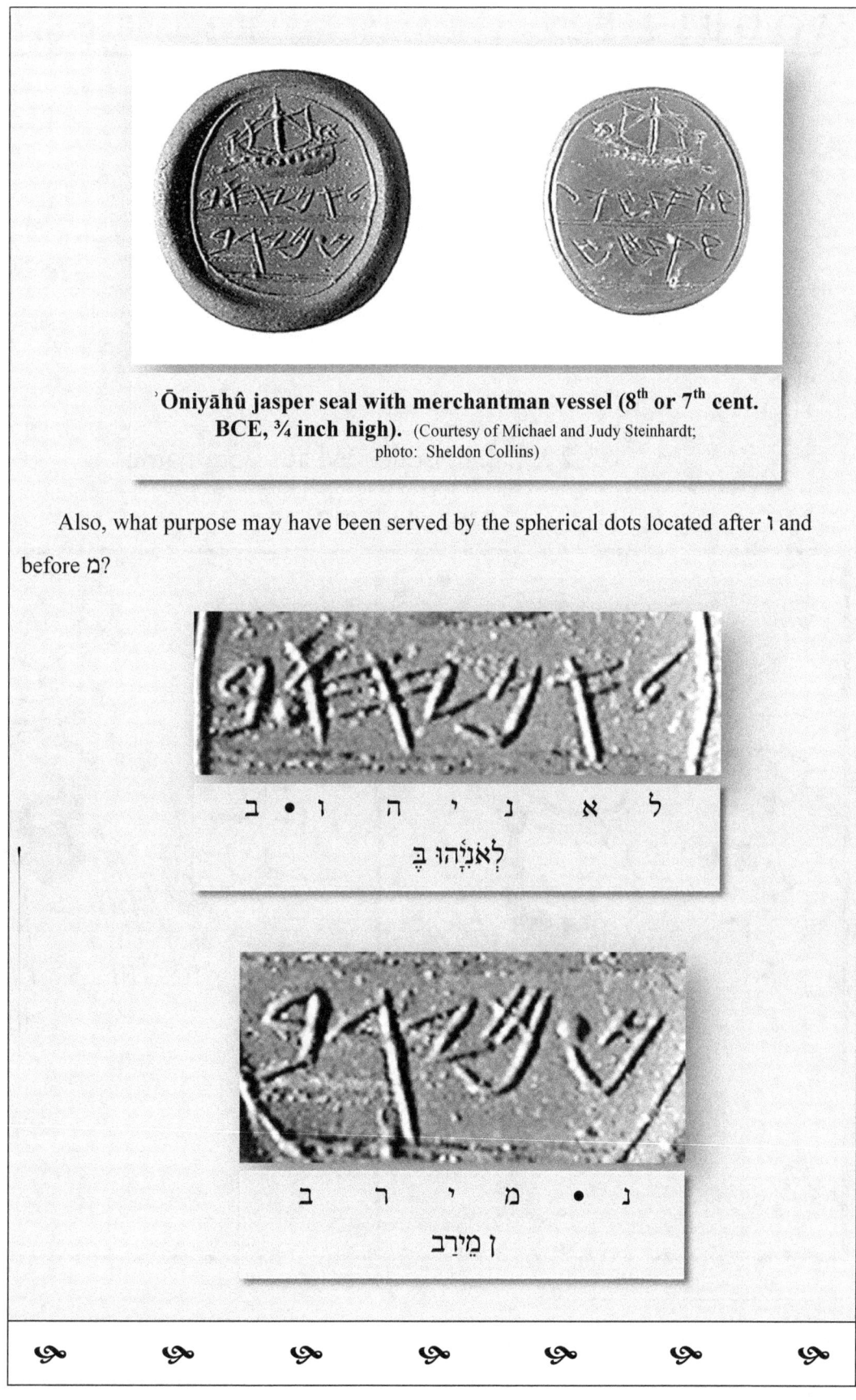

'Ōniyāhû jasper seal with merchantman vessel (8th or 7th cent. BCE, ¾ inch high). (Courtesy of Michael and Judy Steinhardt; photo: Sheldon Collins)

Also, what purpose may have been served by the spherical dots located after ו and before מ?

ל א נ י ה ו • ב

לְאֹנִיָּהוּ בֶּ

נ • מ י ר ב

ן מֵירַב

MODULE 2.2 — Responding to a greeting

	Words for responding			מִלִּים לַעֲנוֹת
my name*	שְׁמִי		Jonah	יוֹנָה
your name* ms, fs	שְׁמֵךְ / (שְׁמֶךָ or) שִׁמְךָ		very (much)*	מְאֹד

2.2 Jonah Episode: What's your name?

נ׳ = יוֹנָה הַנָּבִיא, ע׳ = עֶבֶד

[ע׳] מַה־שְּׁמֶךָ?

[נ׳] שְׁמִי יוֹנָה:

[ע׳] הֲשָׁלוֹם לְךָ יוֹנָה?

[נ׳] אֵין:
צַר־לִי:
צַר־לִי מְאֹד:

---

* By way of reminder, a word whose root or basic form has appeared in previous vocabulary lists will be marked with an asterisk (*). Words without an asterisk are new.

2.2.א. Activity: "How are you (*ms / fs*)?" הֲשָׁלוֹם לָךְ?

INTERACTIVE SKILL: Exchanging greetings

In languages such as English, proper expression requires that each sentence contain a verb. With Semitic languages such as Hebrew, the situation is a bit different—especially with regard to the verb "to be." Although there is a verb "to be" in Hebrew, it often is omitted. Sentences lacking a finite verb (a verb that is configured to accompany a particular person and number)—these sentences earn the classification of "verbless" or "nominal" sentences.

Turn to a classmate and ask how he / she is doing (הֲשָׁלוֹם לָךְ?, cf. 2 Kings 4:26). Notice that the Hebrew version does not employ any verb. If you are curious, follow the references to see how a particular expression (or one closely resembling it) appears in the Hebrew Bible.

2 Kings 4:26	(I'm) fine.		שָׁלוֹם (לִי):
Esth. 8:17, 2 Kings 11:14	I am joyful (*m, f*).		שִׂמְחָה לִי *or* שָׂמֵחַ / שְׂמֵחָה אֲנִי:
1 Sam. 28:15	I'm in (great) distress.		צַר־לִי (מְאֹד):
1 Sam. 19:14	I feel sick (*m, f*).		חֹלֶה / חֹלָה אֲנִי:

Gen. 25:30   I am tired (*m, f*).    עָיֵף / עֲיֵפָה אֲנִי:

2.2.ב. Activity: "How is Jonah doing?"   הֲשָׁלוֹם לְיוֹנָה?

INTERACTIVE SKILL: Reporting whether someone else is doing okay or not

Read over the 2.2 Jonah Episode. Then listen for your instructor's follow-up question, found in the title for this segment.

2.2.ג. May I offer you (*ms*) advice? (Learning vocabulary)

הַאִיעָצְךָ עֵצָה?

What is the best way to learn new vocabulary? Experiment with several to discover what works best for you. The more important techniques are listed first.

1. **Learn it early, review it often.** Cultivate the discipline of beginning to learn a few new words on the first day of each week. Invest frequent, brief periods learning and reviewing, separated by periods of rest or engaging other tasks.

2. **Carry vocabulary cards.** Write a Hebrew word on one side of a small card, with its translation on the other. Keep your cards with you, reviewing when you have a free moment. Sort to the top those words that are giving you problems.

3. **Say it aloud.** Many are auditory learners. Say each word aloud as you review

its meaning.

4. **Visualize it.** Many are visual learners. Associate a mental picture with the word you are learning. The word will be easier to remember if you make the mental picture striking, bizarre, or extreme. If "stone," picture a looming boulder; if "water," picture a towering breaker.

5. **Act it out.** Some are kinesthetic learners. When learning the expression "stand up," repeatedly stand to your feet as you say the word in Hebrew. Physically writing any word in the target language also qualifies as kinesthetic learning.

6. **Associate it with other Hebrew words.** Create a meaningful context for a new word by fashioning a phrase or sentence using other words you already know. If learning "climb," and if you already know "mountain," then say or write, "Climb a mountain!" At the same time, visualize a hiker carrying an enormous backpack precariously clinging to an inverted cliff: "climb!"

7. **Study with a friend.** Many are social learners. Connect with a classmate, whether in-person or through technology, and spend time quizzing each other on vocabulary. Make a game of it.

8. **Make labels.** When learning "chair" or "table," write those words on small slips of paper and tape them to furniture in your home. Is "sun" on the list for this week? Sketch a bright, simple sun, label it with the Hebrew word, and tape it to your mirror. (Take care not to write the English meaning on the label: rely on the object or sketch to remind you of the meaning.)

9. **Link it to sounds in your native language.** With certain words you may be able to create a sound-link between the Hebrew word and a sound or phrase in your native language. For example, since אֶבֶן *rock* sounds like the name "Evan," one might picture a boy (named "**Evan**," naturally), balancing a ridiculously large **boulder** on his head. Since the word מַיִם *water* begins with a sound resembling the possessive pronoun "my," you might picture an impetuous toddler snatching a cup of water from a sibling, declaring: "Mine!" Caution: keep the links as direct as possible, since the effort required to trace a convoluted link will actually inhibit binding word to meaning.

MODULE 2.3 — Describing a person or object

Words for responding — מִלִּים לַעֲנוֹת

Several vocabulary entries below introduce both the target form of the word and related forms as well, thereby giving a more complete picture of a word. Thus in addition to the target form גָּדוֹל *big* (*masculine singular*), you will also find the feminine singular (גְּדוֹלָה), masculine plural (גְּדוֹלִים), and feminine plural (גְּדוֹלוֹת). Italicized abbreviations accompanying the glosses indicate what the forms represent. Not all forms are used in the Jonah episode.

Word root (שֹׁרֶשׁ). With this module the vocabulary lists will begin to include the root (called the שֹׁרֶשׁ) underlying a given verb. The root will appear in brackets and without vowels. The principle consonants (called "radicals") of the שֹׁרֶשׁ *root* will be separated by periods. Thus [ה.ל.כ] is the root of לָלֶכֶת.

You are encouraged to learn a word's root (ה.ל.כ, in this case) as you learn the word itself. The root (שֹׁרֶשׁ) will help simplify memorization, as it will allow you to mentally gather under one שֹׁרֶשׁ the various words that spring from that שֹׁרֶשׁ.

To pronounce the root (שֹׁרֶשׁ) aloud, you may either name the letters singly (ה-ל-כ), or—in most cases—pronounce the שֹׁרֶשׁ as if it were vocalized with "A" vowels: הָלַךְ. This vocalization (with "A" vowels qameṣ and pataḥ) produces the simplest conjugated form of a root (שֹׁרֶשׁ). In the case of הָלַךְ, it means *he walked*. Your instructor can help you recognize those verbs requiring vowels other than "A" class vowels for vocalizing the שֹׁרֶשׁ.

עִיר, עִיר־	city* *f* (*sing. absol., sing. constr.*)	גָּדוֹל, גְּדוֹלָה, גְּדוֹלִים, גְּדוֹלוֹת	big, large, great *ms, fs, mpl, fpl*[a]
קָטָן *or* (קָטֹן)[c], קְטַנָּה, קְטַנִּים, קְטַנּוֹת	small, young *ms, fs, mpl, fpl*	טוֹב, טוֹבָה, טוֹבִים, טוֹבוֹת	good *ms, fs, mpl, fpl*
		כִּי	because, that[b], when, indeed
רַע, רָעָה, רָעִים, רָעוֹת	bad, wicked *ms, fs, mpl, fpl*	כְּלִי, כֵּלִים, כְּלִי־	container, sack, baggage *m* (*sing. absol., pl. absol., sing. constr.*)
		לָמָּה...?	Why?

[a] The abbreviations are as follows: *m*[asculine] *s*[ingular], *f*[eminine] *s*[ingular], *m*[asculine] *pl*[ural], *f*[eminine] *pl*[ural]. These four categories comprise the standard sequence of related forms presented for **adjectives**.

[b] The conjunction כִּי generally introduces a clause, such as "God saw **that** it was good." It is not a demonstrative pronoun (e.g., "The ship reached **that** port city").

[c] For *small ms*, the Hebrew Bible employs קָטֹן roughly as often as it employs קָטָן. When it comes to derived forms, however (i.e., masculine plural, feminine singular, feminine plural), all are supplied by קָטָן, not by קָטֹן.

Words for hearing — מִלִּים לִשְׁמֹעַ

כָּבֵד, כְּבֵדָה, כְּבֵדִים, כְּבֵדוֹת	heavy, oppressive *ms, fs, mpl, fpl*	אֱלֹהִים	God *m*
לָלֶכֶת [ה.ל.כ]	to go (*with prep.* ל)	הֶ..., הַ..., הָ...	(alternate spellings of interrogative particle ...הֲ)[a]
מַה־זֶּה?	What is this?		
סֵפֶר, סֵפֶר־	book, scroll *m*	וְ..., וּ..., וִ..., וַ..., וָ...	and, but (*spelling depends on next syllable*)
עָלַי ל...	I must (*followed by* ל *and infinitive construct*)		
		חָזָק, חֲזָקָה, חֲזָקִים, חֲזָקוֹת	strong, hard, tough *ms, fs, mpl, fpl*
צְרוֹר, צְרוֹר־	pouch, bag *m* (absol., constr.)	יָבֵשׁ, יְבֵשָׁה, יְבֵשִׁים, יְבֵשׁוֹת	dry *ms, fs, mpl, fpl*

[a] Thus notice הֶ in ...הֶחָפֵץ אַתָּה *Do you want...?* (instead of הֲחָפֵץ[‡]). The shift from an "A Class" vowel to an "I/E Class" vowel is known as "dissimilation." Please refer to appendix entry under "2.3 Words for hearing" for more information concerning spelling adjustments associated with the interrogative particle הֲ.

2.3 Jonah Episode: Why are you in trouble?

נ׳ = יוֹנָה הַנָּבִיא, ע׳ = עֶבֶד

[ע׳]   לָמָה? לָמָה צַר לָךְ?

[נ׳]   כִּי עָלַי לָלֶכֶת אֶל־נִינְוֵה:
וְאֵינֶנִּי חָפֵץ לָלֶכֶת אֶל־נִינְוֵה:

[ע׳]   לָמָה?

[נ׳]   כִּי נִינְוֵה עִיר רָעָה: עִיר גְּדוֹלָה נִינְוֵה:
עִיר רָעָה וּגְדוֹלָה נִינְוֵה: וַאֲנִי נְבִיא־
אֱלֹהִים:

UNIT 2 מַה-בַּכְּלִי הַגָּדוֹל? 131

2.3.א. Explanation: "And I have (pieces of) baggage." וְיֵשׁ לִי כֵּלִים:

INTERACTIVE SKILL: Distinguishing between one and more than one

As Jonah warms to the idea of revising his itinerary and sailing to Tarshish, he casually adds another bit of information: וְיֵשׁ לִי כֵּלִים טוֹבִים *and I have some fine (pieces of) luggage.* When adding another element, Hebrew uses the conjunction ו *and.* Attach the word ו directly to the second of the two elements you wish to connect. It will attach to the front of that second element without any intervening space. Thus:

וְיֶשׁ לִי... = ...יֵשׁ לִי + וְ *and I have...*

Since the conjunction וְ will be accompanied by a variety of vowels depending on the following syllable (not limited to a sheva), you will want to review the corresponding appendix entry in order to recognize the conjunction in its various spellings:

וְ..., וָ..., וִ..., וַ..., or וֶ...

Now consider the word describing what Jonah is bringing with him on the trip, namely כֵּלִים *containers*. To this point we have concentrated on nouns that are **singular** in number. כֵּלִים is the **plural** form of the noun כְּלִי. Let's explore how to recognize plural nouns.

Plurals ending in ים.... Many nouns form the plural by adding an ים-ending to the singular form. Thus נָבִיא *prophet* (singular) becomes נְבִיאִים *prophets* (plural), and כְּלִי *container* becomes כֵּלִים in plural.

In the process of **adding a syllable** to the end of the word, often one or more of the preceding vowels will undergo changes to accommodate the increased length of the word—an accommodation that often serves to ease pronunciation. Most typical is the **reduction to sheva** of the first vowel in a three-syllable plural (so נָבִיא *prophet* becomes נְבִיאִים *prophets*).

The reduction to sheva becomes instead a reduction to a ֲ if the first consonant is a **guttural**. Thus אֶבֶן *stone* becomes אֲבָנִים *stones*, and עָוֺן *iniquity* becomes עֲוֺנוֺת *iniquities*.

The two-syllable word כֵּלִים also changed its first vowel. In this case, a sheva in the first syllable of כְּלִי was replaced by a ṣērê.

Often a plural ending in ים... indicates that this is a **masculine** noun (but not always). Conversely, often an וֺת... ending is associated with a **feminine** noun (but not always). In the following table you will find examples of the more typical ים... *masculine* and וֺת... *feminine*, as well as the anomalous ים... *feminine* and וֺת... *masculine*.

Plurals ending in וֺת.... If a word does not form its plural with an ים... ending, it will form its plural with an וֺת... ending. There are only these two options.[15] Thus אֳנִיָּה *ship* becomes אֳנִיּוֺת *ships*. כּוֺס *cup* forms its plural as כּוֺסוֺת *cups*.

As with the addition of an ים... ending, lengthening a word by adding an וֺת... suffix may cause adjustments in preceding vowels.

---

[15] This refers to **absolute plural** forms. Dual forms and masculine plural construct endings in ֵי will be introduced in §3.1 (Words to Hear) and §3.3.ה., respectively.

UNIT 2 מַה־בַּכְּלִי הַגָּדוֹל? 133

The following table collects nouns introduced to this point, showing singular and plural forms. Masculine nouns are on the right; feminine nouns are on the left. To help you recognize vowel changes, clusters of words within a single gender group that undergo similar changes have been gathered together, separated by horizontal lines. Thus נָבִיא is grouped with שָׁלוֹם because their plural forms reduce a qameṣ to a sheva (singular נָבִיא becomes נְבִיאִים in plural).

Feminine nouns ending in וֹת...			Masculine nouns ending in ים...		
Plural	Singular		Plural	Singular	
אֳנִיּוֹת	אֳנִיָּה	ship	כֵּלִים	כְּלִי	container
כֹּסוֹת	כּוֹס	cup	נְבִיאִים	נָבִיא	prophet
			שְׁלוֹמִים	שָׁלוֹם	peace
			כְּסָפִים	כֶּסֶף	silver
			מְלָכִים	מֶלֶךְ	king
			סְפָרִים	סֵפֶר	book, scroll
Feminine nouns ending in ים...			**Masculine nouns ending in וֹת...**		
אֲבָנִים	אֶבֶן	stone	כִּסְאוֹת	כִּסֵּא	seat
עָרִים	עִיר	city	צְרֹרוֹת	צְרוֹר	pouch
			שֻׁלְחָנוֹת	שֻׁלְחָן	table
			שֵׁמוֹת	שֵׁם	name

Irregular plurals. Occasionally a plural form may not be recognizable from the corresponding singular form. For example, אִישׁ *man, person* routinely uses as plural the word אֲנָשִׁים *men, people* (the plural form we might have expected, אִישִׁים, is attested but only rarely). The plural נָשִׁים *women* similarly appears to diverge from its singular counterpart, אִשָּׁה *woman*.[16]

---

[16] אִשָּׁה and נָשִׁים are actually related, since the dagesh in אִשָּׁה conceals a root-נ which reappears in the plural form נָשִׁים.

2.3.ב. Explanation: "Big or small?"   גָּדוֹל אוֹ קָטָן?

INTERACTIVE SKILL: Describing objects with adjectives

You may express a simple description in Hebrew by juxtaposing a noun with an adjective. In the Jonah episode above, the sailor asked whether Jonah was holding כְּלִי טוֹב, *a good [piece of] baggage* (or *a good container*). In simple adjective phrases such as כְּלִי טוֹב (in which the adjective describes the noun **without** forming a sentence),[17] Hebrew will indicate the relationship between noun and adjective with a **threefold connection**—links involving (a) number, (b) gender, and (c) definiteness.[18]

---

[17] When it functions in a phrase that does **not** form a sentence, an adjective is known as "**attributive**" (e.g., "a good container"). In such situations, the adjective merely supplies an "attribute" of the targeted noun. Alternatively, if an

UNIT 2   מַה־בַּכְּלִי הַגָּדוֹל?   135

(a) **The number link (singular): masculine singular phrases (כְּלִי טוֹב).** The first link involves **number**. If the noun is singular, then it requires a singular form of the adjective. If, however, the noun is plural, the adjective must appear in its plural form. Consider the noun כְּלִי in the above adjective phrase, כְּלִי טוֹב. Since כְּלִי is singular, any adjective used to modify it must be singular as well (טוֹב is singular). The opposite of כְּלִי טוֹב might be כְּלִי רַע (notice that רַע is singular, matching כְּלִי).

Now it's your turn. When you take a trip, do you prefer to carry כְּלִי גָּדוֹל or כְּלִי קָטָן? Check the word lists for this module if you are unsure of the meanings for גָּדוֹל or קָטָן. Notice that גָּדוֹל and קָטָן are each (masculine) **singular** adjective forms. Also note that since the adjective does not form a sentence, the adjective must **follow** its noun. So: which do you prefer to carry? Write your answer here:

```
┌─────────────────────────────────────────────────────────────┐
│                                                             │
│                                                             │
│                                                             │
└─────────────────────────────────────────────────────────────┘
```

(a′) **The number link (plural): masculine plural phrases (כֵּלִים טוֹבִים).** Let's return to the sailor onboard his ship. If instead of pointing to Jonah's single bag, the sailor were pointing to a **cluster** of containers that happened to be well-made, he would need to use the **plural** noun form (כְּלִי container, m[asculine] s[ingular], would become כֵּלִים containers, m[asculine] pl[ural]). Consequently any adjective modifying כֵּלִים must be plural as well. In place of טוֹב good, ms, we must use טוֹבִים good, mpl. By placing the adjective after the noun we form an adjective phrase, כֵּלִים טוֹבִים, *good containers*.

It's your turn again. Suppose you are writing a one-act play portraying the plight of refugees. You want to show them fleeing from danger, carrying only a very few suitcases. In your opinion, would it be more realistic to show the actors carrying כֵּלִים טוֹבִים or כֵּלִים רָעִים? (Notice that in each case the adjectives match כֵּלִים since they are *mpl* forms. Also, they appear **after** the noun.) Which seems to you to be more realistic? Write your answer here:

---

actual sentence forms around the adjective (in English supplying the verb "to be"), then an adjective is operating in a "predicative" function (e.g., "A container **is** good" or "A ship **is** large"). As you will discover later, the distinction between attributive and predicative adjectives is **not** marked by spelling. They are spelled the same. Rather, syntax (word order) and the role of the definite article can be helpful in distinguishing a predicative adjective. For now we will concentrate on adjectives in **attributive** settings (those not forming a sentence).

[18] The threefold identification is known as "concord" between noun and adjective.

(b) The gender link: feminine singular phrases (אֳנִיָּה טוֹבָה). The second link connecting an adjective to the noun it modifies involves **gender** agreement. Suppose that the captain wished to have his crew transfer some cargo from his vessel to another ship in order to bring it ashore. He locates a smaller harbor boat to assist with this ship-to-shore transfer. The harbor boat happens to be particularly well-maintained. How would he refer to that boat (and its high quality)? Keep in mind that אֳנִיָּה *ship / boat* is a feminine noun. In place of טוֹב *m[asculine] s[ingular]* he would need to choose טוֹבָה *f[eminine] s[ingular]*, yielding the adjective phrase, אֳנִיָּה טוֹבָה *a good boat*.

According to Jonah's statements in the episode above, what is Nineveh like? Write the abbreviation נ׳ (for נִינְוֵה) above any of these phrases that describes Jonah's assessment of **Nineveh**. The third adjective, חֲזָקָה, is the *fs* form of חָזָק *strong, hard, tough* (see list at the end of this module).

עִיר טוֹבָה	עִיר גְּדוֹלָה	עִיר חֲזָקָה	עִיר רָעָה	עִיר קְטַנָּה

How about Tarshish? Referring to the same five phrases, write the abbreviation ת׳ above any phrase matching the sailor's description of **Tarshish**.

(b′) The gender link: feminine plural phrases (אֳנִיּוֹת טוֹבוֹת). Next, imagine that the captain's crew has discovered not only **one** fine harbor boat offering to ferry freight to shore, but **several** fine boats. Puzzled, his crew may need to ask for clarification. To express that they have discovered not one, but many "**good boats**" the crew will need to modify *boats* (אֳנִיּוֹת *fpl*) with a corresponding form of *good* (טוֹבוֹת *fpl*), arriving at the expression אֳנִיּוֹת טוֹבוֹת *good boats, fpl*.

Now, for your opinion: if you and a dozen friends planned to float down a scenic river together, which of the following would you prefer to hire, and why? Select one of the four noun phrases offered below as your answer, and circle it. Then write your reasoning below (in English). Your answer will vary, depending on how you like to float.

אֳנִיּוֹת גְּדוֹלוֹת	אֳנִיּוֹת חֲזָקוֹת	אֳנִיּוֹת קְטַנּוֹת	אֳנִיּוֹת רָעוֹת

How many of those אֳנִיּוֹת do you suppose you would need, in order to accommodate the thirteen of you? Write the number you have in mind here: _____. Your answer will vary, depending on your selection above.

As you may have realized, the "gender link" was also operating in the earlier examples of "number link," although it was not called to your attention. Thus the **masculine** noun כְּלִי in example (a) above required the **masculine** singular form of the adjective (טוֹב), and כֵּלִים in example (a′) required the **masculine** plural form of the adjective (טוֹבִים).

Spelling changes in adjectives. Before proceeding to the third link (definiteness), we should observe the sort of changes you may encounter when converting a masculine adjective into feminine, or a singular adjective into a plural.

- Convert **masculine** singular to **feminine** singular, by adding ָה....
- Convert **masculine singular** to **masculine plural** by adding ִים....
- Convert **masculine singular** to **feminine plural** by adding וֹת....

The addition of the syllable ָה..., ִים..., or וֹת... may cause preceding vowels to adjust, as noted earlier when singular nouns adjusted vowels when a plural suffix was added.

Unlike nouns, the gender indicators (morphemes) of **adjectives** are **stable**. A plural adjective that ends in ִים... will always be **masculine**, a plural adjective that ends in וֹת... will always be **feminine**, and an adjective that ends in ָה... will always be feminine **singular**. As a result, noun-adjective combinations often produce a degree of end-rhyme, as in **אֳנִיוֹת גְדוֹלוֹת** *big ships*. It is important to remember, however, that it is the actual **gender** of the noun (not the sound of its suffix) that drives the spelling of a modifying adjective. That is why—even though both are *fpl*—the suffixes in the phrase *large cities* will **not** rhyme: עָרִים גְדוֹלוֹת.

See whether you can provide the proper form of the specified adjective to describe the following nouns. Remember that the ending of a noun will not necessarily rhyme with the correct ending of its adjective.

How would you say *large books*?　　　　　　　　　　　　סְפָרִים _____

How would you say *large stones*?　　　　　　　　　　　　אֲבָנִים _____

How would you say *good names*?　　　　　　　　　　　　שֵׁמוֹת _____

How would you say *good cities*?　　　　　　　　　　　　עָרִים _____

(c) The definiteness link. Definiteness is the third link that signals that an adjective modifies a particular noun. When using an adjective to modify an indefinite noun, simply use the adjective with no definite article. That is what the sailor did when he described Tarshish as עִיר טוֹבָה *a good city*. Here are more examples. Notice the **absence** of articles.

צְרוֹר גָּדוֹל	a large pouch (*not* **the** large pouch)
אֳנִיָּה גְּדוֹלָה	a large ship (*not* **the** large ship)
מְלָכִים רָעִים	[some] bad kings (*not* **the** bad kings)
כֹּסוֹת רָעוֹת	[some] bad cups (*not* **the** bad cups)

One simple step can convert the above indefinite phrases to **definite** phrases. See if you can discover what it is:

הַצְּרוֹר הַגָּדוֹל	the large pouch
הָאֳנִיָּה הַגְּדוֹלָה	the large ship
הַמְּלָכִים הָרָעִים	the bad kings
הַכֹּסוֹת הָרָעוֹת	the bad cups

As noted earlier, names are considered so specific that they do not need a definite article in Hebrew in order to qualify as "definite." Although a name needs no article, its adjective does: יוֹנָה הַגָּדוֹל *Big Jonah* (not יוֹנָה גָּדוֹל).

To summarize, adjectives that contribute a simple description (attributive adjectives) must **agree** in **number**, **gender**, and **definiteness**. In addition, they will appear **after** the noun they modify.

Sometimes an adjective may appear in isolation, with no noun for it to modify. Thus טוֹבִים alone may mean *good* [*persons*] (cf. Prov. 2:20). For an explanation of this feature—when an isolated adjective operates as a noun (known as a "substantival" use of the adjective)—please see the appendix entry for this segment.

Toward the beginning of §2.3 you found a table containing many nouns and their various forms. Here is a collection of several **adjectives** together with their various forms.

UNIT 2   מַה־בַּכְּלִי הַגָּדוֹל?

Plural		Singular		Meaning
fem.	*masc.*	*fem.*	*masc.*	
גְּדוֹלוֹת	גְּדוֹלִים	גְּדוֹלָה	גָּדוֹל	great, large, big
טוֹבוֹת	טוֹבִים	טוֹבָה	טוֹב	good
קְטַנּוֹת	קְטַנִּים	קְטַנָּה	קָטָן	small
רָעוֹת	רָעִים	רָעָה	רַע	bad
יְבֵשׁוֹת	יְבֵשִׁים	יְבֵשָׁה	יָבֵשׁ	dry
כְּבֵדוֹת	כְּבֵדִים	כְּבֵדָה	כָּבֵד	heavy, oppressive
חֲזָקוֹת	חֲזָקִים	חֲזָקָה	חָזָק	strong, hard, tough

Adjectives

2.3.ג. Activity: "Correct?"   הֲטוֹבִים דְּבָרֶיךָ / דְּבָרַיִךְ?

INTERACTIVE SKILL: Describing objects, continued

Some of the adjective phrases listed below reflect proper Hebrew expression. In others, the adjective does not match the gender and / or number of the noun. Refer to the above charts to determine which phrases have been expressed correctly. The question found in the heading (הֲטוֹבִים דְּבָרֶיךָ / דְּבָרַיִךְ?) means, literally, "Are your words *2ms / 2fs* good?"

* **Circle** numbers of expressions that are **correct**. **Write** a translation of correct expressions in the space provided.
* **Draw a box** around the **incorrect** phrases. **Replace** the adjective with a correct form, and **translate** the entire phrase, as you have corrected it.

Your translation	Expression
	א. עִיר גְּדוֹלָה
	ב. מֶלֶךְ כָּבֵד
	ג. אֳנִיָּה יָבֵשׁ
	ד. נְבִיאִים חֲזָקִים
	ה. שֵׁמוֹת טוֹבִים
	ו. הַמַּיִם הָרָעִים
	ז. סֵפֶר קְטַנִּים

2.3.ד. Activity: "What do you (*ms*) want?"   מָה אַתָּה חָפֵץ?

INTERACTIVE SKILL: Expressing preferences

Describe to your neighbor something you wish you had. Be creative—include an adjective or two. Remember to pick the adjective form that matches the noun you select (gender, number, and definiteness). If there is something on the list that you especially do **not** want, you may indicate that as well. Using אֵינֶנִּי indicates that **you** are not the one wanting it, while allowing that someone **else** may.

Model

What do you want?	מָה אַתָּה חָפֵץ?	Inquiry (you *ms*)
	מָה אַתְּ חֲפֵצָה?[19]	Inquiry (you *fs*)
I want a little king (i.e., one small enough to control!).	מֶלֶךְ קָטָן אֲנִי חָפֵץ / חֲפֵצָה:	Affirmative reply
I don't want a big name (i.e., I'm not in pursuit of fame).	אֵינֶנִּי חָפֵץ / חֲפֵצָה שֵׁם גָּדוֹל:	Negative reply

Bear in mind that if the **object** you desire is **definite** (as in הַצְּרוֹר הַגָּדוֹל *the* big pouch) it's a good idea to insert אֶת־ before the noun (אֶת־הַצְּרוֹר הַגָּדוֹל אֲנִי חָפֵץ *I want the big pouch*).

To make things more interesting, ask לָמָּה? *Why?* in response to your neighbor's statement of preference. You may respond to a question asking לָמָּה? *Why?* by using your native language.

But what if you want an object that has the **opposite** of one of these qualities? Suppose, for example, that you need to purchase a boat to ferry freight across a modest-sized river. You want a ship that is **not large**, since it will never venture into the open sea. Aside from specifying קְטַנָּה *small fs*, you could describe the desired ship **negatively** as אֳנִיָּה לֹא גְדוֹלָה *a not-large ship* (or, *a ship [that is] not large*). לֹא is the proper negation here (rather than אֵין), since we are negating a single word (גְדוֹלָה).

I want a not-large ship.	אֳנִיָּה לֹא גְדוֹלָה אֲנִי חָפֵץ / חֲפֵצָה:

The combination לֹא-plus-adjective functions rather like a compound word: לֹא טוֹב *not-good*, לֹא גָדוֹל *not-large*, לֹא חָכָם *unwise*.

If you wish to lay more **emphasis** on the fact that the **ship** needs to be small, you may use אֵין to negate the noun (instead of לֹא to negate the adjective). In place of merely a quasi-compound-word like לֹא גְדוֹלָה *not-large*, אֵין will create a virtual relative clause focusing on the ship: אֳנִיָּה אֵינֶנָּה גְדוֹלָה *a ship—it is* (or *that is*) *not large*. As illustrated in the table below, אֵין can appear with or without the relative pronoun אֲשֶׁר:

(a) אֵין plus a **pronominal suffix** (אֵינֶנָּה, first example below)

(b) אֲשֶׁר *that* or *which* followed by אֵין with a pronominal suffix (second example)

---

[19] Did you notice that חָפֵץ adopts a feminine form (חֲפֵצָה) when it is a woman who is saying "I want..."?

I want a ship that is not large (*lit.*, I want a ship, **it** is not large).	אֳנִיָּה אֵינֶנָּה גְדוֹלָה אֲנִי חָפֵץ / חֲפֵצָה:	אֵין with a **pronominal suffix**[20]
I want a ship **that** [it] is not large.	אֳנִיָּה אֲשֶׁר אֵינֶנָּה גְדוֹלָה אֲנִי חָפֵץ / חֲפֵצָה:	אֲשֶׁר followed by אֵין with a pronominal suffix

You will learn more about אֲשֶׁר as relative pronoun (*which*, *that*, or *who*) in §2.4.א.

2.3.ה. Activity: "Where do you (ms) want to go?"

אָנָה[21] אַתָּה חָפֵץ לָלֶכֶת?

INTERACTIVE SKILL: Talking about travel interests

Select two places you would like to go, drawing from the list below. **Write your name** in the "My Choices" column, next to your chosen destinations. Then **interview others** in your class. In the inquiries below, אָנָה means *Where? Whither? To what location?*

Model

Where do you want to go?	אָנָה אַתָּה חָפֵץ לָלֶכֶת?	Inquiry (you *ms*)
	אָנָה אַתְּ חֲפֵצָה לָלֶכֶת?	Inquiry (you *fs*)

Find two people who want to go to different destinations (no duplicates, please). **Write their names** opposite their chosen destination. Some destinations are ancient, others are modern. See if you can recognize them by sounding out the words. Can you guess in response (ז) what is the topographical feature הָר? (Hint: it is plural.) For entry (ח) you may insert a destination of your own design.

---

[20] For a table showing אֵין with a variety of pronominal suffixes, please refer to §3.4.א.

[21] אָנָה *To where* (*whither*)? Cf. Gen. 16:8.

UNIT 2   מַה־בַּכְּלִי הַגָּדוֹל?

Friends' Choices (2)	My Choices (2)	Destinations	
		אֲנִי חָפֵץ / חֲפֵצָה לָלֶכֶת אֶל־תַּרְשִׁישׁ:	א.
		אֲנִי חָפֵץ / חֲפֵצָה לָלֶכֶת אֶל־יְרוּשָׁלַיִם:	ב.
		אֲנִי חָפֵץ / חֲפֵצָה לָלֶכֶת אֶל־רוֹם:	ג.
		אֲנִי חָפֵץ / חֲפֵצָה לָלֶכֶת אֶל־נְיוּ־יוֹרְק:	ד.
		אֲנִי חָפֵץ / חֲפֵצָה לָלֶכֶת אֶל־בֵּית־לָחֶם:[22]	ה.
		אֲנִי חָפֵץ / חֲפֵצָה לָלֶכֶת אֶל־הַמַּיִם:	ו.
		אֲנִי חָפֵץ / חֲפֵצָה לָלֶכֶת אֶל־הָרֵי־אֲרָרָט:	ז.
		אֲנִי חָפֵץ / חֲפֵצָה לָלֶכֶת אֶל...	ח.

2.3.1. Explanation and activity: "The container is small."   הַכְּלִי קָטָן:

INTERACTIVE SKILL: Describing an object in a complete sentence—yet without a verb

In §2.3.ב. you learned to describe objects with the help of an adjective (e.g., אֲנִיָּה יְבֵשָׁה *a dry ship*). Using those same components (noun plus adjective), you can also express a **complete sentence** (without a verb). Read the Hebrew sentences below, and compare each with its translation.

הָאֲבָנִים גְּדוֹלוֹת:	הָאֲנִיָּה יְבֵשָׁה:	הַכְּלִי קָטָן:
The stones [are] large.	The ship [is] dry.	The container [is] small.

---

[22] Can you guess this biblical town name? When not occurring at the end of a phrase, it is spelled בֵּית־לֶחֶם.

You may have noticed something unusual about the Hebrew in these sentences. Although the noun and adjective in each phrase agree in number and gender, the **noun is definite** while **the adjective is not**. This lack of concord in the matter of "definiteness" is how we know that these are not merely phrases, but form complete **sentences**.[23]

Unlike a simple adjective phrase such as הַכּוֹס הַגְּדוֹלָה *the big cup* (an attributive use of the adjective), in the case of these **complete sentences** (predicative use of the adjective), the components may be sequenced **in either order**. The simpler sequence ("unmarked syntax") calls for the noun first, followed by the adjective: הָאֳנִיָּה יְבֵשָׁה *The ship [is] dry*.[24] If, however, we wish to draw special attention to the dry condition of the ship, then we will express the adjective first: יְבֵשָׁה הָאֳנִיָּה ***Dry** is [the quality that particularly characterizes] the ship*.

Try your hand at making an adjective sentence (called a "verbless sentence with predicative adjective"). Aim to compose a sentence that reflects any one of the following three qualities: let it be a statement that is either true, or unusual, or patently preposterous!

---

[23] By the way, in case *neither* noun *nor* adjective have an article, the translation can go either way (either translate as a phrase or as a complete sentence). Thus כְּלִי טוֹב may mean either *a good container* (an attributive use of the adjective, producing only a phrase) or *A container **is** good* (a predicative use of the adjective, forming a complete sentence). Context will help you decide which choice is better.

[24] Regarding noun-adjective as the unmarked syntax is based on the likelihood that when occurring within a larger context, "the ship" would already be a known piece of information, while the fact that the ship "is dry"—this would most likely supply new information. New information conveyed by an unmarked verbless clause normally will appear second. Generally it will constitute the predicate. In contrast, placing it first marks it for special attention (see T. Muraoka, "The Tripartite Nominal Clause Revisited," in *The Verbless Clause in Biblical Hebrew: Linguistic Approaches* [ed., C. Miller; Winona Lake, Indiana: Eisenbrauns, 1999], 205, and A. Niccacci, "Types and Functions of the Nominal Sentence," in *The Verbless Clause in Biblical Hebrew*, 218–220).

UNIT 2   מַה־בַּכְּלִי הַגָּדוֹל?   נִינְוֵה עִיר רָעָה:

2.3.ז. Explanation: "Nineveh is a bad city."

INTERACTIVE SKILL: Using a verbless sentence to give a description, continued

While we're on the topic of "sentences without verbs," you may have noticed that Hebrew can form a sentence simply by juxtaposing two nouns or noun phrases. As with adjective sentences (§2.3.ו.), when translating such a sentence we must supply the verb *to be*. For example:

שֵׁם־הָאֳנִיָּה מֶלֶךְ־הַמַּיִם:	שְׁמִי יוֹנָה:	נִינְוֵה עִיר רָעָה:
The name of the ship is "The King of the Water."	My name is Jonah.	Nineveh is a bad city. (*Not* Nineveh: a city is bad.)

Whenever we supply the verb "to be" we may select its **tense** as well: **past** ("was / were"), **present** ("am / are"), or **future** ("will be"), as dictated by the context.

If you wish to draw attention to a particular part of the sentence, simply move that part **to the front** of the sentence. Suppose, for example, you ran into an old acquaintance unexpectedly, and he recalled your name incorrectly. You could emphasize your actual name by placing it first in the sentence: יוֹנָה שְׁמִי: *"Jonah" is my name.*[25]

English syntax cannot always capture nuances of this sort. Notice, for example, how the following sentence calls attention to the character of the city of Nineveh by locating the adjective phrase **before** the city's name: עִיר רָעָה נִינְוֵה *A bad city* is Nineveh. But such literal word-order makes for rough English. It may be best to employ audible emphasis (if a spoken message) or a distinctive font (if a written message): "Nineveh is a *bad* city."

---

[25] In the verbless sentence שְׁמִי יוֹנָה, the expression "my name" represents that part of the information already known and so comprises the subject. In contrast, the word "Jonah" constitutes the new information, and so comprises the predicate. Thus the unmarked verbless syntax (subject-predicate) would be שְׁמִי יוֹנָה, whereas moving "Jonah" to the front (יוֹנָה שְׁמִי) would create a predicate-subject sequence, marking the word "Jonah" for special attention.

2.3.ח. Did you (*ms*) know that...? (Leather goods)   הֲיָדַ֫עְתָּ כִּי...?

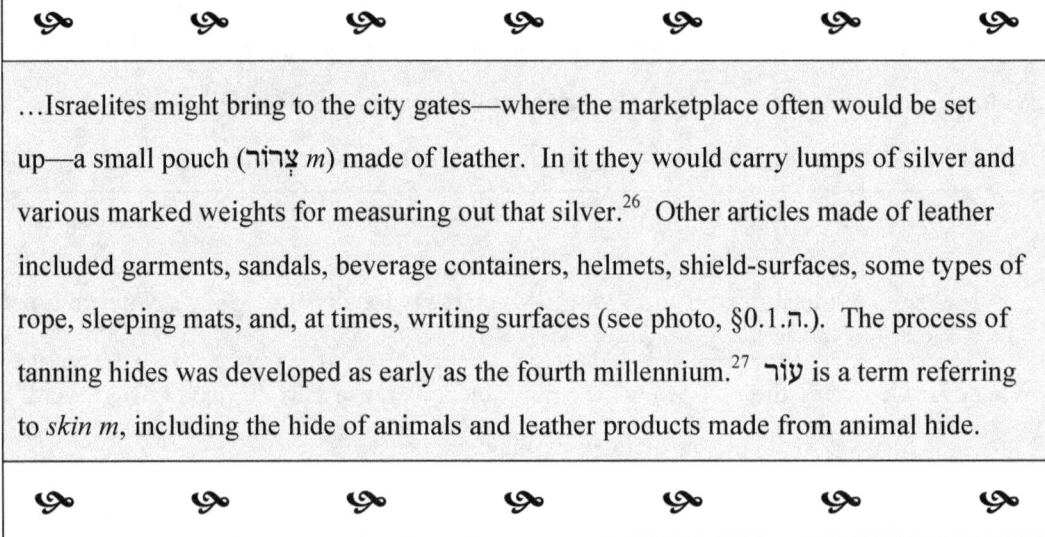

...Israelites might bring to the city gates—where the marketplace often would be set up—a small pouch (צְרוֹר *m*) made of leather. In it they would carry lumps of silver and various marked weights for measuring out that silver.[26] Other articles made of leather included garments, sandals, beverage containers, helmets, shield-surfaces, some types of rope, sleeping mats, and, at times, writing surfaces (see photo, §0.1.ה.). The process of tanning hides was developed as early as the fourth millennium.[27] עוֹר is a term referring to *skin m*, including the hide of animals and leather products made from animal hide.

---

[26] Regarding silver rendered portable for payment, see photo in §7.3.ט.; for weights, see photos in §2.4.ה.

[27] *LBI*, 161–64, and 197.

UNIT 2 — מַה־בַּכְּלִי הַגָּדוֹל? — 147

MODULE 2.4 — Explaining where to find something

Words for responding — מִלִּים לַעֲנוֹת

Note: In addition to these words, it will be important to learn the prepositions presented in the table found in §2.4.א.

אַחֲרֵי	behind, after	עַל	on, upon
אֲשֶׁר	which, since, that, who (*not interrogative*)	שִׂים, שִׂימִי[a] [שׂ.י/ו.מ][b]	Put! *imv, ms, fs*
בְּ...	in, with, by means of		

[a] Some spellings found in the Hebrew Bible depart from custom by not including vowel letters where we would expect them. Such is the case with the *imv fs* of שׂ.י.מ. It is spelled "defectively" without the first י in Jer. 31:21 (שִׂמִי). You are encouraged to learn the "*plene*" (complete) spelling since it will be consistent with related forms (שִׂימִי).

[b] When a שֹׁרֶשׁ *root* displays variable letters (such as י/ו in שׂ.י/ו.מ *to put*, or י/ה in שׁ.ת.י/ה *to drink*), these variable letters are provided (a) to identify the lexical form (the dictionary entry form: שׂ.י.מ or שׁ.ת.ה), also (b) to alert you to the fact that many forms tracing to a variable-letter root will display the alternate letter (GKC §75). Thus the שֹׁרֶשׁ *root* שׂ.י/ו.מ *to put* gives rise both to the imperative שִׂים *Put!* and also to the infinitive לָשׂוּם *to put* (with preposition לְ). You need to be prepared to recognize a variable-letter verb with **either** of the letters. Regarding שׂ.י/ו.מ as a "hollow verb," please see note below concerning ב.ו.א.

Words for hearing — מִלִּים לִשְׁמֹעַ

אוּכַל [י.כ.ל]	I am able	שֹׁאֵל [שׁ.א.ל]	one who is asking *pt, ms*[c]
בּוֹא, בּוֹאִי [ב.ו.א][a]	Enter! Come! *imv, ms, fs*	שֵׁב, שְׁבִי [י.שׁ.ב]	Sit! Dwell! *imv, ms, fs*
לָתֵת [נ.ת.ן]	to give *inf c,* prep לְ[b]	יְבָרֶכְךָ יהוה, יְבָרְכֵךְ יהוה	thank you *m, f*[d]

[a] The verb ב.ו.א belongs to a group known as "hollow verbs" or "monosyllabic verbs." Hollow verbs have a middle-ו or middle-י in the שֹׁרֶשׁ root. This middle-ו or middle-י in hollow verbs is not a genuine consonant, but rather represents a vowel-letter. In some instances that vowel will be וֹ (as in בּוֹא, above). In other instances the middle vowel will be וּ (as in קוּם *Get up!*, from the hollow verb ק.ו.מ) or יִ◌ (as in אָבִין *I understand* from the hollow verb ב.י.נ).

In vocalized forms it is not difficult to recognize that the ו or י is a vowel letter, since there will be no other vowel following the first radical. There is no word such as בָּוֹא‡ with a qameṣ followed directly by a ḥolem-vav, for example). Thus the letter ו in בּוֹא must serve as a vowel-letter (with the ḥolem) following the first radical, ב.

ש.ו/י.מ is another hollow verb, often displaying an I-vowel (as with the imperative שִׂים *Put!*). At other times it displays a U-vowel (as with the infinitive לָשׂוּם *to put*).

In case you are wondering whether a root with a middle-ו or middle-י can ever represent a truly three-consonant verb (as opposed to a hollow verb), the answer is "yes." In §4.3 you will meet the verb יִחְיֶה *he will live*, from the verb ח.י.י/ה (hollow, with a middle-י). The segol directly after the middle-י shows that it is a true consonant, not a vowel-letter.

Also, in §4.4 you will meet the verb ק.ו.י/ה *to hope*. Here the letter ו is a consonant. Notice the segol directly after ו in קֹוֶה *one who hopes*. The segol shows that the ו is a consonant, not a vowel letter.

[b] The designation "*inf c, prep*" indicates that the word לָתֵת consists of two parts: (a) the sort of infinitive that can accept a prefixed preposition (known as an infinitive **construct**), plus (b) a preposition (לְ, in this case). At present, simply learn these meanings. How infinitives operate will be explained more fully at a later point (cf. §§3.1.א. and 5.2.ד.).

[c] Vocabulary entries translated "one who…" represent Hebrew participles (abbreviated *pt*). Often a good starting point when translating a participle is to think of it as representing "a person who is… [insert activity designated by the verb]." Thus שֹׁאֵל is a participle *ms* from the verb "to ask." It means "a person who **is asking**." Your instructor will explain other uses of participles in a future session. In the spelling שֹׁאֵל, please note that there is a ḥolem vowel after the letter šîn.

[d] The Hebrew Bible does not preserve a commonly used, human-to-human expression of gratitude. The word תּוֹדָה, a term that does appear in the Hebrew Bible, involves gratitude toward the divine. Expressions of blessing such as יְבָרֶכְךָ יהוה (lit., *May the* LORD *bless you, ms*) were used in greetings, so reasonably may have been used to wish favor upon another when wishing to convey gratitude.

2.4 Jonah Episode: What's in the pouch?

נ׳ = יוֹנָה הַנָּבִיא, ע׳ = עֶבֶד

UNIT 2 מַה־בִּכְלִי הַגָּדוֹל? 151

[ע׳] לֵךְ אֶל־תַּרְשִׁישׁ בָּאֳנִיַּת־מֶלֶךְ־הַמָּיִם!

2.4.א. Explanation and activity: "Sit (*ms*) on the chair that is behind the table."   שֵׁב עַל־הַכִּסֵּא אֲשֶׁר אַחֲרֵי הַשֻּׁלְחָן:

INTERACTIVE SKILL: Helping guests find a seat

When serving as host, it is a good idea to help guests find a seat. Often this sort of communication will require a prepositional phrase, as in the seaman's instruction to Jonah: שֵׁב עַל־הַכִּסֵּא... *Sit on the chair*.... There are three ways in which prepositions can connect to the next word.

- Some Hebrew prepositions are capable of standing alone, such as אַחֲרֵי *behind*, as in אַחֲרֵי הַשֻּׁלְחָן *behind the table*. These are called **independent** prepositions.
- Other prepositions will only appear **prefixed** to their object, such as בְּ... *in*, as seen in בִּצְרוֹר *in a pouch*.

- Still others—while remaining as independent words—are routinely **joined** to the next word **by a maqqef** (hyphen). Such is the case with עַל־ *upon*, as seen in עַל־הַמַּיִם *upon the water* (cf. appendix for explanation of the maqqef and accentual units). These are termed "proclitic" since they "lean forward" toward the next word.

Here is a handful of the most useful prepositions. Those followed by an ellipsis will only occur **prefixed** to their object (e.g., ...בְּ).

Words for responding / מִלִּים לַעֲנוֹת

מֵעַל [d]	from upon	אַחַר, אַחֲרֵי [a]	behind, after
מִתַּחַת	from under	אֶל־	to, toward
נֶגֶד	opposite, facing [e]	...בְּ	in, with, by means of
עַד־	toward, as far as	בְּתוֹךְ [b]	in the middle of
עַל־	on, upon, against	...כְּ [c]	like (similar to)
עַל־יַד	beside	...לְ	to, for
עִם־	with [together]	לִפְנֵי	before, in front of
תַּחַת	under, instead of	מִן־	from

[a] These two forms have the same meaning (אַחַר, אַחֲרֵי). You will encounter אַחֲרֵי more frequently.

[b] בְּתוֹךְ consists of a preposition (בְּ *in*) and a noun (תּוֹךְ *middle*).

[c] When freestanding, use כְּמוֹ (lit., *like what*) in place of ...כְּ.

[d] When two or more prepositions combine into a single word, they form a "compound preposition" (e.g., מֵעַל, מִתַּחַת, and מֵאֵת).

[e] *Across from*, not necessarily *opposing*.

Please refer to the appendix portion corresponding to this segment in order to learn how the sheva in ...בְּ, ...כְּ, and ...לְ may modify, depending on the next syllable. The appendix also explains how מִן may modify (e.g., through assimilation, often losing the נ when the preposition is attached to the next word).

You recently read several prepositional phrases in the Jonah episode. How quickly can you match each with a proper translation? In the box to the left of each English phrase, please write the alpha-numeral designating the Hebrew phrase which best corresponds to that English phrase.

UNIT 2   מַה־בַּכְּלִי הַגָּדוֹל?

	in a container	אֶל־נִינְוֵה אּ.
	on a chair	בִּכְלִי ב.
	on the table	עַד־תַּרְשִׁישׁ ג.
	to Nineveh	עַל־הַשֻּׁלְחָן ד.
	as far as Tarshish	עַל־כִּסֵּא ה.

Compare the spelling of the first two consonants in each word-pair below. Now compare the translations. Although the consonant ה of the definite article has been lost ("elided"), it has left something behind. Can you isolate the remaining evidence of the definite article in בַּכְּלִי?[28] How about in the phrase בַּלֶּחֶם?[29]

in / with a container	בִּכְלִי
in / with the container	בַּכְּלִי
in / with (some) bread	בְּלֶחֶם
in / with the bread	בַּלֶּחֶם

Did you notice the word אֲשֶׁר (*who*, *which*, or *that*) in the title phrase אֲשֶׁר אַחֲרֵי הַשֻּׁלְחָן *that is behind the table*? אֲשֶׁר introduces additional information concerning a person or object (called a "relative pronoun").[30]

---

[28] Pataḥ vowel following preposition בְּ and dagesh in כְּ of כְּלִי.

[29] Pataḥ vowel following preposition בְּ and dagesh in לְ of לֶחֶם.

[30] In some situations אֲשֶׁר departs from the "relative pronoun" role and instead operates as a conjunction. In those situations it generally introduces an explanation and will be translated *because* or *since*. Begin by translating אֲשֶׁר as *who* or *which* (relative pronoun). Context will help you recognize when it means *because*.

2.4.ב. Activity: "On or under?"   עַל אוֹ תַּחַת?

INTERACTIVE SKILL: Describing where things are located

In this activity you may be asked either **to describe** where an object is located, or you may be asked **to place** an object somewhere indicated by your instructor.

    The "model" below provides a sample of the sort of questions and responses that may emerge in this activity. Additional questions and responses of a similar nature will also be appropriate for this activity.

Model (for describing object)

Where is the bread?	אַיֵּה הַלֶּחֶם?	Inquiry א
The bread is on the table.	הַלֶּחֶם עַל־הַשֻּׁלְחָן:	Reply א
What is in the container?	מַה־בַּכְּלִי?	Inquiry ב
A stone is in the container.	אֶבֶן בַּכְּלִי:	Reply ב

Incidentally, you may be interested in the slight shift of focus that is embedded in these two replies. Notice this principle. In a verbless clause (a clause without a finite verb) one of the ways to detect emphasis is to ask: "What is the new information in this clause?" Then observe where that information appears in the clause. In a simple ("unmarked") sentence, new information will come second. This new information will comprise the predicate. If, however, the speaker wishes to "mark" that new information, it will appear first.

The new information given in response to Inquiry א above (אַיֵּה הַלֶּחֶם?) will disclose **the location** of the bread. To locate that information (עַל־הַשֻּׁלְחָן) in second place will produce an unmarked sentence. Thus the response "הַלֶּחֶם עַל־הַשֻּׁלְחָן" is unmarked, with no special emphasis. If instead we responded, "עַל־הַשֻּׁלְחָן הַלֶּחֶם," we would be drawing particular attention to the location of the bread by mentioning that new information **first**: "On the table is where the bread is located."

For Inquiry ב above, the new information will involve discovering **the commodity** located inside the container. Again, an unmarked response would place this information (אֶבֶן) second (בַּכְּלִי אֶבֶן׃). By answering with the commodity first (אֶבֶן בַּכְּלִי), a bit of attention is drawn to that commodity, as if to say, "**A stone** is what is in the container."

Model (for placing object)

Instruction א	שִׂים / שִׂמִי אֶת־הַלֶּחֶם עַל־הַשֻּׁלְחָן׃	Put the bread on the table.
Instruction ב	שִׂים / שִׂמִי אֶת־הָאֶבֶן בַּכְּלִי׃	Put the stone into the container.

2.4.ג. Activity: "Where's Jonah?"   אַיֵּה יוֹנָה?

INTERACTIVE SKILL: Verifying that you understand a given story

Read through the 2.4 Jonah Episode. Then test your understanding of the Jonah account, up to this point in the story. Based on the story, are the sentences that appear below correct or incorrect?

- If a statement is correct, write "אֱ" (for אֱמֶת *truth*) in the column labeled "שׁ / אֱ." A diamond centered above a letter (as in אֱ) is the Masoretic symbol known as "revia," sometimes used to indicate an abbreviation.
- If a statement is incorrect, write a שׁ (for שֶׁקֶר *falsehood*) in the column.

- Under each statement, write its translation.
- Replace any false statements with a corrected true statement (in Hebrew), using the column labeled "correction." There may be more than one way to correct a false statement.

The first has been completed as an example.

Correction	Translation		שׁ / אֱ
יוֹנָה בָּאֳנִיָּה: הַכֶּסֶף בִּכְלִי:	יוֹנָה בִּכְלִי: *Jonah is in a container.*	א.	שׁ
	יוֹנָה תַּחַת אֳנִיָּה:	ב.	
	הַכֶּסֶף בָּעִיר:	ג.	
	תַּרְשִׁישׁ עַל־יַד מָיִם:	ד.	
	הַכִּסֵּא לִפְנֵי הַמֶּלֶךְ:	ה.	
	בִּצְרוֹר כָּסֶף:	ו.	
	כְּלִי עַל־הַשֻּׁלְחָן:	ז.	
	שָׁלוֹם לְיוֹנָה:	ח.	

UNIT 2 מַה־בַּכְּלִי הַגָּדוֹל?

2.4.ד. Activity: "How is Abram going to the land of Canaan?"
בַּמֶּה הוֹלֵךְ אַבְרָם אֶל־אֶרֶץ־כְּנָעַן?[31]

INTERACTIVE SKILL: Describe how someone is traveling, who or what may be in their party

Note: בַּמֶּה in the heading above is a compound word. Can you tell what two words make up בַּמֶּה? The components are "in / by [means of]" + "What?" Combined, בַּמֶּה means "How?"

As you may recall, early in the biblical account of Abram we learn of his trip from Mesopotamia to Canaan (Genesis 12). Can you picture him as he is making this journey? How is he traveling? Is anyone accompanying him? What is he passing alongside of? Is he wearing anything on his head? Use objects (or names) you have learned thus far, together with prepositions, to paint this imaginary picture. For example:

Model

| Abram is going to the land of Canaan with Sarai. | עִם־שָׂרַי הוֹלֵךְ אַבְרָם אֶל־אֶרֶץ־כְּנָעַן׃ |

Alternatively, you may be asked to form a response to this question:

Model

| How is Sarai going to Egypt? | בַּמֶּה הוֹלֶכֶת שָׂרַי אֶל־מִצְרַיִם? |

The preposition אֶת־. This is a good point at which to introduce a preposition similar to עִם־, namely the preposition אֶת־. The phrase *with Sarai* can be expressed either by עִם־שָׂרַי or by אֶת־שָׂרַי. When

---

[31] The three words comprising the phrase אֶל־אֶרֶץ־כְּנָעַן are linked to each other by the maqqef. Consequently they form one "accentual unit." The primary accent falls on the last word. Any other accent is a secondary accent (here marked with a meteg in אֶרֶץ־).

appearing without pronominal suffixes, אֵת is **spelled the same** as the definite direct object marker אֶת־ (and both are spelled אֵת when lacking the maqqef). Thus, whenever you encounter the word אֶת־ (or אֵת) in the Hebrew Bible it will be important to consider both meanings, and then select the meaning best suited to the context. Happily, when combined **with suffixes** the two words are spelled **differently** (see second table in §3.4.א.).

2.4.ה. Did you (*ms*) know that…? (Weights)   הֲיָדַעְתָּ כִּי...?

…the earliest form of trade involved bartering? Later on, lumps of precious metal such as silver or gold would be weighed on small balance-beam scales for payment (cf. Gen. 23:15-16, photo of silver coil in §7.3.ט.).

Hematite weights from Ur, ranging from one mina (500 gm) to three שֶׁקֶל (25 gm; ca. 1900–1600 BCE). (Courtesy of British Museum)

Sets of graduated weights served to determine the value of precious metal. Some weight-sets found in Babylon roughly dating to 2500-1500 BCE were fabricated from hematite (iron oxide) or stone in the shape of ducks with their head laid back against their body ("duck weights," cf. sketch in 2.4 Jonah Episode, cell 5).

Close-up of stone weights from Lachish (9ᵗʰ–8ᵗʰ cent. BCE). Stone in foreground is inscribed *n-ṣ-p* (5/6 shekel, 10 gm). (Courtesy of British Museum)

Zoomorphic "duck weights" from ancient Mesopotamia, of agate (smallest, 0.2917 gm) and hematite. (Courtesy of Mesopotamian Gallery, the Oriental Institute Museum)

A scale weight is sometimes referred to as an אֶבֶן. The word שֶׁקֶל *shekel m* initially was a unit of weight, not a monetary unit. The פִּים weighed two-thirds of a שֶׁקֶל, while the גֵּרָה *f*, the smallest weight, amounted to one-twentieth of a שֶׁקֶל. The word פֶּלֶס *m* designates a *scale*, as does מֹאזְנַיִם *m*.

Coins were not developed until the seventh century BCE, originating in Lydia (northwest Anatolia). The earliest coins recovered in Israel date to the latter half of the sixth century BCE, minted in Athens, Thasos, and Macedon.[32] The first Judean-minted coins date to about 400 BCE. Authorized by the Persians, some of these coins bear the letters יהד (Yehud).[33]

---

[32] Arie Kindler, "Coins and Currency," *Encyclopaedia Judaica* 5:47–55.

[33] *LBI*, 199. More information concerning weights and measures many be found in §4.2.1.

MODULE 2.5   Sending someone on a trip

(This module does not introduce a new Jonah Episode or present new vocabulary.)

2.5.א. Explanation: "How are you (*ms / fs*)?"   הֲשָׁלוֹם לָךְ?

INTERACTIVE SKILL: Grammar review of prepositional phrases

Here are some other prepositional phrases encountered earlier. In these cases, the preposition is linked to a pronominal suffix. Pronominal suffixes may attach both to inseparable prepositions (such as ...לְ) as well as to independent prepositions (such as עַל־).

How are you? [*lit.*, Is there peace for you?]	הֲשָׁלוֹם לָךְ?
Give to me.	תֵּן / תְּנִי לִי:
I have a stone [*lit.*, There is for me a stone].	יֵשׁ[34] לִי אֶבֶן:
I must [*lit.*, {An obligation is} upon me to] go to Nineveh.	עָלַי לָלֶכֶת אֶל־נִינְוֵה:
You have no stone [*lit.*, There is not for you a stone].	אֵין לְךָ / לָךְ אֶבֶן:
You must [*lit.*, {An obligation is} upon you to] give me silver.	עָלֶיךָ / עָלַיִךְ לָתֵת לִי כָּסֶף:

If you wish to see a more complete picture of pronominal suffixes attached to prepositions, see §3.4.א., or refer to the table of prepositions at the back of this volume (p. 494).

---

[34] You may recall יֵשׁ from the previous unit. יֵשׁ is known as the "predication of existence." Taken alone, it means *there is / are*. If you are familiar with French, you will find יֵשׁ functioning in a manner similar to *il y a*.... The opposite (negation) of יֵשׁ is אֵין, known as the "predication of non-existence," and can be rendered *there is / are no*.

2.5.ב. Activity: "Go (*ms*) to the great city!"   לֵךְ אֶל־הָעִיר הַגְּדוֹלָה:

INTERACTIVE SKILL: Issuing and understanding directions

Do you like to tell others what to do, where to go? Then here is your chance! In groups of three or four, take turns telling each other where to go (and then, to return). Your instructor will explain the "destinations" available in your classroom today. Samples of these destinations may be found under the heading, "Locations / objects," listed below.

Model

Instruction א	לֵךְ / לְכִי אֶל־הָעִיר הַגְּדוֹלָה:	Go to the great city!
Instruction ב	שׁוּב / שׁוּבִי:	Return!

Locations / objects

לֵךְ / לְכִי אֶל־הַדֶּלֶת[35] הַחֲזָקָה:	לֵךְ / לְכִי אֶל־הָעִיר הַגְּדוֹלָה:
לֵךְ / לְכִי אֶל־כִּסֵּא־הַמֶּלֶךְ:	לֵךְ / לְכִי אֶל־עִיר טוֹבָה:
לֵךְ / לְכִי אֶל־אֳנִיַּת־הַמֶּלֶךְ:	לֵךְ / לְכִי אֶל־כְּלִי קָטָן:
לֵךְ / לְכִי אֶל־מֵי[36]־שָׁלוֹם:	לֵךְ / לְכִי אֶל־הָאֶבֶן הָרָעָה:
לֵךְ / לְכִי אֶל־לֶחֶם־הָאִשָּׁה:	לֵךְ / לְכִי אֶל־הַשֻּׁלְחָן הַגָּדוֹל:
לֵךְ / לְכִי אֶל־כֶּסֶף־הָאִישׁ:	לֵךְ / לְכִי אֶל־כִּסֵּא כָּבֵד:

2.5.ג. Do you (*ms*) know the meaning of a word? (Ownership)

<u>הֲיָדַעְתָּ פֵּשֶׁר דָּבָר?</u>

See if you can recognize the difference between these two expressions of ownership:

Indefinite	Definite
(using the preposition לְ)	(using a construct phrase)
אֳנִיָּה לַמֶּלֶךְ הִיא:	אֳנִיַּת־הַמֶּלֶךְ הִיא:
*It is **a** ship of the king.*	*It is **the** ship of the king.*

The statement on the left (with לְ) leaves room for the king to own other ships in addition to the vessel presently being described. In contrast, the statement on the right (with construct phrase) implies that this particular ship is the only vessel owned by the king (e.g., בֵּן לְיִשַׁי *a son* [not *the son*] *of Jesse* in 1 Sam. 16:18, cf. Joüon §130b).

---

[35] דֶּלֶת *door, f.*

[36] מֵי is the construct form of מַיִם.

> Nevertheless, occasionally the context will indicate that a noun must have an indefinite meaning, even though followed by a definite noun (e.g., עִיר בְּנֵי יְהוּדָה *a city* [not *the city*] *of the people of Judah*, Josh. 18:4). Thus אֳנִיָּת־תַּרְשִׁישׁ הִיא may be rendered, "It is a ship of (or from) Tarshish" (Jonah Episode 2.1, cell 3)..

2.5.ד. Activity: "You (*ms*) have to..." עָלֶיךָ...

INTERACTIVE SKILL: Outlining job qualifications

Have you ever needed to explain the qualifications needed for a particular job? In the current activity you will develop this skill. Take, for example, the role of a prophet or prophetess in the ancient world. What do you think a prophet or prophetess should be willing to do? Circle the letter of the responses you would choose to complete the following sentences:

If you are a good prophet…	אִם נָבִיא טוֹב אַתָּה...
If you are a good prophetess…	אִם נְבִיאָה טוֹבָה אַתְּ...

For example, if you believe a good prophet *must* [*be willing to*] *travel*, then complete the sentence with option א below:

Model

If you are a good prophet… you have (to be willing) to travel.	אִם נָבִיא טוֹב אַתָּה... עָלֶיךָ לָלֶכֶת:	Prophet
If you are a good prophetess… you have (to be willing) to travel.	אִם נְבִיאָה טוֹבָה אַתְּ... עָלַיִךְ לָלֶכֶת:	Prophetess

Qualifications

...you have to travel	...עָלֶיךָ / עָלַיִךְ לָלֶכֶת:	א.
...you have to speak	...עָלֶיךָ / עָלַיִךְ לְדַבֵּר:	ב.
...you have to repent, turn	...עָלֶיךָ / עָלַיִךְ לָשׁוּב:	ג.
...you have to give	...עָלֶיךָ / עָלַיִךְ לָתֵת:	ד.
...you have to listen	...עָלֶיךָ / עָלַיִךְ לִשְׁמוֹעַ:	ה.
...you have to... (*make up your own response*)	...עָלֶיךָ / עָלַיִךְ :...	ו.

2.5.ה. Do you (*ms*) know the meaning of a word? (Obligation)

הֲיָדַעְתָּ פֵּשֶׁר דָּבָר?

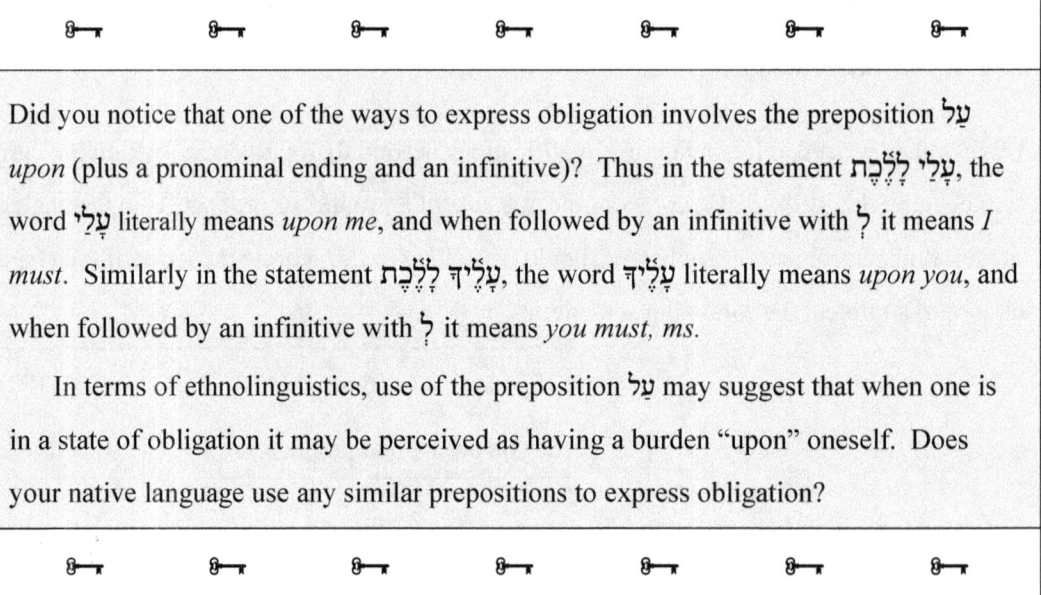

Did you notice that one of the ways to express obligation involves the preposition עַל *upon* (plus a pronominal ending and an infinitive)? Thus in the statement עָלַי לָלֶכֶת, the word עָלַי literally means *upon me*, and when followed by an infinitive with לְ it means *I must*. Similarly in the statement עָלֶיךָ לָלֶכֶת, the word עָלֶיךָ literally means *upon you*, and when followed by an infinitive with לְ it means *you must, ms*.

In terms of ethnolinguistics, use of the preposition עַל may suggest that when one is in a state of obligation it may be perceived as having a burden "upon" oneself. Does your native language use any similar prepositions to express obligation?

2.5.1. Activity: "Place (*ms*)... give (*ms*)...!"   שִׂים... תֵּן...!

INTERACTIVE SKILL: Issuing more complex instructions

Here is another chance to give (or receive) orders! In groups of two or three, take turns asking a classmate to position objects in a particular place. Creativity is encouraged.

Model (with ש.י.מ/ו)

Place a heavy chair on a dry table.	שִׂים / שִׂימִי כִּסֵּא כָּבֵד עַל־שֻׁלְחָן יָבֵשׁ:
Place bread on the king.	שִׂים / שִׂימִי לֶחֶם עַל־הַמֶּלֶךְ:

Alternatively, you may ask a classmate **to give** you something. Add an adjective to make sure they select the particular object you have in mind.

Model (with נ.ת.נ)

Give me the big bag of rocks.	תֵּן / תְּנִי לִי כְּלִי הָאֲבָנִים הַגָּדוֹל:

Note: The correct translation of כְּלִי הָאֲבָנִים הַגָּדוֹל is "the **big bag** of rocks," not "the bag of **big rocks**."[37] This is due to gender, number, and definiteness concord linking "big" and "bag"—both are masculine, singular, and definite. Put another way, it is due to the **lack** of gender and number concord between "big" *ms* and "rocks" *fpl*. Although the adjective "big" describes "bag," it must **follow** the word "rocks" because nothing is permitted to break up the "bag-of-rocks" construct chain. Thus to say *the big bag of rocks*, Hebrew syntax requires a phrase that would literally translate as *the-bag-of-rocks big*.

---

[37] "The bag of big rocks" would read: כְּלִי הָאֲבָנִים הַגְּדֹלוֹת.

2.5.ז. Do you (*ms*) know the meaning of a word? (Greeting)

<u>הֲיָדַ֫עְתָּ פֵּ֫שֶׁר דָּבָר?</u>

When meeting someone it was customary to invoke a blessing as part of the greeting, using the שֹׁ֫רֶשׁ ב.ר.כ. One day as Jehu was riding along in his chariot, he encountered Jehonadab. We read that Jehu "greeted him" (וַיְבָרְכֵ֫הוּ, lit., *and he blessed him*, 2 Kings 10:15). It is clear that the blessing was preliminary, since afterward Jehu proceeded to his main topic: proposing an alliance with Jehonadab. Elsewhere we read of אֱלִישָׁע הַנָּבִיא dispatching his servant Gehazi on an urgent mission—so urgent that he forbade Gehazi from issuing a greeting or responding to a greeting from anyone he may encounter (לֹא תְבָרְכֶ֫נּוּ, lit., *do not bless him*, 2 Kings 4:29). The study of how verbal expression relates to the culture of persons using a given language is known as ethnolinguistics.

You can recognize ב.ר.כ in the Modern Hebrew greeting that a host may extend to a guest when he or she arrives: בָּרוּךְ הַבָּא *ms* (or בְּרוּכָה הַבָּאָה *fs*). Literally this means: *Blessed is the one who enters*. When it occurs in the Hebrew Bible, this expression is part of a temple-entry liturgy (cf. Ps. 118:26). Would any custom of greeting in your culture similarly invoke the beneficence of a deity?

UNIT 2   מַה־בַּכְּלִי הַגָּדוֹל?

You (ms) can read the Bible.[38]   אַתָּה תִּקְרָא אֶת־הַתַּנַ״ךְ:

Selected readings

Together with a prohibition against deceptive oaths, God gave this command to the people.	2.1

$$\text{וְלֹא... חִלַּלְתָּ}^a \text{ אֶת־שֵׁם אֱלֹהֶיךָ}^b$$
אֲנִי יהוה : (Lev. 19:12)   .1

^a וְלֹא... חִלַּלְתָּ [ח.ל.ל] you *ms* must not profane   ^b אֱלֹהֶיךָ your *ms* God *m*

וְלֹא־תִשָּׁבְעוּ בִשְׁמִי לַשָּׁקֶר וְחִלַּלְתָּ אֶת־שֵׁם אֱלֹהֶיךָ אֲנִי יהוה:

Solomon was so rich, it was said that:	2.1

וּכְלֵי^{μa}־הַמֶּלֶךְ שְׁלֹמֹה^b זָהָב^c...: (2 Chron. 9:20)   .2

^a וּכְלֵי וְ + כְּלִי   ^b שְׁלֹמֹה (man's name)   ^c זָהָב gold *m*

וְכֹל כְּלֵי מַשְׁקֵה הַמֶּלֶךְ שְׁלֹמֹה זָהָב...

---

[38] A Hebrew word or phrase in the Selected Readings that has been marked with the symbol ^μ has been modified or substituted to facilitate reading. For that reason, Selected Readings marked with the symbol ^μ often will not fully correspond to what you find in a standard Bible translation for the same passage. The original Hebrew text may be found in smaller font at the bottom of the given selection (provided for informational purposes only). Also, from time to time modern punctuation marks (such as quotation marks or question marks) have been supplied to assist you. The use of ^μ-modified words and modern punctuation marks will gradually disappear as you progress.

Prior to the introduction of standardized coinage, one might purchase goods in the market‑ 2.3
place by weighing out pieces of precious metals. To guard against a double standard, God
prohibited merchants from carrying the following in their weight‑pouch. This verse begins:
"You must not have in your pouch…." (Note that וָאָ֫בֶן is וָאֶ֫בֶן in pause.)

.3 …אֶ֫בֶן וָאָ֫בֶן

(Deut. 25:13): גְּדוֹלָה וּקְטַנָּה

לֹא־יִהְיֶה לְךָ בְּכִיסְךָ אֶ֫בֶן וָאָ֫בֶן גְּדוֹלָה וּקְטַנָּה:

In contrast to many rural communities that Jonah would have been acquainted with… 2.3

.4 נִינְוֵה…עִיר גְּדוֹלָה….

(Jonah 3:3b):

…וְנִינְוֵה הָיְתָה עִיר־גְּדוֹלָה לֵאלֹהִים מַהֲלַךְ שְׁלֹ֫שֶׁת יָמִים:

The man named יַעֲקֹב first encountered his future bride Rachel at a sheep‑watering well. 2.4
Something prevented them from accessing the water, however. (How would the meaning
change if it read הַגְּדֹלָה instead of גְּדֹלָה?)

.5 …וְהָאֶ֫בֶן גְּדֹלָה עַל־פִּי־הַבְּאֵר ᵃ: (Gen. 29:2)

ᵃ פִּי־הַבְּאֵר the mouth of the well *f*

…כִּי מִן־הַבְּאֵר הַהוּא יַשְׁקוּ הָעֲדָרִים וְהָאֶ֫בֶן גְּדֹלָה עַל־פִּי הַבְּאֵר:

UNIT 2   מַה־בַּכְּלִי הַגָּדוֹל?

2.4 Joseph gave this unusual command to his steward after his brothers came to Egypt for grain: "Fill the men's sacks with food…"

6. …וְשִׂים כֶּסֶף־אִישׁ^{a} בְּפִי^b הַכְּלִי^μ: (Gen. 44:1)

^{a}אִישׁ *m* each one (*lit.*, a man) ^{b}בְּפִי *m* in the mouth of

…וְשִׂים כֶּסֶף־אִישׁ בְּפִי אַמְתַּחְתּוֹ:

2.4 Achan paid dearly for his act of deceit at Jericho. Upon his death, they heaped up a pile in the following manner. (Note: be sure to take into consideration the gender and number of גַּל since it will affect how you translate the sentence.)

7. וַיָּקִימוּ^{a} עַל־עָכָן^b גַּל^b־אֲבָנִים גָּדוֹל עַד הַיּוֹם הַזֶּה^c…: (Josh. 7:26)

^{a}וַיָּקִימוּ [ק.ו.מ] then they piled up *mpl* ^{b}גַּל *m* a mound ^{c}עַד ה'… *m* unto this [very] day

וַיָּקִימוּ עָלָיו גַּל־אֲבָנִים גָּדוֹל עַד הַיּוֹם הַזֶּה…:

2.4 When preparing to flee Jerusalem before his rebellious son Absalom, David turned to Ittai (one of his foreign officers) and excused him from the evacuation. This is what David said. (Who is here referred to by הַמֶּלֶךְ? And whom does Ittai believe to be the genuine מֶלֶךְ? Read v. 21 to find out.)

8. …שׁוּב^a וְשֵׁב עִם־הַמֶּלֶךְ…: (2 Sam. 15:19)

^{a}שׁוּב [ש.ו.ב] Return! *imperative ms*

…לָמָּה תֵלֵךְ גַּם־אַתָּה אִתָּנוּ שׁוּב וְשֵׁב עִם־הַמֶּלֶךְ כִּי־נָכְרִי אַתָּה…

2.4 | In a frantic effort to save their storm-threatened ship, the sailors threw...

.9 | ...אֶת־הַכֵּלִים[a] אֲשֶׁר בָּאֳנִיָּה אֶל־הַיָּם... (Jonah 1:5)

[a] כֵּלִים כְּלִי *plural*

וַיִּֽירְא֣וּ הַמַּלָּחִ֗ים וַֽיִּזְעֲקוּ֘ אִ֣ישׁ אֶל־אֱלֹהָיו֒ וַיָּטִ֨לוּ אֶת־הַכֵּלִ֜ים אֲשֶׁ֤ר בָּֽאֳנִיָּה֙ אֶל־הַיָּ֔ם לְהָקֵ֖ל מֵֽעֲלֵיהֶ֑ם וְיוֹנָ֗ה יָרַד֙ אֶל־יַרְכְּתֵ֣י הַסְּפִינָ֔ה וַיִּשְׁכַּ֖ב וַיֵּרָדַֽם׃

2.4 | Solomon's court enjoyed many exotic imports. Here is the reason:

.10 | ...כִּי אֳנִיּוֹת לַמֶּלֶךְ הֹלְכוֹת[a] תַּרְשִׁישׁ עִם עַבְדֵי חוּרָם[b]... (2 Chron. 9:21)

[a] הֹלְכוֹת [ה.ל.כ] *participle fpl* would go to [b] עַבְדֵי חוּרָם the servants of Hyram

כִּֽי־אֳנִיּ֤וֹת לַמֶּ֨לֶךְ֙ הֹלְכ֣וֹת תַּרְשִׁ֔ישׁ עִ֖ם עַבְדֵ֣י חוּרָ֑ם...

2.4 | אֲרָם is the name of ancient Syria. The following strategy was presented by מֶלֶךְ אֲרָם to his chariot officers before the start of a particular battle: "Do not fight..." (continue with the verse below).

(For more information regarding the substantival use of adjectives as seen in this selection, see Appendix §2.3.ב. The word אֶת־ appearing here is likely the preposition [used after ל.ח.מ *to fight* as seen in 1 Sam. 17:9]. But ל.ח.מ may also be construed with אֶת־ the definite direct object marker [cf. 1 Kings 20:25].)

.11 | ...אֶת־הַקָּטֹן אֶת־הַגָּדוֹל כִּי אִם־[a] אֶת־מֶלֶךְ[a] יִשְׂרָאֵל לְבַדּוֹ[b]׃ (2 Chron. 18:30)

[a] כִּי אִם־ *m* only, except [b] לְבַדּוֹ alone, exclusively

UNIT 2   מַה־בַּכְּלִי הַגָּדוֹל?   171

2.5   יִצְחָק had two sons, named יַעֲקֹב and עֵשָׂו. This Bible selection recounts a bitter feud that mushroomed between them. The beginning and end of the verse are translated for you. Please insert your translation of the Hebrew at the point marked "[insert statement here]."

"Then יַעֲקֹב said אֶל־יִצְחָק his father: '[insert statement here], and eat some of my game, so that you may bless me.'"

12. ...אָנֹכִי‎ᵃ עֵשָׂו...קוּם־נָא‎ᵇ שְׁבָ‎ᵘ... (Gen. 27:19)

ᵃ אָנֹכִי אֲנִי   ᵇ נָא   please (or tone of urgency)

וַיֹּאמֶר יַעֲקֹב אֶל־אָבִיו אָנֹכִי עֵשָׂו בְּכֹרֶךָ עָשִׂיתִי כַּאֲשֶׁר דִּבַּרְתָּ אֵלָי קוּם־נָא שְׁבָה וְאָכְלָה מִצֵּידִי בַּעֲבוּר תְּבָרֲכַנִּי נַפְשֶׁךָ:

2.5   When passing through the territory of Esau's descendants, an Israelite messenger negotiated for his people: "I will not venture off the highway. Only sell me food for money…"

13. ...וּמַיִם בַּכֶּסֶף תִּתֶּן‎ᵘ לִי... (Deut. 2:28)

אֹכֶל בַּכֶּסֶף תַּשְׁבִּרֵנִי וְאָכַלְתִּי וּמַיִם בַּכֶּסֶף תִּתֶּן־לִי וְשָׁתִיתִי...:

2.5   Upon noticing that some of his donkeys had wandered off, Kish said to his son שָׁאוּל (who later would become Israel's first king), "Take one of the youths with you…"

14. ...וְקוּם לֵךְ בַּקֵּשׁ‎ᵃ אֶת־הָאֲתֹנֹת‎ᵇ: (1 Sam. 9:3)

ᵃ בַּקֵּשׁ [ב.ק.ש] Search! *imperative ms*   ᵇ אֲתֹנֹת donkeys *f*

קַח־נָא אִתְּךָ אֶת־אַחַד מֵהַנְּעָרִים וְקוּם לֵךְ בַּקֵּשׁ אֶת־הָאֲתֹנֹת:

2.5 Joab, upon learning that one of his soldiers had refrained from killing rebel Absalom, replied: "Why did you not strike him? [If you had, then]…"

15. …וְעָלַי לָתֶת לְךָ֨ᵃ עֲשָׂרָהᵇ כֶּ֖סֶף׃… (2 Sam. 18:11)

לְךָᵃ to you עֲשָׂרָהᵇ ten [pieces] of

…וּמַדּ֨וּעַ לֹֽא־הִכִּית֤וֹ שָׁם֙ אַ֔רְצָה וְעָלַ֗י לָ֤תֶת לְךָ֙ עֲשָׂרָ֣ה כֶ֔סֶף וַחֲגֹרָ֖ה אֶחָֽת׃

עֲקֵדַת יִצְחָק A connected reading: The binding of Isaac (Gen. 22:2)

2. וַיֹּ֨אמֶרᵃ
קַח־נָאᵇ אֶת־בִּנְךָ֤ᶜ
אֶת־יְחִידְךָ֙ᵈ
אֲשֶׁר־אָהַ֣בְתָּᵉ
אֶת־יִצְחָ֔קᶠ
וְלֶךְ־לְךָ֔ᵍ אֶל־אֶ֖רֶץ הַמֹּרִיָּ֑הʰ
וְהַעֲלֵ֤הוּⁱ שָׁם֙ʲ לְעֹלָ֔הᵏ
עַ֚ל אַחַ֣דˡ הֶֽהָרִ֔יםᵐ
אֲשֶׁ֖ר אֹמַ֥רⁿ אֵלֶֽיךָ׃ᵒ (Gen. 22:2)

ואֹ֨מֶרᵃ then he said קַח־נָאᵇ Take! אֶת־בִּנְךָᶜ your son m אֶת־יְחִידְךָᵈ your only one אָהַבְתָּᵉ you love
יִצְחָקᶠ (a person's name) וְלֶךְ־לְךָᵍ and go! אֶרֶץ הַמֹּרִיָּהʰ the land f of Moriah וְהַעֲלֵהוּⁱ and offer him
שָׁםʲ there לְעֹלָהᵏ as a whole burnt offering אַחַדˡ on one (of) הֶהָרִיםᵐ the mountains mpl
אֹמַרⁿ I will say (or tell) אֵלֶיךָᵒ to you

UNIT 3

מָה־אַתָּה עֹשֶׂה?

Talking about the here-and-now

pronouns, participles, and infinitives

This unit will enable you to report events you are currently experiencing, such as:

- what you are doing
- what you see going on around you
- what you need to do
- what you like to do

When talking about someone else, you will be able to describe:

- to whom certain objects belong
- what someone can do with them

MODULE 3.1 — Designating an object and who owns it

Unit 3 JONAH STORY: Jonah gets hungry

Have you ever been a guest and had the awkward experience of being offered food that made you lose your appetite? Or have you ever gotten the unpleasant feeling that your host wished that you would leave rather soon? If so, perhaps you can relate to the next episode in Jonah's travels.

Words for responding — מִלִים לַעֲנוֹת

לָשׂוּם [ש.ו/י.מ]	to put, to place *inf c, prep* לְ	אֹכֵל [א.כ.ל]	one who is eating *pt ms*
לִשְׁכַּב [ש.כ.ב]	to lie down *inf c, prep* לְ	אֵלֶּה	these *m, f*
שֹׁתֶה, שֹׁתָה [ש.ת.י/ה][b]	one who is drinking *pt ms, fs*	הֵם (also הֵמָּה)	they, those *m*
		יָם, יַם- (or יָם)[a]	sea *m*
		לֶאֱכֹל [א.כ.ל]	to eat *inf c, prep* לְ
		לַחְמִי	my bread*
		לִמְצֹא [מ.צ.א]	to find *inf c, prep* לְ

[a] When no maqqef is used, the construct is spelled יָם.

UNIT 3   מָה־אַתָּה עֹשֶׂה?   175

[a] ש.ת.י/ה *to drink* is another variable-letter שֹׁרֶשׁ *root*, like ש.י/ו.מ *to put* in §2.4. It should be noted that a handful of verbs such as ת.מ.ה *to be astounded*, ג.ב.ה *to be high*, מ.ה.ה *to delay* end with a true consonant ה (not a vowel letter ה replacing an original י). This fact is signaled by a dot in the ה, known as a mappiq (Blau §30 and GKC §65n.).

* A word whose root or basic form has appeared in previous vocabulary lists will be marked with an asterisk (*). Words without an asterisk are new or may introduce a new pattern for a familiar root.

Words for hearing   מִלִּים לִשְׁמֹעַ

מִסְפָּר, מִסְפָּרִים, מִסְפַּר־	number *m sing absol, pl absol, sing constr*	אַךְ	but, however, surely
מַר, מָרָה, מָרִים, מָרוֹת	bitter *ms, fs, mpl, fpl*	אָנֹכִי	I (אָנֹֽכִי *when in pause; alternate to* אֲנִי)
מָתוֹק, מְתוּקָה, מְתוּקִים, מְתוּקוֹת	sweet *ms, fs, mpl, fpl*	דְּבַשׁ	honey *m* (דְּבָֽשׁ *when in pause*)
סְלַח־נָא[c], סִלְחִי־נָא	I'm sorry (*lit.*, Forgive!) *imv ms, fs*	יָדַיִם	hands *f dual*[a]
רַךְ, רַכָּה, רַכִּים, רַכּוֹת	soft *ms, fs, mpl, fpl*	יֹרֵד, יֹרֶֽדֶת [י.ר.ד]	one who descends, one who goes down *pt ms, fs*
רָעֵב, רְעֵבָה, רְעֵבִים, רְעֵבוֹת	hungry *ms, fs, mpl, fpl*	לְבַקֵּשׁ	to look for *piel*[b] *inf c, prep* לְ
שְׁכַב, שִׁכְבִי [ש.כ.ב]	Lie down! *imv ms, fs*	לְמַֽעַן	in order to
		לִשְׁתּוֹת [ש.ת.י/ה]	to drink *inf c, prep* לְ

[a] The designation "dual" refers to a specialized plural form—a unit of two. Many paired body parts can be expressed as dual (including ears, eyes, feet, lips). Often a dual form may be rendered, "a pair of..." or "both...." Dual forms close with the characteristic sound "...ַיִם," with accent on the pataḥ. Dual words take plural verbs and

adjectives, rather than requiring specialized dual forms. Words with dual forms may also have traditional plurals (e.g., יָדוֹת *hands* [not limited to a pair]).

ᵇ The piel spelling pattern will be explained in Unit 10. For the time being, simply learn the meaning of the word לְבַקֵּשׁ.

ᶜ Known as an entreating interjection, when associated with asking forgiveness the particle נָא־ appears to soften the request (*Please forgive...*). In other situations it may convey the notion of "I beg you." And in some cases it may be so subtle as to remain untranslatable (cf. Joüon §105c).

UNIT 3 מָה־אַתָּה עָשָׂה? 177

3.1 Jonah Episode: I'm hungry.

נ׳ = יוֹנָה הַנָּבִיא, ע׳ = עֶבֶד

---

[1] The accent moved one syllable *back* from the end of the word because in this sentence the word occurs at the end of a phrase or sentence (אָנֹכִי became אָנֹכִי). This is known as a "pausal" form. There is no change in meaning.

[2] This word also is "in pause" due to its position at the end of the sentence. That is why the accent moved one syllable *back* from the end of the word. In addition, the pataḥ becomes a qameṣ (אַתָּה became אָתָּה). Again, pausal forms bring no change in meaning.

[3] לָחֶם is the pausal form of לֶחֶם.

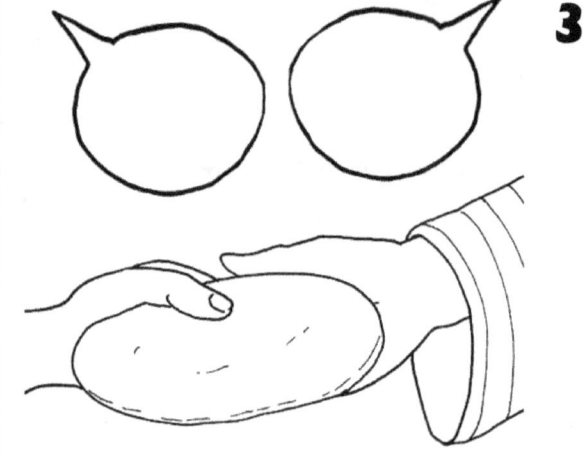

[ע] הִנֵּה לְךָ לָֽחֶם׃

[נ'] יְבָרֶכְךָ יהוה...

[נ'] אֲנִי לֹא אוּכַל לֶאֱכֹל אֶת־הַלֶּחֶם הַזֶּה׃
אֵין רַךְ׃ יָבֵשׁ וְחָזָק הוּא כָּאָֽבֶן׃
הֲזֶה הַלֶּחֶם אֲשֶׁר אַתָּה אֹכֵל?

[ע] טוֹב לִי לָשׂוּם אֶת־הַלֶּחֶם בַּמָּֽיִם׃
הַאַתָּה מְבַקֵּשׁ אֶת־הַמָּֽיִם?

[נ'] אֶת־הַמַּֽיִם אֲנִי מְבַקֵּשׁ׃

מָה־אַתָּה עֹשֶׂה?

8

[נ׳] יְבָרֶכְךָ יהוה... אַךְ מָרִים הַמַּיִם... מָרִים מְאֹד:
הַאַתָּה שָׁתָה אֶת־הַמַּיִם הָאֵלֶּה?

7

[ע׳] לֹא אוּכַל לִמְצֹא מַיִם לָךְ:
מַיִם... מַיִם... מַיִם... אַיֵּה מָיִם?
הִנֵּה מַיִם לָךְ:

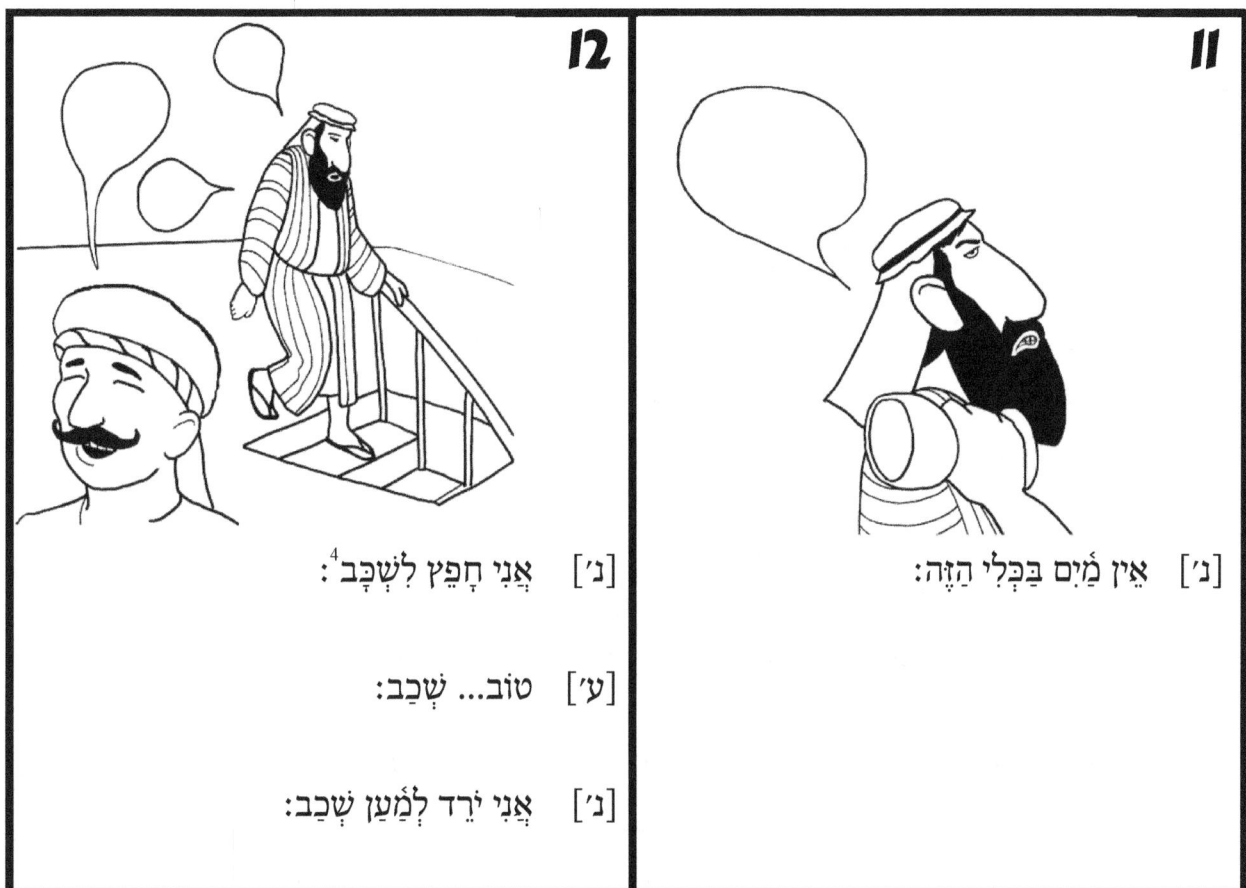

[נ׳] אֵין מַיִם בַּכְּלִי הַזֶּה:

[נ׳] אֲנִי חָפֵץ לִשְׁכָּב[4]:

[ע׳] טוֹב... שְׁכַב:

[נ׳] אֲנִי יֵרֵד לְמַעַן שְׁכַב:

---

[4] A pausal spelling of לִשְׁכַּב.

3.1.א. Activity: "Do you (*ms*) desire to travel?" הֲלָלֶכֶת אַתָּה חָפֵץ?

INTERACTIVE SKILL: Sharing what activities you would desire to do

What sorts of activities do you enjoy? Make note of one or two activities **you** enjoy. Then select two activities you think **your neighbor** may enjoy. Focus on one that you have selected for your neighbor, and ask whether he/she enjoys doing it. Your neighbor will tell you if you guessed correctly (by announcing אֱמֶת *truth*) or not (by announcing שֶׁקֶר *falsehood*). Then reverse roles so your neighbor can learn about you. Here is a sample exchange.

Model

Do you (*ms, fs*) desire to travel?	הֲלָלֶכֶת אַתָּה חָפֵץ / אַתְּ חֲפֵצָה?	Inquiry
True (*lit.* truth)...I (*m, f*) desire to travel.	אֱמֶת... לָלֶכֶת אֲנִי חָפֵץ / חֲפֵצָה:	Reply, if inquiry was correct
False (*lit.* falsehood)...I (*m, f*) do not desire to travel.	שֶׁקֶר... לֹא לָלֶכֶת אֲנִי חָפֵץ / חֲפֵצָה:	Reply, if inquiry was not correct

Did you notice that Hebrew places the activity (such as traveling) directly after the interrogative particle הֲ? In this way Hebrew is able to indicate that it is the **activity** that constitutes the variable in question, rather than the person ("you") or the attitude ("desire"). The question may be paraphrased thus: "Is **traveling** the activity that you desire to engage in, or would you prefer some **other** activity?" Languages such as English are not so agile when attempting to create this sort of focus.

Note concerning negation. Since the focus of the inquiry rests on the activity ("traveling"), we should not be surprised to find that when the reply is negative, the negation will similarly focus on the activity (rather than the person or the attitude). So we find the negative reply expressed thus: לֹא לָלֶכֶת אֲנִי חָפֵץ. When you employ this response, you are leaving open the likelihood that you still desire to do *some activity*, but "traveling" is not the activity you are interested in.

Perhaps you are wondering, "Why do we not negate using אֵין?" In fact, most negated phrases in the Hebrew Bible that involve participles will be negated with אֵין. But if אֵין were used in response to the present dialogue inquiry, it would send a slightly different message. אֵין would shift the attention away from negating the **activity** ("not-traveling," in this case), and would focus instead on negating the **subject** ("not-I"): אֵינֶנִּי חָפֵץ לָלֶכֶת *I am not the one who desires to travel*. Negating the subject (with אֵין) allows that someone **else** may desire to travel, but it is **"not I"** who desire to travel.[5]

Incidentally, this principle (that אֵין negates the subject, often expressed as the pronominal suffix of אֵין) explains why אֵינֶנִּי appears in the 3.3 Jonah Episode expression אֵינֶנִּי אֹהֵב (cell 4), rather than אֲנִי לֹא אֹהֵב. The context of the story presents a contrast between two **subjects**: **God**, on the one hand (who **does** love the people of Nineveh), and **Jonah**, on the other hand (who does **not**). אֵינֶנִּי focuses negation on the **subject** (Jonah), underscoring the contrast between him and God.

If instead we were to say אֲנִי לֹא אֹהֵב, we would shift the negative focus from negating the subject (אֲנִי) to negating the **attitude** (אֹהֵב). It would amount to saying: "I do have an attitude toward the people of Nineveh, but **loving** them is *not* that attitude."

Here, then, are several activities (verbs) to choose from as you engage this activity. Some resulting expressions will be rather bland until you add a bit of color, specifying what it is that you "desire to find" or what it is that you "delight to eat." If you wish, you may use your native language to finish your sentence with a bit of color (e.g., "Do you delight in traveling **to exotic places**?").

לָשׂוּם	to put, place	לְהַשְׁלִיךְ	to throw	לֶאֱכֹל	to eat
לִשְׁכַּב	to lie down	לִמְלֹךְ	to rule	לְבַקֵּשׁ	to look for
לָתֵת	to give	לִמְצֹא	to find	לְדַבֵּר	to talk

If time allows, learn a bit more by returning to one activity your neighbor likes (or does not like) and ask לָמָה? *Why?* You may respond to לָמָה? in your native language.

Two similar words: אֲנִי and אָנֹכִי. Both אֲנִי and אָנֹכִי translate as the pronoun "I." When occurring together, אָנֹכִי tends to be more emphatic. At times, a biblical writer's choice appears to have been based on sound (euphony) rather than sense. Over time, אֲנִי grew to become more common than אָנֹכִי.

Words "in pause." Sometimes you will find אָנֹכִי with a shift of accent: אָנֹכִי, as in the statement רָעֵב אָנֹכִי *I am hungry*. Notice that in this statement, אָנֹכִי appears at the **end** of a sentence. As you may recall from §1.1.ג., words are classified as "**in pause**" or "**pausal**" when they present a change in accent or vocalization due to appearing at the end of a major phrase (including sentence-end). "Pause" refers to the slight break in reading that naturally occurs at the end of a phrase or sentence. Many words undergo

---

[5] If we were to employ אֵין to negate strictly the infinitive (not a pronominal subject), it would convey *there is no* [supply whatever is the verb's topic]. Thus אֵין־לְחֹם means *there is no warmth* (ח.מ.מ *to be warm*, Hag. 1:6).

no change when "in pause." Other words may experience a change either in the **location of the accented syllable**, in the **selection of a vowel**, or in **both accent and vowel**. Neither of these changes alters the meaning of a word.

- **Accent change.** אָנֹכִי, the pronoun *I*, will retract its accent when in pause, so that it reads אָנֹכִי.

- **Vowel change.** כֶּסֶף *silver* will be pronounced כָּסֶף when in pause (as in §2.4). לֶחֶם *bread* becomes לָחֶם. In לְךָ *to you*, both the sheva and qameṣ change, becoming לָךְ (as in §1.1.ו).

- **Accent change and vowel change.** The pronoun אָתָּה is in pause in the question הֲרָעֵב אָתָּה? *Are you hungry?* This word displays both accent change and vowel change (compare the non-pausal spelling, אַתָּה).

3.1.ב. Do you (*ms*) know the meaning…? (לֶחֶם)   הֲיָדַעְתָּ פֵּשֶׁר…?

The word לֶחֶם encompasses more than simply "bread." Strictly speaking, לֶחֶם refers to those grain products that serve as ingredients for bread (wheat, in the case of higher-quality bread, or barley, for lower-quality bread).

Since the main meal (served in the evening) was typically comprised of bread served with seasonal vegetables flavored with herbs, the term לֶחֶם at times would refer to an entire meal. On special occasions, meat might be added (cf. Abram hosting guests in Genesis 18 and Isaac's meal before issuing a blessing in Genesis 27). Consequently we find that א.כ.ל לֶחֶם (lit., *to eat bread*) refers to eating a meal (Gen. 31:54), and ע.ש.ה לֶחֶם (lit., *to make bread*) refers to preparing a meal or a feast (not simply making loaves of bread, Eccl. 10:19). Moreover, if your tribe were to declare metaphorically that "so-and-so is our bread," it would mean that you planned to devour or destroy that adversary (Deut. 7:16).[6]

---

[6] For more information, see W. Dommershausen, "לֶחֶם," 521–29, in *Theological Dictionary of the Old Testament*, vol. 7, English translation (Grand Rapids: Eerdmans, 1995), and J. A. Thompson, "Food and its Preparation," in *Handbook of Life in Bible Times* (Downers Grove, Illinois: Intervarsity Press, 1986), 147–163.

As far as literal bread making is concerned, each household typically would grind its own grain using mortars, hand mills (querns), or larger basalt mills turned by animals. To make wheat bread, the flour was mixed with water, salt, and leaven to yield flat circular loaves about 25 cm in diameter (כִּכָּר *f* or עֻגָה *f*). If made from barley flour, loaves tended to be oblong.

The discovery of fifty-two saddle-querns in a two-story Middle Bronze structure in Jericho suggests that some may have developed grain milling into a commercial enterprise. Comments in Hosea and Jeremiah similarly suggest that some took up baking as an occupation. (cf. Hos. 7:4, and mention of "bakers' street" in Jer. 37:21).

This concave saddle-quern (28 cm long) and polisher stone are typical of grinding implements in use from the Pre-Pottery Neolithic to Roman periods (7500 BCE– 70 CE). (Courtesy of Flora Archaeological Center; photo: B. Hoffman)

What role does bread play in your culture, whether in diet or in metaphoric expression?

3.1.ג. Activity: "Is this the bread that you (*ms*) are eating?"
הֲזֶה הַלֶּחֶם אֲשֶׁר אַתָּה אֹכֵל?

INTERACTIVE SKILL: Identifying which object (among several) a person may be referring to

At times, it is helpful to distinguish which particular object (among several related objects) a person is referring to. For example, if you are a merchant with various כֵּלִים for sale, you will want to know whether the customer who is studying your inventory is interested in a particular sack, cup, or bottle (all of which would fall under the heading כֵּלִים). The conversational activity found here will help you determine **which** כְּלִי the customer wants, distinguishing by use of the word *this*.

Begin by selecting your line of business (top row of "Inventory list" table, below: לֶחֶם, אִישׁ, or כְּלִי). In the case of the אִישׁ-group, consider yourself a well-connected community person who can—for a slight fee—introduce your customer to prominent individuals in these various occupations. Perhaps your customer hopes to secure employment with one of these persons.

After selecting your line of business, familiarize yourself with what you have "in-stock" (see inventory listed in column under respective "business" headings). For example, if you set up shop dealing in כֵּלִים, then you will have the following items for sale: כּוֹס, בַּקְבֻּק, שַׂק, צְרוֹר, and אָרוֹן.

Announce to your neighbor what is your line of business (select one from the top row: לֶחֶם, אִישׁ, or כְּלִי). Now it is up to your neighbor secretly to select one item from your inventory list that he or she is interested in. Then you will attempt to guess which element your neighbor has selected. If your neighbor is a connoisseur of tea or coffee, he or she will likely be more interested in כּוֹס rather than the other כֵּלִים options (such as בַּקְבֻּק, שַׂק, צְרוֹר, or אָרוֹן). Use the inquiry modeled below to see if you correctly deduced which inventory item your neighbor is interested in. Under the כְּלִי column of the Inventory list, point to the word כּוֹס, and then ask:

Model (singular)

Is **this** the container that you (*ms, fs*) find appealing?	הֲזֶה הַכְּלִי אֲשֶׁר אַתָּה חָפֵץ / אַתְּ חֲפֵצָה?	Inquiry (you *ms, fs*)
This is the container [that I find appealing].	זֶה הַכְּלִי:	Affirmative reply
This is **not** the container [that I find appealing].	לֹא זֶה הַכְּלִי:	Negative reply

Naturally, if you select a group other than כְּלִי, you would substitute the appropriate group title in place of כְּלִי. (Do not be concerned with learning new vocabulary found in these groups. The new words are intended simply to provide variety for your selection.)

Inventory list

Here are some nouns to draw from. All of the "Line of business" **headings** are masculine (top row). Use the blanks to fill in the meaning of words already learned.

לֶחֶם	אִישׁ, אֲנָשִׁים	כְּלִי, כֵּלִים
פְּרִי fruit *m*	מֶלֶךְ, מְלָכִים	כּוֹס, כֹּסוֹת
בָּשָׂר, בְּשָׂרִים meat *m*	נָבִיא, נְבִיאִים	בַּקְבּוּק, בַּקְבּוּקִים flask *or* bottle
דָּג, דָּגִים fish *m*	רֹעֶה, רֹעִים shepherd *m*	שַׂק, שַׂקִּים sack *m*
דְּבַשׁ honey from bees *or* date-syrup *m*	יוֹצֵר, יֹצְרִים potter *m*	צְרוֹר, צְרֹרוֹת small bag *m*
גְּבִינָה cheese *f*	מַלְאָךְ, מַלְאָכִים messenger *m*	אָרוֹן, אֲרֹנוֹת chest *or* ark, *m or f*

If you guessed incorrectly but wish to probe further, you may obtain the answer from your friend with this follow-up query:

Model (follow-up)

What do you (*ms, fs*) find appealing?	מַה־חָפֵץ אַתָּה? / מַה־חֲפֵצָה אַתְּ?

After learning what your neighbor is shopping for, **reverse** roles. Now it is your neighbor's turn to guess what inventory item (singular) **you** are interested in.

If time allows, repeat by selecting a **different** item, one from among the **plural** words. Below you will find the same inquiry / reply, modified for **plural**. Notice that זֶה *this* has been replaced by אֵלֶּה *these*. See who can accumulate more guesses that are correct.

Model (plural)

Are **these** the containers you (*ms, fs*) find appealing?	הָאֵלֶה הַכֵּלִים אֲשֶׁר אַתָּה חָפֵץ / אַתְּ חֲפֵצָה?	Inquiry (you *ms, fs*)
These are the containers.	אֵלֶה הַכֵּלִים :	Affirmative reply
These are **not** the containers.	לֹא אֵלֶה הַכֵּלִים :	Negative reply

Demonstrative pronouns (overview)

The words זֶה *this ms,* and אֵלֶּה *these mpl / fpl,* are called "demonstrative pronouns." They operate in a manner similar to adjectives. That is, **a sentence** may form around them (**predicative** use), as in:

$$זֶה\ הַכְּלִי:$$

This is the container.

Alternatively, demonstrative pronouns may simply **modify** a noun (**attributive** use), as in:

$$הַכְּלִי\ הַזֶּה$$

this container

When **merely modifying** a noun (attributive use), the demonstrative pronoun will display these three traits:

(a) It will **follow** the noun.

(b) It will match the noun by appearing with its own **article**.

(c) It will **match** the noun in **gender**.

To this point we have designated only those objects that are **near** (זֶה and אֵלֶּה). The sort of "nearness" suitable for זֶה and אֵלֶּה may include either **time** (for an entity that was recently mentioned in a conversation) or **space** (for an entity near-at-hand).

But what if the entity you wish to designate is **not** immediately present? What if it is separated from the present situation because it occurred either earlier (time) or farther away (space)? The role of **remote**

demonstratives *that* and *those* is supplied by words you already have encountered: independent personal pronouns, third person.[7]

- To designate a **single** remote masculine entity as "*that [object* or *person]...,*" Hebrew uses הוּא (meaning either *he* or *that ms*). Thus הָאִישׁ הַהוּא would mean *that person / man* (employing הוּא as a demonstrative pronoun in an attributive manner).

- To designate a **plural** remote masculine entity as "*those...,*" Hebrew uses הֵם (meaning either *they* or *those mpl*). Thus הַמְּלָכִים הָהֵם would mean *those kings* (another attributive example).

Here are the **masculine** demonstrative pronouns (for **feminine** demonstrative pronouns, cf. §3.2.א):

Masculine demonstrative pronouns

(הָ)אֵ֫לֶּה , (הַ)זֶּה[8]	this, these *ms, mpl*
(הָ)הֵם , (הַ)הוּא	that, those *ms, mpl*

If הַדְּבָרִים means *the words*, can you surmise what אֵ֫לֶּה הַדְּבָרִים means? (Hint: this is a **predicative** usage since אֵ֫לֶּה lacks the article found with הַדְּבָרִים.)[9]

---

[7] An **independent** personal pronoun is one which may stand **alone**, not attached to another word (e.g., אֲנִי *I* or הִיא *she*). In contrast, when a pronoun is **attached** to a word it is called "**suffixed**" (such as the suffix ִי... *me*, in the word לִי *to me*).

[8] Include a dagesh in (הַ)זֶּה only if the definite article is used.

[9] *These are the words [which Moses spoke]...*—this forms the opening line of the Book of Deuteronomy.

3.1.ד. Did you (*ms*) know that…? (Perfumes and spices)   ‏הֲיָדַעְתָּ כִּי...?‏

…the prized aromatic resin known as ‏מֹר‏ *myrrh* derived its name from an adjective that described its bitter flavor: ‏מַר‏ (singular for ‏מָרִים‏)? Like frankincense, myrrh was gathered by tapping shrubs native to southern Arabia and the territory of Somaliland. Since fragrances were suspended in olive oil, in many cases it would be better to render the word *oil* (‏שֶׁמֶן‏) as *scented oil*. Both men and women used scented oil extensively, whether to mask objectionable odors or to protect the skin from dry summer heat.

"Bilbil" perfume juglet (left, Late Bronze [1550–1200 BCE]), pressed-handle juglet (rear, Late Iron [587–330 BCE]), and four-depression cosmetic palette (gypsum, perhaps late 8th cent. BCE, 10 cm square) with mixing tool. (Courtesy of Flora Archaeological Center; photo: B. Hoffman)

Because extensive travel was required to obtain perfumes and spices, they were valued as if they were precious metals. Due to their high value, they were dispensed in tiny juglets and narrow-based pyxides (lidded cosmetic containers).[10]

In a separate use of the adjective ‏מַר‏, consider the depths of grief felt by a bereaved wife and mother as Naomi (*pleasant*) asked her former neighbors now to call her ‏מָרָא‏, a by-form of ‏מָרָה‏ (Ruth 1:20).

---

[10] *LBI*, 280–81 and 347.

3.1.ה. Activity: "Are you (*ms*) seeking to lie down?"

הֲלִשְׁכַּב אַתָּה מְבַקֵּשׁ?

INTERACTIVE SKILL: Conveying personal needs, intentions

For this activity, please refer to the list of verbs located in §3.1.א. (e.g., לֶאֱכֹל *to eat*). Without letting your neighbor see what words you are selecting, **circle** one activity (verb) that **you** wish to do. Next, **draw a box** around one of the activities you think your **neighbor** may wish to do. Find out if you guessed right by asking your neighbor the sort of question modeled below.

You will notice that the **first** term to appear in a sentence, whether in question or reply, is the variable element of the conversation—that activity which a person may be seeking to do. Unlike the rigid word-order (syntax) found in languages like English, Hebrew enjoys considerable flexibility of syntax. Consequently, Hebrew is able to focus attention on various parts of a sentence, depending on the aim of a given situation. Learning to detect emphasis arising from syntax comprises a key advantage of reading the Bible in Hebrew.

Model

Are you (*ms, fs*) seeking **to lie down**? (Is **lying down** what you are seeking to do?)	הֲלִשְׁכַּב אַתָּה מְבַקֵּשׁ / אַתְּ מְבַקֶּשֶׁת?	Inquiry *ms, fs*
I am seeking **to lie down**. (**Lying down** is what I am seeking to do.)	לִשְׁכַּב אֲנִי מְבַקֵּשׁ / מְבַקֶּשֶׁת:	Reply, if guess was **correct** *ms, fs*
I am not seeking **to lie down**. (**Lying down** is not what I am seeking to do. [I am seeking to do something **else**.])	לֹא לִשְׁכַּב אֲנִי מְבַקֵּשׁ / מְבַקֶּשֶׁת:	Reply, if guess was **incorrect** *ms, fs*

3.1.1. Did you (*ms*) know that...? ("Yes")   הֲיָדַעְתָּ כִּי...?

...Biblical Hebrew has no distinct word for "yes"? Instead, when giving an affirmative reply one would restate the inquiry, omitting the question word.

Suppose that someone has asked you: הַאַתָּה מְבַקֵּשׁ אֶת־הַלֶּחֶם: To answer affirmatively you would say either, אֲנִי מְבַקֵּשׁ אֶת־הַלֶּחֶם: *I am seeking some bread*, or you may condense your reply by omitting both the object and the interrogative particle, אֲנִי מְבַקֵּשׁ: *I am seeking*."[11] (Modern Hebrew expresses "yes" with the word כֵּן, a word that in Biblical Hebrew means *it is firm* or *in that fashion*.)

---

[11] E.g., יָדַעְנוּ *We know* comprises the response to Jacob's yes / no ("polar") question in Gen. 29:5: הַיְדַעְתֶּם אֶת־לָבָן בֶּן־נָחוֹר: *Do you know Lābān, son of Nāḥôr?* The spelling יָדָעְנוּ in the reply is pausal for יָדַעְנוּ.

UNIT 3 מַה־אַתָּה עֹשֶׂה? 193

3.1.ז. Explanation: "This water is sweeter than honey."

הַמַּיִם הָאֵלֶּה מְתוּקִים מִדְּבָשׁ:

INTERACTIVE SKILL: Describing one entity by comparing it with something else

When describing something new or unfamiliar, it may be helpful to compare it with another item that is more familiar. Here are two ways one might make a comparison:

(a) "Item א is *like* item ב" (a simile, where two nouns are linked by the word *like*)[12]

(b) "Item א is *larger than* item ב" (associating two nouns with a comparative adjective such as "larger")

Hebrew can generate both of these expressions by using the prepositions ...כְּ and מִן, respectively.

Comparative with מִן		Simile with ...כְּ	
נִינְוֵה גְּדוֹלָה מִתַּרְשִׁישׁ:	Nineveh is **bigger than** Tarshish.	נִינְוֵה כְּתַרְשִׁישׁ:	Nineveh is **like** Tarshish.
טוֹב לֶחֶם מִכֶּסֶף:	**Better** is bread **than** silver.	לֶחֶם כָּאֶבֶן:	Bread is **like** a rock.

The simile with כְּ operates like a simile in English. Precede the second item with ...כְּ.

To form a comparison using מִן, the adjective may either **follow** the first noun (...נִינְוֵה גְּדוֹלָה *Nineveh is bigger*...) or **precede** it (...טוֹב לֶחֶם *Better is bread*...). The adjective is rendered comparative when followed by מִן.

- Incidentally, do you know why there is a dagesh in מִתַּרְשִׁישׁ and מִכֶּסֶף?[13]

- Also, do you recall why נִינְוֵה was described with גְּדוֹלָה (not גָּדוֹל)? (לֶחֶם was described with טוֹב and not טוֹבָה for the same reason.)

See whether you can deduce the meaning of these comparative statements.

---

[12] Similarity may also be expressed by the verb *to resemble* and the preposition ל: ד.מ.י/ה ל...

[13] The dagesh in מִתַּרְשִׁישׁ and מִכֶּסֶף represents the assimilated נ of מִן.

| א. לֶחֶם רַךְ מֵאֶבֶן גְּדוֹלָה: | ב. טוֹב שֵׁם מִכָּסֶף: | ג. לֹא חָזָק הַכִּסֵּא מִן הַשֻּׁלְחָן: |

The comparative with מִן can also mean "too [insert adjective] for…." So we find Jethro cautioning Moses, his son-in-law, against singlehandedly adjudicating cases for all of Israel: כִּי־**כָבֵד מִמְּךָ** הַדָּבָר *For the matter is **too heavy for** you* (Exod. 18:18, מִמְּךָ is מִן plus a *2ms* pronominal suffix).

When a comparative is not strong enough to express what you wish to convey—when you need a superlative—then simply repeat the targeted quality twice. The first will be in construct singular, and the second will be plural, as in these examples.[14]

שִׁיר הַשִּׁירִים	קֹדֶשׁ הַקֳּדָשִׁים	עֶבֶד עֲבָדִים
The supreme song, the Song of Songs	The holiest [space], the Holy of Holies	lowliest of servants, a servant of servants

3.1.ח. Did you (*ms*) know that…? (Diet)   הֲיָדַעְתָּ כִּי...?

…the diet of Israelites was comprised largely of vegetables, legumes, fruit, and nuts? Since it is coarser than חִטָּה *wheat f* and easier to cultivate, שְׂעֹרָה *barley f* comprised the poor person's grain. Grain might be eaten parched or ground daily (see §3.1.ב.) and baked in a beehive-shaped outdoor oven, yielding pita-shaped loaves about 25 cm in diameter.

Typical vegetables included cucumbers, watermelons, onions, leeks, and garlic. Legumes such as lentils, fava beans, and chickpeas were commonly consumed.

---

[14] There are two additional ways to express the superlative. The first involves following the adjective with מִכָּל־ *of all* (e.g., כִּי־אַתֶּם הַמְעַט מִכָּל־הָעַמִּים *…for you were the **fewest** of all the peoples*, Deut. 7:7). The second involves accompanying the adjective (operating as a substantive) with the definite article. Thus Gideon protested being selected as Israel's rescuer, since he felt he was extremely צָעִיר *insignificant*: וְאָנֹכִי הַצָּעִיר בְּבֵית אָבִי... *…and I am the **least significant** (person) in my father's house* (Judg. 6:15b).

Four-handled jug (32 cm tall) with dipping juglet (Iron IIB–C, 900–586 BCE). (Courtesy of Flora Archaeological Center; photo: B. Hoffman)

As regards פְּרִי *fruit m*, dates and figs would have been eaten either fresh or dried and compacted as cakes—excellent for traveler's food. Cultivated עֲנָבִים *grapes m* provided beverage. Pressed olives supplied שֶׁמֶן *oil m* for various uses: cooking, fuel, and cosmetics. Pistachios and almonds are the main nuts mentioned in the Bible.

A typical meal might consist of yogurt poured over a bed of couscous flavored with onions, coriander, and black cumin. חֶמְאָה *yogurt curds f* were produced by churning חָלָב *milk m* in an oblong container made of animal skin or ceramic material. Since utensils were not used, diners would scoop up the dairy and vegetable dish with a piece of pita bread as they relaxed, squatting or reclining on rugs.[15]

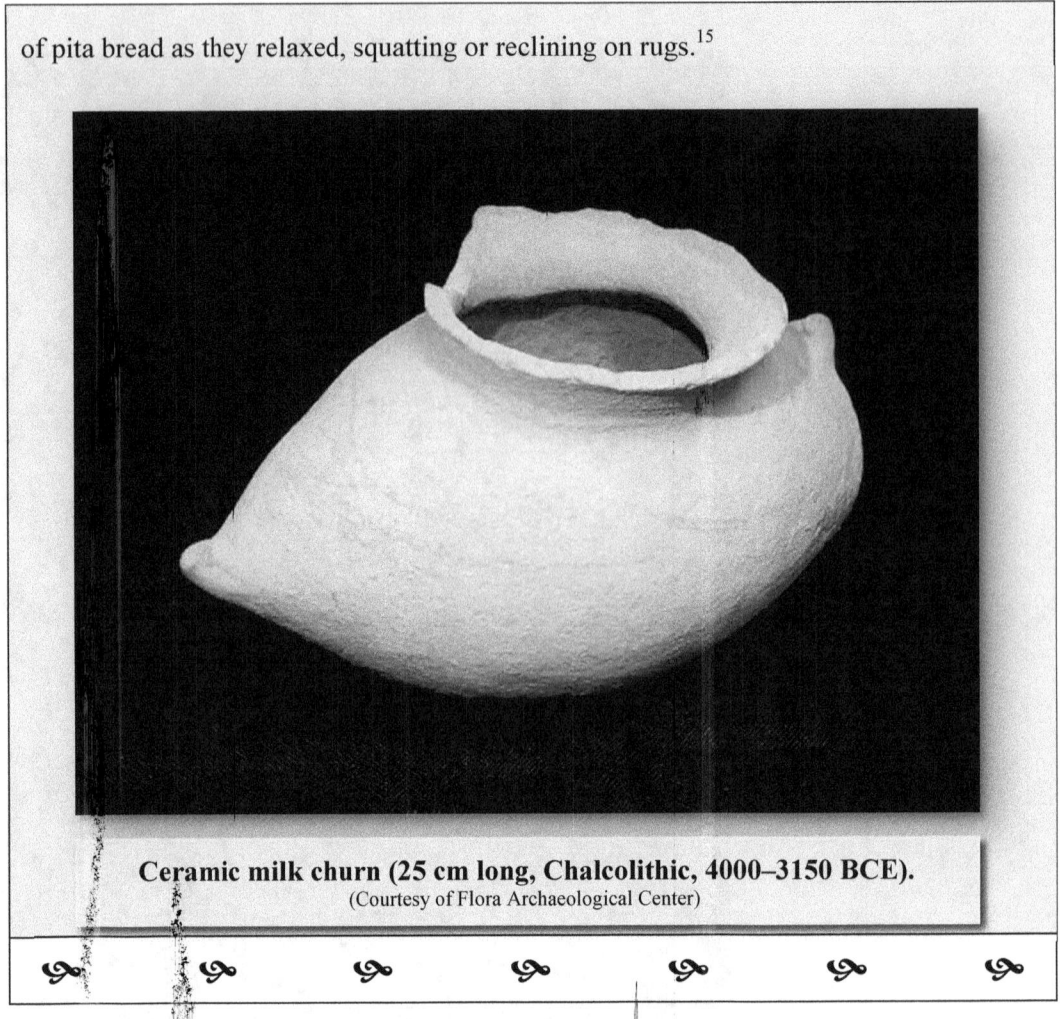

Ceramic milk churn (25 cm long, Chalcolithic, 4000–3150 BCE).
(Courtesy of Flora Archaeological Center)

---

[15] *LBI*, 19, 63, 93–94, and 103–5.

MODULE 3.2 — Discussing job descriptions

מִלִּים לַעֲנוֹת — Words for responding

עֹמֵד, עֹמְדִים [ע.מ.ד]	one who stands *pt ms, mpl*	אֲנַחְנוּ[a]	we
עֹשֶׂה, עֹשִׂים [ע.שׂ.י/ה]	one who does, works *pt ms, mpl*	אֶרֶץ[b], אֲרָצוֹת, אֶרֶץ־, אַרְצוֹת	land, earth *f (sing absol, pl absol, sing constr, pl constr)*
עַתָּה	now	לַעֲבֹר [ע.ב.ר]	to cross over *inf c*, *prep* ל
שֹׁמֵעַ, שֹׁמְעִים [ש.מ.ע]	one who hears, listens *pt ms, mpl*	מִי	Who?
שֹׁמֵר, שֹׁמְרִים [ש.מ.ר]	one who guards, keeps* *pt ms, mpl*	עֹבֵר, עֹבְרִים [ע.ב.ר]	one who crosses over *pt ms, mpl*

[a] When in pause, אֲנַחְנוּ will be spelled אֲנָחְנוּ.

[b] When combined with the article, אֶרֶץ will be vocalized הָאָרֶץ. You also will find it spelled אָרֶץ at the end of a major phrase (pausal form).

מִלִּים לִשְׁמֹעַ — Words for hearing

אֵצֵא [י.צ.א]	I will go out, leave	אֵינְךָ	you are not (*2ms* + אֵין)
גַּדִּיאֵל	Gaddiel (El is my fortune) *name, m*	אֵינֶנּוּ	we are not (אֲנַחְנוּ + אֵין)
הֹלֵךְ, הֹלְכִים [ה.ל.כ]	one who is walking *pt ms, mpl*	אֱלֹהֶיךָ, אֱלֹהֵינוּ	your *ms* God, our God[a]
וַאֲנַחְנוּ	אֲנַחְנוּ *preceded by* וְ		

מָעוֹן	מִן + עָוֹן	זֶה, זֹאת	this* ms, fs
עָוֹן [e]	iniquity m	חֹבֵל	sailor m
עַם, עַמִּים, עַם־, עַמֵּי־ [f]	people m (sing absol, pl absol, sing constr, pl constr)	יָשֵׁן, יְשֵׁנָה, יְשֵׁנִים, יְשֵׁנוֹת	sleeping, asleep adj
		כְּמוֹ	like, similar to
		לָמָּה זֶה לִי...	Of what use to me is...? (lit., Why this to me?)
צֵא, צְאִי [י.צ.א]	Go out! imv ms, fs		
קוֹל, קוֹל־	sound, voice m	לְמַטֵּה זְבוּלֻן	belonging to the tribe of Zebulun
רַב, רַבָּה, רַבִּים, רַבּוֹת	numerous, great, much, many		
רַב, רַבִּים, רַב־, רַבֵּי־	chief, captain m (sing absol, pl absol, sing constr, pl constr)	מְדַבֵּר, מְדַבְּרִים [ד.ב.ר]	one who is speaking piel[b] pt ms, mpl
		מִדְבָּר, מִדְבַּר־	wilderness[c] m
		מְלָאכָה, מְלֶאכֶת־	occupation, business f
רוּחַ, רוּחוֹת, רוּחַ־, רוּחוֹת־	spirit, wind f (sing absol, pl absol, sing constr, pl constr)	מְלַאכְתְּךָ	your ms occupation
		מַה־אַתָּה עֹשֶׂה בָזֶה:	What are you doing ms in this [place]?
שְׁאוֹל	Sheol (netherworld) f	מֵסִיר, מְסִירִים [ס.ו.ר]	one who turns something away from hifil[d] pt ms, mpl

[a] אֱלֹהִים is technically plural. When referring to a non-Israelite deity it may be translated plural (gods, reflecting a polytheistic worldview). When referring to the God of Israel, although the plural spelling is employed, it functions as a singular noun. This singular meaning is substantiated by the fact that when אֱלֹהִים refers to the God of Israel, verbs and adjectives associated with this plural noun are expressed in the singular.

[b] The piel spelling pattern will be explained in Unit 10. For the time being, simply learn the meaning of the word מְדַבֵּר.

^c מִדְבָּר, often rendered *desert*, more accurately designates a steppe region, uninhabited pasturelands, and less frequently represents barren locales dotted with oases.

^d The hifil spelling pattern will be explained in Unit 8.

^e Memorizing the correct pronunciation of the term עָוֹן can help you grow comfortable knowing when the glyph וֹ should be pronounced *vō* (consonant "vav" and vowel "ḥolem") or simply *ô* (vowel "ḥolem-vav"). Notice that the glyph וֹ is immediately preceded by a vowel (qameṣ). Since Hebrew does not allow two vowels in succession, therefore the glyph וֹ may *not* represent the vowel "ḥolem-vav." Consequently, וֹ in עָוֹן represents the consonant "vav" and vowel "ḥolem," *vō*. The word is pronounced *'āvōn*. To recap, whenever you encounter וֹ, check to see what immediately precedes it. If a consonant, then וֹ is *ô*; if a vowel, then it is *vō*.

^f עָם is a monosyllabic noun. Some monosyllabic nouns will double their second consonant when plural (hence the dagesh in עַמִּים). Notice that the pataḥ of עַם strengthens to a qameṣ when it is definite: הָעָם. The customary article הַ ◌ lengthens to become הָ in order to compensate for the fact that the guttural of עַם resists the dagesh of the article.

3.2 Jonah Episode: What are you doing here?

נ׳ = יוֹנָה הַנָּבִיא, ר׳ = רַב־הַחֹבֵל, ע׳ס = עֲבָדִים

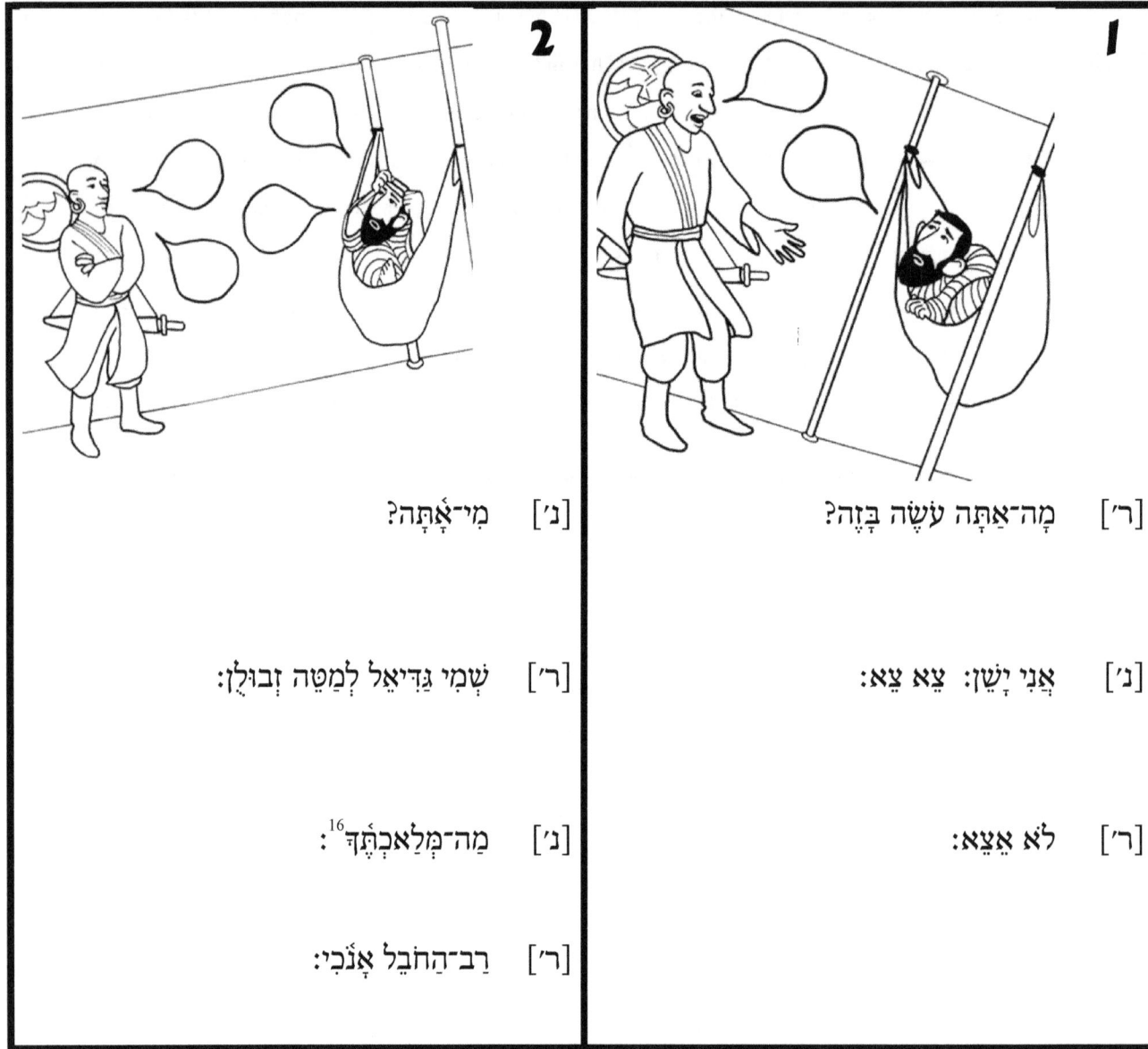

[ר׳] מָה־אַתָּה עֹשֶׂה בָּזֶה?

[נ׳] אֲנִי יָשֵׁן: צֵא צֵא:

[ר׳] לֹא אֵצֵא:

[נ׳] מִי־אָתָּה?

[ר׳] שְׁמִי גַּדִיאֵל לְמַטֵּה זְבוּלֻן:

[נ׳] מַה־מְּלַאכְתֶּךָ:[16]

[ר׳] רַב־הַחֹבֵל אָנֹכִי:

---

[16] מְלַאכְתֶּךָ is a pausal form of מְלַאכְתְּךָ.

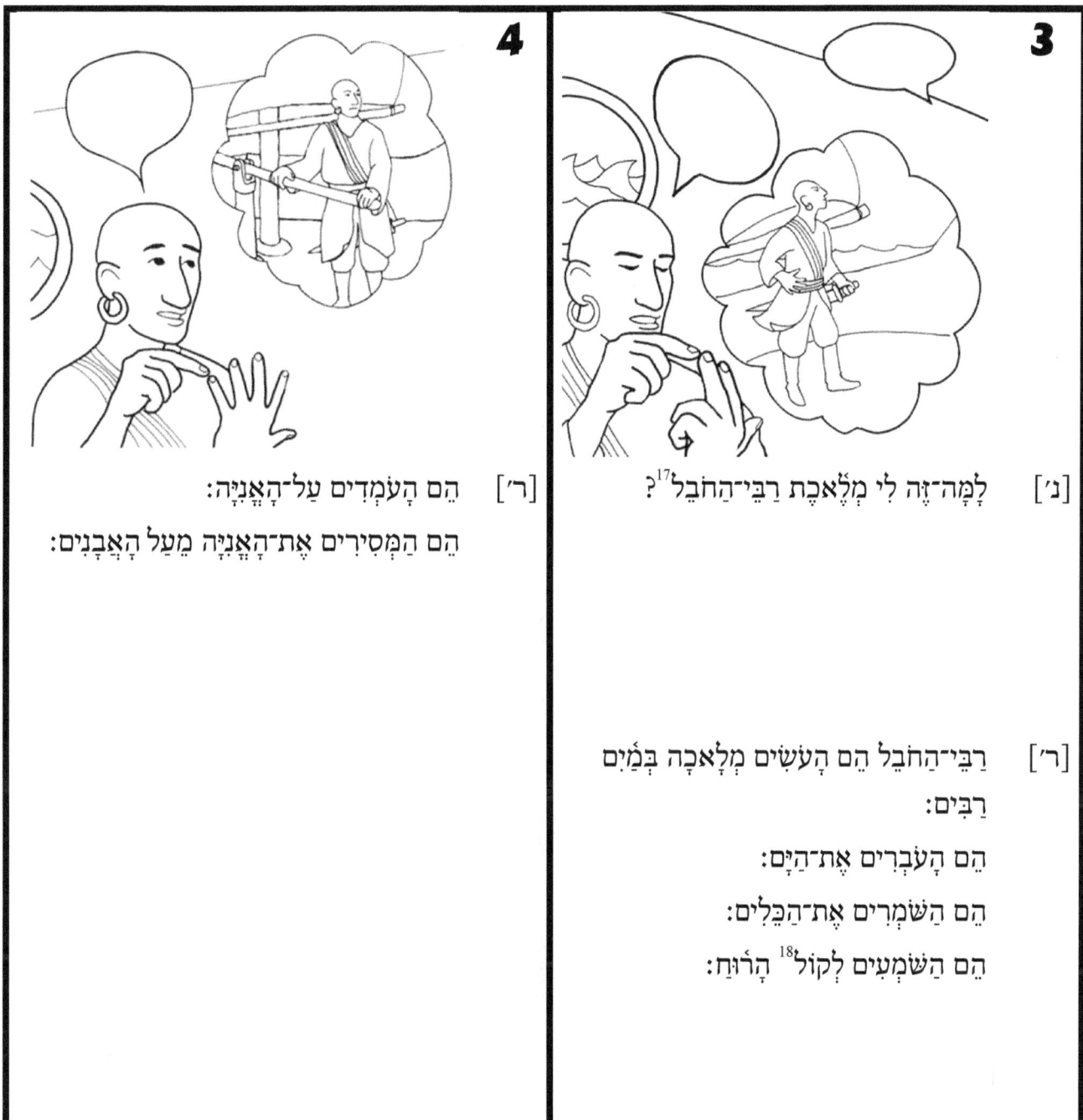

---

[17] רַבֵּי־הַחֹבֵל *sea captains*, lit., *chiefs of the sailor[s]*.

[18] ש.מ.ע לְקוֹל means *to listen to the sound of...* (note preposition לְ).

---

[19] ש.מ.ע בְּקוֹל יהוה means *to obey the LORD* (note the preposition בְּ).

9

[ר׳] וְעַתָּה הַיָּם רַע... רַע מְאֹד:
מַיִם עֹבְרִים עַל־הָאֳנִיָּה:

10

[ע׳ם] הֹלְכִים לַעֲבֹר לִשְׁאוֹל אֲנָחְנוּ:
הַאַתָּה חָפֵץ לַעֲבֹר לִשְׁאוֹל?
אֵינֶנּוּ חֲפֵצִים לַעֲבֹר לִשְׁאוֹל:
וַאֲנַחְנוּ מְדַבְּרִים אֶל־אֱלֹהֵינוּ:

11

[ע׳ם] וְהִנֵּה... לָמָּה זֶּה אֵינְךָ מְדַבֵּר אֶל־אֱלֹהֶיךָ?

3.2.א. Activity: "Are you (*ms*) the one turning this ship away from these rocks?" הַאַתָּה הַמֵּסִיר אֶת־הָאֳנִיָּה הַזֹּאת מֵעַל הָאֲבָנִים הָאֵלֶּה?

INTERACTIVE SKILL: Identifying that particular object, among several, that a person may prefer (expanded from earlier activity)

Make a mental note of one item that you find interesting, drawn from the "Object list" below. Next, select an item from the list that you think your neighbor may be interested in. Using the model dialogue below, find out whether you guessed correctly. Then reverse roles with your neighbor.

Object list

All the objects in this group are **feminine**. Two nouns are new, although you have already met their masculine counterparts (מֶלֶךְ and נָבִיא). Can you recall the meaning of words that are not glossed?

מַלְכָּה, מַלְכוֹת	queen		אֶבֶן, אֲבָנִים
נְבִיאָה, נְבִיאוֹת	prophetess		אֳנִיָּה, אֳנִיּוֹת
עִיר, עָרִים		land	אֶרֶץ, אֲרָצוֹת
רוּחַ, רוּחוֹת	spirit, wind		יָד, יָדַיִם [*dual*] , יָדוֹת [*plural*]

For this activity, you will need the following **feminine** demonstrative pronouns. You will discover that the word אֵלֶּה(הָ) *these* provides the plural for **both** masculine and feminine forms.

If מִצְוֹת means *commandments*, can you surmise what אֵלֶּה הַמִּצְוֹת would mean? (Hint: this is a predicative usage since אֵלֶּה lacks the article found with הַמִּצְוֹת.)[20]

Feminine demonstrative pronouns

(הָ)זֹאת[21], (הָ)אֵלֶּה	this, these *fs, mpl and fpl*
(הָ)הִיא, (הָ)הֵנָּה [*rare*]	that, those *fs, fpl*

Model

Do you (*ms, fs*) prefer this land?	הֶחָפֵץ אַתָּה / הֶחֲפֵצָה אַתְּ אֶת־הָאָרֶץ הַזֹּאת?	Inquiry[22]
I prefer this land.	אֲנִי חָפֵץ / חֲפֵצָה אֶת־הָאָרֶץ הַזֹּאת:	Affirmative reply
I do not prefer this land.	אֵינֶנִּי חָפֵץ / חֲפֵצָה אֶת־הָאָרֶץ הַזֹּאת:	Negative reply

In case the object you offered was **not** preferred, you may inquire further…

What do you (*ms, fs*) prefer?	מָה אַתָּה חָפֵץ / מָה אַתְּ חֲפֵצָה?	Inquiry
I prefer this city.	אֲנִי חָפֵץ / חֲפֵצָה אֶת־הָעִיר הַזֹּאת:	Reply (preferring "city")

Which is more intriguing?

Would you like to practice a bit more with demonstrative pronouns? The following table offers a series of objects, in pairs. For each pair, draw a bold **box** around the one that you find more intriguing. Give the meaning for each Hebrew expression in the space below it. Using your native language, give a one- or two-word reason for your choice in the column to the far left ("Why more intriguing").

---

[20] אֵלֶּה הַמִּצְוֹת would mean *These are the commandments*—a fitting way to close the book of Leviticus (Lev. 27:34).

[21] Include dagesh in (הָ)זֹאת only if definite article is used.

[22] If you wish with greater precision to emphasize *this land* in your question, you may word it as follows: הֲזֹאת הָאָרֶץ אֲשֶׁר אַתָּה חָפֵץ? *Is **this** the land that you prefer?* (cf. Joseph's question in Gen. 43:29).

By the way—some of the expressions below are **incorrect**. Thus, a **plural** demonstrative pronoun may appear where a **singular** is needed, or a **masculine** demonstrative pronoun may appear where there should be a **feminine**. Draw a line through any incorrect forms and write the correct form alongside it. The first has been completed as an example.

Why more intriguing	Change, if needed	Item ב	Change, if needed	Item א
הָאֳנִיּוֹת I chose because I like to sail—perhaps these may be sailboats.	correct as-is Transl. *these ships*	הָאֳנִיּוֹת הָאֵלֶּה	הַזֹּאת Transl. *this rock (corrected for fem. noun)*	הָאֶבֶן הַזֶּה
	Transl.	הָעִיר הַזֹּאת	Transl.	הָאָרֶץ הַזֹּאת .1
	Transl.	הָרוּחַ הַהוּא	Transl.	הָאֳנִיָּה הַהִיא .2
	Transl.	הָאֳנִיּוֹת הָהֵנָּה	Transl.	הַמַּיִם הַזֶּה .3
	Transl.	הַכֶּסֶף הַזֶּה	Transl.	הָאֲבָנִים הָאֵלֶּה .4
	Transl.	הֶעָרִים הָהֵם	Transl.	הַמֶּלֶךְ הַהוּא .5

"These" and "those." It may be helpful to explore briefly how the terms for **nearness** (*this / these*) relate to terms for **remoteness** (*that / those*). Perhaps you noticed in the above exercise that each member of a pair was described at the **same level of nearness**. That is, both options in each pair were described either with the terms *this / these* or else with the terms *that / those*. Unlike languages such as English, Hebrew does not contrast two different objects that are under immediate consideration by describing one as *this* and the other as *that*. Instead, both will be labeled *this* (*one*).

Here is an example of showing the use of "זֹאת... זֹאת...," where English would contrast by using "this… that…." When Laban explains his plan for marrying off both of his sisters to the same man

(Jacob), Laban indicates that one week after Jacob has married "this one" (זֹאת, referring to Leah, whom Jacob unwittingly had just married), he may proceed to marry "this one" (again using זֹאת, but now referring to Rachel, the woman Jacob had intended to marry in the first place, Gen. 29:27).

3.2.ב. Explanation and activity: "And Jonah... what is he doing?"
וְיוֹנָה... מַה־הוּא עֹשֶׂה?

INTERACTIVE SKILL: Live reporting of events as they unfold

Have you ever been in a situation where others relied on you to relay events to them as you watched them unfolding? Perhaps you served as a lookout at a surprise birthday party. Fellow-guests who were in hiding relied on you to report back to them what was going on outside and—especially—the point when the guest-of-honor was actually arriving. Your report may have sounded like this: "She is getting off the bus. She is walking toward the house. Get ready, because now she is walking through the front door!"

In this activity you will serve as a reporter, giving others a live account of events as you observe them transpiring in the experience of Jonah. Think back to Jonah's first encounter with God. Imagine that those events are taking place right now. Report them as they unfold, one action at a time.

Perhaps your report would begin: "Jonah is walking… God is speaking to him…." Don't worry if it sounds segmented or choppy. The style appropriate for this activity actually needs to sound segmented.

How will we assemble our report in Hebrew? Notice the following simple sentences to gather some ideas. Each sentence is built around a participle.[23]

Jonah is walking.	יוֹנָה הֹלֵךְ:
Sarah is walking.	שָׂרָה הֹלֶכֶת:
The king is speaking.	הַמֶּלֶךְ מְדַבֵּר:
The queen is speaking.	הַמַּלְכָּה מְדַבֶּרֶת:

You may have noticed a shift in the second and fourth participles above, due to the gender of the noun that they modify. In the case of Jonah, *walking* was spelled הֹלֵךְ. But in the case of Sarah, it was spelled הֹלֶכֶת.[24] Like adjectives, participles need to **match the noun** they modify in number and gender.[25]

The collection of verbs appearing below provides masculine singular and feminine singular forms to help with your report of Jonah's activities (plural forms will appear in §3.2.ד.). Most verbs have been translated. See if you can fill in the blanks for missing meanings.

---

[23] Later on you will find that participles are very versatile—at times operating in the future as well as in the past. Yet there are numerous instances in the Hebrew Bible when speakers used participles to report on present actions (e.g., Gen. 6:17, 37:13, Exod. 18:6, Num. 14:3, Judg. 14:3, 1 Sam. 14:11, Jer. 37:14, Job 12:3, and Neh. 13:18). Later on you will discover that Hebrew has other ways to express the present tense, in addition to participles.

[24] Less frequently we find *fs* participles ending in הָ◌..., not ת◌◌.... Both forms may be attested for a single verb root. Thus הֹלְכָה appears in Jer. 3:6, while the more common form הֹלֶכֶת appears in Gen. 32:21, with no difference in formal description (parsing) and evidently no difference in meaning.

[25] In fact, grammarians refer to participles as adjectival forms of the verb.

Verbs for your report (*one who is...*)

שֹׁמֵעַ, שֹׁמַעַת	listening, hearing	מֹלֵךְ, מֹלֶכֶת	ruling	אֹכֵל, אֹכֶלֶת	
שֹׁמֵר, שֹׁמֶרֶת	guarding	מֵסִיר, מְסִירָה	removing, diverting something	הֹלֵךְ, הֹלֶכֶת	walking
שֹׁתֶה, שֹׁתָה	drinking	עֹבֵר, עֹבֶרֶת	crossing over	יֹרֵד, יֹרֶדֶת	descending
		עֹמֵד, עֹמֶדֶת	standing	מְבַקֵּשׁ, מְבַקֶּשֶׁת	
		שֹׁאֵל, שֹׁאֶלֶת	asking	מְדַבֵּר, מְדַבֶּרֶת	speaking

Now it's your turn. Draw from the above participles to reconstruct a so-called "live report" of what Jonah is experiencing up to this point in time. Work with a friend to see how many pieces of the story you can recall.

Your retelling may diverge a bit from the standard account. For example—in your version Jonah may be out for a walk when he hears God's voice (see the first sentence, below). Aim for six to eight brief sentences, including the two that are provided below.

Jonah is walking.	יוֹנָה הֹלֵךְ:	א.
God is speaking to Jonah.	אֱלֹהִים מְדַבֵּר אֶל־יוֹנָה:	ב.
		ג.
		ד.
		ה.
		ו.
		ז.

	ח.

Your instructor will explain how to present your finished report.

Other uses for participles. In addition to supplying the verbal component for a sentence (called a predicative use of the participle), a participle may serve (a) as an attribute or (b) as a substantive. When a participle operates in an **attributive** manner, it will describe a noun without forming a sentence (cf. §2.3.ב.).[26] Notice in the example below how the participle שֹׁתֶה *one who is drinking* describes נָבִיא without forming a sentence (חָפֵץ is the verbal element creating the sentence). Like an attributive adjective, an attributive participle will agree with the noun it modifies, not only in number and gender, but in definiteness as well. Since הַנָּבִיא is singular, masculine, and definite in this example, so also is הַשֹּׁתֶה.

The prophet **who is drinking** water [*not some other prophet*] desires to eat bread.	הַנָּבִיא הַשֹּׁתֶה מַיִם חָפֵץ לֶאֱכֹל לָחֶם׃

When a participle does not accompany a noun, it may itself operate as a noun (as a **substantive**). In particular, it will represent an object or person who is characterized by that activity indicated by the participle. Thus, taken alone, שֹׁמֵר can stand as if it were a noun—a thing or person characterized by the action of guarding: *a guard, a keeper*.[27]

one who is guarding (*or* a guard *m, f*)	שֹׁמֵר, שֹׁמֶרֶת
one who is walking (*or* a walker *m, f*)	הֹלֵךְ, הֹלֶכֶת

Cain used שֹׁמֵר in this fashion, in his well-known question, הֲשֹׁמֵר אָחִי אָנֹכִי׃ *Am I my brother's* **keeper**? (The word אָחִי means *my brother*, Gen. 4:9.)

A suggestion for rendering participles. When reading a given passage, if you are unsure whether to treat a participle as standing alone (whether attributive or substantive) or as forming a sentence (predicative), you may find it helpful to begin by rendering the participle as "a thing / person characterized by [fill in the basic verb meaning]." Then proceed to refine your translation as the context may dictate.

---

[26] In the expression, אֵשׁ אֹכְלָה הוּא *he is a consuming fire*, the word *consuming* is a participle attributively modifying the noun *fire* (Deut. 4:24, cf. *IBHS* §37.4).

[27] שֹׁפֵט *a judge* is another example of a substantival participle. Adjectives also may operate as substantives. Thus זָקֵן *old* can also mean *an elderly person*.

A spelling note on participles. After working with participles in the above table, you may have noticed that many participles follow a vocalization pattern of *ḥolem-ṣērê* (◌ֵ◌ֹ) in the masculine. Can you think of a grand vizier in ancient Egypt whose name followed the ◌ֵ...[וֹ]◌ pattern?[28] Feminine patterns often employ a *ḥolem-segol-segol-tav* (◌ֹ◌ֶ◌ֶת) spelling pattern. Learning these two sound patterns will help you recognize many participles when reading the Hebrew Bible.

At times, you will find that the ḥolem vowel in a participle such as מֹלֵךְ will be spelled more fully as מוֹלֵךְ (with a וֹ). Since this more complete spelling (known as the *plene* spelling) does not affect pronunciation or meaning, you should have little difficulty recognizing that both the "*plene*" spelling (מוֹלֵךְ) and the "defective" spelling (מֹלֵךְ) mean *one who rules, ms*. Similarly, both עוֹשֶׂה and עֹשֶׂה mean *one who makes, ms*.[29]

3.2.ג. Do you (*ms*) know the meaning of a word? (Theophoric names)

הֲיָדַעְתָּ פֵּשֶׁר דָּבָר?

As you may have noticed in §1.1.ח., Hebrew names at times would combine a reference to God together with a particular trait. Consider the name גַּדִּיאֵל, for example. If גַּדִּי means "my fortune" and אֵל means "God," can you deduce the meaning of this name?

Such compound names are called "theophoric" (bearing a reference to a deity). Theophoric names were fairly common in Israel, including such men's names as יְהוֹנָתָן (Jonathan: *The LORD gives*) and גְּדַלְיָה (Gedaliah, *Great is the LORD*), as well as women's names such as יוֹכֶבֶד (Jochebed, *The LORD is glorious* or *powerful*) and מִיכַל (Michal, short for מִיכָאֵל, *Who is like God?*).

What about your culture? Does your culture employ theophoric names?

---

[28] The name יוֹסֵף evidently was formed from a participle. It means *one who adds* or *increases*.

[29] In case you are wondering why עֹשֶׂה *one who makes ms* is not spelled עֹשָׂה, the segol resulted from influence of the final ה/י. The participle שֹׁתֶה *one who drinks ms* displays a segol in the last syllable for the same reason.

3.2.ד. Activity: "And what are we (the servants) doing?"

וּמָה אֲנַ֫חְנוּ (הָעֲבָדִים) עֹשִׂים?

INTERACTIVE SKILL: Live reporting of events as they unfold

Imagine that you are a reporter embedded with the sailors. Can you retell the events from **their** vantage point? Speak as if you are one of them, telling their group's story: "We…." As before, aim for six to eight brief sentences including those already provided below.

Unlike Jonah's retelling of the story from his singular perspective (an individual account), in this report you will speak for an entire group of sailors (**plural**). It is up to you to choose whether you will envision the crew as group of men (use masculine forms), a group of women (use feminine forms), or a blend (use masculine forms). You may start with these sentences.

We are servants on a boat.	אֲנַ֫חְנוּ עֲבָדִים עַל־אֳנִיָּה:	.א
We are travelling to Joppa.	אֲנַ֫חְנוּ הֹלְכִים אֶל־יָפוֹ:	.ב
We…	אֲנַ֫חְנוּ…	.ג
		.ד
		.ה
		.ו
		.ז
		.ח

Here are some verbs to draw from. Since there are several sailors onboard, we will need to use plural participles. Feminine plural forms are shown as well.

Verbs for your report (*ones who are...*)

שֹׁאֲלִים, שֹׁאֲלוֹת	מֹלְכִים, מֹלְכוֹת	אֹכְלִים, אֹכְלוֹת
שֹׁמְעִים, שֹׁמְעוֹת	מְסִירִים, מְסִירוֹת	הֹלְכִים, הֹלְכוֹת
שֹׁמְרִים, שֹׁמְרוֹת	עֹבְרִים, עֹבְרוֹת	מְבַקְשִׁים, מְבַקְשׁוֹת
שֹׁתִים, שֹׁתוֹת	עֹמְדִים, עֹמְדוֹת	מְדַבְּרִים, מְדַבְּרוֹת

3.2.ה. Did you (*ms*) know that...? (Burial customs and afterlife)

הֲיָדַעְתָּ כִּי...?

...tombs in the Ancient Near East may consist of a pit or a cave, and may be used for either single or multiple burials? In some tombs the deceased would be laid on a stone bench. After some time had passed, the bones (עֶצֶם, עֲצָמוֹת *f*) would be deposited in a stone ossuary, thus making room on the bench for the next deceased family member.

Since graves (קֶבֶר, קְבָרִים *m*) generally were established outside a city, the discovery of graves for the period 1000–800 BCE has helped to define the perimeter of cities such as Jerusalem, during that era. Pottery, jewelry, and weapons deposited in tombs as part of the burial ceremony have helped archaeologists reconstruct some of the culture of the ancient Near East.[30]

---

[30] *LBI*, 370 and 374–75.

Within the cosmology of ancient Israel, שְׁאוֹל (the realm of the afterlife) was portrayed as located beneath an expansive subterranean ocean. It is described as a realm of darkness (חֹשֶׁךְ *m*, Job 17:13), reached by descending into the depths (תְּהוֹם, תְּהֹמוֹת *m*)—the eventual destination of all alike.

Limestone ossuary (1st cent. CE; 53 cm long, 42 cm high, 26 cm wide). (Courtesy of Flora Archaeological Center)

On the one hand, persons who reside in שְׁאוֹל were perceived as being remote from God. As King and Stager observe, "In Israelite belief the essence of life is the ability to praise God; for the dead in Sheol that was impossible because they had no contact with the divine presence."[31] Nevertheless, Israelites understood God as maintaining sovereignty over this region (Ps. 139:8, Job 26:6, Prov. 15:11). At least one poet was confident that the righteous would not be abandoned there (Ps. 16:10), since God would redeem from שְׁאוֹל the life of one who was devoted to him (Ps. 49:15 [ET v. 14]).[32]

---

[31] *LBI*, 375.

[32] For more information, see L. Wächter, "שְׁאוֹל," *Theological Dictionary of the Old Testament* (English translation; Grand Rapids: Eerdmans, 2004), 14: 239–48.

MODULE 3.3   Describing what people are doing

Words for responding   מִלִּים לַעֲנוֹת

Note: Entries for nouns will often be expanded to present the following four forms (in this order): singular absolute, plural absolute, singular construct, and plural construct (see דָּג and רֹאשׁ below). The spelling of plural constructs will be explained in this module.

מַשְׁלִיךְ, מַשְׁלֶכֶת, מַשְׁלִיכִים, מַשְׁלִיכוֹת [ש.ל.כ]	one who throws *hifil pt ms, fs, mpl, fpl*	אֹהֵב, אֹהֶבֶת, אֹהֲבִים, אֹהֲבוֹת [א.ה.ב]	one who loves *pt ms, fs, mpl, fpl*
		אַתֶּם	you *mpl*
נֶפֶשׁ, נְפָשׁוֹת, נֶפֶשׁ־, נַפְשׁוֹת־	soul, person, life force, throat *f*	אַתֵּנָה, also אַתֵּן	you *fpl*
		דָּג, דָּגִים, דַּג־, דְּגֵי־	fish *m*
רֹאשׁ, רָאשִׁים, רֹאשׁ־, רָאשֵׁי־	head *f*	לְהַשְׁלִיךְ [ש.ל.כ]	to throw *hifil*[a] *inf c*, *prep* לְ
		לָשׁוּב אֶל־ [ש.ו.ב]	to turn self toward, to return to *inf c*, *prep* לְ[b]

[a] The hifil spelling pattern will be explained in Unit 8.

[b] While ש.ו.ב אֶל־ means *to turn self toward*, ש.ו.ב מִן־ or ש.ו.ב מֵעַל would mean *to turn self away from*. Concerning the compound preposition מֵעַל־, the terminal consonant ן of מִן־ is vulnerable to loss before gutturals and ר, leaving behind only a strengthening or lengthening of the ḥireq vowel from מִן to מֵ[וֹ].

Words for hearing   מִלִּים לִשְׁמֹעַ

...הֹלֵךְ וְסֹעֵר [ה.ל.כ, ס.ע.ר]	...is growing stormier *pt ms, pt ms*[a]	אֹיְבִי, אֹיְבַי	my enemy *ms, mpl*
		אֹתִי	me (אֲנִי + אֶת־)

מַה־אַתָּה עֹשֶׂה?

Throw! *hifil imv mpl*	הַשְׁלִיכוּ [ש.ל.כ]	we understand *hifil*	נָבִין [ב.י.נ]
dry land *f*	יַבָּשָׁה	my soul, myself, me	נַפְשִׁי
fool *m*	כְּסִיל, כְּסִילִים	on what account?	עַל־מֶהb
to come, enter, go *inf c, prep* לְ	לָבוֹא [ב.ו.א]		

a When ה.ל.כ is followed by a parallel verb (both participles, or both infinitives absolute, for example) it produces an idiom expressing gradual development of whatever the second verb involves (thus "*growing* stormier," in the expression הֹלֵךְ וְסֹעֵר). Despite the use of the verb ה.ל.כ in Hebrew, the notion of "going" should not be found in translation.

b עַל־מֶה is a pausal spelling of עַל־מָה.

3.3 Jonah Episode: What are you doing?

נ׳ = יוֹנָה הַנָּבִיא, ע׳ם = עֲבָדִים

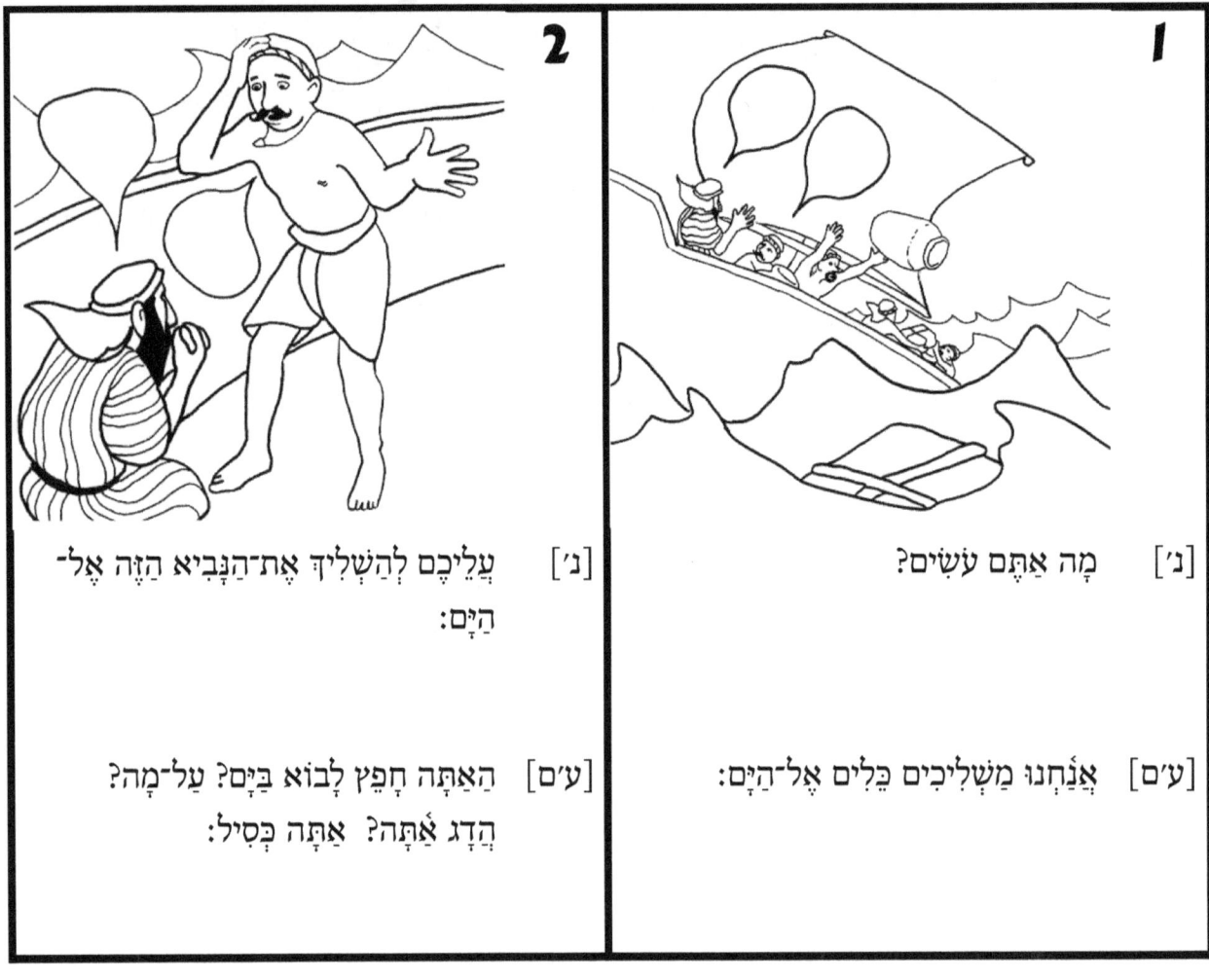

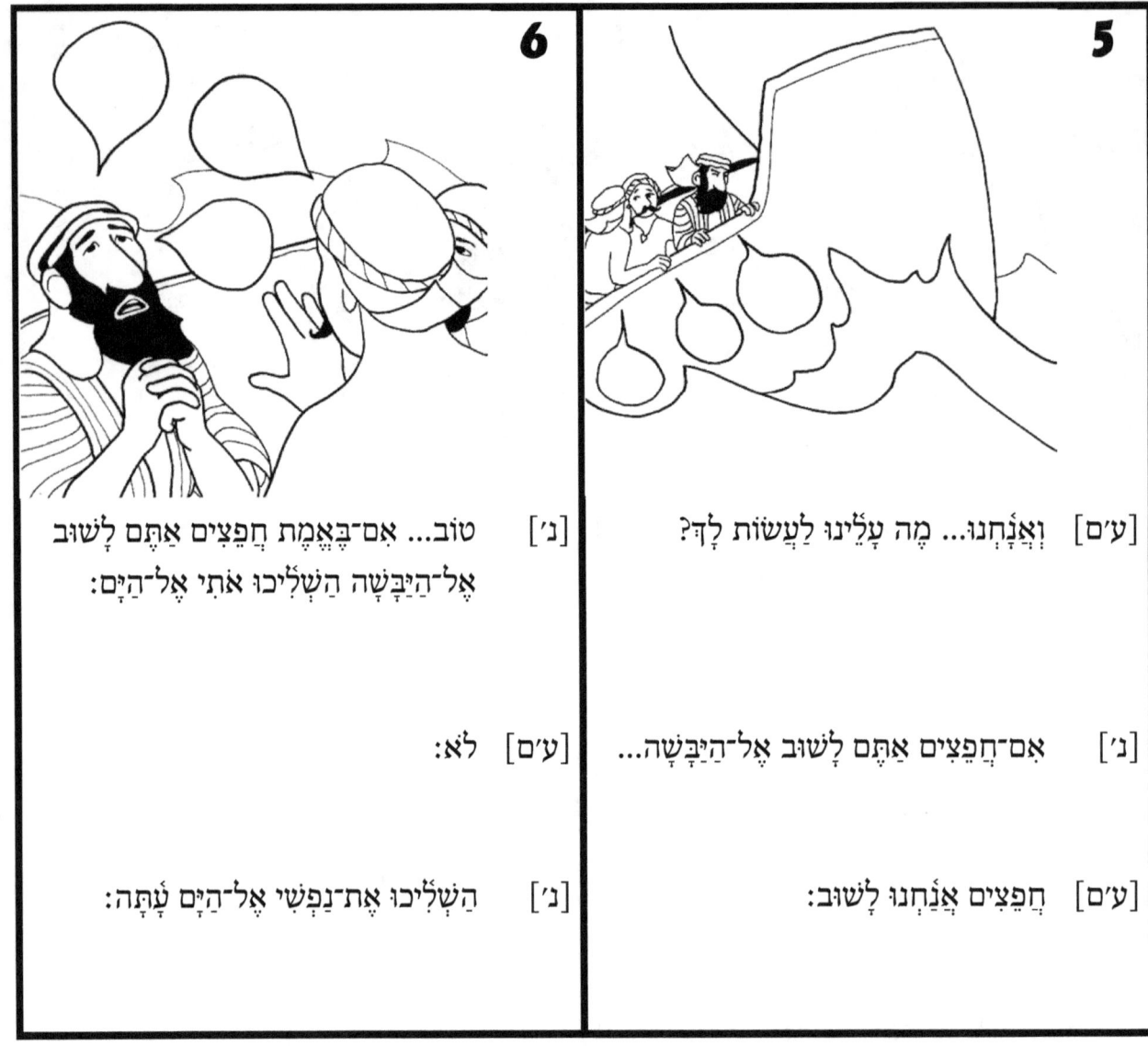

3.3.א. May I offer you (*ms*) advice? (We don't understand)

הַאִיעָצְךָ עֵצָה?

> Do you recall how to indicate when you do not grasp something (לֹא אָבִין, §1.3)? The sailors' expression of collective puzzlement may be useful in case **several** of you need an explanation in class: לֹא נָבִין *We don't understand*.
>
> Alternatively, you may wish to emphasize that your group *does* understand. In that case, say: נָבִין *We understand*.

3.3.ב. Activity: "What in the world are they (*m*) doing?"

מַה־זֶּה הֵם עֹשִׂים?

INTERACTIVE SKILL: Describing what you see people doing

Cluster in groups of three. Choose a verb you would like to act out as a group. If possible, include a physical object as well (see model). Use your imagination to make the scene interesting. After you (as a group) have silently acted out your sentence, the rest of the class will guess what you are doing (in Hebrew, of course!).

Avoid duplicating what a trio before you has already presented. Suggestion: if you volunteer early to present your "act," it will reduce the chances that another will have already used your expression.

Here is a sample small-group action, including a prompt question and response-guess from the audience:

Model

Scene: Have all members of your group climb up on a sturdy table and stand there.

What in the world are they (*m*) doing?	<div dir="rtl">מַה־זֶּה הֵם עֹשִׂים?</div>	Inquiry
They (*m*) are standing on a table.	<div dir="rtl">הֵם עֹמְדִים עַל־שֻׁלְחָן׃</div>	Reply, affirmative
They (*m*) are not standing on a table.	<div dir="rtl">הֵם לֹא עֹמְדִים עַל־שֻׁלְחָן׃</div>	Reply, negative

The negative reply is provided in case you wish to wish to move through a process of elimination, as if to say: "Since they are not doing A and they are not doing B, therefore they must be doing C." Notice that in order to rule out other actions (here expressed as participles like עֹמְדִים), simply express the negation לֹא directly before that activity (לֹא עֹמְדִים). Incidentally, can you see this negation pattern in Jonah's admission: "אַחֲרֵי יהוה אֱלֹהֵי יִשְׂרָאֵל לֹא הֹלֵךְ אָנֹכִי" (3.3. Jonah Episode, cell 3, line 1)? By using לֹא to negate the participle הֹלֵךְ, Jonah drew focus on the **activity** he did **not** engage in ("not **following** the LORD"), rather than using אֵין to draw focus on the **subject** (אֵינֶנִּי הֹלֵךְ, "I am not the one following").[33]

---

[33] Use of אֵין to underscore the divergence between two subjects (Jonah versus the sailors) also occurs in the sailors' words, אֵינֶנּוּ חֲפֵצִים לַעֲבֹר לִשְׁאוֹל. (3.2 Jonah Episode, cell 10, line 3; compare line 2).

מָה־אַתָּה עֹשֶׂה?

Here are several words that lend themselves to being acted-out. Most words below are already in **plural** form. Words in parentheses, however, are in the singular. You will need to **adjust** singular forms to generate the proper plural form to express your guess. A few translations are provided for words you may not recognize.

One who is... / ones who are...

שֹׁכְבִים	מַשְׁלִיכִים	(מְדַבֵּר)	הֹלְכִים
שֹׁמְרִים	נֹתְנִים giving	(מֶלֶךְ)	(יָרַד)
שֹׁתִים	עֹבְרִים	מֹצְאִים	יֹשְׁבִים sitting
שָׂמִים placing	עֹמְדִים	(מֵסִיר)	מְבַקְשִׁים

3.3.ג. Activity: "What are we doing?"   מָה אֲנַחְנוּ עֹשִׂים?

INTERACTIVE SKILL: Telling a group what you think they are doing

Cluster again in groups of three. Choose a verb-and-object that you as a group would like to act out. Refer to the model below. Your tableau for this segment should be different from what you portrayed in the last segment. In addition, it should be different from the tableau presented by any group prior to your group's dramatization.

Here are two adjustments that will distinguish this activity from the last one (§3.3.ב.).

- Instead of having the instructor pose the prompt question, choose one from within your trio to read this question after your brief dramatization is complete. Notice the shift from "What are **they** doing?" in the last activity, to "What are **we** doing?" in this activity.
- The audience will respond, "**You** are..." (rather than, "**They** are...").

Model

Scene: Have all members of your group sit in chairs with cups of water on your heads.

What are we doing?	מָה אֲנַחְנוּ עֹשִׂים?	Inquiry
You (*mpl*) are sitting beneath cups of water.	אַתֶּם יֹשְׁבִים תַּחַת כֹּסוֹת מָיִם:	Reply

Incidentally, were you able to deduce that כֹּסוֹת מָיִם is a construct phrase (*cups of water*), even without a maqqef? In the Hebrew Bible, not all construct phrases are marked by the maqqef.

3.3.ד. Alternative activity: "What are you (*mpl*) doing?" מָה אַתֶּם עֹשִׂים?

INTERACTIVE SKILL: Describing a club or other group activity you are involved in at this moment

What activities are you currently involved in? Reflect on some aspect of your identity, whether as a family member, student, employee, sports enthusiast, connoisseur of music, artist, listener, builder, etc. Now imagine yourself seated with a cluster of those persons sharing the same trait (so that with them you comprise a **group** of students or a **group** of musicians). Imagine that someone who needs to talk with you has interrupted your meeting, called you aside, and asked: מָה אַתֶּם עֹשִׂים? *What are you* [*mpl*] *doing?* How would you reply?

Try to engage some of the larger aims, goals, or ambitions latent within the group that you identify with. Since your answer will be limited to simple Hebrew, it will admittedly only "scratch the surface," likely requiring further explanation in your native language. As an example, the model below imagines that you are gathered with a group that enjoys discussing philosophy.

Model

Sample identity: you are a member of a Philosophy Club. (In order to foster curiosity, do not disclose this "identity affiliation" until *after* someone has asked what you are doing, evoking your reply.)

Inquiry	מָה אַתֶּם עֹשִׂים?	What are you (mpl) doing?
Reply	אֲנַחְנוּ מְדַבְּרִים.	We are talking.
Follow-up inquiry	לָמָּה?	Why?
Follow-up reply		(*In your native language, explain why "talking" characterizes your philosophy club.*)

3.3.ה. Explanation: "Of what value to me is the occupation of sea captains?" לָמָּה־זֶּה לִי מְלֶאכֶת רַבֵּי־הַחֹבֵל?

INTERACTIVE SKILL: Expressing possession, when the items that are owned number more than one

Notice the expression רַבֵּי־הַחֹבֵל *sea captains* (lit., *captains of the sailor*[s]) in the above heading. In an earlier module we learned that adjacent nouns can express possession without any intervening preposition. Thus שֵׁם־הָאֳנִיָּה means *the name of the ship*. Similarly, מֶלֶךְ־הַמַּיִם means *the king of the sea.*

As regards the leading word in these expressions (called a "construct" or "bound" form), to this point we have limited ourselves to singular words: *the name* (not *names*) *of the ship*. Now we will include **plural forms** (as in ...רַבֵּי־ *captains of...*).

Plurals ending in ים...

When the word expressing possession is plural and would normally end in ים..., the ים... ending will be replaced by י... in the construct form. Thus:

רַבִּים *captains* becomes רַבֵּי־ *captains of*, and

נְבִיאִים *prophets* becomes נְבִיאֵי־ *prophets of*.

Here are three more examples. Note that feminine plural nouns ending in ים... follow the same pattern (e.g., עִיר *city f*).

Possessive form (construct state)		Regular form (absolute state)	
אֱלֹהֵי־	God (or gods) of	אֱלֹהִים	God (or gods)
עַמֵּי־	peoples of	עַמִּים	peoples
עָרֵי־	cities of	עָרִים	cities

Can you detect a plural construct found in the opening line of the Book of Exodus: וְאֵלֶּה שְׁמוֹת בְּנֵי יִשְׂרָאֵל? If you guessed בְּנֵי, you are correct. בְּנֵי is the construct of plural noun בָּנִים (from the singular בֵּן son). The phrase means: *These are the names of the sons* (or *people*) *of Israel*. Since יִשְׂרָאֵל is a proper noun, it is definite (even without the definite article). Thus the Book of Exodus came to be known as וְאֵלֶּה שְׁמוֹת, or simply שְׁמוֹת. As it happens, שְׁמוֹת also is a plural construct, as explained in the next paragraph.

Plurals ending in וֹת...

When the entity "belonging to" another (i.e., the entity in construct) is a plural ending in וֹת..., the word often remains unchanged.

Possessive form (construct state)		Regular form (absolute state)	
כִּסְאוֹת־	chairs of	כִּסְאוֹת	chairs
נְבִיאוֹת־	prophetesses of	נְבִיאוֹת	prophetesses

To summarize, then, these are the basic **construct plural** patterns: words ending ִים... become ֵי..., while words ending וֹת... show no change in ending. Having said that, it is not uncommon for some vowels to change in construct forms. For a summary of these construct plural vowel changes, please refer to the corresponding segment in the appendix. Note especially the explanation regarding an initial ḥireq in words such as בִּרְכוֹת־ *blessings of* and similarly in דִּבְרֵי־ *words of*.

3.3.1. Activity: "To whom do those (*m*) belong?" לְמִי־הֵם?

INTERACTIVE SKILL: Expressing possession, when the items that are owned number more than one

Did you ever happen upon something and wonder to whom it belonged? Perhaps you found some chocolates, a few coins, or a stack of dirty dishes! Whose are they?

For this activity, draw lines showing which object (from the column labeled רֹאשׁ *head m* on the right) might belong to (or be at home in the environment of) some other entity. For an "owner" entity, choose from the center column, designated זָנָב *tail m*. The term you select from the רֹאשׁ column will be at the "head" of your construct chain, while the term you select from the זָנָב column will be at the "tail" of your construct chain. In the column on the left, please write the Hebrew phrase you have constructed as a result of combining those two selections, together with a translation of that phrase.

One pair has been completed for you: the plural object דְּגֵי־ reasonably belongs in the environment of הַיָּם. By joining the two words as a construct chain, we compose the phrase, *fishes of the sea*. As you combine various objects in the רֹאשׁ column with owners / environments in the זָנָב column, keep in mind that all the רֹאשׁ objects in this activity are plural.

Since there are fewer objects in the זָנָב column, you may stop as soon as all זָנָב items have been used. After you have finished, (1) select one of the phrases that reminds you of something you have personally experienced, and (2) compare your selection with that of one or two classmates. How do theirs differ?

Combined phrase, with translation	(#)	*Tail* זָנָב	Head רֹאשׁ	
	.1	אֱמֶת (truth)	אַבְנֵי־	א.
			אֱלֹהֵי־	ב.
	.2	אֹהֲבֵי־כֶּסֶף	דְּגֵי־	ג.
			כְּלֵי־	ד.
	.3	בַּעַל) Baal (*or* master	מְדַבְּרֵי־	ה.
			מַלְכֵי־	ו.
	.4	יְהוּדָה	נְבִיאֵי־	ז.
			סִפְרֵי־	ח.

the fish(es) of the sea דְּגֵי־הַיָּם (ג.)	הַיָּם	.5	ט. עַמֵּי־
			י. צָרֵי־
	יִשְׂרָאֵל	.6	יא. רָאשֵׁי־
			יב. שֹׁמְרֵי־
	מְלָכִים	.7	יג. כִּסְאוֹת־
			יד. נְבִיאוֹת־
	סֵפֶר	.8	טו. נַפְשׁוֹת־
			טז. שֻׁלְחֲנוֹת־
	עִיר	.9	יז. שְׁמוֹת־
	שְׁתַּיִם	.10	
	שָׁלוֹם	.11	

Now take any three or four of the phrases that you fashioned above, and string them together to make a very short story. You may supply additional words such as verbs and nouns in your native language in order to hook the phrases together meaningfully. Remember to include a translation of the Hebrew you compose. Here is an example:

> (1) A group of three rulers sat in כִּסְאוֹת־הַמְּלָכִים (the seats of the kings [thrones])...
>
> (2) ...and summoned all נְבִיאֵי־הַבַּעַל (the prophets of [the] Baal).
>
> (3) "You are not מְדַבְּרֵי־שָׁלוֹם (speakers of peace)," they declared.

Write your composition in the spaces below.

3.3.ז. Did you (ms) know that...? (Sea travel)   הֲיָדַעְתָּ כִּי...?

> ...in view of the two-season climate of the Levant, a skilled sailor (חֹבֵל m) would avoid traveling during the stormy conditions prevalent from mid-November to mid-March?
>
> Both written and material evidence attests considerable maritime activity in the ancient world, whether for military or commercial objectives. In Phoenicia (Tyre and Sidon), abundant timber fostered shipbuilding as well as export trade in lumber (עֵץ m).[34]
>
> At least three ship designs were employed in the Levant: (a) the "long" model (warship) with pointed ram at water level, (b) the "round" model (merchant vessel with asymmetrical bow and stern), and (c) the "hippos" (a merchant ship with raised horse-head bow as depicted in the ʾOniyahu seal, §2.1.ח.). The vessels featured twin side-rudders, a configuration still used today by Indonesian shipbuilders. They were propelled by rowing (a double-bank of staggered שָׁטִים oars m), by wind (a tall תֹּרֶן mast m with מִפְרָשׂ a square-sail m), or both by שָׁטִים and by מִפְרָשׂ, depending on the model.[35]
>
> A deep-sea excavation in 1999 revealed two eighth-century BCE Phoenician אֳנִיּוֹת, lying at a depth of 400 meters, some 50 kilometers off the Ashkelon coast. This

---

[34] Ze'ev Yeivin, "Ships and Sailing," *Encyclopaedia Judaica*, vol. 14 (Jerusalem: Keter Publishing House, 1982), 1411a; cf. §6.2.א. regarding an Egyptian lumber voyage in the 11th century BCE.

[35] *LBI*, 86 and 178–82.

discovery has overturned the earlier assumption that navigation in antiquity was limited to cautiously hugging שְׂפַת־הַיָּם *the seashore* (*f*).[36]

---

[36] R.D. Ballard and L.E. Stager, "Iron Age Shipwrecks in Deep Water off Ashkelon, Israel," available at http://web.mit.edu/deeparch/www/publications/papers/BallardEtAl2002.pdf.

UNIT 3　　　　　　　　　　מָה־אַתָּה עָשָׂה?　　　　　　　　　　231

MODULE 3.4　　　　　　　　　　Designating a recipient

Although there is no Jonah Episode for §3.4, several groups of words in this module merit learning thoroughly. They will appear under the heading "Words for responding" in §§3.4.א. and 3.4.ב.

3.4.א. Activity: "King / queen for a day"　　הַמֶּלֶךְ / הַמַּלְכָּה בְּיוֹם אֶחָד
Or: "To whom am I doing this?"　　לְמִי אֲנִי עֹשֶׂה / עָשָׂה אֶת־הַדָּבָר הַזֶּה?

INTERACTIVE SKILL: Designating persons to receive special action

Here is a chance to unleash the repressed ruler within! Your instructor will offer to perform one of the random actions below to someone in the class.

If you are selected as "king for a day," you will be entitled to choose **the person(s) to whom** a random action will be performed. Announce whom you have chosen with dignity and authority (using one of the ל + pronominal suffix forms listed in the table below). In case you want the random action to be performed on **yourself**, simply declare, "לִי!"

After you have issued one edict, your brief rule will come to an end. The crown will then pass to the person you selected as recipient of the random action.

While you are getting accustomed to the spelling of ל... with various pronominal suffixes, take a moment to compare each of the sample words to which suffixes have been added, found in the table below (אֶל, ל..., עַל, and אֵין). They are aligned to the left so that suffixes may be observed more easily. Notice how many suffixes are formed alike (e.g., all first-singular suffixes end in י...).

Words for responding

מִלִּים לַעֲנוֹת

Suffixed pronoun reference table

fs	ms	he, him / she, her	fs	ms	you	c	I, me	
אֵלֶיהָ	אֵלָיו	to him / her	אֵלַיִךְ	אֵלֶיךָ	to you	אֵלַי	to me	אֶל
לָהּ[37]	לוֹ	to him / her	לָךְ	לְךָ	to you	לִי	to me	ל...
עָלֶיהָ	עָלָיו[38]	on him / her	עָלַיִךְ	עָלֶיךָ	on you	עָלַי	on me	עַל
אֵינֶנָּה	אֵינֶנּוּ	he / she is not	אֵינֵךְ	אֵינְךָ	you are not	אֵינֶנִּי	I am not	אֵין
fpl	**mpl**	**them**	**fpl**	**mpl**	**you**	**c**	**we, us**	
אֲלֵיהֶן	אֲלֵיהֶם	to them	אֲלֵיכֶן	אֲלֵיכֶם	to you	אֵלֵינוּ	to us	אֶל
לָהֶן	לָהֶם	to them	לָכֶן	לָכֶם	to you	לָנוּ	to us	ל...
עֲלֵיהֶן	עֲלֵיהֶם	on them	עֲלֵיכֶן	עֲלֵיכֶם	on you	עָלֵינוּ	on us	עַל
אֵינָן	אֵינָם	they are not	אֵינְכֶן	אֵינְכֶם	you are not	אֵינֶנּוּ	we are not	אֵין

The forms above that are associated with the preposition ל... are the forms you will use in this activity. The forms for אֶל *to*, עַל *upon*, and אֵין *is not / are not* have been included for comparison of suffix spellings.

If you wish, you may begin the announcement of whom you have selected to receive your random action by using this expression: מְצַוָּה... / אֲנִי מְצַוֶּה (*I am commanding m, f...*). Complete the statement by designating the recipient with the preposition ל plus an appropriate suffix.

Suggestion: because the structure "preposition-plus-suffixed-pronoun" is so common in Hebrew, many students find it helpful to make special note of the above table for quick reference.

At the end of this segment you will find a similar table showing how pronominal suffixes help to differentiate the spelling of the words אֵת (definite direct object marker) and אֶת (the preposition *with*).

---

[37] Please note that the dot in the ה... of לָהּ is a vital part of the spelling. Without the dot (called a mappiq) you might think that the ה was simply a vowel letter, part of the feminine ending to the noun, rather than a suffixed feminine pronoun. The mappiq causes that final ה to be recognized as a true consonant (to be pronounced with a slight aspiration at the close of the syllable).

[38] The pronunciation of ָיו is the same as וֹ. This sequence (qameṣ-yod-vav) does not produce a diphthong (cf. GKC §8m).

UNIT 3   מָה־אַתָּה עָשָׂה?

For a wider range of prepositions with pronominal suffixes, please consult the preposition table at the back of this volume (p. 494).

Six random actions / questions for Round One (singular)

1. לְמִי אֲנִי נֹתֵן / נֹתֶנֶת לֶחֶם לֶאֱכֹל?

2. לְמִי אֲנִי מַשְׁלִיךְ / מַשְׁלֶכֶת דָּג?

3. עַל־רֹאשׁ מִי אֲנִי שָׂם / שָׂמָה כּוֹס מַיִם?

4. אֶת־מִי אֲנִי מְצַוֶּה / מְצַוָּה לָשֶׁבֶת תַּחַת שֻׁלְחָן?

5. אֶל־מִי אֲנִי מַשְׁלִיךְ / מַשְׁלֶכֶת לֶחֶם לֶאֱכֹל?

6. בִּידֵי־מִי אֲנִי שָׂם / שָׂמָה כֶּסֶף?   Into whose hands...?

Six random actions / questions for Round Two (plural forms)

1. לְמִי אֲנַחְנוּ נֹתְנִים לֶחֶם לֶאֱכֹל?

2. אֶל־מִי אֲנַחְנוּ מַשְׁלִיכִים כִּסֵּא?

3. עַל־רֹאשׁ מִי אֲנַחְנוּ שָׂמִים כּוֹס מַיִם?

4. אֶת־מִי אֲנַחְנוּ מְצַוִּים לַעֲמֹד עַל־יְדֵיהֶם[39]?

5. אֶל־מִי אֲנַחְנוּ מַשְׁלִיכִים לֶחֶם לֶאֱכֹל?

---

[39] עַל־יְדֵיהֶם *on their hands.*

6. ‏אֶת־מִי אֲנַ֫חְנוּ מְצֻוִּים לִשְׁתּוֹת מַ֫יִם כַּדָּג?‏

Words for responding / ‏מִלִּים לַעֲנוֹת‏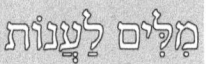

Before leaving this exploration of prepositions with pronominal suffixes, it may be helpful to view side-by-side two words that may be confused due to similar spelling:

(1) ‏אֵת‏ (the preposition *with*)

(2) ‏אֵת‏ (the definite direct object marker)

When **pronominal suffixes** are added, the two words may be easily **distinguished**.

- Watch for a ḥireq vowel in the first syllable and dagesh in ‏ת‏—signals of the preposition ‏אֵת‏ "***with***" (e.g., ‏אִתִּי‏ *with me*).

- When you do **not** find this ḥireq and dagesh (but instead a segol, ḥolem, or ḥolem-vav), it is a sign of the **definite direct object marker** (e.g., ‏אֶתִי‏ or ‏אוֹתִי‏ *me*).

- Note that most forms of the **definite direct object marker** may also be spelled with a ḥolem-vav (e.g., ‏אוֹתִי, אוֹתְךָ, אוֹתָךְ, אוֹתוֹ, אוֹתָהּ, אוֹתָ֫נוּ‏, and ‏אוֹתָם‏).

Distinguishing the preposition ‏אֵת‏ (with) from ‏אֵת‏ (definite direct object marker)

	him / her		you *sing.*		me	
‏אִתָּהּ‏ / ‏אִתּוֹ‏ with him / her		‏אִתָּךְ‏ / ‏אִתְּךָ‏ with you *ms, fs*		‏אִתִּי‏ with me	.א
‏אֹתָהּ‏ / ‏אֹתוֹ‏ him / her		‏אֹתָךְ‏ / ‏אֹתְךָ‏ you *ms, fs*		‏אֹתִי‏ me	.ב
	them		you *pl.*		us	
‏אִתָּן‏ / ‏אִתָּם‏ with them *m, f*		‏אִתְּכֶן‏ / ‏אִתְּכֶם‏ with you *mpl, fpl*		‏אִתָּ֫נוּ‏ with us	.א
‏אֹתָן‏ / ‏אֹתָם‏ them *m, f*		‏אֶתְכֶן‏ / ‏אֶתְכֶם‏ you *mpl, fpl*		‏אֹתָ֫נוּ‏ us	.ב

When spelled **without** a pronominal suffix, we must rely on **context** to distinguish them. Without a pronominal suffix, both are spelled the same: ‏אֵת‏ (or when joined to the next word with a maqqef, ‏אֶת־‏).

3.4.ב. Explanation: "Aren't you (*fpl*) queens?"   הֲלֹא אַתֵּנָה מְלָכוֹת?

INTERACTIVE SKILL: Addressing (or referring to) females, using pronouns

Words for responding   מִלִּים לַעֲנוֹת

We have encountered the following independent feminine pronouns at various points in earlier material. Here they are collected in one place.

אַתֵּנָה (*also* אַתֵּן)	you* *fpl*	אַתְּ [a]	you* *fs*
הֵנָּה [b]	they* *fpl*	הִיא	she*

[a] The form אַתְּ resulted from historic אנת, still evident in Arabic *2fs* pronoun, ʾant.

[b] The *3fpl* pronoun may take the form הֶן... when suffixed to a preposition (e.g., בָּהֶן *in them fpl*). Although Biblical Hebrew attests הֵם as *3mpl* independent pronoun, the analogous form הֵן will not appear as a *3fpl* independent pronoun until Post-Biblical Hebrew.

Feminine plural forms appear only rarely in Biblical Hebrew.[40] Such rare occurrence owes in part to the practice of employing masculine forms when referring to mixed company. Here is a convenient reference table giving the typical spellings for feminine and masculine independent pronouns:

Independent pronoun reference table

	Plural		Singular		
	f	*m*	*f*	*m*	
we	אֲנַחְנוּ		אֲנִי		I
you	אַתֵּנָה	אַתֶּם	אַתְּ	אַתָּה	you
they	הֵנָּה	הֵם	הִיא	הוּא	he, she

---

[40] *You fpl* אַתֵּנָה occurs only five times, including one instance spelled as אַתֵּן; *they 3fpl* הֵנָּה occurs 47 times.

3.4.ג. Explanation: "What can you (*ms*) do with your (*ms*) gadgets?"

מַה־תּוּכַל לַעֲשׂוֹת בְּמַחְשְׁבוֹתֶ֫יךָ ?[41]

INTERACTIVE SKILL: Expressing ownership and functionality of various objects

Early on you may have noticed that in order to indicate when an object belongs to someone or something, Hebrew will attach a pronominal suffix to the end of a noun, as in שְׁמִי *my name* or לַחְמִי *my bread*. Here is a recap of how suffixed pronouns appear when attached to a noun.

---

[41] בְּמַחְשְׁבוֹתֶ֫יךָ is plural of מַחֲשָׁבָה *thought, device, invention, f*, with prefixed preposition בְּ (here meaning *with* or *by means of*) and a pronominal suffix ךָ... *your ms*. If this word is too awkward, your instructor may opt for בִּדְבָרְךָ (or בִּדְבָרֶ֫ךָ in pause, from דָּבָר *word, thing, m*), although דָּבָר as *thing* tends to refer to **events** rather than tangible **objects**).

Keep in mind that it is not the gender of the noun that drives the gender of the suffix. Rather, the gender of the suffix is determined by the person to whom the suffix refers. Notice how the pronominal suffix changes in these two expressions (even though the gender of לֶחֶם remains constant): לַחְמוֹ *his bread* (note the *3ms* suffix), and לַחְמָהּ *her bread* (*3fs* suffix). The gender of the pronominal suffix is determined by the person **owning** the bread, rather than by the gender of **bread**.[42]

Whose name? (noun with pronominal suffixes)

	Plural		Singular		
	f	*m*	*f*	*m*	
our...	שְׁמֵנוּ			שְׁמִי	my...
your...	שְׁמְכֶן	שִׁמְכֶם	שְׁמֵךְ	שִׁמְךָ[43]	your...
their...	שְׁמָן	שְׁמָם	שְׁמָהּ	שְׁמוֹ[44]	his / her...

Whose food? (noun with pronominal suffixes)

	Plural		Singular		
	f	*m*	*f*	*m*	
our...	לַחְמֵנוּ			לַחְמִי	my...
your...	לַחְמְכֶן	לַחְמְכֶם	לַחְמֵךְ	לַחְמְךָ	your...
their...	לַחְמָן	לַחְמָם	לַחְמָהּ	לַחְמוֹ	his / her...

To view a wider range of nouns with pronominal suffixes, please consult the tables for nouns with pronominal suffixes, located at the back of this volume (pp. 482–493).

---

[42] If you are curious why some vowels shift when suffixes are added (e.g., the *ṣērê* in שֵׁם becomes a *sheva* in שְׁמִי or a *ḥireq* in שִׁמְךָ), you will discover the answers as you compare the vowel-change principles found in the appendix entry corresponding to §3.3.ה.

[43] When in pause, שְׁמְךָ becomes שְׁמֶךָ.

[44] Following the letter י the *3ms* suffix appears as ו, rather than וֹ (as in עָלָיו, *upon him*). This applies to words other than prepositions as well.

3.4.ד. Activity: "What can you (*ms*) do with your (*ms*) gadgets?"
מַה־תּוּכַל לַעֲשׂוֹת בְּמַחְשְׁבוֹתֶיךָ?

INTERACTIVE SKILL: Expressing ownership and functionality of various objects (continued)

Today it is likely your neighbor has brought to class something out of the ordinary.

- To discover what the object **is**, ask the **first** question from the model, below.
- To learn what she can **do** with it, ask the **second** question (line 3, below). The hidden talents all around you may surprise you.

Hint: If you know the Hebrew word for the object that you yourself are displaying, please use that word (with pronominal suffix "my")! If you do not know the Hebrew word, don't worry: using the correct name for the object is not vital to this activity. Simply use the all-purpose label מַחְשַׁבְתִּי *my thing*, *device* (see response in line ב, below).

When asked what you can do with your gadget, you may reply in one of two ways.

(1) You may either **describe** your action in simple Hebrew. See line ד, which imagines that the "gadget" is a cell phone: אוּכַל לְדַבֵּר *I am able to speak*.

UNIT 3   מָה־אַתָּה עֹשֶׂה?   239

(2) Or you may invite your inquirer to **watch and see** what you do with that object (use response in line ה in this case, then demonstrate with actions).

Model (for individual)

What do you have?	מַה־יֵּשׁ לְךָ?	Inquiry about object	א.
I have my gadget.	לִי מַחֲשַׁבְתִּי:	Reply	ב.
What are you (ms, fs) able to do with your (ms, fs) gadget?	מַה־תּוּכַל / תּוּכְלִי לַעֲשׂוֹת בְּמַחֲשַׁבְתְּךָ / בְּמַחֲשַׁבְתֵּךְ?	Inquiry about its function	ג.
I am able to speak with you (ms, fs) [if gadget is a cell phone].	אוּכַל לְדַבֵּר אִתְּךָ / אִתָּךְ בְּמַחֲשַׁבְתִּי:	Reply with description	ד.
Watch what I can do with my gadget [follow with demonstration].	רְאֵה / רְאִי מָה אוּכַל לַעֲשׂוֹת בְּמַחֲשַׁבְתִּי:	Reply with demonstration	ה.

Group-to-group conversation: Can you adjust the above expressions for group-to-group conversation? Consult the plural version of the dialogue, provided below. **Hebrew words shaded in gray** still need adjustment from singular to plural so they will match the English words shaded in gray. Take a moment to make those changes. (Plural changes already appear in English words.)

Model (for group)

What do you (mpl) have?	מַה־יֵּשׁ לָכֶם?	Inquiry about what they brought	א.
We have our gadget.	לִי מַחֲשַׁבְתִּי:	Reply	ב.
What are you (mpl, fpl) able to do with your pl gadget?	מַה־תּוּכְלוּ / תּוּכַלְנָה לַעֲשׂוֹת בְּמַחֲשַׁבְתִּי?	Inquiry about what they can do with it	ג.

ד.	Reply with description	נוּכַל לְדַבֵּר אִתְּכֶן בְּמַחֲשַׁבְתִּי:	We are able to speak with you *fpl* with our gadget [if gadget is a cell phone].
ה.	Reply with demonstration	רְאוּ / רְאֶינָה מַה־נוּכַל לַעֲשׂוֹת בְּמַחֲשַׁבְתִּי:	Watch (*mpl*, *fpl*) what we can do with our gadget [follow with demonstration].

You (*ms*) can read the Bible.[45] אַתָּה תִּקְרָא אֶת־הַתנַ״ךְ:

Selected readings

3.1.א. Reuben, the eldest son of Jacob, was devastated to discover that his brothers had already sold Joseph to slave traders. He confronted his brothers with this anguished exclamation and question. (Note that אֵינֶנּוּ is אֵין with a *3ms* pronominal suffix, meaning *he does not exist* or *is no more*. In English the pronoun will become superfluous.)

.1 ..."הַיֶּלֶד[a] אֵינֶנּוּ

וַאֲנִי אָנָה[b] אֲנִי־בָא[c]?" (Gen. 37:30)

[a] יֶלֶד young boy *m*   [b] אָנָה to what place, whither (interrogative)   [c] ב.ו.א *pt ms* come, enter

3.1.א. The fifth book of the Bible contains a powerful oration by מֹשֶׁה, who led Israel out of Egypt. The book introduces his oration with these words.

.2 אֵלֶּה הַדְּבָרִים[a] אֲשֶׁר דִּבֶּר[b] מֹשֶׁה אֶל־כָּל־יִשְׂרָאֵל[c]... (Deut. 1:1a)

[a] דָּבָר word, matter *m*   [b] דִּבֶּר [ד.ב.ר] he spoke   [c] כָּל־ all, every (*qames-hatuf*)

3.1.א. These words suggest how deeply the psalmist desired to follow God.

.3 לַמְּדֵנִי[a] לַעֲשׂוֹת רְצוֹנְךָ[b] כִּי־אַתָּה אֱלוֹהָי[c]... (Ps. 143:10a)

[a] לַמְּדֵנִי [ל.מ.ד] Teach me!   [b] רְצוֹנְךָ desire *ms* (*with 2ms pronominal sfx* "your")

[c] אֱלוֹהָי (*with 1cs pronominal sfx* "my")

---

[45] As noted earlier, a Hebrew word or phrase in the Selected Readings that has been marked with the symbol ᵘ has been modified to facilitate reading. That is why Selected Readings marked with the symbol ᵘ often will not fully correspond to what you find in a standard Bible translation for the same passage.

On account of Joseph's integrity, his master Potiphar concerned himself with virtually nothing in his household. (Notice that due to context, the participle אוֹכֵל [a fuller spelling of אֹכֵל] should be translated as past tense.)   3.1.ג.

4. ...כִּי אִם־הַלֶּחֶם אֲשֶׁר־הוּא אוֹכֵל׃ (Gen. 39:6a)

כִּי אִם־ except   אוֹכֵל אָכַל

During the period following Joshua's conquest, central government in Israel could be described thus: 3.1.ג.

5. בַּיָּמִים הָהֵם אֵין מֶלֶךְ בְּיִשְׂרָאֵל... (Judg. 18:1)

יָמִים days m

God said of his servant, "I have put my words in your mouth..."   3.1.ה.

6. ...לֵאמֹר לְצִיּוֹן "עַמִּי־אָתָּה": (Isa. 51:16)

א.מ.ר to say   צִיּוֹן Zion   עַמִּי my people m

וַלֵּאמֹר לְצִיּוֹן עַמִּי־אָתָּה...

With these words Solomon accounted for the grandeur of the temple (בַּיִת house, m) that he was building.   3.1.ה.

7. וְהַבַּיִת אֲשֶׁר־אֲנִי בוֹנֶה גָּדוֹל
כִּי־גָדוֹל אֱלֹהֵינוּ מִכָּל־הָאֱלֹהִים׃ (2 Chron. 2:4)

בּוֹנֶה [ב.נ.י/ה] one who builds participle ms   כָּל־ all, every

3.1.ה.	How much worth would you place on a "name" (reputation)?	

8. טוֹב שֵׁם מִשֶּׁ֫מֶן[a] טוֹב: (Eccl. 7:1a)

[a] שֶׁ֫מֶן oil, scented oil *m*

3.2.א. When describing the assets of the land of Havilah, the author of Genesis made this statement. (The conjunction in וּזֲהַב is spelled ו and not וְ, since וּזֲהַב developed from וְזָהָב in consequence of the sibilant ז plus sheva.[46] The word הַהוּא was vocalized by the Masoretes with a ḥireq to recommend that it be read as הַהִיא, not as הַהוּא [cf. §8.1.כ].)

9. וּזֲהַב[a] הָאָ֫רֶץ הַהִוא טוֹב:... (Gen. 2:12)

[a] זָהָב gold *m*

3.2.ב. Longing for rescue, the prophet-poet recalls the LORD's mighty deeds of old.

10. ...זְר֫וֹעַ[a] יהוה ...
הֲלוֹא[b] אַתְּ־הִיא... מְחוֹלֶ֫לֶת[c] תַּנִּין[d]: (Isa. 51:9)

[a] זְר֫וֹעַ arm (*metaphor for strength*) *f*   [b] הֲלוֹא הֲ + לֹא   [c] מְחוֹלֶ֫לֶת [ח.ל.ל] one who pierces *f*
[d] תַּנִּין sea monster *m*

...זְרוֹעַ יהוה ע֫וּרִי כִּימֵי קֶ֫דֶם דֹּרוֹת עוֹלָמִים הֲלוֹא אַתְּ־הִיא הַמַּחְצֶ֫בֶת רַ֫הַב מְחוֹלֶ֫לֶת תַּנִּין:

3.2.ב. Although the wicked may flourish for a time, their time will come.

11. [הָרָשָׁע[a]] עֹבֵר וְהִנֵּה אֵינֶ֫נּוּ[b]
וָאֲבַקְשֵׁ֫הוּ[c]
וְאֵינֶ֫נִּי[d] מֹצֵא אוֹתוֹ[c]: (Ps. 37:36)

[a] רָשָׁע wicked person *m*   [b] אֵינֶ֫נּוּ אֵין + הוּא   [c] אוֹתוֹ אֵת־ + הוּא   [d] וְאֵינֶ֫נִּי אֵין + אֲנִי

וַיַּעֲבֹר וְהִנֵּה אֵינֶ֫נּוּ וָאֲבַקְשֵׁ֫הוּ וְלֹא נִמְצָא:

---

[46] GKC §10g and Joüon §9c.

3.2.ב. As the poet was musing, speaking to himself (to his נֶ֫פֶשׁ *soul* or *self, fs*) one day, he employed these two phrases to describe the LORD. (You may recognize the participle סֹלֵחַ since it relates to the expression סְלַח־נָא.)

12. הַסֹּלֵחַ לְכָל־ᵃ עֲוֹנֵכִי ᵇ
     הָרֹפֵא ᶜ לְכָל־ᵃ תַּחֲלֻאָ֑יְכִי ᵈ (Ps. 103:3)

   ᵃ כָּל־ all (*qames-hatuf*) m   ᵇ עָוֹן (*with 2fs pronominal sfx* "your")
   ᶜ ר.פ.א. to heal   ᵈ תַּחֲלֻאִים diseases m (*with 2fs pronominal sfx* "your")

3.2.ג. Grateful for her gift of shelter, the Israelite spies on a reconnaissance mission in Jericho made this pact with a woman named Rahab. (Notice that the participle describes a future time frame, as if to say: "When we shall…." The participle here does not refer to the present time.)

13. הִנֵּה אֲנַחְנוּ בָאִים בָּאָ֑רֶץ... (Josh. 2:18a)

[The verse continues: "…bind this scarlet cord in the window from which you make us descend (i.e., helped us to make our escape)," and expresses a pledge of security for those of her family who remain in her house on the day of battle against Jericho.]

3.2.ג. Have you ever offered good advice, only to have a friend reject it? If so, you may be able to empathize with Jeremiah after he received this response from his audience, toward the close of his ministry. (Concerning אֵינֶ֫נּוּ, the suffix for *1cpl* "we" and *3ms* "he" has the same spelling.)

14. הַדָּבָר אֲשֶׁר אַתָּה ᵘ מְדַבֵּר ᵘ אֵלֵ֫ינוּ בְּשֵׁם יהוה
     אֵינֶ֫נּוּ ᵃ שֹׁמְעִים אֵלֶ֫יךָ ᵇ : (Jer. 44:16)

   ᵃ אֵינֶ֫נּוּ אֵין + אֲנַ֫חְנוּ   ᵇ אֵלֶ֫יךָ אֶל־ + אַתָּה
   הַדָּבָר אֲשֶׁר־דִּבַּ֫רְתָּ אֵלֵ֫ינוּ בְּשֵׁם יהוה אֵינֶ֫נּוּ שֹׁמְעִים אֵלֶ֫יךָ:

3.2.ג.

In the cycles of nature, the writer of Ecclesiastes observed paradox. (When you come to the word וְהַיָּם, experiment with translating the conjunction וְ as an adversative [*yet* or *however*].)

15. כָּל־הַנְּחָלִים^a הֹלְכִים^b אֶל־הַיָּם
   וְהַיָּם אֵינֶנּוּ^{c} מָלֵא^d : (Eccl. 1:7a)

   ^{a} כָּל־ all, every (*qameṣ-ḥaṭuf*) ^{b} נַחַל river *m* ^{c} אֵינֶנּוּ אֵין + הוּא ^{d} מָלֵא full

3.3.ג.

After learning that their lack of faith displayed at the edge of Canaan would bring negative consequences, Israel decided to enter the land, after all. But it was too late. Moses warned against the folly of presumptuous invasion.

(Note that when לָמָּה expands to לָמָּה זֶּה, the entire phrase takes on a rhetorical tone, infused with puzzlement: "Why in the world…?" Thus the term זֶה will not appear in your translation as "this." The word וְהוּא was vocalized by the Masoretes with a ḥireq to recommend that it be read as וְהִיא [cf. §8.1.כ.].)

16. מֹשֶׁה אָמַר^a "לָמָּה זֶּה אַתֶּם עֹבְרִים אֶת־פִּי־יהוה?^{b}
   וְהִוא לֹא תִצְלָח^c" : (Num. 14:41)

   ^{a} א.מ.ר to say ^{b} עֹבְרִים אֶת־פִּי־ [ע.ב.ר] *pt mpl* to overstep, transgress the command of
   ^{c} תִצְלָח [צ.ל.ח] it will succeed *fs*

   וַיֹּאמֶר מֹשֶׁה לָמָּה זֶּה אַתֶּם עֹבְרִים אֶת־פִּי יהוה וְהִוא לֹא תִצְלָח:

3.4.א.

When he set eyes upon his younger brother Benjamin, the Grand Vizier of Egypt inquired:

17. …הֲזֶה אֲחִיכֶם^a הַקָּטֹן
   אֲשֶׁר אֲמַרְתֶּם^b אֵלָי^c:… (Gen. 43:29)

   ^{a} אֲחִיכֶם brother (*with pronominal sfx*) ^{b} אֲמַרְתֶּם [א.מ.ר] you said, told *mpl*
   ^{c} אֵלָי to me (*pausal*)

   וַיִּשָּׂא עֵינָיו וַיַּרְא אֶת־בִּנְיָמִין אָחִיו בֶּן־אִמּוֹ וַיֹּאמֶר הֲזֶה אֲחִיכֶם הַקָּטֹן אֲשֶׁר אֲמַרְתֶּם אֵלָי וַיֹּאמַר אֱלֹהִים יָחְנְךָ בְּנִי:

3.4.א. To underscore the importance of refraining from making any material representation of God, Moses reminded Israel how God did (and did not) present himself during their supreme encounter with him at Mt. Sinai. (When you reach the conjunction in וּתְמוּנָה, experiment with an adversative [*yet* or *however*].)

18. וַיְדַבֵּר יהוה[a] אֲלֵיכֶם מִתּוֹךְ[b] הָאֵשׁ[c]
קוֹל דְּבָרִים[d] אַתֶּם שֹׁמְעִים
וּתְמוּנָה[e] אֵינְכֶם רֹאִים[f]
זוּלָתִי[g] קוֹל: (Deut. 4:12)

[a] וַיְדַבֵּר יהוה and the LORD spoke [b] מִתּוֹךְ from within [c] אֵשׁ *f* fire [d] דָּבָר *m* word, matter
[e] תְּמוּנָה *f* form, visible shape [f] רֹאִים [ר.א.ה/י] *pt mpl* ones who see
[g] זוּלָתִי exclusively, nothing but

וַיְדַבֵּר יהוה אֲלֵיכֶם מִתּוֹךְ הָאֵשׁ קוֹל דְּבָרִים אַתֶּם שֹׁמְעִים וּתְמוּנָה אֵינְכֶם רֹאִים זוּלָתִי קוֹל:

3.4.א. Moses knew that his life was drawing to a close, and that Joshua would lead the Israelites across the Jordan. So he encouraged Joshua with these words. The context makes it clear that the singular pronominal suffix found here refers to Joshua personally, as an individual.

19. וַיהוָה הוּא הַהֹלֵךְ לְפָנֶיךָ[a] הוּא יִהְיֶה עִמָּךְ... (Deut. 31:8a)

[a] לְפָנֶיךָ לִפְנֵי and ךָ *suffix*

3.4.ב. From a window in her house, Rahab was able to lower the spies directly outside the city of Jericho...

20. ...כִּי בֵיתָהּ[a] בְּקִיר[b] הַחוֹמָה וּבַחוֹמָה[c] הִיא יוֹשָׁבֶת: (Josh. 2:15)

[a] בַּיִת, בֵּית־ *m* house [b] קִיר *m* wall [c] חוֹמָה *f* city wall, city enclosure

3.4.ב.	Unaware that their young miracle-son had died, the father was puzzled when his wife suddenly determined to visit the prophet. He asked...	

21. ...״לָ֤מָּה אַ֣תְּ הֹלֶ֤כֶת אֵלָיו֙ הַיּ֔וֹם לֹֽא־חֹ֖דֶשׁ וְלֹ֣א שַׁבָּ֑ת.״
וַתֹּ֖אמֶר, ״שָׁלֽוֹם״: (2 Kings 4:23)

הַיּוֹם [a] today *m*   חֹדֶשׁ [b] new moon festival *m*   שַׁבָּת [c] [seventh day of week] *m / f*

וַתֹּאמֶר [d] and she said [א.מ.ר]

וַיֹּ֗אמֶר מַדּ֨וּעַ אַ֤תְּי הֹלֶ֤כֶת[47] אֵלָיו֙ הַיּ֔וֹם לֹֽא־חֹ֖דֶשׁ וְלֹ֣א שַׁבָּ֑ת וַתֹּ֖אמֶר שָׁלֽוֹם:

3.4.ב.	When King Josiah sought verification from the prophetess Hulda concerning an alarming scroll found in the temple, it was not difficult for his officials to reach her since...	

22. ...הִ֤יא יֹשֶׁ֨בֶת בִּירוּשָׁלִַ֨ם[48a] בַּמִּשְׁנֶ֑ה וַֽיְדַבְּר֖וּ אֵלֶֽיהָ: (2 Kings 22:14)

יְרוּשָׁלִַם [a] [capital of Southern Israel] *m*   מִשְׁנֶה [b] Second District (*of city*) *m*

וַיְדַבְּרוּ [c] and they spoke [ד.ב.ר]

---

[47] In place of the expression אַתִּי הֹלֶכְתִּי, we follow the reading recommended by the Masoretes (omitting the final י in each case, which evidently was an archaic *fs* ending).

[48] Did you notice that there seem to be too many vowels in the final syllable of יְרוּשָׁלִַם? This textual issue is known as a "perpetual *qere*" [from קָרָא *read*]. Masoretes advised pronouncing it as if spelled יְרוּשָׁלַיִם (note the added י) and so vocalized it accordingly, despite the spelling of the consonants (how they were "written" (*ketiv* [כְּתִיב *write*]). This word appears with the full *qere* spelling in a handful of passages (e.g., Jer. 26:18 and Esth. 2:6). Since the *ketiv* / *qere* issue involving יְרוּשָׁלִַם occurs so often, Masoretes did not bother to point out each occurrence in their marginal notes (Masorah Marginalis Parva), expecting instead that readers would memorize how it should be read, "perpetually" (cf. §8.1.ב.).

3.4.ג.   As soon as Jonah's fugitive status came to light, the storm-tossed sailors were brimming with questions. (The word אַרְצֶ֑ךָ is אַרְצְךָ in pause.)

23. ...דַּבֶּר־נָ֤א ᵃ לָ֙נוּ֙...

בַּאֲשֶׁ֧ר לְמִי־ᵇהָרָעָ֥ה הַזֹּ֖את לָ֑נוּ...

וּמֵאַ֣יִן ᶜ בָּ֔א ᵈ אַתָּ֑ה

וּמָ֖ה אַרְצֶֽךָ׃... (Jonah 1:8)

ᵃ דַּבֶּר־נָא [ד.ב.ר] please speak ms   ᵇ בַּאֲשֶׁר לְמִי־ on whose account?   ᶜ וּמֵאַיִן וּ + מִן + אַיֵּה

ᵈ בָּא [ב.ו.א] pt ms

וַיֹּאמְר֣וּ אֵלָ֗יו הַגִּֽידָה־נָּ֣א לָ֔נוּ בַּאֲשֶׁ֧ר לְמִי־הָרָעָ֛ה הַזֹּ֖את לָ֑נוּ מַה־מְּלַאכְתְּךָ֙ וּמֵאַ֣יִן תָּב֔וֹא מָ֣ה אַרְצֶ֔ךָ וְאֵֽי־מִזֶּ֥ה עַ֖ם אָֽתָּה׃

3.4.ד.   For the author of Psalm 136, gratitude was grounded in reason. See whether you can identify this poet's reasons. (Also notice the structure in לֵאלֹהֵי הָאֱלֹהִים; review §3.1.ז. if unsure.)

24. 1.   הוֹד֣וּ ᵃ לַיהוָ֣ה כִּי־ט֑וֹב

כִּ֖י לְעוֹלָ֣ם ᵇ חַסְדּֽוֹ׃ ᶜ

2.   הוֹד֭וּ לֵאלֹהֵ֣י הָאֱלֹהִ֑ים

כִּ֖י לְעוֹלָ֣ם חַסְדּֽוֹ׃ (Ps. 136:1-2)

ᵃ הוֹדוּ [י.ד.ה/ה] give thanks imperative mpl, hifil   ᵇ לְעוֹלָם forever   ᶜ חֶסֶד kindness m

UNIT 3   מָה־אַתָּה עֹשֶׂה?   249

A connected reading: The binding of Isaac (Gen. 22:3-4)   עֲקֵדַת יִצְחָק

3. וַיַּשְׁכֵּם‎ᵃ אַבְרָהָם‎ᵇ בַּבֹּקֶר‎ᶜ
   וַיַּחֲבֹשׁ‎ᵈ אֶת־חֲמֹרוֹ‎ᵉ
   וַיִּקַּח‎ᶠ אֶת־שְׁנֵי נְעָרָיו‎ᵍ אִתּוֹ וְאֵת יִצְחָק בְּנוֹ‎ʰ
   וַיְבַקַּע‎ⁱ עֲצֵי עֹלָה‎ʲ
   וַיָּקָם וַיֵּלֶךְ‎ᵏ אֶל־הַמָּקוֹם‎ˡ
   אֲשֶׁר־אָמַר‎ᵐ־לוֹ הָאֱלֹהִים:

וַיַּשְׁכֵּם ᵃ so he got up early   אַבְרָהָם ᵇ (*a person's name*)   בֹּקֶר ᶜ *m* morning   וַיַּחֲבֹשׁ ᵈ and he saddled   אֶת־ ᵉ

חֲמֹרוֹ *m* his donkey   וַיִּקַּח ᶠ and he took   אֶת־שְׁנֵי נְעָרָיו ᵍ two of his young men   בֵּן ʰ *m* son

וַיְבַקַּע ⁱ and he split   עֲצֵי עֹלָה ʲ wood for a whole burnt offering

וַיָּקָם וַיֵּלֶךְ ᵏ then he got up and went (*the second qameṣ is a qameṣ-ḥaṭuf*)   מָקוֹם ˡ *m* place   אָמַר ᵐ he said

4. בַּיּוֹם‎ᵃ הַשְּׁלִישִׁי‎ᵇ וַיִּשָּׂא‎ᶜ אַבְרָהָם אֶת־עֵינָיו‎ᵈ
   וַיַּרְא‎ᵉ אֶת־הַמָּקוֹם‎ᶠ מֵרָחֹק‎ᵍ:

יוֹם ᵃ *m* day   שְׁלִישִׁי ᵇ third   וַיִּשָּׂא ᶜ then he lifted   עֵינָיו ᵈ his eyes *f dual*   וַיַּרְא ᵉ and he saw

מָקוֹם ᶠ *m* place   מֵרָחֹק ᵍ at a distance

UNIT 4

מַה־יַּעֲשׂוּ מָחָר?

Talking about what they will do tomorrow

יִקְטֹל *conjugation (part 1)*

This unit will enable you to talk about events yet unfolding in the future. You will be able to report:

- what individual people will be doing
- what groups of men or women will be doing

A table located below offers a preview of verb forms often used to express the future. These comprise the "יִקְטֹל conjugation" (also known as the "imperfect" or "prefix" conjugation). These forms will be introduced over the course of Unit 4 and Unit 5.

In this unit you will also expand your facility to describe abilities associated with the human body, such as:

- hearing
- seeing
- eating

The following chart offers a preview of the verb conjugation known as יִקְטֹל. By referring to the outer columns you may anticipate the particular segment when a certain part of the יִקְטֹל conjugation will be introduced. For example, the form meaning "he will guard" will be introduced in §4.3.א. Some elements will not be introduced until Unit 5.

The יִקְטֹל conjugation

Segment	Plural	Singular	Segment
5.1.א.	נִשְׁמֹר we will guard	אֶשְׁמֹר I will guard	5.2.ב.
5.1.ד.	תִּשְׁמְרוּ you will guard *mpl*	תִּשְׁמֹר you will guard *ms*	5.3.א.
5.1.ו.	תִּשְׁמֹרְנָה you will guard *fpl*	תִּשְׁמְרִי you will guard *fs*	5.3.ג.
4.1.א.	יִשְׁמְרוּ they will guard *m*	יִשְׁמֹר he will guard	4.3.א.
4.4.א.	תִּשְׁמֹרְנָה they will guard *f*	תִּשְׁמֹר she will guard	4.5.א.

If you are developing vocabulary cards to learn new words, it may be helpful to design a single card for the יִקְטֹל forms of each שֹׁרֶשׁ. As each new element of the conjugation is introduced, add that part to the card for a given שֹׁרֶשׁ. When you are finished, the יִקְטֹל card for שׁ.מ.ר would resemble the table above (although your vocabulary card would display only Hebrew on one side, with the translation on the other side).

UNIT 4   מַה־יַּעֲשׂוּ מָחָר?

MODULE 4.1   Describing what a group (men or men and women) is about to do

Unit 4 JONAH STORY: Jonah jumps ship

Have you ever suffered a transportation emergency? Perhaps your horse has begun to limp, your car has developed a flat tire, or the airplane you are flying in has run out of fuel. If you are close to home (or taxiing on an airport runway), the disruption may create only a minor inconvenience. But suppose that your emergency occurs when onboard a vessel, with no land in sight!

Words for responding / מִלִּים לַעֲנוֹת

עֶבֶד, עֲבָדִים, עֶבֶד־, עַבְדֵי־	servant, slave, worker *m*	אִישׁ, אֲנָשִׁים, אִישׁ־, אַנְשֵׁי־	man, human* *m*
עֹשֶׂה, עֹשָׂה, עֹשִׂים, עֹשׂוֹת [ע.שׂ.י/ה]	one who makes, does* *pt*	זְרוֹעַ, זְרֹעוֹת, זְרוֹעַ־, זְרֹעֵי־	arm *f* [a]
רֹאשׁ, רָאשִׁים, רֹאשׁ־, רָאשֵׁי־	head *m*	יִכְרְתוּ [כ.ר.ת]	they will cut *mpl*
		יִפְּלוּ [נ.פ.ל]	they will fall *mpl*
		יִשְׁמְרוּ [שׁ.מ.ר]	they will guard* *mpl*

[a] Within the Jonah story, the smaller fish will refer to fins as זְרֹעוֹת. For greater accuracy, you may wish to read סְנַפִּיר *fin(s)*, *m*, in place of זְרֹעוֹת (cf. Lev. 11:9, 10, 12 and Deut. 14:9-10).

Words for hearing / מִלִּים לִשְׁמֹעַ

לֵאמֹר [א.מ.ר]	to say *inf c, prep* ל	הֲלֹא (or) הֲלוֹא...?	Is / will / did not...?
עוֹד [b]	again, more, yet, still	הִשָּׁמֶר לְךָ / הִשָּׁמְרִי לָךְ [שׁ.מ.ר]	Look out (for yourself)! *nifal*[a] *imv ms, fs*
פֶּן־	lest		

253

שְׁלֹשָׁה, שָׁלֹשׁ	three *m, f*	רֹאֶה, רֹאָה, רֹאִים, רֹאוֹת [ר.א.י/ה]	one who sees *pt*

[a] The meaning "to look out" or "to guard oneself" belongs to the nifal spelling of the verb ש.מ.ר. The nifal spelling will be explained further in Unit 7.

[b] In the vast majority of cases, עוֹד operates as a simple adverb—as in עוֹד שְׁלֹשָׁה כֵּלִים *three **more** containers*. עוֹד also may operate in place of a verb, much as יֵשׁ or אֵין, often with a pronominal suffix (e.g., וְשָׁאוּל עוֹדֶנּוּ בַּגִּלְגָּל *but Saul **was still** in Gilgal*, 1 Sam. 13:7b). For a listing of עוֹד with suffixes, please refer to the table of prepositions at the back of this volume (p. 494).

4.1 Jonah Episode: What's that?

ק׳ = הַדָּג הַקָּטָן, ג׳ = הַדָּג הַגָּדוֹל

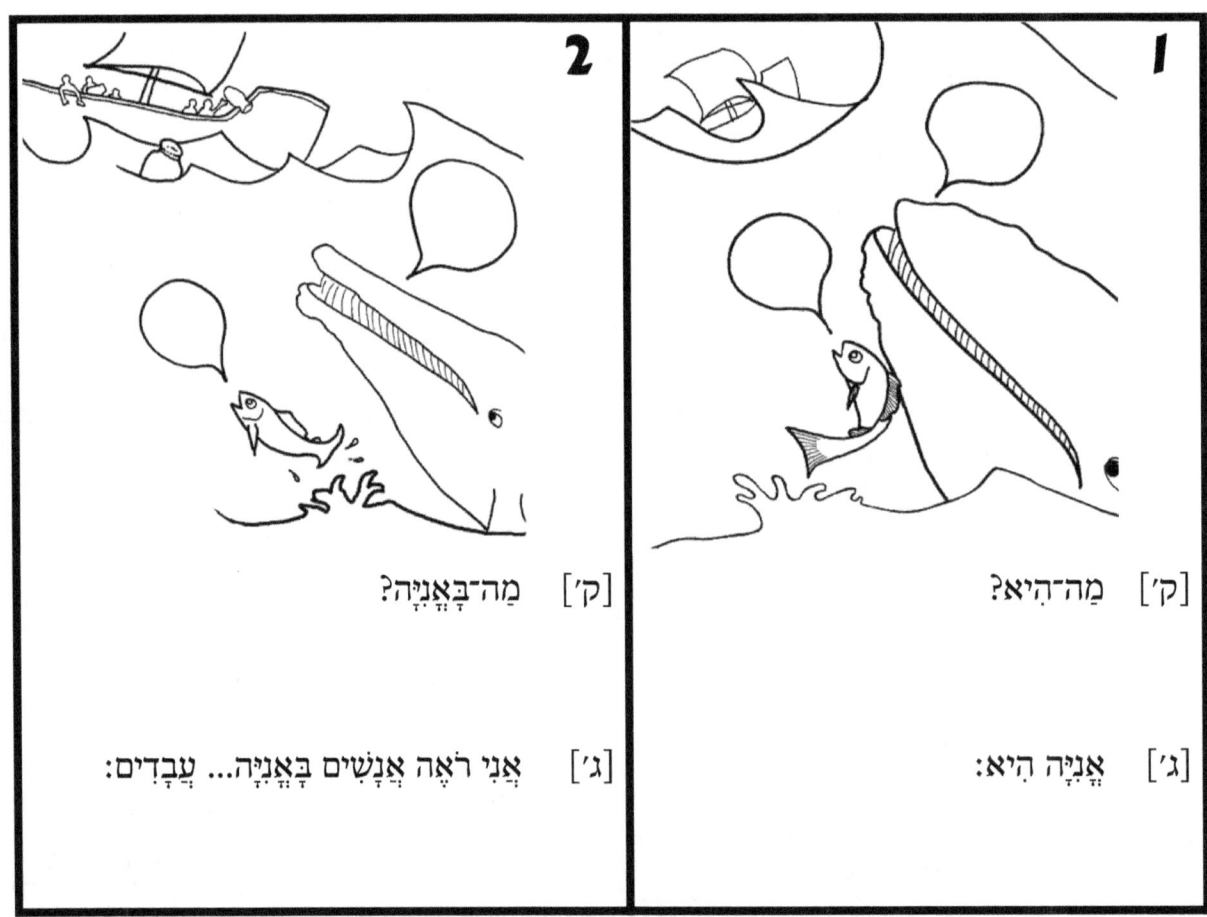

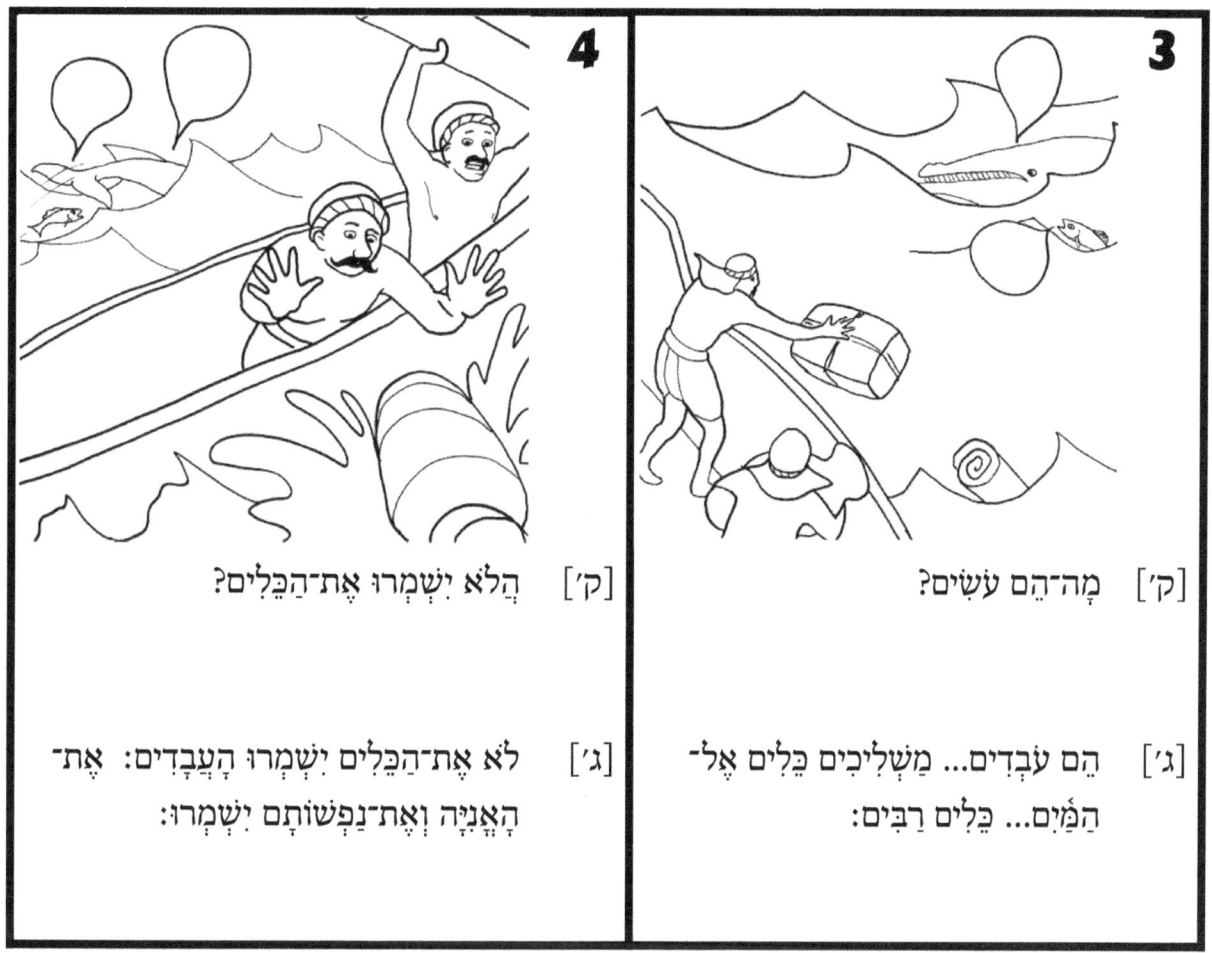

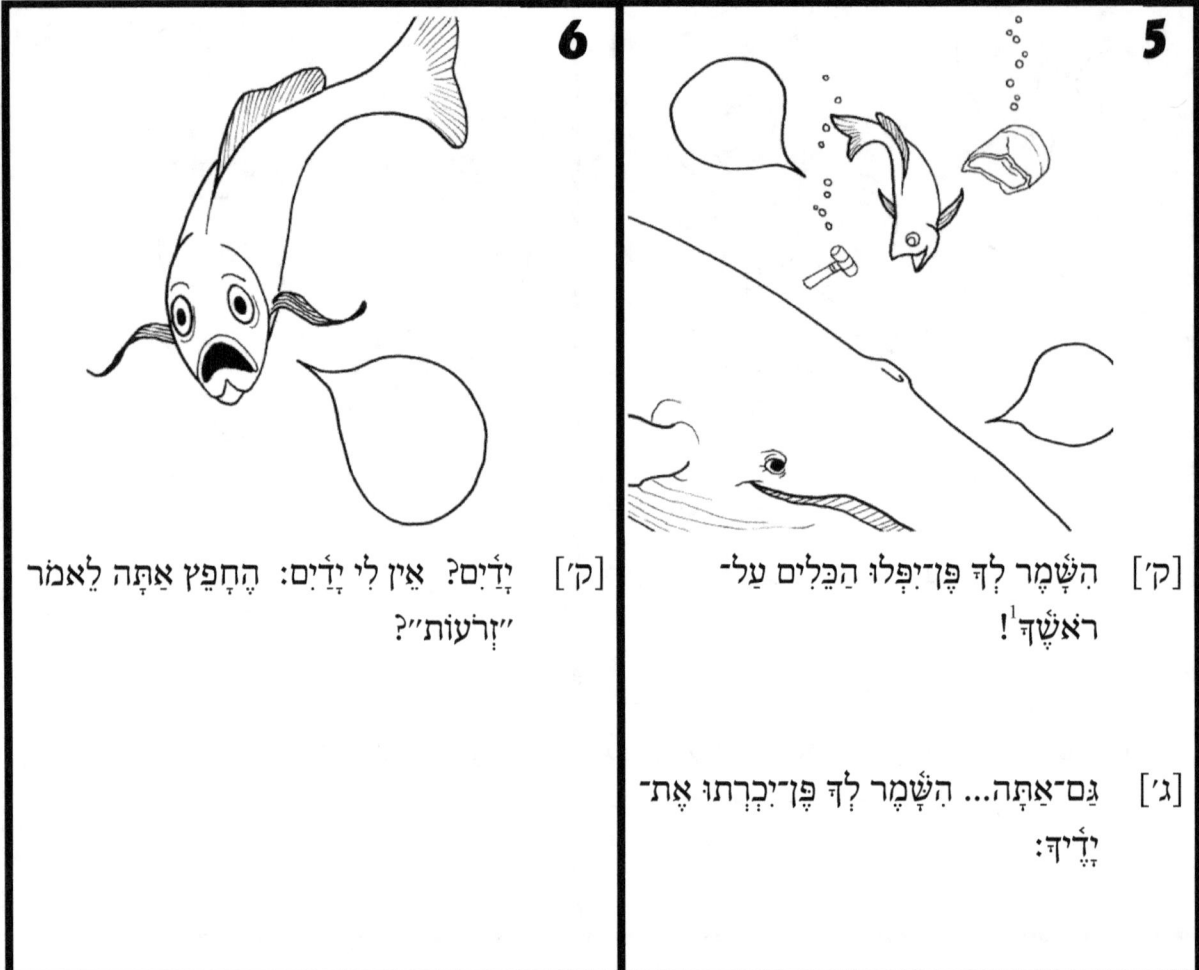

[ק׳] הִשָּׁמֶר לְךָ פֶּן־יִפְּלוּ הַכֵּלִים עַל־רֹאשֶׁךָ¹!

[ג׳] גַּם־אַתָּה... הִשָּׁמֶר לְךָ פֶּן־יִכְרְתוּ אֶת־יָדֶיךָ:

[ק׳] יָדַיִם? אֵין לִי יָדַיִם: הֶחָפֵץ אַתָּה לֵאמֹר "זְרֹעוֹת"?

---

¹ רֹאשֶׁךָ is the pausal form of רֹאשְׁךָ.

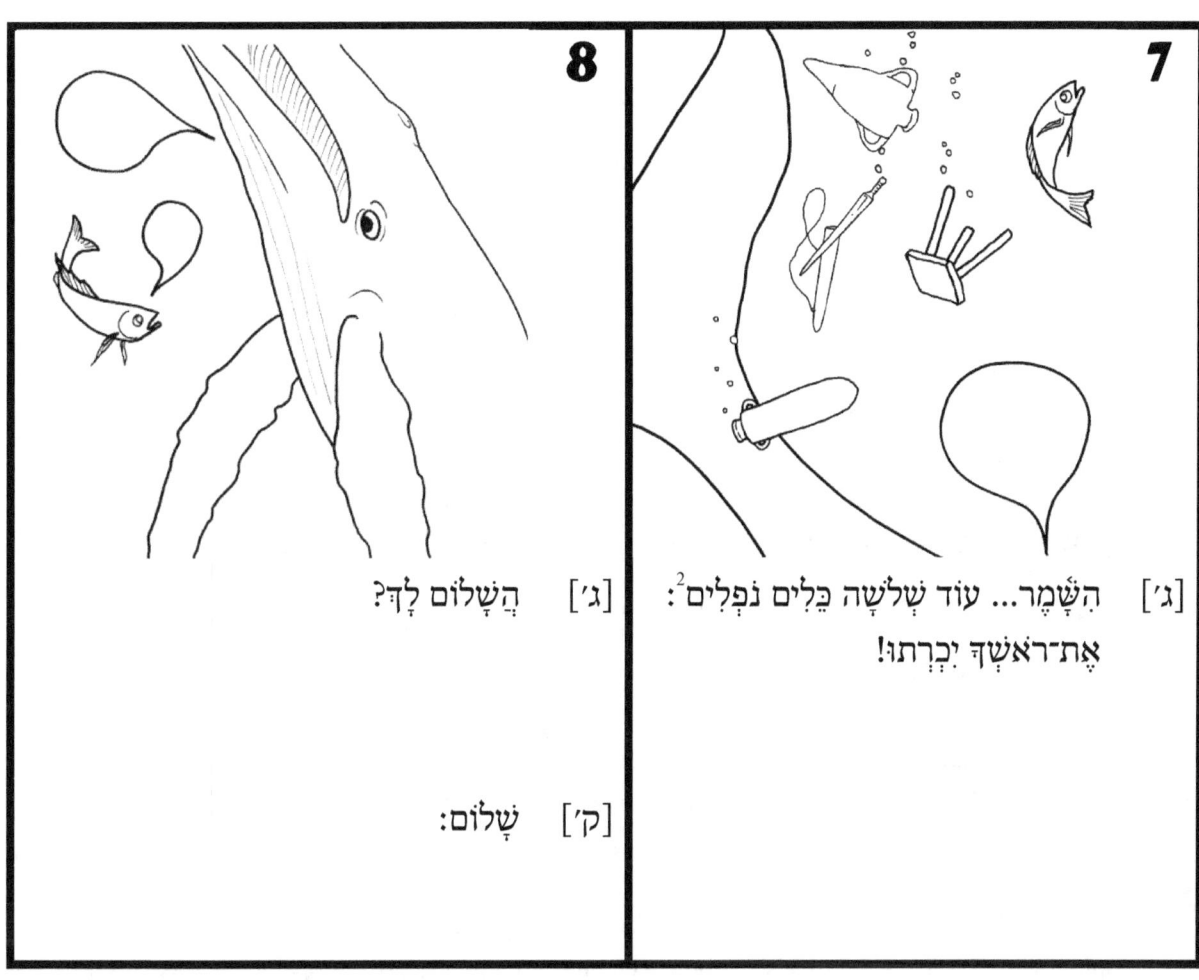

---

[2] In this phrase, נֹפְלִים may operate as an attributive participle (describing the noun) or as a predicative participle (forming a sentence with the noun as subject). Which seems more suitable to the context?

4.1.א. Explanation: "They (*m*) will guard the ship." אֶת־הָאֳנִיָּה יִשְׁמְרוּ׃

INTERACTIVE SKILL: Explaining what you expect a group may do in the future

One of the ways to describe future events in Hebrew may be seen in the term יִשְׁמְרוּ *they (m) will guard*. Perhaps you recognize the fundamental consonants ש.מ.ר in יִשְׁמְרוּ. The pattern seen in יִשְׁמְרוּ is known as the "יִקְטֹל conjugation"[3] for the verb ש.מ.ר.

The following table lists several more verbs that display "they (*m*) will…" forms (3rd masculine plural, abbreviated *3mpl*, similar to יִשְׁמְרוּ *they will guard*).

שֹׁרֶשׁ	יִקְטֹל 3mpl	they (*m*) will…	שֹׁרֶשׁ	יִקְטֹל 3mpl	they (*m*) will…
ש.כ.ב	יִשְׁכְּבוּ	they will lie down	כ.ר.ת	יִכְרְתוּ	they will cut
ש.מ.ע	יִשְׁמְעוּ	they will hear	מ.ל.כ	יִמְלְכוּ	they will rule
ש.מ.ר	יִשְׁמְרוּ	they will guard	מ.צ.א	יִמְצְאוּ	they will find

Did you notice the particulars that signal a **3rd masculine plural** יִקְטֹל form? They are: **a יִ... prefix** followed by **two adjacent shevas** ְ ְ and **ending with a וּ...**, as in יִכְרְתוּ. As you may recall, the first of two adjacent shevas is silent while the second is vocal.

Certain שֹׁרֶשׁ consonants ("radicals") produce changes in how the יִקְטֹל is spelled. Please review the appendix entry for this segment to become familiar with those changes.

Perhaps you are wondering where the pronoun "they" is located, within the form יִשְׁמְרוּ *they will guard*. The pronoun "they" is contained within that specific *3mpl* verb spelling. In fact, when no explicit subject is supplied, **we should supply the pronoun** "they" in our translation.

On the other hand, as soon as a specific subject appears, we must use that explicit subject **rather than supplying** a pronoun.

---

[3] The "יִקְטֹל conjugation" is also known as "long **prefix** conjugation" since it adds a syllable to the front of the verb (unlike the suffix / affix conjugation, to be introduced in Unit 6). Some describe the יִקְטֹל as the "imperfect" conjugation. Concerning יִקְטֹל as future tense, van der Merwe observes: "In most cases the [יִקְטֹל] verb is translated with a *future tense*," (Christo van der Merwe, et al., *A Biblical Hebrew Reference Grammar* [Sheffield: Sheffield Academic Press: 1999], §19.3.1, italics original). Regarding the יִקְטֹל with future meaning as rooted in a sense of contingency arising from other expressed or unexpressed situation, see *IBHS* §31.6.2b.

They (*m*) will guard. (*Supply the pronoun "they," since there is no explicit subject.*)		יִשְׁמְרוּ׃
The servants will guard. (*Do not supply the pronoun "they," since an explicit subject is provided.*)		יִשְׁמְרוּ הָעֲבָדִים׃

4.1.ב. Snapshot of sample verb: יִקְטֹל conjugation *3mpl*

Over time you will grow comfortable with יִקְטֹל forms for each person (1ˢᵗ, 2ⁿᵈ, 3ʳᵈ), for both genders (masculine, feminine), and both numbers (singular, plural). In case you are wondering how the "third masculine plural" (abbreviated *3mpl*) form relates to other יִקְטֹל forms, the following snapshot of the verb ש.מ.ר may be helpful. Non-targeted forms appear in a lighter shade to indicate that you do not need to focus on these at this time.

	Plural	Singular	
First person common plural (masc. and fem.) *1cpl*	נִשְׁמֹר we will guard	אֶשְׁמֹר I will guard	First person common singular (masc. and fem.) *1cs*
Second person masc. plural *2mpl*	תִּשְׁמְרוּ you will guard *mpl*	תִּשְׁמֹר you will guard *ms*	Second person masc. singular *2ms*
Second person fem. plural *2fpl*	תִּשְׁמֹרְנָה you will guard *fpl*	תִּשְׁמְרִי you will guard *fs*	Second person fem. singular *2fs*
Third person masc. plural *3mpl*	יִשְׁמְרוּ they will guard *m*	יִשְׁמֹר he will guard	Third person masc. singular *3ms*
Third person fem. plural *3fpl*	תִּשְׁמֹרְנָה they will guard *f*	תִּשְׁמֹר she will guard	Third person fem. singular *3fs*

4.1.ג. Activity: "What will they (*m*) do?"   מַה־יַּעֲשׂוּ?

INTERACTIVE SKILL: Forecasting how a group will behave

Several "scenarios" are offered below. Without disclosing your selection to your neighbor, **pick one** of these scenarios.

Next, **select a verb** from the table in §4.1.א. (or from verbs found in the appendix for §4.1.א.). It should be a verb that is **suited to the scenario** you have picked out. The verb should depict what your friends or family will typically do in that scenario ("they will…"). To generate more interest, expand your statement to include **additional elements** (such as an object or prepositional phrase).

Word-order (syntax). A יִקְטֹל verb will generally occupy **second position**. It should not stand first in the sentence. Begin with the subject instead. If you wish to draw attention to the object or prepositional phrase, begin with that element, followed by the verb and then the subject.[4] For this particular

---

[4] When a יִקְטֹל form appears first in a prose sentence, it generally signifies a wish (known as a jussive form; cf. §9.4.א.).

conversation, you likely will not need an explicit subject, since "members of my family" is the implied subject (*3mpl*).

Begin the conversation by letting your neighbor pose to you the inquiry found in the model below. After you have responded, see whether your neighbor can guess which scenario you had in mind.

Scenarios

✓ On the beach	✓ With a loaf of bread	✓ In a tree
✓ At work	✓ With a baby	✓ Late at night
✓ When feeling mischievous	✓ In the mountains	✓ During a storm

Model

What will they [*m*, members of your family] do?	מַה־יַּעֲשׂוּ?	Neighbor's inquiry
They (*m*) will lie down on the earth.	עַל הָאָרֶץ יִשְׁכְּבוּ׃	Your reply
(*Use native language to guess scenario.*)	✓ On the beach *or* ✓ Late at night	Neighbor's guess

4.1.ד. Do you (*ms*) know the meaning...? (יָד)　הֲיָדַעְתָּ פֵּשֶׁר...?

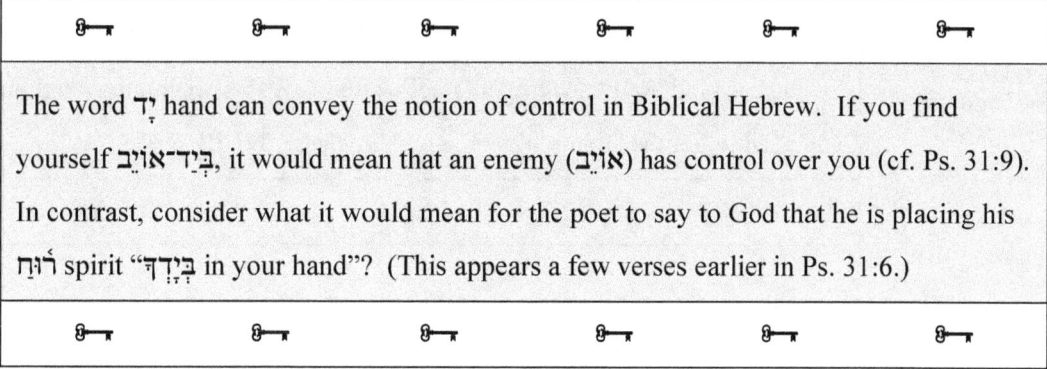

The word יָד hand can convey the notion of control in Biblical Hebrew. If you find yourself בְּיַד־אוֹיֵב, it would mean that an enemy (אוֹיֵב) has control over you (cf. Ps. 31:9). In contrast, consider what it would mean for the poet to say to God that he is placing his רוּחַ spirit "בְּיָדְךָ in your hand"? (This appears a few verses earlier in Ps. 31:6.)

4.1.ה. May I offer you (*ms*) advice? (Clarification)   הַאִיעָצְךָ עֵצָה?

✻ ✻ ✻ ✻ ✻ ✻

The question הֶחָפֵץ אַתָּה לֵאמֹר...? provides a simple way to obtain clarification—right in the middle of class! If addressing a woman, you would ask: הֶחֲפֵצָה אַתְּ לֵאמֹר...?.

Alternatively, you could obtain clarification in this way: הַאַתָּה אֹמֵר...? *Are you saying*...? (or in the feminine: הַאַתְּ אֹמֶרֶת...?).

✻ ✻ ✻ ✻ ✻ ✻

4.1.ו. May I offer you (*ms*) advice? (Attention)   הַאִיעָצְךָ עֵצָה?

✻ ✻ ✻ ✻ ✻ ✻

A call for attention opens one of the most famous verses in the entire Bible: שְׁמַע יִשְׂרָאֵל... *Hear, O Israel*... (Deut. 6:4, known as the Shema). The passage goes on to declare a fundamental principle of biblical theology: that the God of Israel is the sole deity, and that this God alone deserves one's complete devotion.

Just as God used שְׁמַע to get Israel's attention, so also you may call out "שְׁמַע" when you need to get the attention of someone in class. Try it!

✻ ✻ ✻ ✻ ✻ ✻

4.1.ז. Did you (*ms*) know that...? (Pottery) — הֲיָדַעְתָּ כִּי...?

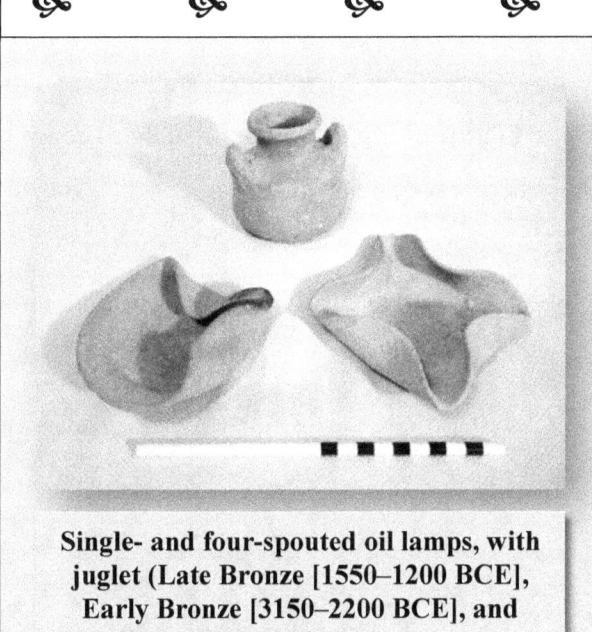

Single- and four-spouted oil lamps, with juglet (Late Bronze [1550–1200 BCE], Early Bronze [3150–2200 BCE], and Late Bronze, respectively). (Courtesy of Flora Archaeological Center)

...due to their durability, fragments of fire-hardened pottery discovered on a given habitation layer of an ancient town ("tell" or mound) often can help archaeologists infer the date of that level? Since the fast pottery wheel came into use in Middle Bronze IIB–C (1750-1550 BCE), vessels displaying fast-turned effects could not date before that era (unless intrusively deposited). Fast-turned effects include the absence of ledge-handles, and less frequent occurrence of flat bottoms.

Similarly, bichrome ware (featuring red-and-black geometric and / or zoomorphic decoration) of a Philistine provenance indicates a date after 1000 BCE, since prior to that point Philistine ware employed only black patterned decoration ("monochrome ware" of Iron Age IB, 1150–1000 BCE).

Pottery production comprised a major industry in certain

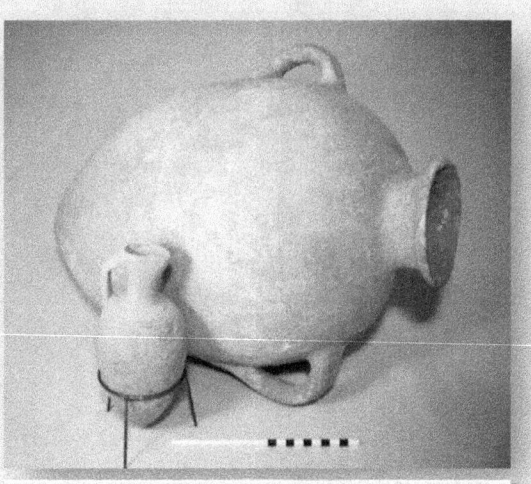

"Canaanite jar" and slender dipping pitcher (Middle Bronze IIA–B [1950–1600 BCE]). (Courtesy of Flora Archaeological Center)

locales. In Zarephath (Phoenician port between Tyre and Sidon), for example, pottery workshops have been uncovered in the "Industrial Quarter" (a sector also evidencing olive-pressing, metalworking, and dying industries). At Megiddo an extensive pottery workshop dating to the Late Bronze and Iron Age (1550-587 BCE) has come to light on the eastern slope of the city—complete with cool-temperature caves (allowing slower drying times). Twenty-two kilns with usage spanning from Late Bronze II to the Persian Era (1400-330 BCE) indicate a large-scale production of pottery wares such as shipping amphorae.

A ubiquitous style of shipping amphora that likely originated in Canaan is the so-called "Canaanite Jar." Ovoid, two-handled, with collar and tapered base, often featuring a 30-liter capacity, vessels of this style were in use by 1900 BCE and continued in use—with minor modifications—into the Islamic era.[5] The related torpedo-profile amphora is an early descendant of the Canaanite Jar (see §4.1.ח.).

In addition to vessels fashioned on wheels, other products produced by the potter included terracotta anthropomorphic and zoomorphic figurines (see §11.2.ז.),

Pavement brick with imprint of the Legio X Fretensis (Tenth Roman Legion Fretensis, 1st cent. CE; 18 cm square, 3 cm thick). (Courtesy of Flora Archaeological Collection)

---

[5] P.E. McGovern and G. Harbottle, "'Hyksos' Trade Connections between Tell el-Dabʿa (Avaris) and the Levant: A Neutron Activation Study of the Canaanite Jar," in *The Hyksos: New Historical and Archaeological Perspectives* (ed. E.D. Oren; Philadelphia: University Museum, 1997), 143.

> loom weights (see §7.5.ה.), tiles, and bricks.[6] Terms that can designate ceramic goods include: נֵר *lamp m*, סִיר *cooking pot m*, חֶרֶשׂ *earthenware* or *potsherd m*, and כְּלִי *container m*.

4.1.ח. Did you (*ms*) know that...? (Amphora and sea transport)

> ...ceramic jars were the preferred containers for maritime transport? In particular, the amphora served as a common shipping container, especially for דָּגָן *grain* or *corn m* and liquids, whether שֶׁמֶן *m* from the olive groves or יַיִן *m* from nearby vineyards.
>
> During the summer of 1999 an offshore survey team led by Robert Ballard and Lawrence Stager explored a Phoenician vessel dating to the eighth century BCE, lying at a depth of 400 meters, some fifty kilometers west of Ashkelon, Israel. Nicknamed *Tanit* by archaeologists (after a Phoenician deity for seafarers), the vessel carried a cargo of 385 wine amphorae, with an estimated aggregate volume of eleven tons.
>
> Small handles shaped like an אֹזֶן *ear m* at the shoulder of an amphora, while unsuitable for lifting so large a volume, were discovered to be ideally suited for stabilizing the container with the help of a guide made of חֶבֶל *rope m*, deep in the cargo hold of הָאֳנִיָּה. A crew of חֹבְלִים *sailors m* would plant the amphora's rounded base upright in a bed of sand or ballast of אֲבָנִים. The vertical taper of the container was well suited to stowage, as it corresponded to the slope of a ship's hull.

---

[6] *LBI*, 134–35 and 138–39. The pavement tile pictured above may have been produced at the Tenth Roman Legion's ceramics workshop located two km west of the Old City of Jerusalem, excavated in 1992. For more information, see Hillel Geva, "Jerusalem-*Binyane Ha'uma* Ceramics Workshop," n.p. [cited 9 November 2013]. Online: http://www.jewishvirtuallibrary.org/jsource/Archaeology/jeruceram.html#1.

The amphorae onboard the *Tanit* were remarkably uniform in size and profile (averaging 69 cm long with a 17.8 liter-capacity)—evidence of a sophisticated production process. To prevent seepage, the containers had been lined with pine pitch. Perhaps this

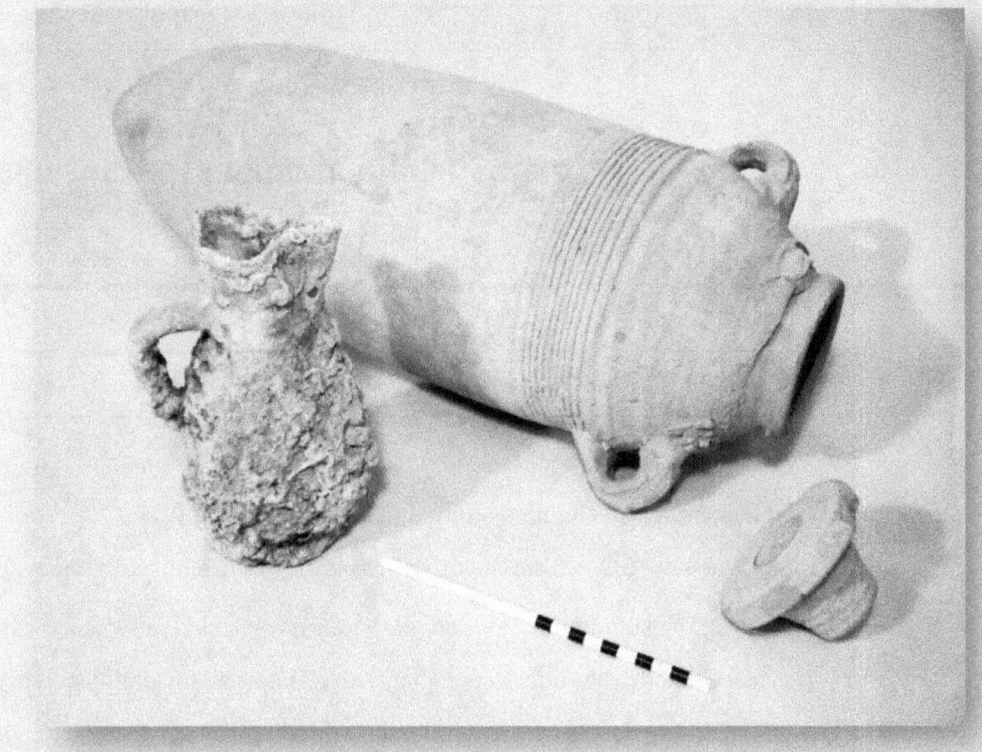

Torpedo-profile amphora with stopper and marine-encrusted pitcher (Hellenistic, 332–53 BCE]). (Courtesy of Flora Archaeological Center)

particular shipment from Palestine was bound for enjoyment along the Nile in מִצְרַיִם, or in the Phoenician colony of Carthage.⁷ Incidentally, the term נֵבֶל *jar m* could designate both ceramic storage containers and also skin-bottles.

---

⁷ P.J. King and L.E. Stager, *Life in Biblical Israel* (Louisville, Kentucky: John Knox, 2001), 179, and R.D. Ballard and L.E. Stager, "Iron Age Shipwrecks in Deep Water off Ashkelon, Israel," http://web.mit.edu/deeparch/www/publications/papers/BallardEtAl2002.pdf, accessed April 19, 2013.

UNIT 4   מַה־יַּעֲשׂוּ מָחָר?

MODULE 4.2   Describing what an object is for

Words for responding — מִלִּים לַעֲנוֹת

לַחֲרוֹת [ח.ר.י/ה]	to be hot	אֹזֶן, אָזְנַיִם[a]	ear f, dual
עַיִן, עֵינַיִם	eye, water-spring f, dual	אִם (אִם־ usually)	if
עֵינָיו	his eyes dual	אֶשְׁאֲלָה לְךָ: [ש.א.ל]	I would [like to][b] ask you a question ms and fs
פֶּה	mouth m		
רֶגֶל, רַגְלַיִם, רֶגֶל־, רַגְלֵי־	foot f, dual	בֵּין	between, among
		דָּבָר, דְּבָרִים, דְּבַר־, דִּבְרֵי־	word, matter, event, thing m

[a] The first syllable of both אֹזֶן and אָזְנַיִם produces an *o* sound. In אָזְנַיִם the first syllable is closed (the sheva is silent) and unaccented, so that the qameṣ is a qameṣ-ḥaṭuf.

[b] The capacity of a יִקְטֹל verb to connote a **desire to do** something will be explained in §5.4.א. (e.g., אִם־אַתָּה תִּקַּח־לְךָ... *If you want to take it*..., 1 Sam. 21:10). The object "a question" is implied by the verb in the statement אֶשְׁאֲלָה לְךָ: (given the context of an inquiry).

Words for hearing — מִלִּים לִשְׁמֹעַ

כּוֹס, כֹּסוֹת, כּוֹס־, כֹּסוֹת־	cup* f	אַף	nose, anger m
		הַר, הָרִים, הַר־, הָרֵי־	mountain m
עֵץ, עֵצִים	tree, wood m		
רְאֵה, רְאִי [ר.א.י/ה]	Look! imv ms, fs	יֶחֱרֶה [ח.ר.י/ה]	he / it will be hot

4.2 Jonah Episode: Look! Man overboard!

ק׳ = הַדָּג הַקָּטֹן, ג׳ = הַדָּג הַגָּדוֹל

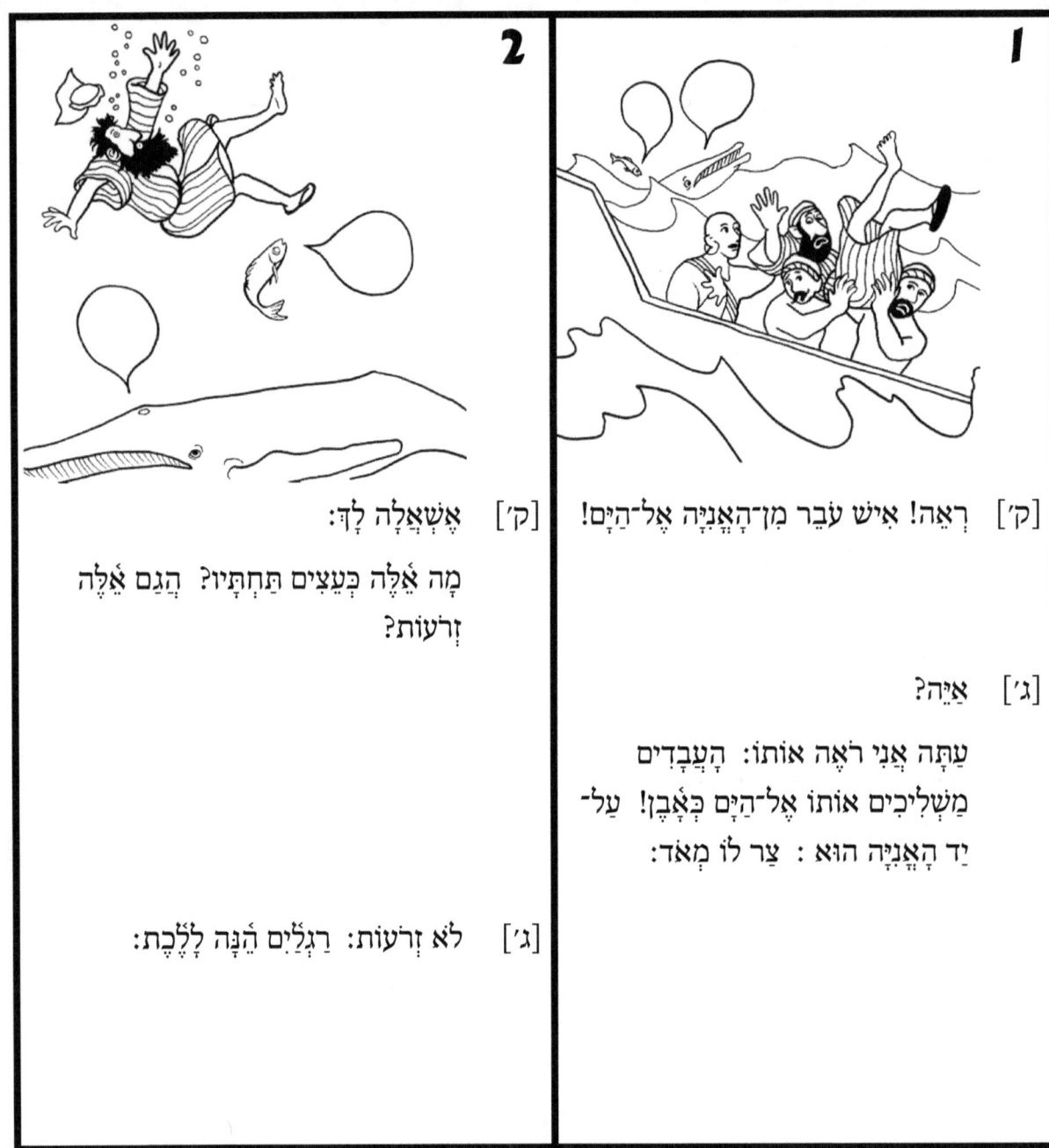

[ק׳]   רְאֵה! אִישׁ עָבַר מִן־הָאֳנִיָּה אֶל־הַיָּם!

[ג׳]   אַיֵּה?

עַתָּה אֲנִי רֹאֶה אוֹתוֹ: הָעֲבָדִים מַשְׁלִיכִים אוֹתוֹ אֶל־הַיָּם כְּאָבֶן! עַל־יַד הָאֳנִיָּה הוּא : צַר לוֹ מְאֹד:

[ק׳]   אֶשְׁאֲלָה לָךְ:

מָה אֵלֶּה כְּעֵצִים תַּחְתָּיו? הֲגַם אֵלֶּה זְרֹעוֹת?

[ג׳]   לֹא זְרֹעוֹת: רַגְלַיִם הֵנָּה לָלֶכֶת:

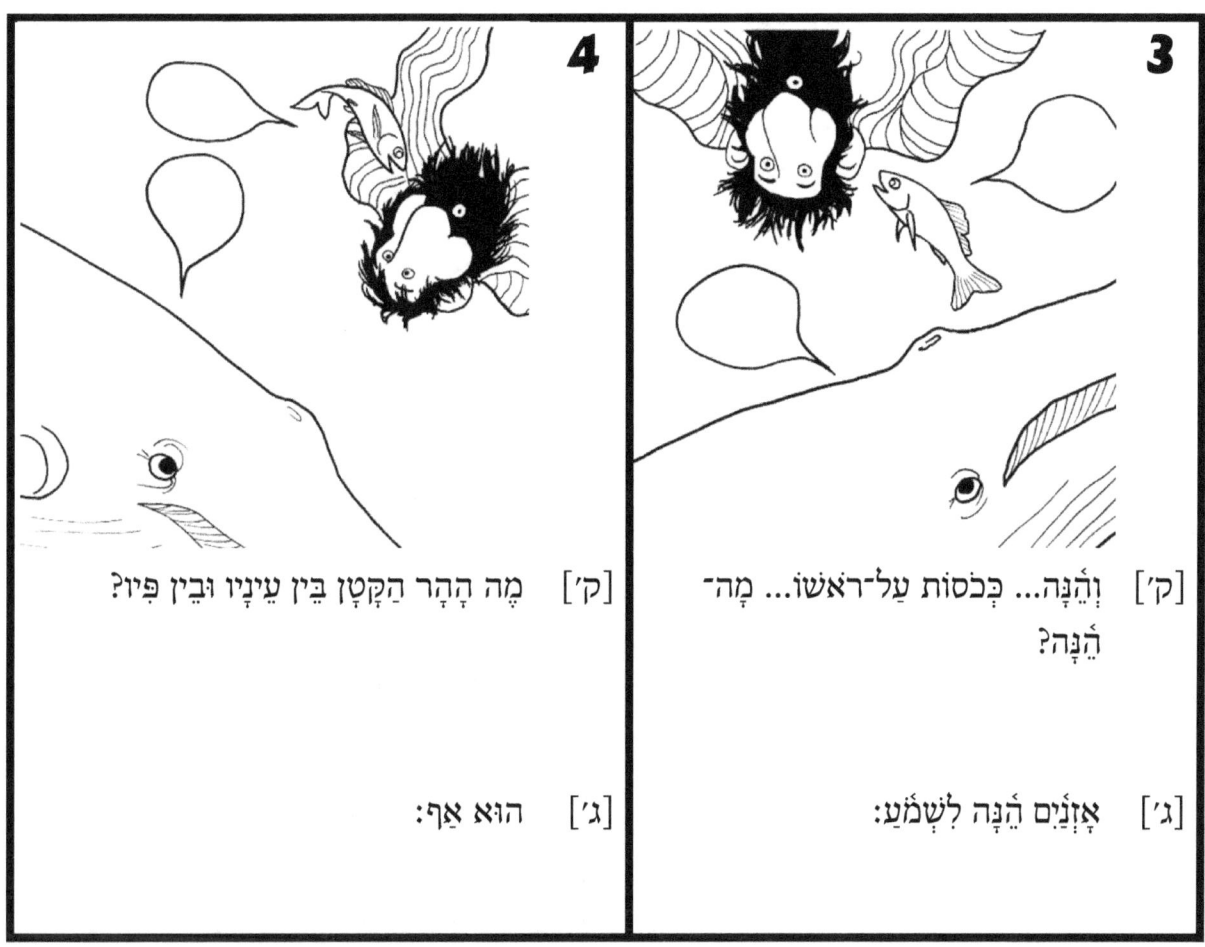

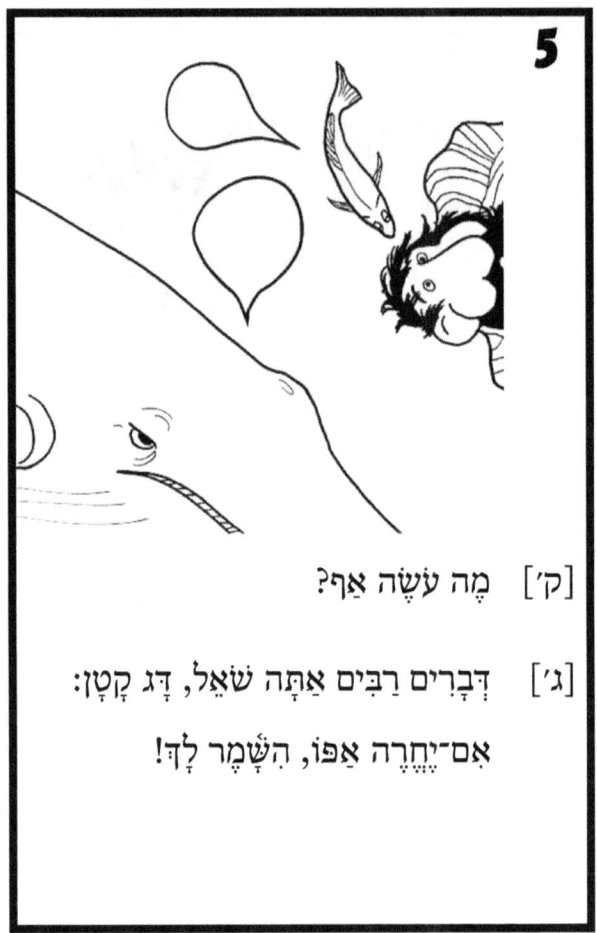

4.2.א. Do you (ms) know the meaning…? (אַף)   הֲיָדַעְתָּ פֵּשֶׁר…?

🔑	🔑	🔑	🔑	🔑	🔑	🔑
The expression יֶחֱרֶה אַפּוֹ *his nose is getting hot* should more idiomatically be expressed "*he is angry.*" The noun אַף *nose* arises from the verb א.נ.פ *to be angry, to snort*.[8] Does your native language associate physical descriptions with particular emotions?						
🔑	🔑	🔑	🔑	🔑	🔑	🔑

---

[8] Incidentally, by comparing the root form א.נ.פ we can better understand why the dagesh ḥazaq (strong dagesh) appears in the פ of the suffixed form אַפּוֹ. The noun אַף conceals a root letter נ that, due to its weakness disappears when there is no suffix, but reappears in the form of a dagesh when a suffix is added (אַפּוֹ).

4.2.ב. Activity (matching): "What does a human do with these?"

מֶה עָשָׂה אָדָם בְּאֵלֶה?[9]

INTERACTIVE SKILL: Explaining how something is used

Have you ever read science fiction? Imagine an extra-terrestrial guest making initial contact with a member of our species. Using flawless Biblical Hebrew, it points to various human appendages and asks: מֶה עָשָׂה אָדָם בְּאֵלֶה?

In the column labeled "עֶצֶם (Noun)" you will find the various appendages that the visitor asked about (numbered 1-7).[10] The column labeled "פֹּעַל (Verb)" offers a collection of actions that you may use when explaining how a particular appendage is used.[11]

The column labeled מֶה עָשָׂה בְּ...? has been left blank. Write the Hebrew alpha-numeral and verb suitable to each appendage. You need only give one action for each appendage. Not all actions will be used. Answers will vary depending on one's imagination.

---

[9] אָדָם *human, Adam.*

[10] עֶצֶם in Biblical Hebrew means *bone, substance, self* (*f*), and has been adopted by grammarians to refer to "noun."

[11] פֹּעַל in Biblical Hebrew means *action* or *deed* (*m*). Grammarians have adopted it to refer to "verb."

פֹּעַל (Verb)		מֶה עָשָׂה בְּ...?	עֶצֶם (Noun)	
לְאַהֲבָה[12]	א.	ח. לִשְׁמֹעַ	אֹזֶן	1.
לֶאֱכֹל	ב.		אַף	2.
לְדַבֵּר	ג.		זֶרַע	3.
לַחֲרוֹת	ד.		עַיִן	4.
לָלֶכֶת	ה.		פֶּה	5.
לַעֲמֹד	ו.		רֹאשׁ	6.
לִרְאוֹת	ז.		רֶגֶל	7.
לִשְׁמֹעַ	ח.			
לִשְׁמֹר	ט.			
לִשְׁתֹּת	י.			
לָתֵת	יא.			

---

[12] In purposes clauses with א.ה.ב, Biblical Hebrew prefers לְאַהֲבָה (preposition plus alternate infinitive or feminine noun for *love*). Less often we encounter purpose clauses with the infinitive לֶאֱהֹב.

4.2.ג. May I offer you (*ms*) advice? (Posing a question) הַאִיעָצְךָ עֵצָה?

> ✼ ✼ ✼ ✼ ✼ ✼
>
> Whether to satisfy curiosity or to get clarification, from time to time everyone needs to ask for more information. Here is the way to indicate in Hebrew that you wish to pose an **informational question** (as opposed to making a request):
>
> - ◆ אֶשְׁאֲלָה לָךְ: *I wish to ask you* [*a question*] (cf. Judg. 8:24).
>
> Conveniently, the pausal form לָךְ will address **either a man or a woman** (*2m/fs*). In case you are posing a question to an entire **group**, use: אֶשְׁאֲלָה לָכֶם: Later on you will learn more precisely how the form אֶשְׁאֲלָה is related to ש.א.ל. *to ask* (cohortatives will be explained in §9.4.ג. and §9.4.ו.).
>
> If you wish to present your question in a **more direct** manner, you may announce it as did King Zedekiah when he confronted his prisoner-prophet Jeremiah. The construction used by Zedekiah dispenses with any tentativeness connoted by אֶשְׁאֲלָה *I wish to ask*. Instead he announces with a rather confrontational tone exactly what is the situation:
>
> - ◆ ...שֹׁאֵל אֲנִי אֹתְךָ דָּבָר *I am asking you a question*[13] (cf. Jer. 38:14a, notice participle שֹׁאֵל and pronominal subject אֲנִי).
>
> Placing the participle first (as Zedekiah does) brings focus to the activity at hand, namely, "asking." Or, given the power-differential between monarch and prisoner, perhaps שֹׁאֵל rather involved "interrogating." The focus on obtaining information grows

---

[13] דָּבָר means *word* or *matter*. As it refers here to "what is being asked," in this context דָּבָר should be translated *question*.

even more intense as the king warns: "Don't hide anything from me!" (v. 14b).

If, on the other hand, you wish to **acknowledge a question** raised by someone else, there are three options.

- מַה־לָּךְ: *What is it?* or *What is your concern?* or *What is the matter?* This response is nonspecific, suitable whether the questioner seeks information or comes with a request that some commodity would be bestowed.[14]
- הֲתִשְׁאָל / הֲתִשְׁאֲלִי אֹתִי דָּבָר: *Would you (like to) ask me something?*[15]
- וְלָמָה אַתָּה שֹׁאֵל / וְלָמָה אַתְּ שֹׁאָלֶת: *And why do you ask?* This response seeks clarification for a question that has already entered the dialogic exchange.[16]

The noun best representing "question" in the sense of "inquiry" is דָּבָר (commonly rendered *word*, *thing*, or *event*).[17] The noun שְׁאֵלָה *f*, while pertaining to the field of "inquiry," is limited to inquiries that present a petition.[18] שְׁאֵלָה does not encompass inquiries that seek only information.

---

[14] Caleb responded to his daughter in this way (Josh. 15:18), as did the Persian king to Esther (Esth. 5:3; cf. Gen. 21:17 and Judg. 18:24).

[15] Cf. הֲשְׁאַלְתִּי in 2 Kings 4:28.

[16] See Solomon's use of וְלָמָה in conversation with his mother (1 Kings 2:22).

[17] For examples of דָּבָר as encompassing the notion of "question" or "topic of inquiry," see Gen. 43:7, 1 Sam. 17:29, and 1 Kings 10:3.

[18] Cf. Esth. 7:2, where it is parallel to בַּקָּשָׁה *entreaty f*.

4.2.ד. Explanation and activity: "What is between his eyes and his mouth?" מַה־הִיא בֵּין עֵינָיו וּבֵין פִּיו?

INTERACTIVE SKILL: How to describe where an object may be found, in relation to two flanking objects

The Hebrew way to describe that an object is located between two other objects involves repeating the word בֵּין *between* twice: "ב is between א *and between* ג."

For example, imagine a skipper spying a large object jutting up from the waves, lying between his vessel and a rocky shore. In order to determine whether he needs to steer around this unknown object, he calls out to a mate perched in the crow's-nest (yes, crow's-nests have been attested in ancient vessels):

What is that, between the ship and [between] the rocks?	מַה־הִיא[19] **בֵּין הָאֳנִיָּה וּבֵין הָאֲבָנִים**?	Skipper's inquiry
It is a big container.	כְּלִי גָּדוֹל הוּא:	Reply

As the sailors scurry to avoid striking the piece of floating freight, a passenger is puzzled by the commotion. He has not yet caught sight of the obstacle. So he asks:

Where is the big container?	אַיֵּה הַכְּלִי הַגָּדוֹל?	Passenger's inquiry
The big container is between the ship and [between] the rocks.	הַכְּלִי הַגָּדוֹל **בֵּין הָאֳנִיָּה וּבֵין הָאֲבָנִים**:	Reply

When expressed only once, בֵּין simply means *among*.

| If (כִּי) there should be a dispute (רִיב) **among** (some) people... (Deut. 25:1) | כִּי־יִהְיֶה רִיב בֵּין אֲנָשִׁים... | |

---

[19] When referring to an unknown object, Hebrew tends to use the feminine (cf. מַה־הִיא, Zech. 5:6). In the reply the gender of the object is known, so the pronoun must conform to that gender (כְּלִי גָּדוֹל הוּא).

Can you deduce the answers to these questions? You may use the glossary if needed.

א. מַה־בֵּין "ס" וּבֵין "פ"?

ב. מִי בֵּין אַבְרָהָם וּבֵין יַעֲקֹב?

ג. מַה־בֵּין שְׁתַּיִם וּבֵין אַרְבַּע?

4.2.ה. Do you (*ms*) know the meaning...? (נֶפֶשׁ)   הֲיָדַעְתָּ פֵּשֶׁר...?

The word נֶפֶשׁ *soul, person f* has an underlying meaning of *throat*, and by extension *life* and *appetite*. When crying out for help, the psalmist declares that floodwaters have reached עַד־נָפֶשׁ (Ps. 69:2 [ET v. 1]; נָפֶשׁ is pausal). To translate נֶפֶשׁ as *soul* in Psalm 69 would miss the point, for the context calls for *throat*. Jonah registered his mortal peril in a similar manner: מַיִם עַד־נֶפֶשׁ (Jonah 2:6).

An awareness of connotations indigenous to נֶפֶשׁ will help us both to enrich our reading of Hebrew and also to guard against the tendency to import non-Hebrew notions associated with *soul* (such as Greek *psyche*) when reading the Hebrew Bible.

4.2.ו. Did you (*ms*) know that...? (Units of measure)   הֲיָדַעְתָּ כִּי...?

...several terms relating to parts of the human body served as units of linear measurement? The אַמָּה *cubit f*, for example, corresponded to the distance from the elbow to the tip of the middle finger (44.4 cm in the short-cubit system). The זֶרֶת *span f*, measured between the farthest fingertips (22.2 cm, or half-cubit). The distance across the base of the fingers comprised the טֶפַח *handbreadth m* (7.4 cm). A single fingerbreadth (אֶצְבַּע *finger f*, 1.85 cm) offered the smallest linear measurement.

One of the larger volumetric units, in contrast, came from the realm of pack animals. The חֹמֶר *homer* (ḥōmer) *m* amounted to 150 dry liters, and stemmed from the carrying-capacity of the typical pack animal—חֲמוֹר *donkey m*.[20] A seventh century Assyrian relief from the North Palace of Nineveh indicates that horses also served as pack animals—at least during hunting expeditions for members of the royal court.

Pack animals on a royal Assyrian hunt (Nineveh, North Palace, 645–635 BCE). (Courtesy of British Museum)

---

[20] *LBI*, 200. See §2.4.ה. for more information concerning weights and measures.

MODULE 4.3   Describing what a man will do

Words for responding   מִלִּים לַעֲנוֹת

יֵשֵׁב [י.ש.ב]	he / it will sit / dwell*	בַּיִת, בָּתִּים[a], בֵּית־, בָּתֵּי־	house *m*
יִשְׁכַּב [ש.כ.ב]	he / it will lie down*	חַיִּים[b]	life *mpl*
פֹּתֵחַ, פֹּתַחַת, פֹּתְחִים, פֹּתְחוֹת [פ.ת.ח]	one who opens *pt*	יָבוֹא [ב.ו.א]	he / it will come, enter, go*
		יִחְיֶה [ח.י.ה]	he / it will live
		יָמוּת [מ.ו.ת]	he / it will die
רָשָׁע, רְשָׁעָה, רְשָׁעִים, רְשָׁעוֹת	evil, wicked	יֵרֵד [י.ר.ד]	he / it will descend*

[a] Although the qameṣ of בָּתִּים occurs in a closed, unaccented syllable, it is not pronounced *o*. This is an exception.

[b] With words such as חַי *life, singular,* Hebrew often employs the plural form (חַיִּים) to convey a singular meaning (*life*, not *lives*). Thus, despite its plural ending, תַּחֲנוּנִים means *supplication* (not *supplications*); similarly עֲשׁוּקִים means *oppression* (not *oppressions*). This feature is known as the plural abstract. A lexicon will inform you when a plural should be treated with a singular meaning.

Words for hearing   מִלִּים לִשְׁמֹעַ

בֹּכֶה, בֹּכָה[b], בֹּכִים, בֹּכוֹת [ב.כ.י/ה]	one who cries *pt*	אֶהְיֶה [ה.י.ה]	I will be
		אַל־[a]	Don't...!
לִבְלֹעַ [ב.ל.ע]	to swallow	אַל־תֵּבְךְּ, אַל־תִּבְכִּי [ב.כ.י/ה]	Don't cry! *ms, fs*
לְעוֹלָם	forever		
מָחָר	tomorrow, next day, in the future *noun m*, also adverb	אַל־תִּירָא, אַל־תִּירְאִי [י.ר.א]	Don't be afraid! *ms, fs*
		בֶּטֶן	belly, stomach *f*

עַל־כֵּן	on this account, therefore	מֵת, מֵתִים מֵתָה, מֵתוֹת [מ.ו.ת]	one who is dying *pt*
קֶבֶר	grave *m*	סוּר, סוּרִי [ס.ו.ר]	Turn!* *imv m, f*
רַק [c]	only	עָזְרֵנִי	Help me! *imv ms* (*note qameṣ-ḥaṭuf*)
שְׁלֹשֶׁת יָמִים	three days *mpl*		
תְּהוֹם	watery depths *f*		

[a] The negation אַל will always directly precede its verb, forming a negative command. It will negate only a יִקְטֹל verb (more precisely, a command form known as "jussive" [cf. §§9.4.א-ב.], that often is indistinguishable from a יִקְטֹל form).

[b] The *pt fs* occurs only once, spelled בּוֹכִיָּה (poetry); most likely it was spelled בֹּכָה in common usage.

[c] After לֹא, רַק may be rendered *except*.

4.3 Jonah Episode: Will he lie in the depths?

ק׳ = הַדָּג הַקָּטֹן, ג׳ = הַדָּג הַגָּדוֹל

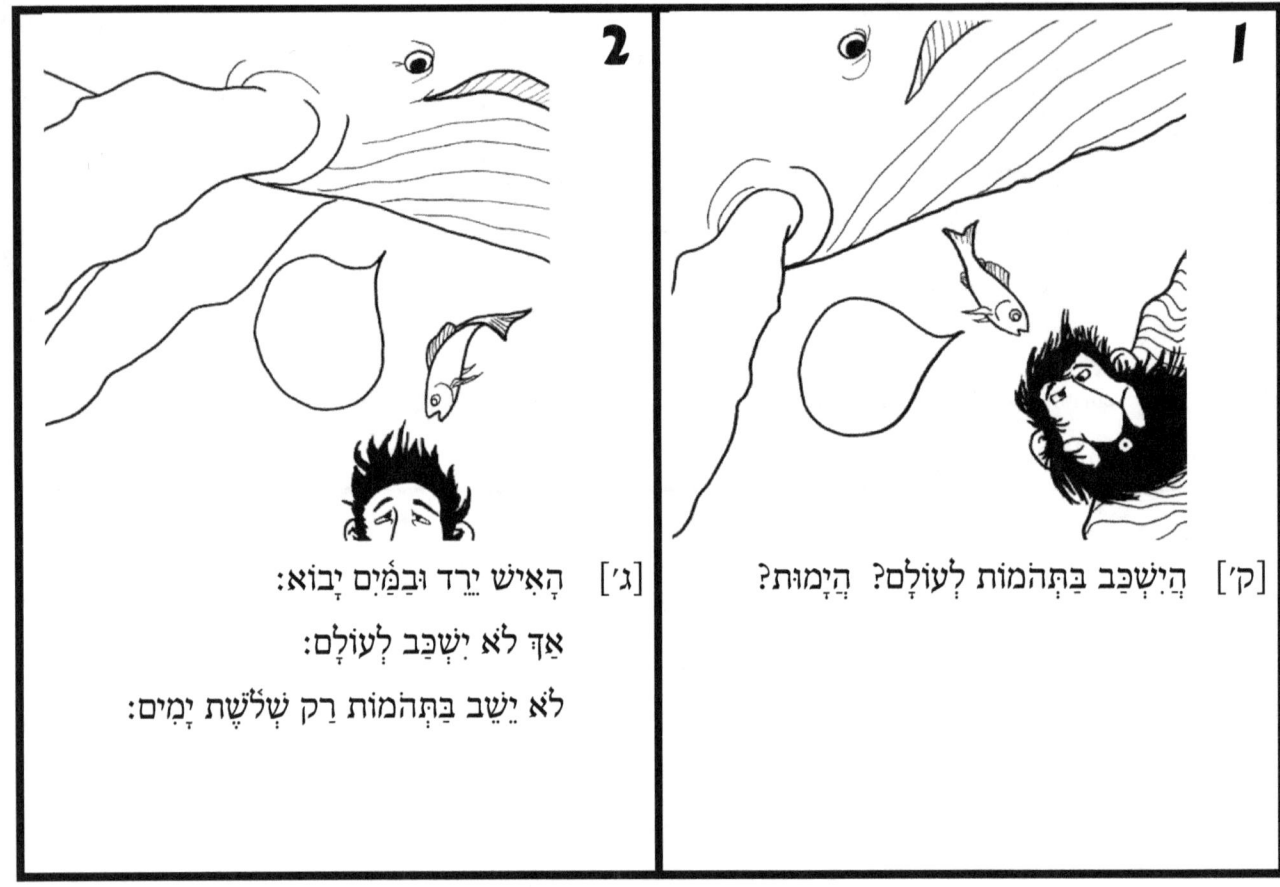

[ק׳] הֲיִשְׁכַּב בַּתְּהֹמוֹת לְעוֹלָם? הֲיָמוּת?

[ג׳] הָאִישׁ יָרַד וּבַמַּיִם יָבוֹא:
אַךְ לֹא יִשְׁכַּב לְעוֹלָם:
לֹא יֵשֵׁב בַּתְּהֹמוֹת רַק שְׁלֹשֶׁת יָמִים:

4

[ק׳] הֲלִבְלֹעַ אוֹתוֹ אַתָּה הֹלֵךְ... כִּשְׁאוֹל... חַיִּים??
אַתָּה דָּג רָשָׁע!
עֲזֹב סוּר מִמֶּנִּי[21]!
וַאֲנִי צַר לִי: אֲנִי בֹכֶה כִּי יָמוּת הָאָדָם:

3

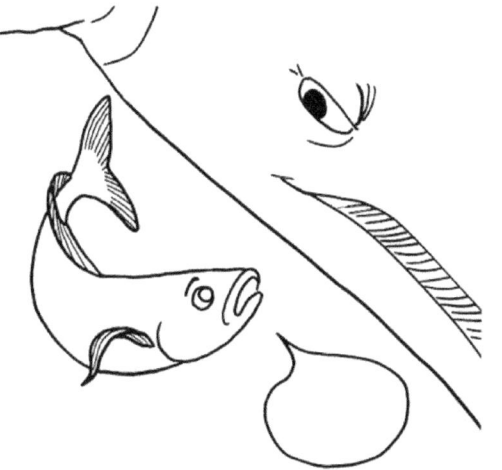

[ק׳] "הוּא יָרַד וּבַמַּיִם יָבוֹא..."
"לֹא לְעוֹלָם יִשְׁכַּב:"
אֵיךְ יֵשֵׁב וְלֹא יָמוּת?
לֹא אָבִין: עָזְרֵנִי:

[ג׳] כִּי אֲנִי הֹלֵךְ לִבְלֹעַ אוֹתוֹ:

---

[21] מִמֶּנִּי is comprised of מִן and אֲנִי.

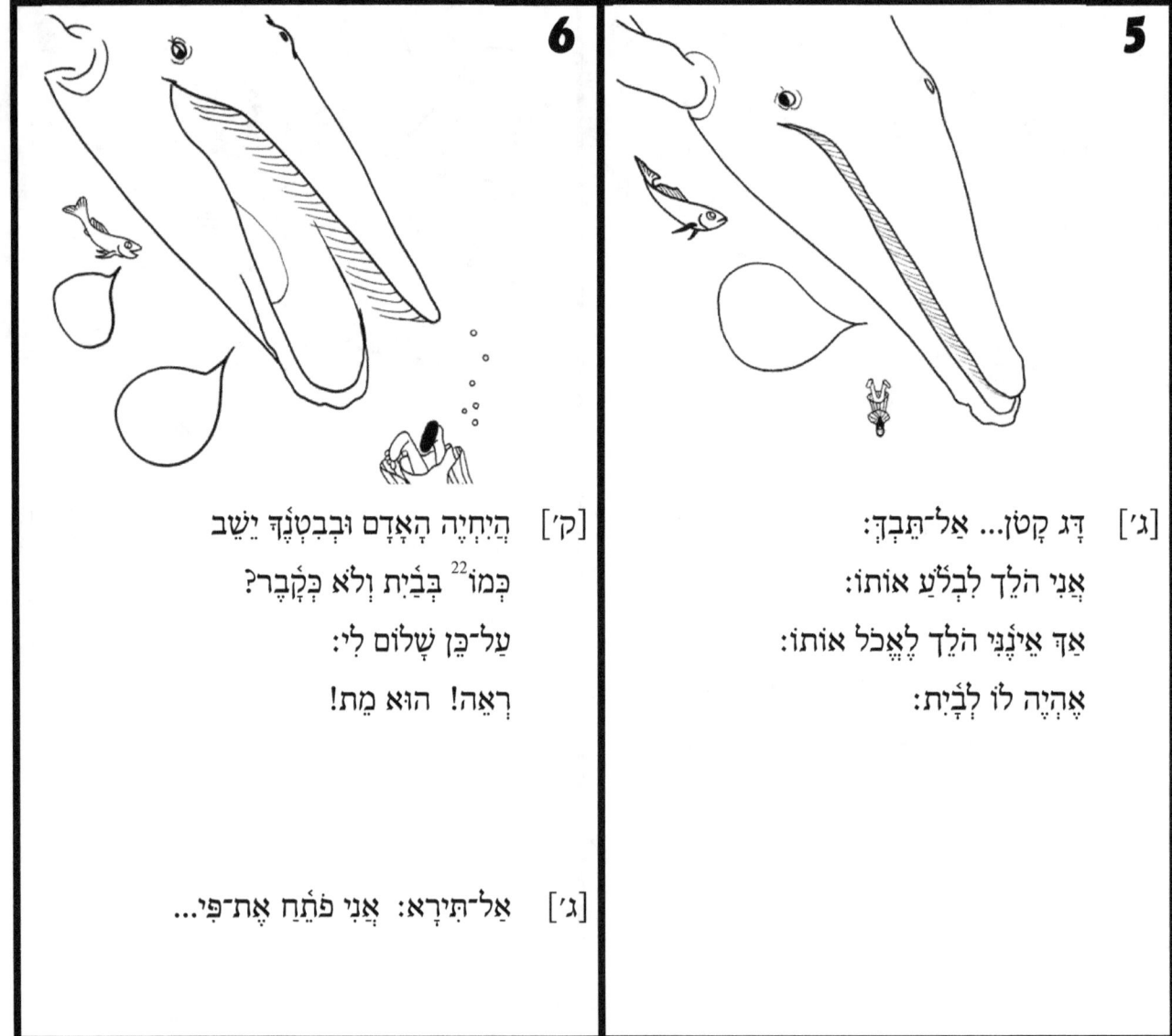

[ג׳] דָּג קָטֹן... אַל־תֵּבְךְּ:
אֲנִי הֹלֵךְ לִבְלֹעַ אוֹתוֹ:
אַךְ אֵינֶנִּי הֹלֵךְ לֶאֱכֹל אוֹתוֹ:
אֶהְיֶה לוֹ לְבָיִת:

[ק׳] הֲיִחְיֶה הָאָדָם וּבְבִטְנְךָ יֵשֵׁב
כְּמוֹ²² בְּבַיִת וְלֹא כְּקֶבֶר?
עַל־כֵּן שָׁלוֹם לִי:
רְאֵה! הוּא מֵת!

[ג׳] אַל־תִּירָא: אֲנִי פֹּתֵחַ אֶת־פִּי...

---

²² כְּמוֹ is the form used for the preposition כְּ when operating as an independent word.

4.3.א. Explanation: "He won't lie down forever." לֹא לְעוֹלָם יִשְׁכַּב:

INTERACTIVE SKILL: Describing how an individual will (or will not) act

In the table below, you will find a handful of verbs letting you describe what an individual will (or will not) do, as in לֹא יִשְׁכַּב *he won't lie down*, *3ms* (third masculine singular). These forms **begin with a יְ... prefix**, just as the *3mpl* forms did in Module 4.1 (יִשְׁכְּבוּ *3mpl*, יִשְׁכַּב *3ms*).

In contrast to *3mpl* forms, a *3ms* form will **omit the ו... suffix**. Also, a *3ms* form will typically supply **a ḥolem as "theme vowel"** after the second שֹׁרֶשׁ consonant (as in יִכְרֹת *he will cut*). ("**Theme vowel**" is the label given to designate the vowel appearing after second שֹׁרֶשׁ consonant [second radical]).

Here are several common verbs that use a ḥolem as theme vowel.

Ḥolem as theme vowel

שֹׁרֶשׁ	יִקְטֹל *3ms*	he will...	שֹׁרֶשׁ	יִקְטֹל *3ms*	he will...
ע.ב.ד	יַעֲבֹד	he will work	ח.שׁ.ב	יַחְשֹׁב	he will think
ע.מ.ד	יַעֲמֹד	he will stand	כ.ר.ת	יִכְרֹת	he will cut
שׁ.מ.ר	יִשְׁמֹר	he will guard	מ.ל.כ	יִמְלֹךְ	he will rule
			נ.פ.ל	יִפֹּל	he will fall

Not all verbs use ḥolem as theme vowel. For example, יִשְׁכַּב *he will lie down* illustrates a verb using a **pataḥ** as theme vowel. Others will use a **ṣērê** (as in יֵרֵד *he will descend* and יֵשֵׁב *he will sit / dwell*), or a **šureq** (as in יָמוּת *he will die*). Suggestions to help you understand these theme vowel variations may be found in the appendix entry corresponding to this segment.

Also, please note the use of לֹא in the expression לֹא יִשְׁכַּב. Hebrew employs לֹא (not אֵין) to negate **finite verb forms** (i.e., verb forms such as יִשְׁכַּב—forms that are so detailed that they indicate a subject with a particular person / gender / number). In contrast, אֵין negates simple verbless expressions (such as אֵין לִי אָבֶן:).

4.3.ב. Snapshot of sample verb: יִקְטֹל conjugation *3ms*

נִשְׁמֹר we will guard	אֶשְׁמֹר I will guard
תִּשְׁמְרוּ you will guard *mpl*	תִּשְׁמֹר you will guard *ms*
תִּשְׁמֹרְנָה you will guard *fpl*	תִּשְׁמְרִי you will guard *fs*
יִשְׁמְרוּ they will guard *m*	**יִשְׁמֹר** **he will guard**
תִּשְׁמֹרְנָה they will guard *f*	תִּשְׁמֹר she will guard

4.3.ג. Activity: "What will Jonah do tomorrow?" מַה־יַּעֲשֶׂה יוֹנָה מָחָר?

INTERACTIVE SKILL: Asking concerning someone's plans

In the last Jonah episode (§4.2), הַדָּג הַקָּטֹן watched as עֲבָדִים tossed אֶת־הַנָּבִיא overboard, into the stormy יָם. In the current episode (§4.3), הַדָּג הַקָּטֹן watches as with one great gulp הַדָּג הַגָּדוֹל provides אֶת־הַנָּבִיא with a new place to spend the night (three nights, actually). Eventually, though, הַנָּבִיא will have to leave this watery apartment. What do you suppose will happen at that point?

  (a) What about הַנָּבִיא—what is the first thing you think that הַנָּבִיא will want to do, once he has been delivered from הַדָּג הַגָּדוֹל?

  (b) And how about הַדָּג הַגָּדוֹל—what will הַדָּג הַגָּדוֹל want to do, when at last he is rid of his internal passenger?

Here are some guidelines to help you speculate concerning their respective plans:

  (a) Your speculations may be either **positive** (*He will…*) or **negative** (*He will not…*).

  (b) Since the model question below uses a יִקְטֹל form (יַעֲשֶׂה), what form should your answer employ?[23]

  (c) In order to make a **simple** statement about the **future** (in order to avoid conveying a wish or hope), you will want to place the verb in **second or third position**. In front of the verb, place one or more of the following:

   (i)   a subject (noun or pronoun)

   (ii)   an object

   (iii) a negative particle (לֹא)

   Then follow with a יִקְטֹל form. Again, a יִקְטֹל verb should **not** be in the **first** position in the sentence when conveying simple future information.[24]

Under each question, write what you think will happen. Then practice the Model א question so that you can ask your neighbor what he or she expects will happen. Needless to say, answers will vary according to your imagination. Please limit yourself to verbs that have been introduced up to this point, such as

---

[23] Your primary statement should rest on a יִקְטֹל form. If you wish to include an infinitive or a participle as part of your reply, it should serve a secondary role, giving information in addition to a יִקְטֹל form.

[24] As you will learn in §9.4.א-ב., a יִקְטֹל form in first position conveys a hope or wish, not a simple future sense.

those found in §4.3.א. (including the appendix). If you look up words in the glossary, only use those marked with the module designation "4.3" or lower.

Model א

What will **Jonah** do tomorrow?	מַה־יַּעֲשֶׂה יוֹנָה מָחָר?	Inquiry about הַנָּבִיא
Tomorrow he will eat a big fish.	הוּא יֹאכַל דָּג גָּדוֹל מָחָר:	Sample reply

Your reply (Hebrew with translation)

Model ב

And (as for) the big fish—what will the fish do tomorrow?	וְהַדָּג הַגָּדוֹל מַה־יַּעֲשֶׂה הַדָּג מָחָר?	Inquiry about הַדָּג הַגָּדוֹל
He will not eat the prophet tomorrow.	לֹא יֹאכַל אֶת־הַנָּבִיא מָחָר:	Sample reply

Your reply (Hebrew with translation)

4.3.ד. Activity: "Put (*ms*) your (*ms*) feet on your (*ms*) hands!"
שִׂים רַגְלֶיךָ עַל־יָדֶיךָ!

INTERACTIVE SKILL: Choreographing a tableau

Have you ever watched as a person or group would swiftly strike a silent pose for dramatic effect (called a "tableau")? Show your grasp of the concept by quickly striking the various poses that your instructor directs. Later, you may choreograph a tableau, directing others to pose.

You will find the following imperative forms helpful in this activity:

שִׂימוּ... Put *mpl*...!	שִׂימִי... Put *fs*...!	שִׂים... Put *ms*...!

Incidentally, the שֹׁרֶשׁ for the command "Put!" is pronounced as a monosyllable, just like the command itself: שִׂים. The שֹׁרֶשׁ is represented as שׂ.י/ו.מ. As mentioned earlier, verbs with a monosyllabic שֹׁרֶשׁ are known as "hollow verbs" (see note on בוֹא in §2.4 Words for hearing, p. 148). The middle letter will be either י (as in ב.י.נ *to understand*, pronounced בִּין), or ו (as in ק.ו.מ *to get up*, pronounced קוּם), or a variable letter ו/י (as in שׂ.י/ו.מ). The variable letter indicates that some forms of that verb will display a middle vowel associated with ו (an O/U-vowel), while other forms of the same verb will display a middle vowel associated with י (an I-vowel).

Here are some hollow verbs you have encountered already:

Module	Sample form	Pronunciation of שֹׁרֶשׁ	שֹׁרֶשׁ (a hollow verb)
§2.4	*Come! or Enter!* בּוֹא	בּוֹא	ב.ו.א
§1.3	*I understand* אָבִין	בִּין	ב.י.נ
§4.3	*he will die* יָמוּת	מוּת	מ.ו.ת
§4.3	*Turn away!* סוּר	סוּר	ס.ו.ר
§1.3	*Get up!* קוּם	קוּם	ק.ו.מ

Module	Sample form	Pronunciation of שֹׁרֶשׁ	שֹׁרֶשׁ (a hollow verb)
§3.3	to turn toward לָשׁוּב אֶל	שׁוּב	ש.ו.ב

And here are some verbs with middle-י or middle-ו, that are *not* hollow verbs. Notice the two-syllable pronunciation of the שֹׁרֶשׁ in each case.

Module	Sample form	Pronunciation of שֹׁרֶשׁ	שֹׁרֶשׁ (*not* a hollow verb)
§4.3	*I will be, become* אֶהְיֶה	הָיָה	ה.י.ה
§4.3	*he will live* יִחְיֶה	חָיָה	ח.י.ה
§3.4	*one who commands* מְצַוֶּה	צָוָה	צ.ו.ה

4.3.ה. May I offer you (*ms*) advice? (Calling for help)   הַאִיעָצְךָ עֵצָה?

Here is an expression that will help you obtain assistance quickly, especially in the context of your language class. Simply call out either עָזְרֵנִי *Help me!* or—especially if seeking assistance from a divine source—הוֹשִׁיעֵנִי *Rescue me!* Try it! Soon those around you will respond with help.

Don't feel embarrassed to ask for assistance—long ago people of great stature used this noble cry (cf. Ps. 109:26, where the poet employed both עָזְרֵנִי and הוֹשִׁיעֵנִי in close succession).[25]

---

[25] According to principles of Hebrew poetry, by virtue of appearing **second** in the parallel structure of Ps. 109:26, הוֹשִׁיעֵנִי may convey more intensity or solemnity than עָזְרֵנִי. Notice that the qameṣ in עָזְרֵנִי is a qameṣ-ḥaṭuf, pronounced *o*.

MODULE 4.4 Describing what a group of women will do

Words for responding — מִלִּים לַעֲנוֹת

נֵר, נֵרוֹת, נֵר־, נֵרוֹת־	lamp *m*	אַאֲמִין [א.מ.נ]	I do / will / would believe *hifil*[a]
שֶׁמֶן, שְׁמָנִים, שֶׁמֶן־, שַׁמְנֵי־	oil (*of olive fruit*), scented oil *m*	אוֹמֵר, אוֹמֶרֶת, אוֹמְרִים, אוֹמְרוֹת [א.מ.ר]	one who says* *pt*
תֵּלַכְנָה [ה.ל.כ]	they will go, walk* *fpl*	דֶּרֶךְ, דְּרָכִים, דֶּרֶךְ־, דַּרְכֵי־	road, way *f or m*
תִּרְאֶינָה [ר.א.י/ה]	they will see* *fpl*	לֵב (*or* לֵבָב), לִבּוֹת, לֵב־, לִבּוֹת־	heart, mind *m* (*alternate spellings*)
תִּשְׁמַעְנָה [ש.מ.ע]	they will hear* *fpl*		

[a] The meaning "believe" belongs to a particular pattern branching off of the basic שֹׁרֶשׁ (the שֹׁרֶשׁ is א.מ.נ in this instance). This pattern (or "stem") is known as the *hifil* pattern (abbreviated *hif*), characterized by some shifts in spelling that will be explained more fully in Unit 8.

Words for hearing — מִלִּים לִשְׁמֹעַ

מַה־לָּךְ?	What is it or what is your concern? *ms and fs*	אוּלַי	perhaps
קֹוֶה, קֹוָה [ק.ו.י/ה]	one who hopes for *pt ms, fs*	אוֹר, אוֹרִים, אוֹר־, אוֹרֵי־	light, brightness *f*
תַּאֲמִין, תַּאֲמִינִי [א.מ.נ]	you do / will / would believe *hifil ms, fs*	בִּהְיוֹת [ה.י.י/ה]	while being* *inf c*, prep בְּ
		חֹשֶׁךְ	darkness *m*
		יְדַבֵּר [ד.ב.ר]	he / it will speak* *piel*

4.4 Jonah Episode: I would like to ask you a question.

ק׳ = הַדָּג הַקָּטֹן, ג׳ = הַדָּג הַגָּדוֹל

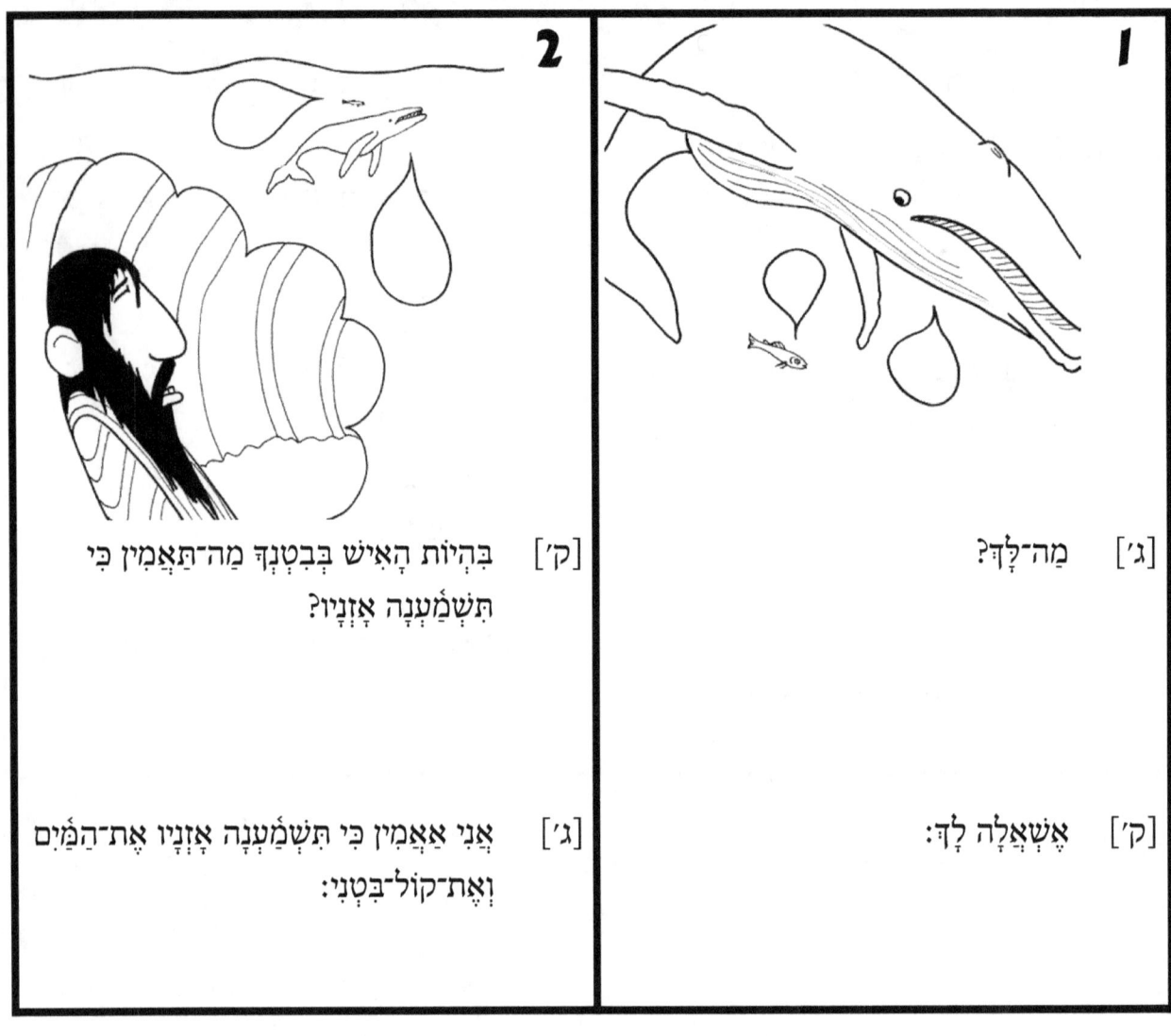

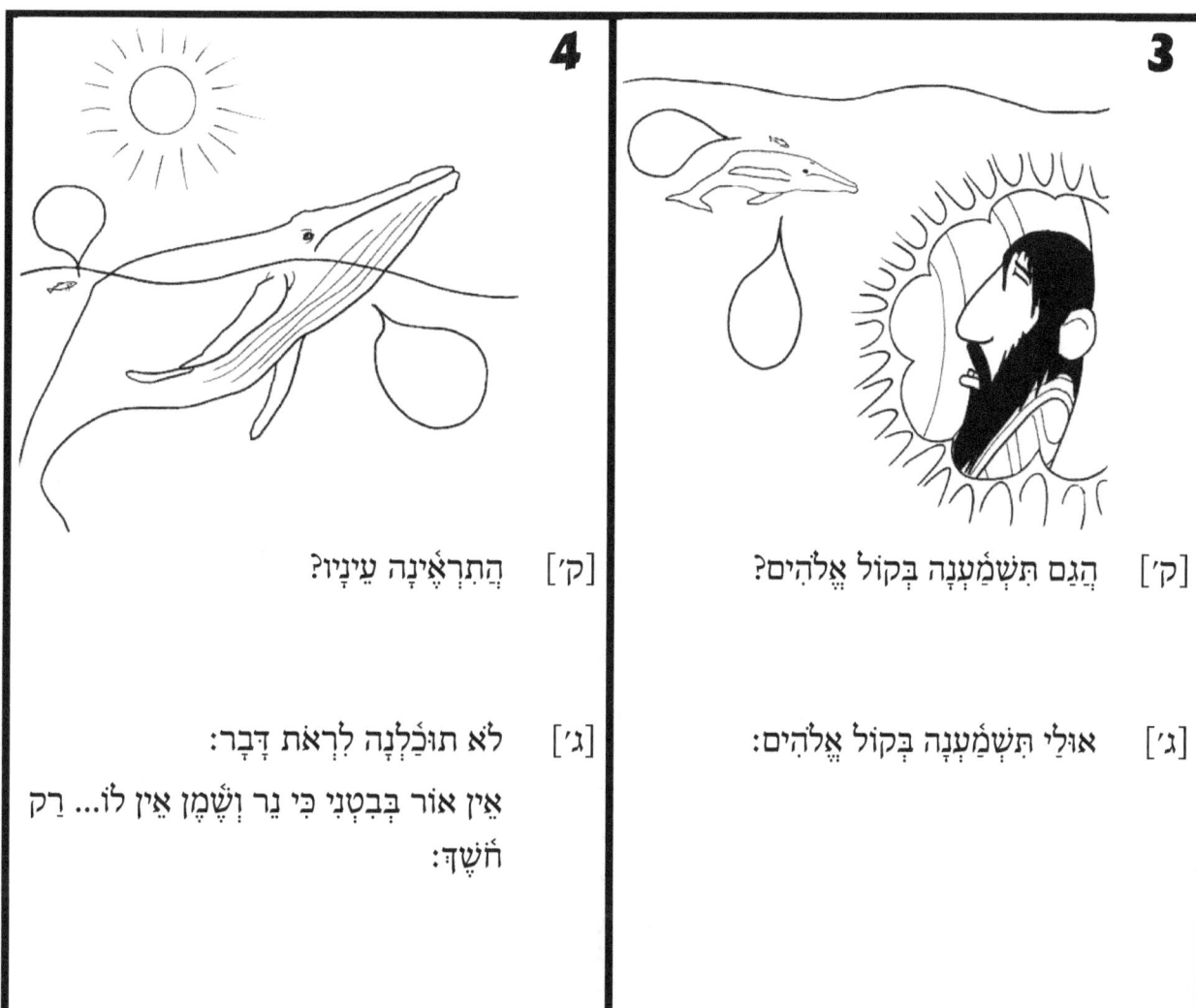

4

[ק׳] הֲתִרְאֶינָה עֵינָיו?

[ג׳] לֹא תוּכַלְנָה לִרְאוֹת דָּבָר:
אֵין אוֹר בְּבִטְנִי כִּי נֵר וְשֶׁמֶן אֵין לוֹ... רַק חֹשֶׁךְ:

3

[ק׳] הֲגַם תִּשְׁמַעְנָה בְּקוֹל אֱלֹהִים?

[ג׳] אוּלַי תִּשְׁמַעְנָה בְּקוֹל אֱלֹהִים:

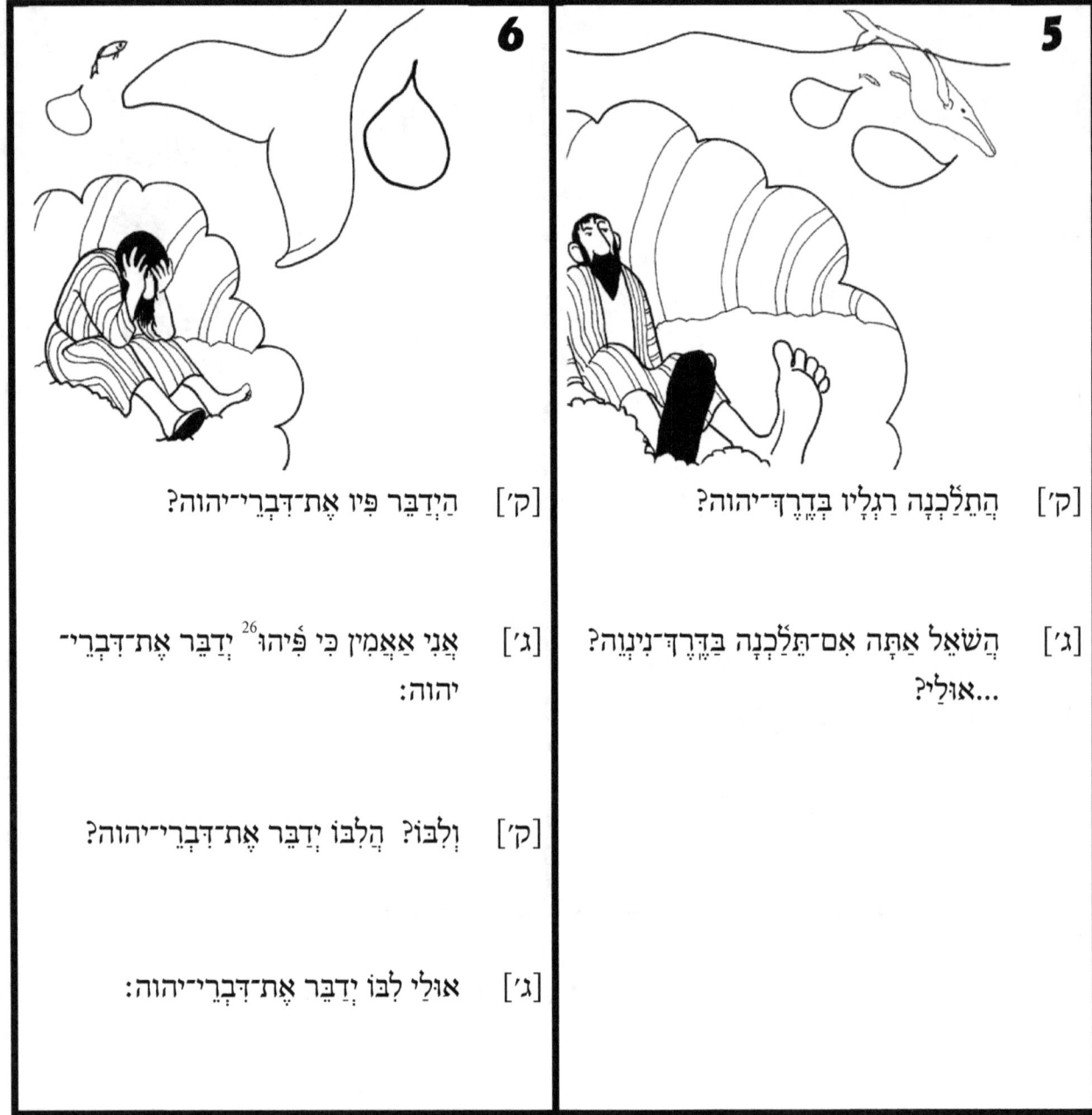

---

[26] פִּיהוּ is the form used for פִּיו when the accent is not on the final syllable.

4.4.א. Explanation: "His ears will hear."   אָזְנָיו תִּשְׁמַ֫עְנָה:

INTERACTIVE SKILL: Describing what several women will do

In order to describe what will be done by a group of women (or a group of feminine-gendered objects such as cities, ships, ears, hands, or feet), you will need the יִקְטֹל *3fpl* form. Although relatively rare in biblical usage, it is not difficult to learn the distinguishing marks of this form.

Fundamentally, the יִקְטֹל *3fpl* form sandwiches the שֹׁ֫רֶשׁ between a prefix ת... and a suffix ...נָה as in תִּשְׁמַ֫עְנָה *they (f) will hear*, or תִּשְׁמֹ֫רְנָה *they (f) will guard*. Concentrate on the spellings provided below to grow familiar with this form. For variations in prefix vowel spellings and theme vowel spellings, please see the two appendix entries corresponding to this segment.

Here is a collection of verbs you may consult for a later activity, alphabetically arranged by שֹׁ֫רֶשׁ. Can you supply the meanings and שָׁרָשִׁים, where they have been omitted?

שֹׁ֫רֶשׁ	יִקְטֹל *3fpl*	they (f) will…	שֹׁ֫רֶשׁ	יִקְטֹל *3fpl*	they (f) will…
י.ר.ד	תֵּרַ֫דְנָה	they will…	א.כ.ל	תֹּאכַ֫לְנָה	they will eat
	תֵּשַׁ֫בְנָה	they will…	א.מ.ן	תַּאֲמִ֫ינָה	they will believe
כ.ר.ת	תִּכְרֹ֫תְנָה	they will…	א.מ.ר	תֹּאמַ֫רְנָה	they will…
	תְּמוּתֶ֫נָה	they will die	ב.ו.א	תָּבֹ֫אינָה	they will…
	תִּמְלֹ֫כְנָה	they will rule	ב.כ.י/ה	תִּבְכֶּ֫ינָה	they will weep
	תִּמְצֶ֫אנָה	they will…		תִּהְיֶ֫ינָה	they will…
נ.פ.ל	תִּפֹּ֫לְנָה	they will…	ה.ל.כ	תֵּלַ֫כְנָה	they will…
	תִּתֵּ֫נָּה	they will…	ח.י.י/ה	תִּחְיֶ֫ינָה	they will live
ס.ו.ר	תָּסֹ֫רְנָה	they will…	י.כ.ל	תּוּכַ֫לְנָה	they will…

שֹׁרֶשׁ	יִקְטֹל 3fpl	they (f) will...
ש.כ.ב	תִּשְׁכַּ֫בְנָה	they will...
ש.ל.כ	תַּשְׁלֵ֫כְנָה ᵃ	they will...
ש.מ.ע	תִּשְׁמַ֫עְנָה	they will...
	תִּשְׁמֹ֫רְנָה	they will...
ש.ת.י/ה	תִּשְׁתֶּ֫ינָה	they will drink

שֹׁרֶשׁ	יִקְטֹל 3fpl	they (f) will...
ע.ב.ד	תַּעֲבֹ֫דְנָה	they will serve, worship
ע.מ.ד	תַּעֲמֹ֫דְנָה	they will...
ק.ו.ם	תָּקֹ֫מְנָה	they will...
ר.א.י/ה	תִּרְאֶ֫ינָה	they will see
	תָּשִׂ֫ימְנָה	they will...

ᵃ The *ṣērê* theme vowel and *pataḥ* prefix vowel in תַּשְׁלֵ֫כְנָה owe to the fact that this is a *hifil* form of the verb. The *hifil* will be explained in greater detail in Unit 8.

4.4.ב. Snapshot of sample verb: יִקְטֹל conjugation *3fpl*

נִשְׁמֹר we will guard	אֶשְׁמֹר I will guard
תִּשְׁמְרוּ you will guard *mpl*	תִּשְׁמֹר you will guard *ms*
תִּשְׁמֹ֫רְנָה you will guard *fpl*	תִּשְׁמְרִי you will guard *fs*
יִשְׁמְרוּ they will guard *m*	יִשְׁמֹר he will guard
תִּשְׁמֹ֫רְנָה **they will guard *f***	תִּשְׁמֹר she will guard

4.4.ג. Activity: "Where's a nose? Here's a nose!" אַיֵּה אַף? הִנֵּה אַף!

INTERACTIVE SKILL: Locating something that another is looking for

Can you locate these body parts?

אֹזֶן	זְרֹעַ	לֵב	עַיִן	רֹאשׁ
אַף	יָד	נֶפֶשׁ	פֶּה	רֶגֶל

Listen for your instructor's inquiry "אַיֵּה [דָּבָר]?" concerning a particular body part. See how quickly you can respond by declaring "הִנֵּה [דָּבָר]!" as you point to that body part.

4.4.ד. Activity: "What should they (f) do? What do you (ms) think?"
מַה־תַּעֲשֶׂינָה? מַה־תֹּאמַר בִּלְבָבְךָ?

INTERACTIVE SKILL: Expressing your opinion concerning what a group you are acquainted with ought to do

Imagine that during the past year you have served as consultant or advisor to one of the following four groups (select a group according to your interest). At the end of the year's relationship, a friend asks you what you think this group (that you have been advising) ought to do. What path of future action would you map out for your advisees?

Four groups (choose one)

נָשִׁים	מְלָכוֹת
A collegiate sports team consisting of six gifted נָשִׁים who are bound for the national playoffs (נָשִׁים serves as a plural for אִשָּׁה.)	An association of four מְלָכוֹת who hope to end hunger among the poor in their lands
עָרִים	נְבִיאוֹת
A consortium of five עָרִים, all of which are suffering an upturn in urban unemployment and crime (עָרִים is the plural of עִיר.)	A group of seven נְבִיאוֹת whose oracles against abuse of power are engendering increasing hostility from persons in authority

The model below imagines that you have served as consultant for the four מְלָכוֹת. After reading over the sample reply, formulate a reply of your own, consistent with whatever group you select. If necessary, you may round out your thoughts using your native language (after employing at least one *3fpl* verb).

For this dialogue, you will need the following expressions:

What should they (f) do? What would you (ms, fs) think / suppose [*lit.,* what would you say in your heart]? (תֹּאמְרִי / תֹּאמַר is 2ms/fs of יִקְטֹל of א.מ.ר.)	מַה־תַּעֲשֶׂינָה? מַה־תֹּאמַר בִּלְבָבְךָ / מַה־תֹּאמְרִי בִּלְבָבֵךְ?
I would think / suppose.... (אֹמַר is יִקְטֹל 1cs of א.מ.ר. *I will say.*)	אֹמַר בְּלִבִּי...

By the way: do you know why we should use a *3fpl* verb in the response? Consider the composition of each of the four groups.

Also, did you notice the connotation associated with the question, "מַה־תַּעֲשֶׂינָה?" Although תַּעֲשֶׂינָה is a יִקְטֹל form (often translated as future indicative, *they will do*), here we are translating it with a **potential** tone (not certain), and with a sense (or "mood") of obligation: *What **should** they (f) do?* As you will discover in §5.4.א., Hebrew prefers the יִקְטֹל when conveying an idea that is more potential than it is certain, such as when expressing a mood of obligation (cf. especially §5.4.א., sub-point 2.1).

Model

What should they (f) do? What would you think / suppose [*lit.*, what would you say in your heart]?	מַה־תַּעֲשֶׂינָה? מַה־תֹּאמַר בִּלְבָבְךָ / מַה־תֹּאמְרִי בִּלְבָבֵךְ?	Inquiry *ms, fs*
I would think / suppose: they (f) should give food to the small ones, and not to the great ones.	אָמַר בְּלִבִּי, תִּתֵּנָּה אֶת־הַלֶּחֶם לַקְּטַנִּים וְלֹא לַגְּדוֹלִים:	Reply (based on מַלְכוּת group)

Incidentally, although we might be inclined to follow אָמַר בְּלִבִּי with כִּי or לֵאמֹר, attested usage omits these words, moving directly from אָמַר בְּלִבִּי to the quotation itself (as shown in the model).

Your reply (Hebrew, with translation)

4.4.ה. Do you (*ms*) know the meaning...? (ש.מ.ע בְּקוֹל־) הֲיָדַעְתָּ פֵּשֶׁר...?

The expression ש.מ.ע בְּקוֹל־ *to listen to (the) voice of*... supplies an idiom meaning *to obey* (cf. Gen. 22:18 and 27:13). Does your native language offer any associations between *listening* and *obeying*?

4.4.1. Activity: "What should they (*f*) do first?" מַה־תַּעֲשֶׂינָה בָּרִאשׁוֹנָה?

INTERACTIVE SKILL: Helping some friends prioritize their work schedule

אֵלֶּה שְׁמוֹת הַמְיַלְּדֹת הָעִבְרִית בְּמִצְרָיִם: שִׁפְרָה שֵׁם הָאַחַת וְשֵׁם הַשֵּׁנִית פּוּעָה:[27]

Perhaps you are acquainted with the story of these two courageous women. Now imagine that you are living as a neighbor in their community. Life has grown so hectic that they have hired you as consultant to help them prioritize their daily schedule. What should they do first, second, etc.?

After accompanying them "on rounds" for a couple of days, you develop some recommendations. Your report consists of five (or more) activities that they **should do**—in order—each day. Begin by **giving the translation** of each word, writing it below the Hebrew. Then proceed to select the activity you are going to recommend that they should do **first** each day. Write "1" alongside that activity in the column labeled "Your priority," with a **brief explanation** (native language). Similarly write "2" for the **second** priority, and so on, up to #5. Conversely, select one activity that you feel they should **not do at all** (or should do only very rarely), and **write לֹא** opposite that activity in the "Your priority" column.[28]

---

[27] These are the names of the Hebrew midwives (הַמְיַלְּדֹת הָעִבְרִית) in Egypt. Šifrâ was the name of the one, and the name of the second was Pû'â (cf. Exod. 1:15).

[28] If you are curious concerning how one would indicate priority with words such as "first," "second," and "third" in Hebrew (called ordinal numbers), see §7.5.א.

Your priority	Activity		Your priority	Activity	
	תֵּרַדְנָה	ח.		תֹּאכַלְנָה	א.
	תִּשְׁכַּבְנָה	ט.		תַּחְשֹׁבְנָה	ב.
	תִּשְׁלֵכְנָה	י.		תְּמוּתֶנָה	ג.
	תִּשְׁמַעְנָה	יא.		תִּמְלֹכְנָה	ד.
	תִּשְׁמֹרְנָה	יב.		תִּמְצֶאנָה	ה.
	תִּשְׁתֶּינָה	יג.		תַּעֲבֹדְנָה	ו.
	תִּתֵּנָּה	יד.		תָּקֹמְנָה	ז.

4.4.ז. Did you (*ms*) know that...? (Olive industry) — הֲיָדַעְתָּ כִּי...?

This roller-style olive press of basalt found at Capernaum may date to Roman times.

...olive oil (שֶׁמֶן *m*) was one of the major exports from the Levant? Egypt was a major importer, since the olive tree does not grow well in the Nile valley. Throughout the Levant, olive oil was used as a dietary staple, for lamp fuel (see §4.1.ז.), lubrication of leather shields, perfume suspension, and for ritual anointing. Oil production presumed a stable economy, since five or six years were required before olive trees (זַיִת *m*) would begin to bear fruit, and thereafter they bore only on alternate years.

Oil was extracted by a two-stage process: first by crushing, then by pressing.

Initially a stone roller would crush the fruit. The crushed fruit was then flooded with hot water. Top-grade virgin oil would float to the surface, where it was skimmed off. Next, the pulp that remained would be placed in baskets and pressed by a wooden lever beam, weighted down as pairs of large pierced stones joined by a rope were slung over one end of the beam. Extracted oil would course downward to the stone base incised with a perimeter catchment groove, then would escape through a spout groove, finally gathering in a sunken receptacle (called a יֶקֶב *m*, also used in wine presses). Stone drums with a drain pierced at the base line were also used in olive oil production.

A venerable olive tree in the Gethsemane grove, east of Old Jerusalem.

Basalt base of lever-beam press with sunken יֶקֶב, Capernaum.

Olive presses are widely documented from Iron Age II (1000–800 BCE). The Philistine city-state of Ekron produced as much as one thousand tons of oil annually, based on the discovery of over 100 such presses.[29]

---

[29] *LBI,* 95–97. Incidentally, the olive orchard known as Gethsemane (גַּת + שֶׁמֶן) likely contained a press as well as olive trees. Taken alone, גַּת *press f* refers to the upper basin of a winepress.

MODULE 4.5   Describing what a woman will do

Words for responding   מִלִּים לַעֲנוֹת

תַּכֶּה [נ.כ.י/ה]	she / it will hit *hifil*[a]
תִּקְרַב [ק.ר.ב]	she / it will draw near
תִּשְׁבֹּר [ש.ב.ר]	she / it will break (something)

[a] The meaning "to hit" belongs to a pattern of נ.כ.י/ה known as *hifil*, to be explained in Unit 8. At present, simply learn the meaning given for this word.

4.5 Jonah Episode: Look out!

ק׳ = הַדָּג הַקָּטֹן

[ק׳] הִשָּׁמֵר! הָאֳנִיָּה תִּקְרַב אֵלֵינוּ... אוֹתְךָ
תַּכֶּה... אֶת־רֹאשְׁךָ תִּשְׁבֹּר!

4.5.א. Explanation: "The ship will come close!" הָאֳנִיָּה תִּקְרַב!

INTERACTIVE SKILL: Describing what an individual woman (or feminine object) will do

Since you already are familiar with the יִקְטֹל *3ms* form, the *3fs* will be easy to recognize. Simply trade the *3ms* יִקְטֹל prefix …יְ for a …תְּ. Thus יִקְרַב *he / it will come close* becomes תִּקְרַב *she / it will come close*. Now you will be able to describe what an individual woman (or feminine-gendered object such as an אֳנִיָּה) is about to do. The *3fs* pattern will be imprinted quickly as you scan sample verbs collected below. The "he will…" verbs are provided simply for comparison.

he will…	she will…		he will…	she will…		he will…	she will…	
יָקוּם	תָּקוּם	get up	יָמוּת	תָּמוּת	die	יֹאמַר	תֹּאמַר	say
יִשְׁבֹּר	תִּשְׁבֹּר	break	יִמְלֹךְ	תִּמְלֹךְ	rule	יַאֲמִין	תַּאֲמִין	believe
יִרְאֶה	תִּרְאֶה	see	יִמְצָא	תִּמְצָא	find	יָבוֹא	תָּבוֹא	come
יָשִׂים	תָּשִׂים	place	יָסוּר	תָּסוּר	turn aside	יִבְכֶּה	תִּבְכֶּה	weep
יַשְׁלִיךְ	תַּשְׁלִיךְ	throw	יַעֲמֹד	תַּעֲמֹד	stand	יוּכַל	תּוּכַל	be able
יִשְׁמַע	תִּשְׁמַע	hear	יִסְלַח	תִּסְלַח	forgive	יַכֶּה	תַּכֶּה	strike
יִשְׁתֶּה	תִּשְׁתֶּה	drink	יִקְרַב	תִּקְרַב	draw near	יִכְרֹת	תִּכְרֹת	cut

If you are wondering why some verbs have a theme vowel of ḥolem (such as תִּמְלֹךְ), while others present different theme vowels (such as a pataḥ in תִּסְלַח), please review the information found in §4.3.א. That same segment (together with the corresponding appendix entry) will remind you why the prefix vowel is generally ḥireq (as in תִּשְׁבֹּר), but may present other vowels as well (such as the qameṣ in תָּשִׂים).

4.5.ב. Snapshot of sample verb: יִקְטֹל conjugation *3fs*

נִשְׁמֹר we will guard	אֶשְׁמֹר I will guard
תִּשְׁמְרוּ you will guard *mpl*	תִּשְׁמֹר you will guard *ms*
תִּשְׁמֹרְנָה you will guard *fpl*	תִּשְׁמְרִי you will guard *fs*
יִשְׁמְרוּ they will guard *m*	יִשְׁמֹר he will guard
תִּשְׁמֹרְנָה they will guard *f*	**תִּשְׁמֹר** **she will guard**

4.5.ג. Activity: "What will she do?"   מַה־תַּעֲשֶׂה?

INTERACTIVE SKILL: Anticipating actions and describing them

In this activity, various women in your class will go through the motions *leading up to* a simple task. Your assignment is to guess what they are *about to do*. For example, if someone picks up a cup, your guess will not be, "She will pick up a cup" (since that is something she has *already* done). Instead, you will predict that—very soon—she will quench her thirst with some water. So you will answer: מַיִם תִּשְׁתֶּה *She will drink some water*.

    Can you guess what question will be used to prompt you to respond—stating what you expect your classmate (*f*) is about to do? If in doubt concerning what the prompt question will be, consider the heading for this segment. And if you are unsure where to find some verbs to help with your reply, consider the collection found in §4.5.א.

    Your instructor may ask you to prepare for this activity by preselecting one action that one of the women in your class might dramatize. Write it on a slip of paper (both Hebrew and English). Your action should involve a simple prop or visual aid (e.g., if "תִּשְׁתֶּה," then bring a cup).

4.5.ד. Activity: "What can you (*ms*) do?" מַה־תּוּכַל לַעֲשׂוֹת?

INTERACTIVE SKILL: Discovering a neighbor's hidden talents

What special ability do you possess? Share it with your classmates when they ask you. If helpful, elaborate briefly in your native language. You may use (but are not limited to using) the verbs found in §3.1.א. and §4.2.ב. Notice that the verbs found in these segments are infinitives construct—the form of a verb that in Hebrew serves to name the activity embodied by a given verb.

Your instructor may conduct this conversation in an inquire-reply-confirm fashion. Thus, after the first person asks the second person, the first person then will confirm what he / she heard the second person say (notice "confirmation," below). Next, the second person will ask a third. Upon hearing the third person's response, the second person will then confirm what he / she heard the third person say.

Model

What can you (*ms, fs*) do?	מַה־תּוּכַל / תּוּכְלִי לַעֲשׂוֹת?	Inquiry (by person א)
I am able to listen (i.e., I can help others by lending a listening ear).	אֲנִי אוּכַל לִשְׁמֹעַ: *or* לִשְׁמֹעַ אוּכַל:	Reply (by person ב)
You (*ms, fs*) are able to listen.	אַתָּה תּוּכַל / אַתְּ תּוּכְלִי לִשְׁמֹעַ:	Confirmation (by person א)

4.5.ה. Activity: "What will the ship do?"   מַה־תַּעֲשֶׂה הָאֳנִיָּה?

INTERACTIVE SKILL: Proposing alternative scenarios

Imagine that you are a screenwriter, charged to invent new material for the Jonah story. What will happen next in this adventure? To be specific, what will the **ship** do? While you are at it, what will the **servants** (sailors) do? And **Jonah**? For that matter, what about the **winds** (רוּחוֹת)?

    There is no need to restrict yourself either to verbs in the above table or to your awareness of how the story ends. Range through previous vocabulary to fashion a captivating next-scene. Then write your responses (with translation) opposite the questions below.

א. מַה־תַּעֲשֶׂה הָאֳנִיָּה?

ב. מַה־יַּעֲשׂוּ הָעֲבָדִים?

ג. מַה־יַּעֲשֶׂה יוֹנָה?

ד. מַה־תַּעֲשֶׂינָה הָרוּחוֹת?

4.5.ו. Activity (drama): "What will the ship do?"   מַה־תַּעֲשֶׂה הָאֳנִיָּה?

INTERACTIVE SKILL: "Reading" a mime

When invited by your instructor, announce which of the four "characters" in §4.5.ה. you will be presenting. Then dramatize what you envision that character doing next (refer to earlier composition).

    If you are in the audience (not acting), notice what action your classmate is performing. Then guess what they had written down in their "screenwriting" for that character.

UNIT 4   מַה־יַּעֲשׂוּ מָחָר?

You (ms) can read the Bible.   אַתָּה תִּקְרָא אֶת־הַתַּנַ״ךְ:

A few of the selections below contain יִקְטֹל forms that venture outside the future indicative meaning that you have learned to this point. These additional meanings available within the יִקְטֹל will be explained in §5.4.א. For the time being, simply employ the notes provided. Some verses employ verbs found in the appendix portions corresponding to this unit.

Selected readings

4.1.א.   God promised a perpetual dynasty to David, on one condition:

.1   ...אִם־יִשְׁמְרוּ בָנֶיךָ^a אֶת־דַּרְכָּם^b לָלֶכֶת לְפָנַי^c בֶּאֱמֶת^d בְּכָל^e־לְבָבָם^f וּבְכָל־נַפְשָׁם...

...then David's lineage would not lose...

...אִישׁ מֵעַל־כִּסֵּא יִשְׂרָאֵל׃ (1 Kings 2:4)

בָּנֶיךָ[a] your sons mpl   דֶּרֶךְ[b] way f (with pronominal suffix)   לְפָנַי[c] (with pronominal suffix)
בֶּאֱמֶת[d] in truth   בְּכָל[e] with all (qameṣ ḥaṭuf)   לֵבָב[f] heart, mind m (with pronominal suffix)

...אִם־יִשְׁמְרוּ בָנֶיךָ אֶת־דַּרְכָּם לָלֶכֶת לְפָנַי בֶּאֱמֶת בְּכָל־לְבָבָם וּבְכָל־נַפְשָׁם לֵאמֹר לֹא־יִכָּרֵת לְךָ אִישׁ מֵעַל כִּסֵּא יִשְׂרָאֵל׃

4.1.א.   Isaiah offered good news on a dark day.

.2   הָעָם הַהֹלְכִים בַּחֹשֶׁךְ^a יִרְאוּ^μ אוֹר^b גָּדוֹל׃...
(Isa. 9:1 [ET v. 2], ^μmodified from original past tense)

חֹשֶׁךְ[a] darkness m   אוֹר[b] light m

הָעָם הַהֹלְכִים בַּחֹשֶׁךְ רָאוּ אוֹר גָּדוֹל...

א.1.4	Here is the strategy of some especially malevolent kidnappers:	
3.	יִבְלָעוּᵘ אוֹתָםᵘ כִּשְׁאוֹל חַיִּיםᵃ....׃ (Prov. 1:12a)	
	חַיִּיםᵃ alive	
	נִבְלָעֵם כִּשְׁאוֹל חַיִּים...	

א.3.4	Upon learning that the infant son born to him and to Bathsheba at last had died, King David made this statement with a sense of finality. (When you reach the conjunction in וְהוּא, experiment with an adversative [*yet* or *however*]. Also, note that אֵלָי is pausal for אֵלַי.)	
4.	...אֲנִי הֹלֵךְ אֵלָיו וְהוּא לֹא־יָשׁוּב אֵלָי׃ (2 Sam. 12:23b)	

א.3.4	According to this statement, the God of Israel hoped that his followers would be...	
5.	...כְּעַבְדִּי דָוִד אֲשֶׁר שָׁמַרᵃ מִצְוֺתַיᵇ וַאֲשֶׁר־הָלַךְᶜ אַחֲרַי בְּכָל־לְבָבוֹᵈ לַעֲשׂוֹת רַק הַיָּשָׁרᵉ בְּעֵינָי׃ (1 Kings 14:8)	
	שָׁמַרᵃ [ש.מ.ר] he guarded, kept מִצְוָהᵇ command *m* (with pronominal sfx) *f*	
	הָלַךְᶜ [ה.ל.כ] he walked לֵבָבᵈ heart, mind *m* הַיָּשָׁרᵉ the right thing *m*	

ד.3.4	When six hundred Danites began to pilfer some religious articles, the priest protested (see question below). They responded with a clandestine offer (their offer follows his question).	
6.	...מָה אַתֶּם עֹשִׂים׃	
	...שִׂים־יָדְךָ עַל־פִּיךָ וְלֵךְ עִמָּנוּ...׃ (Judg. 18:18-19)	

| | מַה־יַּעֲשׂוּ מָחָר? | UNIT 4 |

4.3.ה. Rising waters gave rise to this prayer. (Note that נָ֑פֶשׁ is pausal for נֶ֫פֶשׁ.)

7. הוֹשִׁיעֵ֣נִי אֱלֹהִ֑ים כִּ֤י בָ֖אוּ^{a} מַ֣יִם עַד־נָֽפֶשׁ׃ (Ps. 69:2)

^{a}בָ֖אוּ [ב.ו.א] they have come

4.4.א. This reassurance was extended to those truly seeking guidance:

8. וְאָזְנֶ֨יךָ תִּשְׁמַ֤עְנָה דָבָר֙ מֵֽאַחֲרֶ֣יךָ^{a} לֵאמֹ֔ר זֶ֥ה הַדֶּ֖רֶךְ לְכ֣וּ^{b} בוֹ׃... (Isa. 30:21)

^{a}מֵֽאַחֲרֶ֣יךָ (from) behind you ^{b}לְכוּ [ה.ל.ב] Go! or Walk! pl

4.5.א. Here is a warning against defiant acts, lest serious consequences may follow. (As you may have noticed from a Bible reading in Unit 3, the word הַהוּא at times appears vocalized with a ḥireq. In this way the Masoretes have recommended that it be read as הַהִיא [cf. §8.1.כ]. As indicated in the gloss, וְנִכְרְתָה has a future meaning. Known as a וְקָטַל vav-conversive form, it will be explained in §7.3.ז. The nifal בִּנְיָן also will be explained in Unit 7.)

9. וְהַנֶּ֜פֶשׁ אֲשֶֽׁר־תַּעֲשֶׂ֣ה^a בְּיָ֣ד רָמָ֗ה^b... וְנִכְרְתָ֛ה^c הַנֶּ֥פֶשׁ הַהִ֖וא מִקֶּ֥רֶב^d עַמָּֽהּ׃ (Num. 15:30)

^{a}הַנֶּ֜פֶשׁ אֲ׳ the person f who ... ^{b}רָמָה high fs ^{c}וְנִכְרְתָה it will be cut off nifal fs ^{d}מִקֶּרֶב from among

4.5.א. Can you imagine how much young Samuel anticipated his family's visit, year by year? (Note that the יִקְטֹל form here signals repeated action [iterative], not future statement of fact, since the context stipulates a past time frame. Translate used to... or would [customarily].... Such variations available to יִקְטֹל forms will be explained in §5.4.א.)

10. וּמְעִיל^a קָטֹ֤ן תַּֽעֲשֶׂה־לּוֹ֙ אִמּ֔וֹ^{b}... (1 Sam. 2:19a)

^{a}מְעִיל robe m ^{b}אֵם mother f (dagesh appears with pronominal sfx)

Using a parable, the prophet Nathan told King David of a poor man who was robbed of something very dear to him. (As in 1 Sam. 2:19, the יִקְטֹל forms signal repeated action [iterative], not future statement of fact. Context indicates a past timeframe. Translate as *used to...* or *would* [*customarily*]*...*; cf. §5.4.א.)	4.5.א.

11. ...כִּבְשָׂה אַחַת^a קְטַנָּה אֲשֶׁר... מִפִּתּוֹ^b תֹאכַל וּמִכֹּסוֹ תִשְׁתֶּה... (2 Sam. 12:3)

^aכִּבְשָׂה 'א... one ewe-lamb *f*   ^bפַּת (*dagesh with pronominal sfx*) *f* meager fare *f*

וְלָרָשׁ אֵין־כֹּל כִּי אִם־כִּבְשָׂה אַחַת קְטַנָּה אֲשֶׁר ... מִפִּתּוֹ תֹאכַל וּמִכֹּסוֹ תִשְׁתֶּה...

The poet assures his hearers that when God's followers appeal to his mercy, he responds. (Note that when an adjective with article such as הַטּוֹב does not modify another word, it operates as a substantive: *that which is good*.)	4.5.א.

12. גַּם־יְהוָה יִתֵּן הַטּוֹב וְאַרְצֵנוּ תִּתֵּן יְבוּלָהּ^a: (Ps. 85:13 [ET v. 12])

^aיְבוּל produce (of soil, *with pronominal sfx*) *m*

How would you describe Job's outlook at this point?	4.5.א.

13. ...לֹא־תָשׁוּב עֵינִי לִרְאוֹת טוֹב: (Job 7:7b)

"What goes 'round comes 'round." (Hint: וְגֹלֵל אֶבֶן is a noun phrase, resumed in the next phrase by the pronoun suffixed to אֵלָיו. Experiment by beginning your translation with: *As for one who....*)	4.5.א.

14. ...וְגֹלֵל^a אֶבֶן אֵלָיו תָּשׁוּב: (Prov. 26:27b)

^aג.ל.ל to roll

According to the sage, when all is said and done...	4.5.א.

15. ...וְהָרוּחַ תָּשׁוּב אֶל־הָאֱלֹהִים אֲשֶׁר נְתָנָהּ^a: (Eccl. 12:7b)

^aנְתָנָהּ [נ.ת.נ] he gave it

UNIT 4   מַה־יַּעֲשׂוּ מָחָר?   311

4.5.1. Moses urged Israel to pay close attention to this principle, above all.

16. שְׁמַע יִשְׂרָאֵל יהוה אֱלֹהֵינוּ
יהוה אֶחָד^a: (Deut. 6:4)

אֶחָד^a one, single *m*

A connected reading: The binding of Isaac (Gen. 22:5-6)   עֲקֵדַת יִצְחָק

5. וַיֹּאמֶר^a אַבְרָהָם אֶל־נְעָרָיו^b
שְׁבוּ־לָכֶם^c פֹּה^d עִם־הַחֲמוֹר^e
וַאֲנִי וְהַנַּעַר נֵלְכָה^f עַד־כֹּה^g
וְנִשְׁתַּחֲוֶה^h וְנָשׁוּבָהⁱ אֲלֵיכֶם:

וַיֹּאמֶר^a then he said   נְעָרָיו^b his young men *mpl*   שְׁבוּ־לָכֶם^c as for you, stay! *pl*   פֹּה^d here
חֲמוֹר^e donkey *m*   נֵלְכָה^f we will go   עַד־כֹּה^g over there   וְנִשְׁתַּחֲוֶה^h and we will worship
וְנָשׁוּבָהⁱ and we will return

6. וַיִּקַּח^a אַבְרָהָם אֶת־עֲצֵי הָעֹלָה^b
וַיָּשֶׂם^c עַל־יִצְחָק בְּנוֹ^d
וַיִּקַּח בְּיָדוֹ אֶת־הָאֵשׁ^e וְאֶת־הַמַּאֲכֶלֶת^f
וַיֵּלְכוּ^g שְׁנֵיהֶם^h יַחְדָּוⁱ:

וַיִּקַּח^a then he took   עֲצֵי הָעֹלָה^b wood *mpl* for the whole burnt offering *f*   וַיָּשֶׂם^c and he placed
בְּנוֹ^d his son *m*   אֵשׁ^e fire *m*   מַאֲכֶלֶת^f knife *f*   וַיֵּלְכוּ^g so they went off   שְׁנֵיהֶם^h both of them
יַחְדָּוⁱ together

UNIT 5

מַה־תַּעֲשֶׂה בָּרִאשׁנָה?

Talking about what you will do first

יִקְטֹל *conjugation (part 2), ordinal numbers*

This unit will enable you to talk about your upcoming plans with a friend. You will be able to relate:

* what you as an individual intend to do next
* what your group intends to do
* what those you are talking with are about to do (whether individuals or groups)

Toward the close of this unit, you will encounter several rich nuances available within the יִקְטֹל conjugation. These nuances go beyond simply describing the future, and will include connotations such as beginning an action or sustaining an action (see §5.4.א.).

On the following page you will find the complete יִקְטֹל conjugation for the verb ש.מ.ר. Side columns indicate in what segment a given part will be introduced. A similar table appears toward the end of the unit as well (§5.4.ז.).

The יִקְטֹל conjugation

Segment	Plural	Singular	Segment
5.1.א.	נִשְׁמֹר we will guard	אֶשְׁמֹר I will guard	5.2.ב.
5.1.ד.	תִּשְׁמְרוּ you will guard *mpl*	תִּשְׁמֹר you will guard *ms*	5.3.א.
5.1.ו.	תִּשְׁמֹרְנָה you will guard *fpl*	תִּשְׁמְרִי you will guard *fs*	5.3.ג.
4.1.א.	יִשְׁמְרוּ they will guard *m*	יִשְׁמֹר he will guard	4.3.א.
4.4.א.	תִּשְׁמֹרְנָה they will guard *f*	תִּשְׁמֹר she will guard	4.5.א.

MODULE 5.1 Describing what your group is about to do

Unit 5 JONAH STORY: A shocking surprise for sailors and a prophet

Can you recall a time when a perilous situation resolved itself so smoothly that it left you in shock? Perhaps that is how the sailors felt in this episode.

Words for responding — מִלִּים לַעֲנוֹת

תּוֹרָה, תּוֹרוֹת, תּוֹרַת־, תּוֹרוֹת־	law, instruction *f*	בְּהֵמָה, בְּהֵמוֹת, בֶּהֱמַת־, בַּהֲמוֹת־	animal, cattle *f*
תִּזְכְּרוּ [ז.כ.ר]	you will remember *mpl*	חֵן	grace, favor *m*
תֵּלַכְנָה [ה.ל.כ]	you will go, walk* *fpl*	יוֹם, יָמִים, יוֹם־, יְמֵי־	day *m*
תֵּצְאוּ [י.צ.א]	you will go out, exit *mpl*	כֹּל, כָּל־[a]	every, each, all, the whole…
		נִקַּח [ל.ק.ח]	we will take
		נִשָּׂא [נ.ש.א]	we will lift, carry

[a] כֹּל means "all" when modifying a **plural** entity, but "every / each" when modifying a **singular** entity. כָּל־הַיּוֹם (with article) means *all day [long]*. When joined to next word by maqqef (hyphen), כֹּל is spelled כָּל־. There is no change in pronunciation (כָּל־ is very common example of the qameṣ-ḥaṭuf vowel, pronounced *o*).

Words for hearing — מִלִּים לִשְׁמֹעַ

בֹּקֶר	morning, daybreak, dawn *m*	אָח, אַחִים, אֲחִי־, אֲחֵי־	brother *m*
בְּשׁוּבֵנוּ [ש.ו.ב]	when we return	אַל־תִּירְאוּ [י.ר.א]	Don't be afraid!* (תִּירָאוּ in pause) *mpl*
הָיָה [ה.י.ה/ה]	he / it was*		
הַיּוֹם	today	אֱמֶת	truth *f*

we will call, read	נִקְרָא [ק.ר.א]	sacrifice, ritual feast *m*	זֶבַח, זְבָחִים, זֶבַח־, זִבְחֵי־
women, wives *fpl*	נָשִׁים, נְשֵׁי־	to sacrifice *inf c* with prep ל	לִזְבֹּחַ [ז.ב.ח]
you will believe* *hifil fpl*	תַּאֲמֵנָּה [א.מ.נ]	he became[a] ... one who rescues *hifil pt ms*	הָיָה ... לְמוֹשִׁיעַ [י.ש.ע]
thanks, gratitude *f*	תּוֹדָה		
you will fear* *mpl*	תִּירְאוּ [י.ר.א]	all that happens / happened (*lit.*, finds) *pt fpl*	כָּל־הַמֹּצָאוֹת [מ.צ.א]
you will go, walk* *mpl*	תֵּלְכוּ [ה.ל.כ]		
you will take *mpl*	תִּקְחוּ [ל.ק.ח]	wave, surf, breaker *m*	מִשְׁבָּר, מִשְׁבָּרִים, מִשְׁבַּר־, מִשְׁבְּרֵי־
you will lift, carry *mpl*	תִּשְׂאוּ [נ.ש.א]	we will remember	נִזְכֹּר [ז.כ.ר]
		we will find*	נִמְצָא [מ.צ.א]

[a] The verb ה.י.ה followed by the preposition ל may indicate a relationship or status into which someone has entered. ה.י.ה/ in this circumstance should be rendered *to become*, not simply *to be* (see also §7.4.י.). The *hifil* spelling will be explained in Unit 8. In the expression הָיָה לָנוּ לְמוֹשִׁיעַ (5.1 Jonah Episode, cell 8), the accent in הָיָה has shifted to the the first syllable in order to avoid adjacent accented syllables (הָיָה לָנוּ instead of הָיָה לָנוּ). This shift is known as *nāsôg ʾāḥôr*.

5.1 Jonah Episode: Where is the wind?

ר׳ = רַב הַחֹבֵל, ע׳ס = עֲבָדִים, א׳ = אֱלֹהִים

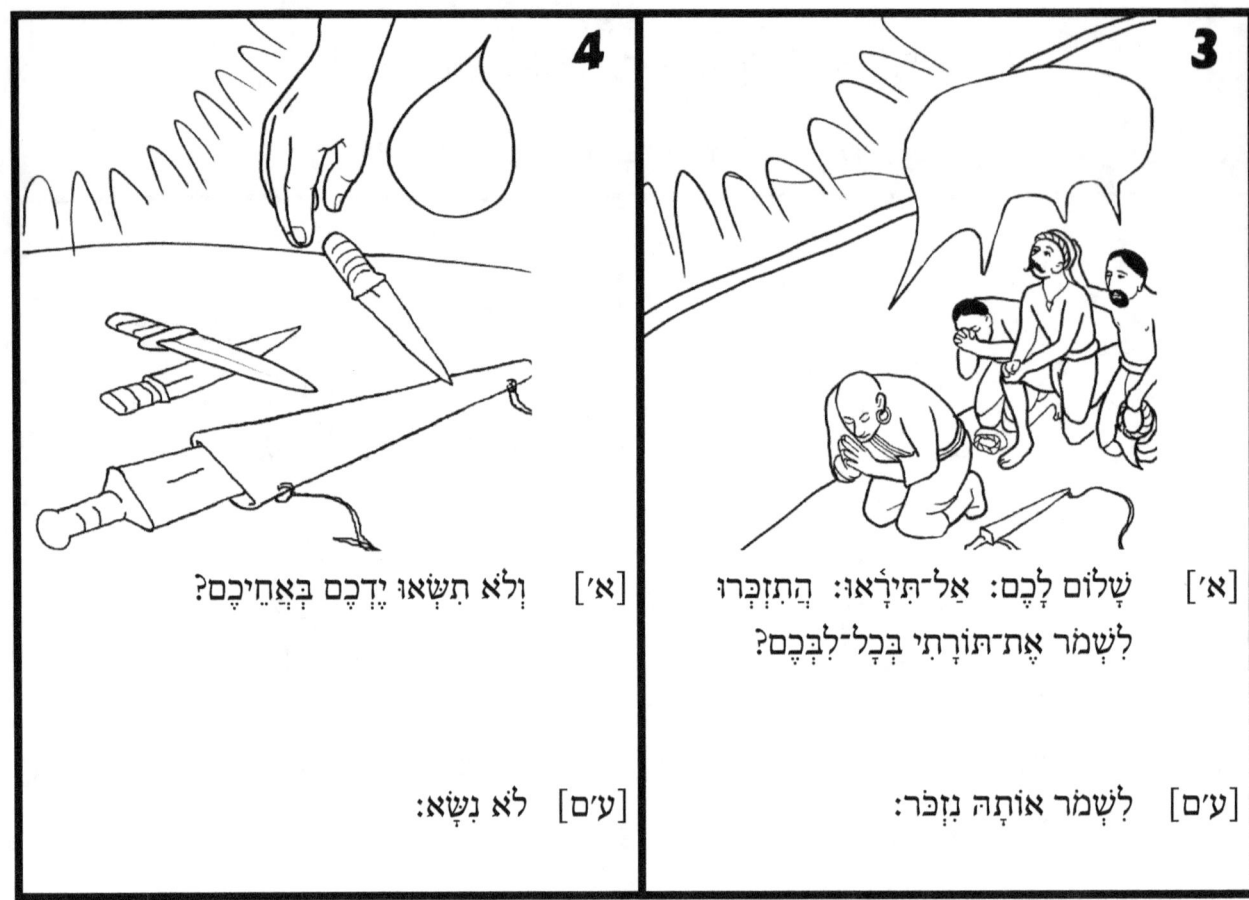

מַה־תַּעֲשֶׂה בָּרִאשׁנָה?

5
[ר׳] הַיּוֹם תֵּצְאוּ מִן הָאֳנִיָּה וּבַיַּבָּשָׁה תֵּלְכוּ:
מַה־תִּקְחוּ עִמָּכֶם לָתֵת לֵאלֹהֵי יִשְׂרָאֵל?

6

[ע׳ס] בְּהֵמָה נִקַּח:
בֶּאֱמֶת חָפֵץ יהוה בְּזִבְחֵי־תוֹדָה:

7

[ע׳ס] בְּשׁוּבֵנוּ לְבָתֵּינוּ נִקְרָא לְנָשֵׁינוּ: "לֹא תַאֲמֵנָּה אֶת כָּל־הַמֹּצָאוֹת אֹתָנוּ בַּיָּם!"

8

[ע׳ס] "בַּבֹּקֶר תֵּלַכְנָה עִמָּנוּ לִזְבֹּחַ לֵאלֹהֵי־יִשְׂרָאֵל כִּי הָיָה לָנוּ לְמוֹשִׁיעַ:"

5.1.א. Explanation: "We will remember to keep it." לִשְׁמֹר אוֹתָהּ נִזְכֹּר:

INTERACTIVE SKILL: Letting friends know what your group plans to do

In order to indicate what your group plans to do (such as, "We will guard the ship" נִשְׁמֹר אֶת־הָאֳנִיָּה), you may begin with the form יִשְׁמֹר *he will guard*, then replace the prefix ...יְ with the prefix ...נְ, resulting in נִשְׁמֹר *we will guard*.

Similarly, the verb ז.כ.ר *remember* becomes נִזְכֹּר *we will remember* (as in the heading for this segment). The "we" forms are described as *1cpl*: first person, common gender (encompassing male and female), and plural.

The theme vowel for the form *we will...* (*1cpl*) will be the same as the theme vowel of the corresponding *he will...* (*3ms*) form of the same verb. Thus since יִבְכֶּה *he will weep* employs a segol theme vowel, so also will the *1cpl* form: נִבְכֶּה *we will weep*. Here are several samples. Third person forms are included for comparison.

מַה־תַּעֲשֶׂה בָּרִאשֹׁנָה?

שֹׁרֶשׁ	יָקְטֹל 3ms	יָקְטֹל 1cpl	we will...	שֹׁרֶשׁ	יָקְטֹל 3ms	יָקְטֹל 1cpl	we will...
ק.ר.ב	יִקְרַב	נִקְרַב	we will approach	ב.כ.י/ה	יִבְכֶּה	נִבְכֶּה	we will weep
ש.ב.ר	יִשְׁבֹּר	נִשְׁבֹּר	we will break (something)	כ.ת.ב	יִכְתֹּב	נִכְתֹּב	we will write
ש.כ.ב	יִשְׁכַּב	נִשְׁכַּב	we will lie down	ס.ל.ח	יִסְלַח	נִסְלַח	we will forgive
ש.ת.י/ה	יִשְׁתֶּה	נִשְׁתֶּה	we will drink	ע.מ.ד	יַעֲמֹד	נַעֲמֹד	we will stand

5.1.ב. Snapshot of sample verb: יָקְטֹל conjugation 1cpl

אֶשְׁמֹר I will guard	נִשְׁמֹר we will guard
תִּשְׁמֹר you will guard ms	תִּשְׁמְרוּ you will guard mpl
תִּשְׁמְרִי you will guard fs	תִּשְׁמֹרְנָה you will guard fpl
יִשְׁמֹר he will guard	יִשְׁמְרוּ they will guard m
תִּשְׁמֹר she will guard	תִּשְׁמֹרְנָה they will guard f

5.1.ג. Activity: "What will you (*mpl*) do today?"   מַה־תַּעֲשׂוּ הַיּוֹם?

INTERACTIVE SKILL: Being able to respond when someone asks what your group plans to do

Form groups of two. Your pair should consist of two males or a male and a female, due to the *mpl* form used for this activity. Drawing on verbs learned up to this point, select one activity you **both** may do later today (actual or outlandishly fictitious). Add detail by supplying an object or prepositional phrase.

As soon as you have agreed on what activity you may engage in later today, find another pair of classmates. Take turns discovering what each other's group plans to do.

Model

What will you (*mpl*) do today?	מַה־תַּעֲשׂוּ הַיּוֹם?	Inquiry
We will find some food to give to the big animal.	נִמְצָא לֶחֶם לָתֵת לַבְּהֵמָה הַגְּדוֹלָה:	Reply

Several suggestions to help simplify the spelling of various *1cpl* forms may be found in the appendix entry corresponding to this segment. Take a moment to look them over.

5.1.ד. Explanation and activity: "What will you (*mpl*) take with you?"
מַה־תִּקְחוּ עִמָּכֶם?

INTERACTIVE SKILL: Asking what a group of your friends plans to do

By now you have acquired quite a few expressions to use when reporting about yourself (you and your friends). To put that in other words: עַתָּה יֵשׁ לָכֶם דְּבָרִים רַבִּים לְדַבֵּר עֲלֵיכֶם.

But others may tire of hearing only about **you** and **your** plans. One simple stroke will enable you to turn the tables to show interest in the activities that **others** are engaged in—beyond simply asking the question, "מַה־תַּעֲשׂוּ?" (as you did in §5.1.ג.).

Begin with a *"they will..."* form (*3mpl*) such as יִרְאוּ *they will see*. To say תִּרְאוּ *you will see* (*2mpl*), replace the prefix ...יְ with ...תִּ: תִּרְאוּ.

Here are several examples. The *3mpl* יִקְטֹל forms have been included for comparison.

שֹׁרֶשׁ	יִקְטֹל *3mpl*	יִקְטֹל *2mpl*	you (*mpl*) will...	שֹׁרֶשׁ	יִקְטֹל *3mpl*	יִקְטֹל *2mpl*	you (*mpl*) will...
ש.ו/י.מ	יָשִׂימוּ	תָּשִׂימוּ	you will place	מ.צ.א	יִמְצְאוּ	תִּמְצְאוּ	you will find
ש.מ.ע	יִשְׁמְעוּ	תִּשְׁמְעוּ	you will hear	ס.ל.ח	יִסְלְחוּ	תִּסְלְחוּ	you will forgive
ש.מ.ר	יִשְׁמְרוּ	תִּשְׁמְרוּ	you will guard	י.צ.א	יֵצְאוּ	תֵּצְאוּ	you will go out
ש.ת.י/ה	יִשְׁתּוּ	תִּשְׁתּוּ	you will drink	נ.ש.א	יִשְׂאוּ	תִּשְׂאוּ	you will lift, take along
נ.ת.נ	יִתְּנוּ	תִּתְּנוּ	you will give	ש.ב.ר	יִשְׁבְּרוּ	תִּשְׁבְּרוּ	you will break (something)

For the activity portion of this segment, work in pairs and begin by selecting one of the following scenarios. Do not disclose your selection to other groups. Later on you will cluster with another pair, using indirect questions to ferret out which scenario the neighboring pair settled on.

Scenarios

✓ When embarking on a hazardous journey, we would…	✓ When very, very hot, we would…	✓ Under a starry sky, we would…
✓ When talking with our boss, we would…	✓ When comforting a sad friend, we would…	✓ At a birthday or wedding celebration, we would…
✓ When playing with children, we would…	✓ When confronting a bully, we would…	✓ Frightened by a ferocious beast, we would…

In a moment you will talk with another pair of classmates, trying to uncover which scenario they have selected. You will accomplish this indirectly, by selecting one activity (a verb), and inquiring how they might perform that activity (in their chosen scenario). In the model below, the verb selected for the inquiry is נ.שׂ.א. The verb you select for your inquiry will be different from נ.שׂ.א.

Model

What will / would you (*mpl*) take along? (תִּשָּׂאוּ *is pausal for* תִּשְׂאוּ.[1])	מַה־תִּשָּׂאוּ?	Inquiry
We will / would take a big rock.	אֶבֶן גְּדֹלָה נִשָּׂא:	Reply

How might this bit of information (that they would "take along a big rock") help you identify their secret scenario? Likely they have been "frightened by a ferocious beast," and so are carrying a rock to use in self-defense.

Using the above verb collection, select a verb (and object or prepositional phrase) to use in your inquiry. If you should choose a verb **not** on this list, for the purposes of this activity please pick a verb that can easily accept a **direct object** or a **prepositional phrase**. Also, since נ.שׂ.א is used in the model above, please select a verb other than נ.שׂ.א for your inquiry.

As soon as you have correctly guessed the scenario chosen by your neighbor-pair, exchange roles to see if they can discover your secretly-selected scenario. If time allows, repeat with a new scenario selection and discovery dialogue.

---

[1] Concerning the presence or absence of dagesh, see explanation for יִשָּׂאוּ in the appendix, §4.1.א., under the heading "Shifting or vanishing consonants…."

5.1.ה. Snapshot of sample verb: יִקְטֹל conjugation *2mpl*

נִשְׁמֹר we will guard	אֶשְׁמֹר I will guard
תִּשְׁמְרוּ **you will guard** *mpl*	תִּשְׁמֹר you will guard *ms*
תִּשְׁמֹרְנָה you will guard *fpl*	תִּשְׁמְרִי you will guard *fs*
יִשְׁמְרוּ they will guard *m*	יִשְׁמֹר he will guard
תִּשְׁמֹרְנָה they will guard *f*	תִּשְׁמֹר she will guard

5.1.1. Explanation and activity: "In the morning you (*fpl*) will go to make a sacrifice..." בַּבֹּקֶר תֵּלַכְנָה לִזְבֹּחַ...

INTERACTIVE SKILL: Asking what a group of your friends plans to do—assuming the group is comprised entirely of women.

Once you have learned how to describe what a group of women are about to do (*3fpl*, as in תֵּלַכְנָה *they will go* or תֹּאמַרְנָה *they will say*), you will also be able to address them directly, with "you-statements." Why is this possible? Because the *you fpl* forms and the *they fpl* forms are spelled the same.

Rather than reprinting these identical forms, please refer back to §4.4.א. to review the forms found there. Notice the list of verbs given in that segment as "they (*f*) will…" *3fpl*. These can be used with equal accuracy as a collection of "you (*f*) will…" *2fpl* forms.

Now you are ready for an activity that will explore whether there is any difference how a particular gender will behave in various scenarios. What you learn may surprise you!

(a) Join with a few others to form a group consisting only of men or only of women.

(b) Together with others in your group, select one of the scenario options found in §5.1.ד.

(c) Select a verb suitable to that scenario.

(d) Using the verb that you have selected, together with the scenario that you have selected, ask the opposite-gender group how they would respond.

(e) Formulate a response on behalf of your own group as well. That is, explain how your group would respond to that same scenario. Responses may be positive (*We would…*) or negative (*We would not…*).

(f) Compare how your group and how the opposite-gender group would respond to the same scenario.

Model

Imagine, for example, that yours is the male group, and you wish to ask the female group concerning the **scenario,** "When comforting a sad friend." The **verb** you select is נ.ת.נ *to give*. After explaining to the other group which scenario you have selected, you then would express your inquiry: "מַה־תִּתֵּנָּה?" (note the use of *2fpl* since you are addressing a group of women). After thinking it over, perhaps they would respond with a reply similar to the one given below. At the same time, you will need to compose a reply reporting on how your own group would respond (using נ.ת.נ). Then you can compare how similar (or divergent) are the responses of your respective groups.

Inquiry	מַה־תִּתֵּנָה?	What will / would you (*fpl*) give?
Reply	לֹא נִתֵּן אֶת־הַבָּסֶף׃ אֶת־הַלֶּחֶם נִתֵּן׃	We would not give silver (*pausal*). We would give food.

5.1.ז. Snapshot of sample verb: יִקְטֹל conjugation *2fpl*

נִשְׁמֹר we will guard	אֶשְׁמֹר I will guard
תִּשְׁמְרוּ you will guard *mpl*	תִּשְׁמֹר you will guard *ms*
תִּשְׁמֹרְנָה **you will guard** *fpl*	תִּשְׁמְרִי you will guard *fs*
יִשְׁמְרוּ they will guard *m*	יִשְׁמֹר he will guard
תִּשְׁמֹרְנָה they will guard *f*	תִּשְׁמֹר she will guard

5.1.ח. Did you (*ms*) know that...? (Body language)   ?...הֲיָדַעְתָּ כִּי

> ...hand gestures carried a variety of meanings in ancient Israel? Lifting one's hand *against* someone (נ.ש.א יָד בְּ...) conveyed hostility (2 Sam. 18:28, 20:21). Lifting one's hand *concerning* something (נ.ש.א יָד לְ...) expressed a formal intent to enter into a solemn oath (Ezek. 20:5), while hands lifted *toward* (נ.ש.א יָד אֶל־) a sanctuary depicted a posture of prayer or supplication (Ps. 28:2, 134:2).[2]
>
> Excavations at the ancient Israelite city of Hazor have unearthed a Canaanite temple from the Late Bronze era (1550–1200 BCE) containing—among other things—a stele featuring two hands stretched upward in prayer. The hands are reaching up toward a deity symbol consisting of a crescent cradling a sun disc, located at the top of the stele.[3]
>
> How many messages may hand gestures convey in your culture?

5.1.ט. Did you (*ms*) know that...? (Musical instruments)   ?...הֲיָדַעְתָּ כִּי

> ...that at least nine musical instruments are referred to in the Hebrew Bible? They range from stringed instruments (asymmetrical כִּנּוֹר *lyre m* and נֵבֶל *harp* or *lute m*), to wind instruments (יוֹבֵל or שׁוֹפָר *ram's horn m*, חֲצֹצְרָה *bugle f*, and חָלִיל *flute m*), and percussion instruments (tambourines, צִלְצְלֵי תְרוּעָה *larger cymbals m* [10 cm diameter]

---

[2] For a graphic depiction of Ashkelon inhabitants with upraised hands supplicating Ramesses II during a siege (preserved in a Karnak temple relief from the 13th century BCE), see Yigael Yadin, *The Art of Warfare in Biblical Lands* (New York: McGraw-Hill, 1963), 1:228.

[3] Yigael Yadin, "Excavations at Hazor," *Biblical Archaeologist* 19:1 (1956): 10 and 12.

and צִלְצְלֵי שָׁמַע *finger cymbals m*).

Vocal and instrumental music played a major role in societal settings as varied as temple worship, harvest celebrations, weddings, and warfare.[4]

Egyptian arched wooden harp (Thebes, New Kingdom [1550–1069 BCE], 60.2 cm). (Courtesy of British Museum)

Byzantine finger cymbals (resembling instruments from 9th cent. Megiddo, 5.5 cm in diameter). (Courtesy of Flora Archaeological Center)

---

[4] *LBI*, pp. 285–91.

5.1.י. Did you (ms) know that...? (Domesticated animals) ‏הֲיָדַעְתָּ כִּי...?

...the goat (עַתּוּד m, עֵז f) was among the most useful of domesticated animals? Goats were an important source of חָלָב milk m (with twice the production of sheep), and also provided meat, coarsely woven clothing, and skins for storing liquids. Other domesti-

Aramean King of Astartu in horse-drawn chariot, captured by Assyrian Tiglath Pileser III (745–727 BCE, from SW palace of Nimrud). (Courtesy of British Museum)

cated animals included בָּקָר cattle m, חֲמוֹר donkey m, פֶּרֶד mule m, סוּס horse m, אֲלָפִים oxen or cattle m, and גָּמָל camel m.

The extent of one's cattle holdings gave an index of one's wealth. Cattle were maintained primarily for milk, seldom for meat. The two-ox team formed the typical draft operation in agriculture.

As early as 3500 BCE

Camels presented to Shalmaneser III as tribute (detail from replica of Black Obelisk, 9th cent. BCE). (Courtesy of Flora Archaeological Center)

donkeys were domesticated, and served both for riding and as the principal pack animal. Mules were the preferred mounts of royalty. The camel was the principal military mount in Assyria, with an average range of 95–120 kilometers per day. In Israel, horses were used primarily for pulling war chariots, not for riding.[5]

Horse-mounted Assyrian Ashurbanipal, on a lion hunt (North Palace, Nineveh, ca. 645–635 BCE). (Courtesy of British Museum)

---

[5] *LBI*, pp. 112–19. For a depiction of a pack animal, see §4.2.ג; for a Judean chariot, see §11.1.ו.

MODULE 5.2

Describing what you yourself are about to do

Words for responding — מִלִּים לַעֲנוֹת

חָדָשׁ, חֲדָשָׁה, חֲדָשִׁים, חֲדָשׁוֹת	new	אִירָא [י.ר.א]	I will be afraid, fear*
תֹּאמַר [א.מ.ר]	you will say* ms	אֵלֵךְ [ה.ל.כ]	I will go*
תֵּלֵךְ [ה.ל.כ]	you will go, walk* ms	אֶמְצָא [מ.צ.א]	I will find*
		אֶשָּׂא [נ.שׂ.א]	I will lift, carry*
תִּשָּׂא [נ.שׂ.א]	you will lift, carry* ms	אֶתֵּן [נ.ת.נ]	I will give*
		בָּשָׂר	meat, flesh m

Words for hearing — מִלִּים לִשְׁמֹעַ

מִצְוָה, מִצְוֹת, מִצְוַת־, מִצְוֹת־	commandment f	אֲהָהּ	Alas…! Ah…!
		אֲדֹנָי	LORD[a]
עֶצֶם, עֲצָמוֹת, עֶצֶם־, עַצְמוֹת־	bone, inner substance, self f	אֶחָד, אַחַת, אֲחָדִים	one, single, same m, f, mpl
שָׂפָה, שְׂפָתַיִם, שְׂפַת־, שִׂפְתֵי־	lip f, dual	אֹכַל [א.כ.ל]	I will eat*
שְׂפַת־הַיָּם	the shore f	אֵרֵד [י.ר.ד]	I will descend, go down*
תָּמוּת [מ.ו.ת]	you will die* ms	אַשְׁלִיךְ [שׁ.ל.כ]	I will throw* hifil
תַּשְׁלִיךְ [שׁ.ל.כ]	you will throw* hifil ms	מוֹת אָמוּת [מ.ו.ת]	I most certainly will die*

[a] The vocalization אֲדֹנָי references יהוה LORD. In contrast, "my lord" would be vocalized אֲדֹנִי.

5.2 Jonah Episode: I'm hungry.

ג׳ = הַדָּג הַגָּדוֹל, נ׳ = יוֹנָה הַנָּבִיא, א׳ = אֱלֹהִים

[ג׳] אֲנִי רָעֵב: אֲנִי חָפֵץ לֶאֱכֹל אֶת־הַנָּבִיא:

[נ׳] הוֹשִׁיעֵנִי יהוה!

[א׳] שְׁמַע הַדָּג הַגָּדוֹל:[6] לֹא תֹאכַל אֶת־הַנָּבִיא: עֲצָמוֹת רַבּוֹת לוֹ וּבְשָׂרוֹ לֹא־טוֹב:

[נ׳] הַלְלוּ יָהּ!! לֹא אִירָא:

---

[6] Did you notice the articles used in הַדָּג הַגָּדוֹל? These indicate the person whom the speaker is addressing, calling that person out by title or position. It is known as the "vocative." You will find it used a couple lines later as the big fish addresses the prophet. Biblical examples of the vocative may be found in 1 Sam. 17:58 and 2 Sam. 14:4.

[ג׳] אַל־תְּדַבֵּר, הַנָּבִיא הַקָּטֹן!
אֲהָהּ אֲדֹנָי! אֲנִי לֹא אֶשָּׂא אֹתוֹ[7] לְעוֹלָם
פֶּן־אָמוּת:
מוֹת אָמוּת אִם־יֵשֵׁב בְּבִטְנִי עוֹד יוֹם
אֶחָד:

[א׳] לֹא תָמוּת, הַדָּג הַגָּדוֹל:
מִצְוָה חֲדָשָׁה אֶתֵּן לָךְ:
בַּבֹּקֶר תִּשָּׂא אֶת־הַנָּבִיא וְעִמּוֹ תֵּלֵךְ אֶל־שְׂפַת־הַיָּם:

---

[7] In addition to stating fact, another shade of meaning available for יִקְטֹל involves conveying "capability" (or its opposite). Due to the context involving pending hardship, the expression לֹא אֶשָּׂא אֹתוֹ may be rendered *I cannot carry him forever* (rather than *I will not carry him forever*). Cf. וַאֲנִי כְחֵרֵשׁ לֹא אֶשְׁמָע *But I am like a deaf person, I cannot hear* (Ps. 38:14a; *IBHS* §31.4).

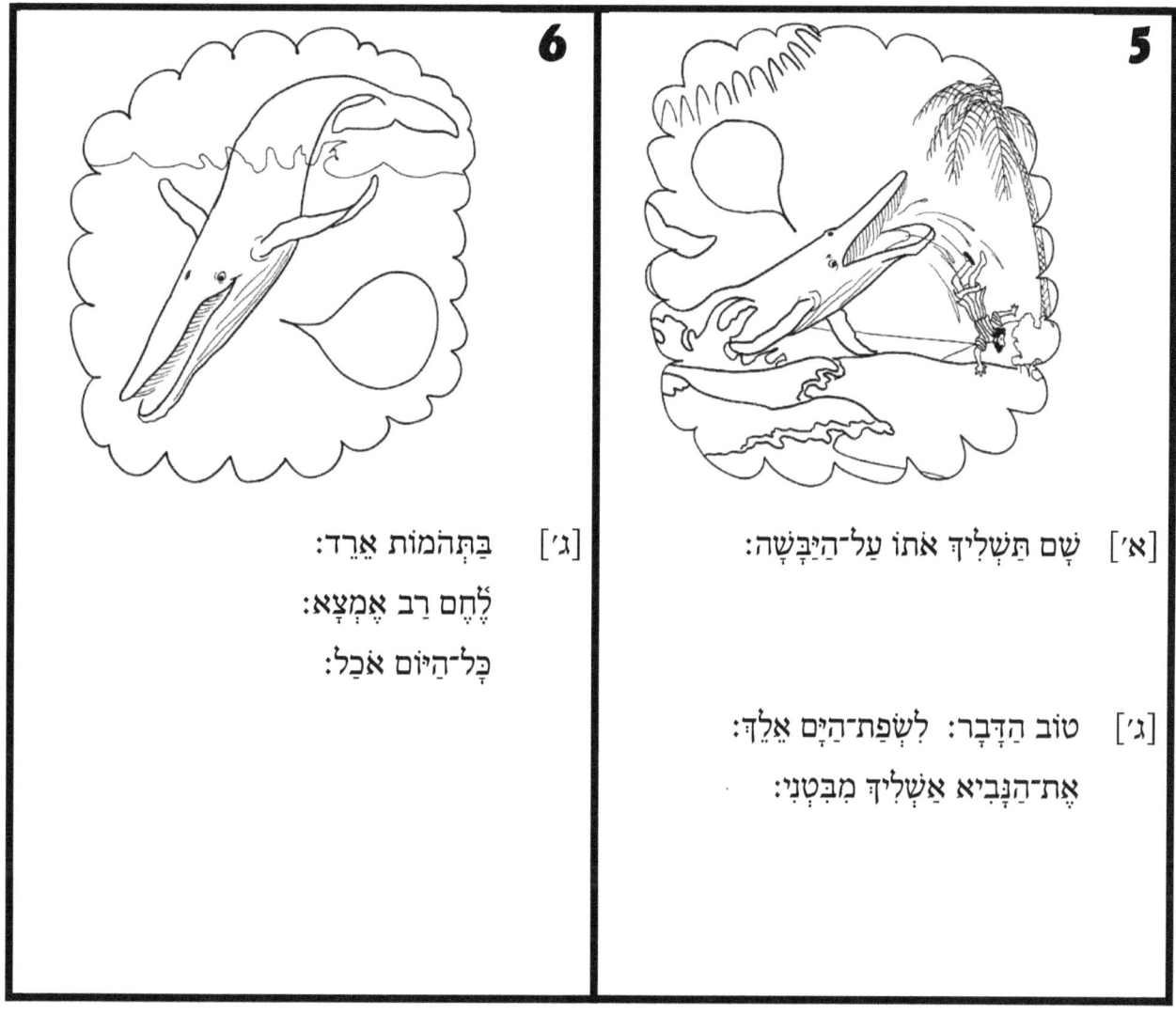

5.2.א. Do you (*ms*) know the meaning of a word? (Protocol idiom)

הֲיָדַעְתָּ פֵּשֶׁר דָּבָר?

On occasion we may discover that the custom of social class has been preserved in an idiom. When a superior (such as a queen) warmly welcomed a subordinate (such as a servant) it was said that she "lifted up the head" (נ.שׂ.א ראשׁ) of her servant. Perhaps protocol dictated that the commoner would actually approach the sovereign with head humbly bowed.

> From this idiom Joseph formed a wordplay when interpreting the divergent dreams of his fellow-prisoners in Egypt. To the cupbearer he announced, ‎יִשָּׂא פַרְעֹה אֶת־רֹאשֶׁךָ... (Gen. 40:13). But to the baker he cautioned, ‎יִשָּׂא פַרְעֹה אֶת־רֹאשְׁךָ מֵעָלֶיךָ... (v. 19). The change in the last word made all the difference!
>
> Consider your own culture. What sort of message may be conveyed by the position of one's head?

5.2.ב. Explanation and activity: "What will you (*ms*, *fs*) do first, tomorrow?" ‎מַה־תַּעֲשֶׂה / תַּעֲשִׂי מָחָר בָּרִאשֹׁנָה?

INTERACTIVE SKILL: Describe to a friend how your typical day will unfold

The Jonah Episode for this module employs a number of first-person statements. Here are a few of the verbs (‎יִקְטֹל, with customary future meaning). As you scan examples in the first table you will discover a distinct pattern that distinguishes a *1cs* form. The *3ms* forms are provided as a point of comparison.

Most *I will...* (*1cs*) verb forms call for a prefix of ‎אֶ..., as evident in this table:

UNIT 5 — מַה־תַּעֲשֶׂה בָּרִאשֹׁנָה?

I will...	יִקְטֹל 1cs	יִקְטֹל 3ms	שֹׁרֶשׁ
I will find	אֶמְצָא	יִמְצָא	מ.צ.א
I will lift	אֶשָּׂא	יִשָּׂא	נ.שׂ.א
I will give	אֶתֵּן	יִתֵּן	נ.ת.ן

Here are several more:

I will...	יִקְטֹל 1cs	יִקְטֹל 3ms	שֹׁרֶשׁ	I will...	יִקְטֹל 1cs	יִקְטֹל 3ms	שֹׁרֶשׁ
I will approach	אֶקְרַב	יִקְרַב	ק.ר.ב	I will write	אֶכְתֹּב	יִכְתֹּב	כ.ת.ב
I will break	אֶשְׁבֹּר	יִשְׁבֹּר	שׁ.ב.ר	I will weep	אֶבְכֶּה	יִבְכֶּה	ב.כ.י/ה
I will lie down	אֶשְׁכַּב	יִשְׁכַּב	שׁ.כ.ב	I will forgive	אֶסְלַח	יִסְלַח	ס.ל.ח
I will drink	אֶשְׁתֶּה	יִשְׁתֶּה	שׁ.ת.י/ה	I will stand	אֶעֱמֹד	יַעֲמֹד	ע.מ.ד

To learn spelling tips for verbs when the שֹׁרֶשׁ begins with א (as in א.כ.ל), or with י (as in י.ר.ד), or when the שֹׁרֶשׁ is hollow (as in מ.ו.ת), please refer to the appendix entry corresponding to this segment.

Now, take a couple of minutes to think through what tomorrow may hold for you. What will you do first? Second? Third? Fill in the list below with brief sentences. Do you remember what מָחָר means? (Hint: it is the day following הַיּוֹם.) Armed with the information that בָּרִאשֹׁנָה means *at first*, you should have little difficulty deciphering the sequence that continues with הַדָּבָר הַשֵּׁנִי.[8]

	א. מָחָר בָּרִאשֹׁנָה...
	ב. הַדָּבָר הַשֵּׁנִי...

---

[8] Can you see a correlation between בָּרִאשֹׁנָה and the Hebrew word for *head* or *top*? Aside from רִאשֹׁנָה (for which see Gen. 13:4), you may find the ordinal numbers "second" through "fourth" used to designate the days of creation (Gen. 1:8, 13, and 19). Incidentally, רִאשֹׁנָה offers a good example of a quiescent or silent א.

ג. הַדָּבָר הַשְּׁלִישִׁי...	

ד. הַדָּבָר הָרְבִיעִי...	

Finally, ask a friend what he / she will do first (second, and third, etc.). Refer to the question found in the heading for this segment in order to fashion your inquiry.

5.2.ג. Snapshot of sample verb: יִקְטֹל conjugation *1cs*

נִשְׁמֹר	אֶשְׁמֹר
we will guard	I will guard
תִּשְׁמְרוּ	תִּשְׁמֹר
you will guard *mpl*	you will guard *ms*
תִּשְׁמֹרְנָה	תִּשְׁמְרִי
you will guard *fpl*	you will guard *fs*
יִשְׁמְרוּ	יִשְׁמֹר
they will guard *m*	he will guard
תִּשְׁמֹרְנָה	תִּשְׁמֹר
they will guard *f*	she will guard

5.2.ד. Explanation: "If he dwells... I will surely die."

אִם־יֵשֵׁב... מוֹת אָמוּת:

INTERACTIVE SKILL: How to express a future certainty

Hebrew can convey emphasis by linking two forms of the same שֹׁרֶשׁ. In the expression מוֹת אָמוּת *I will surely die*, the first word (מוֹת) is an infinitive—a particular infinitive form that stands alone (without prefixed prepositions). It is known as the *infinitive absolute*. When an infinitive absolute (such as מוֹת) precedes a יִקְטֹל form drawn from the same שֹׁרֶשׁ (such as אָמוּת), the whole expression means: *I will surely die*. In the next Jonah episode you will encounter another infinitive absolute used for emphasis, where the two forms share the שֹׁרֶשׁ ש.ו.ב: שׁוֹב אָשׁוּב *I will surely repent*.[9]

Incidentally, did you notice that אִם־יֵשֵׁב should be rendered *If he dwells* or *If he were to dwell* (not *If he will dwell*)? Although this sort of conditional expression looks to the future, English idiom calls for "*dwells*" rather than "*...will dwell*."[10]

---

[9] When an infinitive absolute shares the same שֹׁרֶשׁ with an accompanying finite verb, the structure is referred to as a "paronomastic usage" (wordplay-related). Infinitives construct are also capable of conveying emphasis (combined with a finite קָטַל form, often conveying past tense, as you will learn in Unit 6).

If you are wondering whether any difference in spelling distinguishes infinitives **construct** (the infinitives capable of accepting prefixed prepositions) from the spelling of infinitives **absolute**, the primary rule is that infinitives **absolute** more regularly employ a qameṣ in the first syllable of strong verbs (or, in the case of hollow verbs, a ḥolem or ḥolem-vav: מוֹת is *infinitive absolute* for *to die*, while מוּת is *infinitive construct*). In contrast, infinitives construct begin with a sheva or a reduced vowel (שְׁמֹר rather than שָׁמוֹר). This may be easily observed by scanning the two columns showing infinitives for numerous verbs in the qal reference tables (pp. 511–16).

[10] This sort of conditional statement is known as "real" since it may actually materialize, as opposed to an "irreal" ("contrary-to-fact") conditional. In its "if" clause ("protasis"), an irreal conditional uses the קָטַל conjugation, a conjugation that will be introduced in the next unit.

MODULE 5.3 Discussing plans with a friend

Words for responding — מִלִּים לַעֲנוֹת

תֵּשְׁבִי [י.ש.ב]	you will dwell, sit* fs	אֶעֱלֶה [ע.ל.י/ה]	I will go up
תָּשׁוּב / תָּשׁוּבִי [ש.ו.ב]	you will turn back, return, repent* ms, fs	תְּדַבֵּר [ד.ב.ר]	you will speak* piel ms
		תִּזְכֹּר [ז.כ.ר]	you will remember* ms
תִּשְׁכַּח [ש.כ.ח]	you will forget ms	תַּעֲלֶה [ע.ל.י/ה]	you will go up ms
תִּשְׁמַע [ש.מ.ע]	you will hear* ms	תַּעֲנֶה [ע.נ.י/ה]	you will answer ms
		תַּעֲשִׂי [ע.ש.י/ה]	you will do, make* fs

Words for hearing — מִלִּים לִשְׁמֹעַ

הַכֵּה אַכֶּה [נ.כ.י/ה]	I will surely strike* hifil	אָז	then
		אֶזְבַּח [ז.ב.ח]	I will sacrifice (pausal אֶזְבָּח)
יְרַחֵם [ר.ח.מ]	he will have mercy piel[b]	אֹמַר [א.מ.ר]	I will say*
לָצֵאת [י.צ.א]	to go out* inf c, prep לְ	אֶסְלַח [ס.ל.ח]	I will forgive (pausal אֶסְלָח)
מִי יוֹדֵעַ? [י.ד.ע]	Who knows?		
עָנִי, עֲנִיִּים	oppressed, afflicted, poor ms, mpl	אָשִׂים [ש.ו./י.מ]	I will put*
		בַּעֲבוּר	on account of
		גַּם	also
צְעָקָה, צַעֲקַת־	outcry, scream from despair f	הוֹשִׁיעֵנִי [י.ש.ע]	Rescue me! hifil[a] imv
רֵעַ, רֵעִים, רֵעַ, רֵעִי־	neighbor, friend m		

שׁוֹב אָשׁוּב [שׁ.ו.ב]	I most certainly will turn back, return, repent*

[a] The *hifil* spelling will be explained in Unit 8.

[b] יְרַחֵם belongs to the *piel* spelling, a form that will be explained in Unit 10.

5.3 Jonah Episode: I'm in big trouble!

נ׳ = יוֹנָה הַנָּבִיא, א׳ = אֱלֹהִים

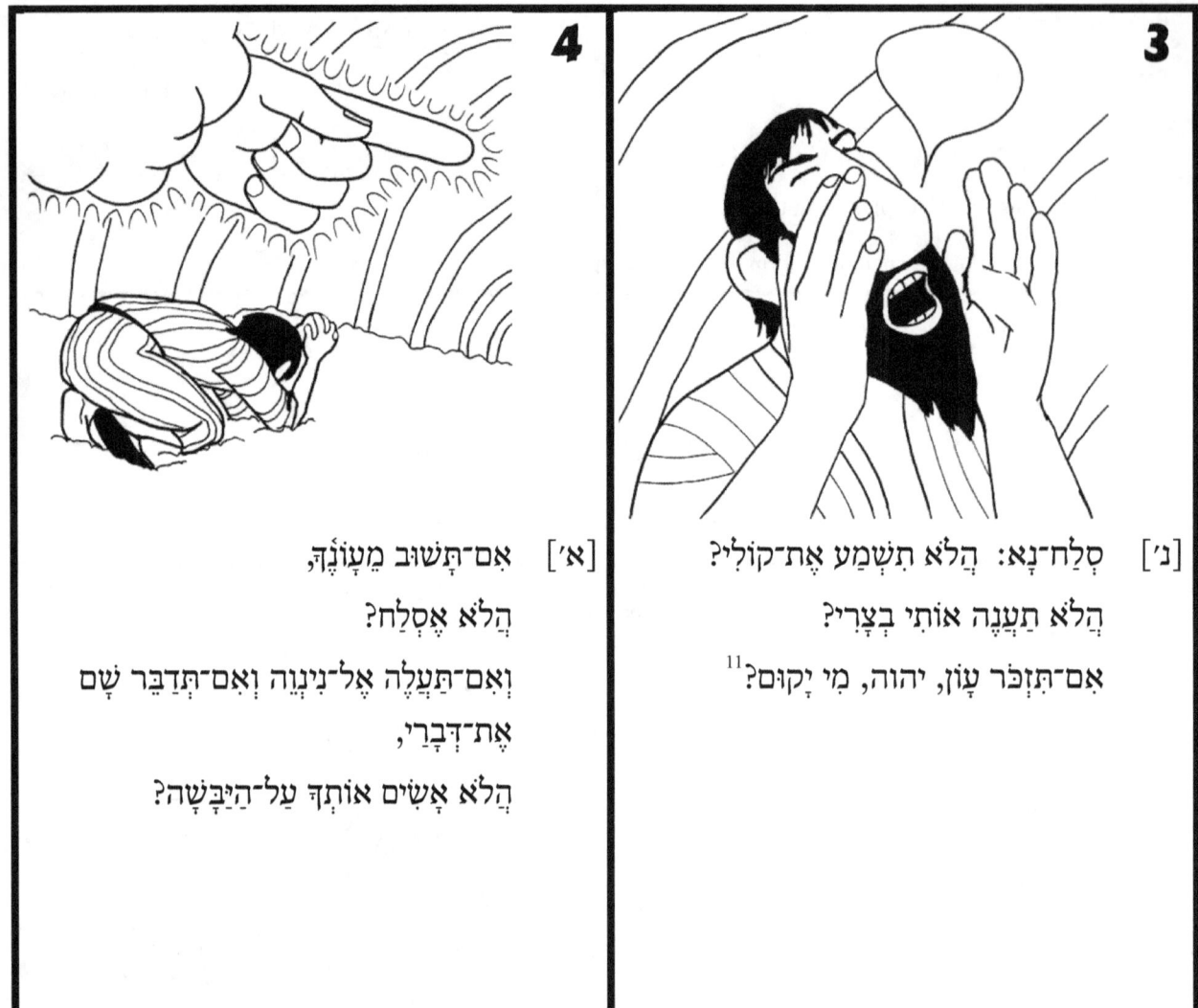

[נ׳] סְלַח־נָא: הֲלֹא תִשְׁמַע אֶת־קוֹלִי?
הֲלֹא תַעֲנֶה אוֹתִי בְּצָרִי?
אִם־תִּזְכֹּר עָוֹן, יהוה, מִי יָקוּם?[11]

[א׳] אִם־תָּשׁוּב מֵעֲוֹנֶךָ,
הֲלֹא אֶסְלַח?
וְאִם־תַּעֲלֶה אֶל־נִינְוֵה וְאִם־תְּדַבֵּר שָׁם אֶת־דְּבָרַי,
הֲלֹא אָשִׂים אוֹתְךָ עַל־הַיַּבָּשָׁה?

---

[11] Which translation seems more fitting for מִי יָקוּם: *Who **will** stand?* or *Who **can** stand?*

---

[12] The question מָה אֹמַר לָעִיר? may initially be translated, *What **will** I say to the city?* Another option offered by יָקְטֹל is called the יָקְטֹל of obligation: *What **should** I say to the city?* Context serves to indicate when we ought to employ the "obligation" option. Cf. *IBHS* §31.4g, also Exod. 4:15.

---

[13] One of the ways oracles refer to a populace is to identify it as "the daughter(s)" or "virgin daughter(s)" of a particular city (e.g., daughter of Tarshish [Isa. 23:10], daughter of Babylon [Isa. 47:1]) or of a nation (e.g., daughters of Moab [Isa. 16:2], daughter of Chaldeans / Babylonians [Isa. 47:1]). Most frequent is the expression "daughter of Zion" (e.g., Isa. 3:16, 17, Jer. 4:31).

5.3.א. Explanation: "Won't you (*ms*) remember me?" הֲלֹא תִזְכֹּר אוֹתִי?

INTERACTIVE SKILL: This information will prepare you for the choices-and-consequences conversation in §5.3.ה.

The *you will 2ms* forms of the יִקְטֹל conjugation are easy to recognize since they are quite similar to the *he will 3ms* forms learned earlier (cf. §4.1.א.). The shift from יִזְכֹּר *he will remember* to תִזְכֹּר *you will remember 2ms* involves substituting the prefix י of *he will* with the prefix ת for *you will 2ms*. Aided by this comparison, אַתָּה תִזְכֹּר this form with little difficulty![14] Notice the correlation between 3rd and 2nd person in the samples below.

שֹׁרֶשׁ	יִקְטֹל *3ms*	יִקְטֹל *2ms*	you (*ms*) will...
ז.כ.ר	יִזְכֹּר	תִזְכֹּר	you will remember
ק.ר.ב	יִקְרַב	תִקְרַב	you will approach
ש.כ.ב	יִשְׁכַּב	תִשְׁכַּב	you will lie down

Perhaps you are wondering how the verbs whose שֹׁרֶשׁ begins with י or נ will be spelled in the *2ms* forms. Here are a few representative samples. Sample verbs ending in ...י/ה and those with ו as the second radical (hollow verbs) are included as well. The adjustments appearing in these so-called "weak" spellings will remind you of adjustments noted in earlier "weak" forms.

שֹׁרֶשׁ	יִקְטֹל *3ms*	יִקְטֹל *2ms*	you (*ms*) will...
י.שׁ.ב	יֵשֵׁב	תֵּשֵׁב	you will sit
ה.ל.כ	יֵלֵךְ	תֵּלֵךְ	you will walk, go
נ.פ.ל	יִפֹּל	תִּפֹּל	you will fall
נ.כ.י/ה	יַכֶּה	תַּכֶּה	you will hit
ב.כ.י/ה	יִבְכֶּה	תִּבְכֶּה	you will weep
ש.ת.י/ה	יִשְׁתֶּה	תִּשְׁתֶּה	you will drink

---

[14] Notice that אַתָּה תִזְכֹּר in the context of this sentence may be treated as a יִקְטֹל of **capability**: *You **will be able** to remember....* Unlike English, no auxiliary verbs are needed to convey this meaning.

	יָקְטֹל 3ms		יָקְטֹל 2ms	you (ms) will…
שֹׁרֶשׁ				
א.ו.ב	יָבוֹא		תָּבוֹא	you will come
שׁ.ו.ב	יָשׁוּב		תָּשׁוּב	you will turn to

5.3.ב. Snapshot of sample verb: יָקְטֹל conjugation *2ms*

נִשְׁמֹר we will guard	אֶשְׁמֹר I will guard
תִּשְׁמְרוּ you will guard *mpl*	**תִּשְׁמֹר** **you will guard *ms***
תִּשְׁמֹרְנָה you will guard *fpl*	תִּשְׁמְרִי you will guard *fs*
יִשְׁמְרוּ they will guard *m*	יִשְׁמֹר he will guard
תִּשְׁמֹרְנָה they will guard *f*	תִּשְׁמֹר she will guard

5.3.ג. Explanation: "If you (*fs*) dwell..." אִם־תֵּשְׁבִי...

INTERACTIVE SKILL: This segment also will prepare you for the choices-and-consequences conversation in §5.3.ה.

With one small step we can shift from talking about "you" *ms* to "you" *fs*. If we take a *you 2ms* form such as תֵּשֵׁב *you* (*ms*) *will dwell* and add the suffix ִי..., the resulting form will be תֵּשְׁבִי *you* (*fs*) *will dwell*. Again, if the masculine form is תִּזְכֹּר *you* (*ms*) *will remember,* then the corresponding feminine form will be תִּזְכְּרִי *you* (*fs*) *will remember*.[15]

As you compare the following *2fs* verbs side-by-side with corresponding *2ms* forms you will recognize the conversion. In fact, with relatively little effort you may be sure that אַתָּה תִּזְכֹּר these forms (unless you are a woman, in which case, אַתְּ תִּזְכְּרִי אוֹתָם)!

שֹׁרֶשׁ	יִקְטֹל *2ms*	יִקְטֹל *2fs*	you (*fs*) will...
ז.כ.ר	תִּזְכֹּר	תִּזְכְּרִי	you will remember
ק.ר.ב	תִּקְרַב	תִּקְרְבִי	you will approach
ש.כ.ב	תִּשְׁכַּב	תִּשְׁכְּבִי	you will lie down
ש.כ.ח	תִּשְׁכַּח	תִּשְׁכְּחִי	you will forget

As for so-called weak verbs like ש.ו.ב or ה.ל.כ, the collection of verbs offered below will give an idea how even these *2fs* forms will follow spelling patterns observed earlier.

שֹׁרֶשׁ	יִקְטֹל *2ms*	יִקְטֹל *2fs*	you (*fs*) will...
י.ש.ב	תֵּשֵׁב	תֵּשְׁבִי	you will sit
ה.ל.כ	תֵּלֵךְ	תֵּלְכִי	you will walk, go
נ.פ.ל	תִּפֹּל	תִּפְּלִי	you will fall
נ.כ.י/ה	תַּכֶּה	תַּכִּי	you will hit
ב.כ.י/ה	תִּבְכֶּה	תִּבְכִּי	you will weep

---

[15] Since this extra syllable (the suffix ִי...) lengthens the entire word, typically what *used to be the last syllable* will reduce its vowel to a sheva (except when the word is in pause). Thus the ḥolem in תִּזְכֹּר becomes a sheva: תִּזְכְּרִי.

שֹׁרֶשׁ	יִקְטֹל 2ms	יִקְטֹל 2fs	you (fs) will...
ע.ש.י/ה	תַּעֲשֶׂה	תַּעֲשִׂי	you will make, do
ש.ת.י/ה	תִּשְׁתֶּה	תִּשְׁתִּי	you will drink
ב.ו.א	תָּבוֹא	תָּבוֹאִי	you will come
ש.ו.ב	תָּשׁוּב	תָּשׁוּבִי	you will turn to

5.3.ד. Snapshot of sample verb: יִקְטֹל conjugation *2fs*

נִשְׁמֹר we will guard	אֶשְׁמֹר I will guard
תִּשְׁמְרוּ you will guard *mpl*	תִּשְׁמֹר you will guard *ms*
תִּשְׁמֹרְנָה you will guard *fpl*	**תִּשְׁמְרִי** **you will guard** *fs*
יִשְׁמְרוּ they will guard *m*	יִשְׁמֹר he will guard
תִּשְׁמֹרְנָה they will guard *f*	תִּשְׁמֹר she will guard

5.3.ה. Activity: "What will I (*or* should I) do if...?"   מָה אֶעֱשֶׂה אִם...?

INTERACTIVE SKILL: Counseling a friend concerning what he or she will do (or should do) tomorrow, if a certain course of action is followed today

This activity will lead you into a rather sophisticated level of conversation—a conversation where you will ponder the future and offer a forecast (or give some advice). Take time to review the introduction thoughtfully.

Imagine that a friend has come to you, seeking your advice. He or she is facing a dilemma and needs your help in forecasting what **consequences** may result from a proposed course of action.

After your friend has informed you of his or her action proposed for today, your task will be to help him forecast what he will do (or should do) tomorrow, as a consequence.

Notice the model below. The first entry is labeled "**Today's action**." Here you will find the course of action proposed by your friend. This entry begins with an "if-clause" (known as a "protasis"). In the model, the proposed course of action has been marked with brackets: "[to break Sarah's big container]."

The second entry is labeled "**Tomorrow's forecast**." Here you will find two sample elements of forecast or advice arising out of "Today's action." This portion of an "if-then" conditional statement is known as the "apodosis." Notice that the advice opens with the word "tomorrow," not with the יִקְטֹל verb. Also note that the term "יִקְטֹל" often is written without vowels (יקטל).

Model

Please adapt the phrases in brackets according to your chosen "action" or "forecast."

		Today's action
If I [were to break Sarah's big container] today, what will / should I do tomorrow?[16]	אִם־הַיּוֹם [אֶשְׁבֹּר כְּלִי־שָׂרָה הַגָּדוֹל], מָה אֶעֱשֶׂה מָחָר?	(friend's proposed course of action)

---

[16] The protasis אִם...אֶשְׁבֹּר may be rendered either as *If... I were to break* (hypothetical), or simply as *If... I break*.

Tomorrow's forecast (two consequences)	אִם־הַיּוֹם [תִּשְׁבֹּר כְּלִי־שָׂרָה הַגָּדוֹל], מָחָר [(א) "סִלְחִי לִי" תֹּאמַר / תֹּאמְרִי לְשָׂרָה] [(ב) וְכֶסֶף תִּתֵּן / תִּתְּנִי לָהּ]:	If you [were to break Sarah's big container] today, tomorrow [(a) you will / should say "Sorry!" to Sarah, and (b) you will / should give her some silver].

Note (1). Have you noticed that this activity frequently offers a translation of either "will" or "should"? Since the connotation of "should" belongs to the range of meanings governed by the יקטל, you may render a יקטל form by either "will" or "should," depending on the context. Thus in the model forecast statement (א) above, it will be up to the reader to determine whether to translate תֹּאמַר לְשָׂרָה as *you **will** say to Sarah* or as *you **should** say to Sarah*.[17]

Note (2). Did you observe the guideline to begin your forecast statements with a word such as מָחָר (rather than beginning with a יקטל verb)? The reason is this: if instead we were to begin with a יקטל verb, we would create the notion: "I firmly hope that you would…."[18] By avoiding יקטל in first position we can maintain the meaning of "you will…" (or "you should…").

Suggestions for "Today's action." Here are some ideas you may wish to draw from when fashioning a "Today's action" proposal ("If today I were to…"). Feel free to range beyond these, using alternate verbs already encountered. You will need to supply an **object** appropriate to the verb you select (such as כְּלִי־שָׂרָה הַגָּדוֹל in the model above). See whether you can recall the meaning of those expressions below for which a gloss has not been supplied. Call out עָזְרֵנִי if you need help.

"Today's action": If I were to...

אִם אֶשְׁכַּח	(can't remember??)	אִם אָשׁוּב	... to turn, return	אִם אֶעֱשֶׂה	... to make	אִם אֶסְלַח		אִם אֶזְכֹּר	... to remember
אִם אֶשְׁמַע	... to listen	אִם אָשִׂים		אִם אֵשֵׁב		אִם אֶעֱלֶה	... to go up	אִם אֹמַר	

Suggestions for "Tomorrow's forecast." For ideas concerning the forecast portion (the two consequence-forecasts that you will fashion), look to the sample verbs found in earlier segments (*2ms* in

---

[17] The "obligation" dimension of the יקטל will be treated more fully in §5.4.א., Part 2.1.

[18] For more on this topic, see the explanation of the "jussive" in §9.5.א.

UNIT 5 מַה־תַּעֲשֶׂה בָּרִאשֹׁנָה? 351

§5.3.א. and *2fs* in §5.3.ג.). Be creative![19] Remember to design your response using the gender appropriate for your neighbor.

Here, then, are the steps for this activity:

(a) Begin by crafting a "**Today's action**" statement of your own.

(b) Include an object, to add interest.

(c) When directed by your instructor, exchange it with that of a neighbor.

(d) Read over the "Today's action" statement received from your neighbor.

(e) Write two (2) statements that will form "**Tomorrow's forecast**"—what you anticipate your neighbor will do (or should do), in view of the "Today's action" that he or she has proposed.

(f) Let your pair of "Tomorrow's forecast" statements begin with a word such as מָחָר, so that the יקטל form *does not appear first* in its "then-clause" (the apodosis).[20]

(g) Each piece of "forecast" should use a different יקטל verb.

---

[19] If you feel strongly about your advice, you may want to reinforce it with the emphatic pattern described earlier (as in מוֹת תָּמוּת). Ask your instructor how to spell the infinitive absolute of a verb you want to emphasize.

[20] Alternatively, you may begin your forecast with a prepositional phrase or an object, placed ahead of the יקטל form. It is also possible to preface the יקטל form with לֹא, so long as the ensuing clause predicts a negative consequence rather than stipulating a negative obligation or wish (e.g., "If... **then you will not see** my face any longer" rather than, "If... **then you should not see** my face any longer…;" cf. Gen. 44:23). Negative obligation or wish will be explained together with the jussive in §9.5.א.

MODULE 5.4 Nuancing messages with ability, possibility, or obligation

This module does not introduce any additional Jonah episodes, מִלִּים לִשְׁמֹעַ, or מִלִּים לַעֲנוֹת.

5.4.א. Explanation: Additional יִקְטֹל meanings

INTERACTIVE SKILL: Nuancing your communication with elements such as ability, possibility, or obligation

To this point we have employed the יקטל conjugation to express plans about the future, just as הַדָּג הַגָּדוֹל did, upon learning that he soon would be free of his internal passenger (from 5.2 Jonah Episode, cell 6):

בַּתְּהֹמוֹת אֵרֵד:
לֶחֶם רַב אֶמְצָא:
כָּל־הַיּוֹם אֹכַל:

However, as we read the Hebrew Bible we discover that the יקטל is not limited to conveying straightforward plans about the future (called "future indicative" expressions). At times the יקטל describes not the future, but the **past**, and in still other contexts it refers to the **present**. In addition, often we find the יקטל departing from fact-telling (indicative) in order to convey messages that in English will require auxiliary words such as *may, should, can, must,* or *customarily would.*[21] These involve a notion of potentiality, not the indicative.

---

[21] Much of the material in this segment has been adapted from *IBHS*, chs. 29 and 31.

To reflect these various meanings available within the יקטל, the material in this segment is divided into four sections. Part 1 will offer various options of tense, Part 2 will treat potentiality and purpose options, and Part 3 will offer a some thoughts concerning how these various meanings may cohere within one conjugation (expanded in the appendix). A final section provides suggestions for navigating the various meanings available within the יקטל (Part 4).

Part 1: Tense options within the יִקְטֹל

As you are aware, the יקטל conjugation can convey the future tense. Yet it is not limited to future tense. In certain situations it may convey a past or a present tense meaning.

To appreciate this range of tense options, please look over the following examples, grouped under headings "Future tense meanings," "Past tense meanings," and "Present tense meanings." Especially notice words in **bold type** (both in the Hebrew column and in the translation column), as these signify the **key יקטל words** within a given verse. Since many Hebrew words in these verses will be new to you, feel free to rely on the translations that have been provided.

Within the translations, you often will find **italicized words**. Italicized words convey **connotations** that are implicit within the יקטל form, ideas that generally require auxiliary expressions when converted into English. By noticing the italicized words you will learn fairly quickly the sorts of connotations available within the יקטל conjugation.

Finally, read over the information in the column labeled "Description." Here you will learn which of the various יקטל meaning-options a given example is illustrating.

Part 1.1: The יִקְטֹל with future tense meanings. You are already familiar with the fact that the יקטל can convey a future meaning, often expressing straightforward statements about the future ("future indicative"). What you may not realize is that when a statement about the future (such as "I shall not be in want") is juxtaposed with a statement about the past or present circumstance (such as "The LORD is my shepherd"), we should weigh the possibility that the **future** statement should be recognized as an **outgrowth** of the past or present circumstance.

There are times when such a connection between a future statement and a preceding circumstance—though valid—may not merit special mention in your translation. But in other instances the connotation may be worth pointing out. Generally this will require inserting an auxiliary expression. See, for example, the auxiliary expression "as a result" in the following translation of Ps. 23:1.[22]

Description	Translation	Hebrew
Future time, showing a relationship between a preceding circumstance and an ensuing consequence	The LORD is my shepherd; *as a result* **I will not be** [or, I am not] **in want** (Ps. 23:1).	יהוה רֹעִי לֹא אֶחְסָר׃

Part 1.2: The יקטל with past tense meanings. The following examples employ יקטל verbs that would not make sense if rendered as future tense. The context calls for a past tense meaning. Yet it is not an isolated, simplistic past. Something more being conveyed—something that the יקטל is uniquely suited to convey.

In the examples below, please notice the words *used to* (in Gen. 2:6a) and *began to* (in 1 Sam. 1:10). The connotations of (a) repeated or customary action (as in *used to*) and (b) incipient action (as in *began to*) are part of the repertoire of the יקטל. And that explains why the writer turned to the יקטל to relate these particular past events.

Description	Translation	Hebrew
Past time, showing repeated (iterative) or customary action	A mist (or stream) *used to* **come up** from the ground… (Gen. 2:6a).	וְאֵד יַעֲלֶה מִן־הָאָרֶץ…׃
Incipient past (the onset of an action)	…she prayed to the LORD and *began to* **weep** bitterly (1 Sam. 1:10).	…וַתִּתְפַּלֵּל עַל־יהוה וּבָכֹה תִבְכֶּה׃

The next two יקטל examples similarly convey the past tense. Notice the use of אָז *then* and [בְּ]טֶרֶם *before*. These two expressions alert us to the likelihood of a past tense meaning.

---

[22] *IBHS* §31.6.2b.

Description	Translation	Hebrew
The word אָז (*then* or *at that time*) routinely produces a past time meaning with יקטל.[23]	At that time Moses **sang**... (Exod. 15:1a).	אָז יָשִׁיר מֹשֶׁה....:
The word (בְּ)טֶרֶם *before* sometimes produces a past time meaning with יקטל.	...and they spent the night there before **they crossed over** (Josh. 3:1b).	...וַיָּלִינוּ שָׁם טֶרֶם יַעֲבֹרוּ:

Part 1.3: The יְקַטֵל with present tense meanings. Here are some cases where neither future nor past translations would be appropriate. In these examples the יקטל carries a **present** meaning. Give particular attention to the italicized words, as these will enrich your awareness of the range of meaning that the יקטל can convey.

Description	Translation	Hebrew
Habitual present	Therefore the Israelites *routinely* **do not eat** the tendon... (Gen. 32:33).	עַל־כֵּן לֹא־יֹאכְלוּ בְנֵי־יִשְׂרָאֵל אֶת־גִּיד....:
Present, showing repeated (iterative) or customary activity	Day after day it [the heavens] *continually* **pours forth** speech... (Ps. 19:3a [ET v. 2a]).	יוֹם לְיוֹם יַבִּיעַ אֹמֶר....:
Incipient present (the onset of an action)	Hear, O LORD, *as I begin to* **call** aloud... (Ps. 27:7).	שְׁמַע־יהוה קוֹלִי אֶקְרָא....:

Part 2: Potentiality within the יִקְטֹל

The realization that the יקטל can operate as past and present tenses (as well as future) is an important discovery. Yet it does not get at the heart of יקטל meaning. It only alerts us to the variety of time settings in which the יקטל can function.

---

[23] When אָז introduces a sentence *not* featuring a יִקְטֹל form, but rather a קָטַל form (to be introduced in the next unit), אָז will convey the meaning *then* in the sense of *the next event that occurred was this* [i.e., *as follows*].

In contrast, one of the principal connotations found in many יקטל uses involves the notion of **potentiality**. For example, consider the potentiality (and inherent uncertainty) of this statement: "Joab ought to travel." Whether or not Joab actually will travel remains uncertain. We only know that the speaker feels that Joab **should** travel. It is an expression of **obligation** (from the speaker's point of view, at least). This would call for the יקטל when rendered into Hebrew (יוֹאָב יֵלֵךְ; compare the example from Ps. 32:8a, below).

The theme of potentiality may be further subdivided into three areas. The first is labeled "**modal**" (mood-related) in order to reflect the subjective tone of these examples. A second group is labeled "**volitional**" to indicate that these examples the involve imposition of one person's will upon another (as in the preceding example concerning Joab traveling). The last group is labeled "**telic**" (expressing purpose)—statements that indicate the intent of a provision or request, without assuring that the intent has been actualized or will be actualized in the future.

Part 2.1: Potentiality as modal. Under modal expressions of potential we will find capability, permission, possibility, deliberation, obligation, and desire.

Description	Translation	Hebrew
Capability	And I am like a deaf person, I *can* **not hear**… (Ps. 38:14).[24]	...וַאֲנִי כְחֵרֵשׁ לֹא אֶשְׁמָע:
Permission	… "My two sons **you** *may* **kill** if I do not bring him back to you…" (Gen. 42:37).	...אֶת־שְׁנֵי בָנַי תָּמִית אִם־לֹא אֲבִיאֶנּוּ אֵלֶיךָ:...

---

[24] Another example of capability connoted by the יְקֹטל may be seen in the following excerpt from poetry: לֹא יָדְעוּ וְלֹא יָבִינוּ *They do not know and **cannot** understand* (Ps. 82:5). Given that both י.ד.ע and ב.י.ן deal with cognition, adding the dimension of incapability (of cognition) in the second parallel member would be consistent with the principle of intensification when moving from the first to the second of parallel members.

In addition to **implying** capability by means of a יְקֹטל form, Hebrew is able to express capability in a more **explicit** manner by combining the auxiliary verb י.כ.ל *to be able* with an infinitive construct. Thus we learn of aged Jacob's dimming eyesight through this comment: לֹא יוּכַל לִרְאוֹת *he was unable to see* (Gen. 48:10a; יוּכַל is the *3ms* יְקֹטל of י.כ.ל).

Possibility (routinely found in the protasis of conditional statements, signaled by אִם [or sometimes כִּי] *if*, or by לוּ *if not*)	... "My two sons you may kill **if I do not bring him back** to you..." (Gen. 42:37).	...אֶת־שְׁנֵי בָנַי תָּמִית אִם־לֹא אֲבִיאֶנּוּ אֵלֶיךָ...
	...and what[ever] **you** *may* **say** [or stipulate] to me, I will give (Gen. 34:11b).	...וַאֲשֶׁר תֹּאמְרוּ אֵלַי אֶתֵּן:
Deliberation (occurs principally with questions)	...*Should* **I go up** into any of the cities of Judah?... (2 Sam. 2:1a).	...הַאֶעֱלֶה בְּאַחַת עָרֵי יְהוּדָה...
Obligation	... and I will teach you concerning the road that **you** *ought to* **travel**... (Ps. 32:8a).	...וְאוֹרְךָ בְּדֶרֶךְ־זוּ תֵלֵךְ:
Desire	...If you *want to* **take** it, take [it]... (1 Sam. 21:10).	...אִם־אֹתָהּ תִּקַּח־לְךָ קַח...

Part 2.2: Potentiality as volitional. The volitional connotation of the יקטל is akin to the modal category above labeled "obligation," except that volitional examples are more insistent. Hence the use of the word "must" in the examples below.

Description	Translation	Hebrew
Positive instruction (generally in a legislative context)	In the presence of the elderly **you will** / *must* **rise**... (Lev. 19:32a).	...מִפְּנֵי שֵׂיבָה תָּקוּם:
Negative instruction (prohibition with לֹא, generally in a legislative context)	**You shall** / *must* **not make** for yourself a idol... (Exod. 20:4a).	...לֹא תַעֲשֶׂה־לְךָ פֶסֶל:

Part 2.3: Potentiality as telic (purpose-related). We are helped in recognizing instances when the יקטל bears a telic ("purpose") connotation, particularly when the יקטל is preceded by words such as לְמַעַן *so that* or פֶּן *lest*.

Description	Translation	Hebrew
After the expression לְמַעַן *so that* (similarly after בַּעֲבוּר *so that*)	So that **they** *may* **believe** that the LORD ... appeared to you (Exod. 4:5).	לְמַעַן יַאֲמִינוּ כִּי־נִרְאָה אֵלֶיךָ יהוה....:
After the word פֶּן *lest* (and similarly after לְבִלְתִּי *lest*)	...but let not the LORD speak [directly] to us, lest **we die** (Exod. 20:19).	וְאַל־יְדַבֵּר עִמָּנוּ אֱלֹהִים פֶּן־נָמוּת :

Part 3: Coherence of varied meanings within the יִקְטֹל

Given such a range of varied meanings, what may lie at the center of the יקטל? Across the centuries scholars have wondered how so many meanings could cohere in a single form.[25] While a consensus has not yet been reached, this conjugation seems to cohere around the notions of **events that are either ongoing or potential** in nature (as opposed to events that are definite, confined, or sure-to-materialize). If you wish to further explore the idea of coherence within יקטל connotations, the appendix discussion corresponding to this segment may interest you.

Part 4: Suggestions for navigating the various יִקְטֹל meanings

On the one hand, so wide an array of יקטל options may feel overwhelming. When reading a given text, how can we be sure of selecting the correct connotation?

On the other hand, this array of translational options opens some very enriching meanings! When used responsibly, the information you have just received can bring to light meanings latent within the text that too often go unnoticed. Here are some steps for responsible reading of יקטל forms.

A. Begin by inferring a simple meaning cast in future time. Often the יקטל conveys straightforward information about the future ("future indicative"). Thus an affirmation such as אֵלֵךְ may mean, quite simply, *I will go* (e.g., Rachel indicating her willingness to accompany Abraham's servant, Gen. 24:58b). To "enrich" the translation of אֵלֵךְ with connotations such as (a) *I will begin to go* or (b) *I must go* or (c) *I will keep on going*—these would depart from the plain sense of the text.

---

[25] See historical overview in *IBHS*, ch. 29.

B. If the context will not allow a future indicative translation, then keep in mind that יקטל at times may best be rendered as past or present, *provided that we employ one of the enriched meanings unique to the* יקטל (such as iterative or incipient).

C. Notice particles and use them to your advantage. If a conditional particle such as אִם or לוּ is present (or sometimes כִּי), then realize that that you have encountered a protasis—an "if" (or "if not") clause. This realization generally allows us (even encourages us) to favor the present tense over the future tense for a smooth English translation (e.g., אִם־יִמְצָא הַלֶּחֶם should generally be rendered, *If he finds food*, and not *If he will find food*). Other helpful particles include אָז, בְּ[טֶרֶם], לְמַעַן, בַּעֲבוּר, and פֶּן.

D. Be attentive to the surrounding genre. Is the text you are reading located in a legislative section, thick with instructions? Then you have a solid reason to experiment with a tone of injunction. Thus a יקטל such as תָּקוּם should be rendered *you must rise*, not simply *you will rise* (as in the Lev. 19:32a example, above).

E. Periodically remind yourself of the modal options. Jot down terms such as *can, may, should, ought* so that you may remind yourself of them easily. When you encounter a יקטל in a context where a simple indicative translation feels inadequate, experiment with modal alternatives.

F. Consult solid Bible translations and scholarly resources. Before proceeding too far with novel renditions, check responsible Bible versions (e.g., *New Revised Standard*, *New American Standard*, *Jewish Publication Society*, *Today's New International Version*). Even better, consult an in-depth commentary (one that devotes an entire volume to each major book of the Bible) or an advanced Hebrew grammar. Often you will discover that scholars have already entered into conversation concerning the very phrase you are exploring, and may confirm or correct your hypothesis. At the same time, do not be stifled if a commentary fails to observe what you have uncovered. Simply be sure you are applying translational principles in a responsible manner.

5.4.ב. Activity: Enriching past Jonah Episodes

INTERACTIVE SKILL: Connotations of ability, possibility, or obligation (continued)

With few exceptions, יקטל expressions employed in the Jonah episodes of Units 4 and 5 were designed to make sense if rendered with a simple future meaning. However, if we were to revisit certain excerpts we would find places where a modal or volitional meaning would fit even better.

Take a look at the excerpts below, and translate them once again. Only this time, experiment by supplying a modal or volitional meaning that may seem to fit the context.

Incidentally, this process of enriching a basic יקטל translation by supplying a modal / volitional meaning is a process you will find yourself repeating from time to time when reading the Hebrew Bible. While at times a suitable enriched meaning will have been captured by one of the standard versions, at other times the richer meaning will have been overlooked.

The first two have been completed for you. Note especially the words in bold font.

Should they not guard the freight?	§4.1, cell 4a	הֲלֹא יִשְׁמְרוּ אֶת־הַכֵּלִים?		א.
Look out lest the freight **may** fall on your head.	§4.1, cell 5a	הִשָּׁמֶר לְךָ פֶּן־יִפְּלוּ הַכֵּלִים עַל־רֹאשֶׁךָ!		ב.
	§4.3, cell 3a	אֵיךְ יֵשֵׁב וְלֹא יָמוּת?		ג.
	§4.4, cell 2a	בִּהְיוֹת הָאִישׁ בְּבִטְנְךָ מַה־תַּאֲמִין כִּי תִשְׁמַעְנָה אָזְנָיו?		ד.
	§5.1, cell 2	אוּלַי נִמְצָא חֵן בְּעֵינֵי־אֱלֹהִים!		ה.
	§5.1, cell 7	"לֹא תַאֲמֶנָה אֵת כָּל־הַמֹּצָאוֹת אֹתָנוּ בַּיָּם!"		ו.
	§5.1, cell 8	"בַּבֹּקֶר תֵּלַכְנָה עִמָּנוּ לִזְבֹּחַ לֵאלֹהֵי־יִשְׂרָאֵל:"		ז.

ח.	לֹא תֹאכַל אֶת־הַנָּבִיא:	§5.2, cell 2a
ט.	אֲנִי לֹא אֶשָּׂא אֹתוֹ לְעוֹלָם פֶּן־אָמוּת:	§5.2, cell 3
י.	...מוֹת אָמוּת אִם־יֵשֵׁב בְּבִטְנִי עוֹד יוֹם אֶחָד:	§5.2, cell 3
יא.	שָׁם תַּשְׁלִיךְ אֹתוֹ עַל־הַיַּבָּשָׁה:	§5.2, cell 5a
יב.	אַךְ אֶשְׁאֲלָה לָךְ:	§5.3, cell 6a
יג.	מָה אָמַר לָעִיר?	§5.3, cell 6a
יד.	לָעִיר הַהִיא תֹּאמַר...	§5.3, cell 6b

Can you think of a more concise and idiomatic way to express—in Hebrew—the verbal element in the following question? It happens to come from 4.1 Jonah Episode, cell 6.

הֶחָפֵץ אַתָּה לֵאמֹר "זְרָעוֹת"?

5.4.ג. Activity: Exploring Judah's plea

INTERACTIVE SKILL: Connotations of ability, possibility, or obligation (a biblical example)

In one of the most moving speeches of the Bible, Judah makes a pathos-filled plea to the Grand Vizier of Egypt, unaware that he is addressing his brother, Joseph. Judah pleads for the release of his youngest brother, Benjamin (Gen. 44:34). The translation provided below is from the *New American Standard Bible*.

Do you find here any phrase that you might translate differently? Circle any phrase(s) you would change, and write your translation in the open space to the left.

כִּי־אֵיךְ אֶעֱלֶה אֶל־אָבִי וְהַנַּעַר אֵינֶנּוּ אִתִּי׃...	"For how shall I go up to my father if the lad [וְהַנַּעַר] is not with me…?" (Gen. 44:34)[26]

5.4.ד. יִקְטֹל conjugation of geminate verbs

Some verbs **duplicate** the **final** radical, as in ס.ב.ב *to surround*, ר.ע.ע *to be evil*, and ח.נ.נ *to show favor*. These are known as **geminate verbs**. Some geminate forms have unique spelling patterns. Please consult the appendix entry corresponding to this segment for spelling patterns of geminate verbs in the יקטל conjugation.

5.4.ה. יִקְטֹל conjugation of stative verbs

By now we have come to expect a **ḥolem** as theme vowel (following the second radical in the יקטל conjugation), as in יִשְׁמֹר or יִכְרֹת.[27] However, some verbs do **not** display the expected ḥolem theme vowel, but employ instead a **pataḥ**.

---

[26] Hint: translations such as those by the Jewish Publication Society, *New Revised Standard Version* and *New International Version* infer a connotation of capability for the opening phrase of Gen. 44:34 (see §5.4.א., part 2.1, above).

[27] Exceptions include III-guttural verbs such as ק.ר.א or פ.ת.ח where the III-guttural consonant inclines the theme vowel to be an A-class vowel: יִקְרָא (never ‡יִקְרֹא) and יִפְתַּח (never ‡יִפְתֹּח). The remaining gutturals ה or ע when appearing as third שֹׁרֶשׁ consonant position also will precipitate a pataḥ theme vowel, whether the verb is stative or not.

Often a **patah** theme vowel in the יקטל conjugation signals a "**stative verb**." "Stative" refers to verbs that describe a state of being (in contrast with verbs where the subject performs an action, known as "fientive" verbs).[28] Among the statives are יִזְקַן *he will be old*, יִיבַשׁ *he will be dry*, and יִישַׁן *he will sleep*. Please refer to the appendix entry corresponding to this segment for more information concerning stative verbs in the יקטל conjugation.

5.4.1. יִקְטֹל forms with an unexpected נ

Certain יקטל forms display an **unexpected** נ either as an extra consonant at the end (known as paragogic נ forms), or with the נ inserted prior to an object suffix (known as energic נ forms). Please refer to the appendix entry corresponding to this segment for further explanation concerning paragogic and energic forms.

---

[28] For a general introduction to stative verbs, see *IBHS* §22.2.1.

5.4.1. Snapshot of sample verb: יִקְטֹל conjugation

נִשְׁמֹר we will guard	אֶשְׁמֹר I will guard
תִּשְׁמְרוּ you will guard *mpl*	תִּשְׁמֹר you will guard *ms*
תִּשְׁמֹרְנָה you will guard *fpl*	תִּשְׁמְרִי you will guard *fs*
יִשְׁמְרוּ they will guard *m*	יִשְׁמֹר he will guard
תִּשְׁמֹרְנָה they will guard *f*	תִּשְׁמֹר she will guard

UNIT 5   מַה־תַּעֲשֶׂה בָּרִאשֹׁנָה?

You (ms) can read the Bible.   אַתָּה תִּקְרָא אֶת־הַתַּנָ"ךְ:

Selected readings

5.1.א. The king of Edom did not want the people of יִשְׂרָאֵל to pass through his territory. So מֹשֶׁה sought to reassure the king with these words. (To visualize the route mentioned in this passage [known as דֶּרֶךְ הַמֶּלֶךְ], you may wish to consult the map of יִשְׂרָאֵל found on p. 565. Contrast this route with דֶּרֶךְ הַיָּם, described in §1.3.ד.)

1. ...לֹא נַעֲבֹר בְּשָׂדֶה^a וּבְכֶרֶם^b
   וְלֹא נִשְׁתֶּה מֵי בְאֵר^c
   דֶּרֶךְ הַמֶּלֶךְ^d נֵלֵךְ...: (Num. 20:17)

^aשָׂדֶה field *m*   ^bכֶּרֶם vineyard *m*   ^cבְּאֵר well *f*
^dדֶּרֶךְ ה'... (*name of the major Damascus - Aqaba trade route*)

5.1.א. When they neared the Promised Land, the people recommended the following strategy. (The general term דָּבָר appearing in the second phrase is further specified by the two clauses beginning אֶת־הַדֶּרֶךְ and וְאֵת הֶעָרִים. We might introduce those clauses: *...in particular, X and Y.* Also, if you have studied §5.4.א., can you suggest modal meanings that may be suitable for נַעֲלֶה and נָבֹא, e.g., *should, desire to, be able to,* or *may*? As in earlier units, the superscript symbol^μ signals a modification from the original text of the verse.)

2. ...אֲנָשִׁים נִשְׁלַח^μ לְפָנֵינוּ
   וְדָבָר^μ יִתְּנוּ^μ לָנוּ^μ אֶת־הַדֶּרֶךְ אֲשֶׁר נַעֲלֶה־בָּהּ
   וְאֵת הֶעָרִים אֲשֶׁר נָבֹא אֲלֵיהֶן: (Deut. 1:22)

נִשְׁלְחָה אֲנָשִׁים לְפָנֵינוּ וְיַחְפְּרוּ־לָנוּ אֶת־הָאָרֶץ וְיָשִׁבוּ אֹתָנוּ דָּבָר אֶת־הַדֶּרֶךְ אֲשֶׁר נַעֲלֶה־בָּהּ וְאֵת הֶעָרִים אֲשֶׁר נָבֹא אֲלֵיהֶן:

5.1.ד.　When Jacob heard that the Grand Vizier of Egypt demanded to see Benjamin before releasing more food, he lamented to his sons: "You have bereaved me of my children!...." (Note that three of Jacob's sons are named in this sentence. If you have studied §5.4.א., can you suggest a modal sense or other enriched meaning that may be suitable for תִּקָּחוּ? Incidentally, if תִּקָּחוּ were not in pause, it would be spelled תִּקְחוּ.)

3.　יוֹסֵף אֵינֶנּוּ וְשִׁמְעוֹן אֵינֶנּוּ
וְאֶת־בִּנְיָמִן תִּקָּחוּ... : (Gen. 42:36)

5.1.ה.　Still unrecognized by his brothers, Joseph spoke these reassuring words when they reported money found in their grain sacks. (If תִּירָאוּ were not in pause, it would be spelled תִּירְאוּ.)

4.　שָׁלוֹם לָכֶם
אַל־תִּירָאוּ : (Gen. 43:23a)

5.1.ו.　Do you recall the painful circumstance experienced by Naomi and her two daughters-in-law? She did not feel she could expect her daughters-in-law to accompany her back to Israel, and so asked them this question. (Note that הַ in הַעוֹד is the spelling of interrogative הֲ when it precedes a guttural.)

5.　לָמָּה תֵלַכְנָה עִמִּי
הַעוֹד־לִי בָנִים: (Ruth 1:11)

עוֹד[a]　again, still, yet

5.1.ג. When Naomi reached Bethlehem she responded to the women's greetings by observing how much her experiences had diverged from the meaning of her given name. Naomi means "pleasant." (Note that מָרָא is an alternate spelling of the adjective מָרָה *fs*. Also note that since a qameṣ is pronounced *o* before a qameṣ-ḥaṭuf, the name Naomi produces two adjacent *o* sounds: *No-omi*.)

6. ...אַל־תִּקְרֶאנָה לִי נָעֳמִי תִּקְרֶאנָֽה⁺ לִי מָרָא... (Ruth 1:20)

...אַל־תִּקְרֶאנָה לִי נָעֳמִי קְרֶאןָ⁺ לִי מָרָא...

5.2.ב. As he lay dreaming one night, Solomon heard God extend this offer. (If you have studied §5.4.א., can you suggest a modal meaning that may be suitable for אֶתֶּן־? Note that אֶתֶּן־ would be spelled אֶתֵּן, were it not for the maqqef—a marker indicating that all words it connects comprise only one accentual unit.)

7. שְׁאַל֙ מָ֣ה⁺ᵇ אֶתֶּן־לָֽךְᵃ: (1 Kings 3:5b)

שְׁאַלᵃ [ש.א.ל] *imperative 2ms*   מָהᵇ *what (interrogative), whatever*²⁹

5.2.ב. Can you identify the reason for this poet's confidence? (Note that רָע is רַע in pause.)

8. גַּםᵃ כִּֽי־אֵלֵ֨ךְ בְּגֵיאᵇ צַלְמָ֡וֶתᶜ לֹא־אִ֘ירָ֤א רָ֗ע
כִּי־אַתָּ֥ה עִמָּדִֽיᵈ:... (Ps. 23:4a)

גַּם כִּיᵃ *although*   גֵּיאᵇ *valley (absol. and constr.) m*
צַלְמָוֶתᶜ *death's shadow, impenetrable gloom m*   עִמָּדִיᵈ *with me*

---

²⁹ When operating in a non-interrogative fashion (similar to the relative pronoun אֲשֶׁר *what* or *that which*), the choice of מָה can bring the connotation of the "unknown," a connotation which is more obvious when it functions in an interrogative capacity ("What...?").

5.2.ב. From the foundation of this affirmation, the poet later will invite his reader to echo his commitment and so enjoy his confidence (see v. 9). (Recall that the preposition ל can mean *concerning* as well as *to*. How might an awareness of the modal meanings for יקטל introduced in §5.4.א. influence our understanding of אֶבְטַח? Consider that the poet could have used a participle instead [אֲנִי בֹּטֵחַ].)

9. אֹמַר לַיהוה מַחְסִי^a וּמְצוּדָתִי^b אֱלֹהַי אֶבְטַח־בּוֹ^c : (Ps. 91:2)

מַחְסֶה^a refuge *m*   מְצוּדָה^b mountain stronghold *f*   ב.ט.ח^c to trust

5.2.ב. Through a parental analogy God conveys a profound degree of unwavering interest.

10. הֲתִשְׁכַּח^a אִשָּׁה... בֶּן־בִּטְנָהּ^b? גַּם־אֵלֶּה תִשְׁכַּחְנָה וְאָנֹכִי לֹא אֶשְׁכָּחֵךְ^d : (Isa. 49:15)

ש.כ.ח^a to forget   בֶּן^b son (*constr.*) *m*   בִּטְנָהּ^c (*pronominal sfx*)
אֶשְׁכָּחֵךְ^d [ש.כ.ח] (*pronominal sfx*)

הֲתִשְׁכַּח אִשָּׁה עוּלָהּ מֵרַחֵם בֶּן־בִּטְנָהּ גַּם־אֵלֶּה תִשְׁכַּחְנָה וְאָנֹכִי לֹא אֶשְׁכָּחֵךְ :

5.3.א. Despite Moses' promise not to trespass beyond the borders of the highway passing through Edom, the king of that region responded with these words. Then he proceeded to marshal a massive army against the Israelites. (If you have become familiar with §5.4.א., can you suggest a modal meaning that may be suitable for this statement?)

11. ...לֹא תַעֲבֹר: (Num. 20:20)

5.3.א. God stipulated that once the Israelites reached the land promised to them, they must worship in prescribed locations. (If you have studied §5.4.א., can you suggest a modal meaning that may be suitable for תִּרְאֶה?)

12. הִשָּׁמֶר לְךָ פֶּן־תַּעֲלֶה עֹלֹתֶיךָ^{a} בְּכָל־מָקוֹם^c אֲשֶׁר תִּרְאֶה: (Deut. 12:13)

^{a}[ע.ל.י/ה] to offer *hifil* (*coincidentally spelled the same as qal "to ascend"*)
^{b}עֹלֹת whole burnt offerings *fpl* ^{c}כָּל־מָקוֹם any place *m*

5.3.ג. Notice Isaiah's mastery of the language, evident from his use of synonymous expressions both rich and rare in order to express an assurance of Zion's profound restoration, following her deep suffering as "a barren woman."

13. אַל־תִּירְאִי^a כִּי־לֹא תֵבוֹשִׁי...
כִּי בֹשֶׁת^b עֲלוּמַיִךְ^{c} תִּשְׁכָּחִי
וְחֶרְפַּת^d אַלְמְנוּתַיִךְ^{e} לֹא תִזְכְּרִי־עוֹד: (Isa. 54:4)

^{a}י.ר.ש to be ashamed ^{b}בֹּשֶׁת (*feelings of*) shame *f* ^{c}עֲלוּמִים youth (*as a stage of life*) *m*
^{d}חֶרְפָּה reproach *f* ^{e}אַלְמָנוּת widowhood *f*

אַל־תִּירְאִי כִּי־לֹא תֵבוֹשִׁי וְאַל־תִּכָּלְמִי כִּי לֹא תַחְפִּירִי כִּי בֹשֶׁת עֲלוּמַיִךְ תִּשְׁכָּחִי וְחֶרְפַּת אַלְמְנוּתַיִךְ לֹא תִזְכְּרִי־עוֹד:

Through Hosea, God extended rich assurances of renewed welcome. (Note concerning בַּעַל: some contexts employ this word without implying a negative aspect in a relationship [cf. Prov. 31:28].)   5.3.ג.

14. וְהָיָה‎ᵃ בַיּוֹם־הַהוּא נְאֻם‎ᵇ־יהוה
    תִּקְרְאִי אִישִׁי
    וְלֹא־תִקְרְאִי־לִי עוֹד בַּעְלִי‎ᶜ: (Hos. 2:18 [ET v. 16])

וְהָיָה‎ᵃ and it shall be, come about *m*   נְאֻם‎ᵇ declares (*lit.*, a declaration of) *m*   בַּעַל‎ᶜ master *m*

A connected reading: The binding of Isaac (Gen. 22:7-8)   עֲקֵדַת יִצְחָק

7. וַיֹּאמֶר‎ᵃ יִצְחָק אֶל־אַבְרָהָם אָבִיו‎ᵇ
   וַיֹּאמֶר אָבִי
   וַיֹּאמֶר הִנֶּנִּי בְנִי‎ᶜ
   וַיֹּאמֶר הִנֵּה הָאֵשׁ‎ᵈ וְהָעֵצִים וְאַיֵּה הַשֶּׂה‎ᵉ לְעֹלָה‎ᶠ:

8. וַיֹּאמֶר אַבְרָהָם
   אֱלֹהִים יִרְאֶה־לּוֹ‎ᵍ הַשֶּׂה לְעֹלָה בְּנִי
   וַיֵּלְכוּ‎ʰ שְׁנֵיהֶם‎ⁱ יַחְדָּו‎ʲ:

וַיֹּאמֶר‎ᵃ then he said   אָבִיו‎ᵇ his father *m*   בְּנִי‎ᶜ my son *m*   אֵשׁ‎ᵈ fire *m*   שֶׂה‎ᵉ an individual sheep or goat *m*
עֹלָה‎ᶠ whole burnt offering *f*   ר.א.ה/י.ר.ה‎ᵍ ...to select something for oneself   וַיֵּלְכוּ‎ʰ so they went
שְׁנֵיהֶם‎ⁱ both of them   יַחְדָּו‎ʲ together

UNIT 6

מֶה עָשִׂיתָ אֶתְמוֹל:

Sharing memories of yesterday

קָטַל *conjugation*

This unit will enable you to talk with friends concerning things that you (or they) have experienced or heard about—whether those events transpired during the day that has just concluded, or in the distant past. You will be able to relate:

- personal experiences
- group events that you participated in
- experiences that happened to other persons

In this unit we will employ the "קָטַל" conjugation to express past events. The following table offers a preview, showing the verb forms that you will encounter in this unit and where you will meet them. For קָטַל connotations other than past tense, please see §6.5.א.

The קָטַל conjugation

Segment	Plural	Singular	Segment
6.4.ב.	שָׁמַ֫רְנוּ we guarded	שָׁמַ֫רְתִּי I guarded	6.1.ד.
6.3.ו.	שְׁמַרְתֶּם you guarded *mpl*	שָׁמַ֫רְתָּ you guarded *ms*	6.3.א.
6.4.ד.	שְׁמַרְתֶּן you guarded *fpl*	שָׁמַרְתְּ you guarded *fs*	6.3.ג.
6.2.ה.	שָׁמְרוּ they guarded	שָׁמַר he guarded	6.1.א.
		שָׁמְרָה she guarded	6.2.ב.

As suggested for יִקְטֹל words, it may be helpful to devote an entire vocabulary card to the various קָטַל forms of each שֹׁ֫רֶשׁ, adding forms as they are introduced. Your קָטַל vocabulary card for the verb ש.מ.ר would look like the table above except that Hebrew would appear on one side, with the translation appearing on the other side.

UNIT 6   מֶה עָשִׂיתָ אֶתְמוֹל׃   373

MODULE 6.1   Explaining what you did, in contrast to what a friend did

Unit 6 JONAH STORY: Jonah wakes up on the beach

Have you ever fallen into a sleep so deep that—when at last you awakened—it was difficult to get your bearings? That is how Jonah must have felt on this particular day.

Note: Since the Hebrew Bible does not employ modern punctuation marks, we will begin to reduce the use of these marks this point forward. One piece of authentic punctuation to which you have grown accustomed is the סוֹף פָּסוּק *sôf pāsûq* (׃). The Hebrew Bible allows only one סוֹף פָּסוּק per verse, located at the verse's end. In this textbook we will at times use the סוֹף פָּסוּק more than once within a single cell of a Jonah Episode, in an effort to ease comprehension of a longer statement.

The Masoretes indicated breaks of thought within a verse by a system of symbols called cantillation marks. You will be introduced to some of the more important cantillation marks at the outset of the Bible readings at the end of this unit.

Words for responding — מִלִּים לַעֲנוֹת

בַּת, בָּנוֹת, בַּת־, בְּנוֹת־	daughter *f*	אָב, אָבוֹת, אֲבִי־ (*or* אַב־), אֲבוֹת־	father *m*
זָכַרְתִּי [ז.כ.ר]	I remembered*		
חַי, חַיָּה, חַיִּים, חַיּוֹת	alive*	אָדָם, אֲדַם־ (*or* אָדָם־)	man, humankind, Adam *m*
לָקַח [ל.ק.ח]	he took*		
		אֵם, אֵם־	mother *f*
מָקוֹם, מְקוֹמוֹת, מְקוֹם־, מְקוֹמוֹת־	place, location *m*	בָּאתִי [ב.ו.א]	I came, entered*
		בֵּן, בָּנִים, בֶּן־[a], בְּנֵי־	son *m*

[a] בֶּן־ may also be spelled בִּן־.

Words for hearing — מִלִּים לִשְׁמֹעַ

אוֹי לִי	Woe is me!	אֹהֶל, אֹהָלִים, אֹהֶל־, אָהֳלֵי־[a]	tent *m*
אֲמִתַּי	Amittai *m* (*name*)		

מָצָאתִי [מ.צ.א]	I found*	אֶפְרַיִם	Ephraim m (name)
מֵרָחֹק	at a distance	אֶתְמוֹל	yesterday
מֵת [מ.ו.ת]	he is dead or has died*	בָּאָה [ב.ו.א]	one who comes, enters pt fs
נָתַן [נ.ת.נ]	he gave*	גַּת הַחֵפֶר	Gath-Hepher pn loc[b]
סֹבְבִים [ס.ב.ב]	ones who surround pt mpl	הָלַכְתִּי [ה.ל.כ]	I went, traveled*
סַפֵּר, סַפְּרִי [ס.פ.ר]	Tell! Recount! piel[c] imv ms, fs	וַיְהִי הַיּוֹם...	One day… (lit., And the day was…)
עָבַרְתִּי [ע.ב.ר]	I crossed over, trespassed*	חֻלְדָּה	Hulda (feminine name)
עָנִיתִי [ע.נ.י/ה]	I answered, replied*	יֹדֵעַ, יֹדַעַת, יֹדְעִים, יֹדְעוֹת [י.ד.ע]	one who knows,* pt
פָּקַח [פ.ק.ח]	he opened (eyes)	יָפוֹ	Joppa pn loc
רָאָה [ר.א.י/ה]	he saw*	יְרוּשָׁלַם (also spelled יְרוּשָׁלַיִם)	Jerusalem pn loc
רְאֵה, רְאִי [ר.א.י/ה]	Look!* imv ms, fs		
רָאִיתִי [ר.א.י/ה]	I saw*	כָּל־הַמֹּצָאוֹת אוֹתָךְ	all that happens or happened to you (pausal for אוֹתָךְ)
שָׂמֵחַ, שְׂמֵחָה, שְׂמֵחִים, שְׂמֵחוֹת	rejoicing, joyful		
שָׁמַעְתִּי [ש.מ.ע]	I heard*	לָקַחְתִּי [ל.ק.ח]	I took*
תַּרְשִׁישָׁה	toward Tarshish	מַה־לְּךָ פֹה:	What are you doing here?

[a] For אֹהֳלִי, keep in mind that both a qameṣ-ḥaṭuf and an immediately preceding qameṣ are pronounced o.

[b] גַּת הַחֵפֶר is situated between יָם כִּנֶּרֶת and הַיָּם הַגָּדוֹל (see map of יִשְׂרָאֵל, p. 565). "Pn loc" means "proper noun of location," signaling a place name that may vary in gender depending on how it is used (cf. GKC 122.i).

[c] The piel spelling of verbs will be explained in Unit 10.

6.1 Jonah Episode: Who are you?

חֻלְדָּה = שֵׁם אִשָּׁה, אֲמִתַּי = שֵׁם אִישׁ

[חֻלְדָּה] א. הִנֵּה אִישִׁי מָצָאתִי דָבָר: מַה־זֶּה:

[אֲמִתַּי] ב. אֵינֶנִּי יֹדֵעַ: אוּלַי אָדָם הוּא:

[חֻלְדָּה] ג. אַאֲמִין כִּי אָדָם הוּא: אוֹ כִּי הָיָה אָדָם: אַאֲמִין כִּי עַתָּה מֵת:

[אֲמִתַּי] ד. לֹא: רְאִי: פָּקַח אֶת־עֵינָיו: חַי הוּא:

[נ׳] א. אַיֵּה הַדָּג הַגָּדוֹל:

מַה־שֵּׁם־הַמָּקוֹם הַזֶּה:

אֵיךְ בָּאתִי אֶל־הַמָּקוֹם הַזֶּה:

וּמִי אַתֶּם:

[אֲמִתַּי] ב. הִנֵּה רָאִיתִי דָּג גָּדוֹל מֵרָחֹק וְהוּא שָׂמֵחַ מְאֹד: אָז יָרַד בַּתְּהֹמוֹת:

3

א. [חֻלְדָּה] אֲנַחְנוּ עֹמְדִים עַל־שְׂפַת־הַיָּם עַל־יַד יָפוֹ:

ב. [אֲמִתַּי] בֵּיתֵנוּ בֶּהָרִים הַסֹּבְבִים אֶת־גַּת הַחֵפֶר: שְׁמִי אֲמִתַּי וְשֵׁם־אִשְׁתִּי חֻלְדָּה בַּת־אֶפְרַיִם:

ג. [נ׳] הַאַתָּה אֲמִתַּי: הַאַתְּ חֻלְדָּה בַּת־אֶפְרַיִם: אַתֶּם אָבִי וְאִמִּי:

[חֻלְדָּה] א. יוֹנָה בְּנִי: הֲשָׁלוֹם לָךְ: מַה־לְּךָ פֹה:

[נ׳] ב. עָבַרְתִּי אֶת־מִצְוֺת־יהוה:

[אֲמִתַּי] ג. לָמָּה בְנִי: סַפֶּר לָנוּ אֶת כָּל־הַמֹּצָאוֹת אוֹתְךָ:

מֶה עָשִׂיתָ אֶתְמוֹל?

5

[נ׳] א. וַיְהִי הַיּוֹם וַאֲנִי יֹשֵׁב בְּאָהֳלִי וְאֶת־קוֹל־יהוה שָׁמַעְתִּי לֵאמֹר לֵךְ אֶל־נִינְוֵה:

[אֲמִתַּי] ב. הַאַתְּ שָׁמַעַתְּ חֻלְדָּה: דְּבַר־יהוה הָיָה אֵלָיו:

[נ׳] ג. אַךְ עָנִיתִי לֵאמֹר לֹא אֵלֵךְ אֶל־נִינְוֵה:

[חֻלְדָּה] ד. לֹא תֵלֵךְ: אוֹי לִי:

[נ׳] א. זָכַרְתִּי כִּי רָאִיתִי בְיָפוֹ אֳנִיָּה בָּאָ֫ה¹ תַּרְשִׁישָׁה:

[נ׳] ב. לָקַחְתִּי כֶּסֶף וְיָמָּה הָלַכְתִּי:

[נ׳] ג. כַּאֲשֶׁר רָאָה רַב הַחֹבֵל כִּי יֶשׁ־כֶּסֶף בִּצְרוֹרִי אֶת־הַכֹּל לָקַח מִמֶּ֫נִּי וְלֶחֶם יָבֵשׁ נָתַן לִי:

---

¹ An accent on the final syllable (ultima) is shown to distinguish בָּאָ֫ה as *pt fs* from בָּ֫אָה, a *3fs* קָטַל form (see §6.2). As a participle, בָּאָ֫ה describes present activity or an ongoing attribute of the אֳנִיָּה, while the קָטַל form בָּ֫אָה would indicate what the אֳנִיָּה has done. The initial dagesh in בָּאָ֫ה is omitted because of the word's close association with the preceding word אֳנִיָּה, a word that ends in an open syllable.

UNIT 6   מָה עָשִׂיתָ אֶתְמוֹל: 381

6.1.א. Explanation: "He descended into the depths."   יָרַד בַּתְּהֹמוֹת:

INTERACTIVE SKILL: Describing how someone behaved

To describe what some male has done (*3ms* קָטַל conjugation), simply vocalize the שרש as follows (שרש is shorthand for שֹׁרֶשׁ, sometimes written simply as שרש):

- Place a **qameṣ** vowel following the **first consonant** of the שרש
- Place a **pataḥ** vowel following the **second consonant**.[2]

Thus י.ר.ד becomes יָרַד *he went down, descended*.

שרש	קָטַל *3ms*	he...	שרש	קָטַל *3ms*	he...
נ.פ.ל	נָפַל	... fell down	א.כ.ל	אָכַל	... ate
ע.ב.ר	עָבַר	... crossed over	ה.ל.כ	הָלַךְ	... went
ק.ו.מ	קָם	... got up	ז.כ.ר	זָכַר	... remembered
ש.ב.ר	שָׁבַר	... broke	י.ר.ד	יָרַד	... went down
ש.כ.ב	שָׁכַב	... reclined	כ.ת.ב	כָּתַב	... wrote
ש.י/ו.מ	שָׂם	... put	ל.ק.ח	לָקַח	... took

Did you notice how the so-called hollow verbs behaved in the table above?[3] For additional examples of קָטַל *3ms* with a hollow verb (where the middle שרש radical is actually a vowel-letter, either ו or י), please refer to the appendix entry for this segment.

In the table below, notice that when either י/ה or א appear as the **final radical**, the last syllable takes a qameṣ (instead of a pataḥ).[4]

---

[2] The קָטַל conjugation also goes by the label "perfect" conjugation since it often conveys a sense of completed action. Alternatively it may be called the "suffix" conjugation, since it adds syllables only to the end of the verb.

[3] When the second שרש radical is a vowel-letter (ו as in ק.ו.מ, or י as in ש.י/ו.מ) the verb is termed "hollow." For קָטַל *3ms* forms, hollow verbs yield a monosyllable, generally with a qameṣ vowel (e.g., קָם and שָׂם, above).

[4] An א as third radical in the שרש becomes silent or "quiescent," so that the pataḥ lengthens to a qameṣ since it occurs in an open syllable (as in מָצָא). In cases such as בָּנָה where the third radical appears as a ה, that ה is not

III-ה/י Verbs and III-א Verbs

שרש	קָטַל 3ms	he...	שרש	קָטַל 3ms	he...
ע.שׂ.י/ה	עָשָׂה	... made	ב.נ.י/ה	בָּנָה	... built
ר.א.י/ה	רָאָה	... saw	מ.צ.א	מָצָא	... found
שׁ.ת.י/ה	שָׁתָה	... drank	ק.ר.א	קָרָא	... called out

6.1.ב. Snapshot of sample verb: קָטַל conjugation *3ms*

שָׁמַרְנוּ we guarded	שָׁמַרְתִּי I guarded
שְׁמַרְתֶּם you guarded *mpl*	שָׁמַרְתָּ you guarded *ms*
שְׁמַרְתֶּן you guarded *fpl*	שָׁמַרְתְּ you guarded *fs*
שָׁמְרוּ they guarded	שָׁמַר he guarded
	שָׁמְרָה she guarded

actually a root consonant, but is a vowel-letter, helping to represent the preceding qameṣ (a vowel that arose as a lengthening of the pataḥ in verbs that are historically III-י or III-ו cf. Joüon §79a). This contrasts verbs such as ת.מ.ה (*to be amazed*), where the final ה is actually a root consonant (cf. note following מִלִּים לַעֲנוֹת in §3.1).

UNIT 6   מָה עָשִׂיתָ אֶתְמוֹל: 383

6.1.ג. Activity: "What did the man do?"   מָה עָשָׂה הָאָדָם:

INTERACTIVE SKILL: Describing how someone behaved (in particular, when describing a man or a boy)

See how quickly you can describe in Hebrew what someone has done, whether you saw it in an illustration or in a classmate's dramatization.

    Note concerning word order for קָטַל expressions: In the case of קָטַל clauses, the **verb** routinely appears **first**, followed by any of these elements: (a) the subject (if explicitly expressed), (b) ל-plus-pronoun (indirect object), (c) direct object, and (d) any adverbial component. The sequence of those additional elements may vary, depending on the portion to which the speaker or writer wishes to draw attention. In short, special attention is being drawn to any word that appears before a verb expressed as a קָטַל (excepting those words that are obliged to precede the verb, such as אָז, כֹּה, and לֹא).[5]

6.1.ד. Explanation: "I took some silver and I went toward [the] sea." לָקַחְתִּי כֶּסֶף וְיָמָּה הָלַכְתִּי:

INTERACTIVE SKILL: Retelling something memorable that you have done

To express *I took* (*1cs* קָטַל conjugation), begin with a *3ms* form such as לָקַח *he took*, then add the suffix ־ְתִּי in this manner: לָקַח + ־ְתִּי = לָקַחְתִּי *I took*. Please note that the accent rests on the second-from-last syllable (called "penultimate").

    As with *1cs* of the יִקְטֹל conjugation, similarly with the קָטַל conjugation the first person form has a "common" gender, serving both feminine and masculine speakers. Here are several examples. The *3ms* form is included as a reference point.

---

[5] Cf. *IBH* §45, also van der Merwe §46.1.1 and §47.1d. This contrasts the syntax of יִקְטֹל indicative clauses, where the verb does **not** come first. A יִקְטֹל in first position tends to be a jussive form (cf. §4.1.ג. and §9.4.א.).

I...	קָטַל 1cs	he...	שֹׁרֶשׁ		I...	קָטַל 1cs	he...	שֹׁרֶשׁ
... ate	אָכַלְתִּי	אָכַל	א.כ.ל		... fell down	נָפַלְתִּי	נָפַל	נ.פ.ל
... went	הָלַכְתִּי	הָלַךְ	ה.ל.כ		... crossed over	עָבַרְתִּי	עָבַר	ע.ב.ר
... remembered	זָכַרְתִּי	זָכַר	ז.כ.ר		... got up	קַמְתִּי[6]	קָם	ק.ו.מ
... went down	יָרַדְתִּי	יָרַד	י.ר.ד		... broke	שָׁבַרְתִּי	שָׁבַר	שׁ.ב.ר
... wrote	כָּתַבְתִּי	כָּתַב	כ.ת.ב		... reclined	שָׁכַבְתִּי	שָׁכַב	שׁ.כ.ב
... took	לָקַחְתִּי	לָקַח	ל.ק.ח		... put	שַׂמְתִּי	שָׂם	שׂ.ו/י.מ

Since the קָטַל conjugation makes changes only to the **suffix** of the word, we don't need to worry about making accommodations when certain consonants appear at the beginning of the שֹׁרֶשׁ. Thus the following words require **no** special attention: words beginning with א (such as אָכַל or אָמַר), with ה (such as הָלַךְ), with י (such as יָרַד), with נ (such as נָפַל), and with ע (such as עָבַר).

The next few paragraphs will help you know how to express the קָטַל conjugation when the שֹׁרֶשׁ **concludes** with certain consonants. For example, when a שֹׁרֶשׁ ends in י/ה, a ִי routinely appears after the second radical (with no additional third radical). Thus בָּנָה *he built* becomes בָּנִיתִי *I built*.[7]

	III-ה/י Verbs		
I...	קָטַל 1cs	he...	שֹׁרֶשׁ
... built	בָּנִיתִי	בָּנָה	ב.נ.י/ה
... saw	רָאִיתִי	רָאָה	ר.א.י/ה
... drank	שָׁתִיתִי	שָׁתָה	שׁ.ת.י/ה

What do you suppose will happen when the final שֹׁרֶשׁ consonant is a ת (as in כָּרַת *he cut*) or a נ (as in נָתַן *he gave*)? If you guessed, "a dagesh will take its place," you are right!

---

[6] Notice that the *3ms* form קָם and שָׂם each reduced the qameṣ vowel to a pataḥ in order to produce the *1cs* forms קַמְתִּי and שַׂמְתִּי.

[7] This shift from ה to י illustrates why roots ending in ה are often presented with an alternative final consonant: ב.נ.י/ה.

III-נ/ת Verbs

שרש	he...	קָטַל 1cs	I...
כ.ר.ת	כָּרַת	כָּרַ֫תִּי	... cut
נ.ת.נ	נָתַן	נָתַ֫תִּי	... gave

Now let's consider verbs ending in א. To develop a *1cs* form, simply add ...תִי to the *3ms* form. Thus מָצָא *he found* becomes מָצָ֫אתִי *I found*. Notice that ...תִי has no dagesh, since it is preceded by an open syllable.[8]

III-א Verbs

שרש	he...	קָטַל 1cs	I...
מ.צ.א	מָצָא	מָצָ֫אתִי	... found
נ.ש.א	נָשָׂא	נָשָׂ֫אתִי	... lifted

---

[8] The sheva typically following the third radical of a *1cs* form (as in זָכַ֫רְתִּי) does not appear in a III-guttural verb (א, ה, ח, ע, and in similar fashion ר) since these letters to varying degrees will resist being vocalized with a silent sheva.

6.1.ה. Snapshot of sample verb: קָטַל conjugation *1cs*

שָׁמַ֫רְנוּ we guarded	שָׁמַ֫רְתִּי I guarded
שְׁמַרְתֶּם you guarded *mpl*	שָׁמַ֫רְתָּ you guarded *ms*
שְׁמַרְתֶּן you guarded *fpl*	שָׁמַרְתְּ you guarded *fs*
שָׁמְרוּ they guarded	שָׁמַר he guarded
	שָׁמְרָה she guarded

6.1.1. Explanation: "A ship bound for Tarshish" אֳנִיָּה בָּאָה תַרְשִׁ֫ישָׁה

INTERACTIVE SKILL: Describing an itinerary

Did you notice the ה ָ... suffix in תַרְשִׁ֫ישָׁה? Known as a "ה-locative" (or "directional ה"), this suffix indicates **motion in a particular direction**. In this case it indicates motion toward Tarshish and would be translated *toward Tarshish*. The phrase אֳנִיָּה בָּאָה תַרְשִׁ֫ישָׁה would be rendered: *a ship bound for Tarshish*. The ה ָ... suffix functions just as the suffix "-ward" in English expressions "homeward" and "skyward."

UNIT 6 — מֶה עָשִׂיתָ אֶתְמוֹל׃

The ה-locative suffix may be added to a city name (as in תִּרְשִׁישָׁה), a nation (as in מִצְרַיְמָה *toward Egypt*), a region (as in מִזְרָחָה *eastward, toward [the] sunrise*), or an object (as in הַמִּזְבֵּחָה *toward the altar*). The word may appear with or without the definite article (הַמִּזְבֵּחָה contains the article). Notice that the addition of this syllable does not change where the accent rests (so אֶרֶץ becomes אַרְצָה).

A number of ה-locative words have been collected below, many with underlying nouns and their meanings. See if you can supply missing information in the blank areas, whether giving the underlying Hebrew noun, its translation, or the translation of the ה-locative word. Your translation should reflect whether or not an article was included.

	חוּץ	מִזְבֵּחַ	הַר	בַּיִת	אֹהֶל	אֶרֶץ	Noun alone
	outside *m*	altar *f*					
יָמָּה	חוּצָה	הַמִּזְבֵּחָה	הָהָרָה	הַבַּיְתָה	הָאֹהֱלָה	אַרְצָה	Noun with הָ... suffix
seaward, westward					toward the tent	toward earth	
צָפוֹן	פֶּתַח	פַּדַּן אֲרָם	נֶגֶב	מִצְרַיִם		יְרוּשָׁלַם	Noun alone
north *f*	doorway *m*	Paddan Aram	arid south region *m*	Egypt *f*			
צָפֹנָה	פֶּתְחָה	פַּדֶּנָה אֲרָם	נֶגְבָּה	מִצְרַיְמָה	מִדְבָּרָה	יְרוּשָׁלְָמָה	Noun with הָ... suffix
			toward [the] south				
		שַׁעַר	שָׁם	שְׁאוֹל		קֶדֶם	Noun alone
		gate *m*				east *m*	
		שַׁעְרָה	שָׁמָּה	שְׁאֹלָה		קֵדְמָה	Noun with הָ... suffix

Now, direct your attention to God's statement to Abram after his nephew Lot separated from him (see below). Use the footnotes to understand selected phrases. Watch for ה-locative terms. What sort of emotions may have stirred within Abram as he heard these words?

You will find that Masoretic cantillation marks have been retained in this excerpt so you may begin to notice how they assist reading by calling attention to accented syllables. Notice especially the penultimate accentuation of ה-locatives such as צָפֹנָה. Several comments at the start of Unit 6 Selected Readings will begin to explain how cantillation marks can help us recognize groups of thought.

וַיהוָ֣ה אָמַ֣ר אֶל־אַבְרָ֗ם אַחֲרֵי֙ הִפָּֽרֶד־ל֣וֹט מֵֽעִמּ֔וֹ⁹ שָׂ֣א נָ֤א עֵינֶ֨יךָ֙ וּרְאֵ֔ה מִן־הַמָּק֖וֹם אֲשֶׁר־אַתָּ֣ה שָׁ֑ם צָפֹ֥נָה וָנֶ֖גְבָּה וָקֵ֥דְמָה וָיָֽמָּה׃

כִּ֧י אֶת־כָּל־הָאָ֛רֶץ אֲשֶׁר־אַתָּ֥ה רֹאֶ֖ה לְךָ֣ אֶתְּנֶ֑נָּה¹⁰ וּֽלְזַרְעֲךָ֖¹¹ עַד־עוֹלָֽם׃ (Gen. 13:14-15)

6.1.ז. Do you (*ms*) know the meaning...? (תְּהוֹם) הֲיָדַ֫עְתָּ פֶּ֫שֶׁר....:

The term תְּהוֹם conveys more than simply "watery depths." Within its range of meaning lies the notion of watery abyss and primeval ocean, with all the terror that such chaos typically would imply for frail humans. Babylonians associated this realm with a powerful water-deity known as Tiamat (etymologically related to תְּהוֹם). But for biblical writers, תְּהוֹם simply comprised one element within the larger cosmos, all of which came under the rule of the creator-God of Israel (Gen. 1:2).

---

⁹ אַחֲרֵי֙ הִפָּֽרֶד־ל֣וֹט מֵֽעִמּ֔וֹ *after Lot separated from him.*

¹⁰ אֶתֵּן + אֹתָהּ.

¹¹ וּֽלְזַרְעֲךָ֖ *and to your descendants.*

UNIT 6 מֶה עָשִׂיתָ אֶתְמוֹל: 389

6.1.ח. Activity: "What did you (*ms*) do yesterday?" מֶה עָשִׂיתָ אֶתְמוֹל:

INTERACTIVE SKILL: Learn how to respond when someone asks what you did recently

Begin by recalling some interesting event or activity you participated in yesterday (or in the more distant past), whether actual or outlandishly fictitious. Please restrict yourself to verbs learned up to this point (including the present lesson). Add a bit of detail by including an object or a prepositional phrase.

Then locate a dialogue partner. Use the inquiry below to find out what your partner did recently. Then exchange roles.

Model

What did you (*ms, fs*) do yesterday?	מֶה עָשִׂיתָ / עָשִׂית אֶתְמוֹל:	Inquiry
I swallowed a big fish.	בָּלַעְתִּי דָּג גָּדוֹל:	Reply

6.1.ט. Did you (*ms*) know that...? (Village settlement) הֲיָדַעְתָּ כִּי....:

... the settlement pattern within Israelite עָרִים or חֲצֵרִים *villages m* was largely the product of networks in the מִשְׁפָּחָה *clan* (or *extended family f*)? King and Stager explain:

> [The Israelite town or village] seems to lack rational organization, consisting of densely packed houses hidden behind featureless courtyard walls, with streets and alleys that lead nowhere.... It is not spatial order derived from some external principles but order emanating from internal social organization, based on neighborhoods coalescing around families and larger units of kinship, patron-client relationships, and other forms of alliance. What looks like utter chaos to an outsider makes a great deal of sense to those who belong there.[12]

This density of village settlement may be seen in Deir el-Medina, a craftsman village

---

[12] *LBI*, 12-15, where you will find site plans of several tells. For a sample village plan, see the excavation diagram of Tell en-Naṣbeh (ancient Mizpeh) at http://www.arts.cornell.edu/jrz3/siteplan.htm.

adjacent to the Valley of the Kings, opposite Thebes along the Nile. See if can locate Thebes in the map of the Ancient Near East at the back of your textbook, where it goes by its biblical name "נֹא" (p. 564).

The tight network of house walls and lanes in the foreground of Deir el-Medina conveys a sense of residential density (founded in the 15th century BCE, adjacent to the Valley of the Kings, Egypt).

According to 2 Kings 14:25, גַּת הַחֵפֶר was the hometown of יוֹנָה (גַּת suggests that the town may have been known for a winepress). Excavation has shown that גַּת הַחֵפֶר was among the עָרִים of lower Galilee that suffered a break in occupation beginning in the late eighth century BCE—corresponding closely to the Assyrian invasions under פּוּל (Tiglath Pileser III, 745–727 BCE). גַּת הַחֵפֶר was not occupied again until the Persian Era (beginning in 539 BCE with the fall of the kingdom of בָּבֶל [Babylon] to כּוֹרֶשׁ [Cyrus II]).[13]

---

[13] Z. Gal, "Israel in Exile," *Biblical Archaeology Review* 24:03 (May / June 1993), available at http://www.cojs.org/pdf/israel_in_exile.pdf (accessed April 29, 2013). If you are wondering how a preliminary archaeological site report appears, you wish to look over the Gath-Hepher report (available at http://www.hadashot-esi.org.il/report_detail_eng.asp?id=2109&mag_id=119).

גַּת הַחֵפֶר was located in the region of מַטֵּה זְבוּלֻן. The heraldic emblem of זְבוּלֻן happens to have been an אֳנִיָּה of the sailing sort (cf. Gen. 49:13). If you wish, you may locate גַּת הַחֵפֶר in the map of יִשְׂרָאֵל found on p. 565.

6.1.י. Did you (*ms*) know that...? (Birth)   הֲיָדַעְתָּ כִּי...:

...when the day arrived for a יֶלֶד *child m* to be born (יוֹם הֻוָּלֶדֶת), the אֵם *mother* might take her place on a "birthing-stool"? Since the term for this piece of furniture is dual in number (אָבְנַיִם *a pair of stones*, Exod. 1:16), some suppose that it may literally have consisted of two parts.[14]

The same dual noun (אָבְנַיִם) is used to describe the potter's two-part fast-wheel. An upper wheel held the raw clay that the potter was throwing. The rotation of the upper plate was propelled by kicking a lower wheel that was connected to the upper by a vertical axle. Upon the אָבְנַיִם the earthen creation eventually would be unveiled.

In one of Jeremiah's oracles the concept of "fashioning of people" mixes metaphorically with the work of a יוֹצֵר *potter* as he works at his אָבְנַיִם (Jer. 18:3-6, the only other use of אָבְנַיִם in the Hebrew Bible). This conjunction of people-fashioning and pottery raises the question of whether אָבְנַיִם in the birth process may be metaphorical or even euphemistic. If so, אָבְנַיִם may have come to be associated with giving birth in order to liken a mother to a master-artisan who over time fashions and eventually unveils an intricately-crafted creation. The place where the maternal artisan eventually unveils her work would be, as a master-potter, upon the אָבְנַיִם.

Soon after being born, the infant would be bathed (ר.ח.צ.). Afterward the child would be rubbed with מֶלַח *salt m*, and wrapped in cloths (ח.ת.ל., see Ezekiel 16).

---

[14] *LBI*, 52–53. The first vowel in אָבְנַיִם is a qameṣ-ḥaṭuf.

6.1.כ. Did you (*ms*) know that...? (Marriage)   הֲיָדְעְתָּ כִּי...:

...when a man wished to marry, he would pay a bride-price to his future חֹתֵן *father-in-law m*? Both אִישׁ ל.ק.ח אִשָּׁה and אִישׁ נ.שׂ.א אִשָּׁה mean "to marry."

In the שִׁמְשׁוֹן story, the proposal was arranged by the parents (Judg. 14:1-5). The bride-to-be would become betrothed to the man (א.ר.שׂ *to betroth*), initiating a period of engagement that was almost as binding as the marriage itself. The marriage ceremony was civil, not religious, with formal attainment of marriage occurring when the bejeweled bride entered the bridegroom's household. A generous מִשְׁתֶּה *feast m* would follow, with festivities lasting as long as two weeks.[15]

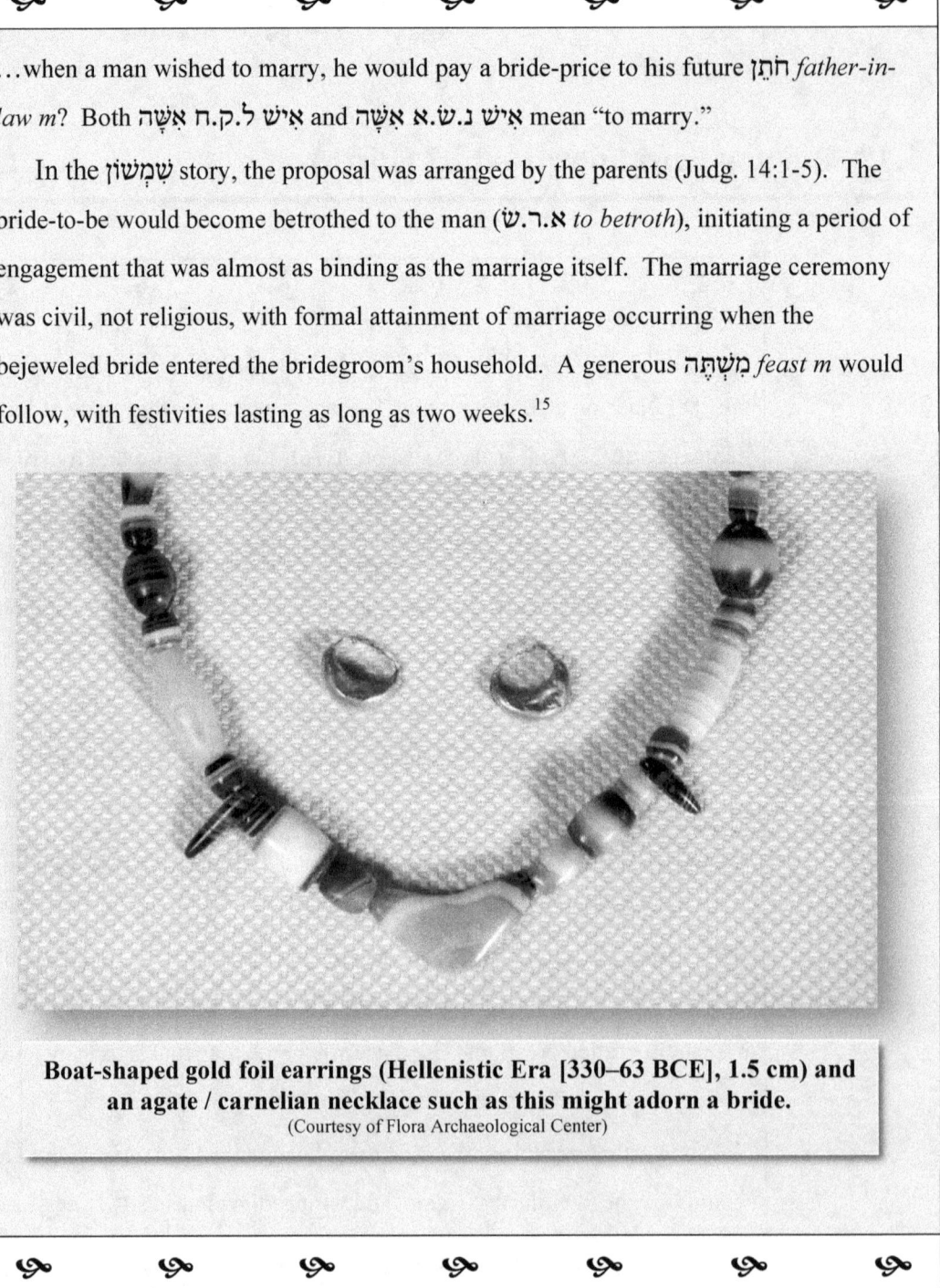

Boat-shaped gold foil earrings (Hellenistic Era [330–63 BCE], 1.5 cm) and an agate / carnelian necklace such as this might adorn a bride.
(Courtesy of Flora Archaeological Center)

---

[15] *LBI*, 54–56; see also §6.3.ח. For אִישׁ ל.ק.ח אִשָּׁה, cf. Deut. 24:1; for אִישׁ נ.שׂ.א אִשָּׁה, cf. Ruth 1:4.

MODULE 6.2 — Describing what was done by a woman, or by a group of people

Words for responding — מִלִּים לַעֲנוֹת

קָרְאוּ [ק.ר.א]	they encountered, met, called, read [a]	אָבוּ [א.ב.י/ה]	they were willing
רָדְפָה [ר.ד.פ]	she pursued	בָּאָה [ב.ו.א]	she came, entered*
שָׁלַח [ש.ל.ח]	he sent	יָצְאָה [י.צ.א]	she went out*
שָׂמוּ [ש.ו/י.מ]	they put, placed*	יִרְאָה, יִרְאַת־	fear, dread f
		יָרְאוּ [י.ר.א]	they feared
		עָלְתָה [ע.ל.י/ה]	she went up*

[a] Two different verbs share a single שֹׁרֶשׁ spelling, namely ק.ר.א. The one means *to encounter, to meet* (a by-form of ק.ר.י/ה). The other means *to call, to read*. Often these two שָׁרָשִׁים will spell a specific form identically (homonyms). That is why קָרְאוּ can mean either *they called / read* or *they encountered / met*. In such situations, look to the context to determine the better meaning. Some forms are distinct, such as the infinitive construct: קְרֹא *to call / read*, in contrast with קְרַאת *to encounter / meet*.

Words for hearing — מִלִּים לִשְׁמֹעַ

הִשְׁלִיבוּנִי [ש.ל.כ]	they threw me* *hifil*	אֵת (or אֶת־)	(marker of definite direct object)*
יָרְדָה [י.ר.ד]	she descended* (*pausal* יָרֵדָה)	בַּעֲבֹר [ע.ב.ר]	when (entity) is or was crossing over *inf c, prep* בְּ
כִּמְלֹאת [מ.ל.א]	as soon as (entity) is / was / will be full *inf c, prep* בְּ	דִּבַּרְתִּי [ד.ב.ר]	I spoke* *piel*
		הִשְׁלִיכָה [ש.ל.כ]	she threw* *hifil*

רָדַף [ר.ד.פ]	he pursued	לְהִשָּׁבֵר [ש.ב.ר]	to be broken up* *nifal inf c, prep* לְ
שָׁאַלְתִּי [ש.א.ל]	I asked, requested*	לַיְלָה, לֵילוֹת, לֵיל-, לֵילוֹת-	night *m*
תַּשְׁלִיכוּנִי [ש.ל.כ]	you *mpl* will / must throw me* *hifil*	לְפָנָי [a]	לְפָנַי *pausal form**
		לָקְחָה [ל.ק.ח]	she took*
		נָשְׂאָה [נ.ש.א]	she lifted up*
		נָשְׂאוּ [נ.ש.א]	they lifted up*

[a] The wishbone-shaped symbol under לְפָנָי is a Masoretic mark indicating a major pause, called an atnaḥ (see introduction to Selected Readings for this unit).

6.2 Jonah Episode: It was a terrible storm!

[נ׳] א. וַיְהִי[16] כִּמְלֹאת[17] הָאֳנִיָּה אֶת־הַכֵּלִים יָצְאָה מֵהָעִיר[18]:

[נ׳] ב. אֶת־הַמַּיִם לִשְׁתּוֹת שָׁאַלְתִּי וְלֹא שָׂמוּ מַיִם לְפָנַי וּבַצַּר־לִי יָרַדְתִּי וְלֹא אָכַלְתִּי:

---

[16] A new narrative segment often opens with וַיְהִי (lit., *and it was* or *and it came to pass*). Sometimes וַיְהִי is best rendered "now," as in this instance: *Now after the servants had....*

[17] When כְּ introduces an *inf c* (as in כִּמְלֹאת) it may be rendered *as soon as*. In contrast, בְּ before an *inf c* is more general, so should be rendered *when* in the sense of *while* or *after*. See 1 Kings 4:22 for an example of כְּ and 1 Kings 16:11 for an example of both prepositions operating in close proximity.

[18] מֵהָעִיר consists of מִן + הָעִיר.

[נ'] א. בַּלַּיְלָה בָּאָה רוּחַ גְדוֹלָה אֲשֶׁר שָׁלַח אֹתָהּ אֱלֹהִים אֶל־הַיָּם׃

[נ'] ב. רָדְפָה הָרוּחַ אֶת הָאֳנִיָּה׃ אֵיךְ לְקָחָה אֹתָהּ וְאֵיךְ נָשְׂאָה אֹתָהּ׃ וּבַתְּהֹמוֹת הִשְׁלִיכָה אֹתָהּ׃

[נ'] ג. אֶל־הַשָּׁמַיִם עָלְתָה וְעַד־שְׁאוֹל יָרְדָה׃

[נ'] ד. וַיְהִי בַּעֲבֹר הַמִּשְׁבָּרִים עַל־הָאֳנִיָּה וַעֲבָדִים יָרְאוּ יִרְאָה גְדוֹלָה׃

[נ'] ה. גַּם נָשְׂאוּ עֵינֵיהֶם גַּם קָרְאוּ אֶל־אֱלֹהֵיהֶם׃

UNIT 6 מֶה עָשִׂיתָ אֶתְמוֹל: 397

3

[נ׳] א. דִּבַּ֫רְתִּי אֲלֵיהֶם לֵאמֹר תַּשְׁלִיכֻ֫נִי אֶל־הַיָּם:

[נ׳] ב. לֹא־אָבוּ בָּרִאשׁוֹנָה וּבָאַחֲרֹנָה הִשְׁלִיכֻ֫נִי אֶל־הַיָּם:

6.2.א. Did you (*ms*) know that...? (The voyage of Wenamun) הֲיָדַ֫עְתָּ כִּי...:

...there is an account מִמִּצְרַ֫יִם known as "The Tale of Wenamun"? It recounts a hazardous sea voyage during the 11th century BCE. The journey was launched to procure lumber from Lebanon for the "great noble bark of Amen-Re."

For its part, יִשְׂרָאֵל showed relatively little interest in the maritime industry, likely

> due to lack of access to significant ports. The אֳנִי fleet (m and f) that was commissioned by שְׁלֹמֹה Solomon represented an exception to this trend. This אֳנִי was cooperatively staffed by sailors from both יִשְׂרָאֵל and from צֹר Tyre. It operated out of the יַם־סוּף Red Sea port of עֶצְיוֹן־גֶּבֶר (1 Kings 9:26-28).[19]

> ✥ ✥ ✥ ✥ ✥ ✥ ✥

6.2.ב. Explanation: "The ship… left the city." הָאֳנִיָּה… יָצְאָה מֵהָעִיר:

INTERACTIVE SKILL: Retelling what was done by a woman (or a feminine-gendered object, such as a ship)

To describe what a woman (or feminine-gendered object) has done, convert a *3ms* form such as יָצָא *he went out* to יָצְאָה *she went out*. In the examples that follow, notice how consistent this spelling pattern is.

Pronunciation hint: The sheva now following the second radical in words such as יָצְאָה is **vocal**, not silent. In the tables this is indicated by a small vertical stroke to the left of the first qames, called a meteg: יָצְאָה.[20] When pronounced slowly you will be able to hear three distinct syllables: יָ-צְ-אָה.[21]

Here is a sampling of verbs. Some translations have been omitted to help stretch your memory.

---

[19] Concerning the voyage of Wenamun, see Miriam Lichtheim, *Ancient Egyptian Literature: Volume II: The New Kingdom* (Berkeley: University of California Press, 1973-80), 224. Concerning the maritime industry, see §3.3.ז.

[20] Thus any *beged-kefet* letter following the sheva will *not* take on a dagesh. While the meteg does appear in the Masoretic Text, like many other cantillation marks it generally is omitted within this textbook.

[21] When a word normally ends in sheva + consonant + long-vowel (such as סָרָה… in שָׁמְרָה *she guarded*), the sheva will be replaced by the full vowel customary for that syllable when the word occurs in pause (שָׁמָרָה).

UNIT 6 — מֶה עָשִׂיתָ אֶתְמוֹל:

שֹׁרֶשׁ	he...	she...		שֹׁרֶשׁ	he...	she...	
מ.צ.א	מָצָא	מָצְאָה	...	א.כ.ל	אָכַל	אָכְלָה	... ate
נ.פ.ל	נָפַל	נָפְלָה	... fell down	ה.ל.כ	הָלַךְ	הָלְכָה	...
נ.שׂ.א	נָשָׂא	נָשְׂאָה	...	ז.כ.ר	זָכַר	זָכְרָה	... remembered
ע.ב.ר	עָבַר	עָבְרָה	... crossed over	י.ר.ד	יָרַד	יָרְדָה	...
שׁ.ב.ר	שָׁבַר	שָׁבְרָה	...	כ.ר.ת	כָּרַת	כָּרְתָה	... cut
שׁ.כ.ב	שָׁכַב	שָׁכְבָה	... reclined	כ.ת.ב	כָּתַב	כָּתְבָה	... wrote
שׁ.מ.ר	שָׁמַר	שָׁמְרָה	...	ל.ק.ח	לָקַח	לָקְחָה	...

Since the so-called "hollow verbs" (such as ק.ו.מ and שׁ.י/ו.מ) have only one syllable in *3ms* (קָם or שָׂם) the feminine form appears a bit shorter than we might expect. Even so, the characteristic הָ ending persists for the *3fs*. The accent falls on the penultimate syllable, as shown here.

Hollow Verbs

שֹׁרֶשׁ	he...	she...	
ק.ו.מ	קָם	קָ֫מָה	... got up
מ.ו.ת	מֵת	מֵ֫תָה	... died
שׁ.ו/י.מ	שָׂם	שָׂ֫מָה	... put

When we come to verbs whose third consonant is י/ה (known as III-י/ה verbs), we discover a new element surfacing in *3fs* spellings: the suffix תָה.... Thus בָּנְתָה means *she built* (from ב.נ.י/ה). Additional examples appear in the table below.

For any wondering where the suffix ת came from, it may be of interest to know that in reality it is not a new element, since historically the *3fs* of all קָטַל verbs would have contained a suffix with ת (just as *1cs*, *2ms*, and *2fs*).[22] With *3fs* in Biblical Hebrew the historic ת normally is lost—except in the case of III-י/ה verbs.

---

[22] This fact becomes clear when comparing Arabic, a Semitic language that still uses the feminine ending –*t* to this day.

III-י/ה Verbs

שֹׁרֶשׁ	he...	she...	
ב.נ.י/ה	בָּנָה	בָּנְתָה	...
ע.שׂ.י/ה	עָשָׂה	עָשְׂתָה	...
ר.א.י/ה	רָאָה	רָאֲתָה	... saw
שׁ.ת.י/ה	שָׁתָה	שָׁתְתָה	... drank

6.2.ג. Snapshot of sample verb: קָטַל conjugation *3fs*

שָׁמַ֫רְנוּ we guarded	שָׁמַ֫רְתִּי I guarded
שְׁמַרְתֶּם you guarded *mpl*	שָׁמַ֫רְתָּ you guarded *ms*
שְׁמַרְתֶּן you guarded *fpl*	שָׁמַ֫רְתְּ you guarded *fs*
שָׁמְרוּ they guarded	שָׁמַר he guarded
	שָׁמְרָה she guarded

UNIT 6   מָה עָשִׂיתָ אֶתְמוֹל: 401

6.2.ד. Activity: "What did the mother do?"   מָה עָשְׂתָה הָאֵם:

INTERACTIVE SKILL: Describing the traits of an effective mother

Have you ever watched a mother do something special to benefit her child? Describe what you remember seeing as you respond to this question: "What did you see her do?" You may include mothers from the animal kingdom.

You may use a negation if you wish, saying "she did not…." For negation, simply begin with לֹא... followed by the *3fs* קָטַל verb of your choosing.

The prompt question employs two קָטַל forms you will meet in §§6.3.א. and 6.3.ג.: רָאִיתָ *you saw 2ms* and רָאִית *you saw 2fs*. You will find that the question ends with אֹתָה *it*—referring to what she did. Called a "resumptive pronominal suffix," this reference back to what she did becomes redundant in English, so will not be translated. "It" (אֹתָה) is feminine because Hebrew prefers the feminine for general, indeterminate objects.

Model

What did you see her do (*lit.,* What did you see, that she did it *f*)?	מָה רָאִיתָ / רָאִית אֲשֶׁר עָשְׂתָה אֹתָה?	Inquiry
She wrote to her daughter when she lived in a far country.	כָּתְבָה לְבִתָּהּ בְּשִׁבְתָּהּ בְּאֶרֶץ רְחֹקָה:	Reply

The *3fs* suffix ָהּ... in לְבִתָּהּ refers to the mother. While in בְּשִׁבְתָּהּ the *3fs* suffix ָהּ... could conceivably refer either to the daughter or to the mother (both are *3fs*), the daughter is preferred since it is the nearer (more recent) eligible antecedent.

Alternate activity

Similar to an earlier activity (when you described what you saw a man do), now see how quickly you can describe what a woman (or feminine object) has done, whether in an illustration or in a pose acted out by a classmate. Follow your teacher's instructions.

6.2.ה. Explanation: "They called out to their gods." :קָרְאוּ אֶל־אֱלֹהֵיהֶם

INTERACTIVE SKILL: Describing what several people in a group have done

Compare קָרָא *he called* and קָרְאוּ *they called*. Simply by reducing the second vowel to a vocal sheva, and by adding the suffix וּ... we can convert the subject from *he* (ms) to *they* (cpl). You can detect the *3cpl* spelling pattern easily in the table below. Some translations are left blank to encourage you to draw on your memory.

Pronunciation hint: As with *3fs* forms such as אָכְלָה *she ate*, so also in a *3mpl* form such as אָכְלוּ *they ate*, a meteg accompanying the first qameṣ vowel reminds us that the following sheva will be **vocal**. When pronounced slowly you will be able to hear three distinct syllables: אָ־כְ־לוּ.

שֹׁרֶשׁ	he...	they...		שֹׁרֶשׁ	he...	they...	
מ.צ.א	מָצָא	מָצְאוּ	...found	א.כ.ל	אָכַל	אָכְלוּ	...
נ.פ.ל	נָפַל	נָפְלוּ	...	ה.ל.ב	הָלַךְ	הָלְכוּ	...went
נ.שׂ.א	נָשָׂא	נָשְׂאוּ	...lifted	ז.כ.ר	זָכַר	זָכְרוּ	...
ע.ב.ר	עָבַר	עָבְרוּ	...	י.ר.ד	יָרַד	יָרְדוּ	...went down
שׁ.ב.ר	שָׁבַר	שָׁבְרוּ	...broke	כ.ר.ת	כָּרַת	כָּרְתוּ	...
שׁ.כ.ב	שָׁכַב	שָׁכְבוּ	...	כ.ת.ב	כָּתַב	כָּתְבוּ	...
שׁ.מ.ר	שָׁמַר	שָׁמְרוּ	...	ל.ק.ח	לָקַח	לָקְחוּ	...took

"Hollow verbs" will simply add וּ... to the *3ms* base (such as קָם or שָׂם), as seen in the next table. Notice that the accent falls on the first syllable.

מֶה עָשִׂיתָ אֶתְמוֹל:

Hollow Verbs

שֹׁרֶשׁ	he...	they...	
ב.ו.א	בָּא	בָּאוּ	...came, entered
ס.ו.ר	סָר	סָרוּ	...turned
ק.ו.מ	קָם	קָמוּ	...
מ.ו.ת	מֵת	מֵתוּ	...died
שׂ.ו/י.מ	שָׂם	שָׂמוּ	...put

In the case of III-ה/י verbs, the *3cpl* suffix וּ... completely replaces the last שֹׁרֶשׁ letter (as in אָבוּ, from א.ב.י/ה). Here are a few samples.

III-ה/י Verbs

שֹׁרֶשׁ	he...	they...	
א.ב.י/ה	אָבָה	אָבוּ	...were willing
ב.נ.י/ה	בָּנָה	בָּנוּ	...
ע.ל.י/ה	עָלָה	עָלוּ	...went up
ע.נ.י/ה	עָנָה	עָנוּ	...answered
ע.שׂ.י/ה	עָשָׂה	עָשׂוּ	...made
ר.א.י/ה	רָאָה	רָאוּ	...
שׁ.ת.י/ה	שָׁתָה	שָׁתוּ	...

6.2.1. Snapshot of sample verb: קָטַל conjugation *3cpl*

שָׁמַרְנוּ we guarded	שָׁמַרְתִּי I guarded
שְׁמַרְתֶּם you guarded *mpl*	שָׁמַרְתָּ you guarded *ms*
שְׁמַרְתֶּן you guarded *fpl*	שָׁמַרְתְּ you guarded *fs*
שָׁמְרוּ they guarded	שָׁמַר he guarded
	שָׁמְרָה she guarded

6.2.2. Activity: "What did they (*m*) do to him?"   מֶה עָשׂוּ לוֹ:

INTERACTIVE SKILL: Recounting a practical joke

Have you ever seen a group play a practical joke on one of their friends? Perhaps you only heard about it second-hand, or saw it in a drama. Using simple Hebrew, describe what they did. If you cannot remember one, simply make one up and pretend that you heard about it.

For the sake of learning, please describe the event as, "**They** did so and so…" (not "**We** did so and so…"), even though you may have been one of the perpetrators.

UNIT 6   מָה עָשִׂיתָ אֶתְמוֹל: 405

MODULE 6.3   Getting clarification from a friend concerning what he or she has been doing

Words for responding — מִלִּים לַעֲנוֹת

נָתַתְּ [נ.ת.נ]	you gave* fs	הָלַכְתְּ [ה.ל.כ]	you went* fs
עֲבַרְתֶּם [ע.ב.ר]	you crossed over* mpl	הָלַכְתָּ [ה.ל.כ]	you went* ms
קָנִית [ק.נ.י/ה]	you bought, acquired, created fs	זָהָב, זְהַב-	gold m
		חָשַׁבְתָּ [ח.ש.ב]	you thought, supposed* ms
שְׁמַעְתֶּם [ש.מ.ע]	you heard* mpl	כָּבְדוּ [כ.ב.ד]	they are mighty* a
		לַאֲבֹד [א.ב.ד]	to perish inf c, prep לְ

[a] Verbs that describe a **condition** (such as "to be mighty") rather than an action (like "to run") often convey a present tense connotation in the קָטַל conjugation. Called stative verbs, these are discussed briefly in §6.5.ג., and more fully in the appendix section for that same segment.

Words for hearing — מִלִּים לִשְׁמֹעַ

חֶרֶב, חֲרָבוֹת, חֶרֶב-, חַרְבוֹת-	sword f	א.מ.ר בְּלֵב (or בִּלְבָב)	to think (lit., to say in [one's] heart [plus pronominal suffix])
חָשַׁבְתִּי [ח.ש.ב]	I thought, supposed*		
יָרֵאתָ [י.ר.א]	you were afraid* ms		
מִלְחָמָה, מִלְחָמוֹת, מִלְחֶמֶת-, מִלְחֲמוֹת-	war, battle f	בְּהַשְׁלִיכָם [ש.ל.כ]	when they threw (lit., in their throwing)* hifil inf c, prep בְּ
שָׁנָה, שָׁנִים (or שָׁנוֹת), שְׁנַת-, שְׁנֵי- (or שְׁנוֹת-)	year f	חַיִל, חֲיָלִים, חֵיל-, חֵילֵי-	army, wealth, might m

6.3 Jonah Episode: Why didn't you go to Nineveh?

[חֻלְדָּה] א.   לָמָּה לֹא הָלַכְתָּ לְנִינְוֵה:

[נ׳] ב.   הַאַתֶּם עֲבַרְתֶּם בְּדֶרֶךְ־נִינְוֵה:

[אֲמִתַּי] ג.   אֲנִי לֹא עָבַרְתִּי:

חֻלְדָּה הֲלֹא־אַתְּ הָלַכְתְּ אֶל־נִינְוֵה בַּשָּׁנָה הַזֹּאת:

מֶה עָשִׂיתָ אֶתְמוֹל:

א. [אֲמִתַּי] נָתַתְּ לִי חֶרֶב־זָהָב אֲשֶׁר קָנִית מִשָּׁם: הֲלֹא תִזְכֹּר:

ב. [חֶלְדָּה] עַתָּה אֶזְכֹּר: חָשַׁבְתִּי עִם־נִינְוֵה אַנְשֵׁי־חַיִל:

ג. [נ׳] הֵם אַנְשֵׁי־חַיִל: אַךְ הֲלֹא שְׁמַעְתֶּם אֶת־אֲשֶׁר עָשׂוּ לָנוּ עַבְדֵי־מַלְכְּכֶם: נָפְלוּ עָלֵינוּ בְמִלְחָמָה:

[חֻלְדָּה] א. סַפֶּר לָנוּ אֶת־אֲשֶׁר אָמַרְתָּ בִּלְבָבְךָ בְּהַשְׁלִיכְכֶם אֹתְךָ בַּיָּם:
הֲלֹא יָרֵאתָ בִּלְבָבֶךָ:

[אֲמִתַּי] ב. הֲלֹא חָשַׁבְתָּ לַאֲבֹד:
אוּלַי דָּג גָּדוֹל יֹאכַל אֹתְךָ:

[נ׳] ג. הֵן אָמַרְתִּי בְּלִבִּי אָבֹד אֲבַד בַּיָּם: טוֹב לִי לָמוּת מִלֶּכֶת אֶל־נִינְוֵה:

UNIT 6   מָה עָשִׂיתָ אֶתְמוֹל:

6.3.א. Explanation: "Why didn't you (*ms*) travel to Nineveh?"

לָמָּה לֹא הָלַכְתָּ לְנִינְוֵה:

INTERACTIVE SKILL: Telling (or asking) a man what he has done

Once you are comfortable remembering how to say הָלַכְתִּי *I travelled*, you will have no trouble describing to a friend what you saw him do: *you travelled* (*2ms*). Merely replace the תִּי... suffix of the *1cs* form with a תָּ... suffix, so that הָלַכְתִּי *I travelled* becomes הָלַכְתָּ *you travelled* (*2ms*). Here are some examples to help you communicate.

he...	I...	you *ms*...		he...	I...	you *ms*...	
עָבַר	עָבַרְתִּי	עָבַרְתָּ	... crossed over	אָבַד	אָבַדְתִּי	אָבַדְתָּ	... perished
פָּתַח	פָּתַחְתִּי	פָּתַחְתָּ	... opened[23]	אָכַל	אָכַלְתִּי	אָכַלְתָּ	... ate
קָם [ק.ו.מ]	קַמְתִּי	קַמְתָּ	... got up	זָכַר	זָכַרְתִּי	זָכַרְתָּ	... remembered
רָדַף	רָדַפְתִּי	רָדַפְתָּ	... pursued	חָשַׁב	חָשַׁבְתִּי	חָשַׁבְתָּ	... thought, supposed
שָׁבַר	שָׁבַרְתִּי	שָׁבַרְתָּ	... broke	יָדַע	יָדַעְתִּי	יָדַעְתָּ	... knew
שָׁכַב	שָׁכַבְתִּי	שָׁכַבְתָּ	... reclined	יָרַד	יָרַדְתִּי	יָרַדְתָּ	... went down
שָׁלַח	שָׁלַחְתִּי	שָׁלַחְתָּ	... sent	כָּתַב	כָּתַבְתִּי	כָּתַבְתָּ	... wrote
שָׂם [שׂ.ו./י.מ]	שַׂמְתִּי	שַׂמְתָּ	... put	לָקַח	לָקַחְתִּי	לָקַחְתָּ	... took
שָׁמַע	שָׁמַעְתִּי	שָׁמַעְתָּ	... heard	נָפַל	נָפַלְתִּי	נָפַלְתָּ	... fell

    When the שֹׁרֶשׁ ends with ה/י the *2ms* suffix begins with a י (just as with "I" forms [*1cs*]). Thus בָּנִיתִי *I built* becomes בָּנִיתָ *you built*.

---

[23] The more common verb for *to open* is shown here (פ.ת.ח). For *opening* (of eyes), פ.ק.ח is preferred.

III-ה/י Verbs

he...	I...	you *ms*...	
בָּנָה	בָּנִיתִי	בָּנִיתָ	... built
קָנָה	קָנִיתִי	קָנִיתָ	... bought, acquired, created
רָאָה	רָאִיתִי	רָאִיתָ	... saw
שָׁתָה	שָׁתִיתִי	שָׁתִיתָ	... drank

A final נ or ת in the שרש will disappear, leaving behind only a strong (doubling) dagesh in the suffix, as with כָּרַתָּ *you cut*. The נ or ת is said to "assimilate" with the ensuing consonant.

III-נ or III-ת Verbs

he...	I...	you *ms*...	
כָּרַת	כָּרַתִּי	כָּרַתָּ	... cut
נָתַן	נָתַתִּי	נָתַתָּ	... gave

In addition, a final א usually grows quiescent, resulting in a qameṣ vowel for the consonant just prior (מָצָאתָ *you found*). The final א is silent also when it follows the ṣērê of stative verbs, as with יָרֵאתָ *you are / were afraid* and שָׂנֵאתָ *you hate / hated*.

III-א Verbs

he...	I...	you *ms*...	
בָּא [ב.ו.א]	בָּאתִי	בָּאתָ	... came, entered
יָרֵא	יָרֵאתִי	יָרֵאתָ	... are / were afraid
מָצָא	מָצָאתִי	מָצָאתָ	... found
נָשָׂא	נָשָׂאתִי	נָשָׂאתָ	... lifted
שָׂנֵא	שָׂנֵאתִי	שָׂנֵאתָ	... hate / hated

UNIT 6   מֶה עָשִׂיתָ אֶתְמוֹל: 411

6.3.ב. Snapshot of sample verb: קָטַל conjugation *2ms*

שָׁמַרְנוּ we guarded	שָׁמַרְתִּי I guarded
שְׁמַרְתֶּם you guarded *mpl*	**שָׁמַרְתָּ** **you guarded *ms***
שְׁמַרְתֶּן you guarded *fpl*	שָׁמַרְתְּ you guarded *fs*
שָׁמְרוּ they guarded	שָׁמַר he guarded
	שָׁמְרָה she guarded

6.3.ג. Explanation: "Didn't you (*fs*) go to Nineveh?"

הֲלֹא־אַתְּ הָלַכְתְּ אֶל־נִינְוֵה:[24]

INTERACTIVE SKILL: Telling (or asking) a woman what she has done

As with the יִקְטֹל conjugation, now also with the קָטַל conjugation, the transition from talking about "you" *2ms* to "you" *2fs* is very simple. Merely replace the suffix תָּ... with תְּ.... Thus הָלַכְתָּ *you went* (*2ms*) becomes הָלַכְתְּ *you went* (*2fs*). The last syllable תְּ will sound like the *–ed* in the English word *"locked."*

---

[24] Please note that in the model sentence beginning this section (הֲלֹא־אַתְּ הָלַכְתְּ...) the independent personal pronoun אַתְּ is not required for the קָטַל conjugation. In this sentence it lends emphasis to the pronominal subject.

Here is a sampling of verbs. As with other collections, some translations have been omitted to help stretch your memory.

he...	you *ms*...	you *fs*...		he...	you *ms*...	you *fs*...	
נָתַן	נָתַתָּ	נָתַתְּ	... gave	אָבַד	אָבַדְתָּ	אָבַדְתְּ	... perished
עָבַר	עָבַרְתָּ	עָבַרְתְּ	...	אָכַל	אָכַלְתָּ	אָכַלְתְּ	...
פָּתַח	פָּתַחְתָּ	פָּתַחְתְּ	... opened	זָכַר	זָכַרְתָּ	זָכַרְתְּ	... remembered
קָם [ק.ו.מ]	קַמְתָּ	קַמְתְּ	... got up	חָשַׁב	חָשַׁבְתָּ	חָשַׁבְתְּ	...
רָדַף	רָדַפְתָּ	רָדַפְתְּ	... pursued	יָרַד	יָרַדְתָּ	יָרַדְתְּ	... went down
שָׁבַר	שָׁבַרְתָּ	שָׁבַרְתְּ	...	כָּרַת	כָּרַתָּ	כָּרַתְּ	... cut
שָׁכַב	שָׁכַבְתָּ	שָׁכַבְתְּ	... reclined	כָּתַב	כָּתַבְתָּ	כָּתַבְתְּ	... wrote
שָׁלַח	שָׁלַחְתָּ	שָׁלַחְתְּ	... sent	לָקַח	לָקַחְתָּ	לָקַחְתְּ	...
שָׂם [ש.ו./י.מ]	שַׂמְתָּ	שַׂמְתְּ	... put	נָפַל	נָפַלְתָּ	נָפַלְתְּ	...

When the שרש ends with ה/י the *2fs* suffix begins with a י (just as with *2ms* forms). Thus בָּנִיתָ *you built* (*ms*) becomes בָּנִית *you built* (*fs*).

III-ה/י Verbs

he...	you *ms*...	you *fs*...	
בָּנָה	בָּנִיתָ	בָּנִית	... built
קָנָה	קָנִיתָ	קָנִית	... bought, acquired
רָאָה	רָאִיתָ	רָאִית	...
שָׁתָה	שָׁתִיתָ	שָׁתִית	...

Since a ב.ו.א with its final א produces בָּאתָ *you came, entered* (*ms*), the *2fs* form will simply be בָּאת, with neither dagesh nor sheva in the ת.

III-א Verbs

he...	you *ms*...	you *fs*...	
בָּא [ב.ו.א]	בָּאתָ	בָּאת	...
יָרֵא	יָרֵאתָ	יָרֵאת	... are / were afraid[25]
יָצָא	יָצָאתָ	יָצָאת	...
מָצָא	מָצָאתָ	מָצָאת	...
נָשָׂא	נָשָׂאתָ	נָשָׂאת	... lifted

When the consonant ע comprises the third radical (as in ש.מ.ע), the ע resists the sheva generally found in that third radical, preferring a pataḥ instead. Thus *you listened* (*2fs*) is pronounced שָׁמַעַתְּ. You will not find it spelled שָׁמַעְתְּ‡.

III-ע Verbs

he...	you *ms*...	you *fs*...	
יָדַע	יָדַעְתָּ	יָדַעַתְּ	... know / knew[26]
שָׁמַע	שָׁמַעְתָּ	שָׁמַעַתְּ	... heard

---

[25] The קטל conjugation of the verb י.ר.א may operate either as present tense or as past, depending on the context.

[26] Like י.ר.א, the קטל conjugation of the verb י.ד.ע may operate either as present tense or as past, depending on the context.

6.3.ד. Snapshot of sample verb: קָטַל conjugation *2fs*

שָׁמַ֫רְנוּ we guarded	שָׁמַ֫רְתִּי I guarded
שְׁמַרְתֶּם you guarded *mpl*	שָׁמַ֫רְתָּ you guarded *ms*
שְׁמַרְתֶּן you guarded *fpl*	**שָׁמַרְתְּ** **you guarded *fs***
שָׁמְרוּ they guarded	שָׁמַר he guarded
	שָׁמְרָה she guarded

6.3.ה. Activity: "Why didn't you (*ms*, *fs*) travel the road to Nineveh?"

לָ֫מָּה לֹא הָלַ֫כְתָּ / הָלַ֫כְתְּ לְנִינְוֵה:

INTERACTIVE SKILL: Following up a friend's reported activities by asking whether he / she did not do something else

Your neighbor is about to tell you two (2) things he / she did yesterday. As you listen to them, think of something additional that your neighbor did not mention doing. Acting surprised, ask whether he / she did **not** do this **additional** activity. Start the process by asking what was done yesterday (Inquiry א). Then follow up with an "Inquiry ב" (of your own design, beginning with הֲלֹא).

In anticipation of your neighbor asking what you did yesterday, please write down two (2) things that you were involved with. Try to make them interesting, unusual, and, if necessary, quite fictitious.

UNIT 6   מֶה עָשִׂיתָ אֶתְמוֹל:

Model

What did you do (*ms, fs*) yesterday?	מֶה עָשִׂיתָ / עָשִׂית אֶתְמוֹל:	Inquiry א
I built a house. I sat in it.	בָּנִיתִי בַּיִת: יָשַׁבְתִּי בּוֹ:	Reply א
Didn't you (*ms, fs*) throw rocks upon your neighbor's house?	הֲלֹא הִשְׁלַכְתָּ / הִשְׁלַכְתְּ אֲבָנִים עַל־בֵּית־רֵעֲךָ / רֵעֵיךְ:	Inquiry ב
I did (*or* did not) throw rocks at my neighbor's house. I threw [bread, silver...].	(לֹא) הִשְׁלַכְתִּי אֲבָנִים עַל־בֵּית־רֵעִי: הִשְׁלַכְתִּי [לֶחֶם, כֶּסֶף...]:	Reply ב

6.3.1. Explanation: "Didn't you (*mpl*) hear what they did to us?"
הֲלֹא שְׁמַעְתֶּם אֶת־אֲשֶׁר עָשׂוּ לָנוּ:

INTERACTIVE SKILL: Telling (or asking) a group of people what they have done

In the question ...הֲלֹא שְׁמַעְתֶּם *Didn't you* (*2mpl*) *hear...?* we discover how to converse with a group of people regarding what they did in the past. This form (*2mpl*) resembles the first person שָׁמַעְתִּי *I heard*, with two changes. First, the initial vowel of the שרש weakens from qameṣ שָׁ... to sheva שְׁ....[27] Second, in place of the ...תִּי suffix we find ...תֶּם. As is customary for most Hebrew words, once again the accent falls on the final syllable (marked in these tables only as a learning aid). Thus שָׁמַעְתִּי *I heard* becomes שְׁמַעְתֶּם *you heard* (*2mpl*). The following sample verbs display these markers.

---

[27] This change is known as "propretonic reduction," meaning that the vowel located two syllables before the accented ("tone") syllable is weakened (cf. Appendix §0.4.ד.).

I...	you mpl...		I...	you mpl...	
נָפַ֫לְתִּי	נְפַלְתֶּם	... fell	הִשְׁלַ֫כְתִּי	הִשְׁלַכְתֶּם	... threw
נָשָׂ֫אתִי	נְשָׂאתֶם	... lifted	זָכַ֫רְתִּי	זְכַרְתֶּם	... remembered
נָתַ֫תִּי	נְתַתֶּם	... gave	יָדַ֫עְתִּי	יְדַעְתֶּם	... knew
פָּתַ֫חְתִּי	פְּתַחְתֶּם	...	יָרֵ֫אתִי	יְרֵאתֶם	...
רָדַ֫פְתִּי	רְדַפְתֶּם	... pursued	יָרַ֫דְתִּי	יְרַדְתֶּם	... went down
שָׁבַ֫רְתִּי	שְׁבַרְתֶּם	... broke	כָּרַ֫תִּי	כְּרַתֶּם	... cut
שָׁכַ֫בְתִּי	שְׁכַבְתֶּם	...	כָּתַ֫בְתִּי	כְּתַבְתֶּם	... wrote
שָׁלַ֫חְתִּי	שְׁלַחְתֶּם	... sent	לָקַ֫חְתִּי	לְקַחְתֶּם	...
			מָצָ֫אתִי	מְצָאתֶם	... found

Here are more verbs with the same changes from "I" to "you" *2mpl*. Can you detect what trait the שָׁרָשִׁים of these verbs have in common?[28] Fill it in, using the blank at the top of the table.

Your title for this group of verbs: _____

I...	you mpl...		I...	you mpl...	
רָאִ֫יתִי	רְאִיתֶם	... saw	בָּנִ֫יתִי	בְּנִיתֶם	... built
שָׁתִ֫יתִי	שְׁתִיתֶם	... drank	קָנִ֫יתִי	קְנִיתֶם	... bought, acquired

Do you notice anything distinct about the spelling in this next group of verbs? Pay particular attention to the vowels.[29]

---

[28] If you guessed, "The שרש of each ends with י/ה," you are correct. As with verbs whose שרש ends in א, no dagesh appears here in the suffix תֶם.... (For III-א examples, please see verbs מְצָאתֶם and נְשָׂאתֶם in the table above.)

[29] Did you notice that the first vowel only reduces to a ḥatef-pataḥ (rather than a pure sheva) when it follows a guttural consonant (א, ה, ח, ע)?

Your title for this group of verbs: _____

I...	you mpl...		I...	you mpl...	
הָלַכְתִּי	הֲלַכְתֶּם	... went	אָמַרְתִּי	אֲמַרְתֶּם	... said
חָשַׁבְתִּי	חֲשַׁבְתֶּם	... thought	אָבַדְתִּי	אֲבַדְתֶּם	... perished
עָבַרְתִּי	עֲבַרְתֶּם	... crossed over	אָכַלְתִּי	אֲכַלְתֶּם	... ate

A later activity will direct you to draw on the *2mpl* verbs presented in these tables (see §6.4.ו.).

6.3.ז. Snapshot of sample verb: קָטַל conjugation *2mpl*

שָׁמַרְנוּ we guarded	שָׁמַרְתִּי I guarded
שְׁמַרְתֶּם you guarded *mpl*	שָׁמַרְתָּ you guarded *ms*
שְׁמַרְתֶּן you guarded *fpl*	שָׁמַרְתְּ you guarded *fs*
שָׁמְרוּ they guarded	שָׁמַר he guarded
	שָׁמְרָה she guarded

6.3.ח. Did you (*ms*) know that...? (Metallurgy)   הֲיָדַעְתָּ כִּי...:

...that 250 ancient mines yielding נְחֹשֶׁת *copper f* (also refers to *bronze*) have been discovered at Feinan, Jordan, dating to the 4th millennium (approx. 55 km south of the Dead Sea and 22 km east of the Israeli border)? Copper mineshafts reaching as much as 35 meters deep have been found at Timnaʻ (in the Arabah valley, 25 km north of the Gulf of Aqaba and approx. 165 km SSW of Feinan). נְחֹשֶׁת was used to fashion chisels, mace heads, wands, crowns, trays, cauldrons, and bowls

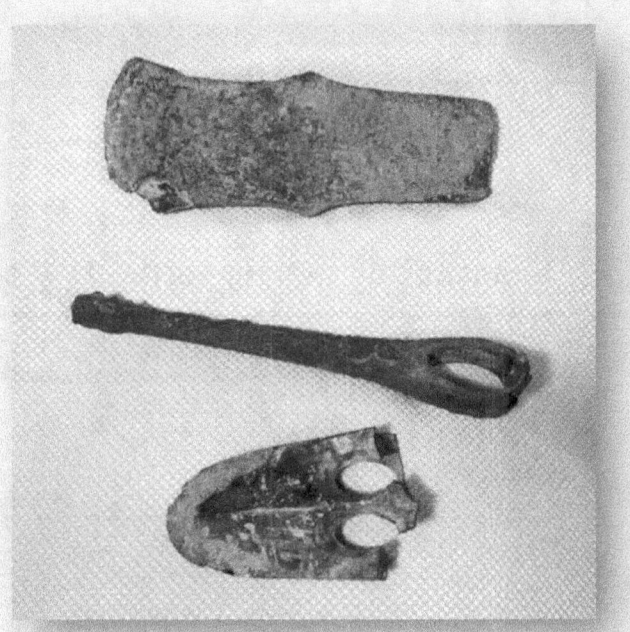

Axe blades of נְחֹשֶׁת, ranging from 8.5 to 16 cm in length. The bottom specimen (from Antioch area of Turkey) resembles a molded blade from Megiddo Stratum XIV (1850–1800 BCE). (Courtesy of Flora Archaeological Center)

Embossed frontlet of gold foil (Iron II [1000–800 BCE]). (Courtesy of Flora Archaeological Center; photo: B. Hoffman)

(see weapons in §10.2.ב.). To fashion bronze (90% copper, 10% tin), it was necessary to import בְּדִיל *tin m* from sources such as Afghanistan or the Taurus Mountains in Turkey.

Due to its ability to hold

an edge, by the tenth century בַּרְזֶל *iron m* overtook נְחֹשֶׁת *bronze f* as the principal metal—especially for smaller objects such as axes, plowpoints, and swords, while נְחֹשֶׁת continued in use for statues and vessels. Although furnace technology did not allow for casting בַּרְזֶל (heating to 2,793 degrees Fahrenheit is required for melting בַּרְזֶל), as the heated בַּרְזֶל came into contact with גַּחֶלֶת *burning charcoal f* it would develop a steel surface. A steel pick with an oak handle dating to the eleventh century BCE was found in Upper Galilee.

As to זָהָב, since אֶרֶץ־יִשְׂרָאֵל lacked native deposits of this precious metal, בְּנֵי־יִשְׂרָאֵל were obliged to obtain it from sources in מִצְרַיִם *Egypt f* and the Arabian peninsula. Jewelry recovered from caches in קְבָרִים dated 1600-1200 BCE (in Tell el-ʿAjjul, south-west of עַזָּה *Gaza*) includes crescents, pendants, earrings, toggle pins, and bracelets—all made of זָהָב (see also §6.1.ב.)

Unlike זָהָב, it was routinely necessary לִצְרוֹף *to refine / smelt* ore containing כֶּסֶף. כֶּסֶף came into common use as a precious metal during the third millennium, whether for jewelry or as a medium of exchange

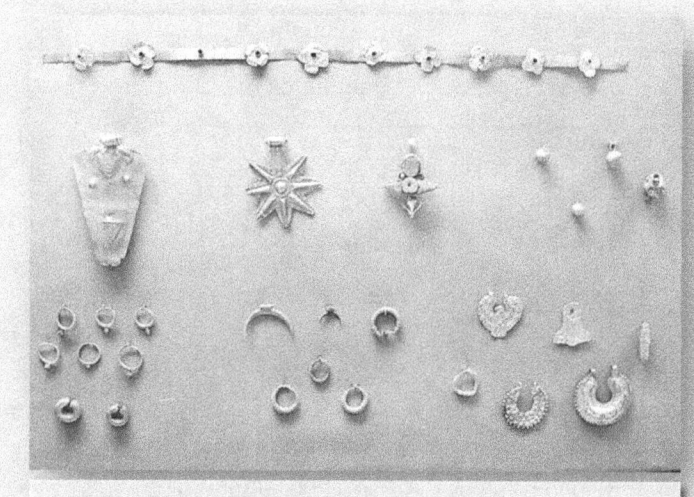

Jewelry of זָהָב from 16ᵗʰ century BCE Tell el-ʿAjjul, southwest of Gaza. (Courtesy of British Museum)

(payment consisting of broken jewelry or cut pieces of silver, known as *Hacksilber*, cf. §7.3.ט.). The Taurus Mountains (called by סַרְגוֹן *Sargon* of Akkad, "Silver Mountains") served as a significant source of כֶּסֶף in the ancient world.[30]

---

[30] Some suppose that Tarshish with its tin exports (Ezek. 27:12) corresponds to Tarsus of Turkey rather than the Phoenician colony of Tartessus in southwest Spain (*LBI*, 165–74, esp. 166).

MODULE 6.4 Interviewing a group to learn what they have been involved in, and why

Words for responding — מִלִּים לַעֲנוֹת

יְרַדְתֶּן [י.ר.ד]	you descended* fpl	בָּאנוּ [ב.ו.א]	we came, entered*
פָּקַדְנוּ [פ.ק.ד]	we visited, inspected, inflicted, appointed	בִּקַּשְׁתִּי [ב.ק.שׁ]	I searched* piel
		דִּבַּרְנוּ [ד.ב.ר]	we spoke* piel
פְּקַדְתֶּן [פ.ק.ד]	you visited, inspected, inflicted, appointed fpl	הֲלַכְתֶּן [ה.ל.כ]	you went* fpl
		זָקֵן, זְקֵנָה, זְקֵנִים, זְקֵנוֹת	old
		יְלַדְתֶּן [י.ל.ד]	you gave birth to fpl
		יָצָאנוּ [י.צ.א]	we went out*

Words for hearing — מִלִּים לִשְׁמֹעַ

מֵאַיִן...:	from where...?	אַחֲרֵי הִשְׁלִיךְ הָעֲבָדִים	after the servants threw
קְשֵׁה-עֹרֶף	stiff-necked, stubborn	בְּרֶדֶת [י.ר.ד]	when [something] descended / descends / will descend* inf c, בְּ prep
רָם, רָמָה, רָמִים, רָמוֹת [ר.ו.מ]	one who is high, exalted		
שָׁבוּ [שׁ.ו.ב]	they returned*		
		הִשְׁלִיךְ [שׁ.ל.כ]	to throw* hifil inf c
		כִּי אִם	but rather

6.4 Jonah Episode: As the fish descended...

Note: מְסַפֵּר designates lines spoken by a narrator (*piel pt ms* of ס.פ.ר *to recount, rehearse*).

[מְסַפֵּר]   א.   וַיְהִי בְּרֶדֶת הַדָּגִים בַּתְּהֹמוֹת וְהִנֵּה רָאוּ דָג זָקֵן: דִּבֶּר הַדָּג הַזֶּה לֵאמֹר...

[זָקֵן]   ב.   מֵאַיִן תָּבֹאוּ:   בִּקַּשְׁתִּי אֶתְכֶם יָמִים רַבִּים:

א. [גָּדוֹל] יָצָאנוּ לִמְצֹא לֶחֶם וְהִנֵּה לֹא מָצָאנוּ לֶחֶם כִּי אִם־רוּחוֹת גְּדֹלוֹת מָצְאוּ אֹתָנוּ:

ב. [גָּדוֹל] דִּבַּרְנוּ לָרוּחוֹת לֵאמֹר לָמָּה הֲלַכְתֶּן וְעָלֵינוּ יְרַדְתֶּן:

לָמָּה פְּקַדְתֶּן אֶת־הָרָעָה הַזֹּאת עָלֵינוּ:

לָמָּה יְלַדְתֶּן מִשְׁבָּרִים אֲשֶׁר רָמִים מִן־הָאֳנִיָּה:

מֶה עָשִׂיתָ אֶתְמוֹל:

3

[גָּדוֹל / א. עָנוּ הָרוּחוֹת לֵאמֹר לֹא עֲלֵיכֶם פְּקַדְנוּ אֹתָם כִּי אִם־עַל־אָדָם אֶחָד
רוּחוֹת] וְעַל־אָדָם קְשֵׁה־עֹרֶף בָּאנוּ כִּי עָלָיו שָׁלַח אֹתָנוּ הָאֱלֹהִים:

[קָטָן] ב. שָׁבוּ הָרוּחוֹת אֶל־הַשָּׁמַיִם אַחֲרֵי הִשְׁלִיךְ הָעֲבָדִים אֶת הַנָּבִיא מִן הָאֳנִיָּה:

6.4.א. Explanation and activity: "As the fish descended..."

וַיְהִי בְּרֶדֶת הַדָּגִים...

INTERACTIVE SKILL: Describing background situation (setting the scene) when telling a story

To describe a parallel or background situation, Hebrew often employs a preposition followed by an infinitive construct, as in בְּרֶדֶת הַדָּגִים *as the fish descended* (lit., *in the descending of the fish*).[31] רֶדֶת is the infinitive construct of ד.ר.י.. In storytelling, the expression וַיְהִי *and it came to pass* generally will introduce such a clause, thereby casting it in past time.[32] It is not always necessary to translate וַיְהִי.

How would you complete the following background situations? The first has been finished for you. Please write your ending in the column labeled "Your completion." Then round out the "Translation" column by adding the English version of your "completion."

Note: Each of the translations on the left has assigned a particular time frame for the situation. A different time frame could have been selected, with equal faithfulness to the Hebrew (due to the absence of any time indicator such as "וַיְהִי"). Therein lies the versatility of an "infinitive"—it is time-flexible.

Translation	Your completion	Background situation
As the fish descended… **an old fish saw them.**	... וְדָג זָקֵן רָאָה אֹתָם:	א. בְּרֶדֶת הַדָּגִים...
As the people walked beneath the sun…		ב. בְּלֶכֶת הָאֲנָשִׁים תַּחַת הַשֶּׁמֶשׁ...
As soon as the woman saw her friends…		ג. כִּרְאוֹת הָאִשָּׁה אֶת־רֵעֶיהָ...

---

[31] This is known as a temporal clause. Often the ensuing main statement (i.e., what follows the temporal clause) will employ a form you will meet in the next unit, known as a וַיִּקְטֹל form.

[32] וַיְהִי is from ה.י.ה *to be*, and is expressed as a וַיִּקְטֹל form. The וַיִּקְטֹל will be explained Unit 7, and וַיְהִי in §7.1.א.

UNIT 6   מֶה עָשִׂיתָ אֶתְמוֹל:

As soon as you (ms) lift a big rock…		ד. כְּשֵׂאתְךָ אֶבֶן גְּדֹלָה…

Notice that when employing a pronoun to identify the **person** who is doing an activity named by an infinitive construct, Hebrew may **attach the pronoun** directly to the infinitive construct, as in example #ד: כְּשֵׂאתְךָ = כְּ + שְׂאֵת + ךָ *as soon as you (ms) lift*. Similarly, if example #ג had only a pronominal subject ("as soon as **she** saw" instead of "as soon as **the woman** saw"), we could attach the pronoun "she" directly to the infinitive רְאוֹת in this fashion: כִּרְאוֹתָהּ (cf. Gen. 39:13-14, where Potiphar's wife raised a cry "as soon as she saw" that Joseph had escaped her clutches).

6.4.ב. Explanation: "We went out to find some food." יָצָאנוּ לִמְצֹא לֶחֶם:

INTERACTIVE SKILL: Making a progress report on behalf of a group that you are a part of

When reporting on behalf of a group you belong to, you will want make a number of "we" statements (*1cpl*). It is easy to form these if you begin with the "I" forms (*1cs*). Remove the תִּי... suffix, replacing it with נוּ.... Thus יָצָאתִי *I went out* will become יָצָאנוּ *we went out*.

Here is a cluster of these forms for use in future communication. A few translations have been omitted. Can you recall their meanings?

	I…	we…			I…	we…	
	חָשַׁבְתִּי	חָשַׁבְנוּ	… thought		אָכַלְתִּי	אָכַלְנוּ	… ate
	יָדַעְתִּי	יָדַעְנוּ	… knew		אָמַרְתִּי	אָמַרְנוּ	… said
	רָאִיתִי	רָאִינוּ	…		בָּנִיתִי	בָּנִינוּ	… built
	יָרַדְתִּי	יָרַדְנוּ	… went down		הָלַכְתִּי	הָלַכְנוּ	… went
	כָּתַבְתִּי	כָּתַבְנוּ	… wrote		הִשְׁלַכְתִּי	הִשְׁלַכְנוּ	… threw
	לָקַחְתִּי	לָקַחְנוּ	…		זָכַרְתִּי	זָכַרְנוּ	… remembered

I...	we...	
רָאִיתִי	רָאִינוּ	... saw
רָדַפְתִּי	רָדַפְנוּ	... pursued
שָׁבַרְתִּי	שָׁבַרְנוּ	... broke
שָׁכַבְתִּי	שָׁכַבְנוּ	...
שָׁלַחְתִּי	שָׁלַחְנוּ	... sent
שָׁתִיתִי	שָׁתִינוּ	... drank

I...	we...	
מָצָאתִי	מָצָאנוּ	... found
נָפַלְתִּי	נָפַלְנוּ	... fell
נָשָׂאתִי	נָשָׂאנוּ	... lifted
עָבַרְתִּי	עָבַרְנוּ	... crossed over
פָּתַחְתִּי	פָּתַחְנוּ	...
קָנִיתִי	קָנִינוּ	... bought, acquired

As with "I" forms, the accent falls on the **second-to-last** syllable (penultima), rather than the last syllable (ultima). How do you suppose the verb כ.ר.ת *to cut off* will form its first person plural?[33] What about the verb נ.ת.נ?[34]

6.4.ג. Snapshot of sample verb: קָטַל conjugation *1cpl*

שָׁמַרְנוּ we guarded	שָׁמַרְתִּי I guarded
שְׁמַרְתֶּם you guarded *mpl*	שָׁמַרְתָּ you guarded *ms*
שְׁמַרְתֶּן you guarded *fpl*	שָׁמַרְתְּ you guarded *fs*
שָׁמְרוּ they guarded	שָׁמַר he guarded
	שָׁמְרָה she guarded

---

[33] If you proposed כָּרַתְנוּ *we [did] cut*, you are correct.

[34] If you deduced נָתַנּוּ *we gave* (note the dagesh forte in second נ), then you are right again.

6.4.ד. Explanation: "Why have you (*fpl*) descended against us?"

לָמָה עָלֵינוּ יְרַדְתֶּן:

INTERACTIVE SKILL: Describing to a group of women what they have done

Once you are accustomed to the masculine plural form of "you," the feminine plural for "you" will follow easily. Simply replace the final ם... of a word such as יְרַדְתֶּם *you descended* (*mpl*) with the letter ן..., resulting in יְרַדְתֶּן *you descended* (*fpl*). The accent will rest on this suffix: יְרַדְתֶּֽן. The pattern will appear clearly as you compare masculine and feminine forms in the table below. Can you recall the meaning of verbs that have not been translated?

you *mpl*...	you *fpl*...		you *mpl*...	you *fpl*...	
נְפַלְתֶּם	נְפַלְתֶּן	... fell	אֲמַרְתֶּם	אֲמַרְתֶּן	... said
נְתַתֶּם	נְתַתֶּן	... gave	יְדַעְתֶּם	יְדַעְתֶּן	... knew
נְשָׂאתֶם	נְשָׂאתֶן	...	זְכַרְתֶּם	זְכַרְתֶּן	...
פְּקַדְתֶּם	פְּקַדְתֶּן	... visited, inflicted	יְלַדְתֶּם	יְלַדְתֶּן	... gave birth
פְּתַחְתֶּם	פְּתַחְתֶּן	...	יְרֵאתֶם	יְרֵאתֶן	... were afraid
רְדַפְתֶּם	רְדַפְתֶּן	... pursued	יְרַדְתֶּם	יְרַדְתֶּן	... went down
שְׁבַרְתֶּם	שְׁבַרְתֶּן	...	כְּרַתֶּם	כְּרַתֶּן	... cut
שְׁכַבְתֶּם	שְׁכַבְתֶּן	... lay down	כְּתַבְתֶּם	כְּתַבְתֶּן	... wrote
שְׁלַחְתֶּם	שְׁלַחְתֶּן	... sent	לְקַחְתֶּם	לְקַחְתֶּן	... took
שְׁמַעְתֶּם	שְׁמַעְתֶּן	...	מְצָאתֶם	מְצָאתֶן	...

This ן/ם... shift holds true for other verbs as well, including I-guttural (such as א.כ.ל, ה.ל.כ, ח.ש.ב, and ע.ב.ד) and III-י/ה (such as ב.נ.י/ה, ק.נ.י/ה, ר.א.י/ה, and ש.ת.י/ה).

I-Guttural verbs, III-ה/י verbs

you mpl...	you fpl...		you mpl...	you fpl...	
עֲבַרְתֶּם	עֲבַרְתֶּן	...	אֲכַלְתֶּם	אֲכַלְתֶּן	...
קְנִיתֶם	קְנִיתֶן	... bought, acquired	בְּנִיתֶם	בְּנִיתֶן	... built
רְאִיתֶם	רְאִיתֶן	... saw	הֲלַכְתֶּם	הֲלַכְתֶּן	...
שְׁתִיתֶם	שְׁתִיתֶן	...	חֲשַׁבְתֶּם	חֲשַׁבְתֶּן	... thought

6.4.ה. Snapshot of sample verb: קָטַל conjugation *2fpl*

שָׁמַ֫רְנוּ we guarded	שָׁמַ֫רְתִּי I guarded
שְׁמַרְתֶּם you guarded *mpl*	שָׁמַ֫רְתָּ you guarded *ms*
שְׁמַרְתֶּן **you guarded *fpl***	שָׁמַרְתְּ you guarded *fs*
שָׁמְרוּ they guarded	שָׁמַר he guarded
	שָׁמְרָה she guarded

UNIT 6   מֶה עָשִׂיתָ אֶתְמוֹל:

6.4.1. Activity: "What did you (*mpl*, *fpl*) do yesterday?"

מֶה עֲשִׂיתֶם / עֲשִׂיתֶן אֶתְמוֹל:

INTERACTIVE SKILL: Interviewing groups of men or women concerning their recent activities[35]

Begin this activity by teaming up with one partner. After you have selected an action to pantomime (with **both** of you performing the action **together**), connect with another pair (the "observers") and let them interview you.

Let's suppose, for example, that the activity you and your partner claim to have performed yesterday was this: you claim to have *built a house out of stones*. The conversation would then begin as the "observers" interview you with an opening question: מֶה עֲשִׂיתֶם/ן אֶתְמוֹל:

You will respond by silently recreating the event, pretending together to place one stone upon another, until you have constructed a habitable home. The "observers" then will surmise from your drama: בְּנִיתֶם/ן בַּיִת בָּאֲבָנִים: *You (pl) built a house out of stones*. Refer to §6.3.1. to refresh your memory concerning *you mpl* forms.

Indicate whether their "observation" was correct. Please respond with a full sentence (not simply שֶׁקֶר / אֱמֶת):: בָּנִינוּ בַּיִת בָּאֲבָנִים... אֱמֶת

Then reverse roles, interviewing the pair who served as observers, asking concerning an activity that they claim to have performed yesterday.

Note that if the pair of classmates whom you are addressing is **comprised only of females**, you will want to address them with a feminine form (ן...).

Model

Inquiry (by observers)	מֶה עֲשִׂיתֶם / עֲשִׂיתֶן:	What did you (*mpl*, *fpl*) do?
Response		(*Respond by pantomiming an activity, such as pretending to build a stone house.*)

---

[35] In the case of a mixed group, use masculine form.

You (*mpl / fpl*) built a house of stones.	בְּנִיתֶם / בְּנִיתֶן בַּיִת בַּאֲבָנִים:	Assertion (by observers)
(*The above assertion represents what an observer-team may surmise, after watching the action recreated by you and your actor-partner.*)		
True (*lit.*, truth). We built a house of stones.	אֱמֶת: בָּנִינוּ בַּיִת בַּאֲבָנִים:	Verification (by actors)
False (*lit.*, falsehood). We did not build a house of stones.	שֶׁקֶר: לֹא בָנִינוּ בַּיִת בַּאֲבָנִים:	Denial (by actors)

6.4.ז. Activity: "What did you (*mpl, fpl*) do yesterday?"

מָה עֲשִׂיתֶם / עֲשִׂיתֶן אֶתְמוֹל:

INTERACTIVE SKILL: Interviewing groups of men or women concerning how they have responded in good times or bad[36]

Have you ever wondered how others might respond during times of prosperity (or alternatively, during times of hardship)? You will be able to learn just that, through this conversation.

Join with a partner and determine what you would like to learn about another pair of classmates. You may inquire how they would respond either in good times (use דָּבָר א֎ *Issue / question #*א below) or their response in difficult times (use דָּבָר ב *Issue / question #*ב below).[37] Then seek out another pair of classmates and pose your question to them. Before they respond, they will ask you one of these two questions in order to start you and your partner thinking of your response.

Develop a מַעֲנֶה *answer m* that you and your partner can agree upon, and then express that מַעֲנֶה to your inquirers.

---

[36] In the case of a mixed group, use masculine form.

[37] The small diamond above the א in א֎ דָּבָר is a Masoretic mark indicating that the consonant stands for something else, such as a numeral.

UNIT 6 — מֶה עָשִׂיתָ אֶתְמוֹל׃

Note: To refer to "prosperity" and "misery," use the abstract terms הַטּוֹב and הָרָעָה, respectively. Refer to §6.3.1. to refresh your memory concerning *you mpl* forms. For *you fpl* forms, see §6.4.1.

Model

דָּבָר א	מֶה עֲשִׂיתֶם / עֲשִׂיתֶן בְּמָצְאֲכֶם/ן[38] אֶת־הַטּוֹב׃	What have you (*mpl, fpl*) done when prosperity has befallen you (*lit.*, when you found prosperity)?
מַעֲנֶה א	בְּמָצְאֵנוּ אֶת־הַטּוֹב כֶּסֶף נָתַנּוּ לְרֵעֵינוּ׃	When prosperity has befallen us (*lit.*, when we found prosperity), we gave silver to our friends.
דָּבָר ב	מֶה עֲשִׂיתֶם / עֲשִׂיתֶן בְּמָצְאֲכֶם/ן אֶת־הָרָעָה׃	What have you (*mpl, fpl*) done when misery has befallen you (*lit.*, when you found misery)?
מַעֲנֶה ב	בְּמָצְאֵנוּ אֶת־הָרָעָה עִם־מִשְׁפְּחוֹתֵינוּ[39] בָּכִינוּ׃	When misery has befallen us (*lit.*, when we found misery), we wept with our families.

---

[38] Notice the qameṣ-ḥaṭuf in בְּמָצְאֲכֶם *inf c* (pronounced *o*, as also in בְּמָצְאֵנוּ of the next sentence).

[39] מִשְׁפָּחָה *family f.*

MODULE 6.5 Adding story layers in reporting, and sapiential expressions

(No new Jonah Episode is introduced in this module.)

6.5.א. Explanation: Additional קָטַל meanings

INTERACTIVE SKILL: Adding depth to your reports by relating events that occurred (or will have occurred) prior to the scenario being described

With expressions such as שָׁבוּ הָרוּחוֹת אֶל־הַשָּׁמַיִם, we have seen that the קָטַל conjugation is useful when reporting events belong to a past timeframe. However, just as the יִקְטֹל can do much more than describe future events, so also the קָטַל can do more than describe past events in a simple fashion.

Continuing with the **past** timeframe, קָטַל can portray both **recent past** (simple past) as well as **remote past** (pluperfect). Turning to the **present** timeframe, קָטַל can present a **routine principle** (gnomic or proverbial perfect).

In the **future** timeframe, קָטַל can signify a forthcoming event marked with high **certitude** (prophetic perfect), and can also help distinguish preliminary future events from those events that are in the more remote future. Examples of each of these may be found below.

Part 1: Past tense meanings

The first example below (Gen. 3:10a) shows what a simple past looks like. In this instance a simple past is appropriate. In the remaining examples, however, merely to render with a simple past would not capture the sense of the original context. Simple past renditions in these cases would have read: "she heard," "the LORD visited," "God heard," "Who heard," and "If we did not delay," respectively.

UNIT 6 — מֶה עָשִׂיתָ אֶתְמוֹל׃

Description	Translation	Hebrew
Simple past (preterite)	...**I heard** the sound of you in the garden (Gen. 3:10a).	...אֶת־קֹלְךָ שָׁמַעְתִּי בַגָּן[40]
Remote past (pluperfect, locates an event in the more distant past, relative to other actions in the same narrative)	So she arose... from the fields of Moab for **she had heard**... that the LORD **had visited** his people... (Ruth 1:6).	וַתָּקָם הִיא... מִשְּׂדֵי מוֹאָב כִּי שָׁמְעָה... כִּי־פָקַד יְהוָה אֶת־עַמּוֹ...
Definite past (present perfect)	...Do not be afraid, for God **has heard** the lad's voice... (Gen. 32:17b).	...אַל־תִּירְאִי כִּי־שָׁמַע אֱלֹהִים אֶל־קוֹל הַנַּעַר...
Indefinite past	Who **has ever heard** such a thing? (Isa. 66:8a).	...מִי־שָׁמַע כָּזֹאת
Irreal (contrary-to-fact) condition, past[42]	If we **had not delayed**, by now we would have already gone back twice (Gen. 43:10).	כִּי לוּלֵא[41] הִתְמַהְמָהְנוּ כִּי־עַתָּה שַׁבְנוּ זֶה פַעֲמָיִם׃

Part 2: Present tense meanings

Here are some קָטַל examples where a present meaning is more fitting than a past indicative.

Description	Translation	Hebrew
Gnomic or proverbial present	The appetite of a laborer **labors** for him, for his mouth **keeps up** the pressure (Prov. 16:26).	נֶפֶשׁ עָמֵל עָמְלָה לּוֹ כִּי־אָכַף עָלָיו פִּיהוּ׃
Ingressive present (beginning or becoming)	Will I actually give birth though **I have grown old**? (Gen. 18:13).	...הַאַף אֻמְנָם אֵלֵד וַאֲנִי זָקַנְתִּי׃

---

[40] Masoretic cantillation marks have been retained in these examples. You may ignore them for the present.

[41] The term [לוּ]לֵא is rendered, *If...not*....

[42] Irreal (contrary-to-fact) conditional expressions resemble the time sequence of a pluperfect, since they depict an event in the remote past (the protasis) and another event in the nearer past (the apodosis). Since the protasis did not materialize (it was "irreal," or "contrary-to-fact"), the apodosis did not transpire either. In irreal conditional statements of a past nature, both protasis and apodosis employ קָטַל forms. The term [לוּ]לֵא *if not* often introduces an irreal condition (cf. *IBHS* §38e).

In the above examples the flavor of the קָטַל is retained not by tense, but by aspect. In the saying from Proverbs 16, use of the קָטַל conveys that the principle is marked by certitude, by definiteness. To capture the sense of certitude in a proverbial saying it is customary in English to employ the present tense (as in "labors" and "keeps up").

In the above example from Genesis 18 we encounter a stative verb in the קָטַל. Stative verbs (verbs dealing with a state of being rather than an action) in the קָטַל routinely have a present tense meaning.[43] It is not uncommon for statives in the קָטַל to also carry a sense of beginning or becoming (sometimes called "ingressive," as with זָקַנְתִּי *I have grown old*).

Part 3: Future tense meanings

In the following קָטַל examples, notice that a future timeframe is called for.

Description	Translation	Hebrew
Future perfect (describes a future event that will have transpired, by the time that a more remotely future event has taken place)	And you will eat and you will be satisfied and you will bless the LORD your God concerning the good land that **he will have given** to you (Deut. 8:10b).	וְאָכַלְתָּ וְשָׂבָעְתָּ וּבֵרַכְתָּ אֶת־יְהוָה אֱלֹהֶיךָ עַל־הָאָרֶץ הַטֹּבָה אֲשֶׁר נָתַן־לָךְ:
Prophetic perfect (perfective of confidence)	...a star **will make its way** out of Jacob... (Num. 24:17).	...דָּרַךְ כּוֹכָב מִיַּעֲקֹב...

Part 4: Suggestions for navigating the various קָטַל meanings

In many cases a given קָטַל verb will carry a simple past meaning. The past tense is a good starting point for translating קָטַל.

At the same time, take note of the setting in which this קָטַל event takes place. Is it **prior** to another, more salient past-event? If so, then in English the first event should be made more remote (e.g., *she had heard* from the example in Ruth 1:6 given above).

Or, is the קָטַל event **proverbial** in nature? If so, cast it as present tense in English (e.g., *The appetite of a laborer labors for him*, from Prov. 16:26, above).

---

[43] By way of reminder, the following are some of the more common concepts represented by stative verbs in Hebrew: *to be old, to sleep, to be heavy, to love, to hate, to be high, to be great.*

Alternatively, does the קָטַל event issue from a **prophetic oracle**, portraying a future that the prophet anticipates with a high degree of certitude? If so, then the English will call for the future tense.

This brief recap does not include all the options illustrated above. For still more options please consult grammar resources.[44]

To sum up, it will be important to keep in mind that the קָטַל, like the יִקְטֹל, does not serve primarily to signal tense, but to signal **aspect**. The aspectual element that the קָטַל brings to our attention is this:

- A קָטַל verb-event tends to signal a greater measure of **definiteness** or **certitude** than would be connoted, had the communicator employed a יִקְטֹל form.
- A יִקְטֹל, in contrast, tends to signal that an event is either **currently in progress** or is **potential** in nature.[45]

6.5.ב. קָטַל conjugation of geminate verbs

As noted toward the close of the previous unit (§5.4.ד.), some verbs duplicate their final שרש consonant, as in ס.ב.ב *to surround*, ר.ע.ע *to be evil*, and ח.נ.נ *to show favor*. These verbs are known as geminates. Some geminate forms have unique spelling patterns. Please see the appendix entry corresponding to this segment for spelling patterns of geminate verbs in the קָטַל conjugation.

---

[44] Much of the above material has been adapted from *IBHS*, ch. 30. Additional principles may be found there, as well as in Joüon §112 and in van der Merwe §19.2.

[45] You may wish to review to the יִקְטֹל component of this explanation in §5.4.א.

6.5.ג. קָטַל conjugation of stative verbs

The יִקְטֹל spelling for a group of verbs known as "stative" was introduced in §5.4.ה. For the קָטַל spelling of stative verbs such as כָּבֵד *he is heavy* or קָטֹן *he is small*, please refer to the appendix entry corresponding to this segment.

6.5.ד. Snapshot of sample verb: קָטַל conjugation

שָׁמַ֫רְנוּ we guarded	שָׁמַ֫רְתִּי I guarded
שְׁמַרְתֶּם you guarded *mpl*	שָׁמַ֫רְתָּ you guarded *ms*
שְׁמַרְתֶּן you guarded *fpl*	שָׁמַרְתְּ you guarded *fs*
שָׁמְרוּ they guarded	שָׁמַר he guarded
	שָֽׁמְרָה she guarded

UNIT 6   מֶה עָשִׂיתָ אֶתְמוֹל:

You (*ms*) can read the Bible.   אַתָּה תִּקְרָא אֶת־הַתַּנַ״ךְ:

Masoretic accents

The Masoretes developed a sophisticated system of accents appearing above and below the consonants to help group phrases within each Bible verse. These marks also determine voice modulation when chanting the Hebrew Bible (called cantillation marks or trope). By paying attention to a few of the higher-order accents you can discover how earlier readers distinguished phrases.

To help you develop this skill, some of the verses below include a few accents that are either more influential or more common (such as the atnaḥ [◌] in אָמַר, Gen. 21:1, the first Selected reading). Several of the following accents have been retained in selected readings below. There are two types of accents: disjunctive and conjunctive.[46]

- The **disjunctive accents** (accents that signal a **separation** following the word in which they appear) are these, in descending order of disjunctive strength (i.e., the first accent listed here makes the **most** decisive break following the word in which it appears): *silluq* [◌] with *sof pasuq* [:], *atnaḥ* [◌], *segolta* [◌], *zaqef parvum* [◌], *revia* [◌], *tifḥa* [◌], and *tevir* [◌].
- The **conjunctive accents** (accents that signal a **union** with the ensuing word) are these, in descending order of conjunctive strength: *munaḥ* [◌], *mereka* [◌] and *darga* [◌]. The accents shown here are neither exhaustive nor consecutive, only sequential.

---

[46] The cantillation marks presented here apply to all books of the Hebrew Bible except Job, Psalms, and Proverbs. Many marks applying to these three books are the same as those used for the larger group. At the back of the textbook you will find a listing of both sets of cantillation marks.

When a given accent first appears in the various selections below, a brief comment will explain that accent. Please refer to the supplemental section entitled "Masoretic Accents" for a fuller listing of accents and an explanation of how they operate (volume II, pp. 410–15).

Selected readings

A number of the verses included with this unit contain a form that appears to involve a conjunction followed by a verb in the יִקְטֹל conjugation: וַ + יֹאמַר (with a two additional changes). Known as a וַיִּקְטֹל verb form (or "imperfect vav-consecutive"), it functions to convey simple action in past time ("preterit"), usually in a narrative sequence (i.e., story telling). This special component of Biblical Hebrew will be explained more thoroughly in the next unit.

6.1.א.   A childless woman waited long for this visit.

1.   (Gen. 21:1) : וַיהוה פָּקַד אֶת־שָׂרָה כַּאֲשֶׁר אָמָר ᵃ וַיַּעַשׂ ᵇ יהוה לְשָׂרָה כַּאֲשֶׁר דִּבֵּר ᶜ

   כַּאֲשֶׁר ᵃ just as   וַיַּעַשׂ ᵇ [ע.שׂ.י/ה] and he did   דִּבֵּר ᶜ [ד.ב.ר] he said

The atnaḥ [֑] in אָמָר marks a major break in thought. The silluq [֣] in דִּבֵּר accompanies the verse-end sof pasuq [׃].

6.1.א.   Aged Jacob already had lost one son, so…. (Notice attention drawn to the object of שָׁלַח, since that object has been placed before the verb.)

2.   וְאֶת־בִּנְיָמִין אֲחִי ᵃ יוֹסֵף לֹא־שָׁלַח יַעֲקֹב אֶת־אֶחָיו ᵇ כִּי אָמַר פֶּן־יִקְרָאֶנּוּ ᶜ אָסוֹן ᵈ :

   (Gen. 42:4)

   אֲחִי ᵃ brother m, constr   אֶת־ ᵇ with   ק.ר.א ᶜ to befall, to happen to (3ms pronominal sfx)

   אָסוֹן ᵈ harm m

The zaqef parvum [֔] in יוֹסֵף and אָמַר marks a weaker break than the atnaḥ [֑] in אֶחָיו.

UNIT 6 — מֶה עָשִׂיתָ אֶתְמוֹל׃

6.1.א.

At a critical point, Samuel asked Saul a question.

3. וַיֹּאמֶרᵃ שְׁמוּאֵל הַחֵפֶץ לַיהוה בְּעֹלוֹתᵇ,ᶜ וּזְבָחִים כִּשְׁמֹעַ בְּקוֹל יהוה הִנֵּה שְׁמֹעַ מִזֶּבַח טוֹב לְהַקְשִׁיבᵈ מֵחֵלֶב אֵילִיםᵉ׃ (1 Sam. 15:22)

ᵃ וַיֹּאמֶר [א.מ.ר] and he said   ᵇ הַחֵפֶץ לַיהוה בְּ… Is the LORD pleased with…?
ᶜ עֹלָה whole burnt offering *t*   ᵈ הַקְשִׁיב [ק.ש.ב] to pay attention *hifil inf c*
ᵉ חֵלֶב אֵילִים fat of rams *m*

The *revia* [◌̇] in שְׁמוּאֵל marks a weaker break than the *zaqef parvum* [◌̈] in וּזְבָחִים and טוֹב.

6.1.א.

Would you ever employ a rhetorical question in an attempt to snap an adversary out of unwarranted anger? Weary of running from Saul, David raised these questions.

4. אַחֲרֵי מִי יָצָא מֶלֶךְ יִשְׂרָאֵל אַחֲרֵי מִי אַתָּה רֹדֵף אַחֲרֵי כֶּלֶבᵃ מֵת אַחֲרֵי פַּרְעֹשᵇ אֶחָדᶜ׃ (1 Sam. 24:15)

ᵃ כֶּלֶב dog *m*   ᵇ פַּרְעֹשׁ flea *m*   ᶜ אֶחָד a single

6.1.א.

Late in Saul's reign he entered a dark season.

5. וַיִּשְׁאַלᵃ שָׁאוּל בַּיהוָה וְלֹא עָנָהוּ יהוה גַּם בַּחֲלֹמוֹתᵇ גַּם בָּאוּרִיםᶜ גַּם בַּנְּבִיאִם׃ (1 Sam. 28:6)

ᵃ וַיִּשְׁאַל [ש.א.ל] and he asked, inquired⁴⁷   ᵇ חֲלוֹם dream *m*
ᶜ אוּרִים Urim (*ceremonial stones for oracular inquiry*) *nifal pt*

The *darga* [◌̣] in גַּם moderately joins it to the next word, while the *tevir* [◌̣] in בַּחֲלֹמוֹת weakly separates it from the next (*tevir* is weaker than *revia* [◌̇]). The *mereka* [◌̣] in גַּם joins to the next word with greater force than does a *darga* [◌̣]. The *tifḥa* [◌̣] in בָּאוּרִים separates from the next (with a disjunctive force one grade weaker than *revia* [◌̇]).

---

⁴⁷ When ש.א.ל is followed by the preposition בְּ plus a reference to God, it generally means to request a divine oracle.

6.1.א.	Despite a recent supernatural display, the loyal prophet now hid in a cave to elude Queen Jezebel. There God asked him this question.

6. וְהִנֵּה דְבַר־יהוה אֵלָיו וַיֹּאמֶר^a לוֹ מַה־לְּךָ פֹה אֵלִיָּהוּ^{b}: (1 Kings 19:9)

   וַיֹּאמֶר [א.מ.ר]^a and he said אֵלִיָּהוּ^{b} (a man's name)

6.1.ג.	After murdering his brother, this person tried to cloak his guilt with ignorance.

7. וַיֹּאמֶר^a יהוה אֶל־קַיִן^b אֵי^c הֶבֶל^d אָחִיךָ וַיֹּאמֶר לֹא יָדַעְתִּי הֲשֹׁמֵר אָחִי אָנֹכִי: (Gen. 4:9)

  וַיֹּאמֶר [א.מ.ר]^a and he said קַיִן^b (name of one of Adam's sons) אֵי אַיֵּה^c
  הֶבֶל^d (name of Adam's second son)

6.1.ד.	Samuel filled a unique role for the entire nation of Israel on this particular day.

8. וּשְׁמוּאֵל רָאָה אֶת־שָׁאוּל וַיהוה עָנָהוּ הִנֵּה הָאִישׁ אֲשֶׁר אָמַרְתִּי אֵלֶיךָ זֶה יַעְצֹר^a בְּעַמִּי: (1 Sam. 9:17)

  ע.צ.ר בְּ^{a} ... to keep in check (*usual meaning*), to rule (*meaning in this context*)

6.2.ב.	When asked whether he had eaten the prohibited fruit, Adam gave this reply.

(The word נָתַתָּה ends in a "paragogic [lengthening] ה." Translate as if spelled נָתַתָּ, here in the sense of "to place" or "to set." Read הוא as היא [a Masoretic "perpetual *qere* [קְרֵי]," also called "*qere perpetuum*"].)

9. וַיֹּאמֶר^a הָאָדָם הָאִשָּׁה אֲשֶׁר נָתַתָּה עִמָּדִי^b הִוא נָתְנָה־לִּי מִן־הָעֵץ וָאֹכֵל^c: (Gen. 3:12)

  וַיֹּאמֶר [א.מ.ר]^a and he said עִמָּדִי^b beside *or* accompanying me וָאֹכֵל [א.כ.ל]^c and I ate

UNIT 6 מָה עָשִׂיתָ אֶתְמוֹל: 441

6.2.ב. Abram and his wife were experiencing a painful disappointment.

10. וְשָׂרַיᵃ אֵשֶׁת אַבְרָם לֹא יָלְדָה לוֹ וְלָהּ שִׁפְחָהᵇ מִצְרִיתᶜ וּשְׁמָהּ הָגָר: (Gen. 16:1)

ᵃ שָׂרַי (*woman's name*) ᵇ שִׁפְחָה maid *f* ᶜ מִצְרִית Egyptian person *f*

6.2.ב. As the plagues mounted up, counselors around the Egyptian ruler grew incredulous. (What word after וְיַעַבְדוּ has a similar sound? What may the author have implied by this assonance? [Admittedly, it is unlikely that these words were linked assonantly in Egyptian.] The term וְיַעַבְדוּ has the connotation "so may they [serve or worship]" since it is a וְיִקְטֹל form, known as an indirect jussive.⁴⁸)

11. וַיֹּאמְרוּᵃ עַבְדֵי פַרְעֹה אֵלָיו עַד־מָתַיᵇ יִהְיֶה זֶה לָנוּ לְמוֹקֵשׁᶜ שַׁלַּחᵈ אֶת־הָאֲנָשִׁים וְיַעַבְדוּᵉ אֶת־יהוה אֱלֹהֵיהֶם הֲטֶרֶםᶠ תֵּדַע כִּי אָבְדָה מִצְרָיִם: (Exod. 10:7)

ᵃ וַיֹּאמְרוּ and they said ᵇ עַד־מָתַי How long? ᶜ מוֹקֵשׁ snare *m*
ᵈ שַׁלַּח Let go free! *piel imv ms* ᵉ וְיַעַבְדוּ so may they serve *or* worship
ᶠ הֲטֶרֶם Do [you] not yet...?

6.2.ה. As if overcome by curiosity, God decided to pay a visit to the construction site.

12. וַיֵּרֶדᵃ יהוה לִרְאֹת אֶת־הָעִיר וְאֶת־הַמִּגְדָּלᵇ אֲשֶׁר בָּנוּ בְּנֵי הָאָדָם: (Gen. 11:5)

ᵃ וַיֵּרֶד [י.ר.ד] and he came down ᵇ מִגְדָּל tower *m*

6.2.ה. As Moses contemplated the assignment God was giving to him, he asked God an important question—not unlike a question Jacob asked of his supernatural wrestler. But unlike Jacob, Moses was granted an answer.

---

⁴⁸ Cf. §9.4.א., n.

13. וַיֹּאמֶר מֹשֶׁה אֶל־הָאֱלֹהִים הִנֵּה אָנֹכִי בָא אֶל־בְּנֵי יִשְׂרָאֵל וְאָמַרְתִּי^a לָהֶם אֱלֹהֵי אֲבוֹתֵיכֶם שְׁלָחַנִי^b אֲלֵיכֶם וְאָמְרוּ^c־לִי מַה־שְּׁמוֹ מָה אֹמַר אֲלֵהֶם:

14. וַיֹּאמֶר אֱלֹהִים אֶל־מֹשֶׁה אֶהְיֶה אֲשֶׁר אֶהְיֶה וַיֹּאמֶר כֹּה תֹאמַר לִבְנֵי יִשְׂרָאֵל אֶהְיֶה שְׁלָחַנִי אֲלֵיכֶם: (Exod. 3:13-14)

וְאָמַרְתִּי^a	and I will say⁴⁹	[א.מ.ר]
שְׁלָחַנִי^b	[ש.ל.ח] (1cs obj.)	
וְאָמְרוּ^c	and they will say	[א.מ.ר]

6.2.ה. The community of Bethlehem was so impressed by the character of Ruth that—recalling two matriarchs—they offered this blessing to Boaz at the news of his upcoming wedding.

14. וַיֹּאמְרוּ^a כָּל־הָעָם אֲשֶׁר־בַּשַּׁעַר^b וְהַזְּקֵנִים^c עֵדִים^d יִתֵּן^e יהוה אֶת־הָאִשָּׁה הַבָּאָה^f אֶל־בֵּיתֶךָ כְּרָחֵל וּכְלֵאָה אֲשֶׁר בָּנוּ שְׁתֵּיהֶם^g אֶת־בֵּית יִשְׂרָאֵל:... (Ruth 4:11)

וַיֹּאמְרוּ^a	and they said	[א.מ.ר]	שַׁעַר^b	[city] gate *m*	זְקֵנִים^c *mpl* elders
עֵדִים^d	[We are] witnesses	יִתֵּן^e [נ.ת.ן]	May he grant *jussive*⁵⁰	בָּאָה^f [ב.ו.א] *pt fs*
שְׁתֵּיהֶם^g	the two of them			

6.2.ה. What can we learn about this poet's worldview, based on how he describes the storm? (עָבְרוּ is a pausal form.)

15. ...כָּל־מִשְׁבָּרֶיךָ וְגַלֶּיךָ^a עָלַי עָבָרוּ: (Ps. 42:8b [ET v. 7])

גַּל^a	wave *m*

6.3.א. Before departing on a journey to find a bride for Isaac, the servant tasked with this responsibility posed a question to his master, Abraham.

---

⁴⁹ See §7.3.ז. for an explanation "וְקָטַל" forms (וְאָמַרְתִּי and וְאָמְרוּ).

⁵⁰ Jussive expresses a wish or volition (to be explained in §§9.4.א and ב).

16. וַיֹּאמֶר֩ אֵלָ֨יו הָעֶ֜בֶד אוּלַ֗י לֹא־תֹאבֶ֤ה הָֽאִשָּׁה֙ לָלֶ֣כֶת אַחֲרַ֔י אֶל־הָאָ֖רֶץ הַזֹּ֑את הֶֽהָשֵׁ֤ב אָשִׁיב֙ אֶת־בִּנְךָ֔ אֶל־הָאָ֖רֶץ אֲשֶׁר־יָצָ֥אתָ מִשָּֽׁם׃ (Gen. 24:5)

^a וַיֹּאמֶר [א.מ.ר] and he said

^b הֶהָשֵׁב אָשִׁיב must I bring back [*lit.*, shall I surely bring back]...?   ^c מִשָּׁם from there

---

6.3.ג. What woman would not treasure a commendation such as this? (We might expect the first two words to appear in reversed order. Can you sense any difference achieved by the poetic expression as it stands?)

17. רַבּ֥וֹת בָּנ֖וֹת עָ֣שׂוּ⁵¹ חָ֑יִל וְ֝אַ֗תְּ עָלִ֥ית עַל־כֻּלָּֽנָה^a׃ (Prov. 31:29)

^a כֻּלָּנָה all (*with 3fpl sfx*)

6.3.ד. Have you ever served as a go-between, relaying messages between your friends and a highly influential person? Moses did.

18. אָנֹכִ֞י עֹמֵ֣ד בֵּין־יְהוָ֣ה וּבֵֽינֵיכֶ֗ם בָּעֵ֤ת^a הַהִוא^b לְהַגִּ֥יד^c לָכֶ֖ם אֶת־דְּבַ֣ר יְהוָ֑ה כִּ֤י יְרֵאתֶם֙ מִפְּנֵ֣י^d הָאֵ֔שׁ^e וְלֹֽא־עֲלִיתֶ֥ם בָּהָ֖ר... (Deut. 5:5)

^a עֵת time *f*   ^b הִוא (*3fs personal pronoun, signified by ḥireq*)⁵²

^c לְהַגִּיד to announce *hifil inf c, prep*   ^d מִפְּנֵי before   ^e אֵשׁ fire *f*

6.4.א. Rebekah's long journey from her home in Mesopotamia to Canaan passed without recorded comment. Then something on the horizon caught her attention....

---

⁵¹ The penultimate accent in חָ֑יִל produces a recessive accent in עָ֣שׂוּ (contrast the customary עָשׂ֑וּ). Called *nāsôg ʾāḥôr*, this shift prevents accented syllables from occurring adjacent to each other.

⁵² See footnote for הוא in selection #9, above.

19. וַתֹּאמֶר^a אֶל־הָעֶבֶד מִי־הָאִישׁ הַלָּזֶה^b הַהֹלֵךְ בַּשָּׂדֶה^c לִקְרָאתֵנוּ^d וַיֹּאמֶר^e הָעֶבֶד הוּא
אֲדֹנִי^f וַתִּקַּח^g הַצָּעִיף^h וַתִּתְכָּסⁱ: (Gen. 24:65)

^aוַתֹּאמֶר [א.מ.ר.] and she said   ^bהָאִישׁ הַלָּזֶה that man over yonder   ^cשָׂדֶה field *m*

^dלִקְרָאתֵנוּ [ק.ר.א] to meet us *inf c, prep (1cpl sfx)*   ^eוַיֹּאמֶר [א.מ.ר.] and he said

^fאָדוֹן lord, master *m*   ^gוַתִּקַּח [ל.ק.ח] and she took   ^hצָעִיף veil *f*

ⁱוַתִּתְכָּס [כ.ס.י/ה] and covered herself *hitpael*

6.4.ב. Past hardships endured during slavery under Pharaoh appear to have been forgotten when food supplies were running low in the wilderness. (Recall that the קטל of stative verbs such as ז.כ.ר should be translated in the present tense; cf. §6.5.א.)

20. זָכַרְנוּ אֶת־הַדָּגָה^a אֲשֶׁר־נֹאכַל בְּמִצְרַיִם^b חִנָּם^c:... (Num. 11:5)

^aדָּגָה fish (*collective*) *f*   ^bמִצְרַיִם Egypt *f*   ^cחִנָּם freely

6.4.ב. Can you discern the Philistines' motive for invading Judah on this occasion?

21. וַיֹּאמְרוּ^a אִישׁ^b יְהוּדָה לָמָה^c עֲלִיתֶם עָלֵינוּ וַיֹּאמְרוּ לֶאֱסוֹר^d אֶת־שִׁמְשׁוֹן^e עָלִינוּ
לַעֲשׂוֹת לוֹ כַּאֲשֶׁר^f עָשָׂה לָנוּ: (Judg. 15:10)

^aוַיֹּאמְרוּ [א.מ.ר.] and they said   ^bאִישׁ (*singular, yet treat as group*)   ^cלָמָה why

^dלֶאֱסוֹר [א.ס.ר.] to bind *inf c, prep*   ^eשִׁמְשׁוֹן (*man's name*)   ^fכַּאֲשֶׁר just as

6.4.ג. Dismayed by the treatment received from his father-in-law, Jacob conferred with his wives, rehearsing how his relationship with their father had unraveled. (Again, the קטל of stative verbs such as י.ד.ע should be translated as present tense; cf. §6.5.א.)

22. וְאַתֵּנָה יְדַעְתֶּן כִּי בְּכָל־כֹּחִי^a עָבַדְתִּי אֶת־אֲבִיכֶן: (Gen. 31:6)

^aכֹּחַ strength *m*

UNIT 6 מֶה עָשִׂיתָ אֶתְמוֹל: 445

6.5.א. Notice how the imagery of light contrasts darkness in this oracle of hope.

23. 1. קוּמִי אוֹרִי^a כִּי בָא אוֹרֵךְ^{b} וּכְבוֹד^c יהוה עָלַיִךְ זָרָח^d:

2. כִּי־הִנֵּה הַחֹשֶׁךְ יְכַסֶּה^e־אֶרֶץ וַעֲרָפֶל^f לְאֻמִּים^g

וְעָלַיִךְ יִזְרַח יהוה וּכְבוֹדוֹ עָלַיִךְ יֵרָאֶה^h: (Isa. 60:1-2)

[א.ו.ר]^a to dawn, become bright *imv fs*   אוֹר^b light, brightness *m and f*
כָּבוֹד^c glory, honor *m*   [ז.ר.ח]^d to shine, go forth   [כ.ס.י/ה]^e to cover, conceal *piel*
עֲרָפֶל^f darkness, gloom, cloud *m*   לְאֻמִּים^g peoples *m*
יֵרָאֶה^h [ר.א.ה/י] it will be seen, revealed *nifal*

עֲקֵדַת יִצְחָק   A connected reading: The binding of Isaac (Gen. 22:9-10)

9. וַיָּבֹאוּ^{a} אֶל־הַמָּקוֹם אֲשֶׁר אָמַר־לוֹ הָאֱלֹהִים

וַיִּבֶן^b שָׁם אַבְרָהָם אֶת־הַמִּזְבֵּחַ^{c}

וַיַּעֲרֹךְ^{d} אֶת־הָעֵצִים

וַיַּעֲקֹד^e אֶת־יִצְחָק בְּנוֹ

וַיָּשֶׂם^f אֹתוֹ עַל־הַמִּזְבֵּחַ מִמַּעַל^g לָעֵצִים:

10. וַיִּשְׁלַח^h אַבְרָהָם אֶת־יָדוֹ

וַיִּקַּח^i אֶת־הַמַּאֲכֶלֶת^j לִשְׁחֹט^k אֶת־בְּנוֹ:

וַיָּבֹאוּ^{a} then they came   וַיִּבֶן^b and he built   מִזְבֵּחַ^{c} altar *m*   וַיַּעֲרֹךְ^{d} and he arranged
וַיַּעֲקֹד^e and he bound *or* trussed   וַיָּשֶׂם^f and he placed   מִמַּעַל^g on top of   וַיִּשְׁלַח^h and he reached out
וַיִּקַּח^i and he took   מַאֲכֶלֶת^j knife *f*   ש.ח.ט^k to slaughter (*for sacrifice*)

Reference Materials

Volume I Reference Materials

Appendix for units 0–6 449

Pronominal (object) suffixes 481

    With nouns 482   With verbs 495

    With prepositions and particles 494

Verbs (Qal בִּנְיָן) 501

Glossaries 517

    Hebrew-English 518   English-Hebrew 541

Maps 563

    Ancient Near East 564   Israel 565

Volume II Reference Materials

Appendix for units 7–11 377

Syntax summary 395

Masoretic accents 410

Indices 417

    Culture 418   Illustration 427

    Grammar 420   Scripture reference 429

Resources 433

Pronominal (object) suffixes 437

- Nouns with suffixes 438
- Prepositions and particles with suffixes 450
- Verbs with suffixes 451

Verbs 457

- Qal בִּנְיָן 458
- Nifal בִּנְיָן 474
- Hifil בִּנְיָן 481
- Hofal בִּנְיָן 487
- Piel בִּנְיָן 491
- Pual בִּנְיָן 498
- Hitpael בִּנְיָן 502

Glossaries 507

- Hebrew-English 508
- English-Hebrew 531

Maps 553

- Ancient Near East 554
- Israel 555

APPENDIX | דְּבָרִים נוֹסָפִים[a]

For units 0-6 | [a] נוֹסָפִים added, *nifal* [י.ס.פ.]

To find an appendix entry, locate the heading in the appendix that matches the heading of the corresponding segment. When a single segment heading spans more than one appendix entry, separate subheadings will designate secondary entries (cf. multiple subheadings under §2.4.א., below).

0.2.ד. Do you (*ms*) know how to read? (Vowel letters) הֲיָדַעְתָּ לִקְרֹא?

Matres lectionis. The letter ה likely was adopted as a *mater lectionis* (vowel letter) since it often was associated with an *ah* sound (as in the very common word הַ...⊙, meaning "the"). As a result, scribes began adding ה to the end of a word as a vowel letter in places where they wanted readers to remember to pronounce a long *ah* sound. Occasionally other sounds are also associated with ה as a *mater lectionis*.

Similarly scribes began to insert a י where they wanted to remind readers to pronounce a long *ee* or *ei* sound. The vowel letter ו was inserted to signal an *ou* or *oh* sound.

Since vowel letters accounted only for long vowels, this system of notation left many sounds unrepresented. In the second stage of development (from 500-700 CE), various groups of Masoretic scribes designed no fewer than three different systems to represent vowels: Tiberian, Babylonian, and Palestinian.[1] Over time, the Tiberian system gained widest acceptance. Perhaps its finest example is the Aleppo codex, vocalized by Aaron Ben Asher in approximately 925 CE. Thus you will be learning Tiberian vocalization in this course, and Hebrew Bible editions such as we will study (equipped with vowels) are said to present the "Masoretic Text."

---

[1] See Emmanuel Tov, Textual *Criticism of the Hebrew Bible* (3d ed.; Minneapolis: Fortress Press, 2012), 39–47, Angel Sáenz-Badillos, *A History of the Hebrew Language* (trans. John Elwolde; Cambridge: Cambridge University Press: 1993), 105–11, and Joshua Blau, *A Grammar of Biblical Hebrew* (2d ed.; Wiesbaden: Otto Harrassowitz, 1993), §3.1.

With the addition of these vowel points, a vowel letter ה became הָ as in אֲדָמָה 'ădāmâ "soil" (note that there is no vowel after the vowel letter ה). Additional qameṣ or pataḥ vowels (for example) also were inserted below consonants wherever a word called for an *ah* sound, even apart from the long vowel indicated by ה.

Thus, following the vowel point ִ you may find a *mater lectionis* י resulting in ִי, where י is serving as part of the vowel, not a separate consonant.² Similarly, י may appear with ֵ as ֵי, a long O-vowel may appear as וֹ, and a U-vowel may be represented by וּ.

Some words have been preserved, spelled both with a *mater lectionis* and without it. Those spellings that include the vowel-consonant are termed "*scriptio plene*" (fully written, as in יוֹצֵא), while spellings lacking the vowel-consonant are termed "*scriptio defective*" (not fully written, as in יֹצֵא).

0.4.ד. Explanation: Simple and compound shevas

Propretonic reduction. Soon you will discover that as plural endings or pronominal suffixes cause words to grow longer, vowels located in early syllables tend to grow shorter. Thus when a singular form דָּבָר *dābār* [word] lengthens to add a plural ending ִים..., the first vowel reduces from דָּ *dā* to דְּ *dĕ*, resulting in דְּבָרִים *dĕbārîm* [words]. This transformation regularly happens with either ָ or ֵ occur in open syllables that in the new, lengthened word are now located two syllables before the accented (or "tonic") syllable. This vowel transformation is known as propretonic reduction.

Pretonic reduction. With some words the propretonic vowel will not admit the sort of reduction described above. The ḥolem of שֹׁפֵט, for example, belongs to the category of vowels known as "unchangeably long." When such a word adds a syllable at the end, since the propretonic vowel cannot reduce to sheva, then a ָ or a ֵ occurring in the **pretonic** syllable (one syllable removed from the accented syllable) **may reduce instead**. Thus the ֵ has become a sheva in the plural form שֹׁפְטִים.

Since gutturals (א, ה, ח, and ע) resist a ְ, in situations where a vowel reduction would normally follow a guttural with a vocal ְ, we often find either ֲ or ֱ instead (e.g., חֲמוֹר *ḥămôr* [donkey] or אֱמֹר *'ĕmōr* [to say].

---

² Not every occurrence of ḥireq-yod involves a *mater lectionis* י. As you will learn later, the yod in דְּבָרֶיךָ, for example, specifies the plural (*your words* instead of *your word*).

APPENDIX　　　　　　　　　　דְּבָרִים נוֹסָפִים　　　　　　　　　　451

0.4.ח. Explanation: Syllable division

Vowel letters and syllable division. Like other vowel letters, the י in לִי is part of the vowel. It does not supply a syllable-closing consonant. When functioning as vowel letters, א, ה, ו, and י similarly do not close a syllable. You can tell these are functioning as vowel letters (not consonants) when they are not followed by a vowel of their own. In the table of words appearing later in this note, observe that א, ה, ו, and י are *not directly followed* by vowels. Note the following table:

פֶּה	מִי	מָה	לוּ	לוֹ	לֹא	הִיא	הוּא	בּוֹא	בּוֹ	בָּא
peh	mî	mâ	lû	lô	lōʾ	hîʾ	hûʾ	bôʾ	bô	bāʾ

The connection between vowel letters and syllable division is this: vowel letters at the end of a syllable **do not produce a closed syllable**. They merely serve as part of the vowel. Thus all the words in the table above consist of open syllables (Cv).

It is customary to preserve vowel letters א and ה when transliterating, even though they do not close a syllable. Thus בָּא is rendered *bāʾ* (not simply *bā*), and פֶּה is rendered *peh* (not *pe*). Where a vowel is followed by a vowel-letter (such as הָ◌ and י◌), the vowel-letter is actually part of the vowel. Consequently the vowel-plus-vowel-letter will be represented by a single symbol: *â* represents הָ◌ (not transliterated *āh*) and *î* represents י◌ (not transliterated *iy*), as shown in earlier transliteration tables.

2.1.א. Explanation: "The king"　　　　הַמֶּלֶךְ

Spelling variations in the definite article. Hebrew will indicate the definite article most often by attaching ...הַ◌ to the front of a word, with the dagesh indicating a doubling of the first consonant of that word. Thus מֶלֶךְ *king* becomes הַמֶּלֶךְ *the king*. If Hebrew script did not employ the dagesh as an abbreviation for the doubled letter, הַמֶּלֶךְ would be written הַמְמֶלֶךְ‡.

Sometimes the article is spelled הַ... (omitting the dagesh) or הָ... (omitting the dagesh and substituting a qameṣ in place of the pataḥ). The first letter of the word to which the article is attached determines these variations. In particular, variations appear when that word begins with one of the guttural consonants (א, ה, ח, and ע), or else the consonant ר. Gutturals (and ר) routinely resist the dagesh, evidently due to the difficulty of preserving in customary speech a phoneme produced by doubling: ...אא..., ...הה..., ...חח..., ...עע..., or ...רר...). The consonant-plus-sheva would tend to be lost.

Four variations arise when the definite article encounters an initial guttural or ר.

(1) When the first letter resists doubling, the energy intended for doubling often transforms the previous vowel. The previous vowel in this case would be the pataḥ of the article הַ. In words beginning with א (such as אֶבֶן), with ע (such as עֶבֶד), or with ר (such as רֹאשׁ), the definite article with the ensuing dagesh הַ...ּ becomes הָ.... Note the transformation of pataḥ into qameṣ and the omission of the dagesh in the examples below. The shift from dagesh to lengthening the previous vowel is called "**compensatory lengthening**."

With definite article		**Without** definite article	
הָאֶבֶן	the stone	אֶבֶן	a stone
הָעֶבֶד	the servant	עֶבֶד	a servant
הָרֹאשׁ	the head	רֹאשׁ	a head

(2) Another tip concerning spelling the article involves words beginning with ה (as in הֶבֶל) or with ח (as in חֹשֶׁךְ)—so long as the first vowel of the word is not a qameṣ (see next point below). In these cases the usual article הַ...ּ becomes simply הַ... (with neither a compensatory lengthening of the vowel from pataḥ to qameṣ, nor any dagesh following the article). This accommodation is known as "**virtual gemination**."

With definite article		**Without** definite article	
הַהֶבֶל	the breath, vanity	הֶבֶל	(some) breath, vanity
הַחֹשֶׁךְ	the darkness	חֹשֶׁךְ	(some) darkness

(3) When a qameṣ follows an initial ה (as in הָרִים), an initial ח (as in חָמָס), or an initial ע (as in עָרִים), the vowel of the article changes from pataḥ to segol. Since ה, ח, and ע are gutturals, they resist the dagesh. Thus *the mountains* would be rendered as הֶהָרִים (rather than the spelling הַהָרִים‡, a spelling that would never occur). Conversion of the article's pataḥ (הַ...) to a segol (הֶ...) for the sake of variation is known as dissimilation.[3]

---

[3] In words such as הָהָר *the mountain* and הָעָם *the people*, just the opposite occurs—the qameṣ of the article (a case of compensatory lengthening) influences the first vowel of the noun הַר or עַם, transforming a pataḥ into a qameṣ, thus matching the definite article (a transformation known as assimilation). These exceptions are related to the fact

דְּבָרִים נוֹסָפִים

With definite article		Without definite article	
הֶהָרִים	the mountains	הָרִים	mountains
הֶחָמָס	the violence	חָמָס	(some) violence
הֶעָרִים	the cities	עָרִים	cities

(4) Finally, you will encounter words such as הַיְאֹר *the Nile* and הַמְבַקְשִׁים *the searchers*, where the first consonant of the word resists doubling, even though it is neither a guttural nor ר. This rule operates when the first letter (after the article ה) has a sheva and is one of these consonants: a sibilant (with an *s* sound), ק, נ, מ, ל, י, or ו.[4]

In summary, then, the definite article generally will appear as הַ... . But do not be surprised if it fails to display a dagesh, or if a vowel other than a pataḥ follows the ה (especially when the word begins with a guttural or ר).[5]

2.3 Words for hearing   מִלִּים לִשְׁמֹעַ

Spelling adjustments in the interrogative particle הֲ. The interrogative particle הֲ can appear with a vowel other than ◌ֲ. For example, it employs a ◌ָ in the question, ...הֶחָפֵץ אַתָּה *Do you want...?* Here are four factors that will alter the vowel of the interrogative ה.

(1) **Generally** it is spelled הֲ, as in הֲיֵשׁ לְךָ לֶחֶם? *Do you have (some) food?*

(2) Before a **sheva**, the ◌ֲ lengthens to ◌ַ, as in הַמְבַקֵּשׁ אַתָּה מַיִם? *Are you looking for (some) water?*

(3) Before a **guttural** (א, ה, ח, or ע), the ◌ֲ similarly lengthens to ◌ַ, as in הַאַתָּה הָאִישׁ אֲשֶׁר מְבַקֵּשׁ לֶחֶם? *Are you the man who is looking for (some) food?*

(4) Before a **guttural vocalized with a** ◌ָ, the הֲ becomes הֶ, as in הֶחָפֵץ אַתָּה לָלֶכֶת לָעִיר? *Do you want to go to the city?*[6]

---

that the syllable containing the assimilated vowel occurs in the accented syllable—a principle which also would account for a qameṣ following the א of הָאָרֶץ *the earth* (cf. *IBHS* §13.3).

[4] Some have found the following mnemonic expression helpful for recalling this collection of consonants: "**skin 'em alive.**"

[5] For more information concerning variables involving the definite article, see *IBHS* §13.3.

2.3.א. Explanation: "And I have (pieces of) baggage." וְיֶשׁ לִי כֵּלִים:

Spelling variations in the conjunction וְ. The conjunction "and" attaches to the front of the ensuing word and generally is spelled וְ. Depending on the initial letter of the following word it may display the following adjustments to ease pronunciation:

Example	וְ	Feature
וְדָוִד and David	וְ	Basic spelling
וּמֶלֶךְ and a king	וּ	Followed by ב, מ, or פ (known as labial consonants)
וּנְבִיאִים and prophets	וּ	Followed by a consonant with a ◌ְ
וִיהוּדָה and Judah	וִי	Followed by יְ
וַעֲרָבָה and desert steppe	וַ	Followed by a guttural having a compound sheva (ו reproduces the primary vowel from that compound sheva)
וֶאֱכֹל and eat!⁷	וֶ	(same)
וָחֳלִי and sickness	וָ⁸	(same)

---

⁶ For further information regarding the interrogative particle, see Joüon §102.

⁷ An exception to this occurs regularly with אֱלֹהִים God. Notice the ṣērê (not segol) and quiescent א in וֵאלֹהִים *and God*. A ṣērê also appears when אֱלֹהִים is preceded by prepositions: בֵּאלֹהִים (*in / by*...), כֵּאלֹהִים (*like*...), and לֵאלֹהִים (*to / for*...).

⁸ The qameṣ in וָ is a qameṣ-ḥatuf due to the ensuing ḥatef-qameṣ. Both are pronounced *o*.

2.3.ב. Explanation: "Big or small?" גָּדוֹל אוֹ קָטָן?

Substantival adjectives. When no noun is present for an adjective to modify, the adjective may operate as if it were a noun (known as a "substantival adjective"). In such situations, the noun represents either the **abstract idea** associated with the noun, or a **generic person or object** suitable for the context. For example, when Abram advises Sarai, "Do to her [Hagar] that which is good in your eyes," the expression "that which is good" represents the adjective הַטּוֹב (literally "the good," Gen. 16:6). Since there is no noun present for טוֹב to modify, it serves as a substantive and refers to the **abstract notion** of "what is good."

In contrast, when Jehoshaphat charged the leaders to execute with integrity their role as arbiters, he closed by saying, "…and may the LORD be with the good" (הַטּוֹב, 2 Chron. 19:11). Here again there is no noun present for טוֹב to modify. Given this context (inaugurating leaders), "the good" refers to a "good **person**" rather than an abstract notion of goodness. Other examples of substantival adjectives include הֶחָכָם *the wise person* (Eccl. 2:16), הָרַע [*the*] *wickedness*, *m* (Num. 32:13, also הָרָעָה *f* in Exod. 10:10), הַקָּטֹן *the insignificant person* and הַגָּדוֹל *the important person* (both in 2 Chron. 18:30).[9]

2.4.א. Explanation and activity: "Sit (*ms*) on the chair that is behind the table." שֵׁב עַל־הַכִּסֵּא אֲשֶׁר אַחֲרֵי הַשֻּׁלְחָן׃

Maqqef and accentual units

Two or more words joined by a maqqef possess a single primary-accented syllable among them, as if they formed one long word (e.g., עַל־הַמַּיִם). Thus, when a word such as a preposition is joined with a maqqef to the following word, the first word (called "proclitic") will not have a primary accent of its own.[10]

Two types of vowels occurring *before* a maqqef will undergo a change. A ṣērê will become a segol (thus לֵךְ *Go! ms*, becomes לֶךְ־, as in the expression לֶךְ־לְךָ [*You, yourself*] *go!*). A ḥolem will become a qameṣ-ḥaṭuf (so that שְׁמֹר *Guard! ms*, becomes שְׁמָר־נָא *Guard, now!*).

---

[9] See *IBH* §23, and *IBHS* §14.3.3d.

[10] The proclitic word may, however, be marked with an infralinear vertical stroke (called a meteg) to indicate a secondary accent (e.g., note the meteg below the first א in אַחֲרֵי־שָׁאוּל *after Saul*).

How the sheva in ...בְּ, ...כְּ, and ...לְ may modify, depending on the next syllable

A word of explanation will help you work with the inseparable prepositions (...בְּ, ...כְּ, and ...לְ). Generally the sheva will be retained. However, since the sheva is extremely weak, it can be affected by—and even resemble—the first vowel of the next word.

(1) When attached to a word beginning with **a guttural and a compound vowel** (also known as a half-vowel: ◌ֲ, ◌ֱ, or ◌ֳ), the preposition adopts the corresponding **full** vowel (regarding gutturals, see §0.4.א.). Thus we find:

בְּ + אֲשֶׁר = בַּאֲשֶׁר *in which*

בְּ + אֱמֶת = בֶּאֱמֶת *in truth, really*[11]

בְּ + אֳנִיָּה = בָּאֳנִיָּה *in a ship*[12]

(2) When attached to a word whose first vowel is **a sheva**, the preposition's sheva becomes a ḥireq (as with any double sheva at the start of a word). Thus:

בְּ + צְרוֹר = בִּצְרוֹר *in a pouch*

(3) When attached to a word that **begins with ...יְ**, the sheva will combine with יְ to become a ḥireq-yod. Thus:

בְּ + יְהוּדָה = בִּיהוּדָה *in Judah*

How מִן may modify

In certain situations the preposition מִן will lose (assimilate) the letter נ and will prefix the remaining מ to the next word:

(1) **Before יְ:** the preposition מִן becomes ...מִ (מִיהוּדָה *from Judah*).

(2) **Before ר and gutturals:** מִן often becomes ...מֵ (מֵרָעָה *from evil*, מֵעִיר *from a city*).

(3) **Before the definite article הַ:** since the definite article ◌ַה involves a guttural, it may transform a preceding מִן to ...מֵ (as in מֵהַמֶּלֶךְ *from the king*). Yet we also find examples with no assimilation of the נ, only a maqqef linking the preposition to a definite noun (as in מִן־הַמֶּלֶךְ *from the king*).

---

[11] With the compound segol of אֱלֹהִים the situation is a bit different since a ṣērê will appear, rendering the א quiescent: בֵּאלֹהִים.

[12] Before a ◌ֳ vowel (pronounced *o*), the ◌ָ in בָּ is a qameṣ-ḥatuf, so is also pronounced *o*.

(4) **Before other consonants:** the נ may be assimilated, leaving behind a dagesh (מִמֶּ֫לֶךְ *from a king*).

3.3.ה. Explanation: "Of what value to me is the occupation of sea captains?" לָמָּה־זֶּה לִי מְלֶ֫אכֶת רַבֵּי־הַחֹבֵל?

Construct plural vowel changes. The following two principles govern vowel changes that occur when a plural noun moves from absolute state to construct state.[13]

(1) An unaccented **qameṣ** or **ṣērê** is often replaced by a **sheva**.

If the absolute plural ends in וֹת...			If the absolute plural ends in ים...			
Construct plural	Absolute plural	Absolute singular	Construct plural	Absolute plural	Absolute singular	Principle
שְׂדוֹת־ fields of	שָׂדוֹת fields	שָׂדֶה field	דִּבְרֵי־[14] words of	דְּבָרִים words	דָּבָר word	unaccented **qameṣ**-to-sheva shift
בִּרְכוֹת־[15] blessings of	בְּרָכוֹת blessings	בְּרָכָה blessing	דְּגֵי־ fish(es) of	דָּגִים fish(es)	דָּג fish	unaccented **qameṣ**-to-sheva shift
שְׁמוֹת־ names of	שֵׁמוֹת names	שֵׁם name	כְּלֵי־ containers of	כֵּלִים containers	כְּלִי container	unaccented **ṣērê**-to-sheva shift

---

[13] Adapted from *IBH* §§5, 76.

[14] Because the qameṣ-turned-sheva was located after another vocal sheva, it caused the first to become a ḥireq. Hebrew does not allow adjacent vocal shevas, likely because they are extremely difficult to articulate.

[15] Again, the first of two vocal shevas will become a ḥireq.

(2) Those initial vowels that are latent in nouns such as אֶבֶן, כֶּסֶף, מֶלֶךְ, סֵפֶר, and שֵׁבֶט will reappear in construct plurals. A shift of qameṣ-to-sheva also occurs in all of these.

If the absolute plural ends in וֹת...			If the absolute plural ends in ִים...			Principle
Construct plural	Absolute plural	Absolute singular	**Construct plural**	Absolute plural	Absolute singular	
אַרְצוֹת־ lands of	אֲרָצוֹת lands	אֶרֶץ land	אַבְנֵי־ stones of	אֲבָנִים stones	אֶבֶן stone	latent **initial** **pataḥ**; unaccented qameṣ-to-sheva shift
חַרְבוֹת־ swords of	חֲרָבוֹת swords	חֶרֶב sword	כַּסְפֵּי־ silver-pieces of	כְּסָפִים silver-pieces	כֶּסֶף silver	latent **initial** **pataḥ**; unaccented qameṣ-to-sheva shift
נַפְשׁוֹת־ souls / persons of	נְפָשׁוֹת souls / persons	נֶפֶשׁ soul / person	מַלְכֵי־ kings of	מְלָכִים kings	מֶלֶךְ king	latent **initial** **pataḥ**; unaccented qameṣ-to-sheva shift
			סִפְרֵי־ scrolls of	סְפָרִים scrolls	סֵפֶר scroll	latent **initial** **ḥireq**; unaccented qameṣ-to-sheva shift
			שִׁבְטֵי־ tribes of	שְׁבָטִים tribes	שֵׁבֶט tribe	(same)

4.1.א. Explanation: "They (*m*) will guard the ship." אֶת־הָאֳנִיָּה יִשְׁמְרוּ׃

Variations in יקטל spelling, *3mpl.* It will be important to review these variations in order to build a mental framework for spelling patterns that diverge from the standard vocalization found with verbs such as ש.מ.ר. The approach employed in this learning process involves repeated exposure rather than rote memorization of paradigms. Nearly all verbs found below you already have encountered in the Jonah episode.

APPENDIX   דְּבָרִים נוֹסָפִים

To recap what we have seen with a verb such as ש.מ.ר, the יִקְטֹל *3mpl* uses sheva (ְ) vowels (as well as a י prefix and a וּ suffix). When followed by a sheva, certain consonants prove quite weak and so shift or vanish as a result. First-radicals consisting of א, י, or נ are treated in the first table below, followed by a table dealing with verbs having a guttural ה, ח, or ע in first position.

Shifting or vanishing consonants in first position, preceded by a prefix: א, י, and נ[16]

Pattern	שֹׁרֶשׁ	יִקְטֹל *3mpl*	Tip
I-א	א.כ.ל eat	יֹאכְלוּ	An initial consonant א remains visible but becomes silent, pairing a ḥolem vowel with the י.
	א.מ.ר say	יֹאמְרוּ	
I-י	י.ר.ד descend	יֵרְדוּ	An initial consonant י combines with the prefix י to produce a stronger vowel (ṣērê instead of pataḥ).[17]
	י.ש.ב sit	יֵשְׁבוּ	
[I-י]	ה.ל.כ walk	יֵלְכוּ	הָלַךְ is a pseudo I-י verb (it behaves as a I-י verb in the יִקְטֹל conjugation; see previous comment).

---

[16] "First position" refers to the first of the three consonants in any שֹׁרֶשׁ. Thus א.כ.ל is known as a "I-א verb" since the first position is occupied by an א. Similarly ע.ל.ה/י is known as a "III-ה/י verb" since the third position is occupied by ה/י. Some prefer the convention of labeling these three positions according to the first, second, and third consonants of Modern Hebrew term for "verb"—פָּעַל. According to this convention, a "I-א verb" would be labeled "פ״א," and a "III-ה/י verb" would be labeled "ל״ה/י."

[17] The verb י.כ.ל is an irregular I-י, producing the *3mpl* יקטל form יוּכְלוּ *they will be able.*

Pattern	שֹׁרֶשׁ	3mpl יִקְטֹל	Tip
I-נ	נ.פ.ל fall	יִפְּלוּ	An initial נ vanishes, usually leaving behind a dagesh in the second consonant. (When the second שֹׁרֶשׁ consonant is a sibilant [with an *s* sound], ק, נ, מ, ל, י, or ו, the dagesh may be omitted when followed by a sheva, as in יִשְׂאוּ.)[18]
	נ.שׂ.א lift	יִשְׂאוּ	
	נ.ת.נ give	יִתְּנוּ	

Gutturals ה, ח, or ע in first position, preceded by a prefix[19]

Pattern	שֹׁרֶשׁ	3mpl יִקְטֹל	Tip
I-ח	ח.שׁ.ב think	יַחְשְׁבוּ	An initial consonant ח remains visible, takes a customary sheva and also influences the vowel under the prefix יְ... to become a pataḥ (one of the A-class vowels), replacing the customary ḥireq. Gutturals prefer A-class vowels (ַ, ֲ, ֶ).
I-ע	ע.ב.ד work	יַעַבְדוּ	An initial ע resists customary reduction to sheva, retaining a pataḥ instead. It is responsible for a pataḥ appearing in the prefix as well.[20]
	ע.מ.ד stand	יַעַמְדוּ	

The next table treats *3mpl* יִקְטֹל in verbs whose middle radical is either ו or י. These are called hollow verbs.

---

[18] Cf. Joüon §18m.

[19] א is a guttural as well, but varies between using a ḥolem in the first syllable (see א.כ.ל example) or a pataḥ (preferred by other gutturals). Check each verb to be certain.

[20] There is another verb you have encountered which takes a pataḥ as the prefix vowel, but not due to a guttural as the first radical. The verb is יַשְׁלִיכוּ *they will throw* (from שׁ.ל.כ). In this case, the prefix pataḥ owes to the spelling known as "hifil," a verb stem you will learn about in Unit 8.

APPENDIX   דְּבָרִים נוֹסָפִים

Hollow verbs: ו or י in second position

Notice that instead of the usual prefix syllable of יִ..., the hollow verbs consistently use יָ....

שֹׁרֶשׁ	יִקְטֹל 3mpl	שֹׁרֶשׁ	יִקְטֹל 3mpl
ב.ו.א come	יָבוֹאוּ	ק.ו.מ get up	יָקוּמוּ
מ.ו.ת die	יָמוּתוּ	שׂ.ו/י.מ place	יָשִׂימוּ
ס.ו.ר turn from	יָסוּרוּ		

ה/י in third position

The so-called "III-ה/י" consonant proves too frail to persist. Thus in the case of the verb ב.כ.י/ה, in place of יִבְכִּיוּ‡ we find simply יִבְכּוּ *they will weep*.[21] (Incidentally, one's ability to recognize III-ה/י verbs simply by their first two שֹׁרֶשׁ consonants is a good indication that one has mastered III-ה/י verbs.) Thus when we read ...בכ... we should suspect this may trace to ב.כ.י/ה and recall the meaning "to weep." Similarly, when we see ...שת... we should propose a meaning associated with "to drink."

שֹׁרֶשׁ	יִקְטֹל 3mpl	שֹׁרֶשׁ	יִקְטֹל 3mpl
ב.כ.י/ה weep	יִבְכּוּ	ר.א.י/ה see	יִרְאוּ
ה.י.י/ה be	יִהְיוּ	שׁ.ת.י/ה drink	יִשְׁתּוּ
ח.י.י/ה live	יִחְיוּ		

---

[21] Verbs classed III-ה/י were historically either III-י or III-ו. Where י or ו was dropped at the end of a word, the letter ה was supplied as an orthographic signal of the long vowel which preceded it (cf. GKC §75a). So they became known as III-ה verbs. To acknowledge that the י of historically III-י verbs often resurfaces, they became more accurately labeled III-ה/י. Only occasionally does the ו of a historically III-ו verb resurface (e.g., שָׁלֵו, *pt ms* of ש.ל.ה [historically שׁ.ל.ו] *to rest*, which is classed loosely with III-ה/י verbs). Concerning verbs that are truly III-ה, see note following the list of מִלִּים לַעֲנוֹת in §3.1.

4.3.א. Explanation: "He won't lie down forever." לֹא לְעוֹלָם יִשְׁכַּב:

Variations in יקטל **spelling,** *3ms*. A ḥolem most often serves as the vowel following the second שֹׁרֶשׁ consonant (theme vowel) for יְקֹטל verb forms. Notice the ḥolem as theme vowel in these examples: יִכְרֹת and יִשְׁמֹר). Yet some verbs will employ a **theme vowel other than ḥolem**. The following remarks will help explain why that is the case.

Qameṣ or pataḥ theme vowel

Tip	יקטל 3ms	שֹׁרֶשׁ	Pattern
Just as I-gutturals produce an A-class vowel in the **prefix** (3mpl יַעֲמְדוּ), similarly III-gutturals produce an A-class vowel in the **final syllable**.	יִמְצָא	מ.צ.א find	III-guttural
	יִשְׁמַע	ש.מ.ע hear	
Other verbs similarly have an A-class theme vowel, including many stative verbs.²²	יֹאכַל	א.כ.ל eat	Statives and other verbs
	יוּכַל	י.כ.ל be able	
	יִשְׁכַּב	ש.כ.ב lie down	

---

²² "Stative" identifies a verb that describes a state of being (e.g., to be small, to be great, to be able, to be asleep, or to be old) rather than describing an action. Stative verbs may include psychological conditions (e.g., to love, to hate, or to fear). In contrast to statives, verbs which describe an action are known as "fientive"—a category which accounts for most verbs (e.g., to find, to come, or to get up). Statives in the above list include י.כ.ל and ש.כ.ב. For more information concerning statives, please refer to §§6.5.א. (Part 2) and 6.5.ג., also Appendix §§5.4.ה. and 6.5.ג.

APPENDIX — דְּבָרִים נוֹסָפִים

Ṣērê theme vowel

Tip	יִקְטֹל 3ms	שֹׁרֶשׁ	Pattern
When a ṣērê appears in the first syllable (as with I-י verbs), a second ṣērê appears as theme vowel.	יֵרֵד	י.ר.ד descend	I-י
	יֵשֵׁב	י.שׁ.ב sit	
ה.ל.כ behaves as a pseudo "I-י" verb in the יִקְטֹל conjugation, with a ṣērê theme vowel.	יֵלֵךְ	ה.ל.כ walk	[I-י]
נ.ת.נ also employs a ṣērê. Note that the first נ disappears, leaving a dagesh in the second consonant.	יִתֵּן	נ.ת.נ give	Statives and other verbs

Theme vowel involving י or ו in hollow verbs

Hollow verbs are simple since the middle שֹׁרֶשׁ consonant is closely connected to the theme vowel. Thus the theme vowel for the *3ms* יִקְטֹל of a II-ו verb will be either וֹ or וּ. The theme vowel for a II-י/ו verb will be יִ. Notice also the qameṣ as יִקְטֹל prefix vowel for hollow verbs.

יִקְטֹל 3ms	שֹׁרֶשׁ	יִקְטֹל 3ms	שֹׁרֶשׁ
יָקוּם	ק.ו.מ get up	יָבוֹא	ב.ו.א come
יָשִׂים	שׂ.ו/י.מ place	יָמוּת	מ.ו.ת die
		יָסוּר	ס.ו.ר turn from

Segol theme vowel: III-י/ה verbs

A III-י/ה will produce a segol in the final syllable.

שֹׁרֶשׁ	יִקְטֹל 3ms	שֹׁרֶשׁ	יִקְטֹל 3ms
ב.כ.י/ה weep	יִבְכֶּה	ר.א.י/ה see	יִרְאֶה
ה.י.י/ה be	יִהְיֶה	ש.ת.י/ה drink	יִשְׁתֶּה
ח.י.י/ה live	יִחְיֶה		

4.3.ד. Activity: "Put your feet on your hands!"   שִׂים רַגְלֶיךָ עַל־יָדֶיךָ!

"Head and shoulders, knees and toes" song. Are you familiar with the children's song, "Head and Shoulders, Knees and Toes"? If so, you may enjoy trying it in Hebrew. Point to body parts when they occur in the song. Begin slowly, as the Hebrew version requires that the tune accommodate several extra syllables. Increase the tempo as you grow familiar with the words. בֶּרֶךְ (f)is the singular of בִּרְכַּיִם. It identifies the joint half way between your רֶגֶל and your hip.

רֹאשׁ יָדַיִם בִּרְכַּיִם וְרַגְלַיִם (בִּרְכַּיִם וְרַגְלַיִם)

רֹאשׁ יָדַיִם בִּרְכַּיִם וְרַגְלַיִם (בִּרְכַּיִם וְרַגְלַיִם)

עֵינַיִם אָזְנַיִם וּפֶה וְאַף

רֹאשׁ יָדַיִם בִּרְכַּיִם וְרַגְלַיִם (בִּרְכַּיִם וְרַגְלַיִם)

4.4.א. Explanation: "His ears will hear." אָזְנָיו תִּשְׁמַ֫עְנָה׃

Part 1 of יקטל spelling, *3fpl*: Variations in spelling the prefix vowel

Pattern	שֹׁ֫רֶשׁ	יִקְטֹל *3fpl*	Tip
Standard	ש.מ.ר guard	תִּשְׁמֹ֫רְנָה	Recall that the **basic prefix** vowel is **ḥireq**.
	כ.ר.ת write	תִּכְרֹ֫תְנָה	
I-guttural	ע.ב.ד serve	תַּעֲבֹ֫דְנָה	A I-guttural verb will produce a **pataḥ prefix** vowel.
	ע.מ.ד stand	תַּעֲמֹ֫דְנָה	
I-י	י.ר.ד descend	תֵּרַ֫דְנָה	A I-י verb will produce a **ṣērê prefix** vowel.
	י.ש.ב sit	תֵּשַׁ֫בְנָה	
I-א	א.כ.ל eat	תֹּאכַ֫לְנָה	A I-א verb will produce a **ḥolem prefix** vowel.
	א.מ.ר say	תֹּאמַ֫רְנָה	

Part 2 of יקטל spelling, *3fpl*: Variations in spelling the theme vowel

Tip	*3fpl* יקטל	שֹׁרֶשׁ	Pattern
Recall that the **basic theme** vowel is **ḥolem**.	תִּשְׁמֹרְנָה	ש.מ.ר guard	Standard
	תִּכְתֹּבְנָה	כ.ת.ב write	
A nearby **guttural** can produce a pataḥ **middle** vowel.	תִּשְׁמַעְנָה	ש.מ.ע listen	III-guttural
A III-ה/י verb will convert to a י, yielding a suffix of ◌ֶינָה....	תִּבְכֶּינָה	ב.כ.י/ה weep	III-י/ה
	תִּרְאֶינָה	ר.א.י/ה see	
Hollow verbs will imitate **either** III-י/ה with a suffix of [י]◌ֶנָה....	תָּבֹאנָה	ב.ו.א come	II-ו/י
	תְּמוּתֶנָה	מ.ו.ת die	
...Or hollow verbs will imitate the "basic" pattern (ḥolem).	תָּסֹרְנָה	ס.ו.ר turn from	II-ו/י (cont.)
	תָּקֹמְנָה	ק.ו.מ rise	
	תְּשִׂימֶנָה	ש.ו/י.מ place	

5.1.ג. Activity: "What will you (*mpl*) do today?"   מַה־תַּעֲשׂוּ הַיּוֹם?

Variations in יקטל spelling, *1cpl*. The *1cpl* form mimics the *3ms* form quite universally (exchanging the prefix ...י in favor of נ...). This even holds true for a שֹׁרֶשׁ beginning with נ..., as seen below. Again, *3ms* forms are provided as an anchor-point. Just as the initial נ in *3ms* forms will assimilate with the next

APPENDIX — דְּבָרִים נוֹסָפִים

consonant (marking it with a dagesh), so does the initial נ in *1cpl* forms. Thus we find נִשָּׂא (not נִנְשָׂא‡). Since the verb ל.ק.ח behaves as a I-נ verb, it appears here as well.

I-נ verbs (also ל.ק.ח)

שֹׁרֶשׁ	יִקְטֹל *3ms*	יִקְטֹל *1cpl*	we will…
נ.ת.נ	יִתֵּן	נִתֵּן	give
ל.ק.ח	יִקַּח	נִקַּח	take

שֹׁרֶשׁ	יִקְטֹל *3ms*	יִקְטֹל *1cpl*	we will…
נ.כ.י/ה	יַכֶּה	נַכֶּה[23]	hit
נ.פ.ל	יִפֹּל	נִפֹּל	fall
נ.שׂ.א	יִשָּׂא	נִשָּׂא	lift

I-י verbs

If the שֹׁרֶשׁ begins with …י the trend simply continues (*1cpl* imitates *3ms*). Thus we find נֵשֵׁב (not נִישַׁב‡). Since it operates like a I-י verb in the יִקְטֹל conjugation, ה.ל.כ is included below.

שֹׁרֶשׁ	יִקְטֹל *3ms*	יִקְטֹל *1cpl*	we will…
י.צ.א	יֵצֵא	נֵצֵא	go out
י.שׁ.ב	יֵשֵׁב	נֵשֵׁב	sit
ה.ל.כ	יֵלֵךְ	נֵלֵךְ	walk, go

Hollow verbs

What about so-called hollow verbs? Once again a trend set by *3ms* forms will continue: a qameṣ vowel in the first syllable, with the middle radical ו/י operating as a vowel.

שֹׁרֶשׁ	יִקְטֹל *3ms*	יִקְטֹל *1cpl*	we will…
שׂ.י/ו.מ	יָשִׂים	נָשִׂים	place
שׁ.ו.ב	יָשׁוּב	נָשׁוּב	turn to

שֹׁרֶשׁ	יִקְטֹל *3ms*	יִקְטֹל *1cpl*	we will…
ב.ו.א	יָבוֹא	נָבוֹא	come
מ.ו.ת	יָמוּת	נָמוּת	die
ס.ו.ר	יָסוּר	נָסוּר	turn away

---

[23] The verb meaning *to hit* is formed in the *hifil* בִּנְיָן, and for this reason employs a pataḥ as first vowel. The שֹׁרֶשׁ נ.כ.י/ה is not attested in the qal בִּנְיָן.

5.2.ב. Explanation and activity: "What will you (*ms, fs*) do first, tomorrow?" מַה־תַּעֲשֶׂה / תַּעֲשִׂי מָחָר בָּרִאשֹׁנָה?

Variations in יקטל spelling, *1cs*. For *1cs* יקטל forms, when the שֹׁרֶשׁ already begins with an א..., the א of the prefix coalesces with the א of the שֹׁרֶשׁ, as in אֹכַל *I will eat* (not אֹאכַל‡).

שֹׁרֶשׁ	יְקַטֵּל *3ms*	יְקַטֵּל *1cs*	I will...
א.כ.ל	יֹאכַל	אֹכַל	eat
א.מ.ר	יֹאמַר	אֹמַר	say

In case the שֹׁרֶשׁ begins with a י..., the prefix א simply replaces the original initial י and supplies a ṣērê vowel to accompany it, as in אֵרֵד *I will descend* (not אֱיְרֹד‡). The verb ה.ל.כ behaves as if it were a I-י verb in the יקטל conjugation.

שֹׁרֶשׁ	יְקַטֵּל *3ms*	יְקַטֵּל *1cs*	I will...
י.ר.ד	יֵרֵד	אֵרֵד	descend
ה.ל.כ	יֵלֵךְ	אֵלֵךְ	go

In the case of י.ר.א, the first consonant י persists *in addition to the prefix* (instead of being replaced by the prefix consonant). A ḥireq follows the prefix consonant (rather than the customary ṣērê seen in אֵרֵד).

שֹׁרֶשׁ	יְקַטֵּל *3ms*	יְקַטֵּל *1cs*	I will...
י.ר.א	יִירָא	אִירָא	be afraid

Hollow verbs in the *1cs* are spelled as found in other forms. A qameṣ vowel appears in the prefix, and the middle radical contributes to a vowel.

שֹׁרֶשׁ	יְקַטֵּל *3ms*	יְקַטֵּל *1cs*	I will...
מ.ו.ת	יָמוּת	אָמוּת	die
שׂ.י/ו.מ	יָשִׂים	אָשִׂים	place

5.4.א. Explanation: Additional יִקְטֹל meanings

What connotation may lie at the center of the יִקְטֹל?

At the outset, it is vital to realize that Hebrew belongs to a group of languages in which conjugated verbs are particularly concerned with signaling whether an event possesses one of two qualities: either (a) an **ongoing / potential quality** or (b) a **definite / assured quality**.[24] Such languages are said to be concerned with the "aspect" rather than the "tense" of an event. English is a tense-related language, since from its conjugated verbs one can easily detect whether an action is located in the past, the present, or the future.

Returning to Hebrew, if we briefly review the meanings available for the יִקְטֹל, it becomes evident that they belong to the "ongoing / potential action" side of the aspect discussion. Recall for a moment the modal and volitional options available within the יִקְטֹל, such as "can," "may," "should," and "must." We observed that these belong to the realm of potentiality. By definition, what is "potential" is not yet completed, not assured. It remains possible, but lacks certitude.

Consider also the "habitual present," "iterative," and "customary past" meanings available to the יִקְטֹל. These belong to the realm of what is yet "ongoing," not to the more confined realm of the "assured." Similarly an inceptive verb (beginning an action) is ongoing in the sense that, while its onset is known, we do not know whether or when it may finish. It remains open-ended, at least as far as the inceptive verb is concerned.

The only major category remaining to be accounted for is the future indicative—straightforward statements about the future. While the יִקְטֹל may govern future indicatives due to a measure of dependence on past or present circumstances (recall observations by Waltke and O'Connor concerning Ps. 23:1, as noted in §5.4.א.), we should exercise caution lest such an inference of sequential or temporal orientation would risk obscuring the language's more fundamental commitment to distinctions of aspect.

Rather than inferring that future indicative belongs to the יִקְטֹל due to a connection with antecedent events, it may be simpler to recognize יִקְטֹל as the default conduit of future indicative for the following reason. By nature of their futurity, such statements are, from a finite human vantage, unbounded with

---

[24] R. Buth describes יִקְטֹל as referring to "*indefinite* events (future or imperfective or potential or repetitive)," while קָטַל refers to "*definite* events (that is, past or perfective or decisive or contrary to the fact)" (emphases original, "The Hebrew Verb in Current Discussions," *Journal of Translation and Textlinguistics* 5:2 [1992]: 103).

regard to aspect. They remain unassured. They belong to the realm of intention, of potentiality. Whether they will ever materialize cannot yet be positively ascertained by the speaker. In short, they lack certitude.

If we are correct in identifying certitude / incertitude as a major distinction of aspect for Hebrew, as an aspectual language Hebrew should apply this distinction irrespective of temporal dimensions. That is, we should find **incertitude** signaled (through יִקְטֹל) **across the temporal spectrum** (past, present, and future). Similarly we should find **certitude** signaled (through קָטַל) **across the temporal spectrum**.[25]

As regards the **past** time frame, the יִקְטֹל conveys incertitude in the sense of discontinuation, seen in expressions such as וְאֵד יַעֲלֶה מִן־הָאָרֶץ *A stream **used to come up** from the ground* [*but no longer does so*] (Gen. 2:6).[26]

As regards the **present** time frame, יִקְטֹל serves to express incipient events, as in כִּי־אֵלֶיךָ אֶתְפַּלָּל *...for to you I **begin to pray*** (Ps. 5:3). While the beginning of such an action is indisputable, certitude concerning extent of duration beyond inception would remain in question.[27] In addition, we have noticed that modal and volitional expressions with their inherent uncertainty often operate in the present.

As regards the **future** time frame, יִקְטֹל frequently expresses future indicative with its inherent uncertainty. Modal expressions with their sense of potentiality may also operate in a future setting. Thus we may detect an emphasis on incertitude (also encompassing non-durability, dynamic iterativity) in the choice of the יִקְטֹל to represent situations past, present, and future.

The קָטַל, in contrast, deals with the realm of **certitude**. As regards the **past** time frame, events whose certitude is established by virtue of having transpired commonly are expressed by the קָטַל. When a writer or speaker wishes to depict an established condition that obtains in the **present**, the קָטַל again

---

[25] Aspectual languages such as Hebrew possess two conjugations, each belonging to opposing ends of the aspect-spectrum. The one you have already met, the יִקְטֹל (or "imperfect" or "prefix") conjugation. The other is known as the קָטַל (or "perfect," "affix") conjugation, to be introduced in the next unit. The קָטַל is mentioned here to provide by contrast a clearer picture of the central meaning of the יִקְטֹל.

[26] *IBHS* §31.2. Incipient uses of the יִקְטֹל may be shown for the past as well (see regarding 1 Sam. 1:10 in §5.4.א.). Some uncertainty surrounds the meaning of אֵד, ranging from "freshwater stream" to a "mist."

[27] The use of יִקְטֹל for present iterative may link to this incipient present, since attention is drawn to the dynamic quality of the action (whether beginning or recurring, in contrast to a durable sense of certitude), as in יִפְרְצֵנִי פֶרֶץ עַל־פְּנֵי־פָרֶץ *Again and again he bursts upon me...* (Job 16:14). The case of the present habitual יִקְטֹל is similar.

may serve to convey that certitude, as in אָמַר נָבָל בְּלִבּוֹ אֵין אֱלֹהִים *A fool says in his heart, "There is no God,"* Ps. 14:1a.[28] Finally, when a writer or speaker wishes to describe an event belonging to **future** time—an event that is sure to transpire—the קָטַל serves this time frame as well.[29] Thus it appears that the register of certitude operated as a major factor determining whether a biblical communicator employed either the יִקְטֹל or the קָטַל, regardless of time frame.

While the above observations neither exhaust the topic nor resolve all the puzzles surrounding יִקְטֹל and קָטַל, it is hoped that these remarks may help you cultivate a sensitivity concerning the sort of vector along which conjugated Hebrew expressions tended to travel—a vector that is primarily preoccupied **not** with issues of **time**, but rather of **aspect**. In addition, the sort of aspect that hangs in balance concerns, to a significant degree, the question of **whether a given event was marked by certitude** (also durability, non-iterativity) **or by non-certitude** (also non-durability, iterativity).

5.4.ד. יִקְטֹל conjugation of geminate verbs

Since we have met the complete יִקְטֹל conjugation for standard verbs such as ש.מ.ר, it would be a good idea to become aware of another relatively small group of verbs—those characterized by doubled final consonants. These are called geminates. They are bound together only by this double-consonant feature (not by any shared meaning).

You have not yet encountered any geminates. One will turn up in the next unit: סֹבְבִים *ones that surround, pt mpl*, from the verb ס.ב.ב. (§6.1). The יִקְטֹל conjugation for ס.ב.ב appears below. Since two distinct geminate spelling patterns are attested, in this table both are shown for the same verb, side-by-side and separated by a comma.[30] The second pattern represents the doubled consonant by a dagesh in the second שרש consonant (as in תָּסֹבִּי *you will surround, fs*), while the first pattern either accounts for the

---

[28] Such an expression with קָטַל in the present is known as the "proverbial" or "gnomic perfect" (cf. Isa. 40:7).

[29] The use of קָטַל with a future time frame is known as the "prophetic perfect" ("prophetic קָטַל") or "perfective of confidence" (*IBHS* §30.5.1). It is instructive to observe that biblical statements about future events having certitude commonly are distinguished by their source. Whereas human-sourced statements about the future tend to be relegated to verbal forms connoting potentiality (יִקְטֹל), future statements with certitude (קָטַל) tend to be attributed to an extra-human source.

[30] For further explanation of geminate variations, see Appendix §6.4.ה. and *IBH* §126.

doubled consonant by a dagesh in the first שרש consonant (e.g., תִּסְּבִי *you will surround, fs*), or fails to represent the doubled consonant at all (e.g., אָסֹב *I will surround*). Both spellings have the same meaning.

ס.ב.ב	
נָסֹב, נִסֹּב we will surround	אָסֹב, אֶסֹּב I will surround
תָּסֹבּוּ, תִּסְּבוּ you will surround *mpl*	תָּסֹב, תִּסֹּב you will surround *ms*
תְּסֻבֶּינָה, תִּסֹּבְנָה you will surround *fpl*	תָּסֹבִּי, תִּסְּבִי you will surround *fs*
יָסֹבּוּ, יִסְּבוּ they will surround *m*	יָסֹב, יִסֹּב he will surround
תְּסֻבֶּינָה, תִּסֹּבְנָה they will surround *f*	תָּסֹב, תִּסֹּב she will surround

5.4.ה. יִקְטֹל conjugation of stative verbs

In the introduction to stative verbs found in Appendix §4.3.א., it was observed that statives often employ a pataḥ theme vowel in יקטל forms (rather than a ḥolem). Here are several examples. Notice that many of these have no guttural or ר that might otherwise account for the pataḥ.[31]

You will notice a new conjugation column labeled "קָטַל *3ms*." קָטַל forms (often depicting a past time frame) will be explained more fully in Unit 6. The *3ms* forms have been included here to help you grow accustomed to the presence of a ṣērê theme vowel as characteristic of many statives in the קָטַל conjugation (for a complete קָטַל stative conjugation, see Appendix §6.5.ג.).

---

[31] See extensive treatment of statives in *IBHS* §22.2.1–3.

Verbs showing typical stative vocalization in יִקְטַל

The following are stative verbs (*3ms* forms). Notice the standard pattern of a pataḥ theme vowel in יִקְטַל and a ṣērê theme vowel in קָטֵל, not influenced by gutturals or ר.

3ms קָטֵל	*3ms* יִקְטַל	שֹׁרֶשׁ	he will...
זָקֵן	יִזְקַן	ז.כ.נ	be *or* become old
יָבֵשׁ	יִיבַשׁ	י.ב.שׁ	be dry
יָשֵׁן	יִישַׁן	י.שׁ.נ	sleep
כָּבֵד	יִכְבַּד	כ.ב.ד	be heavy

Exception (1): Fientive verbs appearing with typically-stative vocalization in יִקְטַל

Please notice that, despite the pataḥ theme vowel in the יקטל forms below, these are non-stative verbs, known as "fientive."

3ms קָטַל	*3ms* יִקְטַל	שֹׁרֶשׁ	he will...
יָרַשׁ	יִירַשׁ	י.ר.שׁ	inherit
יָנַק	יִינַק	י.נ.ק	suck

Exception (2): Statives appearing with typically-fientive theme vowels in יִקְטֹל

Now notice that, despite the O-class theme vowel characteristic of fientives in יקטל, the following are actually stative, as indicated by the ṣērê as קטל theme vowel.

3ms קָטֵל	*3ms* יִקְטֹל	שֹׁרֶשׁ	he will...
בֹּשׁ	יֵבוֹשׁ	י.ב.שׁ	be ashamed
חָפֵץ	יַחְפֹּץ	ח.פ.צ	delight in
נָבֵל	יִבּוֹל	נ.ב.ל	languish, decay

Exception (3): Statives appearing with atypical vocalization in קָטַל (but typical stative vocalization in יִקְטֹל)

קָטַל 3ms	יִקְטֹל 3ms	שֹׁרֶשׁ	he will...
קָטֹן [32]	יִקְטַן	ק.ט.נ	be small
גָּדַל	יִגְדַּל	ג.ד.ל	be great
שָׁכַב	יִשְׁכַּב	ש.כ.ב	recline

You will find below a full יקטל conjugation of ק.ט.נ *to be* or *become small*. Notice the pataḥ theme vowel.

ק.ט.נ	
אֶקְטַן	נִקְטַן
I will be small	we will be small
תִּקְטַן	תִּקְטְנוּ
you will be small *ms*	you will be small *mpl*
תִּקְטְנִי	תִּקְטֹנָּה
you will be small *fs*	you will be small *fpl*
יִקְטַן	יִקְטְנוּ
he will be small	they will be small *m*
תִּקְטַן	תִּקְטֹנָּה
she will be small	they will be small *f*

---

[32] The *3ms* קָטַל conjugation spelling קָטֹן reminds us of the adjective spelling קָטֹן. Some have described stative verbs as "conjugated adjectives" (Joüon §41b). When discussing statives in Akkadian (another Semitic language) N.J.C. Kouwenberg describes them as as "a relatively transparent combination of a nominal / adjectival stem and person [sic] affixes of nominal or pronominal descent" (*The Akkadian Verb and Its Semitic Background* [Winona Lake, Indiana: Eisenbrauns, 2010], 176).

5.4.1. יִקְטֹל forms with an unexpected נ

As you read the Hebrew Bible, occasionally you will discover a יקטל form with an unexpected נ, located either at the end or just prior to an object suffix. The following paragraphs and tables will help you grow accustomed to these forms.

Forms with a terminal נ

A יקטל form that ends with an unexpected נ is termed a "paragogic" or lengthened form. Compare the following examples, where standard forms appear to the left of the נ-bearing counterparts.

Standard form	Paragogic form (with נ)	שֹׁרֶשׁ	Meaning of paragogic form
תֶּאֱהָבוּ	תֶּאֱהָבוּן	א.ה.ב	you will love, *mpl*
יֹאחֲזוּ	יֹאחֲזוּן	א.ח.ז	they will grasp, *mpl*
תִּשְׁמְעוּ	תִּשְׁמְעוּן	ש.מ.ע	you will hear, *mpl*

Regarding meaning, forms with a paragogic נ forms might convey a measure either of emphasis or of contrast, when compared with expressions employing the standard form.[33] They occur primarily in *2mpl, 2fs,* and—most commonly—*3mpl* יקטל conjugations.

Forms with a נ before a suffix

You may also encounter a יקטל form having a suffixed pronominal object, in which that suffix may begin with an unexpected נ. These are known as "energic" forms. Sometimes the inserted נ is plainly visible (unassimilated, as with the ב.ר.כ example, below). At other times the נ may absorb the ensuing suffix consonant (as in ש.מ.ר example), or else may itself be absorbed by the ensuing consonant (as with נ.כ.ה/י).

---

[33] As to "contrast" associated with the paragogic נ, J. Hoftijzer explains that the contrast may involve "exceptions to normal practice, contradictions, deviations from normal expectation,…[and] statements…which are contrary to the wishes…of other people" (*Nun Paragogicum,* 55–56, quoted in *IBHS* §31.7.1). This sense of contrast tends to be more significant in poetry than in prose.

Standard form	Forms with infixed נ	שֹׁרֶשׁ	Meaning of paragogic form
יְבָרְכֵהוּ	יְבָרְכֶנְהוּ unassimilated נ	ב.ר.כ	he will bless him
יַכְּכָה	יַכֶּכָּה pronominal suffix absorbs the נ (נ + כ < כּ)	נ.כ.י/ה	he will strike you, *ms*
יִשְׁמְרֵהוּ	יִשְׁמְרֶנּוּ the נ absorbs consonant of pronominal suffix (נ + ה < נּ)	שׁ.מ.ר	he will keep him

In contrast to the paragogic-נ forms, energic forms evidently convey no distinctive meaning when compared with their standard counterparts.[34]

6.1.א. Explanation: "He descended into the depths." יָרַד בַּתְּהֹמוֹת:

Variations in קָטַל spelling, *3ms*. The *3ms* קָטַל of hollow verbs (where the middle consonant is either ו or י) will produce a one-syllable form, generally having a qameṣ after the first consonant. Use the table below to become familiar with this spelling.

שֹׁרֶשׁ	קָטַל *3ms*	he...	שֹׁרֶשׁ	קָטַל *3ms*	he...
שׁ.ו.ב	שָׁב	...turned to	ב.ו.א	בָּא	...came
שׂ.ו/י.ם	שָׂם	...placed	ס.ו.ר	סָר	...turned away
			ק.ו.ם	קָם	...got up

Some verbs, such as the stative verb מוּת, use a different vowel for *3ms*: מֵת *he died*.

---

[34] By comparing other Semitic languages we learn that this pattern originally involved inserting the syllable *-an-* between a verb and its pronominal suffix (*IBHS* §31.7.2).

6.5.ב. קָטַל conjugation of geminate verbs

Since Unit 6 has presented the complete קטל conjugation for standard verbs such as ש.מ.ר, this is an appropriate time to become familiar with geminates: those verbs that employ the same consonant for both the second and third שרש consonants. We will continue to use ס.ב.ב, the geminate verb modeled for the יקטל in Appendix §5.4.ד. To review a קטל verb table of ס.ב.ב *to surround*, please see below. The verb ת.מ.מ *to be complete* is also a geminate, but at certain points will depart from the ס.ב.ב model. Those divergences are shown in brackets within the table for ס.ב.ב. An explanation of ת.מ.מ follows the tables.

When the geminated consonant is a guttural (as in ר.ע.ע *to be evil*), the spelling will change slightly (see table for ר.ע.ע, below). With the exception of *3ms* רַע, a qames will replace the customary pataḥ in the first syllable.

ר.ע.ע		ס.ב.ב	
רְעוֹנוּ we were evil	רְעוֹתִי I was evil	סַבּוֹנוּ we surrounded	סַבּוֹתִי I surrounded
רְעוֹתֶם you were evil *mpl*	רְעוֹתָ you were evil *ms*	סַבּוֹתֶם you surrounded *mpl*	סַבּוֹתָ you surrounded
רְעוֹתֶן you were evil *fpl*	רְעוֹת you were evil *fs*	סַבּוֹתֶן you surrounded *fpl*	סַבּוֹת you surrounded *fs*
רָעוּ they were evil	רַע he was evil	סָבְבוּ [תַּמּוּ][35] they surrounded	סָבַב [תַּם] he surrounded
	רָעָה she was evil		סָבְבָה [תַּמָּה][36] she surrounded

From the table displaying ס.ב.ב you may have noticed that geminated consonants at times are represented by a **single letter with a dagesh** (as in סַבּוֹתִי *I surrounded*). This spelling with a dagesh is

---

[35] Spelled סָבֲבוּ in some manuscripts. The fact that a ◌ָ often appears (rather than the sheva customary for קָטַל *3fs* and *3cpl*) owes to the repetition of the consonant (cf. Joüon §82a [n. 4]).

[36] Spelled סָבֲבָה in some manuscripts.

regarded as the "normal" condition. In other parts of the conjugation, the geminated consonants appear as two separate letters (as in סָבַב *he surrounded*). A form spelled with two separate letters is called a "dissociated" form, since the two letters do not coalesce but remain distinct, due to an intervening vowel. There is no difference in meaning between a normal and a dissociated spelling of the same שרש.

At times you may encounter a geminate שרש that uses a compressed spelling (called "reduced") for *3ms*, while using a "normal" spelling (with dagesh) in *3fs* and *3mpl*. For example, ת.מ.מ *to be complete* in *3ms* is spelled תַּם (never תָּמַם, a form we might have expected on analogy with סָבַב). These reduced spellings have been inserted in the above table for ס.ב.ב, in brackets.

What distinguishes geminate verbs using the reduced spellings is this: they involve "conditions of being" (such as "being complete"), rather than actions (such as "surrounding"). They belong to the group of verbs called "stative." The קָטַל conjugation of stative verbs (whether geminate or non-geminate) is explained in Appendix §6.5.ג.

6.5.ג. קָטַל conjugation of stative verbs

The יקטל conjugation of stative verbs was presented in Appendix §5.4.ה, using the verb ק.ט.נ *to be* or *become small*. This segment will present the קטל conjugation of stative.

The sound of the קטל conjugation of ק.ט.נ may remind you of the more common spelling of its corresponding adjective, קָטוֹן, since the verb frequently will share the "A-vowel, O-vowel pattern" (as in the *3ms* form: קָטֹן *he was small*). This verb-adjective similarity provides further support for a notion observed earlier: stative verbs often function as if they were conjugated adjectives.

In addition to the A-O vowel sequence found in verbs such as ק.ט.נ, some stative verbs imitate the more familiar A-A vowel pattern of ש.מ.ר (except in *3ms*, where a ṣērê will appear, as in כָּבֵד *he is heavy*).[37] Consequently כ.ב.ד appears below as a second pattern.[38]

Concerning the translation of stative verbs, the קטל connotation of a completed action or condition often will best be rendered as a **present tense** (rather than the customary past tense translation). To

---

[37] The ṣērê is latent in other parts of the stative conjugation, as evident from the *3fs* כָּבְדָה, which in pause is spelled כָּבֵדָה (Gen. 18:20 and Judges 20:34, respectively).

[38] Some stative verbs are vocalized in קָטַל like many fientives (qameṣ-pataḥ). Examples include שָׁכַב *he reclined* and גָּדַל *he is great*. See further in Appendix §5.4.ה. (Exception [3]).

revisit the two examples above, often קָטֹן should be rendered by present tense as *he is small* (not *he was small*), and כָּבֵד often should be rendered *he is heavy* (not *he was heavy*). That will explain the use of present tense in the glosses below.

ק.ט.נ	
קָטֹנּוּ we are small	קָטֹנְתִּי I am small
קְטָנְתֶּם[39] you are small *mpl*	קָטֹנְתָּ you are small *ms*
קְטָנְתֶּן you are small *fpl*	קָטֹנְתְּ you are small *fs*
קָטְנוּ they are small	קָטֹן he is small
	קָטְנָה she is small

כ.ב.ד	
כָּבַדְנוּ we are heavy	כָּבַדְתִּי I am heavy
כְּבַדְתֶּם you are heavy *mpl*	כָּבַדְתָּ you are heavy *ms*
כְּבַדְתֶּן you are heavy *fpl*	כָּבַדְתְּ you are heavy *fs*
כָּבְדוּ they are heavy	כָּבֵד he is heavy
	כָּבְדָה she is heavy

---

[39] The qameṣ in קְטָנְתֶּם and in קְטָנְתֶּן is a qameṣ-ḥaṭuf, pronounced *o*.

Pronominal (Object) Suffixes

With nouns 482

With prepositions and particles 494

With verbs 495

Reference §§3.4.ג., 3.4.א., and 8.2.ד.

Pronominal (Object) Suffixes with Nouns

A full array of words combined with suffixes is provided to make it easier for you to express yourself. First you will find a list of nouns with suffixes, followed by prepositions with suffixes, concluding with verbs combined with suffixes (conjugated forms, infinitives, and imperatives).

Concerning nouns, most employ both singular and plural forms; a few do not. While many forms found below are attested in the Hebrew Bible, some are not and so have been extrapolated. When the Hebrew Bible attests more than one spelling for a given form, the dominant pattern has been selected (e.g., שְׁאֵלְתִי is shown in place of שְׁאֵלָתִי). Preference generally has been given to *plene* (full) forms over *defectiva* (deficient) forms (thus שְׁנוֹתֵיכֶם rather than שְׁנֹתֵיכֶם).

The maqqef (dash) is employed below to signal construct forms. The Hebrew Bible does not always follow construct forms with a maqqef. Spellings below may vary from construct forms in the Hebrew that are followed by a maqqef.

To conserve space, 2nd and 3rd plural endings are compressed. Thus the entry אֲבִיכֶם/ן under the column heading **2m/fpl** indicates that the 2mpl form is אֲבִיכֶם, while the 2fpl form is אֲבִיכֶן.

their… 3m/fpl	your… 2m/fpl	our… 1cpl	her… 3fs	his… 3ms	your… 2fs	your… 2ms	my… 1cs	Def.	Constr.	Absol.	
אֲבִיהֶם/ן	אֲבִיכֶם/ן	אָבִינוּ	אָבִיהָ	אָבִיו	אָבִיךְ	אָבִיךָ	אָבִי	father *m*	אֲבִי-	אָב	.1
אֲבוֹתֵיהֶם/ן	אֲבוֹתֵיכֶם/ן	אֲבוֹתֵינוּ	אֲבוֹתֶיהָ	אֲבוֹתָיו	אֲבוֹתַיִךְ	אֲבוֹתֶיךָ	אֲבוֹתַי		אֲבוֹת-	אָבוֹת	
אֶבְיוֹנָם/ן	אֶבְיוֹנְכֶם/ן	אֶבְיוֹנֵנוּ	אֶבְיוֹנָהּ	אֶבְיוֹנוֹ	אֶבְיוֹנֵךְ	אֶבְיוֹנְךָ	אֶבְיוֹנִי	poor person *m*	אֶבְיוֹן-	אֶבְיוֹן	.2
אֶבְיוֹנֵיהֶם/ן	אֶבְיוֹנֵיכֶם/ן	אֶבְיוֹנֵינוּ	אֶבְיוֹנֶיהָ	אֶבְיוֹנָיו	אֶבְיוֹנַיִךְ	אֶבְיוֹנֶיךָ	אֶבְיוֹנַי		אֶבְיוֹנֵי-	אֶבְיוֹנִים	
אַבְנָם/ן	אַבְנְכֶם/ן	אַבְנֵנוּ	אַבְנָהּ	אַבְנוֹ	אַבְנֵךְ	אַבְנְךָ	אַבְנִי	stone *f*	אֶבֶן-	אֶבֶן	.3
אַבְנֵיהֶם/ן	אַבְנֵיכֶם/ן	אֲבָנֵינוּ	אֲבָנֶיהָ	אֲבָנָיו	אֲבָנַיִךְ	אֲבָנֶיךָ	אֲבָנַי		אַבְנֵי-	אֲבָנִים	
אֲדוֹנָם/ן	אֲדוֹנְכֶם/ן	אֲדוֹנֵנוּ	אֲדוֹנָהּ	אֲדוֹנוֹ	אֲדוֹנֵךְ	אֲדוֹנְךָ	אֲדוֹנִי	lord *m*	אֲדוֹן-	אָדוֹן	.4
אֲדוֹנֵיהֶם/ן	אֲדוֹנֵיכֶם/ן	אֲדוֹנֵינוּ	אֲדוֹנֶיהָ	אֲדוֹנָיו	אֲדוֹנַיִךְ	אֲדוֹנֶיךָ	אֲדוֹנַי		אֲדוֹנֵי-	אֲדוֹנִים	

NOUNS — Pronominal Suffixes

their... 3m/fpl	your... 2m/fpl	our... 1cpl	her... 3fs	his... 3ms	your... 2fs	your... 2ms	my... 1cs	Def.	Constr.	Absol.	
אָהֳלָם/ן אָהֳלֵיהֶם/ן	אָהָלְכֶם/ן אָהֳלֵיכֶם/ן	אָהֳלֵנוּ אָהֳלֵינוּ	אָהֳלָהּ אָהֳלֶיהָ	אָהֳלוֹ אָהֳלָיו	אָהֳלֵךְ אָהֳלַיִךְ	אָהָלְךָ אָהֳלֶיךָ	אָהֳלִי אָהָלַי	tent *m*	אֹהֶל- אָהֳלֵי-	אֹהֶל אֹהָלִים	.5
אֹיְבָם/ן אֹיְבֵיהֶם/ן	אֹיִבְכֶם/ן אֹיְבֵיכֶם/ן	אֹיְבֵנוּ אֹיְבֵינוּ	אֹיְבָהּ אֹיְבֶיהָ	אֹיְבוֹ אֹיְבָיו	אֹיִבֵךְ אֹיְבַיִךְ	אֹיִבְךָ אֹיְבֶיךָ	אֹיְבִי אֹיְבַי	enemy *m*	אֹיֵב- אֹיְבֵי-	אֹיֵב אֹיְבִים	.6
אוֹרָם	אוֹרְכֶם	אוֹרֵנוּ	אוֹרָהּ	אוֹרוֹ	אוֹרֵךְ	אוֹרְךָ	אוֹרִי	light *f*	אוֹר-	אוֹר	.7
אָזְנָם אָזְנֵיהֶם	אָזְנְכֶם אָזְנֵיכֶם	אָזְנֵנוּ אָזְנֵינוּ	אָזְנָהּ אָזְנֶיהָ	אָזְנוֹ אָזְנָיו	אָזְנֵךְ אָזְנַיִךְ	אָזְנְךָ אָזְנֶיךָ	אָזְנִי אָזְנַי	ear *f* dual	אֹזֶן- אָזְנֵי-	אֹזֶן אָזְנַיִם	.8
אֲחִיהֶם/ן אֲחֵיהֶם/ן	אֲחִיכֶם/ן אֲחֵיכֶם/ן	אָחִינוּ אַחֵינוּ	אָחִיהָ אַחֶיהָ	אָחִיו אֶחָיו	אָחִיךְ אַחַיִךְ	אָחִיךָ אַחֶיךָ	אָחִי אַחַי	brother *m*	אֲחִי- אֲחֵי-	אָח אַחִים	.9
אִישָׁם אַנְשֵׁיהֶם	אִישְׁכֶם אַנְשֵׁיכֶם	אִישֵׁנוּ אֲנָשֵׁינוּ	אִישָׁהּ אֲנָשֶׁיהָ	אִישׁוֹ אֲנָשָׁיו	אִישֵׁךְ אֲנָשַׁיִךְ	אִישְׁךָ אֲנָשֶׁיךָ	אִישִׁי אֲנָשַׁי	man *m*	אִישׁ- אַנְשֵׁי-	אִישׁ אֲנָשִׁים	.10
אֱלֹהֵיהֶם	אֱלֹהֵיכֶם	אֱלֹהֵינוּ	אֱלֹהֶיהָ	אֱלֹהָיו	אֱלֹהַיִךְ	אֱלֹהֶיךָ	אֱלֹהַי	God, gods	אֱלֹהֵי-	אֱלֹהִים	.11
אַלְמְנוֹתָם/ן אַלְמְנוֹתֵיהֶם/ן	אַלְמְנוֹתְכֶם/ן אַלְמְנוֹתֵיכֶם/ן	אַלְמְנוֹתֵנוּ אַלְמְנוֹתֵינוּ	אַלְמָנָתָהּ אַלְמְנוֹתֶיהָ	אַלְמָנָתוֹ אַלְמְנוֹתָיו	אַלְמָנָתֵךְ אַלְמְנוֹתַיִךְ	אַלְמָנָתְךָ אַלְמְנוֹתֶיךָ	אַלְמָנָתִי אַלְמְנוֹתַי	widow *f*	אַלְמְנַת- אַלְמְנוֹת-	אַלְמָנָה אַלְמָנוֹת	.12
אַלְפֵיהֶם	אַלְפֵיכֶם	אֲלָפֵינוּ	אֲלָפֶיהָ	אֲלָפָיו	אֲלָפַיִךְ	אֲלָפֶיךָ	אֲלָפַי	cattle *mpl*	אַלְפֵי-	אֲלָפִים	.13
אִמָּם	אִמְּכֶם	אִמֵּנוּ	אִמָּהּ	אִמּוֹ	אִמֵּךְ	אִמְּךָ	אִמִּי	mother *f*	אֵם-	אֵם	.14
אֲמִתָּם	אֲמִתְּכֶם	אֲמִתֵּנוּ	אֲמִתָּהּ	אֲמִתּוֹ	אֲמִתֵּךְ	אֲמִתְּךָ	אֲמִתִּי	truth *f*	אֲמִתּ-	אֱמֶת	.15
אֳנִיֹּתָם	אֳנִיֹּתְכֶם	אֳנִיֹּתֵנוּ	אֳנִיָּתָהּ	אֳנִיָּתוֹ	אֳנִיָּתֵךְ	אֳנִיָּתְךָ	אֳנִיָּתִי	ship *f*	אֳנִיַּת-	אֳנִיָּה	.16
אַפָּם	אַפְּכֶם	אַפֵּנוּ	אַפָּהּ	אַפּוֹ	אַפֵּךְ	אַפְּךָ	אַפִּי	nose *m*	אַף-	אַף	.17

their... 3m/fpl	your... 2m/fpl	our... 1cpl	her... 3fs	his... 3ms	your... 2fs	your... 2ms	my... 1cs	Def.	Constr.	Absol.	
אֲרוֹנָם/ן אֲרוֹנוֹתָם/ן	אֲרוֹנְכֶם/ן אֲרוֹנוֹתֵיכֶם/ן	אֲרוֹנֵנוּ אֲרוֹנוֹתֵינוּ	אֲרוֹנָהּ אֲרוֹנוֹתֶיהָ	אֲרוֹנוֹ אֲרוֹנוֹתָיו	אֲרוֹנֵךְ אֲרוֹנוֹתַיִךְ	אֲרוֹנְךָ אֲרוֹנוֹתֶיךָ	אֲרוֹנִי אֲרוֹנוֹתַי	chest, ark *m*	אֲרוֹן אֲרוֹנוֹת-	אָרוֹן אֲרוֹנוֹת	.18
אַרְצָם/ן אַרְצוֹתָם/ן	אַרְצְכֶם/ן אַרְצוֹתֵיכֶם/ן	אַרְצֵנוּ אַרְצוֹתֵינוּ	אַרְצָהּ אַרְצוֹתֶיהָ	אַרְצוֹ אַרְצוֹתָיו	אַרְצֵךְ אַרְצוֹתַיִךְ	אַרְצְךָ אַרְצוֹתֶיךָ	אַרְצִי אַרְצוֹתַי	land *f*	אֶרֶץ־ אַרְצוֹת-	אֶרֶץ אֲרָצוֹת	.19
אִשְׁתָּם/ן	אֶשְׁתְּכֶם/ן	אִשְׁתֵּנוּ	אִשְׁתָּהּ	אִשְׁתּוֹ	אִשְׁתֵּךְ	אִשְׁתְּךָ	אִשְׁתִּי	woman *f*	אֵשֶׁת־	אִשָּׁה	.20
בִּגְדָּם/ן	בִּגְדְּכֶם/ן	בִּגְדֵּנוּ	בִּגְדָּהּ	בִּגְדוֹ	בִּגְדֵּךְ	בִּגְדְּךָ	בִּגְדִי	garment *m*	בֶּגֶד־	בֶּגֶד	.21
בְּהֶמְתָּם/ן בַּהֲמוֹתָם/ן	בְּהֶמְתְּכֶם/ן בַּהֲמוֹתֵיכֶם/ן	בְּהֶמְתֵּנוּ בַּהֲמוֹתֵינוּ	בְּהֶמְתָּהּ בַּהֲמוֹתֶיהָ	בְּהֶמְתּוֹ בַּהֲמוֹתָיו	בְּהֶמְתֵּךְ בַּהֲמוֹתַיִךְ	בְּהֶמְתְּךָ בַּהֲמוֹתֶיךָ	בְּהֶמְתִּי בַּהֲמוֹתַי	animal *m*	בֶּהֱמַת־ בַּהֲמוֹת-	בְּהֵמָה בְּהֵמוֹת	.22
בִּטְנָם/ן	בִּטְנְכֶם/ן	בִּטְנֵנוּ	בִּטְנָהּ	בִּטְנוֹ	בִּטְנֵךְ	בִּטְנְךָ	בִּטְנִי	belly *f*	בֶּטֶן־	בֶּטֶן	.23
בֵּיתָם/ן	בֵּיתְכֶם/ן	בֵּיתֵנוּ	בֵּיתָהּ	בֵּיתוֹ	בֵּיתֵךְ	בֵּיתְךָ	בֵּיתִי	house *m*	בֵּית־	בַּיִת	.24
בָּמָתָם/ן בָּמוֹתָם/ן	בָּמַתְכֶם/ן בָּמוֹתֵיכֶם/ן	בָּמָתֵנוּ בָּמוֹתֵינוּ	בָּמָתָהּ בָּמוֹתֶיהָ	בָּמָתוֹ בָּמוֹתָיו	בָּמָתֵךְ בָּמוֹתַיִךְ	בָּמָתְךָ בָּמוֹתֶיךָ	בָּמָתִי בָּמוֹתַי	high place *f*	בָּמַת־ בָּמוֹת-	בָּמָה בָּמוֹת	.25
בְּנָם/ן	בִּנְכֶם/ן	בְּנֵנוּ	בְּנָהּ	בְּנוֹ	בְּנֵךְ	בִּנְךָ	בְּנִי	son *m*	בֶּן־	בֵּן	.26
בְּקָרָם/ן	בְּקַרְכֶם/ן	בְּקָרֵנוּ	בְּקָרָהּ	בְּקָרוֹ	בְּקָרֵךְ	בְּקָרְךָ	בְּקָרִי	cattle *m*	בְּקַר-	בָּקָר	.27
בְּרִיתָם/ן	בְּרִיתְכֶם/ן	בְּרִיתֵנוּ	בְּרִיתָהּ	בְּרִיתוֹ	בְּרִיתֵךְ	בְּרִיתְךָ	בְּרִיתִי	covenant *f*	בְּרִית-	בְּרִית	.28
בִּרְכָּם/ן	בִּרְכְּכֶם/ן	בִּרְכֵּנוּ	בִּרְכָּהּ	בִּרְכּוֹ	בִּרְכֵּךְ	בִּרְכְּךָ	בִּרְכִּי	knee *f*	בֶּרֶךְ-	בֶּרֶךְ	.29
בְּשָׂרָם/ן	בְּשַׂרְכֶם/ן	בְּשָׂרֵנוּ	בְּשָׂרָהּ	בְּשָׂרוֹ	בְּשָׂרֵךְ	בְּשָׂרְךָ	בְּשָׂרִי	meat *m*	בְּשַׂר-	בָּשָׂר	.30

Pronominal Suffixes

their... 3m/fpl	your... 2m/fpl	our... 1cpl	her... 3fs	his... 3ms	your... 2fs	your... 2ms	my... 1cs	Def.	Constr.	Absol.	
בָּתָּם/ן	בִּתְּכֶם/ן	בִּתֵּנוּ	בִּתָּהּ	בִּתּוֹ	בִּתֵּךְ	בִּתְּךָ	בִּתִּי	daughter *f*	בַּת־	בַּת	.31
בְּנוֹתָם/ן	בְּנוֹתֵיכֶם/ן	בְּנוֹתֵינוּ	בְּנוֹתֶיהָ	בְּנוֹתָיו	בְּנוֹתַיִךְ	בְּנוֹתֶיךָ	בְּנוֹתַי		בְּנוֹת־	בָּנוֹת	
גְּבוּלָם/ן	גְּבוּלְכֶם/ן	גְּבוּלֵנוּ	גְּבוּלָהּ	גְּבוּלוֹ	גְּבוּלֵךְ	גְּבוּלְךָ	גְּבוּלִי	border *m*	גְּבוּל־	גְּבוּל	.32
גְּבוּלֵיהֶם/ן	גְּבוּלֵיכֶם/ן	גְּבוּלֵינוּ	גְּבוּלֶיהָ	גְּבוּלָיו	גְּבוּלַיִךְ	גְּבוּלֶיךָ	גְּבוּלַי		גְּבוּלֵי־	גְּבוּלִים	
דְּבָרָם/ן	דְּבַרְכֶם/ן	דְּבָרֵנוּ	דְּבָרָהּ	דְּבָרוֹ	דְּבָרֵךְ	דְּבָרְךָ	דְּבָרִי	word, thing *m*	דְּבַר־	דָּבָר	.33
דְּגָם/ן	דְּגַכֶם/ן	דָּגֵנוּ	דָּגָהּ	דָּגוֹ	דָּגֵךְ	דָּגְךָ	דָּגִי	fish *m*	דַּג־	דָּג	.34
דּוֹרָם/ן	דּוֹרְכֶם/ן	דּוֹרֵנוּ	דּוֹרָהּ	דּוֹרוֹ	דּוֹרֵךְ	דּוֹרְךָ	דּוֹרִי	generation *m*	דּוֹר־	דּוֹר	.35
דַּלְתוֹתָם/ן	דַּלְתוֹתֵיכֶם/ן	דַּלְתוֹתֵינוּ	דַּלְתוֹתֶיהָ	דַּלְתוֹתָיו	דַּלְתוֹתַיִךְ	דַּלְתוֹתֶיךָ	דַּלְתוֹתַי	door *f*	דַּלְתוֹת־	דְּלָתוֹת	.36
דָּמָם/ן	דִּמְכֶם/ן	דָּמֵנוּ	דָּמָהּ	דָּמוֹ	דָּמֵךְ	דָּמְךָ	דָּמִי	blood *m*	דַּם־	דָּם	.37
דַּרְכָּם/ן	דַּרְכְּכֶם/ן	דַּרְכֵּנוּ	דַּרְכָּהּ	דַּרְכּוֹ	דַּרְכֵּךְ	דַּרְכְּךָ	דַּרְכִּי	road *m, f*	דֶּרֶךְ־	דֶּרֶךְ	.38
הָרָם/ן	הַרְכֶם/ן	הָרֵנוּ	הָרָהּ	הָרוֹ	הָרֵךְ	הָרְךָ	הָרִי	mountain *m*	הַר־	הַר	.39
זִבְחָם/ן	זִבְחֲכֶם/ן	זִבְחֵנוּ	זִבְחָהּ	זִבְחוֹ	זִבְחֵךְ	זִבְחֲךָ	זִבְחִי	sacrifice *m*	זֶבַח־	זֶבַח	.40
זְהָבָם/ן	זְהַבְכֶם/ן	זְהָבֵנוּ	זְהָבָהּ	זְהָבוֹ	זְהָבֵךְ	זְהָבְךָ	זְהָבִי	gold *m*	זְהַב־	זָהָב	.41
זְרוֹעָם/ן	זְרוֹעֲכֶם/ן	זְרוֹעֵנוּ	זְרוֹעָהּ	זְרוֹעוֹ	זְרוֹעֵךְ	זְרוֹעֲךָ	זְרוֹעִי	arm *f*	זְרוֹעַ־	זְרוֹעַ	.42

their... 3m/fpl	your... 2m/fpl	our... 1cpl	her... 3fs	his... 3ms	your... 2fs	your... 2ms	my... 1cs	Def.	Constr.	Absol.	
זַרְעָם/ן זַרְעֵיהֶם/ן	זַרְעֲכֶם/ן זַרְעֵיכֶם/ן	זַרְעֵנוּ זְרָעֵינוּ	זַרְעָהּ זְרָעֶיהָ	זַרְעוֹ זְרָעָיו	זַרְעֵךְ זְרָעַיִךְ	זַרְעֲךָ זְרָעֶיךָ	זַרְעִי זְרָעַי	descendants m	זֶרַע־ זַרְעֵי־	זֶרַע זְרָעִים	.43
חָדְשָׁם/ן חָדְשֵׁיהֶם/ן	חָדְשְׁכֶם/ן חָדְשֵׁיכֶם/ן	חָדְשֵׁנוּ חֳדָשֵׁינוּ	חָדְשָׁהּ חֳדָשֶׁיהָ	חָדְשׁוֹ חֳדָשָׁיו	חָדְשֵׁךְ חֳדָשַׁיִךְ	חָדְשְׁךָ חֳדָשֶׁיךָ	חָדְשִׁי חֳדָשַׁי	month m	חֹדֶשׁ־ חָדְשֵׁי־	חֹדֶשׁ חֳדָשִׁים	.44
חַטָּאתָם/ן חַטֹּאתֵיהֶם/ן	חַטַּאתְכֶם/ן חַטֹּאתֵיכֶם/ן	חַטָּאתֵנוּ חַטֹּאתֵינוּ	חַטָּאתָהּ חַטֹּאתֶיהָ	חַטָּאתוֹ חַטֹּאתָיו	חַטָּאתֵךְ חַטֹּאתַיִךְ	חַטָּאתְךָ חַטֹּאתֶיךָ	חַטָּאתִי חַטֹּאתַי	sin f	חַטַּאת־ חַטֹּאת־	חַטָּאת חַטָּאוֹת	.45
חַיָּם/ן	חַיְּכֶם/ן	חַיֵּנוּ	חַיֶּהָ	חַיָּיו	חַיַּיִךְ	חַיֶּיךָ	חַיַּי	life m	חַיֵּי־	חַיִּים	.46
חֵילָם/ן חֵילֵיהֶם/ן	חֵילְכֶם/ן חֵילֵיכֶם/ן	חֵילֵנוּ חֵילֵינוּ	חֵילָהּ חֵילֶיהָ	חֵילוֹ חֵילָיו	חֵילֵךְ חֵילַיִךְ	חֵילְךָ חֵילֶיךָ	חֵילִי חֵילַי	army m	חֵיל־ חֵילֵי־	חַיִל חֲיָלִים	.47
חֲמָסָם/ן חֲמָסֵיהֶם/ן	חֲמַסְכֶם/ן חֲמָסֵיכֶם/ן	חֲמָסֵנוּ חֲמָסֵינוּ	חֲמָסָהּ חֲמָסֶיהָ	חֲמָסוֹ חֲמָסָיו	חֲמָסֵךְ חֲמָסַיִךְ	חֲמָסְךָ חֲמָסֶיךָ	חֲמָסִי חֲמָסַי	violence m	חֲמַס־ חַמְסֵי־	חָמָס חֲמָסִים	.48
חַסְדָּם/ן חַסְדֵּיהֶם/ן	חַסְדְּכֶם/ן חַסְדֵּיכֶם/ן	חַסְדֵּנוּ חֲסָדֵינוּ	חַסְדָּהּ חֲסָדֶיהָ	חַסְדּוֹ חֲסָדָיו	חַסְדֵּךְ חֲסָדַיִךְ	חַסְדְּךָ חֲסָדֶיךָ	חַסְדִּי חֲסָדַי	kindness m	חֶסֶד־ חַסְדֵי־	חֶסֶד חֲסָדִים	.49
חַרְבָּם/ן חַרְבוֹתָם/ן	חַרְבְּכֶם/ן חַרְבוֹתֵיכֶם/ן	חַרְבֵּנוּ חַרְבוֹתֵינוּ	חַרְבָּהּ חַרְבוֹתֶיהָ	חַרְבּוֹ חַרְבוֹתָיו	חַרְבֵּךְ חַרְבוֹתַיִךְ	חַרְבְּךָ חַרְבוֹתֶיךָ	חַרְבִּי חַרְבוֹתַי	sword f	חֶרֶב־ חַרְבוֹת־	חֶרֶב חֲרָבוֹת	.50
יָדָם/ן יְדֵיהֶם/ן	יֶדְכֶם/ן יְדֵיכֶם/ן	יָדֵנוּ יָדֵינוּ	יָדָהּ יָדֶיהָ	יָדוֹ יָדָיו	יָדֵךְ יָדַיִךְ	יָדְךָ יָדֶיךָ	יָדִי יָדַי	hand f dual	יַד־ יְדֵי־	יָד יָדַיִם	.51
יוֹמָם/ן יְמֵיהֶם/ן	יוֹמְכֶם/ן יְמֵיכֶם/ן	יוֹמֵנוּ יָמֵינוּ	יוֹמָהּ יָמֶיהָ	יוֹמוֹ יָמָיו	יוֹמֵךְ יָמַיִךְ	יוֹמְךָ יָמֶיךָ	יוֹמִי יָמַי	day m	יוֹם־ יְמֵי־	יוֹם יָמִים	.52
יֵינָם/ן	יֵינְכֶם/ן	יֵינֵנוּ	יֵינָהּ	יֵינוֹ	יֵינֵךְ	יֵינְךָ	יֵינִי	wine m	יֵין־	יַיִן	.53
יַלְדָּם/ן יַלְדֵיהֶם/ן	יַלְדְּכֶם/ן יַלְדֵיכֶם/ן	יַלְדֵּנוּ יְלָדֵינוּ	יַלְדָּהּ יְלָדֶיהָ	יַלְדּוֹ יְלָדָיו	יַלְדֵּךְ יְלָדַיִךְ	יַלְדְּךָ יְלָדֶיךָ	יַלְדִּי יְלָדַי	child m	יֶלֶד־ יַלְדֵי־	יֶלֶד יְלָדִים	.54
יִרְאָתָם/ן	יִרְאַתְכֶם/ן	יִרְאָתֵנוּ	יִרְאָתָהּ	יִרְאָתוֹ	יִרְאָתֵךְ	יִרְאָתְךָ	יִרְאָתִי	fear f	יִרְאַת־	יִרְאָה	.55

Pronominal Suffixes

their... 3m/fpl	your... 2m/fpl	our... 1cpl	her... 3fs	his... 3ms	your... 2fs	your... 2ms	my... 1cs	Def.	Constr.	Absol.	
חַבְלָם/ן	חַבְלְכֶם/ן	חַבְלֵנוּ	חַבְלָהּ	חַבְלוֹ	חַבְלֵךְ	חַבְלְךָ	חַבְלִי	cord *m*	חֶבֶל־	חֶבֶל	.56
חַבְלֵיהֶם/ן	חַבְלֵיכֶם/ן	חֲבָלֵינוּ	חֲבָלֶיהָ	חֲבָלָיו	חֲבָלַיִךְ	חֲבָלֶיךָ	חֲבָלַי		חַבְלֵי־	חֲבָלִים	
כְּבוֹדָם/ן	כְּבוֹדְכֶם/ן	כְּבוֹדֵנוּ	כְּבוֹדָהּ	כְּבוֹדוֹ	כְּבוֹדֵךְ	כְּבוֹדְךָ	כְּבוֹדִי	glory *m*	כְּבוֹד־	כָּבוֹד	.57
כֹּהֲנָם/ן	כֹּהֲנְכֶם/ן	כֹּהֲנֵנוּ	כֹּהֲנָהּ	כֹּהֲנוֹ	כֹּהֲנֵךְ	כֹּהֲנְךָ	כֹּהֲנִי	priest *m*	כֹּהֵן־	כֹּהֵן	.58
כֹּהֲנֵיהֶם/ן	כֹּהֲנֵיכֶם/ן	כֹּהֲנֵינוּ	כֹּהֲנֶיהָ	כֹּהֲנָיו	כֹּהֲנַיִךְ	כֹּהֲנֶיךָ	כֹּהֲנַי		כֹּהֲנֵי־	כֹּהֲנִים	
כּוֹסָם/ן	כּוֹסְכֶם/ן	כּוֹסֵנוּ	כּוֹסָהּ	כּוֹסוֹ	כּוֹסֵךְ	כּוֹסְךָ	כּוֹסִי	cup *f*	כּוֹס־	כּוֹס	.59
כּוֹסוֹתָם/ן	כּוֹסוֹתֵיכֶם/ן	כּוֹסוֹתֵינוּ	כּוֹסוֹתֶיהָ	כּוֹסוֹתָיו	כּוֹסוֹתַיִךְ	כּוֹסוֹתֶיךָ	כּוֹסוֹתַי		כּוֹסוֹת־	כּוֹסוֹת	
כֹּחָם/ן	כֹּחֲכֶם/ן	כֹּחֵנוּ	כֹּחָהּ	כֹּחוֹ	כֹּחֵךְ	כֹּחֲךָ	כֹּחִי	strength *m*	כֹּחַ־	כֹּחַ	.60
שַׂקָּם/ן	שַׂקְּכֶם/ן	שַׂקֵּנוּ	שַׂקָּהּ	שַׂקּוֹ	שַׂקֵּךְ	שַׂקְּךָ	שַׂקִּי	sack *m*	שַׂק־	שַׂק	.61
שַׂקֵּיהֶם/ן	שַׂקֵּיכֶם/ן	שַׂקֵּינוּ	שַׂקֶּיהָ	שַׂקָּיו	שַׂקַּיִךְ	שַׂקֶּיךָ	שַׂקַּי		שַׂקֵּי־	שַׂקִּים	
כִּסְאָם/ן	כִּסְאֲכֶם/ן	כִּסְאֵנוּ	כִּסְאָהּ	כִּסְאוֹ	כִּסְאֵךְ	כִּסְאֲךָ	כִּסְאִי	chair *m*	כִּסֵּא־	כִּסֵּא	.62
כִּסְאוֹתֵיהֶם/ן	כִּסְאוֹתֵיכֶם/ן	כִּסְאוֹתֵינוּ	כִּסְאוֹתֶיהָ	כִּסְאוֹתָיו	כִּסְאוֹתַיִךְ	כִּסְאוֹתֶיךָ	כִּסְאוֹתַי		כִּסְאוֹת־	כִּסְאוֹת	
כְּסִילָם/ן	כְּסִילְכֶם/ן	כְּסִילֵנוּ	כְּסִילָהּ	כְּסִילוֹ	כְּסִילֵךְ	כְּסִילְךָ	כְּסִילִי	fool *m*	כְּסִיל־	כְּסִיל	.63
כְּסִילֵיהֶם/ן	כְּסִילֵיכֶם/ן	כְּסִילֵינוּ	כְּסִילֶיהָ	כְּסִילָיו	כְּסִילַיִךְ	כְּסִילֶיךָ	כְּסִילַי		כְּסִילֵי־	כְּסִילִים	
כַּסְפָּם/ן	כַּסְפְּכֶם/ן	כַּסְפֵּנוּ	כַּסְפָּהּ	כַּסְפּוֹ	כַּסְפֵּךְ	כַּסְפְּךָ	כַּסְפִּי	money *m*	כֶּסֶף־	כֶּסֶף	.64
כַּסְפֵּיהֶם/ן	כַּסְפֵּיכֶם/ן	כַּסְפֵּינוּ	כַּסְפֶּיהָ	כַּסְפָּיו	כַּסְפַּיִךְ	כַּסְפֶּיךָ	כַּסְפַּי		כַּסְפֵּי־	כְּסָפִים	
לִבָּם/ן	לִבְּכֶם/ן	לִבֵּנוּ	לִבָּהּ	לִבּוֹ	לִבֵּךְ	לִבְּךָ	לִבִּי	heart *m*	לֵב־	לֵב	.65
לִבּוֹתֵיהֶם/ן	לִבּוֹתֵיכֶם/ן	לִבּוֹתֵינוּ	לִבּוֹתֶיהָ	לִבּוֹתָיו	לִבּוֹתַיִךְ	לִבּוֹתֶיךָ	לִבּוֹתַי	(alt. sing.)	לִבּוֹת־	לִבּוֹת	
לַחְמָם/ן	לַחְמְכֶם/ן	לַחְמֵנוּ	לַחְמָהּ	לַחְמוֹ	לַחְמֵךְ	לַחְמְךָ	לַחְמִי	bread *m*	לֶחֶם־	לֶחֶם	.66
מְגִלָּתָם/ן	מְגִלַּתְכֶם/ן	מְגִלָּתֵנוּ	מְגִלָּתָהּ	מְגִלָּתוֹ	מְגִלָּתֵךְ	מְגִלָּתְךָ	מְגִלָּתִי	scroll *f*	מְגִלַּת־	מְגִלָּה	.67
מְגִלּוֹתֵיהֶם/ן	מְגִלּוֹתֵיכֶם/ן	מְגִלּוֹתֵינוּ	מְגִלּוֹתֶיהָ	מְגִלּוֹתָיו	מְגִלּוֹתַיִךְ	מְגִלּוֹתֶיךָ	מְגִלּוֹתַי		מְגִלּוֹת־	מְגִלּוֹת	
מוֹתָם/ן	מוֹתְכֶם/ן	מוֹתֵנוּ	מוֹתָהּ	מוֹתוֹ	מוֹתֵךְ	מוֹתְךָ	מוֹתִי	death *m*	מוֹת־	מָוֶת	.68

	their... 3m/fpl	your... 2m/fpl	our... 1cpl	her... 3fs	his... 3ms	your... 2fs	your... 2ms	my... 1cs	Def.	Constr.	Absol.	
	מִזְבְּחָם/ן מִזְבְּחוֹתָם/ן	מִזְבַּחֲכֶם/ן מִזְבְּחוֹתֵיכֶם/ן	מִזְבְּחֵנוּ מִזְבְּחוֹתֵינוּ	מִזְבְּחָהּ מִזְבְּחוֹתֶיהָ	מִזְבְּחוֹ מִזְבְּחוֹתָיו	מִזְבַּחֵךְ מִזְבְּחוֹתַיִךְ	מִזְבַּחֲךָ מִזְבְּחוֹתֶיךָ	מִזְבְּחִי מִזְבְּחוֹתַי	altar f	מִזְבַּח־ מִזְבְּחוֹת־	מִזְבֵּחַ מִזְבְּחוֹת	.69
	מַחְשְׁבֹתָם/ן	מַחְשְׁבֹתֵיכֶם/ן	מַחְשְׁבֹתֵינוּ	מַחְשְׁבֹתֶיהָ	מַחְשְׁבֹתָיו	מַחְשְׁבֹתַיִךְ	מַחְשְׁבֹתֶיךָ	מַחְשְׁבֹתַי	thought, plan f	מַחְשְׁבוֹת־	מַחֲשָׁבוֹת	.70
	מֵימָם/ן	מֵימֵיכֶם/ן	מֵימֵינוּ	מֵימֶיהָ	מֵימָיו	מֵימַיִךְ	מֵימֶיךָ	מֵימַי	water m	מֵי־	מַיִם	.71
	מַלְאָכָם/ן	מַלְאַכְכֶם/ן	מַלְאָכֵנוּ	מַלְאָכָהּ	מַלְאָכוֹ	מַלְאָכֵךְ	מַלְאָכֲךָ	מַלְאָכִי	messenger m	מַלְאַךְ־	מַלְאָךְ	.72
	מַלְכָּם/ן	מַלְכְּכֶם/ן	מַלְכֵּנוּ	מַלְכָּהּ	מַלְכּוֹ	מַלְכֵּךְ	מַלְכְּךָ	מַלְכִּי	king m	מֶלֶךְ־	מֶלֶךְ	.73
	מַלְכָּתָם/ן	מַלְכַּתְכֶם/ן	מַלְכָּתֵנוּ	מַלְכָּתָהּ	מַלְכָּתוֹ	מַלְכָּתֵךְ	מַלְכָּתְךָ	מַלְכָּתִי	queen f	מַלְכַּת־	מַלְכָּה	.74
	מַתְּנוֹתָם/ן	מַתְּנוֹתֵיכֶם/ן	מַתְּנוֹתֵינוּ	מַתְּנוֹתֶיהָ	מַתְּנוֹתָיו	מַתְּנוֹתַיִךְ	מַתְּנוֹתֶיךָ	מַתְּנוֹתַי	gift f	מַתְּנוֹת־	מַתָּנוֹת	.75
	מִסְפָּרָם/ן	מִסְפַּרְכֶם/ן	מִסְפָּרֵנוּ	מִסְפָּרָהּ	מִסְפָּרוֹ	מִסְפָּרֵךְ	מִסְפָּרְךָ	מִסְפָּרִי	number m	מִסְפַּר־	מִסְפָּר	.76
	מַעֲנָתָם/ן	מַעֲנַתְכֶם/ן	מַעֲנָתֵנוּ	מַעֲנָתָהּ	מַעֲנָתוֹ	מַעֲנָתֵךְ	מַעֲנָתְךָ	מַעֲנָתִי	answer f	מַעֲנַת־	מַעֲנָה	.77
	מְעָרָתָם/ן	מְעָרַתְכֶם/ן	מְעָרָתֵנוּ	מְעָרָתָהּ	מְעָרָתוֹ	מְעָרָתֵךְ	מְעָרָתְךָ	מְעָרָתִי	cave f	מְעָרַת־	מְעָרָה	.78
	מַעֲשָׂם/ן	מַעֲשֵׂיכֶם/ן	מַעֲשֵׂנוּ	מַעֲשָׂהּ	מַעֲשֵׂהוּ	מַעֲשֵׂךְ	מַעֲשְׂךָ	מַעֲשִׂי	work, deed f	מַעֲשֵׂה־	מַעֲשֶׂה	.79
	מִצְוֺתָם/ן	מִצְוֺתֵיכֶם/ן	מִצְוֺתֵינוּ	מִצְוֺתֶיהָ	מִצְוֺתָיו	מִצְוֺתַיִךְ	מִצְוֺתֶיךָ	מִצְוֺתַי	commandment f	מִצְוֺת־	מִצְוֺת	.80

Pronominal Suffixes

	their... 3m/fpl	your... 2m/fpl	our... 1cpl	her... 3fs	his... 3ms	your... 2fs	your... 2ms	my... 1cs	Def.	Constr.	Absol.	
	מְקוֹמָם/ מְקוֹמוֹתָם	מְקוֹמְכֶם/ מְקוֹמוֹתֵיכֶם	מְקוֹמֵנוּ	מְקוֹמָהּ	מְקוֹמוֹ	מְקוֹמֵךְ	מְקוֹמְךָ	מְקוֹמִי	place *m*	מְקוֹם- מְקוֹמוֹת-	מָקוֹם מְקוֹמוֹת	.81
	מִרְמָתָם	מִרְמַתְכֶם	מִרְמָתֵנוּ	מִרְמָתָהּ	מִרְמָתוֹ	מִרְמָתֵךְ	מִרְמָתְךָ	מִרְמָתִי	deceit *f*	מִרְמַת	מִרְמָה	.82
	מַשָּׂאָם	מַשַּׂאֲכֶם	מַשָּׂאֵנוּ	מַשָּׂאָהּ	מַשָּׂאוֹ	מַשָּׂאֵךְ	מַשָּׂאֲךָ	מַשָּׂאִי	burden *m*	מַשָּׂא-	מַשָּׂא	.83
	מִשְׁפְּחוֹתָם	מִשְׁפַּחְתְּכֶם	מִשְׁפַּחְתֵּנוּ	מִשְׁפַּחְתָּהּ	מִשְׁפַּחְתּוֹ	מִשְׁפַּחְתֵּךְ	מִשְׁפַּחְתְּךָ	מִשְׁפַּחְתִּי	family *f*	מִשְׁפַּחַת- מִשְׁפְּחוֹת-	מִשְׁפָּחָה מִשְׁפָּחוֹת	.85
	מִשְׁפָּטָם	מִשְׁפַּטְכֶם	מִשְׁפָּטֵנוּ	מִשְׁפָּטָהּ	מִשְׁפָּטוֹ	מִשְׁפָּטֵךְ	מִשְׁפָּטְךָ	מִשְׁפָּטִי	judgment *m*	מִשְׁפַּט-	מִשְׁפָּט	.86
	נְבִיאָם	נְבִיאֲכֶם	נְבִיאֵנוּ	נְבִיאָהּ	נְבִיאוֹ	נְבִיאֵךְ	נְבִיאֲךָ	נְבִיאִי	prophet *m*	נְבִיא-	נָבִיא	.87
	נְבִיאָתָם	נְבִיאַתְכֶם	נְבִיאָתֵנוּ	נְבִיאָתָהּ	נְבִיאָתוֹ	נְבִיאָתֵךְ	נְבִיאָתְךָ	נְבִיאָתִי	prophetess *f*	נְבִיאַת-	נְבִיאָה	.88
	נִגְעָם	נִגְעֲכֶם	נִגְעֵנוּ	נִגְעָהּ	נִגְעוֹ	נִגְעֵךְ	נִגְעֲךָ	נִגְעִי	plague *m*	נֶגַע-	נֶגַע	.89
	נִדְרָם	נִדְרְכֶם	נִדְרֵנוּ	נִדְרָהּ	נִדְרוֹ	נִדְרֵךְ	נִדְרְךָ	נִדְרִי	vow *m*	נֶדֶר-	נֶדֶר	.90
	נַחֲלָתָם	נַחֲלַתְכֶם	נַחֲלָתֵנוּ	נַחֲלָתָהּ	נַחֲלָתוֹ	נַחֲלָתֵךְ	נַחֲלָתְךָ	נַחֲלָתִי	property *f*	נַחֲלַת-	נַחֲלָה	.91

their... 3mf/pl	your... 2mf/pl	our... 1cpl	her... 3fs	his... 3ms	your... 2fs	your... 2ms	my... 1cs	Def.	Constr.	Absol.	
נִפְלְאֹתָם/ן	נִפְלְאֹתֵיכֶם/ן	נִפְלְאֹתֵינוּ	נִפְלְאֹתֶיהָ	נִפְלְאֹתָיו	נִפְלְאֹתַיִךְ	נִפְלְאֹתֶיךָ	נִפְלְאֹתַי	miraculous acts f	נִפְלְאוֹת־	נִפְלָאוֹת	.92
נַפְשָׁם/ן	נַפְשְׁכֶם/ן	נַפְשֵׁנוּ	נַפְשָׁהּ	נַפְשׁוֹ	נַפְשֵׁךְ	נַפְשְׁךָ	נַפְשִׁי	soul, person f	נֶפֶשׁ־	נֶפֶשׁ	.93
סֻכֹּתָם/ן	סֻכֹּתְכֶם/ן	סֻכֹּתֵינוּ	סֻכָּתָהּ	סֻכָּתוֹ	סֻכָּתֵךְ	סֻכָּתְךָ	סֻכָּתִי	hut f	סֻכַּת־	סֻכָּה	.94
סִפְרָם/ן	סִפְרְכֶם/ן	סִפְרֵנוּ	סִפְרָהּ	סִפְרוֹ	סִפְרֵךְ	סִפְרְךָ	סִפְרִי	book m	סֵפֶר־	סֵפֶר	.95
סִתְרָם/ן	סִתְרְכֶם/ן	סִתְרֵנוּ	סִתְרָהּ	סִתְרוֹ	סִתְרֵךְ	סִתְרְךָ	סִתְרִי	hiding place m	סֵתֶר־	סֵתֶר	.96
עַבְדָּם/ן	עַבְדְּכֶם/ן	עַבְדֵּנוּ	עַבְדָּהּ	עַבְדּוֹ	עַבְדֵּךְ	עַבְדְּךָ	עַבְדִּי	servant m	עֶבֶד־	עֶבֶד	.97
עֲבֹדָתָם/ן	עֲבֹדַתְכֶם/ן	עֲבֹדָתֵנוּ	עֲבֹדָתָהּ	עֲבֹדָתוֹ	עֲבֹדָתֵךְ	עֲבֹדָתְךָ	עֲבֹדָתִי	work f	עֲבֹדַת־	עֲבֹדָה	.98
עֲוֹנָם/ן	עֲוֹנְכֶם/ן	עֲוֹנֵנוּ	עֲוֹנָהּ	עֲוֹנוֹ	עֲוֹנֵךְ	עֲוֹנְךָ	עֲוֹנִי	iniquity m	עֲוֹן־	עָוֹן	.99
עוֹפָם/ן	עוֹפְכֶם/ן	עוֹפֵנוּ	עוֹפָהּ	עוֹפוֹ	עוֹפֵךְ	עוֹפְךָ	עוֹפִי	bird(s) m	עוֹף־	עוֹף	.100
עֲטַרְתָּם/ן	עֲטַרְתְּכֶם/ן	עֲטַרְתֵּנוּ	עֲטַרְתָּהּ	עֲטַרְתּוֹ	עֲטַרְתֵּךְ	עֲטַרְתְּךָ	עֲטַרְתִּי	crown f	עֲטֶרֶת־	עֲטָרָה	.101
עֵינָם/ן	עֵינְכֶם/ן	עֵינֵנוּ	עֵינָהּ	עֵינוֹ	עֵינֵךְ	עֵינְךָ	עֵינִי	eye f	עֵין־	עַיִן	.102
עִירָם/ן	עִירְכֶם/ן	עִירֵנוּ	עִירָהּ	עִירוֹ	עִירֵךְ	עִירְךָ	עִירִי	city f	עִיר־	עִיר	.103
עֹלָתָם/ן	עֹלַתְכֶם/ן	עֹלָתֵנוּ	עֹלָתָהּ	עֹלָתוֹ	עֹלָתֵךְ	עֹלָתְךָ	עֹלָתִי	burnt offering f	עֹלַת־	עֹלָה	.104

Pronominal Suffixes

	their... 3m/fpl	your... 2m/fpl	our... 1cpl	her... 3fs	his... 3ms	your... 2fs	your... 2ms	my... 1cs	Def.	Constr.	Absol.	
	עַמָּם/ן	עַמְּכֶם/ן	עַמֵּנוּ	עַמָּהּ	עַמּוֹ	עַמֵּךְ	עַמְּךָ	עַמִּי	people *m*	עַם־	עַם	.105
	עַמֵּיהֶם/ן	עַמֵּיכֶם/ן	עַמֵּינוּ	עַמֶּיהָ	עַמָּיו	עַמַּיִךְ	עַמֶּיךָ	עַמַּי		עַמֵּי־	עַמִּים	
	עֵצָם	עֵצְכֶם	עֵצֵנוּ	עֵצָהּ	עֵצוֹ	עֵצֵךְ	עֵצְךָ	עֵצִי	tree *m*	עֵץ־	עֵץ	.106
	עֲצֵיהֶם	עֲצֵיכֶם	עֲצֵינוּ	עֲצֶיהָ	עֵצָיו	עֲצַיִךְ	עֲצֶיךָ	עֵצַי		עֲצֵי־	עֵצִים	
	עֲצָתָם	עֲצַתְכֶם	עֲצָתֵנוּ	עֲצָתָהּ	עֲצָתוֹ	עֲצָתֵךְ	עֲצָתְךָ	עֲצָתִי	counsel *f*	עֲצַת־	עֵצָה	.107
	עֲצוֹתֵיהֶם	עֲצוֹתֵיכֶם	עֲצוֹתֵינוּ	עֲצוֹתֶיהָ	עֲצוֹתָיו	עֲצוֹתַיִךְ	עֲצוֹתֶיךָ	עֲצוֹתַי		עֲצוֹת־	עֵצוֹת	
	עַצְמָם	עַצְמְכֶם	עַצְמֵנוּ	עַצְמָהּ	עַצְמוֹ	עַצְמֵךְ	עַצְמְךָ	עַצְמִי	bone *f*	עֶצֶם־	עֶצֶם	.108
	עַצְמוֹתֵיהֶם	עַצְמוֹתֵיכֶם	עַצְמוֹתֵינוּ	עַצְמוֹתֶיהָ	עַצְמוֹתָיו	עַצְמוֹתַיִךְ	עַצְמוֹתֶיךָ	עַצְמוֹתַי		עַצְמוֹת־	עֲצָמוֹת	
	עִתָּם	עִתְּכֶם	עִתֵּנוּ	עִתָּהּ	עִתּוֹ	עִתֵּךְ	עִתְּךָ	עִתִּי	time *f*	עֵת־	עֵת	.109
	עִתֵּיהֶם	עִתֵּיכֶם	עִתֵּינוּ	עִתֶּיהָ	עִתָּיו	עִתַּיִךְ	עִתֶּיךָ	עִתַּי		עִתֵּי־	עִתִּים	
	פִּיהֶם	פִּיכֶם	פִּינוּ	פִּיהָ	פִּיו	פִּיךְ	פִּיךָ	פִּי	mouth *m*	פִּי־	פֶּה	.110
	פְּנֵיהֶם	פְּנֵיכֶם	פָּנֵינוּ	פָּנֶיהָ	פָּנָיו	פָּנַיִךְ	פָּנֶיךָ	פָּנַי	face(s) *mpl*	פְּנֵי־	פָּנִים	.111
	פְּסִילֵיהֶם	פְּסִילֵיכֶם	פְּסִילֵינוּ	פְּסִילֶיהָ	פְּסִילָיו	פְּסִילַיִךְ	פְּסִילֶיךָ	פְּסִילַי	idol *m*	פְּסִילֵי־	פְּסִילִים	.112
	פַּעֲמָם	פַּעַמְכֶם	פַּעֲמֵנוּ	פַּעֲמָהּ	פַּעֲמוֹ	פַּעֲמֵךְ	פַּעַמְךָ	פַּעֲמִי	occurrence, step *f*	פַּעַם־	פַּעַם	.113
	פִּשְׁעָם	פִּשְׁעֲכֶם	פִּשְׁעֵנוּ	פִּשְׁעָהּ	פִּשְׁעוֹ	פִּשְׁעֵךְ	פִּשְׁעֲךָ	פִּשְׁעִי	transgression *f*	פֶּשַׁע־	פֶּשַׁע	.114
	צֹאנָם	צֹאנְכֶם	צֹאנֵנוּ	צֹאנָהּ	צֹאנוֹ	צֹאנֵךְ	צֹאנְךָ	צֹאנִי	flock *f*	צֹאן־	צֹאן	.115
	צִדְקָתָם	צִדְקַתְכֶם	צִדְקָתֵנוּ	צִדְקָתָהּ	צִדְקָתוֹ	צִדְקָתֵךְ	צִדְקָתְךָ	צִדְקָתִי	righteousness *f*	צִדְקַת־	צְדָקָה	.116
	צוּרָם	צוּרְכֶם	צוּרֵנוּ	צוּרָהּ	צוּרוֹ	צוּרֵךְ	צוּרְךָ	צוּרִי	rock, cliff *m*	צוּר־	צוּר	.117

their... 3m/fpl	your... 2m/fpl	our... 1cpl	her... 3fs	his... 3ms	your... 2fs	your... 2ms	my... 1cs	Def.	Constr.	Absol.	
צִלָּם/ן צִלְלָתָם/ן	צִלְּכֶם/ן צִלְלַתְכֶם/ן	צִלֵּנוּ צִלְלָתֵנוּ	צִלָּהּ צִלְלָתָהּ	צִלּוֹ צִלְלָתוֹ	צִלֵּךְ צִלְלָתֵךְ	צִלְּךָ צִלְלָתְךָ	צִלִּי צִלְלָתִי	shadow *m*	צֵל- צִלְלַת-	צֵל צְלָלִים	.118
צָרָם/ן	צָרְכֶם/ן	צָרֵנוּ	צָרָהּ	צָרוֹ	צָרֵךְ	צָרְךָ	צָרִי	distress *m*	צַר-	צַר	.119
קִבְרָם/ן	קִבְרְכֶם/ן	קִבְרֵנוּ	קִבְרָהּ	קִבְרוֹ	קִבְרֵךְ	קִבְרְךָ	קִבְרִי	grave *m*	קֶבֶר-	קֶבֶר	.120
קָדְשָׁם/ן	קָדְשְׁכֶם/ן	קָדְשֵׁנוּ	קָדְשָׁהּ	קָדְשׁוֹ	קָדְשֵׁךְ	קָדְשְׁךָ	קָדְשִׁי	holiness	קֹדֶשׁ-	קֹדֶשׁ	.121
קוֹלָם/ן	קוֹלְכֶם/ן	קוֹלֵנוּ	קוֹלָהּ	קוֹלוֹ	קוֹלֵךְ	קוֹלְךָ	קוֹלִי	voice *m*	קוֹל-	קוֹל	.122
רָאשָׁם/ן	רֹאשְׁכֶם/ן	רֹאשֵׁנוּ	רֹאשָׁהּ	רֹאשׁוֹ	רֹאשֵׁךְ	רֹאשְׁךָ	רֹאשִׁי	head *m*	רֹאשׁ-	רֹאשׁ	.123
רַגְלָם/ן	רַגְלְכֶם/ן	רַגְלֵנוּ	רַגְלָהּ	רַגְלוֹ	רַגְלֵךְ	רַגְלְךָ	רַגְלִי	foot *f*	רֶגֶל-	רֶגֶל	.124
רַגְלֵיהֶם/ן	רַגְלֵיכֶם/ן	רַגְלֵינוּ	רַגְלֶיהָ	רַגְלָיו	רַגְלַיִךְ	רַגְלֶיךָ	רַגְלַי	dual	רַגְלֵי-	רַגְלַיִם	.125
רוּחָם/ן	רוּחֲכֶם/ן	רוּחֵנוּ	רוּחָהּ	רוּחוֹ	רוּחֵךְ	רוּחֲךָ	רוּחִי	spirit *f*	רוּחַ-	רוּחַ	.126
רֵעָם/ן	רֵעֲכֶם/ן	רֵעֵנוּ	רֵעָהּ	רֵעוֹ	רֵעֵךְ	רֵעֲךָ	רֵעִי	friend *m*	רֵעַ-	רֵעַ	.127
רָעָתָם/ן	רָעַתְכֶם/ן	רָעָתֵנוּ	רָעָתָהּ	רָעָתוֹ	רָעָתֵךְ	רָעָתְךָ	רָעָתִי	evil, misery *f*	רָעַת-	רָעָה	.128
שְׁאֵלָתָם/ן	שְׁאֵלַתְכֶם/ן	שְׁאֵלָתֵנוּ	שְׁאֵלָתָהּ	שְׁאֵלָתוֹ	שְׁאֵלָתֵךְ	שְׁאֵלָתְךָ	שְׁאֵלָתִי	question *f*	שְׁאֵלַת-	שְׁאֵלָה שְׁאֵלוֹת	
שְׂדוֹתָם/ן	שְׂדוֹתֵיכֶם/ן	שְׂדוֹתֵינוּ	שְׂדוֹתֶיהָ	שְׂדוֹתָיו	שְׂדוֹתַיִךְ	שְׂדוֹתֶיךָ	שְׂדוֹתַי	field *f*	שְׂדוֹת-	שָׂדוֹת	.129

	their... 3m/fpl	your... 2m/fpl	our... 1cpl	her... 3fs	his... 3ms	your... 2fs	your... 2ms	my... 1cs	Def.	Constr.	Absol.	
	שָׁחְדָּם/ן	שָׁחְדְּכֶם/ן	שָׁחְדֵּנוּ	שָׁחְדָּהּ	שָׁחְדּוֹ	שָׁחְדֵּךְ	שָׁחְדְּךָ	שָׁחְדִּי	bribe m	שֹׁחַד־	שֹׁחַד	.130
	שְׁלוֹמָם/ן	שְׁלוֹמְכֶם/ן	שְׁלוֹמֵנוּ	שְׁלוֹמָהּ	שְׁלוֹמוֹ	שְׁלוֹמֵךְ	שְׁלוֹמְךָ	שְׁלוֹמִי	peace m	שְׁלוֹם־	שָׁלוֹם	.131
	שְׁלוֹמוֹתֵיהֶם/ן	שְׁלוֹמוֹתֵיכֶם/ן	שְׁלוֹמוֹתֵינוּ	שְׁלוֹמוֹתֶיהָ	שְׁלוֹמוֹתָיו	שְׁלוֹמוֹתַיִךְ	שְׁלוֹמוֹתֶיךָ	שְׁלוֹמוֹתַי		שְׁלוֹמוֹת־	שְׁלוֹמוֹת	
	שֻׁלְחָנָם/ן	שֻׁלְחַנְכֶם/ן	שֻׁלְחָנֵנוּ	שֻׁלְחָנָהּ	שֻׁלְחָנוֹ	שֻׁלְחָנֵךְ	שֻׁלְחָנְךָ	שֻׁלְחָנִי	table m	שֻׁלְחַן־	שֻׁלְחָן	.132
	שֻׁלְחֲנוֹתֵיהֶם/ן	שֻׁלְחֲנוֹתֵיכֶם/ן	שֻׁלְחֲנוֹתֵינוּ	שֻׁלְחֲנוֹתֶיהָ	שֻׁלְחֲנוֹתָיו	שֻׁלְחֲנוֹתַיִךְ	שֻׁלְחֲנוֹתֶיךָ	שֻׁלְחֲנוֹתַי		שֻׁלְחֲנוֹת־	שֻׁלְחָנוֹת	
	שְׁמָם/ן		שְׁמֵנוּ	שְׁמָהּ	שְׁמוֹ	שְׁמֵךְ	שִׁמְךָ	שְׁמִי	name m	שֵׁם־	שֵׁם	.133
	שְׁמוֹתָם/ן	שְׁמוֹתֵיכֶם/ן	שְׁמוֹתֵינוּ	שְׁמוֹתֶיהָ	שְׁמוֹתָיו	שְׁמוֹתַיִךְ	שְׁמוֹתֶיךָ	שְׁמוֹתַי		שְׁמוֹת־	שֵׁמוֹת	
	שְׁנָתָם/ן	שְׁנַתְכֶם/ן	שְׁנָתֵנוּ	שְׁנָתָהּ	שְׁנָתוֹ	שְׁנָתֵךְ	שְׁנָתְךָ	שְׁנָתִי	year f	שְׁנַת־	שָׁנָה	.134
	שַׁעְרָם/ן	שַׁעַרְכֶם/ן	שַׁעֲרֵנוּ	שַׁעְרָהּ	שַׁעֲרוֹ	שַׁעֲרֵךְ	שַׁעַרְךָ	שַׁעֲרִי	gate m	שַׁעַר־	שַׁעַר	.135
	שְׂפָתָם/ן	שְׂפַתְכֶם/ן	שְׂפָתֵנוּ	שְׂפָתָהּ	שְׂפָתוֹ	שְׂפָתֵךְ	שְׂפָתְךָ	שְׂפָתִי	lip f	שְׂפַת־	שָׂפָה	.136
	שִׂפְתוֹתֵיהֶם/ן	שִׂפְתוֹתֵיכֶם/ן	שִׂפְתוֹתֵינוּ	שִׂפְתוֹתֶיהָ	שִׂפְתוֹתָיו	שִׂפְתוֹתַיִךְ	שִׂפְתוֹתֶיךָ	שִׂפְתוֹתַי	dual	שִׂפְתֵי־	שְׂפָתַיִם	
	שַׂקָּם/ן	שַׂקְּכֶם/ן	שַׂקֵּנוּ	שַׂקָּהּ	שַׂקּוֹ	שַׂקֵּךְ	שַׂקְּךָ	שַׂקִּי	sack, sackcloth m	שַׂק־	שַׂק	.137
	שִׁקְרָם/ן	שִׁקְרְכֶם/ן	שִׁקְרֵנוּ	שִׁקְרָהּ	שִׁקְרוֹ	שִׁקְרֵךְ	שִׁקְרְךָ	שִׁקְרִי	falsehood m	שֶׁקֶר־	שֶׁקֶר	.138
	שָׂרָם/ן	שַׂרְכֶם/ן	שָׂרֵנוּ	שָׂרָהּ	שָׂרוֹ	שָׂרֵךְ	שָׂרְךָ	שָׂרִי	commander, prince m	שַׂר־	שַׂר	.139
	תּוֹרָתָם/ן	תּוֹרַתְכֶם/ן	תּוֹרָתֵנוּ	תּוֹרָתָהּ	תּוֹרָתוֹ	תּוֹרָתֵךְ	תּוֹרָתְךָ	תּוֹרָתִי	law f	תּוֹרַת־	תּוֹרָה	.140
	תְּחִנָּתָם/ן	תְּחִנַּתְכֶם/ן	תְּחִנָּתֵנוּ	תְּחִנָּתָהּ	תְּחִנָּתוֹ	תְּחִנָּתֵךְ	תְּחִנָּתְךָ	תְּחִנָּתִי	supplication m	תְּחִנַּת־	תְּחִנָּה	.141

Pronominal (Object) Suffixes with Prepositions and Particles

...them 3m/fpl	...you 2m/fpl	...us 1cpl	...her 3fs	...him 3ms	...you 2fs	...you 2ms	...me 1cs	Def.		
אַחֲרֵיהֶם/ן	אַחֲרֵיכֶם/ן	אַחֲרֵינוּ	אַחֲרֶיהָ	אַחֲרָיו	אַחֲרַיִךְ	אַחֲרֶיךָ	אַחֲרַי	after, behind	אַחֲרֵי	1.
אֵינָם/ן	אֵינְכֶם/ן	אֵינֶנּוּ	אֵינֶנָּה	אֵינֶנּוּ	אֵינֵךְ	אֵינְךָ	אֵינֶנִּי	there is not	אֵין	2.
אֲלֵיהֶם/ן	אֲלֵיכֶם/ן	אֵלֵינוּ	אֵלֶיהָ	אֵלָיו	אֵלַיִךְ	אֵלֶיךָ	אֵלַי	to	אֶל	3.
אֹתָם/ן	אֶתְכֶם/ן	אֹתָנוּ	אֹתָהּ	אֹתוֹ	אֹתָךְ	אֹתְךָ	אֹתִי	[def. dir. object]	אֵת	4.
אִתָּם/ן	אִתְּכֶם/ן	אִתָּנוּ	אִתָּהּ	אִתּוֹ	אִתָּךְ	אִתְּךָ	אִתִּי	with	אֵת	5.
בָּהֶם, בָּם/ן	בָּכֶם/ן	בָּנוּ	בָּהּ	בּוֹ	בָּךְ	בְּךָ	בִּי	in, by means of	בְּ...	6.
בֵּינֵיהֶם/ן	בֵּינֵיכֶם/ן	בֵּינֵינוּ	בֵּינָהּ	בֵּינוֹ	בֵּינֵךְ	בֵּינְךָ	בֵּינִי	between, among	בֵּין	7.
בִּלְעָדָם/ן	בִּלְעַדְכֶם/ן	בִּלְעָדֵנוּ	בִּלְעָדֶיהָ	בִּלְעָדָיו	בִּלְעָדַיִךְ	בִּלְעָדֶיךָ	בִּלְעָדַי	without	בִּלְעֲדֵי	8.
בְּתוֹכָם/ן	בְּתוֹכְכֶם/ן	בְּתוֹכֵנוּ	בְּתוֹכָהּ	בְּתוֹכוֹ	בְּתוֹכֵךְ	בְּתוֹכְךָ	בְּתוֹכִי	in the middle of	בְּתוֹךְ	9.
הִנָּם/ן	הִנְּכֶם/ן	הִנֶּנּוּ, הִנְּנוּ	הִנָּהּ	הִנּוֹ	הִנֵּךְ	הִנְּךָ	הִנְנִי, הִנֶּנִּי	behold	הִנֵּה	10.
כָּהֶם/ן, כְּמוֹהֶם/ן	כָּכֶם/ן, כְּמוֹכֶם/ן	כָּמוֹנוּ	כָּמוֹהָ	כָּמוֹהוּ	כָּמוֹךְ	כָּמוֹךָ	כָּמוֹנִי	like, as	כְּ..., כְּמוֹ	11. 12.
לָהֶם/ן	לָכֶם/ן	לָנוּ	לָהּ	לוֹ	לָךְ	לְךָ	לִי	to, for	לְ...	13.
לִפְנֵיהֶם/ן	לִפְנֵיכֶם/ן	לְפָנֵינוּ	לְפָנֶיהָ	לְפָנָיו	לְפָנַיִךְ	לְפָנֶיךָ	לְפָנַי	before, in front of	לִפְנֵי	14.
מֵהֶם/ן	מִכֶּם/ן	מִמֶּנּוּ	מִמֶּנָּה	מִמֶּנּוּ	מִמֵּךְ	מִמְּךָ	מִנִּי, מִמֶּנִּי	from, than	מִן	15.
מִנְהֶם/ן				מִנֵּהוּ						16.
נֶגְדָּם/ן	נֶגְדְּכֶם/ן	נֶגְדֵּנוּ	נֶגְדָּהּ	נֶגְדּוֹ	נֶגְדֵּךְ	נֶגְדְּךָ	נֶגְדִּי	opposite	נֶגֶד	17.
סְבִיבוֹתֵיהֶם/ן	סְבִיבוֹתֵיכֶם/ן	סְבִיבוֹתֵינוּ	סְבִיבוֹתֶיהָ	סְבִיבוֹתָיו	סְבִיבוֹתַיִךְ	סְבִיבוֹתֶיךָ	סְבִיבוֹתַי	around	סָבִיב	18.
עֲדֵיהֶם/ן	עֲדֵיכֶם/ן	עָדֵינוּ	עָדֶיהָ	עָדָיו	עָדַיִךְ	עָדֶיךָ	עָדַי	as far as	עַד	19.
עוֹדָם/ן	עוֹדְכֶם/ן	עוֹדֶנּוּ	עוֹדֶנָּה	עוֹדֶנּוּ	עוֹדָךְ	עוֹדְךָ	עוֹדִי, עוֹדֶנִּי	still, yet	עוֹד	20. 21.
עֲלֵיהֶם/ן	עֲלֵיכֶם/ן	עָלֵינוּ	עָלֶיהָ	עָלָיו	עָלַיִךְ	עָלֶיךָ	עָלַי	on	עַל	22.
עַל־יָדָם/ן	עַל־יֶדְכֶם/ן	עַל־יָדֵנוּ	עַל־יָדָהּ	עַל־יָדוֹ	עַל־יָדֵךְ	עַל־יָדְךָ	עַל־יָדִי	beside	עַל־יַד	23.
עִמָּם/ן	עִמָּכֶם/ן	עִמָּנוּ	עִמָּהּ	עִמּוֹ	עִמָּךְ	עִמְּךָ	עִמִּי	together with	עִם	24.
תַּחְתָּם/ן	תַּחְתֵּיכֶם/ן	תַּחְתֵּינוּ	תַּחְתֶּיהָ	תַּחְתָּיו	תַּחְתַּיִךְ	תַּחְתֶּיךָ	תַּחְתַּי	under	תַּחַת	25.

PRONOMINAL (OBJECT) SUFFIXES WITH VERBS

Isolated Pronominal (Object) Suffixes, shown with Sample 3ms קטל Form[1]					
Suffix alone	**3ms קטל with suffixes**	**Meaning**	**Suffix alone**	**3ms קטל with suffixes**	**Meaning**
־ֿנוּ	שְׁמָרָֿנוּ	he guarded us	־ַֿנִי	שְׁמָרַֿנִי	he guarded me
־ְכֶם	שְׁמַרְכֶם	he guarded you *mpl*	־ְךָ	שְׁמָרְךָ	he guarded you *ms*
־ְכֶן	שְׁמַרְכֶן	he guarded you *fpl*	־ֵךְ	שְׁמָרֵךְ	he guarded you *fs*
־ָם	שְׁמָרָם	he guarded them *m*	־וֹ, ־ָֿהוּ	שְׁמָרוֹ, שְׁמָרָֿהוּ[2]	he guarded him / it
־ָן	שְׁמָרָן	he guarded them *f*	־ָהּ	שְׁמָרָהּ	he guarded her / it

Isolated Pronominal (Object) Suffixes, shown with Sample 3ms יקטל Form					
Suffix alone	**3ms יקטל with suffixes**	**Meaning**	**Suffix alone**	**3ms יקטל with suffixes**	**Meaning**
־ֿנוּ	יִשְׁמְרֵֿנוּ	he will guard us	־ֵֿנִי	יִשְׁמְרֵֿנִי	he will guard me
־ְכֶם	יִשְׁמָרְכֶם	he will guard you *mpl*	־ְךָ	יִשְׁמָרְךָ[3], יִשְׁמְרֶֿךָּ[4]	he will guard you *ms*
־ְכֶן	יִשְׁמָרְכֶן	he will guard you *fpl*	־ֵךְ	יִשְׁמְרֵךְ	he will guard you *fs*
־ָם	יִשְׁמְרֵם	he will guard them *m*	־ֵֿהוּ	יִשְׁמְרֵֿהוּ, יִשְׁמְרֶֿנּוּ, יִשְׁמְרוֹ	he will guard him / it
־ֵן	יִשְׁמְרֵן	he will guard them *f*	־ֶֿהָ	יִשְׁמְרֶֿהָ, יִשְׁמְרֶֿנָּה	he will guard her / it

---

[1] Cf. §8.2.ד.

[2] The hollow verb שׂ.י.מ attests both suffixes: שָׂמוֹ (Ezek. 17:4) and שָׂמָהוּ (Ezek. 7:20), both meaning *he placed him*; the verb ש.מ.ר only attests שְׁמָרוֹ *he guarded him*. III-ה/י verbs employ ־ָֿהוּ (e.g., רָאָֿהוּ *he saw him*).

[3] Note the qameṣ-ḥaṭuf in יִשְׁמָרְךָ, יִשְׁמָרְכֶם, and יִשְׁמָרְכֶן.

[4] The following forms display an energic נ: יִשְׁמְרֶֿךָּ, יִשְׁמְרֶֿנּוּ, and יִשְׁמְרֶֿנָּה.

Infinitive Construct	Pronominal (Object) Suffixes with Complete קטל Conjugation for Strong Verbs in Qal בִּנְיָן[5]								Object Suffix
to guard...	they guarded...	you (2mpl) guarded...[6]	we guarded...	she guarded...	he guarded...	you (2fs) guarded...	you (2ms) guarded...	I guarded...	
[לְ]שְׁמֹר	שָׁמְרוּ	שְׁמַרְתֶּם	שָׁמַרְנוּ	שָׁמְרָה	שָׁמַר	שָׁמַרְתְּ	שָׁמַרְתָּ	שָׁמַרְתִּי	[without suffix]
[לְ]שָׁמְרִי	שְׁמָרוּנִי	שְׁמַרְתּוּנִי	N/A	שְׁמָרַתְנִי	שְׁמָרַנִי	שְׁמַרְתִּינִי	שְׁמַרְתַּנִי	N/A	...me
[לְ]שָׁמְרְךָ	שְׁמָרוּךָ	N/A	שְׁמַרְנוּךָ	שְׁמָרַתְךָ	שְׁמָרְךָ	N/A	N/A	שְׁמַרְתִּיךָ	...you (2ms)
[לְ]שָׁמְרֵךְ	שְׁמָרוּךְ	N/A	שְׁמַרְנוּךְ	שְׁמָרַתְךְ	שְׁמָרֵךְ	N/A	N/A	שְׁמַרְתִּיךְ	...you (2fs)
[לְ]שָׁמְרוֹ	שְׁמָרוּהוּ	שְׁמַרְתּוּהוּ	שְׁמַרְנוּהוּ	שְׁמָרַתְהוּ	שְׁמָרָהוּ[8] / שְׁמָרוֹ	שְׁמַרְתִּיהוּ	שְׁמַרְתּוֹ	שְׁמַרְתִּיהוּ[7] / שְׁמַרְתִּיו	...him / it
[לְ]שָׁמְרָהּ	שְׁמָרוּהָ	שְׁמַרְתּוּהָ	שְׁמַרְנוּהָ	שְׁמָרַתָּה	שְׁמָרָהּ	שְׁמַרְתִּיהָ	שְׁמַרְתָּהּ	שְׁמַרְתִּיהָ	...her / it
[לְ]שָׁמְרֵנוּ	שְׁמָרוּנוּ	שְׁמַרְתּוּנוּ	N/A	שְׁמָרַתְנוּ	שְׁמָרָנוּ	שְׁמַרְתִּינוּ	שְׁמַרְתָּנוּ	שְׁמַרְתִּינוּ	...us
[לְ]שָׁמְרְכֶם	שְׁמָרוּכֶם	N/A	שְׁמַרְנוּכֶם	שְׁמָרַתְכֶם	שְׁמָרְכֶם	N/A	N/A	שְׁמַרְתִּיכֶם	...you (2mpl)
[לְ]שָׁמְרְכֶן	שְׁמָרוּכֶן	N/A	שְׁמַרְנוּכֶן	שְׁמָרַתְכֶן	שְׁמָרְכֶן	N/A	N/A	שְׁמַרְתִּיכֶן	...you (2fpl)
[לְ]שָׁמְרָם	שְׁמָרוּם	שְׁמַרְתּוּם	שְׁמַרְנוּם	שְׁמָרַתַם	שְׁמָרָם	שְׁמַרְתִּים	שְׁמַרְתָּם	שְׁמַרְתִּים	...them (3mpl)
[לְ]שָׁמְרָן	שְׁמָרוּן	שְׁמַרְתּוּן	שְׁמַרְנוּן	שְׁמָרַתַן	שְׁמָרָן	שְׁמַרְתִּין	שְׁמַרְתָּן	שְׁמַרְתִּין	...them (3fpl)

---

[5] Forms that would be reflexive in meaning (I do something to myself, you do something to yourself) are omitted ("N/A") since Hebrew routinely employs a distinct בִּנְיָן to express reflexivity (e.g., the hitpael בִּנְיָן). For more details concerning pronominal object suffixes with the קטל conjugation, cf. GKC §§58 – 61 and *IBH* §§184 – 90.

[6] The קטל 2mpl base to which suffixed pronouns are added is שְׁמַרְתּוּ (cf. GKC §59). It is difficult to conjecture whether 2fpl קטל forms with an object suffix would have been distinct from comparable 2mpl forms, since no 2fpl forms with object suffixes are attested in the Hebrew Bible. In the case of יקטל forms, we find masculine some forms serving for feminine (see note, below).

[7] Some verbs attest both suffix forms (e.g., וּנְתַתִּיהוּ in Judg. 4:7, and וּנְתַתִּיו in 1 Sam. 1:11 or Ezek. 7:20).

[8] The hollow verb ש.י.מ attests both suffixes: שָׂמוֹ (Ezek. 17:4) and שָׂמָהוּ (Ezek. 7:20), both meaning *he placed him*; the verb ש.מ.ר only attests שְׁמָרוֹ *he guarded him*.

Pronominal Suffixes

Infinitive Construct	Pronominal (Object) Suffixes with Complete קטל Conjugation for III-ה/י Verbs in Qal בִּנְיָן								
to acquire…[9]	they acquired…	you (2mpl) acquired…	we acquired…	she acquired…	he acquired…	you (2fs) acquired…	you (2ms) acquired…	I acquired…	Object Suffix
[לִ]קְנוֹת	קָנוּ	קְנִיתֶם[10]	קָנִינוּ	קָנְתָה	קָנָה	קָנִית	קָנִיתָ	קָנִיתִי	[without suffix]
[לִ]קְנוֹתִי	קָנוּנִי	קְנִיתוּנִי	N/A	קָנַתְנִי	קָנַנִי	קְנִיתִנִי	N/A	N/A	…me
[לִ]קְנוֹתְךָ	קָנוּךָ	N/A	קְנִינוּךָ	קָנַתְךָ	קָנְךָ	N/A	N/A	קְנִיתִיךָ	…you (2ms)
[לִ]קְנוֹתֵךְ	קָנוּךְ	N/A	קְנִינוּךְ	קָנַתְךְ	קָנָךְ	N/A	N/A	קְנִיתִיךְ	…you (2fs)
[לִ]קְנוֹתוֹ	קָנוּהוּ	קְנִיתוּהוּ	קְנִינוּהוּ	קָנַתְהוּ / קָנָתוֹ	קָנָהוּ	קְנִיתִיהוּ	קְנִיתוֹ[11]	קְנִיתִיהוּ / קְנִיתִיו	…him / it
[לִ]קְנוֹתָהּ	קָנוּהָ	קְנִיתוּהָ	קְנִינוּהָ	קָנָתָהּ	קָנָהּ	קְנִיתִיהָ	קְנִיתָהּ	קְנִיתִיהָ	…her / it
[לִ]קְנוֹתֵנוּ	קָנוּנוּ	קְנִיתוּנוּ	N/A	קָנַתְנוּ	קָנָנוּ	קְנִיתָנוּ	קְנִיתָנוּ	קְנִיתִינוּ	…us
[לִ]קְנוֹתְכֶם	קָנוּכֶם	N/A	קְנִינוּכֶם	קָנַתְכֶם	קָנָכֶם	N/A	N/A	קְנִיתִיכֶם	…you (2mpl)
[לִ]קְנוֹתְכֶן	קָנוּכֶן	N/A	קְנִינוּכֶן	קָנַתְכֶן	קָנָכֶן	N/A	N/A	קְנִיתִיכֶן	…you (2fpl)
[לִ]קְנוֹתָם	קָנוּם	קְנִיתוּם	קְנִינוּם	קָנָתַם	קָנָם	קְנִיתִים	קְנִיתָם	קְנִיתִים	…them (3mpl)
[לִ]קְנוֹתָן	קָנוּן	קְנִיתוּן	קְנִינוּן	קָנָתַן	קָנָן	קְנִיתִין	קְנִיתָן	קְנִיתִין	…them (3fpl)

---

[9] The infinitive construct often appears with defective spelling (e.g., [לִ]קְנֹת instead of [לִ]קְנוֹת).

[10] The קטל 2mpl base to which suffixed pronouns are added is קְנִיתוּ (cf. GKC §59).

[11] On analogy with piel כִּסִּיתוֹ (Ps. 104:6).

Object Suffix	I will guard...	you (2ms) / she (3fs) will guard...	you (2fs) will guard...	he will guard...	we will guard...	you (2mpl) will guard...[13]	they (3mpl) will guard...
[without suffix]	אֶשְׁמֹר	תִּשְׁמֹר	תִּשְׁמְרִי	יִשְׁמֹר	נִשְׁמֹר	תִּשְׁמְרוּ	יִשְׁמְרוּ
...me	N/A	תִּשְׁמְרֵנִי	תִּשְׁמְרִינִי	יִשְׁמְרֵנִי	N/A	תִּשְׁמְרוּנִי	יִשְׁמְרוּנִי[14]
...you (2ms)	אֶשְׁמָרְךָ	N/A	N/A	יִשְׁמָרְךָ	נִשְׁמָרְךָ	N/A	יִשְׁמְרוּךָ
...you (2ms, energic נ)[15]	אֶשְׁמָרֶךָּ	N/A	N/A		נִשְׁמָרֶךָּ		
...you (2fs)	אֶשְׁמְרֵךְ	N/A	N/A	יִשְׁמְרֵךְ	נִשְׁמְרֵךְ	N/A	יִשְׁמְרוּךְ
...him / it	אֶשְׁמְרֵהוּ	תִּשְׁמְרֵהוּ	תִּשְׁמְרֵיהוּ	יִשְׁמְרֵהוּ	נִשְׁמְרֵהוּ	תִּשְׁמְרֵהוּ	יִשְׁמְרוּהוּ
...him / it (energic נ)	אֶשְׁמְרֶנּוּ	תִּשְׁמְרֶנּוּ		יִשְׁמְרֶנּוּ יִשְׁמְרוֹ	נִשְׁמְרֶנּוּ		יִשְׁמְרֻנוּ[16]
...her / it		תִּשְׁמְרֶהָ	תִּשְׁמְרֶיהָ	יִשְׁמְרֶהָ	נִשְׁמְרֶהָ	תִּשְׁמְרוּהָ	יִשְׁמְרוּהָ
...her / it (energic נ)	אֶשְׁמְרֶנָּה	תִּשְׁמְרֶנָּה		יִשְׁמְרֶנָּה	נִשְׁמְרֶנָּה	תִּשְׁמְרֶנָּה	יִשְׁמְרוּנָה
...us	אֶשְׁמְרֵנוּ	תִּשְׁמְרֵנוּ	תִּשְׁמְרִינוּ	יִשְׁמְרֵנוּ	N/A	תִּשְׁמְרֵנוּ	יִשְׁמְרוּנוּ
...you (2mpl)	אֶשְׁמָרְכֶם	N/A	N/A	יִשְׁמָרְכֶם	נִשְׁמָרְכֶם	N/A	יִשְׁמְרוּכֶם
...you (2fpl)	אֶשְׁמָרְכֶן	N/A	N/A	יִשְׁמָרְכֶן	נִשְׁמָרְכֶן	N/A	יִשְׁמְרוּכֶן
...them (3mpl)	אֶשְׁמְרֵם	תִּשְׁמְרֵם	תִּשְׁמְרִים	יִשְׁמְרֵם	נִשְׁמְרֵם	תִּשְׁמְרוּם	יִשְׁמְרוּם
...them (3fpl)	אֶשְׁמְרֵן	תִּשְׁמְרֵן	תִּשְׁמְרִין	יִשְׁמְרֵן	נִשְׁמְרֵן	תִּשְׁמְרוּן	יִשְׁמְרוּן

---

[12] For more details concerning pronominal object suffixes with the יקטל conjugation, cf. *IBH* §192.

[13] Evidently the *2mpl* forms with suffixes served for *3fpl* as well (cf. Job 19:15 and Jer. 2:19). Perhaps they served for *2fpl* as well (since the base form is the same as *3fpl*), although no יקטל *2fpl* verbs with object suffixes are attested.

[14] III-א verbs tend to employ a nunated form: יִמְצָאֻנְגִי *they will find me*.

[15] The force of the energic (or epenthetic) nun is only phonetic, not semantic (Joüon §61f, p. 160).

[16] The *3ms* suffix נוּ- is attested for the qal בִּנְיָן only in יִלְכְּדֻנוֹ *they will capture him* (Prov. 5:22).

Pronominal Suffixes

Pronominal (Object) Suffixes with Complete יקטל Conjugation for III-ה/י Verbs in Qal בִּנְיָן							
they (3mpl) will acquire…	you (2mpl) will acquire…[17]	we will acquire…	he will acquire…	you (2fs) will acquire…	you (2ms) / she (3fs) will acquire…	I will acquire…	Object Suffix
יִקְנוּ	תִּקְנוּ	נִקְנֶה	יִקְנֶה	תִּקְנִי	תִּקְנֶה	אֶקְנֶה	[without suffix]
יִקְנוּנִי	תִּקְנוּנִי	N/A	יִקְנֵנִי	תִּקְנִינִי	תִּקְנֵנִי	N/A	…me
יִקְנוּךָ	N/A	נִקְנְךָ	יִקְנְךָ	N/A	N/A	אֶקְנְךָ	…you (2ms)
N/A	N/A	נִקְנֶךָּ	יִקְנֶךָּ	N/A	N/A	אֶקְנֶךָּ	…you (2ms, energic נ)
יִקְנוּךְ	N/A	נִקְנֵךְ	יִקְנֵךְ	N/A	N/A	אֶקְנֵךְ	…you (2fs)
יִקְנוּהוּ	תִּקְנוּהוּ	נִקְנֵהוּ[19]	יִקְנֵהוּ	תִּקְנֵהוּ	[note 18]	אֶקְנֵהוּ	…him / it
			יִקְנֶנּוּ		תִּקְנֶנּוּ	אֶקְנֶנּוּ	…him / it (energic נ)
יִקְנוּהָ	תִּקְנוּהָ		יִקְנֶהָ	תִּקְנֶהָ	תִּקְנֶהָ		…her / it
		נִקְנֶנָּה	יִקְנֶנָּה			אֶקְנֶנָּה	…her / it (energic נ)
יִקְנוּנוּ	תִּקְנוּנוּ	N/A	יִקְנֵנוּ	תִּקְנֵנוּ	תִּקְנֵנוּ	אֶקְנֵנוּ	…us
יִקְנוּכֶם	N/A	נִקְנְכֶם	יִקְנְכֶם	N/A	N/A	אֶקְנְכֶם	…you (2mpl)
יִקְנוּכֶן	N/A	נִקְנְכֶן	יִקְנְכֶן	N/A	N/A	אֶקְנְכֶן	…you (2fpl)
יִקְנוּם	תִּקְנוּם	נִקְנֵם	יִקְנֵם	תִּקְנִים	תִּקְנֵם	אֶקְנֵם	…them (3mpl)
יִקְנוּן	תִּקְנוּן	נִקְנֵן	יִקְנֵן	תִּקְנֵן	תִּקְנֵן	אֶקְנֵן	…them (3fpl)

---

[17] See previous note concerning *2mpl* forms and *3fpl* forms with suffixes.

[18] A blank field among the nunated and non-nunated rows suggests that, based on attested spellings, convention may have preferred certain forms to the exclusion of other nearly-equivalent forms. Thus, in the absence of any non-nunated forms attested for III-ה/י qal יקטל *2ms* with a *2ms* suffix (forms that would have been spelled תִּקְנֵהוּ), perhaps convention dictated that only the corresponding nunated form תִּקְנֶנּוּ was used.

Among the nunated and non-nunated rows, when a field is left blank, it suggests that since a particular form is not attested—but its alternative (nunated or non-nunated) is attested, perhaps only the alternative was employed.

[19] A nunated form is attested in the hifil (נַשְׁקֶנּוּ *we will cause him to drink*, Gen. 19:34), although not in the qal.

Pronominal (Object) Suffixes with Imperatives									
III-Guttural Qal Verbs			**III-י/ה Qal Verbs**			**Strong Qal Verbs**			
Send! (2mpl)	Send! (2fs)	Send! (2ms)	Acquire! (2mpl)	Acquire! (2fs)	Acquire! (2ms)	Guard! (2mpl)[21]	Guard! (2fs)[20]	Guard! (2ms)	Object Suffix
שִׁלְחוּ	שִׁלְחִי	שְׁלַח	קְנוּ	קְנִי	קְנֵה	שִׁמְרוּ	שִׁמְרִי	שְׁמֹר	[without suffix]
שְׁלָחוּנִי	שְׁלָחִינִי	שְׁלָחֵנִי	קְנוּנִי	קְנִינִי	קְנֵנִי	שָׁמְרוּנִי	שָׁמְרִינִי	שָׁמְרֵנִי[22]	...me
שְׁלָחוּהוּ	שְׁלָחִיהוּ	שְׁלָחֵהוּ	קְנוּהוּ	קְנִיהוּ	קְנֵהוּ	שָׁמְרוּהוּ	שָׁמְרִיהוּ	שָׁמְרֵהוּ	...him / it
שְׁלָחוּהָ	שְׁלָחִיהָ	שְׁלָחֶנָּה	קְנוּהָ	קְנִיהָ	קְנֶנָּה	שָׁמְרוּהָ	שָׁמְרִיהָ	שָׁמְרֶהָ, שָׁמְרָה	...her / it
שְׁלָחוּנוּ	שְׁלָחִינוּ	שְׁלָחֵנוּ	קְנוּנוּ	קְנִינוּ	קְנֵנוּ	שָׁמְרוּנוּ	שָׁמְרִינוּ	שָׁמְרֵנוּ	...us
שְׁלָחוּם	שְׁלָחִים	שְׁלָחֵם	קְנוּם	קְנִים	קְנֵם	שָׁמְרוּם	שָׁמְרִים	שָׁמְרֵם	...them (3mpl)
שְׁלָחוּן	שְׁלָחִין	שְׁלָחֵן	קְנוּן	קְנִין	קְנֵן	שָׁמְרוּן	שָׁמְרִין	שָׁמְרֵן	...them (3fpl)

---

[20] While the Hebrew Bible gives ample evidence for feminine imperatives, none appear with object suffixes.

[21] *Fpl* imperatives with suffixes do not appear in this table since, on analogy with יקטל indicative forms, they evidently were served by *mpl* imperative forms with suffixes (see earlier note, GKC §61f).

[22] When accompanied by a pronominal object suffix, the first syllable in ש.מ.ר imperative forms will comprise a closed syllable. Thus the qameṣ vowel in forms such as שָׁמְרֵנִי is a qameṣ-ḥaṭuf.

Verbal Array for Qal בִּנְיָן

(shown with ש.מ.ר, meaning *guard* in qal בִּנְיָן)

Command Forms

fpl	mpl	fs	ms	
נִשְׁמְרָה let's guard		אֶשְׁמְרָה may I guard		cohort.
שְׁמֹרְנָה guard!	שִׁמְרוּ guard!	שִׁמְרִי guard!	שְׁמֹר guard!	imv.
תִּשְׁמֹרְנָה may they guard	יִשְׁמְרוּ may they guard	תִּשְׁמֹר may she guard	יִשְׁמֹר may he guard	jussive

Infinitives

to guard	שָׁמוֹר	inf. absolute
to guard	[לְ]שְׁמֹר	inf. construct

Participles

fpl	mpl	fs	ms
שֹׁמְרוֹת	שֹׁמְרִים	שֹׁמֶרֶת שֹׁמְרָה	שֹׁמֵר
ones who guard		one who guards	

יקטל

נִשְׁמֹר we will guard	אֶשְׁמֹר I will guard
תִּשְׁמְרוּ you will guard *mpl*	תִּשְׁמֹר you will guard *ms*
תִּשְׁמֹרְנָה you will guard *fpl*	תִּשְׁמְרִי you will guard *fs*
יִשְׁמְרוּ they will guard *m*	יִשְׁמֹר he will guard
תִּשְׁמֹרְנָה they will guard *f*	תִּשְׁמֹר she will guard

קטל

שָׁמַרְנוּ we guarded	שָׁמַרְתִּי I guarded
שְׁמַרְתֶּם you guarded *mpl*	שָׁמַרְתָּ you guarded *ms*
שְׁמַרְתֶּן you guarded *fpl*	שָׁמַרְתְּ you guarded *fs*
שָׁמְרוּ they guarded	שָׁמַר he guarded
	שָׁמְרָה she guarded

Conjugation of Selected Verbs in Qal בִּנְיָן קטל

3cpl	2m/fpl	1cpl	3fs	3ms	2fs	2ms	1cs	שרש	Qal Def.
אָבְדוּ	אֲבַדְתֶּם/ן	אָבַדְנוּ	אָבְדָה	אָבַד	אָבַדְתְּ	אָבַדְתָּ	אָבַדְתִּי	א.ב.ד	to perish
אָהֲבוּ	אֲהַבְתֶּם/ן	אָהַבְנוּ	אָהֲבָה	אָהַב	אָהַבְתְּ	אָהַבְתָּ	אָהַבְתִּי	א.ה.ב	to love
אָכְלוּ	אֲכַלְתֶּם/ן	אָכַלְנוּ	אָכְלָה	אָכַל	אָכַלְתְּ	אָכַלְתָּ	אָכַלְתִּי	א.כ.ל	to eat
אָמְרוּ	אֲמַרְתֶּם/ן	אָמַרְנוּ	אָמְרָה	אָמַר	אָמַרְתְּ	אָמַרְתָּ	אָמַרְתִּי	א.מ.ר	to say
אָסְפוּ	אֲסַפְתֶּם/ן	אָסַפְנוּ	אָסְפָה	אָסַף	אָסַפְתְּ	אָסַפְתָּ	אָסַפְתִּי	א.ס.פ	to gather
בָּאוּ	בָּאתֶם/ן	בָּאנוּ	בָּאָה	בָּא	בָּאת	בָּאתָ	בָּאתִי	ב.ו.א	to come, enter
בּוֹשׁוּ	בּוֹשְׁתֶּם/ן	בֹּשְׁנוּ	בּוֹשָׁה	בּוֹשׁ	בֹּשְׁתְּ	בֹּשְׁתָּ	בֹּשְׁתִּי	ב.ו.שׁ	to be ashamed
בָּנוּ	בַּנְתֶּם/ן	בַּנּוּ	בָּנָה	בִּין	בַּנְתְּ	בַּנְתָּ	בִּינֹתִי	ב.י.נ	to understand
בָּכוּ	בְּכִיתֶם/ן	בָּכִינוּ	בָּכְתָה	בָּכָה	בָּכִית	בָּכִיתָ	בָּכִיתִי	ב.כ.י/ה	to weep
בָּלְעוּ	בְּלַעְתֶּם/ן	בָּלַעְנוּ	בָּלְעָה	בָּלַע	בָּלַעַתְּ	בָּלַעְתָּ	בָּלַעְתִּי	ב.ל.ע	to swallow
בָּנוּ	בְּנִיתֶם/ן	בָּנִינוּ	בָּנְתָה	בָּנָה	בָּנִית	בָּנִיתָ	בָּנִיתִי	ב.נ.י/ה	to build
גָּנְבוּ	גְּנַבְתֶּם/ן	גָּנַבְנוּ	גָּנְבָה	גָּנַב	גָּנַבְתְּ	גָּנַבְתָּ	גָּנַבְתִּי	ג.נ.ב	to steal
דָּרְשׁוּ	דְּרַשְׁתֶּם/ן	דָּרַשְׁנוּ	דָּרְשָׁה	דָּרַשׁ	דָּרַשְׁתְּ	דָּרַשְׁתָּ	דָּרַשְׁתִּי	ד.ר.שׁ	to investigate
הָיוּ	הֱיִיתֶם/ן	הָיִינוּ	הָיְתָה	הָיָה	הָיִית	הָיִיתָ	הָיִיתִי	ה.י.י/ה	to be, become
הָלְכוּ	הֲלַכְתֶּם/ן	הָלַכְנוּ	הָלְכָה	הָלַךְ	הָלַכְתְּ	הָלַכְתָּ	הָלַכְתִּי	ה.ל.כ	to go, walk
זָבְחוּ	זְבַחְתֶּם/ן	זָבַחְנוּ	זָבְחָה	זָבַח	זָבַחַתְּ	זָבַחְתָּ	זָבַחְתִּי	ז.ב.ח	to sacrifice
זָכְרוּ	זְכַרְתֶּם/ן	זָכַרְנוּ	זָכְרָה	זָכַר	זָכַרְתְּ	זָכַרְתָּ	זָכַרְתִּי	ז.כ.ר	to remember
חָזְקוּ	חֲזַקְתֶּם/ן	חָזַקְנוּ	חָזְקָה	חָזַק	חָזַקְתְּ	חָזַקְתָּ	חָזַקְתִּי	ח.ז.ק	to be strong
חָטְאוּ	חֲטָאתֶם/ן	חָטָאנוּ	חָטְאָה	חָטָא	חָטָאת	חָטָאתָ	חָטָאתִי	ח.ט.א	to sin, miss
חָיוּ	חֲיִיתֶם/ן	חָיִינוּ	חָיְתָה	חָיָה	חָיִית	חָיִיתָ	חָיִיתִי	ח.י.י/ה	to live
חָסוּ	חֲסִיתֶם/ן	חָסִינוּ	חָסְתָה	חָסָה	חָסִית	חָסִיתָ	חָסִיתִי	ח.ס.י/ה	to take refuge
חָרוּ	חֲרִיתֶם/ן	חָרִינוּ	חָרְתָה	חָרָה	חָרִית	חָרִיתָ	חָרִיתִי	ח.ר.י/ה	to be hot
חָשְׁבוּ	חֲשַׁבְתֶּם/ן	חָשַׁבְנוּ	חָשְׁבָה	חָשַׁב	חָשַׁבְתְּ	חָשַׁבְתָּ	חָשַׁבְתִּי	ח.שׁ.ב	to think, suppose
טָמְאוּ	טְמֵאתֶם/ן	טָמֵאנוּ	טָמְאָה	טָמֵא	טָמֵאת	טָמֵאתָ	טָמֵאתִי	ט.מ.א	to be defiled
טָעֲמוּ	טְעַמְתֶּם/ן	טָעַמְנוּ	טָעֲמָה	טָעַם	טָעַמְתְּ	טָעַמְתָּ	טָעַמְתִּי	ט.ע.מ	to taste
יָדְעוּ	יְדַעְתֶּם/ן	יָדַעְנוּ	יָדְעָה	יָדַע	יָדַעַתְּ	יָדַעְתָּ	יָדַעְתִּי	י.ד.ע	to know
יָכְלוּ	יְכָלְתֶּם/ן	יָכֹלְנוּ	יָכְלָה	יָכֹל	יָכֹלְתְּ	יָכֹלְתָּ	יָכֹלְתִּי	י.כ.ל	to be able
יָלְדוּ	יְלַדְתֶּם/ן	יָלַדְנוּ	יָלְדָה	יָלַד	יָלַדְתְּ	יָלַדְתָּ	יָלַדְתִּי	י.ל.ד	to give birth
יָנוּ	יְנִיתֶם/ן	יָנִינוּ	יָנְתָה	יָנָה	יָנִית	יָנִיתָ	יָנִיתִי	י.נ.י/ה	to oppress
יָסְפוּ	יְסַפְתֶּם/ן	יָסַפְנוּ	יָסְפָה	יָסַף	יָסַפְתְּ	יָסַפְתָּ	יָסַפְתִּי	י.ס.פ	to do again
יָצְאוּ	יְצָאתֶם/ן	יָצָאנוּ	יָצְאָה	יָצָא	יָצָאת	יָצָאתָ	יָצָאתִי	י.צ.א	to go out

Conjugation of Selected Verbs in Qal בִּנְיָן קטל

3cpl	2m/fpl	1cpl	3fs	3ms	2fs	2ms	1cs	שרש	Qal Def.
יָרְאוּ	יְרֵאתֶם/ן	יָרֵאנוּ	יָרְאָה	יָרֵא	יָרֵאת	יָרֵאתָ	יָרֵאתִי	י.ר.א	to be afraid
יָרְדוּ	יְרַדְתֶּם/ן	יָרַדְנוּ	יָרְדָה	יָרַד	יָרַדְתְּ	יָרַדְתָּ	יָרַדְתִּי	י.ר.ד	to descend
יָרְשׁוּ	יְרַשְׁתֶּם/ן	יָרַשְׁנוּ	יָרְשָׁה	יָרַשׁ	יָרַשְׁתְּ	יָרַשְׁתָּ	יָרַשְׁתִּי	י.ר.שׁ	to cause to inherit
יָשְׁבוּ	יְשַׁבְתֶּם/ן	יָשַׁבְנוּ	יָשְׁבָה	יָשַׁב	יָשַׁבְתְּ	יָשַׁבְתָּ	יָשַׁבְתִּי	י.שׁ.ב	to sit, dwell
כָּבְדוּ	כְּבַדְתֶּם/ן	כָּבַדְנוּ	כָּבְדָה	כָּבֵד	כָּבַדְתְּ	כָּבַדְתָּ	כָּבַדְתִּי	כ.ב.ד	to be heavy, mighty
כָּלוּ	כְּלִיתֶם/ן	כָּלִינוּ	כָּלְתָה	כָּלָה	כָּלִית	כָּלִיתָ	כָּלִיתִי	כ.ל.י/ה	to waste away
כָּנְסוּ	כְּנַסְתֶּם/ן	כָּנַסְנוּ	כָּנְסָה	כָּנַס	כָּנַסְתְּ	כָּנַסְתָּ	כָּנַסְתִּי	כ.נ.ס	to collect
כָּרְתוּ	כְּרַתֶּם/ן	כָּרַתְנוּ	כָּרְתָה	כָּרַת	כָּרַתְּ	כָּרַתָּ	כָּרַתִּי	כ.ר.ת	to cut
כָּתְבוּ	כְּתַבְתֶּם/ן	כָּתַבְנוּ	כָּתְבָה	כָּתַב	כָּתַבְתְּ	כָּתַבְתָּ	כָּתַבְתִּי	כ.ת.ב	to write
לָבְשׁוּ	לְבַשְׁתֶּם/ן	לָבַשְׁנוּ	לָבְשָׁה	לָבֵשׁ	לָבַשְׁתְּ	לָבַשְׁתָּ	לָבַשְׁתִּי	ל.ב.שׁ	to wash
לָכְדוּ	לְכַדְתֶּם/ן	לָכַדְנוּ	לָכְדָה	לָכַד	לָכַדְתְּ	לָכַדְתָּ	לָכַדְתִּי	ל.כ.ד	to capture
לָמְדוּ	לְמַדְתֶּם/ן	לָמַדְנוּ	לָמְדָה	לָמַד	לָמַדְתְּ	לָמַדְתָּ	לָמַדְתִּי	ל.מ.ד	to learn
לָקְחוּ	לְקַחְתֶּם/ן	לָקַחְנוּ	לָקְחָה	לָקַח	לָקַחְתְּ	לָקַחְתָּ	לָקַחְתִּי	ל.ק.ח	to take, accept
מֵתוּ	מַתֶּם/ן	מֵתְנוּ	מֵתָה	מֵת	מַתְּ	מַתָּ	מַתִּי	מ.ו.ת	to die
מָלְאוּ	מְלֵאתֶם/ן	מָלֵאנוּ	מָלְאָה	מָלֵא	מָלֵאת	מָלֵאתָ	מָלֵאתִי	מ.ל.א	to be full
מָלְכוּ	מְלַכְתֶּם/ן	מָלַכְנוּ	מָלְכָה	מָלַךְ	מָלַכְתְּ	מָלַכְתָּ	מָלַכְתִּי	מ.ל.ב	to rule
מָצְאוּ	מְצָאתֶם/ן	מָצָאנוּ	מָצְאָה	מָצָא	מָצָאת	מָצָאתָ	מָצָאתִי	מ.צ.א	to find
נָטוּ	נְטִיתֶם/ן	נָטִינוּ	נָטְתָה	נָטָה	נָטִית	נָטִיתָ	נָטִיתִי	נ.ט.י/ה	to stretch out
נָפְלוּ	נְפַלְתֶּם/ן	נָפַלְנוּ	נָפְלָה	נָפַל	נָפַלְתְּ	נָפַלְתָּ	נָפַלְתִּי	נ.פ.ל	to fall
נָשְׂאוּ	נְשָׂאתֶם/ן	נָשָׂאנוּ	נָשְׂאָה	נָשָׂא	נָשָׂאת	נָשָׂאתָ	נָשָׂאתִי	נ.שׂ.א	to lift, carry
נָתְנוּ	נְתַתֶּם/ן	נָתַנּוּ	נָתְנָה	נָתַן	נָתַתְּ	נָתַתָּ	נָתַתִּי	נ.ת.נ	to give
סָבְבוּ	סַבּוֹתֶם/ן	סַבּוֹנוּ	סָבְבָה	סָבַב	סַבּוֹת	סַבּוֹתָ	סַבּוֹתִי	ס.ב.ב	to surround
סָרוּ	סַרְתֶּם/ן	סַרְנוּ	סָרָה	סָר	סַרְתְּ	סַרְתָּ	סַרְתִּי	ס.ו.ר	to turn self aside
סָלְחוּ	סְלַחְתֶּם/ן	סָלַחְנוּ	סָלְחָה	סָלַח	סָלַחְתְּ	סָלַחְתָּ	סָלַחְתִּי	ס.ל.ח	to forgive
סָפְרוּ	סְפַרְתֶּם/ן	סָפַרְנוּ	סָפְרָה	סָפַר	סָפַרְתְּ	סָפַרְתָּ	סָפַרְתִּי	ס.פ.ר	to count
עָבְדוּ	עֲבַדְתֶּם/ן	עָבַדְנוּ	עָבְדָה	עָבַד	עָבַדְתְּ	עָבַדְתָּ	עָבַדְתִּי	ע.ב.ד	to serve, worship
עָבְרוּ	עֲבַרְתֶּם/ן	עָבַרְנוּ	עָבְרָה	עָבַר	עָבַרְתְּ	עָבַרְתָּ	עָבַרְתִּי	ע.ב.ר	to cross over
עָזְבוּ	עֲזַבְתֶּם/ן	עָזַבְנוּ	עָזְבָה	עָזַב	עָזַבְתְּ	עָזַבְתָּ	עָזַבְתִּי	ע.ז.ב	to abandon
עָזְרוּ	עֲזַרְתֶּם/ן	עָזַרְנוּ	עָזְרָה	עָזַר	עָזַרְתְּ	עָזַרְתָּ	עָזַרְתִּי	ע.ז.ר	to help
עָלוּ	עֲלִיתֶם/ן	עָלִינוּ	עָלְתָה	עָלָה	עָלִית	עָלִיתָ	עָלִיתִי	ע.ל.י/ה	to go up

Conjugation of Selected Verbs in Qal בִּנְיָן קטל									
3cpl	2m/fpl	1cpl	3fs	3ms	2fs	2ms	1cs	שרש	Qal Def.
עָמְדוּ	עֲמַדְתֶּם/ן	עָמַדְנוּ	עָמְדָה	עָמַד	עָמַדְתְּ	עָמַדְתָּ	עָמַדְתִּי	ע.מ.ד	to stand
עָנוּ	עֲנִיתֶם/ן	עָנִינוּ	עָנְתָה	עָנָה	עָנִית	עָנִיתָ	עָנִיתִי	ע.נ.י/ה	to answer
עָשׂוּ	עֲשִׂיתֶם/ן	עָשִׂינוּ	עָשְׂתָה	עָשָׂה	עָשִׂית	עָשִׂיתָ	עָשִׂיתִי	ע.שׂ.י/ה	to make, do
פָּנוּ	פְּנִיתֶם/ן	פָּנִינוּ	פָּנְתָה	פָּנָה	פָּנִית	פָּנִיתָ	פָּנִיתִי	פ.נ.י/ה	to turn
פָּקְדוּ	פְּקַדְתֶּם/ן	פָּקַדְנוּ	פָּקְדָה	פָּקַד	פָּקַדְתְּ	פָּקַדְתָּ	פָּקַדְתִּי	פ.ק.ד	to visit
פָּתְחוּ	פְּתַחְתֶּם/ן	פָּתַחְנוּ	פָּתְחָה	פָּתַח	פָּתַחְתְּ	פָּתַחְתָּ	פָּתַחְתִּי	פ.ת.ח	to open
קָבְצוּ	קְבַצְתֶּם/ן	קָבַצְנוּ	קָבְצָה	קָבַץ	קָבַצְתְּ	קָבַצְתָּ	קָבַצְתִּי	ק.ב.צ	to assemble self
קָדְשׁוּ	קְדַשְׁתֶּם/ן	קָדַשְׁנוּ	קָדְשָׁה	קָדַשׁ	קָדַשְׁתְּ	קָדַשְׁתָּ	קָדַשְׁתִּי	ק.ד.שׁ	to be holy
קִוּוּ	קִוִּיתֶם/ן	קִוִּינוּ	קִוְּתָה	קִוָּה	קִוִּית	קִוִּיתָ	קִוִּיתִי	ק.ו.י/ה	to hope
קָמוּ	קַמְתֶּם/ן	קַמְנוּ	קָמָה	קָם	קַמְתְּ	קַמְתָּ	קַמְתִּי	ק.ו.ם	to stand up
קָטְנוּ	קְטָנְתֶּם/ן	קָטֹנּוּ	קָטְנָה	קָטֹן	קָטֹנְתְּ	קָטֹנְתָּ	קָטֹנְתִּי	ק.ט.נ	to be small
קָנוּ	קְנִיתֶם/ן	קָנִינוּ	קָנְתָה	קָנָה	קָנִית	קָנִיתָ	קָנִיתִי	ק.נ.י/ה	to buy
קָרְאוּ	קְרָאתֶם/ן	קָרָאנוּ	קָרְאָה	קָרָא	קָרָאת	קָרָאתָ	קָרָאתִי	ק.ר.א	to call, read
קָרְאוּ	קְרָאתֶם/ן	קָרָאנוּ	קָרְאָה	קָרָא	קָרָאת	קָרָאתָ	קָרָאתִי	ק.ר.א	to meet
קָרְבוּ	קְרַבְתֶּם/ן	קָרַבְנוּ	קָרְבָה	קָרַב	קָרַבְתְּ	קָרַבְתָּ	קָרַבְתִּי	ק.ר.ב	to draw near
רָאוּ	רְאִיתֶם/ן	רָאִינוּ	רָאֲתָה	רָאָה	רָאִית	רָאִיתָ	רָאִיתִי	ר.א.י/ה	to see
רָדְפוּ	רְדַפְתֶּם/ן	רָדַפְנוּ	רָדְפָה	רָדַף	רָדַפְתְּ	רָדַפְתָּ	רָדַפְתִּי	ר.ד.פ	to pursue
רָמוּ	רַמְתֶּם/ן	רַמְנוּ	רָמָה	רָם	רַמְתְּ	רַמְתָּ	רַמְתִּי	ר.ו.ם	to be high
רָבוּ	רַבְתֶּם/ן	רַבְנוּ	רָבָה	רָב	רַבְתְּ	רַבְתָּ	רַבְתִּי	ר.י.ב	to contend
רָעוּ	רְעִיתֶם/ן	רָעִינוּ	רָעֲתָה	רָעָה	רָעִית	רָעִיתָ	רָעִיתִי	ר.ע.י/ה	to graze
רָעוּ	רְעוֹתֶם/ן	רָעוֹנוּ	רָעָה	רַע	רָעוֹת	רָעוֹתָ	רָעוֹתִי	ר.ע.ע	to be evil
שָׁאֲלוּ	שְׁאַלְתֶּם/ן	שָׁאַלְנוּ	שָׁאֲלָה	שָׁאַל	שָׁאַלְתְּ	שָׁאַלְתָּ	שָׁאַלְתִּי	שׁ.א.ל	to inquire, request
סָבְבוּ	סַבּוֹתֶם/ן	סַבּוֹנוּ	סָבְבָה	סָבַב	סַבּוֹת	סַבּוֹתָ	סַבּוֹתִי	ס.ב.ב	to go around
שָׁבְרוּ	שְׁבַרְתֶּם/ן	שָׁבַרְנוּ	שָׁבְרָה	שָׁבַר	שָׁבַרְתְּ	שָׁבַרְתָּ	שָׁבַרְתִּי	שׁ.ב.ר	to break
שָׁבוּ	שַׁבְתֶּם/ן	שַׁבְנוּ	שָׁבָה	שָׁב	שַׁבְתְּ	שַׁבְתָּ	שַׁבְתִּי	שׁ.ו.ב	to return
שָׂמוּ	שַׂמְתֶּם/ן	שַׂמְנוּ	שָׂמָה	שָׂם	שַׂמְתְּ	שַׂמְתָּ	שַׂמְתִּי	שׂ.ו./י.ם	to place
שָׁכְבוּ	שְׁכַבְתֶּם/ן	שָׁכַבְנוּ	שָׁכְבָה	שָׁכַב	שָׁכַבְתְּ	שָׁכַבְתָּ	שָׁכַבְתִּי	שׁ.כ.ב	to lie down
שָׁכְחוּ	שְׁכַחְתֶּם/ן	שָׁכַחְנוּ	שָׁכְחָה	שָׁכַח	שָׁכַחְתְּ	שָׁכַחְתָּ	שָׁכַחְתִּי	שׁ.כ.ח	to forget
שָׁכְנוּ	שְׁכַנְתֶּם/ן	שָׁכַנּוּ	שָׁכְנָה	שָׁכַן	שָׁכַנְתְּ	שָׁכַנְתָּ	שָׁכַנְתִּי	שׁ.כ.נ	to inhabit
שָׁלְחוּ	שְׁלַחְתֶּם/ן	שָׁלַחְנוּ	שָׁלְחָה	שָׁלַח	שָׁלַחְתְּ	שָׁלַחְתָּ	שָׁלַחְתִּי	שׁ.ל.ח	to send
שָׁמְעוּ	שְׁמַעְתֶּם/ן	שָׁמַעְנוּ	שָׁמְעָה	שָׁמַע	שָׁמַעַתְּ	שָׁמַעְתָּ	שָׁמַעְתִּי	שׁ.מ.ע	to hear

Conjugation of Selected Verbs in Qal בִּנְיָן קטל										
3cpl	2m/fpl	1cpl	3fs	3ms	2fs	2ms	1cs	שרש	Qal Def.
שָׁמְרוּ	שְׁמַרְתֶּם/ן	שָׁמַרְנוּ	שָׁמְרָה	שָׁמַר	שָׁמַרְתְּ	שָׁמַרְתָּ	שָׁמַרְתִּי	ש.מ.ר	to guard
שָׂנְאוּ	שְׂנֵאתֶם/ן	שָׂנֵאנוּ	שָׂנְאָה	שָׂנֵא	שָׂנֵאת	שָׂנֵאתָ	שָׂנֵאתִי	ש.נ.א	to hate
שָׁתוּ	שְׁתִיתֶם/ן	שָׁתִינוּ	שָׁתְתָה	שָׁתָה	שָׁתִית	שָׁתִיתָ	שָׁתִיתִי	ש.ת.י/ה	to drink
תָּפְשׂוּ	תְּפַשְׂתֶּם/ן	תָּפַשְׂנוּ	תָּפְשָׂה	תָּפַשׂ	תָּפַשְׂתְּ	תָּפַשְׂתָּ	תָּפַשְׂתִּי	ת.פ.שׂ	to grab

יִקְטֹל Conjugation of Selected Verbs in Qal בִּנְיָן

apocopated 3ms	3mpl	2/3fpl	2mpl	1cpl	3ms	2fs	2ms/3fs	1cs	שֹׁרֶשׁ	Qal Def.
	יֹאבְדוּ	תֹּאבַדְנָה	תֹּאבְדוּ	נֹאבַד	יֹאבַד	תֹּאבְדִי	תֹּאבַד	אֹבַד	א.ב.ד	to perish
	יֶאֱהֲבוּ	תֶּאֱהַבְנָה	תֶּאֱהֲבוּ	נֶאֱהַב	יֶאֱהַב	תֶּאֱהֲבִי	תֶּאֱהַב	אֶאֱהַב	א.ה.ב	to love
	יֹאכְלוּ	תֹּאכַלְנָה	תֹּאכְלוּ	נֹאכַל	יֹאכַל	תֹּאכְלִי	תֹּאכַל	אֹכַל	א.כ.ל	to eat
	יֹאמְרוּ	תֹּאמַרְנָה	תֹּאמְרוּ	נֹאמַר	יֹאמַר	תֹּאמְרִי	תֹּאמַר	אֹמַר	א.מ.ר	to say
	יֶאַסְפוּ	תֶּאֱסֹפְנָה	תֶּאַסְפוּ	נֶאֱסֹף	יֶאֱסֹף	תֶּאַסְפִי	תֶּאֱסֹף	אֶאֱסֹף	א.ס.פ	to gather
	יָבֹאוּ	תָּבֹאנָה	תָּבֹאוּ	נָבוֹא	יָבוֹא	תָּבוֹאִי	תָּבוֹא	אָבוֹא	ב.ו.א	to come, enter
וַיֵּבוֹשׁ	יֵבוֹשׁוּ	תֵּבוֹשֶׁנָה	תֵּבוֹשׁוּ	נֵבוֹשׁ	יֵבוֹשׁ	תֵּבוֹשִׁי	תֵּבוֹשׁ	אֵבוֹשׁ	ב.ו.שׁ	to be ashamed
וַיָּבֶן	יָבִינוּ	תְּבִינֶינָה	תָּבִינוּ	נָבִין	יָבִין	תָּבִינִי	תָּבִין	אָבִין	ב.י.נ	to understand
וַיֵּבְךְּ	יִבְכּוּ	תִּבְכֶּינָה	תִּבְכּוּ	נִבְכֶּה	יִבְכֶּה	תִּבְכִּי	תִּבְכֶּה	אֶבְכֶּה	ב.כ.ה/י	to weep
	יִבְלְעוּ	תִּבְלַעְנָה	תִּבְלְעוּ	נִבְלַע	יִבְלַע	תִּבְלְעִי	תִּבְלַע	אֶבְלַע	ב.ל.ע	to swallow
וַיִּבֶן	יִבְנוּ	תִּבְנֶינָה	תִּבְנוּ	נִבְנֶה	יִבְנֶה	תִּבְנִי	תִּבְנֶה	אֶבְנֶה	ב.נ.ה/י	to build
	יִגְנְבוּ	תִּגְנֹבְנָה	תִּגְנְבוּ	נִגְנֹב	יִגְנֹב	תִּגְנְבִי	תִּגְנֹב	אֶגְנֹב	ג.נ.ב	to steal
	יִדְרְשׁוּ	תִּדְרֹשְׁנָה	תִּדְרְשׁוּ	נִדְרֹשׁ	יִדְרֹשׁ	תִּדְרְשִׁי	תִּדְרֹשׁ	אֶדְרֹשׁ	ד.ר.שׁ	to investigate
וַיְהִי	יִהְיוּ	תִּהְיֶינָה	תִּהְיוּ	נִהְיֶה	יִהְיֶה	תִּהְיִי	תִּהְיֶה	אֶהְיֶה	ה.י.ה/י	to be, become
וַיֵּלֶךְ	יֵלְכוּ	תֵּלַכְנָה	תֵּלְכוּ	נֵלֵךְ	יֵלֵךְ	תֵּלְכִי	תֵּלֵךְ	אֵלֵךְ	ה.ל.כ	to go, walk
	יִזְבְּחוּ	תִּזְבַּחְנָה	תִּזְבְּחוּ	נִזְבַּח	יִזְבַּח	תִּזְבְּחִי	תִּזְבַּח	אֶזְבַּח	ז.ב.ח	to sacrifice
	יִזְכְּרוּ	תִּזְכֹּרְנָה	תִּזְכְּרוּ	נִזְכֹּר	יִזְכֹּר	תִּזְכְּרִי	תִּזְכֹּר	אֶזְכֹּר	ז.כ.ר	to remember
	יֶחֶזְקוּ	תֶּחֱזַקְנָה	תֶּחֶזְקוּ	נֶחֱזַק	יֶחֱזַק	תֶּחֶזְקִי	תֶּחֱזַק	אֶחֱזַק	ח.ז.ק	to be strong
וַיֶּחֱטָא	יֶחֶטְאוּ	תֶּחֱטֶאנָה	תֶּחֶטְאוּ	נֶחֱטָא	יֶחֱטָא	תֶּחֶטְאִי	תֶּחֱטָא	אֶחֱטָא	ח.ט.א	to sin, miss
וַיְחִי	יִחְיוּ	תִּחְיֶינָה	תִּחְיוּ	נִחְיֶה	יִחְיֶה	תִּחְיִי	תִּחְיֶה	אֶחְיֶה	ח.י.ה/י	to live
וַיַּחַס	יֶחֱסוּ	תֶּחֱסֶינָה	תֶּחֱסוּ	נֶחֱסֶה	יֶחֱסֶה	תֶּחֱסִי	תֶּחֱסֶה	אֶחֱסֶה	ח.ס.ה/י	to take refuge
וַיֵּחַם	יֵחַמּוּ	תֵּחַמְנָה	תֵּחַמּוּ	נֵחַם	יֵחַם	תֵּחַמִּי	תֵּחַם	אֵחַם	ח.מ.ם	to be hot

יִקְטֹל Conjugation of Selected Verbs in Qal בָּנָה

וַיִּקְטֹל apocopated 3ms	3mpl	2/3fpl	2mpl	1cpl	3ms	2fs	2ms/3fs	1cs	שׁרשׁ	Qal Def.
	יַחְשְׁבוּ	תַּחְשֹׁבְנָה	תַּחְשְׁבוּ	נַחְשֹׁב	יַחְשֹׁב	תַּחְשְׁבִי	תַּחְשֹׁב	אֶחְשֹׁב	ח.שׁ.ב	to think, suppose
	יִטְמְאוּ	תִּטְמֶאנָה	תִּטְמְאוּ	נִטְמָא	יִטְמָא	תִּטְמְאִי	תִּטְמָא	אֶטְמָא	ט.מ.א	to be defiled
	יִטְעֲמוּ	תִּטְעַמְנָה	תִּטְעֲמוּ	נִטְעַם	יִטְעַם	תִּטְעֲמִי	תִּטְעַם	אֶטְעַם	ט.ע.ם	to taste
	יֵדְעוּ	תֵּדַעְנָה	תֵּדְעוּ	נֵדַע	יֵדַע	תֵּדְעִי	תֵּדַע	אֵדַע	י.ד.ע	to know
	יוּכְלוּ	תּוּכַלְנָה	תּוּכְלוּ	נוּכַל	יוּכַל	תּוּכְלִי	תּוּכַל	אוּכַל	י.כ.ל	to be able
	יֵלְדוּ	תֵּלַדְנָה	תֵּלְדוּ	נֵלֵד	יֵלֵד	תֵּלְדִי	תֵּלֵד	אֵלֵד	י.ל.ד	to give birth
	יוֹנוּ		תּוֹנוּ	נוֹנֶה	יוֹנֶה	תּוֹנִי	תּוֹנֶה	אוֹנֶה	י.נ.ה/י	to oppress
	יֹסִפוּ	תֹּסַפְנָה	תֹּסִפוּ	נֹסֵף	יֹסֵף	תֹּסִפִי	תֹּסֵף	אֹסֵף	י.ס.פ	to do again
	יֵצְאוּ	תֵּצֶאנָה	תֵּצְאוּ	נֵצֵא	יֵצֵא	תֵּצְאִי	תֵּצֵא	אֵצֵא	י.צ.א	to go out
	יִירְאוּ	תִּירֶאנָה	תִּירְאוּ	נִירָא	יִירָא	תִּירְאִי	תִּירָא	אִירָא	י.ר.א	to be afraid
וַיֵּרֶד	יֵרְדוּ	תֵּרַדְנָה	תֵּרְדוּ	נֵרֵד	יֵרֵד	תֵּרְדִי	תֵּרֵד	אֵרֵד	י.ר.ד	to descend
	יוֹרִישׁוּ	תּוֹרַשְׁנָה	תּוֹרִישׁוּ	נוֹרִישׁ	יוֹרִישׁ	תּוֹרִישִׁי	תּוֹרִישׁ	אוֹרִישׁ	י.ר.שׁ	to cause to inherit
וַיֵּשֶׁב	יֵשְׁבוּ	תֵּשַׁבְנָה	תֵּשְׁבוּ	נֵשֵׁב	יֵשֵׁב	תֵּשְׁבִי	תֵּשֵׁב	אֵשֵׁב	י.שׁ.ב	to sit, dwell
	יִכְבְּדוּ	תִּכְבַּדְנָה	תִּכְבְּדוּ	נִכְבַּד	יִכְבַּד	תִּכְבְּדִי	תִּכְבַּד	אֶכְבַּד	כ.ב.ד	to be heavy, mighty
וַיֵּלֶךְ	יֵלְכוּ	תֵּלַכְנָה	תֵּלְכוּ	נֵלֵךְ	יֵלֵךְ	תֵּלְכִי	תֵּלֵךְ	אֵלֵךְ	ה/י.ל.ך	to waste away
	יִכְנְסוּ	תִּכְנֹסְנָה	תִּכְנְסוּ	נִכְנֹס	יִכְנֹס	תִּכְנְסִי	תִּכְנֹס	אֶכְנֹס	כ.נ.ס	to collect
	יִכְרְתוּ	תִּכְרֹתְנָה	תִּכְרְתוּ	נִכְרֹת	יִכְרֹת	תִּכְרְתִי	תִּכְרֹת	אֶכְרֹת	כ.ר.ת	to cut
	יִכְתְּבוּ	תִּכְתֹּבְנָה	תִּכְתְּבוּ	נִכְתֹּב	יִכְתֹּב	תִּכְתְּבִי	תִּכְתֹּב	אֶכְתֹּב	כ.ת.ב	to write
	יִכְבְּסוּ	תִּכְבַּסְנָה	תִּכְבְּסוּ	נִכְבַּס	יִכְבַּס	תִּכְבְּסִי	תִּכְבַּס	אֲכַבֵּס	כ.ב.שׁ	to wash
	יִלְכְּדוּ	תִּלְכֹּדְנָה	תִּלְכְּדוּ	נִלְכֹּד	יִלְכֹּד	תִּלְכְּדִי	תִּלְכֹּד	אֶלְכֹּד	ל.כ.ד	to capture

יִקְטֹל Conjugation of Selected Verbs in Qal בִּנְיָן

apocopated 3ms	3mpl	2/3fpl	2mpl	1cpl	3ms	2fs	2ms/3fs	1cs	שרש	Qal Def.
	יִלְמְדוּ	תִּלְמַדְנָה	תִּלְמְדוּ	נִלְמַד	יִלְמַד	תִּלְמְדִי	תִּלְמַד	אֶלְמַד	ל.מ.ד	to learn
יִקַּח	יִקְחוּ	תִּקַּחְנָה	תִּקְחוּ	נִקַּח	יִקַּח	תִּקְחִי	תִּקַּח	אֶקַּח	ל.ק.ח	to take, accept
	יָמֻתוּ	תְּמֻתֶֽנָה	תָּמֻתוּ	נָמוּת	יָמוּת	תָּמוּתִי	תָּמוּת	אָמוּת	מ.ו.ת	to die
	יִמְלְאוּ	תִּמְלֶאנָה	תִּמְלְאוּ	נִמְלָא	יִמְלָא	תִּמְלְאִי	תִּמְלָא	אֶמְלָא	מ.ל.א	to be full
	יִמְלְכוּ	תִּמְלֹכְנָה	תִּמְלְכוּ	נִמְלֹךְ	יִמְלֹךְ	תִּמְלְכִי	תִּמְלֹךְ	אֶמְלֹךְ	מ.ל.ך	to rule
	יִמְצְאוּ	תִּמְצֶאנָה	תִּמְצְאוּ	נִמְצָא	יִמְצָא	תִּמְצְאִי	תִּמְצָא	אֶמְצָא	מ.צ.א	to find
יֵט	יִטּוּ	תִּטֶּינָה	תִּטּוּ	נִטֶּה	יִטֶּה	תִּטִּי	תִּטֶּה	אֶטֶּה	נ.ט.ה/י	to stretch out
	יִפְּלוּ	תִּפֹּלְנָה	תִּפְּלוּ	נִפֹּל	יִפֹּל	תִּפְּלִי	תִּפֹּל	אֶפֹּל	נ.פ.ל	to fall
	יִשְׂאוּ	תִּשֶּׂאנָה	תִּשְׂאוּ	נִשָּׂא	יִשָּׂא	תִּשְׂאִי	תִּשָּׂא	אֶשָּׂא	נ.ש.א	to lift, carry
	יִתְּנוּ	תִּתֵּנָּה	תִּתְּנוּ	נִתֵּן	יִתֵּן	תִּתְּנִי	תִּתֵּן	אֶתֵּן	נ.ת.ן	to give
יָסֹב	יָסֹבּוּ	תְּסֻבֶּֽינָה	תָּסֹבּוּ	נָסֹב	יָסֹב	תָּסֹבִּי	תָּסֹב	אָסֹב	ס.ב.ב	to surround
	יָסֻרוּ	תְּסֻרֶֽינָה	תָּסֻרוּ	נָסוּר	יָסוּר	תָּסוּרִי	תָּסוּר	אָסוּר	ס.ו.ר	to turn self aside
	יִסְלְחוּ	תִּסְלַחְנָה	תִּסְלְחוּ	נִסְלַח	יִסְלַח	תִּסְלְחִי	תִּסְלַח	אֶסְלַח	ס.ל.ח	to forgive
	יִסְפְּרוּ	תִּסְפֹּרְנָה	תִּסְפְּרוּ	נִסְפֹּר	יִסְפֹּר	תִּסְפְּרִי	תִּסְפֹּר	אֶסְפֹּר	ס.פ.ר	to count
	יַעַבְדוּ	תַּעֲבֹדְנָה	תַּעַבְדוּ	נַעֲבֹד	יַעֲבֹד	תַּעַבְדִי	תַּעֲבֹד	אֶעֱבֹד	ע.ב.ד	to serve, worship
	יַעַבְרוּ	תַּעֲבֹרְנָה	תַּעַבְרוּ	נַעֲבֹר	יַעֲבֹר	תַּעַבְרִי	תַּעֲבֹר	אֶעֱבֹר	ע.ב.ר	to cross over
	יַעַזְבוּ	תַּעֲזֹבְנָה	תַּעַזְבוּ	נַעֲזֹב	יַעֲזֹב	תַּעַזְבִי	תַּעֲזֹב	אֶעֱזֹב	ע.ז.ב	to abandon
	יַעְזְרוּ	תַּעְזֹרְנָה	תַּעְזְרוּ	נַעְזֹר	יַעְזֹר	תַּעְזְרִי	תַּעְזֹר	אֶעְזֹר	ע.ז.ר	to help
יַעַל	יַעֲלוּ	תַּעֲלֶינָה	תַּעֲלוּ	נַעֲלֶה	יַעֲלֶה	תַּעֲלִי	תַּעֲלֶה	אֶעֱלֶה	ע.ל.ה/י	to go up
	יַעַמְדוּ	תַּעֲמֹדְנָה	תַּעַמְדוּ	נַעֲמֹד	יַעֲמֹד	תַּעַמְדִי	תַּעֲמֹד	אֶעֱמֹד	ע.מ.ד	to stand

יִקְטֹל Conjugation of Selected Verbs in Qal בִּנְיָן

יִקְטֹל apocopated 3ms	3mpl	2/3fpl	2mpl	1cpl	3ms	2fs	2ms/3fs	1cs	שֶׁרֶשׁ	Qal Def.
יַעַן	יַעֲנוּ	תַּעֲנֶינָה	תַּעֲנוּ	נַעֲנֶה	יַעֲנֶה	תַּעֲנִי	תַּעֲנֶה	אֶעֱנֶה	ע.נ.ה/י	to answer
יַעַשׂ	יַעֲשׂוּ	תַּעֲשֶׂינָה	תַּעֲשׂוּ	נַעֲשֶׂה	יַעֲשֶׂה	תַּעֲשִׂי	תַּעֲשֶׂה	אֶעֱשֶׂה	ע.שׂ.ה/י	to make, do
יִפֶן	יִפְנוּ	תִּפְנֶינָה	תִּפְנוּ	נִפְנֶה	יִפְנֶה	תִּפְנִי	תִּפְנֶה	אֶפְנֶה	פ.נ.ה/י	to turn
	יִפְקְדוּ	תִּפְקֹדְנָה	תִּפְקְדוּ	נִפְקֹד	יִפְקֹד	תִּפְקְדִי	תִּפְקֹד	אֶפְקֹד	פ.ק.ד	to visit
	יִפְתְּחוּ	תִּפְתַּחְנָה	תִּפְתְּחוּ	נִפְתַּח	יִפְתַּח	תִּפְתְּחִי	תִּפְתַּח	אֶפְתַּח	פ.ת.ח	to open
	יִקָּבְצוּ	תִּקָּבַצְנָה	תִּקָּבְצוּ	נִקָּבֵץ	יִקָּבֵץ	תִּקָּבְצִי	תִּקָּבֵץ	אֶקָּבֵץ	ק.ב.צ	to assemble self
	יִקְדְּשׁוּ	תִּקְדַּשְׁנָה	תִּקְדְּשׁוּ	נִקְדַּשׁ	יִקְדַּשׁ	תִּקְדְּשִׁי	תִּקְדַּשׁ	אֶקְדַּשׁ	ק.ד.שׁ	to be holy
	יְקַוּוּ	תְּקַוֶּינָה	תְּקַוּוּ	נְקַוֶּה	יְקַוֶּה	תְּקַוִּי	תְּקַוֶּה	אֲקַוֶּה	ק.ו.ה/י	to hope
יָקָם	יָקוּמוּ	תְּקוּמֶינָה	תָּקוּמוּ	נָקוּם	יָקוּם	תָּקוּמִי	תָּקוּם	אָקוּם	ק.ו.ם	to stand up
	יִקְטְנוּ	תִּקְטַנָּה	תִּקְטְנוּ	נִקְטַן	יִקְטַן	תִּקְטְנִי	תִּקְטַן	אֶקְטַן	ק.ט.נ	to be small
יִקֶן	יִקְנוּ	תִּקְנֶינָה	תִּקְנוּ	נִקְנֶה	יִקְנֶה	תִּקְנִי	תִּקְנֶה	אֶקְנֶה	ק.נ.ה/י	to buy
	יִקְרְאוּ	תִּקְרֶאנָה	תִּקְרְאוּ	נִקְרָא	יִקְרָא	תִּקְרְאִי	תִּקְרָא	אֶקְרָא	ק.ר.א	to call, read, meet
יִקְרַב	יִקְרְבוּ	תִּקְרַבְנָה	תִּקְרְבוּ	נִקְרַב	יִקְרַב	תִּקְרְבִי	תִּקְרַב	אֶקְרַב	ק.ר.ב	to draw near
יֵרֶא	יִרְאוּ	תִּרְאֶינָה	תִּרְאוּ	נִרְאֶה	יִרְאֶה	תִּרְאִי	תִּרְאֶה	אֶרְאֶה	ר.א.ה/י	to see
יִרְדֹּף	יִרְדְּפוּ	תִּרְדֹּפְנָה	תִּרְדְּפוּ	נִרְדֹּף	יִרְדֹּף	תִּרְדְּפִי	תִּרְדֹּף	אֶרְדֹּף	ר.ד.פ	to pursue
יָרֹם	יָרוּמוּ	תְּרוּמֶינָה	תָּרוּמוּ	נָרוּם	יָרוּם	תָּרוּמִי	תָּרוּם	אָרוּם	ר.ו.ם	to be high
יָרֶב	יָרִיבוּ	תְּרִיבֶינָה	תָּרִיבוּ	נָרִיב	יָרִיב	תָּרִיבִי	תָּרִיב	אָרִיב	ר.י.ב	to contend
	יִרְעוּ	תִּרְעֶינָה	תִּרְעוּ	נִרְעֶה	יִרְעֶה	תִּרְעִי	תִּרְעֶה	אֶרְעֶה	ר.ע.ה/י	to graze
	יֵרְעוּ	תֵּרַעְנָה	תֵּרְעוּ	נֵרַע	יֵרַע	תֵּרְעִי	תֵּרַע	אֵרַע	ר.ע.ע	to be evil
	יִשְׁאֲלוּ	תִּשְׁאַלְנָה	תִּשְׁאֲלוּ	נִשְׁאַל	יִשְׁאַל	תִּשְׁאֲלִי	תִּשְׁאַל	אֶשְׁאַל	שׁ.א.ל	to inquire, request
	יִשְׁבְּרוּ	תִּשְׁבֹּרְנָה	תִּשְׁבְּרוּ	נִשְׁבֹּר	יִשְׁבֹּר	תִּשְׁבְּרִי	תִּשְׁבֹּר	אֶשְׁבֹּר	שׁ.ב.ר	to break

יִקְטֹל Conjugation of Selected Verbs in Qal בִּנְיָן

יִקְטֹל apocopated 3ms	3mpl	2/3fpl	2mpl	1cpl	3ms	2fs	2ms/3fs	1cs	שֶׁרֶשׁ	Qal Def.
וַיִּ֫שֶׁב	יָשׁ֫וּבוּ	תָּשֹׁ֫בְנָה	תָּשׁ֫וּבוּ	נָשׁוּב	יָשׁוּב	תָּשׁ֫וּבִי	תָּשׁוּב	אָשׁוּב	שׁ.ו.ב	to turn
וַיָּ֫שֶׂם	יָשִׂ֫ימוּ	תְּשִׂימֶ֫נָה	תָּשִׂ֫ימוּ	נָשִׂים	יָשִׂים	תָּשִׂ֫ימִי	תָּשִׂים	אָשִׂ֫ים	שׂ.י.ם/ש.ו.ם	to place
	יִשְׁכְּבוּ	תִּשְׁכַּ֫בְנָה	תִּשְׁכְּבוּ	נִשְׁכַּב	יִשְׁכַּב	תִּשְׁכְּבִי	תִּשְׁכַּב	אֶשְׁכַּב	שׁ.כ.ב	to lie down
	יִשְׁכְּחוּ	תִּשְׁכַּ֫חְנָה	תִּשְׁכְּחוּ	נִשְׁכַּח	יִשְׁכַּח	תִּשְׁכְּחִי	תִּשְׁכַּח	אֶשְׁכַּח	שׁ.כ.ח	to forget
	יִשְׁכְּנוּ	תִּשְׁכֹּ֫נָּה	תִּשְׁכְּנוּ	נִשְׁכֹּן	יִשְׁכֹּן	תִּשְׁכְּנִי	תִּשְׁכֹּן	אֶשְׁכֹּן	שׁ.כ.ן	to inhabit
	יִשְׁלְחוּ	תִּשְׁלַ֫חְנָה	תִּשְׁלְחוּ	נִשְׁלַח	יִשְׁלַח	תִּשְׁלְחִי	תִּשְׁלַח	אֶשְׁלַח	שׁ.ל.ח	to send
	יִשְׁמְעוּ	תִּשְׁמַ֫עְנָה	תִּשְׁמְעוּ	נִשְׁמַע	יִשְׁמַע	תִּשְׁמְעִי	תִּשְׁמַע	אֶשְׁמַע	שׁ.מ.ע	to hear
	יִשְׁמְרוּ	תִּשְׁמֹ֫רְנָה	תִּשְׁמְרוּ	נִשְׁמֹר	יִשְׁמֹר	תִּשְׁמְרִי	תִּשְׁמֹר	אֶשְׁמֹר	שׁ.מ.ר	to guard
	יִשְׂנְאוּ	תִּשְׂנֶ֫אנָה	תִּשְׂנְאוּ	נִשְׂנָא	יִשְׂנָא	תִּשְׂנְאִי	תִּשְׂנָא	אֶשְׂנָא	שׂ.נ.א	to hate
וַיֵּ֫שְׁתְּ	יִשְׁתּוּ	תִּשְׁתֶּ֫ינָה	תִּשְׁתּוּ	נִשְׁתֶּה	יִשְׁתֶּה	תִּשְׁתִּי	תִּשְׁתֶּה	אֶשְׁתֶּה	שׁ.ת.ה/י	to drink
	יִתְפְּשׂוּ	תִּתְפֹּ֫שְׂנָה	תִּתְפְּשׂוּ	נִתְפֹּשׂ	יִתְפֹּשׂ	תִּתְפְּשִׂי	תִּתְפֹּשׂ	אֶתְפֹּשׂ	ת.פ.שׂ	to grab

QAL בִּנְיָן　　　　Verbs

Infinitives, Participles, and Command Forms for Selected Verbs in Qal בִּנְיָן

	Command Forms					Participles			Infinitives		Root
juss 3ms[2]	cohort 1cs	imv fpl	imv mpl	imv fs	imv ms	fpl	mpl	fs	ms	inf c	inf ab[1]	
	אֶאֱרֹד	אֱרֹדְנָה	אִרְדוּ	אִרְדִי	אֱרֹד	אֹרְדוֹת	אֹרְדִים	אֹרֶדֶת	אֹרֵד	אֱרֹד	אָרוֹד	שרש
	אֶאֱהַב	אֱהַבְנָה	אֶהֱבוּ	אֶהֱבִי	אֱהַב	אֹהֲבוֹת	אֹהֲבִים	אֹהֶבֶת	אֹהֵב	אֱהֹב	אָהוֹב	א.ה.ב
	אֶאֶכְלָה	אֱכֹלְנָה	אִכְלוּ	אִכְלִי	אֱכֹל	אֹכְלוֹת	אֹכְלִים	אֹכֶלֶת, אֹכְלָה	אֹכֵל	אֲכֹל[3]	אָכוֹל	א.כ.ל
	אֶאֱמֹר	אֱמֹרְנָה	אִמְרוּ	אִמְרִי	אֱמֹר	אֹמְרוֹת	אֹמְרִים	אֹמֶרֶת	אֹמֵר	אֱמֹר	אָמוֹר	א.מ.ר
	אֶאֱסֹף	אֱסֹפְנָה	אִסְפוּ	אִסְפִי	אֱסֹף	אֹסְפוֹת	אֹסְפִים	אֹסֶפֶת	אֹסֵף	אֱסֹף	אָסוֹף	א.ס.ף
יָבֹא	אָבוֹא	בֹּאנָה	בֹּאוּ	בֹּאִי	בֹּא	בָּאוֹת	בָּאִים	בָּאָה	בָּא	בֹּא	בּוֹא	ב.ו.א
	אָבוֹשָׁה	בֹּשְׁנָה	בֹּשׁוּ	בּוֹשִׁי	בּוֹשׁ	בּוֹשׁוֹת	בּוֹשִׁים	בּוֹשָׁה	בּוֹשׁ	בּוֹשׁ	בּוֹשׁ	ב.ו.ש
יָבֶן	אָבִינָה	בֵּנָּה	בִּינוּ	בִּינִי	בִּין	בָּנוֹת	בָּנִים	בָּנָה	בֵּן	בִּין	בּוֹן	ב.י.ן
	אֶבְנֶה	בְּנֶינָה	בְּנוּ	בְּנִי	בְּנֵה	בֹּנוֹת	בֹּנִים	בֹּנָה[5]	בֹּנֶה	בְּנוֹת[4]	בָּנֹה	ב.נ.ה/י
	אֶבְגַּד	בְּגֹדְנָה	בִּגְדוּ	בִּגְדִי	בְּגֹד	בֹּגְדוֹת	בֹּגְדִים	בֹּגֶדֶת	בֹּגֵד	בְּגֹד	בָּגוֹד	ב.ג.ד
יִבֶן	אֶבְנֶה	בְּנֶינָה	בְּנוּ	בְּנִי	בְּנֵה	בֹּנוֹת	בֹּנִים	בֹּנָה	בֹּנֶה	בְּנוֹת	בָּנֹה	ב.נ.ה/י

[1] The theme vowel of *inf absol* is fundamentally a holem-vav. It may reduce to holem, as when the *inf absol* operates as tautological or paronomastic infinitive, followed directly by finite form of the same שׁרשׁ.

[2] Most hollow verbs and III-ה/י verbs employ a shortened form for the jussive, with a retracted the accent. A qameṣ in the final syllable of these forms will be a qameṣ-ḥaṭuf. Verbs that are I-י similarly have only two syllables in the jussive 3m/fs, and employ a retracted accent.

[3] When prefixed by a preposition, this form is spelled לֶאֱכֹל[לְ].

[4] When prefixed by a preposition, any infinitive construct with a beged-kefet letter as second שׁרשׁ consonant will take a dagesh (e.g., לִבְנוֹת[לְ]).

[5] Attested בֹּנִיָּה in poetry, likely בֹּנָה in common use.

Infinitives, Participles, and Command Forms for Selected Verbs in Qal בִּנְיָן

	Command Forms					Participles				Infinitives		Root
juss 3ms[2]	cohort 1cs	imv fpl	imv mpl	imv fs	imv ms	fpl	mpl	fs	ms	inf c	inf ab[1]	
	אֶגְנֹב	גְּנֹבְנָה	גִּנְבוּ	גִּנְבִי	גְּנֹב	גֹּנְבוֹת	גֹּנְבִים	גֹּנֶבֶת	גֹּנֵב	גְּנֹב	גָּנוֹב	ג.נ.ב
	אֶדְרְשָׁה	דְּרֹשְׁנָה	דִּרְשׁוּ	דִּרְשִׁי	דְּרֹשׁ	דֹּרְשׁוֹת	דֹּרְשִׁים	דֹּרֶשֶׁת	דֹּרֵשׁ	דְּרֹשׁ	דָּרוֹשׁ	ד.ר.שׁ
יְחִי	אֶחְיֶה	חְיֶינָה	חְיוּ	חְיִי	חְיֵה	חֹיוֹת	חַיִּים	חוֹיָה	חַי	חְיוֹת	חָיֹה	ח.י/י.ה
	אֶזְכְּרָה	זְכֹרְנָה	זִכְרוּ	זִכְרִי	זְכֹר	זֹכְרוֹת	זֹכְרִים	זֹכֶרֶת	זֹכֵר	זְכֹר	זָכוֹר	ז.כ.ר
	אֵרְדָה	רֵדְנָה	רְדוּ	רְדִי	רֵד	יוֹרְדוֹת	יוֹרְדִים	יוֹרֶדֶת	יוֹרֵד	רֶדֶת	יָרוֹד	י.ר.ד
	אֶפְדֶּה	פְּדֶינָה	פְּדוּ	פְּדִי	פְּדֵה	פֹּדוֹת	פֹּדִים	פֹּדָה	פֹּדֶה	פְּדוֹת	פָּדֹה	פ.ד.ה
יֵצֵא	N/A	צֶאנָה	צְאוּ	צְאִי	צֵא	יֹצְאוֹת	יֹצְאִים	יוֹצֵאת	N/A	צֵאת	יָצֹא	י.צ.א
	אֶסֹּבָּה	סֹבְנָה	סֹבּוּ	סֹבִּי	סֹב	סֹבְבוֹת			סֹבֵב	סֹב	סָבוֹב	ס.ב/ב.ב
יָקֹם	אָקוּמָה	קֹמְנָה	קוּמוּ	קוּמִי	קוּם	קָמוֹת	קָמִים	קָמָה	קָם	קוּם	קוֹם	ק.ו/ו.מ
	אֶשְׁמְרָה	שְׁמֹרְנָה	שִׁמְרוּ	שִׁמְרִי	שְׁמֹר	שֹׁמְרוֹת	שֹׁמְרִים	שֹׁמֶרֶת	שֹׁמֵר	שְׁמֹר	שָׁמוֹר	שׁ.מ.ר
	אֶעֶבְדָה	עֲבֹדְנָה	עִבְדוּ	עִבְדִי	עֲבֹד	עֹבְדוֹת	עֹבְדִים	עֹבֶדֶת	עֹבֵד	עֲבֹד	עָבוֹד	ע.ב.ד
	אֶעְדְּעָה	עֲדַעְנָה	דְּעוּ	דְּעִי	דַּע	יֹדְעוֹת	יֹדְעִים	יֹדַעַת	יֹדֵעַ	דַּעַת	יָדֹעַ	י.ד.ע
	אֶגְלֶה	גְּלֶינָה	גְּלוּ	גְּלִי	גְּלֵה	גֹּלוֹת	גֹּלִים	גֹּלָה	גֹּלֶה	גְּלוֹת	גָּלֹה	ג.ל.ה
	אָבִינָה	בִּנָּה	בִּינוּ	בִּינִי	בִּין	בָּנוֹת	בָּנִים	בָּנָה	בָּן	בִּין	בּוֹן	ב.י/י.ן
	אָסֻפָּה	סֹפְנָה	סֹפּוּ	סֹפִּי	סֹף	סֹפוֹת	סֹפִים	סֹפָה	סֹף	סוֹף	סוֹף	ס.פ
	אֶצְאָה	צֶאנָה	צְאוּ	צְאִי	צֵא	יֹצְאוֹת	יֹצְאִים	יֹצֵאת	יֹצֵא	צֵאת	יָצֹא	י.צ.א

בִּנְיָן QAL Verbs 513

Infinitives, Participles, and Command Forms for Selected Verbs in Qal בִּנְיָן

	Command Forms						Participles				Infinitives		Root
juss 3ms[2]	cohort 1cs	imv fpl	imv mpl	imv fs	imv ms	fpl	mpl	fs	ms	inf c	inf ab[1]	שֶׁרֶשׁ
	אֶשָּׁא	שֶּׂאנָה	שְׂאוּ	שְׂאִי	שָׂא	נֹשְׂאוֹת	נֹשְׂאִים	נֹשֵׂאת	נֹשֵׂא	שְׂאֵת	נָשֹׂא	נ.שׂ.א
יֵרֵד	אֵרְדָה	רֵדְנָה	רְדוּ	רְדִי	רֵד	יֹרְדוֹת	יֹרְדִים	יֹרֶדֶת	יֹרֵד	רֶדֶת	יָרוֹד	י.ר.ד
	אֵשְׁבָה	שֵׁבְנָה	שְׁבוּ	שְׁבִי	שֵׁב	יֹשְׁבוֹת	יֹשְׁבִים	יֹשֶׁבֶת	יֹשֵׁב	שֶׁבֶת	יָשׁוֹב	י.שׁ.ב
יֵדַע	אֵדְעָה	דַּעְנָה	דְּעוּ	דְּעִי	דַּע	יֹדְעוֹת	יֹדְעִים	יֹדַעַת	יֹדֵעַ	דַּעַת	N/A	י.ד.ע
												ח.ד.ל
יָלֹן	אָלִינָה	לֹנָּה	לִינוּ	לִינִי	לִין	לָנוֹת	לָנִים	לָנָה	לָן	לוּן	לוֹן	ל./ל.י.ן
	אָקוּמָה	קֹמְנָה	קוּמוּ	קוּמִי	קוּם	קָמוֹת	קָמִים	קָמָה	קָם	קוּם	קוֹם	ק.ו.מ
	אָרוּצָה	רֹצְנָה	רוּצוּ	רוּצִי	רוּץ	רָצוֹת	רָצִים	רָצָה	רָץ	רוּץ	רוֹץ	ר.ו.צ
	אֶבְנֶה	בְּנֶינָה	בְּנוּ	בְּנִי	בְּנֵה	בֹּנוֹת	בֹּנִים	בֹּנָה	בֹּנֶה	בְּנוֹת	בָּנוֹ	ב.נ.ה
	אֶלְכְּדָה	לְכֹדְנָה	לִכְדוּ	לִכְדִי	לְכֹד	לֹכְדוֹת	לֹכְדִים	לֹכֶדֶת	לֹכֵד	לְכֹד	לָכוֹד	ל.כ.ד
	אֶלְמְדָה	לְמֹדְנָה	לִמְדוּ	לִמְדִי	לְמַד	לֹמְדוֹת	לֹמְדִים	לֹמֶדֶת	לֹמֵד	לְמֹד	לָמוֹד	ל.מ.ד
	אֶמְצְאָה	מְצֶאנָה	מִצְאוּ	מִצְאִי	מְצָא	מֹצְאוֹת	מֹצְאִים	מֹצֵאת	מֹצֵא	מְצֹא	מָצוֹא	מ.צ.א
תַּחַת	אַחְזְקָה	חֲזַקְנָה	חִזְקוּ	חִזְקִי	חֲזַק	חֲזָקוֹת	חֲזָקִים	חֲזָקָה	חָזָק	חֲזֹק	חָזֹק	ח.ז.ק
	אֶעְבְדָה	עֲבֹדְנָה	עִבְדוּ	עִבְדִי	עֲבֹד	עֹבְדוֹת	עֹבְדִים	עֹבֶדֶת	עֹבֵד	עֲבֹד	עָבוֹד	ע.ב.ד
	אֶאֱסֹף	אֱסֹפְנָה	אִסְפוּ	אִסְפִי	אֱסֹף	אֹסְפוֹת	אֹסְפִים	אֹסֶפֶת	אֹסֵף	אֱסֹף	אָסוֹף	א.ס.פ
יֵלֵךְ	אֵלְכָה	לֵכְנָה	לְכוּ	לְכִי	לֵךְ	הֹלְכוֹת	הֹלְכִים	הֹלֶכֶת	הֹלֵךְ	לֶכֶת	הָלוֹךְ	ה.ל.ך
	אֹכְלָה	אֱכֹלְנָה	אִכְלוּ	אִכְלִי	אֱכֹל	אֹכְלוֹת	אֹכְלִים	אֹכֶלֶת	אֹכֵל	אֱכֹל	אָכוֹל	א.כ.ל
	אֹמְרָה	אֱמֹרְנָה	אִמְרוּ	אִמְרִי	אֱמֹר	אֹמְרוֹת	אֹמְרִים	אֹמֶרֶת	אֹמֵר	אֱמֹר	אָמוֹר	א.מ.ר

Infinitives, Participles, and Command Forms for Selected Verbs in Qal בִּנְיָן

Command Forms					Participles				Infinitives		Root
juss 3ms[2]	cohort 1cs	imv fpl	imv mpl	imv fs	imv ms	fpl	mpl	fs	ms	inf c	inf ab[1]	
יֵרֶד	אֵרְדָה	רֵדְנָה	רְדוּ	רְדִי	רֵד	יֹרְדוֹת	יֹרְדִים	יֹרֶדֶת	יֹרֵד	רֶדֶת	יָרֹד	י.ר.ד
יִקָּה	אֶקְחָה	קַחְנָה	קְחוּ	קְחִי	קַח	לֹקְחוֹת	לֹקְחִים	לֹקַחַת	לֹקֵחַ	קַחַת	לָקֹחַ	ל.ק.ח
	אֶסְלְחָה	סְלַחְנָה	סִלְחוּ	סִלְחִי	סְלַח	סֹלְחוֹת	סֹלְחִים	סֹלַחַת	סֹלֵחַ	סְלֹחַ	סָלֹחַ	ס.ל.ח
	אֶסְפְּרָה	סְפַרְנָה	סִפְרוּ	סִפְרִי	סְפַר	סֹפְרוֹת	סֹפְרִים	סֹפֶרֶת	סֹפֵר	סְפֹר	סָפֹר	ס.פ.ר
	אֶבְדְּלָה	בְּדַלְנָה	בִּדְלוּ	בִּדְלִי	בְּדַל	בֹּדְלוֹת	בֹּדְלִים	בֹּדֶלֶת	בֹּדֵל	בְּדֹל	בָּדֹל	ב.ד.ל
	אֶבְחֲרָה	בְּחַרְנָה	בַּחֲרוּ	בַּחֲרִי	בְּחַר	בֹּחֲרוֹת	בֹּחֲרִים	בֹּחֶרֶת	בֹּחֵר	בְּחֹר	בָּחֹר	ב.ח.ר
אֵלֵךְ	אֵלְכָה	לֵכְנָה	לְכוּ	לְכִי	לֵךְ	הֹלְכוֹת	הֹלְכִים	הֹלֶכֶת	הֹלֵךְ	לֶכֶת	הָלוֹךְ	ה.ל.ך/הלך
	אָקוּמָה	קֹמְנָה	קוּמוּ	קוּמִי	קוּמִי	קָמוֹת	קָמִים	קָמָה	קָם	קוּם	קוֹם	ק.ו.מ/קום
יָשֵׂם	אָשִׂימָה	שֵׂמְנָה	שִׂימוּ	שִׂימִי	שִׂים	שָׂמוֹת	שָׂמִים	שָׂמָה	שָׂם	שִׂים	שׂוֹם	שׂ.י.מ/שׂים
יָבֹא	אָבוֹאָה	בֹּאנָה	בֹּאוּ	בֹּאִי	בֹּא	בָּאוֹת	בָּאִים	בָּאָה	בָּא	בּוֹא	בּוֹא	ב.ו.א
	אֶבְנֶה	בְּנֶינָה	בְּנוּ	בְּנִי	בְּנֵה	בֹּנוֹת	בֹּנִים	בֹּנָה	בֹּנֶה	בְּנוֹת	בָּנֹה	ב.נ.ה

QAL בִּנְיָן　　　　　　　　　　　Verbs　　　　　　　　　　　515

Infinitives, Participles, and Command Forms for Selected Verbs in Qal בִּנְיָן

	Command Forms					Participles			Infinitives		Root
juss 3ms[2]	cohort 1cs	imv fpl	imv mpl	imv fs	imv ms	fpl	mpl	fs	ms	inf c	inf ab[1]	
	אֶכְבְּדָה	כְּבַדְנָה	כִּבְדוּ	כִּבְדִי	כְּבַד	כְּבֵדוֹת	כְּבֵדִים	כְּבֵדָה	כָּבֵד	כְּבֹד	כָּבוֹד	שׁרב
	אֶקְדְּשָׁה	קְדַשְׁנָה	N/A[6]	קִדְשִׁי	use piel	קְדֵשׁוֹת	קְדֵשִׁים	קְדֵשָׁה	קָדֵשׁ	קְדֹשׁ	קָדוֹשׁ	ק.ד.שׁ
	use piel	use piel	use piel	use piel	use piel					use piel		ק/י.ד.ה
יָקֹם	אָקוּמָה	קֹמְנָה	קוּמוּ	קוּמִי	קוּם	קָמוֹת	קָמִים	קָמָה	קָם	קוּם	קוֹם	ק.ו.ם
	אֶקְרְאָה	קְרֶאנָה	קִרְאוּ	קִרְאִי	קְרָא	קֹרְאוֹת	קֹרְאִים	קֹרְאָה	קֹרֵא	קְרֹא	קָרֹא	ק/י.ר.ה to call
	אֶקְרְאָה	קְרֶאנָה	קִרְאוּ	קִרְאִי	קְרָא	קֹרְאוֹת	קֹרְאִים	קֹרְאָה	קֹרֵא	קְרֹא	קָרֹא	ק.ר.א to meet
	אֶרְדְּפָה	רְדֹפְנָה	רִדְפוּ	רִדְפִי	רְדֹף	רֹדְפוֹת	רֹדְפִים	רֹדְפָה	רֹדֵף	רְדֹף	רָדוֹף	ר.ד.ף
יֵצֵא	אֵצְאָה	צֶאנָה	צְאוּ	צְאִי	צֵא	יֹצְאוֹת	יֹצְאִים	יֹצְאָה	יֹצֵא	צֵאת	יָצֹא[7]	י.צ.א/ה
יָקֹ֫ם[8]	אָקוּמָה	קֹמְנָה	קוּמוּ	קוּמִי	קוּם	קָמוֹת	קָמִים	קָמָה	קָם	קוּם	קוֹם	ק.ו.ם
יָר֫וּ	אָרוּצָה	רֹצְנָה	רוּצוּ	רוּצִי	רוּץ	רָצוֹת	רָצִים	רָצָה	רָץ	רוּץ	רוֹץ	ר.ו.ץ
	אֶרְבֶּה	רְבֶינָה	רְבוּ	רְבִי	רְבֵה	רֹבוֹת	רֹבִים	רֹבָה	רֹבֶה	רְבוֹת	רָבֹה	ר/י.ב.ה
	אֶשְׁאֲלָה	שְׁאַלְנָה	שַׁאֲלוּ	שַׁאֲלִי	שְׁאַל	שֹׁאֲלוֹת	שֹׁאֲלִים	שֹׁאֲלָה	שֹׁאֵל	שְׁאֹל	שָׁאוֹל	שׁ.א.ל

---

[1] The injunction "be holy" is expressed by ה.י.ה followed by a form of the adjective קָדוֹשׁ (cf. Lev. 11:44, 45, 19:2). In בִּנְיָנִים such as piel and hitpael, ק.ד.שׁ attests standard imperatives.

[7] Also יָצוֹא.

[8] If spelled with retracted accent, יָקָ֫ם. Attested usage prefers the form shown above (without the retracted accent).

Infinitives, Participles, and Command Forms for Selected Verbs in Qal בִּנְיָן

	Command Forms						Participles				Infinitives		Root
juss 3ms[2]	cohort 1cs	imv fpl	imv mpl	imv fs	imv ms	fpl	mpl	fs	ms	inf c	inf ab[1]	
	אֶשְׁמְרָה	שְׁמֹרְנָה	שִׁמְרוּ	שִׁמְרִי	שְׁמֹר	שֹׁמְרוֹת	שֹׁמְרִים	שֹׁמֶרֶת	שֹׁמֵר	שְׁמֹר	שָׁמוֹר	ש.מ.ר
יְשֵׁב	אֵשְׁבָה	שֵׁבְנָה	שְׁבוּ	שְׁבִי	שֵׁב	יֹשְׁבוֹת	יֹשְׁבִים	יֹשֶׁבֶת	יֹשֵׁב	שֶׁבֶת	יָשׁוֹב	י.ש.ב
יָקֹם	אָקוּמָה	קֹמְנָה	קוּמוּ	קוּמִי	קוּם	קָמוֹת	קָמִים	קָמָה	קָם	קוּם	קוֹם	ק.ו/י.ם
	אֶבְנֶה	בְּנֶינָה	בְּנוּ	בְּנִי	בְּנֵה	בֹּנוֹת	בֹּנִים	בֹּנָה	בֹּנֶה	בְּנוֹת	בָּנֹה	ב.נ.ה
	אֶעֱבֹדָה	עֲבֹדְנָה	עִבְדוּ	עִבְדִי	עֲבֹד	עֹבְדוֹת	עֹבְדִים	עֹבֶדֶת	עֹבֵד	עֲבֹד	עָבוֹד	ע.ב.ד
	אֶבְחֲרָה	בְּחַרְנָה	בַּחֲרוּ	בַּחֲרִי	בְּחַר	בֹּחֲרוֹת	בֹּחֲרִים	בֹּחֶרֶת	בֹּחֵר	בְּחֹר	בָּחוֹר	ב.ח.ר
	אֶשְׁמְעָה	שְׁמַעְנָה	שִׁמְעוּ	שִׁמְעִי	שְׁמַע	שֹׁמְעוֹת	שֹׁמְעִים	שֹׁמַעַת	שֹׁמֵעַ	שְׁמֹעַ	שָׁמוֹעַ	ש.מ.ע
	אֹכְלָה	אֱכֹלְנָה	אִכְלוּ	אִכְלִי	אֱכֹל	אֹכְלוֹת	אֹכְלִים	אֹכֶלֶת	אֹכֵל	אֱכֹל	אָכוֹל	א.כ.ל
יִצֹּר	אֶצְּרָה	צֹרְנָה	צְרוּ	צְרִי	צֹר	נֹצְרוֹת	נֹצְרִים	נֹצֶרֶת	נֹצֵר	נְצֹר	נָצוֹר	נ.צ/י.ר
	אֶגְּשָׁה	גַּשְׁנָה	גְּשׁוּ	גְּשִׁי	גַּשׁ	נֹגְשׁוֹת	נֹגְשִׁים	נֹגֶשֶׁת	נֹגֵשׁ	גֶּשֶׁת	נָגוֹשׁ	נ.ג.שׁ

Glossaries

Hebrew-English.................. 518

English-Hebrew.................. 541

GLOSSARY

לַחְקוֹר‎ᵃ מִלִּים‎ᵇ

ᵃ ח.ק.ר to search
ᵇ מִלָּה f word, utterance

Hebrew / English   יְהוּדִית / אַנְגְּלִית

Introductory notes

(1) A word whose letters are separated by periods (e.g., א.ה.ב) signifies the underlying שֹׁרֶשׁ *root*. When a שֹׁרֶשׁ comprises an entire entry, the root meaning is given. Thus א.ה.ב is defined as "love."

(2) When no בִּנְיָן *stem* is specified for a verbal form, the meaning offered reflects the qal בִּנְיָן.

(3) Verbal forms preceded by ו have generally been rendered "and…" or "then…."

(4) Imperative, participle, and adjective entries will list related forms in this sequence: masculine singular, feminine singular, masculine plural, feminine plural.

(5) Noun entries will list related forms in this sequence: singular absolute, plural absolute, singular construct, plural construct.

(6) Abbreviations introduced earlier in the textbook continue in the glossary, including "*pn loc*" (proper noun of location, for place names that can vary with regard to gender; cf. GKC §122.i).

(7) Meanings found here support readings in this textbook. The glossary is not intended as a substitute for standard lexica when reading the Hebrew Bible.

א

perish *qal* (6.3), destroy *hifil* (9.3) .... א.ב.ד
be willing (6.2) .... א.ב.ה/י
love (3.3) .... א.ה.ב
delay *piel* (10.2) .... א.ח.ר
eat *qal* (3.1), be devoured *qal passive* (11.1) .... א.כ.ל

believe *hifil* (4.4), be faithful, reliable, ... א.מ.נ
   established *nifal* (7.4)
say (5.3) .... א.מ.ר
think, say in one's heart (4.3, ... א.מ.ר בְּלֵב, בְּלֵבָב
   6.3)
gather *qal* (7.2) be gathered *nifal and pual* .... א.ס.פ
   (8.2, 11.1)
bind *qal*, be bound *nifal* (7.3) .... א.ס.ר
I do / will / would believe *hifil* (4.4) .... אַאֲמִין [א.מ.נ]

HEBREW GLOSSARY — יְהוּדִית

father *m* (6.1)	אָב, אָבוֹת, אֲבִי־ *or* אַב־, אֲבוֹת־
they were willing (6.2)	אָבוּ [א.ב.י/ה]
poor, needy (9.3)	אֶבְיוֹן, ־־, אֶבְיוֹנִים, ־־
I (can) understand (1.3)	אָבִין [ב.י.נ]
stone *f* (1.1)	אֶבֶן, אֲבָנִים, אֶבֶן־, אַבְנֵי־
I will speak *piel* (9.1)	אֲדַבֵּר [ד.ב.ר]
Edom *m* (map of Israel)	אֱדוֹם
lord *m* (10.1)	אָדוֹן, אֲדוֹנִים, אֲדוֹן־, אֲדֹנֵי־
man, humankind, Adam *m* (6.1)	אָדָם, אֲדַם־ *or* אָדָם־
Lord GOD (8.1)	אֲדֹנָי יהוה
I will (*or* am resolved to) seek cohort. (9.4)	אֶדְרְשָׁה [ד.ר.שׁ]
Love! *imv* (9.3)	אֱהַב, אֶהֱבִי, אֶהֱבוּ, אֶהֱבָנָה [א.ה.ב]
one who loves *pt* (3.3)	אֹהֵב, אֹהֶבֶת, אֹהֲבִים, אֹהֲבוֹת [א.ה.ב]
love *f* (10.3)	אַהֲבָה, אַהֲבַת־
Alas…! Ah…! (5.2)	אֲהָהּ
I will be (4.3)	אֶהְיֶה [ה.י.ה]
tent *m* (6.1)	אֹהֶל, אֹהָלִים, אֹהֶל־, אָהֳלֵי־
woe, alas (8.2)	אוֹי
Woe is me (6.1)	אוֹי לִי
enemy *m* (3.3)	אוֹיֵב, אוֹיְבִים, אוֹיֵב־, אוֹיְבֵי־
I am able (2.4)	אוּכַל [י.כ.ל]
perhaps (4.4)	אוּלַי
wickedness, disaster *m* (9.4)	אָוֶן, אוֹנִים, אוֹן־, אוֹנֵי־
Ur of the Chaldeans *m* (map of ANE)	אוּר כַּשְׂדִּים
light, brightness *f* (4.4)	אוֹר, אוֹרִים
then, at that time (5.3)	אָז
I will sacrifice abundantly, repeatedly *piel* (10.2)	אֲזַבֵּחַ [ז.ב.ח]
I will sacrifice *qal* (5.3)	אֶזְבַּח [ז.ב.ח]
ear *f* (4.2)	אֹזֶן, אָזְנַיִם, אֹזֶן־, אָזְנֵי־
his ears *f* (4.4)	אָזְנָיו
brother *m* (5.1)	אָח, אַחִים, אֲחִי־, אֲחֵי־
one, single, same *m* (5.2)	אֶחָד, אַחַת, אֲחָדִים
behind *or* after (2.4)	אַחַר, אַחֲרֵי
different, foreign (9.5)	אַחֵר, אַחֶרֶת, אֲחֵרִים, אֲחֵרוֹת
later on (6.2)	אַחֲרוֹן
my enemy, my enemies (3.3)	אֹיְבִי, אֹיְבַי
Where is…? (2.1)	אַיֵּה…?
How would one say …. "[דָּבָר]"? in Judean "[word]"? (2.1)	אֵיךְ יֹאמְרוּ בִּיהוּדִית "[דָּבָר]"?
How…? (4.3)	אֵיךְ…?
there is not, there are not *constr* (1.1)	אֵין[1]
I do not have (1.1)	אֵין לִי
you do not have *ms* (1.1)	אֵין לְךָ
you *ms* are not, you do not (3.2)	אֵינְךָ
I am not, I do not (1.3)	אֵינֶנִּי
we are not, we do not; he is not, he does not (3.2)	אֵינֶנּוּ
I will fear, be afraid (5.2)	אִירָא [י.ר.א]
man, person *m* (1.1)	אִישׁ, אֲנָשִׁים, אִישׁ־, אַנְשֵׁי־
but, however, surely (3.1)	אַךְ
I will eat *qal* (5.2)	אֹכַל [א.כ.ל]
one who eats *pt* (3.1)	אֹכֵל, אֹכְלָה, אֹכְלִים, אֹכְלוֹת [א.כ.ל]
they were devoured *qal passive* (11.1)	אֻכְּלוּ [א.כ.ל]
Do not…! (4.3)	אַל־
to, toward (2.4)	אֶל
god(s) *or* God *m* (2.3, 8.1)	אֵל, אֱלֹהִים, אֵל־, אֱלֹהֵי־
please do not (*plus jussive*)… (10.2)	אַל־נָא
Don't cry! *m, f* (4.3)	אַל־תֵּבְךְּ, אַל־תִּבְכִּי [ב.כ.י/ה]

---

[1] The absolute form is אַיִן.

Don't be afraid! ...... [י.ר.א] אַל־תִּירָא, תִּירְאִי, תִּירְאוּ	ashes *m* (9.3) .... אֵפֶר
ms, fs, mpl (4.3, 5.1)	Ephraim *m* (6.1) .... אֶפְרַיִם
Do not go out! *mpl* (7.4) .... [י.צ.א] אַל־תֵּצְאוּ	I will go out, leave (3.2) .... [י.צ.א] אֵצֵא
these *m and f* (3.1) .... אֵלֶּה	purple (material) *m* (8.1) .... אַרְגָּמָן
your *ms* God (3.2) .... אֱלֹהֶיךָ	I will descend, go down (5.2) .... [י.ר.ד] אֵרֵד
God *m* (2.3) .... אֱלֹהִים, אֱלֹהֵי־	chest, ark *m* (7.3) .... אָרוֹן, אֲרוֹן
our God *m* (3.2) .... אֱלֹהֵינוּ	lion *m* (7.5) .... אֲרִי, אֲרָיוֹת, אֲרִי־, אֲרָיוֹת־
to us (4.5) .... אֵלֵינוּ	Aram [Syria] *m* (map of Ancient Near East) .... אֲרָם
I will go (5.2) .... [ה.ל.כ] אֵלֵךְ	Mesopotamia *m* (map of Ancient Near East) ... אֲרַם נַהֲרַיִם
widow *f* (7.3) .... אַלְמָנָה, אַלְמְנַת־, אַלְמָנוֹת, אַלְמְנוֹת־	land, earth *f* (3.2) .... אֶרֶץ, אֲרָצוֹת, אֶרֶץ־, אַרְצוֹת־
cattle *m* (10.2) .... אֲלָפִים	Cyprus, the land of *pn loc* (map of ANE) .... אֶרֶץ כִּתִּים
if (4.2) .... אִם	fire *f* (9.2) .... אֵשׁ
mother *f* (6.1) .... אֵם, אִמּוֹת, אֵם־, אִמּוֹת־	I will lift, carry (5.2) .... [נ.שׂ.א] אֶשָּׂא
I will find (5.2) .... [מ.צ.א] אֶמְצָא	I would like to ask you *ms and fs* .... אֶשְׁאֲלָה לְךָ:
Say! *imv* (9.1) ... אֱמֹר, אִמְרִי, אִמְרוּ, אֱמֹרְנָה [א.מ.ר]	(a question), *also for making a request* (4.2)
I will say (5.3) .... [א.מ.ר] אֹמַר	Ashdod *pn loc* (8.2) .... אַשְׁדּוֹד
one who .... אֹמֵר, אֹמֶרֶת, אֹמְרִים, אֹמְרוֹת [א.מ.ר]	Ashdodite (8.2) .... אַשְׁדּוֹדִי
says *pt* (4.4)	woman *f* (1.1) .... אִשָּׁה, נָשִׁים, אֵשֶׁת־, נְשֵׁי־
truth *f* (5.1) .... אֱמֶת	I will (am resolved to) turn *cohort.* (9.4) . [שׁ.ו.ב] אָשׁוּבָה
Amittai, *masculine name* (6.1) .... אֲמִתַּי	Asshur *pn loc* (map of Ancient Near East) .... אַשּׁוּר
please *or* oh! (*as a sigh*, 10.1) .... אָנָּא *or* אָנָּה	I will put (5.3) .... [שׂ.ו/י.מ] אָשִׂים
To where? Whither? (2.3) .... אָנָה...?	I will throw (5.2) .... [שׁ.ל.כ] אַשְׁלִיךְ
we *c* (3.2) .... אֲנַחְנוּ	I will repay *piel* (10.1) .... [שׁ.ל.מ] אֲשַׁלֵּם
I *c* (1.3) .... אֲנִי	guilty (7.5) .... אָשֵׁם, אֲשֵׁמָה, אֲשֵׁמִים, אֲשֵׁמוֹת
ship *f* (2.1) .... אֳנִיָּה, אֳנִיּוֹת, אֳנִיַּת־, אֳנִיּוֹת־	I will cause to hear *hifil* (8.1) .... [שׁ.מ.ע] אַשְׁמִיעַ
I *c* (3.1) .... אָנֹכִי	which, that, who (*not interrogative*), since (2.4) .... אֲשֶׁר
men *m* (4.1, cf. אִישׁ) .... אֲנָשִׁים, אַנְשֵׁי־	אֵת *when written without maqqef dash* (6.2) .... אֵת
I will forgive (5.3) .... [ס.ל.ח] אֶסְלַח	with (2.4) .... אֵת, אֶת־
I will go up, ascend (5.3) .... [ע.ל.י/ה] אֶעֱלֶה	a particle preceding a definite direct object, ... אֵת, אֶת־
nose, anger *m* (4.2) .... אַף, אַפַּיִם	*untranslatable* (2.1)
his nose *m* (4.2) .... אַפּוֹ	you *fs* (1.3) .... אַתְּ
faces (bowed) to the ground (11.2) .... אַפַּיִם אָרְצָה	you *ms* (1.3) .... אַתָּה

HEBREW GLOSSARY — יְהוּדִית

her, it *object form* (3.4)	אוֹתָהּ or אֹתָהּ
him, it *object form* (3.4)	אוֹתוֹ or אֹתוֹ
me *object form* (3.3)	אוֹתִי or אֹתִי
you *object form, fs* (3.4)	אוֹתָךְ or אֹתָךְ
you *object form, ms* (3.4)	אוֹתְךָ or אֹתְךָ
you *object form, mpl* (3.4)	אֶתְכֶם
you *object form, fpl* (3.4)	אֶתְכֶן
them *object form, mpl* (3.4)	אוֹתָם or אֹתָם
you *mpl* (3.3)	אַתֶּם
yesterday (6.1)	אֶתְמוֹל
them *object form, fpl* (3.4)	אֹתָן
I will give (5.2)	אֶתֵּן [נ.ת.ן]
you *fpl* (3.3)	אַתֵּנָה, *also* אַתֵּן
us *object form, mpl* (3.4)	אוֹתָנוּ or אֹתָנוּ

ב

come, enter *qal* (2.4), bring *hifil* (8.1), be brought *hofal* (11.2)	א.ו.ב
be ashamed (10.2)	ב.ו.שׁ
understand (1.3)	ב.י.נ
cry (4.3)	ב.כ.י/ה
swallow (4.3)	ב.ל.ע
build *qal* (7.1), be built *nifal* (7.3)	ב.נ.י/ה
look for, seek *piel* (1.3)	ב.ק.שׁ
bless *piel* (10.1), be blessed *qal passive* (7.3), be blessed *pual* (11.1)	ב.ר.כ
in, with, by means of (2.4)	בְּ
she came, entered (6.2)	בָּאָה [ב.ו.א]
finally, at last (4.4)	בָּאַחֲרוֹן, בָּאַחֲרֹנָה
really (1.1)	בֶּאֱמֶת
we came (6.4)	בָּאנוּ [ב.ו.א]
well *f* (7.1)	בְּאֵר, בְּאֵרֹת, בְּאֵר־, בְּאֵרֹת־
Beer Sheba *pn loc* (map of Israel)	בְּאֵר שֶׁבַע
I came, entered (6.1)	בָּאתִי [ב.ו.א]
Babylon *pn loc* (7.4)	בָּבֶל
garment *m* (7.5)	בֶּגֶד, בְּגָדִים, בֶּגֶד־, בִּגְדֵי־
while he was speaking *piel inf c, prep, 3ms suffix* (8.2)	בְּדַבְּרוֹ [ד.ב.ר]
when it is / was reported *hofal inf c, prep* (11.3)	בְּהֻגַּד [נ.ג.ד]
while being *inf c, prep* (4.4)	בִּהְיוֹת [ה.י.ה]
while he is *inf c, prep, 3ms sfx* (9.4)	בִּהְיוֹתוֹ [ה.י.ה]
animal, cattle *f* (5.1)	בְּהֵמָה, בְּהֵמוֹת, בֶּהֱמַת־, בַּהֲמוֹת־
when they threw you *pl hifil inf c* (6.3)	בְּהַשְׁלִיכָם [שׁ.ל.כ]
Enter! Come! *imv* (2.4)	בּוֹא, בּוֹאִי, בּוֹאוּ, בּוֹאֶנָה [ב.ו.א]
belly, stomach *f* (4.3)	בֶּטֶן
my belly, stomach *f* (4.3)	בִּטְנִי
before *in time* (8.1)	בְּטֶרֶם
between, among (4.2)	בֵּין
house *m* (4.3)	בַּיִת, בָּתִּים, בֵּית־, בָּתֵּי־
Bethel *pn loc* (map of Israel)	בֵּיתְאֵל
Weep for! *imv* (9.3)	בְּכֵה, בְּכִי, בְּכוּ, בְּכֶינָה [ב.כ.י/ה] לְ
one who weeps, cries *pt* (4.3)	בֹּכֶה, בּוֹכִיָּה / בֹּכָה, בֹּכִים, בֹּכוֹת [ב.כ.י/ה]
one who swallows (4.3)	בֹּלֵעַ, בֹּלַעַת, בֹּלְעִים, בֹּלְעוֹת [ב.ל.ע]
not I, apart from me (11.1)	בִּלְעָדַי
except for (7.3)	בִּלְתִּי

high place *cultic mound*, *f* (9.2)	בָּמָה, בָּמוֹת, בָּמַת־, בָּמֳתֵי־
son *m* (6.1)	בֵּן, בָּנִים, בֶּן־, בְּנֵי־
on account of (5.3)	בַּעֲבוּר
when (entity) is / was crossing over *inf c*, *prep* (6.2)	בַּעֲבֹר [ע.ב.ר]
morning, daybreak, dawn *m* (5.1)	בֹּקֶר
cattle, herd *m* (9.2)	בָּקָר, בְּקָרִים, בְּקַר־, בִּקְרֵי־
he looked for, searched, sought *piel* (1.5)	בִּקֵּשׁ [ב.ק.שׁ]
I looked for, searched, sought *piel* (6.4)	בִּקַּשְׁתִּי [ב.ק.שׁ]
firstly, at first (5.2)	בָּרִאשׁוֹנָה
fourthly (5.2)	בָּרְבִיעִית
when (it) descended / descends / will descend *inf c* (6.4)	בְּרֶדֶת [י.ר.ד]
one who is ... blessed *qal passive pt* (7.3)	בָּרוּךְ, בְּרוּכָה, בְּרוּכִים, בְּרוּכוֹת [ב.ר.כ]
covenant *f* (8.1)	בְּרִית, בְּרִית־
knee *f* (4.3)	בֶּרֶךְ, בִּרְכַּיִם, בֶּרֶךְ־, בִּרְכֵּי־
he blessed *piel* (10.1)	בֵּרַךְ [ב.ר.כ]
as I was / am /will be grazing *inf c* ... with *prep* (7.5)	בִּרְעוֹתִי [ר.ע.י/ה]
when we return (5.1)	בְּשׁוּבֵנוּ [שׁ.ו.ב]
secondly (5.2)	בַּשֵּׁנִית
meat, flesh *m* (5.2)	בָּשָׂר, בְּשָׂרִים, בְּשַׂר־
I am ashamed (10.2)	בֹּשְׁתִּי [ב.ו.שׁ]
daughter *f* (6.1)	בַּת, בָּנוֹת, בַּת־, בְּנוֹת־
in the middle of, among (2.4)	בְּתוֹךְ

ג

reveal, uncover *piel* (10.1)	ג.ל.י/ה
steal *qal* (7.5), be stolen *nifal* (10.2)	ג.נ.ב
border *m* (11.1)	גְּבוּל, גְּבוּלִים, גְּבוּל־, גְּבוּלֵי־
Gaddiel, *masculine name* (3.2)	גַּדִּיאֵל
big, large, great (2.3)	גָּדוֹל, גְּדוֹלָה, גְּדוֹלִים, גְּדוֹלוֹת
nation, people *m* (11.1)	גּוֹי, גּוֹיִם, גּוֹי־, גּוֹיֵי־
he uncovered, revealed *piel* (10.1)	גִּלָּה [ג.ל.י/ה]
he stole (7.5)	גָּנַב [ג.נ.ב]
also (5.3)	גַּם
Gath-Hepher *pn loc* (6.1)	גַּת הַחֵפֶר

ד

speak *piel* (2.4), be spoken *pual* (11.1)	ד.ב.ר
investigate (7.4)	ד.ר.שׁ
he spoke *piel* (10.1)	דִּבֶּר [ד.ב.ר]
to speak *piel inf c* (9.5)	דַּבֵּר [ד.ב.ר]
plague *m*, *perhaps bubonic* (8.2)	דֶּבֶר
Tell, speak! *piel* *imv* (9.2)	דַּבֵּר, דַּבְּרִי, דַּבְּרוּ, דַּבֵּרְנָה [ד.ב.ר]
word, matter, event, thing *m* (4.2)	דָּבָר, דְּבָרִים, דְּבַר־, דִּבְרֵי־
we spoke *piel* (6.4)	דִּבַּרְנוּ [ד.ב.ר]
I spoke *piel* (6.2)	דִּבַּרְתִּי [ד.ב.ר]
honey *m* (3.1)	דְּבַשׁ
fish *m* (3.3)	דָּג, דָּגִים, דַּג־, דְּגֵי־
Dagon, *deity name* (8.2)	דָּגוֹן
generation *m* (10.2)	דּוֹר, דֹּרוֹת, דּוֹר־, דֹּרֹת־
door *f* (2.4)	דֶּלֶת, דְּלָתוֹת, דֶּלֶת־, דַּלְתוֹת־
blood *m* (11.1)	דָּם, דָּמִים, דַּם־, דְּמֵי־
Damascus *pn loc* (map of Ancient Near East)	דַּמֶּשֶׂק
Know! *imv* (9.2)	דַּע, דְּעִי, דְּעוּ, דֵּעְנָה [י.ד.ע]

HEBREW GLOSSARY — יְהוּדִית

road, way *m or f* (4.4)	דֶּרֶךְ, דְּרָכִים, דֶּרֶךְ־, דַּרְכֵּי־
Way of the Sea, the *m or f* (map of Israel, note)	דֶּרֶךְ הַיָּם
King's Highway, the *m or f* (map of Israel)	דֶּרֶךְ הַמֶּלֶךְ
to investigate *inf c* (7.4)	דְּרֹשׁ [ד.ר.שׁ]
Investigate! Seek! *imv* (9.2)	דְּרֹשׁ, דִּרְשִׁי, דִּרְשׁוּ, דְּרֹשְׁנָה [ד.ר.שׁ]

ה

be, become (4.3)	ה.י./ה
go, walk *qal* (3.2), walk about *piel* (10.1), walk back and forth, roam *hitpael* (11.3)	ה.ל.כ
praise *piel* (10.3), be praised *pual* (11.1)	ה.ל.ל
be overturned *nifal* (7.5)	ה.פ.ח
the (2.1)	הַ◌ּ..., הַ..., הָ..., הֶ...
question mark, interrogative particle (1.1)	הֲ... / הַ...
Destroy! *hifil imv* (9.3)	הַאֲבֵד, הַאֲבִידִי, הַאֲבִידוּ, הָאֲבֵדְנָה [א.ב.ד]
he brought *hifil* (8.1)	הֵבִיא [ב.ו.א]
to be reported *hofal inf c* (11.3)	הֻגַּד [נ.ג.ד]
he, it, that (one) *m* (2.1)	הוּא
I caused you *ms* to know (8.1)	הוֹדַעְתִּיךָ [י.ד.ע]
Alas! (8.1)	הוֹי
he was killed *hofal* (7.3)	הוּמַת [מ.ו.ת]
they were brought *hofal* (11.2)	הוּבְאוּ [ב.ו.א]
I caused you *ms* to go out *hifil* (8.1)	הוֹצֵאתִיךָ [י.צ.א]
I caused to inherit *hifil* (8.1)	הוֹרַשְׁתִּי [י.ר.שׁ]
I caused to inhabit *hifil* (8.1)	הוֹשַׁבְתִּי [י.שׁ.ב]
he rescued *hifil* (8.1)	הוֹשִׁיעַ [י.שׁ.ע]
Rescue me! Help me! *ms* (5.3)	הוֹשִׁיעֵנִי [י.שׁ.ע]
she, it, that one *f* (2.1)	הִיא
Nile, the *m* (map of Ancient Near East)	הַיְאֹר
Jabbok River, the *pn loc* (map of Israel)	הַיַּבֹּק
he was (5.1)	הָיָה [ה.י./ה]
today *m* (5.1)	הַיּוֹם
Mediterranean Sea, the *m* (maps)	הַיָּם [הַגָּדוֹל]
Jordan River, the *pn loc* (map of Israel)	הַיַּרְדֵּן
I will surely strike *hifil* (5.3)	הַכֵּה אַכֶּה [נ.כ.י/ה]
I struck, hit *hifil* (8.1)	הִכֵּיתִי [נ.כ.י/ה]
she struck, hit *hifil* (7.1)	הִכְּתָה [נ.כ.י/ה]
Is / will / did not...? (4.1)	הֲלֹא, הֲלוֹא...?
Lebanon *pn loc* (map of Ancient Near East)	הַלְּבָנוֹן
Clothe (someone)! *hifil imv* (9.2)	הַלְבֵּשׁ, הַלְבִּישִׁי, הַלְבִּישׁוּ, הַלְבֵּשְׁנָה [ל.ב.שׁ]
to fight *nifal inf absol and inf c* (7.4, 8.2)	הִלָּחֵם [ל.ח.מ]
one who walks *pt* (3.2)	הֹלֵךְ, הֹלְכָה, הֹלְכִים, הֹלְכוֹת [ה.ל.כ]
growing stormier *both pt ms* (3.3)	הוֹלֵךְ וְסֹעֵר [ה.ל.כ, ס.ע.ר]
she walked about *piel* (10.1)	הִלְּכָה [ה.ל.כ]
you walked *fs* (6.3)	הָלַכְתְּ [ה.ל.כ]
you went *ms* (6.3)	הָלַכְתָּ [ה.ל.כ]
I walked about *piel* (10.2)	הִלַּכְתִּי [ה.ל.כ]
I went, traveled *qal* (6.1)	הָלַכְתִּי [ה.ל.כ]
you went *fpl* (6.4)	הֲלַכְתֶּן [ה.ל.כ]
they, those *m*, *alternate forms with same meaning* (3.1)	הֵם, הֵמָּה
he put to death, killed *hifil* (8.1)	הֵמִית [מ.ו.ת]
his being found *nifal inf c, suffix* (9.4)	הִמָּצְאוֹ [מ.צ.א]
indeed (11.2)	הֵן
behold, here is (2.1)	הִנֵּה
they, those *f* (3.4)	הֵנָּה
you removed *hifil ms* (8.1)	הֲסִירֹתָ [ס.ו.ר]

Remove! *hifil imv* (9.2)	הָסֵר, הָסִירִי, הָסִירוּ, הָסֵרְנָה [ס.ו.ר]
he caused (someone) to ascend *hifil* (8.1)	הֶעֱלָה [ע.ל.י/ה]
he caused (someone) to fall *hifil* (8.1)	הִפִּיל [נ.פ.ל]
he delivered, snatched *hifil* (8.1)	הִצִּיל [נ.צ.ל]
you established *hifil ms* (8.1)	הֲקִימוֹתָ [ק.ו.מ]
he caused (someone) to come near *hifil* (8.1)	הִקְרִיב [ק.ר.ב]
mountain *m* (4.2)	הַר, הָרִים, הַר־, הָרֵי־²
Mt. Carmel *pn loc* (map of Israel)	הַר־הַכַּרְמֶל
Mt. Hermon *pn loc* (map of Ancient Near East)	הַר־חֶרְמוֹן
Mt. Sinai *pn loc* (map of Ancient Near East)	הַר־סִינַי
he showed, revealed *hifil* (8.1)	הֶרְאָה [ר.א.י/ה]
you have multiplied *hifil ms* (8.1)	הִרְבִּיתָ [ר.ב.י/ה]
he brought back *hifil* (8.1)	הֵשִׁיב [ש.ו.ב]
How are you *ms, fs*? (1.1)	הֲשָׁלוֹם לְךָ [לָךְ]?
he threw *hifil* (3.3)	הִשְׁלִיךְ [ש.ל.כ]
she threw *hifil* (6.2)	הִשְׁלִיכָה [ש.ל.כ]
to throw *hifil inf c* (6.4)	הַשְׁלִיךְ [ש.ל.כ]
Throw! *hifil imv mpl* (3.3)	הַשְׁלִיכוּ [ש.ל.כ]
they threw me *hifil* (6.2)	הִשְׁלִיכוּנִי [ש.ל.כ]
they were thrown *hofal* (11.2)	הֻשְׁלְכוּ *or* הָשְׁלְכוּ [ש.ל.כ]
Look out! Guard yourself! *nifal imv* (4.1)	הִשָּׁמֵר, הִשָּׁמְרִי, הִשָּׁמְרוּ, הִשָּׁמַרְנָה [ש.מ.ר]
you caused (someone) to hear, you announced *hifil ms* (8.1)	הִשְׁמַעְתָּ [ש.מ.ע]
I caused (someone) to hear, I announced *hifil* (8.1)	הִשְׁמַעְתִּי [ש.מ.ע]

ו

and, *various spellings, depending on next syllable* (2.3)	וְ..., וּ..., וַ..., וָ..., וֶ...
and may I sing *or* play an instrument *piel cohort.* (10.3)	וַאֲזַמְּרָה [ז.מ.ר]
and bless! *piel imv ms* (10.2)	וּבָרֵךְ [ב.ר.כ]
and we will strike *hifil* (7.4)	וְהִכִּינוּ [נ.כ.י/ה]
and I will strike, hit *hifil* (8.1)	וְהִכֵּיתִי [נ.כ.י/ה]
and we will praise *piel* (10.3)	וְהִלַּלְנוּ [ה.ל.ל]
and he may kill *hifil* (8.2)	וְהֵמִית [מ.ו.ת]
and he said (7.1)	וַיֹּאמֶר [א.מ.ר]
then they gathered together *nifal* (8.2)	וַיֵּאָסְפוּ [א.ס.פ]
and he was bound, tied *nifal* (7.3)	וַיֵּאָסֵר [א.ס.ר]
and he came (7.1)	וַיָּבֹא [ב.ו.א]
and he built (7.1)	וַיִּבֶן [ב.נ.י/ה]
and he declared, announced *hifil* (7.1)	וַיַּגֵּד [נ.ג.ד]
and he approached (7.1)	וַיִּגַּשׁ [נ.ג.ש]
and it was spoken *pual* (11.1)	וַיְדֻבַּר [ד.ב.ר]
and he spoke *piel* (10.1)	וַיְדַבֵּר [ד.ב.ר]
and there was (7.1)	וַיְהִי [ה.י.י/ה]
One day... (6.1)	וַיְהִי הַיּוֹם
and it came to pass (6.4)	וַיְהִי
and they were brought *hofal* (11.2)	וַיּוּבְאוּ [ב.ו.א]
then he did (an activity) again *hifil* (7.2)	וַיּוֹסֶף [י.ס.פ]
and it was thought, supposed *nifal* (7.4)	וַיֵּחָשֵׁב [ח.ש.ב]
and they were cut *nifal* (7.3)	וַיִּכָּרְתוּ [כ.ר.ת]

---

² Alternative plural construct הַרְרֵי־.

HEBREW GLOSSARY — יְהוּדִית — 525

and he wrote at the dictation of (10.1)	וַיִּכְתֹּב מִפִּי [כ.ת.ב]
and he went (7.1)	וַיֵּלֶךְ [ה.ל.כ]
and he found (7.1)	וַיִּמְצָא [מ.צ.א]
and he prophesied *nifal* (7.4)	וַיִּנָּבֵא [נ.ב.א]
and he was lifted, carried *nifal* (7.3)	וַיִּנָּשֵׂא [נ.ש.א]
so it was recounted *pual* (11.1)	וַיְסֻפַּר [ס.פ.ר]
and they worked (7.1)	וַיַּעַבְדוּ [ע.ב.ד]
so he answered (7.2)	וַיַּעַן [ע.נ.י/ה]
and he caused (someone) to fall *hifil* shortened (8.2)	וַיַּפֵּל [נ.פ.ל]
then he turned (9.4)	וַיִּפֶן [פ.נ.י/ה]
and he went out (7.1)	וַיֵּצֵא [י.צ.א]
then he took (7.2)	וַיִּקַּח [ל.ק.ח]
and he got up (7.1)	וַיָּקָם [ק.ו.מ]
so they appeared *nifal* (7.4)	וַיֵּרָאוּ [ר.א.י/ה]
and may he return *qal jussive* (9.4)	וְיָשֹׁב [ש.ו.ב]
and they swore an oath *nifal* (7.4)	וַיִּשָּׁבְעוּ [ש.ב.ע]
and he lay down (7.1)	וַיִּשְׁכַּב [ש.כ.ב]
then he put (7.2)	וַיָּשֶׂם [ש.ו/י.מ]
and he drank (7.1)	וַיֵּשְׁתְּ [ש.ת.י/ה]
and they worshipped, bowed down *hishtafel* (11.2)	וַיִּשְׁתַּחֲווּ [ח.ו.י/ה]
and he walked back and forth, roamed, lived *hitpael* (11.3)	וַיִּתְהַלֵּךְ [ה.ל.כ]
and he fortified himself, took courage *hitpael* (11.3)	וַיִּתְחַזֵּק [ח.ז.ק]
and he stationed himself *hitpael* (11.3)	וַיִּתְיַצֵּב [י.צ.ב]
and he / it was given *qal passive* (11.1)	וַיֻּתַּן
and he prayed *hitpael* (11.3)	וַיִּתְפַּלֵּל [פ.ל.ל]
and he grabbed (7.1)	וַיִּתְפֹּשׂ [ת.פ.ש]
and they consecrated themselves *hitpael* (11.3)	וַיִּתְקַדְּשׁוּ [ק.ד.ש]
and we defiled ourselves *nifal* (10.2)	וְנִטְמֵאנוּ [ט.מ.א]
then we struck *hifil* (8.2)	וַנַּךְ [נ.כ.י/ה]
and they will be captured *nifal* (7.4)	וְנִלְכְּדוּ [ל.כ.ד]
and I will exalt *polel* (10.3)	וְרוֹמַמְתִּי [ר.ו.מ]
and you have been compassionate *piel ms* (10.2)	וְרִחַמְתָּ [ר.ח.מ]
then she did [an activity] again *hifil* (7.2)	וַתּוֹסֶף [י.ס.פ]
but she missed, sinned (7.2)	וַתֶּחֱטָא [ח.ט.א]
and she hit *hifil* (7.1)	וַתַּךְ [נ.כ.י/ה]
and they were finished *pual f* (11.1)	וַתְּכֻלֶּינָה [כ.ל.י/ה]
and may it cover *piel jussive 3fs* (10.3)	וּתְכַס [כ.ס.י/ה]
and she was broken *nifal* (7.3)	וַתִּשָּׁבֵר [ש.ב.ר]
so it was at rest *f* (11.2)	וַתִּשְׁקֹט [ש.ק.ט]

ז

sacrifice *qal* (5.1), sacrifice abundantly, repeatedly *piel* (10.2)	ז.ב.ח
remember (5.1)	ז.כ.ר
sing (or play an instrument) *piel* (10.3)	ז.מ.ר
this *f* (3.2)	זֹאת
to sacrifice abundantly, repeatedly *piel inf absol* (10.2)	זַבֵּחַ [ז.ב.ח]
sacrifice, ritual feast *m* (5.1)	זֶבַח, זְבָחִים, זֶבַח־, זִבְחֵי־
this *m* (3.2)	זֶה
gold *m* (6.3)	זָהָב, זְהַב־
I remembered (6.1)	זָכַרְתִּי [ז.כ.ר]
old (6.4)	זָקֵן, זְקֵנָה, זְקֵנִים, זְקֵנוֹת
arm *f* (4.1)	זְרוֹעַ, זְרֹעוֹת, זְרוֹעַ־, זְרֹעֵי־

descendants, seed *m* (9.5)	זֶרַע, זְרָעִים, זֶרַע־ *or* [זֶרַע], זַרְעֵי־
your arm *ms, fs* (4.1)	זְרֹעֲךָ, זְרֹעֵךְ

ח

worship, bow down *hishtafel* (11.2)	ח.ו.ה/י
strong (2.3), be strong *qal*, make strong *piel*, fortify oneself *hitpael* (11.3)	ח.ז.ק
sin, miss (7.4)	ח.ט.א
live (4.3)	ח.י.ה/י
take refuge (10.3)	ח.ס.ה/י
be hot (4.2)	ח.ר.ה/י
think, suppose, be on the verge of *qal*, be thought, be supposed *nifal* (7.4)	ח.ש.ב
sailor *m* (3.2)	חֹבֵל
Tigris River *pn loc* (map of Ancient Near East)	חִדֶּקֶל
new (5.2)	חָדָשׁ, חֲדָשָׁה, חֲדָשִׁים, חֲדָשׁוֹת
month *m* (8.1)	חֹדֶשׁ, חֳדָשִׁים, חֹדֶשׁ־, חָדְשֵׁי־
outside *m* (when *pl*: open fields, streets, 7.1)	חוּץ, חוּצוֹת, חוּץ־, חוּצוֹת־
strong, hard, tough (2.3)	חָזָק, חֲזָקָה, חֲזָקִים, חֲזָקוֹת
sin, sin-offering *f* (7.1)	חַטָּאת, חַטָּאוֹת, חַטַּאת־, חַטֹּאות־
alive (6.1)	חַי, חַיָּה, חַיִּים, חַיּוֹת
life *m* (4.3)	חַי, חַיִּים, חַי־ *or* [חֵי], חַיֵּי־
animal (wild) *f* (8.1)	חַיָּה, חַיּוֹת, חַיַּת־, חַיּוֹת־
army, wealth, might *m* (6.3)	חַיִל, חֲיָלִים, חֵיל־, חֵילֵי־
Hulda *feminine name* (6.1)	חֻלְדָּה
to fight *nifal inf absol* (7.4)	הִלָּחֵם [ל.ח.מ]
heat *m* (7.1)	חֹם, חָם־
violence *m* (10.2)	חָמָס, חֲמָסִים, חֲמַס־, חַמְסֵי־
grace, favor *m* (5.1)	חֵן
gracious (10.2)	חַנּוּן
kindness, steadfast love *m* (7.1)	חֶסֶד, חֲסָדִים, חֶסֶד־, חַסְדֵי־
one who takes refuge *pt* (10.3)	חֹסֶה, חֹסָה, חֹסִים, חֹסוֹת [ח.ס.ה/י]
desire, delight in, prefer, be willing *verbal adj* (1.3)	חָפֵץ, חֲפֵצָה, חֲפֵצִים, חֲפֵצוֹת
sword *f* (6.3)	חֶרֶב, חֲרָבוֹת, חֶרֶב־, חַרְבוֹת־
you thought, supposed *ms* (6.3)	חָשַׁבְתָּ [ח.ש.ב]
I thought, supposed (6.3)	חָשַׁבְתִּי [ח.ש.ב]
darkness *m* (4.4)	חֹשֶׁךְ

ט

be *or* become defiled *qal*, defile oneself *nifal*, defile something *piel* (10.2)	ט.מ.א
taste (9.5)	ט.ע.מ
good (2.3)	טוֹב, טוֹבָה, טוֹבִים, טוֹבוֹת
we defiled *piel* (10.2)	טִמֵּאנוּ [ט.מ.א]

י

be led, be brought *hofal* (11.2)	י.ב.ל
be dry (2.3)	י.ב.שׁ
know *qal* (5.3), be known *nifal* (7.3), make known, cause to know *hifil* (8.1)	י.ד.ע
be able (2.4)	י.כ.ל
give birth *qal* (6.4), be born *pual* (11.1)	י.ל.ד
oppress (7.1)	י.נ.ה/י

HEBREW GLOSSARY   יְהוּדִית   527

establish *qal*, be founded *pual* (11.1)	י.ס.ד
do [some activity] again *qal* and *hifil* (7.2)	י.ס.פ
go out *qal* (5.1), cause to go out *hifil* (8.1)	י.צ.א
station oneself *hitpael* (11.3)	י.צ.ב
fear, be afraid *qal* (5.2), be feared *nifal* (10.1)	י.ר.א
descend, go down (3.1)	י.ר.ד
cause to inherit *hifil* (8.1)	י.ר.שׁ
sit, dwell *qal* (4.3), cause to inhabit *hifil* (8.1)	י.שׁ.ב
rescue, help *hifil* (4.3)	י.שׁ.ע
Nile, the *m* (map of Ancient Near East)	יְאֹר [הַ]
he will come, he will enter (4.3)	יָבוֹא [ב.ו.א]
Jabbok River, the *pn loc* (map of Israel)	יַבֹּק [הַ]
May the LORD bless you *ms, fs* (1.1)	יְבָרֶכְךָ / יְבָרְכֵךְ יהוה [ב.ר.כ]
dry (2.3)	יָבֵשׁ, יְבֵשָׁה, יְבֵשִׁים, יְבֵשׁוֹת
dry land *f* (3.3)	יַבָּשָׁה
it will be revealed *nifal m* (7.5)	יִגָּלֶה [ג.ל.י/ה]
hand *f* (3.1)	יָד, יָדַיִם (*dual*), יָדוֹת (*plural*), יַד־, יְדֵי־
he will speak *piel* (4.4)	יְדַבֵּר [ד.ב.ר]
one who knows (6.1)	יֹדֵעַ, יֹדַעַת, יֹדְעִים, יֹדְעוֹת [י.ד.ע]
Judah *pn loc* (map of Israel)	יְהוּדָה
the LORD *divine name* (1.2)[3]	יהוה
May the LORD protect you *ms, fs* (1.2)	יִשְׁמָרְךָ / יִשְׁמְרֵךְ יהוה [שׁ.מ.ר]
the LORD God of hosts (8.1)	יהוה אֱלֹהֵי צְבָאוֹת
he / it will / would be known *nifal* (7.4)	יִוָּדַע [י.ד.ע]
day *m* (5.1)	יוֹם, יָמִים, יוֹם־, יְמֵי־

---

[3] Sometimes vocalized יְהֹוָה.

he will be put to death *hofal* (11.2)	יוּמַת [מ.ו.ת]
one who oppresses ... *pt* (7.1)	יוֹנֶה, יוֹנָה, יוֹנִים, יוֹנוֹת [י.נ.י/ה]
Jonah *m* (2.2)	יוֹנָה
he will rescue us *hifil* (8.2)	יוֹשִׁיעֵנוּ [י.שׁ.ע]
he will live (4.3)	יִחְיֶה [ח.י.י/ה]
he will be hot (4.2)	יֶחֱרֶה [ח.ר.י/ה]
he will think (4.3)	יַחְשֹׁב [ח.שׁ.ב]
they will taste *mpl* (9.5)	יִטְעֲמוּ [ט.ע.מ]
wine *m* (7.1)	יַיִן, יֵין־
he will hit *hifil* (4.5)	יַכֶּה [נ.כ.י/ה]
he will come to an end, reach completion (8.1)	יִכְלֶה [כ.ל.י/ה]
they may be established *or* regarded as *nifal* (10.3)	יִכּוֹנוּ [כ.ו.נ]
he will cut (4.3)	יִכְרֹת [כ.ר.ת]
they will cut *m* (4.1)	יִכְרְתוּ [כ.ר.ת]
child, boy *m* (7.5)	יֶלֶד, יְלָדִים, יֶלֶד־, יַלְדֵי־
you gave birth to *fpl* (6.4)	יְלַדְתֶּן [י.ל.ד]
sea, west *m* (3.1)	יָם, יַם־ *or* יָם־, יַמִּים
Dead [Salt] Sea, the *m* (map of Israel)	יָם הַמֶּלַח
Sea of Chinnereth [Galilee], the *m* (map of Israel)	יָם־כִּנֶּרֶת
Red [Reed] Sea, the *m* (map of Ancient Near East)	יָם־סוּף
he will die (4.3)	יָמוּת [מ.ו.ת]
he will rule (4.3)	יִמְלֹךְ [מ.ל.כ]
they will rule *m* (4.1)	יִמְלְכוּ [מ.ל.כ]
they will find *m* (4.1)	יִמְצְאוּ [מ.צ.א]
you oppressed *ms* (7.1)	יָנִיתָ [י.נ.י/ה]
he will work (4.3)	יַעֲבֹד [ע.ב.ד]
he will forsake *qal indicative*, may he forsake *qal jussive* (9.4)	יַעֲזֹב [ע.ז.ב]
he will stand (4.3)	יַעֲמֹד [ע.מ.ד]

because (7.4)	יַעַן [אֲשֶׁר]
he will do, make (4.3)	יַעֲשֶׂה [ע.שׂ.י/ה]
they will do m (4.1)	יַעֲשׂוּ [ע.שׂ.י/ה]
Joppa pn loc (6.1)	יָפוֹ
he will fall (4.3)	יִפֹּל [נ.פ.ל]
may he appoint hifil jussive (9.4)	יַפְקֵד [פ.ק.ד]
they will fall m (4.1)	יִפְּלוּ [נ.פ.ל]
she went out (6.2)	יָצְאָה [י.צ.א]
we went out (6.4)	יָצָאנוּ [י.צ.א]
he will be called nifal (7.1)	יִקָּרֵא [ק.ר.א]
Let them be summoned! nifal jussive mpl (7.4)	יִקָּרְאוּ [ק.ר.א]
fear, dread f (6.2)	יִרְאָה, יִרְאַת־
they feared (6.2)	יָרְאוּ [י.ר.א]
you were afraid ms (6.3)	יָרֵאתָ [י.ר.א]
he will descend (4.3)	יֵרֵד [י.ר.ד]
one who descends, one who goes down pt (3.1)	יֹרֵד, יֹרְדָה / יֹרֶדֶת, יֹרְדִים, יֹרְדוֹת [י.ר.ד]
she descended (6.2)	יָרְדָה [י.ר.ד]
Jordan River, the pn loc (map of Israel)	יַרְדֵּן [ה]
you descended fpl (6.4)	יְרַדְתֶּן [י.ר.ד]
he will have or show mercy piel (5.3)	יְרַחֵם [ר.ח.מ]
Jerusalem pn loc (6.1) (also spelled יְרוּשָׁלַיִם)	יְרוּשָׁלַםִ
Jericho pn loc (map of Israel)	יְרִיחוֹ
there is / are (1.1)	יֵשׁ, יֶשׁ־
he will sit, dwell (4.3)	יֵשֵׁב [י.שׁ.ב]
one who sits, one who dwells pt (3.3)	יֹשֵׁב, יֹשֶׁבֶת, יֹשְׁבִים, יֹשְׁבוֹת [י.שׁ.ב]
he will bring back or answer hifil (11.3)	יָשִׁיב [י.שׁ.ב]
he will lie down (4.3)	יִשְׁכַּב [שׁ.כ.ב]
they will lie down m (4.1)	יִשְׁכְּבוּ [שׁ.כ.ב]
they will hear m (4.1)	יִשְׁמְעוּ [שׁ.מ.ע]
he will guard (4.3)	יִשְׁמֹר [שׁ.מ.ר]
they will guard m (4.1)	יִשְׁמְרוּ [שׁ.מ.ר]
May he protect you fs (1.2)	יִשְׁמְרֵךְ
May he protect you ms (1.2)	יִשְׁמָרְךָ
sleeping adj (3.2)	יָשֵׁן, יְשֵׁנָה, יְשֵׁנִים, יְשֵׁנוֹת
he / it would be poured out or shed nifal (11.1)	יִשָּׁפֵךְ [שׁ.פ.כ]
Israel m (5.1)	יִשְׂרָאֵל

ב

be heavy, mighty (2.3, 6.3)	כ.ב.ד
be solid, firm, established nifal (7.4)	כ.ו.נ
come to an end, waste away qal (8.1), finish, complete piel (10.3), be finished pual (11.1)	כ.ל.י/ה
cover, hide piel (10.1), be covered nifal (7.3); be covered pual (11.1)	כ.ס.י/ה
cover, atone piel (10.1)	כ.פ.ר
cut (4.3)	כ.ר.ת
write (10.1), be written qal passive (11.1)	כ.ת.ב
like or as (2.4)	כְּ..., כְּמוֹ
because, when (10.1)	כַּאֲשֶׁר
heavy, rich, mighty, oppressive (2.3)	כָּבֵד, כְּבֵדָה, כְּבֵדִים, כְּבֵדוֹת
they are mighty (6.3)	כָּבְדוּ [כ.ב.ד]
glory, heaviness m (11.1)	כָּבוֹד, כְּבוֹד־
thus, in this manner (7.2)	כֹּה
priest m (7.4)	כֹּהֵן, כֹּהֲנִים, כֹּהֵן־, כֹּהֲנֵי־
cup f (1.1)	כּוֹס, כֹּסוֹת, כּוֹס־, כֹּסוֹת־
strength m (8.2)	כֹּחַ, כֹּחַ־
because, that, when, indeed (2.3)	כִּי

HEBREW GLOSSARY — יְהוּדִית

but rather (6.4)	כִּי אִם
every, each, all, the whole (5.1)	כָּל־, כֹּל
all that happens or happened pt fpl (6.1)	כָּל־הַמֹּצָאוֹת [מ.צ.א]
he finished, completed piel (10.3)	כִּלָּה [כ.ל.י/ה]
container, sack, utensil, vessel m (2.3)	כְּלִי, כֵּלִים, כְּלִי־ כְּלֵי־
all of them (7.2)	כֻּלָּם
like, similar to (3.2)	כְּמוֹ
as soon as [entity] is / was full inf c, prep (6.2)	כִּמְלֹאת [מ.ל.א]
so, thus (11.1)	כֵּן
chair, seat m (2.1)	כִּסֵּא, כִּסְאוֹת, כִּסֵּא־, כִּסְאוֹת־
fool m (3.3)	כְּסִיל, כְּסִילִים
silver, money m (2.1)	כֶּסֶף, כְּסָפִים, כֶּסֶף־, כַּסְפֵּי־
Cover! Atone! piel imv ms (10.2)	כַּפֵּר [כ.פ.ר]
Carchemish pn loc (map of Ancient Near East)	כַּרְכְּמִישׁ
that which is written* qal passive pt (11.1)	כָּתוּב, כְּתוּבָה, כְּתוּבִים, כְּתוּבוֹת

ל

wear qal (8.1 passive, 9.3 active), clothe hifil (9.2), be clothed hofal (11.2)	ל.ב.שׁ
fight nifal (7.3)	ל.ח.מ
capture qal; be captured, trapped nifal (7.1)	ל.כ.ד
learn qal, teach, train piel (10.1)	ל.מ.ד
take (5.1), be taken pual (11.1)	ל.ק.ח
to, for (1.1)	לְ
not (1.1)	לֹא
to perish inf c, prep (6.3)	לֶאֱבֹד [א.ב.ד]
to love inf c, prep (4.2)	לֶאֱהֹב [א.ה.ב]
to eat inf c, prep (3.1)	לֶאֱכֹל [א.כ.ל]
to say inf c, prep (4.1)	לֵאמֹר [א.מ.ר]
Lebanon pn loc (map of Ancient Near East)	לְבָנוֹן [הַ]
to look for piel inf c, prep (3.1)	לְבַקֵּשׁ [ב.ק.שׁ]
heart, mind m (4.4)	לֵב ׀ לֵבָב, לִבּוֹת, לֵב־, לְבוֹת־
to enter, come, go inf c, prep (3.3)	לָבוֹא [ב.ו.א]
one who is clothed in qal passive pt (8.1)	לָבוּשׁ, לְבוּשָׁה, לְבוּשִׁים, לְבוּשׁוֹת [ל.ב.שׁ]
Wear! Put on! qal imv (9.3)	לְבַשׁ, לִבְשִׁי, לִבְשׁוּ, לְבַשְׁנָה [ל.ב.שׁ]
to swallow inf c, prep (4.3)	לִבְלֹעַ [ב.ל.ע]
to speak piel inf c, prep (2.4)	לְדַבֵּר [ד.ב.ר]
to announce hifil inf c, prep (8.1)	לְהַגִּיד [נ.ג.ד]
to prophesy nifal inf c, prep (7.1)	לְהִנָּבֵא [נ.ב.א]
to be broken up nifal inf c, prep (6.2)	לְהִשָּׁבֵר [שׁ.ב.ר]
to return (something) hifil inf c, prep (7.4)	לְהָשִׁיב [שׁ.ו.ב]
to throw hifil inf c, prep (3.3)	לְהַשְׁלִיךְ [שׁ.ל.כ]
if irreal condition (7.3)	לוּ or לוּלֵא
tablet, board m (11.1)	לוּחַ, לוּחוֹת, לוּחַ־, לוּחוֹת־
to sacrifice qal inf c, prep (5.1)	לִזְבֹּחַ [ז.ב.ח]
bread m (1.1)	לֶחֶם, לֶחֶם־
my bread m (3.1)	לַחְמִי
to be hot inf c, prep (4.2)	לַחֲרוֹת [ח.ר.י/ה]
to/for me (1.1)	לִי
night m (6.2)	לַיְלָה, לֵילוֹת, לֵיל־, לֵילוֹת־
to/for you ms, fs (1.1)	לְךָ, לָךְ
Go to…! imv ms, fs (1.3)	לֵךְ אֶל...! לְכִי אֶל...! [ה.ל.כ]
Go in peace! imv ms, fs (1.2)	לֵךְ / לְכִי לְשָׁלוֹם [ה.ל.כ]
Lachish pn loc (map of Israel)	לָכִישׁ

therefore (8.1)	לָכֵן
to cover, atone for *piel inf c, prep* (10.1)	לְכַפֵּר [כ.פ.ר]
to go *inf c, prep* (1.3)	לָלֶכֶת [ה.ל.כ]
he taught, trained *piel* (10.1)	לִמַּד [ל.מ.ד]
Why? (2.3)	לָמָּה...?
Of what use to me is...? (3.2)	לָמָּה זֶּה לִי...?
belonging to the tribe of Zebulun (3.2)	לְמַטֵּה זְבוּלֻן
Whose? To whom? (2.1)	לְמִי...?
to rule *inf c, prep* (3.1)	לִמְלֹךְ [מ.ל.כ]
so that (3.1)	לְמַעַן
to find *inf c, prep* (3.1)	לִמְצֹא [מ.צ.א]
to rest *inf c, prep* (7.1)	לָנוּחַ [נ.ו.ח]
to recount *piel inf c, prep* (10.2)	לְסַפֵּר [ס.פ.ר]
to cross over *inf c, prep* (3.2)	לַעֲבֹר [ע.ב.ר]
forever (4.3)	לְעוֹלָם
to help us *inf c, prep* (7.3)	לְעָזְרֵנוּ [ע.ז.ר]
to stand *inf c, prep* (4.2)	לַעֲמֹד [ע.מ.ד]
to afflict *piel inf c, prep* (10.2)	לְעַנּוֹת [ע.נ.י/ה]
to answer, reply *inf c, prep* (7.1)	לַעֲנוֹת [ע.נ.י/ה]
to do, make *inf c, prep* (3.4)	לַעֲשׂוֹת [ע.שׂ.י/ה]
before me *pausal* (6.2)	לְפָנָי
before, in front of (2.4)	לִפְנֵי
to go out *inf c, prep* (5.3)	לָצֵאת [י.צ.א]
he took (6.1)	לָקַח [ל.ק.ח]
it was taken *qal passive m* (11.1)	לֻקַּח [ל.ק.ח]
she took (6.2)	לָקְחָה [ל.ק.ח]
I took (6.1)	לָקַחְתִּי [ל.ק.ח]
to call, read *inf c, prep* (1.2)	לִקְרֹא [ק.ר.א]
to draw near *inf c, prep* (5.1)	לִקְרוֹב [ק.ר.ב]
to see *inf c, prep* (4.2)	לִרְאוֹת [ר.א.י/ה]
to contend *qal inf c, prep* (11.3)	לָרִיב [ר.י.ב]
to turn (or return) self toward, to repent to *inf c, prep* (3.3)	לָשׁוּב אֶל [שׁ.ו.ב]
to put, to place *inf c, prep* (3.1)	לָשׂוּם [שׂ.ו/י.מ]
tongue, language *m* (2.1)	לָשׁוֹן, לְשֹׁנוֹת לְשׁוֹן־, לְשֹׁנוֹת־
to lie down *inf c, prep* (3.1)	לִשְׁכַּב [שׁ.כ.ב]
to listen *inf c, prep* (2.4)	לִשְׁמֹעַ [שׁ.מ.ע]
to keep, to guard *inf c, prep* (4.2)	לִשְׁמֹר [שׁ.מ.ר]
to drink *inf c, prep* (3.1)	לִשְׁתּוֹת [שׁ.ת.י/ה]
to give *inf c, prep* (2.4)	לָתֵת [נ.ת.נ]

die *qal* (4.3), kill, put to death *hifil* (8.1), be put to death *hofal* (11.2)	מ.ו.ת
be full *qal* (6.2), be filled *nifal* (7.3), fill *piel* (10.2)	מ.ל.א
rule (4.3)	מ.ל.כ
find (3.1), be found *nifal* (7.3)	מ.צ.א
very *or* much (2.2)	מְאֹד
anything (11.1)	מְאוּמָה
from where...? (6.4)	מֵאַיִן...?
one who looks for, seeks *piel pt* (1.3)	מְבַקֵּשׁ, מְבַקֶּשֶׁת, מְבַקְשִׁים, מְבַקְשׁוֹת [ב.ק.שׁ]
blessed *pual pt* (11.1)	מְבֹרָךְ, מְבֹרֶכֶת, מְבֹרָכִים, מְבֹרָכוֹת [ב.ר.כ]
Megiddo *pn loc* (map of Israel)	מְגִדּוֹ
messenger, one who announces *hifil pt* (8.1)	מַגִּיד, מַגֶּדֶת, מַגִּידִים, מַגִּידוֹת [נ.ג.ד]
wilderness *m* (3.2)	מִדְבָּר, מִדְבַּר־
one who speaks *pt* (3.2)	מְדַבֵּר, מְדַבְּרָה, מְדַבְּרִים, מְדַבְּרוֹת [ד.ב.ר]
What? (1.1)	מַה, מַה־, מָה, מֶה

HEBREW GLOSSARY — יְהוּדִית

What is this? (1.1)	מַה־זֶּה?
What are you doing here? (6.1)	מַה־לְּךָ פֹה?
What is your ms/fs concern? (4.4)	מַה־לָּךְ?
What is your fpl concern? (7.3)	מַה־לָּהֶנָה:
What is your ms name? (1.1)	מַה־שְּׁמֶךָ?
Moab pn loc (map of Israel)	מוֹאָב
one who rescues hifil pt ms (5.1)	מוֹשִׁיעַ [י.ש.ע]
I most certainly will die (5.2)	מוֹת אָמוּת [מ.ו.ת]
death m (8.1)	מָוֶת, מוֹתִים, מוֹת, מוֹתֵי־
altar f (9.2)	מִזְבֵּחַ, מִזְבְּחוֹת, מִזְבַּח, מִזְבְּחוֹת־
tomorrow, next day, in the future m and adverb (4.3)	מָחָר
thought, intent, plan f (9.4)	מַחֲשָׁבָה, מַחֲשָׁבוֹת, מַחֲשֶׁבֶת, מַחְשְׁבֹת־
Who? (3.2)	מִי...?
Who knows? (5.3)	מִי יוֹדֵעַ? [י.ד.ע]
water mpl (2.1)	מַיִם, מֵי־
one who strikes, smites hifil pt (7.1)	מַכֶּה, מַכָּה, מַכִּים, מַכּוֹת [נ.כ.י/ה]
one who is covered pual pt (11.1)	מְכֻסֶּה, מְכֻסָּה, מְכֻסִּים, מְכֻסּוֹת [כ.ס.י/ה]
messenger m (9.5)	מַלְאָךְ, מַלְאָכִים, מַלְאַךְ־, מַלְאֲכֵי־
occupation, business f (3.2)	מְלָאכָה, מְלָאכוֹת, מְלֶאכֶת־, מְלַאכוֹת־
we filled piel (10.2)	מִלֵּאנוּ [מ.ל.א]
one who is clothed in pual pt, ms (11.2)	מְלֻבָּשׁ [ל.ב.שׁ]
war, battle f (6.3)	מִלְחָמָה, מִלְחָמוֹת, מִלְחֶמֶת־, מִלְחֲמוֹת־
king m (2.1)	מֶלֶךְ, מְלָכִים, מֶלֶךְ־, מַלְכֵי־
queen f (9.1)	מַלְכָּה, מַלְכוֹת, מַלְכַּת־, מַלְכוֹת־
on the next day (8.1)	מִמָּחֳרָת
from me (4.3)	מִמֶּנִּי
from (2.4) (before gutturals and ר)	מִן (מֵ...)
gift f (11.1)	מִנְחָה, מְנָחוֹת, מִנְחַת־, מִנְחוֹת־
one who turns something away from hifil pt (3.2)	מֵסִיר, מְסִירָה, מְסִירִים, מְסִירוֹת [ס.ו.ר]
one who recounts, narrator piel pt ms (6.4)	מְסַפֵּר [ס.פ.ר]
number m (3.1)	מִסְפָּר, מִסְפָּרִים, מִסְפַּר־, מִסְפְּרֵי־
a little (of something), a few (7.3)	מְעַט, מְעַטִּים
from upon (2.4)	מֵעַל
answer m (7.1)	מַעֲנֶה, מַעֲנוֹת, מַעֲנֵה־, מַעֲנוֹת־
cave f (7.3)	מְעָרָה, מְעָרוֹת, מְעָרַת־, מְעָרוֹת־
work, deed m (8.1)	מַעֲשֶׂה, מַעֲשִׂים, מַעֲשֵׂה־, מַעֲשֵׂי־
Memphis pn loc (map of Ancient Near East)	מֹף
I found (6.1)	מָצָאתִי [מ.צ.א]
one who commands piel pt (3.4)	מְצַוֶּה, מְצַוָּה, מְצַוִּים, מְצַוּוֹת [צ.ו.י/ה]
commandment f (5.2)	מִצְוָה, מִצְוֹת, מִצְוַת־, מִצְוֹת־
Egypt f (8.1)	מִצְרַיִם
place, location m (6.1)	מָקוֹם, מְקֹמוֹת, מְקוֹם־, מְקֹמוֹת־
bitter (3.1)	מַר, מָרָה, מָרִים, מָרוֹת
height, elevated place m (8.1)	מָרוֹם, מְרוֹמִים, מְרוֹם־, מְרוֹמֵי־
at a distance (6.1)	מֵרָחוֹק
deceit f (8.1)	מִרְמָה, מִרְמוֹת, מִרְמַת־, מִרְמֹת־
burden, oracle, pronouncement m (7.1)	מַשָּׂא, מַשָּׂאוֹת, מַשָּׂא־, מַשְׂאוֹת־
wave, surf, breaker m (5.1)	מִשְׁבָּר, מִשְׁבָּרִים, מִשְׁבְּרֵי־
proverb m (11.2)	מָשָׁל, מְשָׁלִים, מְשַׁל־, מִשְׁלֵי־
one who throws hifil pt (3.3)	מַשְׁלִיךְ, מַשְׁלִיכָה, מַשְׁלִיכִים, מַשְׁלִיכוֹת [שׁ.ל.כ]

מִשְׁפָּחָה, מִשְׁפָּחוֹת, מִשְׁפַּחַת־, מִשְׁפְּחוֹת־ .... clan, family *f* (7.5)

מִשְׁפָּט, מִשְׁפָּטִים, מִשְׁפַּט־, מִשְׁפְּטֵי־ .... judgment, judicial decision *m* (8.1)

מְשָׁרֵת [ש.ר.ת] .... personal servant *piel pt m* (9.1)

מֵת [מ.ו.ת] .... he is dead *or* has died (6.1)

מֵת, מֵתִים מֵתָה, מֵתוֹת [מ.ו.ת] ..... one who is dying *pt* (4.3)

מָתוֹק, מְתוּקָה, מְתוּקִים, מְתוּקוֹת .... sweet (3.1)

מִתַּחַת .... from under (2.4)

נ

נ.ב.א .... prophesy *nifal* (7.1)

נ.ג.ד .... declare, announce *hifil* (7.1), be reported *hofal* (11.3)

נ.ג.שׁ .... approach (7.1)

נ.ו.ח .... rest (7.1)

נ.ט.י/ה .... stretch out (something) *qal* (9.2)

נ.כ.י/ה .... strike *hifil* (5.3), be struck *hofal* (11.2)

נ.פ.ל .... fall *qal* (4.3), cause to fall *hifil* (8.1)

נ.צ.ל .... deliver, snatch *hifil* (8.1)

נ.שׂ.א .... lift, carry *qal* (5.1), be lifted *nifal* (7.3), raise high *piel* (10.1)

נ.ת.ן .... give *qal* (2.4), be given *nifal and qal passive* (7.3, 11.1)

נָא .... please, so (9.4)

נֹא .... Thebes [No] *pn loc* (map of Ancient Near East)

נֶאֱכַל [א.כ.ל] .... he was eaten *nifal* (7.3)

נְאֻם יהוה .... declares the LORD (8.1)

נֶאֱמָן, נֶאֱמֶנֶת, נֶאֱמָנִים, נֶאֱמָנוֹת [א.מ.נ] .... one who is faithful, reliable, established *nifal pt* (7.4)

נֶאֱסַר [א.ס.ר] .... he was bound, imprisoned *nifal* (7.3)

נָבוֹאָה [ב.ו.א] .... Let's come, enter! *cohort.* (9.4)

נָבִיא, נְבִיאִים, נְבִיא־, נְבִיאֵי־ .... prophet *m* (1.3)

נְבִיאָה, נְבִיאוֹת, נְבִיאַת־, נְבִיאוֹת־ .... prophetess *f* (2.4)

נָבִין [ב.י.נ] .... we understand *hifil* (3.3)

נִבְנָה [ב.נ.י/ה] .... he was built *nifal* (7.3)

נֶגֶב .... south-country, south *m* (map of Israel)

נִגְנְבוּ [ג.נ.ב] .... they were stolen *nifal* (10.2)

נֶגַע, נְגָעִים, נֶגַע־, נִגְעֵי־ .... plague, affliction *m* (8.1)

נֶדֶר, נְדָרִים, נֶדֶר־, נִדְרֵי־ .... vow *m* (10.2)

נִדְרְשָׁה [ד.ר.שׁ] .... Let's seek *cohort. pl.* (9.4)

נוֹדַע [י.ד.ע] .... he was known *nifal* (7.3)

נוֹצִיא [י.צ.א] .... we will cause (something) to go out *hifil* (8.2)

נוֹרָא, נוֹרָאָה, נוֹרָאִים, נוֹרָאוֹת [י.ר.א] .... feared *nifal pt* (10.1)

נִזְכֹּר [ז.כ.ר] .... we will remember (5.1)

נַחֲלָה, נְחָלוֹת, נַחֲלַת־, נְחָלֹת־ .... property, inheritance *f* (8.1)

נֶהְפָּךְ, נֶהְפֶּכֶת, נֶהְפָּכִים, נֶהְפָּכוֹת [ה.פ.כ] ... one who is *or* has been overturned *nifal pt* (7.5)

נְטֵה, נְטִי, נְטוּ, נְטֵינָה [נ.ט.י/ה] .. Stretch out! *imv* (9.2)

נִינְוֵה .... Nineveh *pn loc* (1.3)

נָהָל .... river *or* stream *m* (map of Ancient Near East)

נְהַר־פְּרָת .... Euphrates River, the *pn loc* (map of ANE)

נָכוֹן [כ.ו.נ] ..... correct *nifal* (2.3); he was established, set up *nifal* (7.3)

נָכוֹן, נְכוֹנָה, נְכוֹנִים, נְכוֹנוֹת [כ.ו.נ] .... one who is solid, firm *nifal pt* (7.4)

נִכְסָה [כ.ס.י/ה] .... he was covered *nifal* (7.3)

we will cover *piel* (10.1)	נְכַסֶּה [כ.ס.י/ה]
he was cut *nifal* (7.3)	נִכְרַת [כ.ר.ת]
to fight *nifal inf absol* (7.4)	נִלְחֹם [ל.ח.מ]
we would fight *nifal* (7.3)	נִלָּחֲמְנוּ [ל.ח.מ]
he was trapped *nifal* (7.3)	נִלְכַּד [ל.כ.ד]
you were trapped *ms nifal* (7.1)	נִלְכַּדְתָּ [ל.כ.ד]
Let's go! *cohort.* (7.5)	נֵלְכָה [ה.ל.כ]
he was caught *nifal* (7.3)	נִלְקַח [ל.ק.ח]
he was filled *nifal* (7.3)	נִמְלָא [מ.ל.א]
he was found *nifal* (7.3)	נִמְצָא [מ.צ.א]
we will find *qal* (5.1)	נִמְצָא [מ.צ.א]
he hid himself, was hidden *nifal* (7.3)	נִסְתַּר [ס.ת.ר]
you hid yourself, were hidden *nifal ms* (7.1)	נִסְתַּרְתָּ [ס.ת.ר]
we will cause (something) to go up *hifil* (8.2)	נַעֲלֶה [ע.ל.י/ה]
he was done, made *nifal* (7.3)	נַעֲשָׂה [ע.ש.י/ה]
Fall! *imv* (9.2)	נְפֹל, נִפְלִי, נִפְלוּ, נְפֹלְנָה [נ.פ.ל]
miraculous acts *nifal pt fpl* (10.2)	נִפְלָאוֹת, נִפְלְאוֹת־ [פ.ל.א]
soul, person, life force, throat *f* (3.3)	נֶפֶשׁ, נְפָשׁוֹת, נֶפֶשׁ־, נַפְשׁוֹת־
my soul, myself, me *f* (3.3)	נַפְשִׁי
their *mpl* soul, themselves (4.1)	נַפְשָׁם
we will set apart, consecrate *piel* (10.2)	נְקַדֵּשׁ [ק.ד.ש]
we will take (5.1)	נִקַּח [ל.ק.ח]
innocent (11.1)	נָקִי, נְקִיָּה, נְקִיִּם, נְקִיּוֹת
we will call, read (5.1), Let's call! *cohort.* (9.4)	נִקְרָא [ק.ר.א]
lamp *m* (4.4)	נֵר, נֵרוֹת, נֵר־, נֵרוֹת־
one who lifts, one who carries *pt* (5.3)	נֹשֵׂא, נֹשְׂאָה, נֹשְׂאִים, נֹשְׂאוֹת [נ.ש.א]
he raised high *piel* (10.1)	נִשֵּׂא [נ.ש.א]
he was lifted, taken away *nifal* (7.3)	נִשָּׂא [נ.ש.א]
we will lift, we will carry *qal* (5.1)	נִשָּׂא [נ.ש.א]
she lifted up (6.2)	נָשְׂאָה [נ.ש.א]
they lifted up (6.2)	נָשְׂאוּ [נ.ש.א]
he / it survived, was left over *nifal* (7.3)	נִשְׁאַר [ש.א.ר]
we (will) swear *nifal* (7.3)	נִשָּׁבַע [ש.ב.ע]
he was broken *nifal* (7.3)	נִשְׁבַּר [ש.ב.ר]
Let's repent! *cohort.* (8.2)	נָשׁוּבָה [ש.ו.ב]
we will cause (something) to return *hifil* (8.2)	נָשִׁיב [ש.ו.ב]
women (or wives, *f*, 5.1)	נָשִׁים, נְשֵׁי־
I was sent *nifal* (8.1)	נִשְׁלַחְתִּי [ש.ל.ח]
we will fulfill, repay *piel* (10.2)	נְשַׁלֵּם [ש.ל.מ]
he was heard *nifal* (7.3)	נִשְׁמַע [ש.מ.ע]
he was guarded *or* he guarded himself *nifal* (7.3)	נִשְׁמַר [ש.מ.ר]
he was poured out *nifal m* (7.3)	נִשְׁפַּךְ [ש.פ.כ]
they (beverages) were drunk *nifal* (11.1)	נִשְׁתּוּ [ש.ת.י/ה]
he gave (6.1)	נָתַן [נ.ת.ן]
he was given, put, or placed *nifal* (7.3)	נִתַּן [נ.ת.ן]
you gave *fs* (6.3)	נָתַתְּ [נ.ת.ן]

ס

surround (6.1)	ס.ב.ב
close *qal*, be closed *pual* (11.1)	ס.ג.ר
turn something away, remove *hifil* (3.2)	ס.ו.ר
forgive (5.3)	ס.ל.ח

count *qal*, recount *piel* (6.1), be recounted, reported *pual* (11.1)	ס.פ.ר
hide self, be hidden *nifal* (7.1)	ס.ת.ר
ones who surround *pt mpl* (6.1)	סֹבְבִים [ס.ב.ב]
around (environs *fpl substantive*, 7.1)	סָבִיב, סְבִיבָה, סְבִיבִים, סְבִיבוֹת
Turn! *imv m, f* (4.3)	סוּר, סוּרִי
hut *f* (7.1)	סֻכָּה, סֻכּוֹת, סֻכַּת־, סֻכּוֹת־
I am sorry (*lit.*, please forgive, 3.1)	סְלַח־נָא, סִלְחִי־נָא [ס.ל.ח]
Tell! Recount! *piel imv ms, fs* (6.1)	סַפֵּר, סַפְּרִי [ס.פ.ר]
book, scroll *m* (2.3)	סֵפֶר, סְפָרִים, סֵפֶר־, סִפְרֵי־
hiding place *m* (7.3)	סֵתֶר, סְתָרִים, סֵתֶר־, סִתְרֵי־

work, worship (4.3)	ע.ב.ד
cross over (3.2)	ע.ב.ר
abandon, forsake (7.1)	ע.ז.ב
help (4.3)	ע.ז.ר
go up, ascend *qal* (5.3), cause to go up *hifil* (8.1)	ע.ל.ה/י
stand (4.2)	ע.מ.ד
afflict *piel* (10.2)	ע.נ.ה/י
answer *qal* (5.3)	ע.נ.ה/י
do, make (4.3), be made, be done *nifal* (7.3)	ע.ש.ה/י
servant, slave, worker *m* (4.1)	עֶבֶד, עֲבָדִים, עֶבֶד־, עַבְדֵי־
work (*of labor or worship*) *f* (11.1)	עֲבוֹדָה, עֲבֹדַת־
one who crosses over *pt* (3.2)	עֹבֵר, עֹבְרָה, עֹבְרִים, עֹבְרוֹת [ע.ב.ר]
Hebrew person (8.1)	עִבְרִי, עִבְרִיָּה, עִבְרִים, עִבְרִית
I crossed over, trespassed (6.1)	עָבַרְתִּי [ע.ב.ר]
you crossed over *mpl* (6.3)	עֲבַרְתֶּם [ע.ב.ר]
cord, rope *m* (7.3)	עֲבֹת, עֲבֹתִים *or* עֲבֹתוֹת, עֲבֹתִי־, עֲבֹתוֹת־ *or* עֲבֹתוֹת־
toward, as far as (2.4)	עַד
future, perpetuity *m* (10.3)	עַד
again, more, yet, still (4.1)	עוֹד
world, eternity *m* (4.3)	עוֹלָם
iniquity *m* (3.2)	עָוֹן, עֲוֹנוֹת, עֲוֹן־, עֲוֹנוֹת־
bird(s), flying insect(s) *m* (8.1)	עוֹף, עוֹף־
he abandoned (7.1)	עָזַב [ע.ז.ב]
Gaza *pn loc* (map of Israel)	עַזָּה
Help me! *imv ms* (4.3)	עָזְרֵנִי [ע.ז.ר]
crown *f* (8.1)	עֲטָרָה, עֲטָרוֹת, עֲטֶרֶת, עֲטֶרֶת־
eye, spring *f* (4.2)	עַיִן, עֵינַיִם, עֵין־, עֵינֵי־
his eyes *f* (4.2)	עֵינָיו
city *f* (2.1)	עִיר, עָרִים, עִיר־, עָרֵי־
on, upon (2.4)	עַל
beside (2.4)	עַל־יַד
on this account, therefore (4.3)	עַל־כֵּן
on what account (3.3)	עַל־מֶה
burnt offering *f* (11.2)	עֹלָה, עֹלוֹת, עֹלַת־, עֹלוֹת־
upon me (2.3)	עָלַי
I must *followed by inf c* (2.3),	עָלַי ל
you must *fs*... (...be sure [to]..., 1.3)	עָלַיִךְ ל
you must *ms*...(...be sure [to]..., 1.3)	עָלֶיךָ ל
you must *mpl*... (...be sure [to]..., 3.3)	עֲלֵיכֶם ל
we must...(...be sure [to]..., 3.3), upon us	עָלֵינוּ ל
she went up (6.2)	עָלְתָה [ע.ל.ה/י]
with [together] (2.4)	עִם
people *m* (3.2)	עַם, עַמִּים, עַם־, עַמֵּי־

HEBREW GLOSSARY — יְהוּדִית — 535

עֹמֵד, עֹמְדָה, עֹמְדִים, עֹמְדוֹת [ע.מ.ד]	one who stands (3.2)
עֲמֹד, עִמְדִי, עִמְדוּ, עֲמֹדְנָה [ע.מ.ד]	Stand! *imv* (9.1)
עַמּוֹן	Ammon *pn loc* (map of Israel)
עָנִי, עֲנִיָּה, עֲנִיִּים, עֲנִיּוֹת	oppressed, afflicted, poor (5.3)
עָנִיתִי [ע.נ.י/ה]	I answered, replied (6.1)
עֵץ, עֵצִים, עֵץ־, עֲצֵי־	tree, wood *m* (4.2)
עֵצָה, עֵצוֹת, עֲצַת־, עֲצוֹת־	counsel, advice *f* (7.5)
עֶצֶם, עֲצָמוֹת, עֶצֶם־, עַצְמוֹת־	bone, inner substance, self *f* (5.2)
עֹשֶׂה, עֹשָׂה, עֹשִׂים, עֹשׂוֹת [ע.שׂ.י/ה]	one who does, makes (3.2)
עֲשׂוֹת [ע.שׂ.י/ה]	to do *inf c* (8.1)
עֵת, עִתִּים, עֶת־ [עֵת or] עִתֵּי־	time, point in time, occasion *f* (7.2)
עַתָּה	now (3.2)

פ.ל.א	be difficult, marvelous *nifal* (10.2)
פ.ל.ט	save, deliver *piel* (10.3)
פ.ל.ל	pray *hitpael* (11.3)
פ.נ.י/ה	turn (9.4)
פ.ק.ד	visit, inspect, inflict, appoint *qal* (6.4), appoint *hifil* (9.4)
פ.ק.ח	open (eyes, 6.1)
פ.ת.ח	open (4.3)
פֶּה, פִּיוֹת, פִּי־, פִּיוֹת־	mouth *m* (4.2)
פִּי	my mouth *m* (4.3)
פִּיו	his mouth *m* (4.2)
פַּלֵּט, פַּלְטִי, פַּלְטוּ, פַּלֵּטְנָה [פ.ל.ט]	Save, deliver! *piel imv* (10.3)
פְּלֶשֶׁת	Philistia *pn loc* (map of Israel)
פְּלִשְׁתִּי	Philistine person (8.2)
פֶּן	lest (4.1)
פָּנִים, פְּנֵי־	face(s) *m* (9.5)
פֶּסֶל, פְּסִילִים, פֶּסֶל־, פְּסִילֵי־	idol *m* (9.3)
פְּקַדְנוּ [פ.ק.ד]	we visited, inspected, inflicted, appointed (6.4)
פְּקַדְתֶּן [פ.ק.ד]	you visited, inspected, inflicted, appointed *fpl* (6.4)
פַּעַם, פְּעָמִים, פַּעַם־, פַּעֲמֵי־	time, occurrence, step *f* (7.2)
פָּקַח [פ.ק.ח]	he opened (eyes, 6.1)
פֶּשַׁע, פְּשָׁעִים, פֶּשַׁע־, פִּשְׁעֵי־	transgression *m* (10.1)
פָּתַח [פ.ת.ח]	he opened (6.1)
פֶּתַח, פְּתָחִים, פֶּתַח־, פִּתְחֵי־	entrance, doorway, opening *m* (7.5)
פֹּתֵחַ, פֹּתַחַת, פֹּתְחִים, פֹּתְחוֹת [פ.ת.ח]	one who opens *pt* (4.3)

צ

צ.ו.י/ה	command *piel* (3.4, 10.1), be commanded *pual* (11.1)
צֵא, צְאִי, צְאוּ, צֶאנָה [י.צ.א]	Go out! *imv* (3.1)
צֹאן, צֹאנִים, צֹאן־, צֹאנֵי־	flock(s), small cattle and sheep *f* (7.5)
צַדִּיק, צַדִּיקִים	righteous, true to one's community, innocent (legally and morally) (10.2)
צְדָקָה, צְדָקוֹת, צִדְקַת־, צִדְקוֹת־	righteousness *f* (11.1)

he commanded *piel* (10.1) .... [צ.ו.י/ה] צִוָּה	meet, encounter *qal* (6.2) .... ק.ר.א[4]
he was commanded *pual* (11.1) ....[צ.ו.י/ה] צֻוָּה	draw near *qal* (4.5), cause to come near, offer .... ק.ר.ב
rock, cliff *m* (10.3) .... צוּר, צֻרִים, צוּר־, צוּרֵי־	*hifil* (8.1)
his command, he commanded *piel inf c* ... [צ.ו.י/ה] צַוֹּתוֹ	Gather (what .... [ק.ב.צ] קַבֵּץ, קַבְּצִי, קַבְּצוּ, קַבֶּצְנָה
(10.1)	has been scattered)! *piel imv* (10.3)
Sidon *pn loc* (map of Ancient Near East) .... צִידוֹן	Gather .... [ק.ב.צ] קְבֹץ, קִבְצִי, קִבְצוּ, קְבֹצְנָה
shadow *m* (11.3) .... צֵל	(assemble selves)! *qal imv* (9.1)
Tanis *pn loc* (map of Ancient Near East) .... צֹעַן	grave *m* (4.3) .... קֶבֶר, קְבָרִים, קֶבֶר־, קִבְרֵי־
outcry, scream from despair *f* (5.3) .... צְעָקָה, צַעֲקַת־	east, front, primeval time *m* (map of ANE) .... קֶדֶם
north *f* (map of Ancient Near East) .... צָפוֹן	former, eastern, ancient ones *collective* (11.2) .... קַדְמֹנִי
I am in distress (1.1) .... צַר לִי	holiness, sanctuary, ... קֹדֶשׁ, קָדָשִׁים, קֹדֶשׁ־, קָדְשֵׁי־
Tyre *pn loc* (map of Ancient Near East) .... צֹר	sacred object *m* (8.1)
bag, little pack *m* (2.3) . צְרוֹר, צְרוֹרוֹת, צְרוֹר־, צְרוֹרוֹת־	assembly, congregation .... קָהָל, קְהָלִים, קְהַל־, קְהָלֵי־
narrow *adj*, or distress .... צַר, צָרִים, צַר־, צָרֵי־	*m* (7.5)
substantive (1.1)	one who hopes .... [ק.ו.י/ה] קוֶֹה, קוָֹה, קוִֹים, קוֹוֹת
	qal pt (4.4)

	they hoped *piel* (10.1) .... [ק.ו.י/ה] קִוּוּ
	we waited, hoped *piel* (10.2) .... [ק.ו.י/ה] קִוִּינוּ
gather, assemble selves *qal* (9.1); gather what .... ק.ב.צ	you hoped *piel ms* (10.1) .... [ק.ו.י/ה] קִוִּיתָ
has been scattered *piel* (10.3)	sound, voice *m* (3.2) .... קוֹל, קוֹלוֹת, קוֹל־, קוֹלוֹת־
be holy *qal*, make holy, consecrate *piel*, ... ק.ד.ש	Get up! (1.3) .... [ק.ו.מ] קוּם, קוּמִי, קוּמוּ, קֹמְנָה
consecrate oneself *hitpael* (11.3)	small, young (2.3) ... קָטֹן / קָטָן, קְטַנָּה, קְטַנִּים, קְטַנּוֹת
hope *qal*, hope *piel* (10.1) .... ק.ו.י/ה	smoke, incense *f* (10.3) .... קְטֹרֶת, קְטֹרֶת־
get up *qal* (1.3), establish *hifil* (8.1) .... ק.ו.מ	you bought, acquired, created *fs* (6.3) ..... [ק.נ.י/ה] קָנִית
be small, become small *qal* (5.3) .... ק.ט.נ	Call! Read! .... קְרָא, קִרְאִי, קִרְאוּ, קְרֶאןָ [ק.ר.א]
buy, acquire, create (6.3) .... ק.נ.י/ה	Encounter! *imv* (7.1, 9.1)
call, read *qal* (5.1), be called *nifal* (7.1) .... ק.ר.א	they called, met, encountered (6.2) .... [ק.ר.א] קָרְאוּ

---

[4] In forms where the spelling of the homonymous ק.ר.א would overlap, both meanings may be offered (*to call* and *to meet*).

HEBREW GLOSSARY — יְהוּדִית

Draw near! imv (9.2)	קְרַב, קִרְבִי, קִרְבוּ, קִרְבְנָה [ק.ר.ב]
near (9.4)	קָרוֹב
hard (6.4)	קָשֶׁה, קָשָׁה, קָשִׁים, קָשׁוֹת
stiff-necked, stubborn (6.4)	קְשֵׁה-עֹרֶף

ר

see, look qal (4.2), appear nifal (7.4), show, reveal hifil (8.1)	ר.א.י/ה
multiply or make numerous hifil (8.1)	ר.ב.י/ה
pursue (6.2)	ר.ד.פ
be high, exalted (6.4)	ר.ו.מ
have or show mercy, be compassionate piel (5.3)	ר.ח.מ
contend qal (11.3)	ר.י.ב
graze (7.5)	ר.ע.י/ה
be evil (5.3)	ר.ע.ע
he saw (6.1)	רָאָה [ר.א.י/ה]
Look! imv (4.2)	רְאֵה, רְאִי, רְאוּ [ר.א.י/ה]
one who sees pt (4.1)	רֹאֶה, רֹאָה, רֹאִים, רֹאוֹת [ר.א.י/ה]
I saw (6.1)	רָאִיתִי [ר.א.י/ה]
head m (3.3)	רֹאשׁ, רָאשִׁים, רֹאשׁ-, רָאשֵׁי-
first, former, foremost (7.5)	רִאשׁוֹן, רִאשׁוֹנָה, רִאשׁוֹנִים, רִאשׁוֹנוֹת
your ms head (4.1)	רֹאשְׁךָ
numerous, great, much, many adj (3.2)	רַב, רַבָּה, רַבִּים, רַבּוֹת
chief, captain m (3.2)	רַב, רַבִּים, רַב-, רַבֵּי-
sea captain (lit., captain of the sailor[s] m, 3.2)	רַב הַחֹבֵל, רַבֵּי-הַחֹבֵל
foot f (4.2)	רֶגֶל, רַגְלַיִם, רֶגֶל-, רַגְלֵי-
my foot f (4.4)	רַגְלִי
his feet f (4.4)	רַגְלָיו
to pursue inf absol (7.4)	רָדוֹף [ר.ד.פ]
he pursued (6.2)	רָדַף [ר.ד.פ]
she pursued (6.2)	רָדְפָה [ר.ד.פ]
spirit, wind f (3.2)	רוּחַ, רוּחוֹת, רוּחַ-, רוּחוֹת-
compassionate (10.3)	רַחוּם
he was compassionate piel (8.2)	רִחַם [ר.ח.מ]
compassion, mercy mpl (10.1)	רַחֲמִים, רַחֲמֵי-
you showed compassion piel (10.1)	רִחַמְתָּ [ר.ח.מ]
empty (7.3)	רֵיק, רֵיקָה, רֵיקִים, רֵיקוֹת
soft (3.1)	רַךְ, רַכָּה, רַכִּים, רַכּוֹת
one who is high, exalted pt (6.4)	רָם, רָמָה, רָמִים, רָמוֹת [ר.ו.מ]
bad, wicked (2.3)	רַע, רָעָה, רָעִים, רָעוֹת
neighbor, friend m (5.3)	רֵעַ, רֵעִים, רֵעַ-, רֵעֵי-
hungry (3.1)	רָעֵב, רְעֵבָה, רְעֵבִים, רְעֵבוֹת
evil, misery f (7.1)	רָעָה, רָעוֹת, רָעַת-, רָעוֹת-
only (4.3)	רַק
evil, wicked (4.3)	רָשָׁע, רְשָׁעָה, רְשָׁעִים, רְשָׁעוֹת

שׂ, שׁ

ask, request (2.4)	שׁ.א.ל
be left over, survive nifal (7.3)	שׁ.א.ר
swear an oath nifal (7.3)	שׁ.ב.ע
break qal (4.5), be broken nifal (7.3), shatter piel (10.2)	שׁ.ב.ר
be destroyed pual (11.1)	שׁ.ד.ד

return *qal* (5.1), cause to return, bring back, answer *hifil* (8.1)	ש.ו.ב
put, place (2.4)	ש.י/ו.מ
lie down (3.1)	ש.כ.ב
forget (5.3)	ש.כ.ח
dwell, inhabit (8.1)	ש.כ.נ
send *qal*, be sent *nifal* (8.1), set free, send away *piel* (10.1), be sent away *pual* (11.1)	ש.ל.ח
throw *hifil* (5.2), be thrown *hofal* (11.2)	ש.ל.כ
repay *piel* (10.1), be repaid *pual* (11.1)	ש.ל.מ
hear, listen *qal* (2.4), be heard *nifal* (7.3), cause to hear *hifil* (8.1)	ש.מ.ע
obey the Lord (3.2)	ש.מ.ע בְּקוֹל יהוה
listen to the sound of (3.2)	ש.מ.ע לְקוֹל
guard *qal* (1.2), look out, beware, be guarded, or guard oneself *nifal* (4.1, 7.3)	ש.מ.ר
hate (8.1)	ש.נ.א
pour out, shed *qal*, be poured out, be shed *nifal* (11.1)	ש.פ.כ
be at rest (11.2)	ש.ק.ט
drink *qal* (3.1), be drunk (*beverage*) *nifal* (11.1)	ש.ת.ה/י
Lift! *imv* (9.2)	שָׂא, שְׂאִי, שְׂאוּ, שְׂאֶנָה [נ.ש.א]
Sheol, netherworld *f* (3.2)	שְׁאוֹל
one who inquires, requests *pt* (2.4)	שׁוֹאֵל, שֹׁאֶלֶת, שֹׁאֲלִים, שֹׁאֲלוֹת [ש.א.ל]
I asked, requested (6.2)	שָׁאַלְתִּי [ש.א.ל]
Sit! Dwell! *imv* (1.3)	שֵׁב, שְׁבִי, שְׁבוּ, שֵׁבְנָה [י.ש.ב]
they returned (6.4)	שָׁבוּ [ש.ו.ב]
seven *m, f* (7.3)	שִׁבְעָה, שֶׁבַע
Break! *imv* (9.2)	שְׁבֹר, שִׁבְרִי, שִׁבְרוּ, שְׁבֹרְנָה [ש.ב.ר]
we shattered *piel* (10.2)	שִׁבַּרְנוּ [ש.ב.ר]
field *m* (7.1)	שָׂדֶה, שָׂדוֹת *or* שָׂדִים, שְׂדֵה־, שְׂדוֹת־, *or* שְׂדֵ־
I most certainly will turn back, return, repent (5.3)	שׁוֹב אָשׁוּב [ש.ו.ב]
Turn back! Return! *imv* (9.2)	שׁוּב, שׁוּבִי, שׁוּבוּ, שֹׁבְנָה [ש.ו.ב]
bribe *m* (7.5)	שֹׁחַד, שֹׁחַד־
Put! Place! Set! *imv* (2.4)	שִׂים, שִׂמִי, שִׂמוּ, שִׂימֶינָה [ש.ו/י.מ]
to lie down *inf c* (3.1)	שְׁכַב [ש.כ.ב]
Lie down! *imv* (3.1)	שְׁכַב, שִׁכְבִי, שִׁכְבוּ, שְׁכַבְנָה [ש.כ.ב]
one who is bereaved *pt* (7.5)	שֹׁכֵל, שֹׁכְלִים, שֹׁכֶלֶת, שֹׁכְלוֹת [ש.כ.ל]
one who dwells, inhabits (8.1)	שֹׁכֵן, שֹׁכֶנֶת, שֹׁכְנִים, שֹׁכְנוֹת [ש.כ.נ]
I am fine (1.1)	שָׁלוֹם לִי
peace, well-being as greeting, *m* (1.1)	שָׁלוֹם, שְׁלוֹמִים, שְׁלוֹם־, שְׁלוֹמֵי־
he sent (6.2)	שָׁלַח [ש.ל.ח]
he set free, sent away *piel* (10.1)	שִׁלַּח [ש.ל.ח]
to send away *piel inf absol* (10.3)	שַׁלֵּחַ [ש.ל.ח]
they were sent away *pual* (11.1)	שֻׁלְּחוּ [ש.ל.ח]
table *m* (2.1)	שֻׁלְחָן, שֻׁלְחָנוֹת, שֻׁלְחַן־, שֻׁלְחֲנוֹת־
third (7.5)	שְׁלִישִׁי, שְׁלִישִׁית
three (4.1)	שְׁלֹשָׁה, שָׁלֹשׁ
three days *mpl* (4.3)	שְׁלֹשֶׁת יָמִים
there (5.2)	שָׁם
one who puts, places, or sets *pt* (3.4)	שָׂם, שָׂמָה, שָׂמִים, שָׂמוֹת [ש.ו/י.מ]
name *m* (1.1)	שֵׁם, שֵׁמוֹת, שֶׁם־ *or* שֵׁם־, שְׁמוֹת־
they put, placed (6.2)	שָׂמוּ [ש.ו/י.מ]

HEBREW GLOSSARY יְהוּדִית

שָׂמֵחַ, שְׂמֵחָה, שְׂמֵחִים, שְׂמֵחוֹת [ש.מ.ח] rejoicing, joyful *pt* (6.1)

שְׁמִי my name *m* (1.1)

שָׁמַיִם, שְׁמֵי- sky, heavens *m* (8.1)

שְׁמֵךְ your *fs* name (1.1)

שִׁמְךָ or [שְׁמֶךָ] your *ms* name (1.1)

שֶׁמֶן, שְׁמָנִים, שֶׁמֶן־, שְׁמָנֵי- oil, scented oil *m* (4.4)

שְׁמַע, שִׁמְעִי, שִׁמְעוּ, שְׁמַעְנָה [ש.מ.ע] Hear! Listen! *imv* (5.2)

שֹׁמֵעַ, שֹׁמַעַת, שֹׁמְעִים, שֹׁמְעוֹת [ש.מ.ע] one who hears, listens *pt* (3.2)

שָׁמַעְתִּי [ש.מ.ע] I heard (6.1)

שְׁמַעְתֶּם [ש.מ.ע] you heard *mpl* (6.3)

שֹׁמֵר, שֹׁמְרָה, שֹׁמְרִים, שֹׁמְרוֹת [ש.מ.ר] one who guards, keeps *pt* (3.2)

שֹׁמְרוֹן Samaria *pn loc* (map of Israel)

שֶׁמֶשׁ sun *m and f* (7.1)

שֹׂנֵא, שֹׂנֵאת, שֹׂנְאִים, שֹׂנְאוֹת [ש.נ.א] one who hates *pt* (8.1)

שְׁנֵה־נָא, שְׁנִי־נָא, שְׁנוּ־נָא, שְׁנֶינָה־נָא [ש.נ.י/ה] Repeat, please! *imv ms, fs* (1.3)

שָׁנָה, שָׁנִים / שָׁנוֹת, שְׁנַת, שְׁנֵי- / שְׁנוֹת- year *f* (6.3)

שֵׁנִי, שֵׁנִית second (in order, 7.1)

שְׁנַיִם, שְׁתַּיִם, שְׁנֵי-, שְׁתֵּי- two *dual* (7.5)

שַׁעַר, שְׁעָרִים, שַׁעַר־, שַׁעֲרֵי- gate *m* (8.1)

שָׂפָה, שְׂפָתַיִם, שְׂפַת־, שִׂפְתֵי- lip *f* (5.2)

שְׂפַת־הַיָּם shore, the *f* (5.2)

שַׂק, שַׂקִּים, שַׂק־, שַׂקֵּי- sack, sackcloth *m* (9.2)

שֶׁקֶל, שְׁקָלִים, שֶׁקֶל־, שִׁקְלֵי- shekel, *unit of money, of weight*, *m* (7.5)

שֶׁקֶר, שְׁקָרִים, שֶׁקֶר־, שִׁקְרֵי- falsehood *m* (3.1)

שַׂר, שָׂרִים, שַׂר־, שָׂרֵי- commander, leader, prince *m* (7.1)

שַׂרְאֶצֶר Shareṣer, *an Assyrian name*, *m* (10.1)

שֹׁתֶה, שֹׁתָה, שֹׁתִים, שֹׁתוֹת [ש.ת.י/ה] one who is drinking *pt* (3.1)

ת

ת.פ.שׁ grab (7.1)

לֶאֱבֹד [א.ב.ד] to perish *inf c, prep* (6.3)

תֹּאכַל [א.כ.ל] you will eat *ms* (5.2)

תַּאֲמִין, תַּאֲמִינִי [א.מ.נ] you do / will / would believe *hifil ms, fs* (4.4)

תַּאֲמֵנָּה [א.מ.נ] you will believe *hifil fpl* (5.1)

תֹּאמַר [א.מ.ר] you will say *ms* (5.2)

תִּבְכֶּה [ב.כ.י/ה] you will cry *ms* (4.3)

תְּדַבֵּר [ד.ב.ר] you will speak *piel ms* (5.3)

תְּהוֹם, תְּהוֹמוֹת, תְּהוֹם־, תְּהוֹמוֹת- watery depths *f* (4.3)

תּוּכַל [י.כ.ל] you are able *ms* (3.4)

תּוּכְלוּ [י.כ.ל] you are able *mpl* (3.4)

תּוּכְלִי [י.כ.ל] you are able *fs* (3.4)

תּוּכַלְנָה [י.כ.ל] you are able *fpl* (3.4)

תּוֹדָה thanks, gratitude *m* (5.1)

תּוֹרָה, תּוֹרוֹת, תּוֹרַת־, תּוֹרוֹת- law, instruction *f* (5.1)

תּוֹרָתִי my law, instruction (5.1)

תִּזְכֹּר [ז.כ.ר] you will remember *ms* (5.3)

תִּזְכְּרוּ [ז.כ.ר] you will remember *mpl* (5.1)

תַּחֲנוּן, תַּחֲנוּנִים, תַּחֲנוּן־, תַּחֲנוּנֵי- [ח.נ.נ] supplication, request *m* (10.3)

תַּחַת under, instead of (2.4)

תִּירְאוּ [י.ר.א] you will fear *mpl* (5.1)

she will hit (4.5) .... [נ.כ.י/ה] תַּכֶּה	you will take *mpl* (5.1) .... תִּקְחוּ [ל.ק.ח]
you will go, walk *ms* (5.2) .... תֵּלֵךְ [ה.ל.כ]	she will draw near (4.5) .... תִּקְרַב [ק.ר.ב]
you will go, walk *mpl* (5.1) .... תֵּלְכוּ [ה.ל.כ]	they will see *f* (4.4) .... תִּרְאֶינָה [ר.א.י/ה]
they will go, walk *f* (4.4) .... תֵּלַכְנָה [ה.ל.כ]	Tarshish *pn loc* (1.3) .... תַּרְשִׁישׁ
you will go, walk *fpl* (5.1) .... תֵּלַכְנָה [ה.ל.כ]	toward Tarshish *f* (6.1) .... תַּרְשִׁישָׁה
you will die *ms* (5.2) .... תָּמוּת [מ.ו.ת]	you will lift, carry *ms* (5.2) .... תִּשָּׂא [נ.שׂ.א]
recently (6.3) .... תְּמֹל שִׁלְשֹׁם	you will lift, carry *mpl* (5.1) .... תִּשְׂאוּ [נ.שׂ.א]
Give *ms* to me! *imv* (1.1) .... תֵּן לִי [נ.ת.נ]	you will sit, dwell *fs* (5.3) .... תֵּשְׁבִי [י.שׁ.ב]
Give *fs* to me! *imv* (1.1) .... תְּנִי לִי [נ.ת.נ]	she will break (4.5) .... תִּשְׁבֹּר [שׁ.ב.ר]
you will go up *ms* (5.3) .... תַּעֲלֶה [ע.ל.י/ה]	you will return *ms* (5.3) .... תָּשׁוּב [שׁ.ו.ב]
you will answer *ms* (5.3) .... תַּעֲנֶה [ע.נ.י/ה]	you will return *fs* (5.3) .... תָּשׁוּבִי [שׁ.ו.ב]
she will do, make (4.5) .... תַּעֲשֶׂה [ע.שׂ.י/ה]	you will forget *ms* (5.3) .... תִּשְׁכַּח [שׁ.כ.ח]
you will do, make *mpl* (5.1) .... תַּעֲשׂוּ [ע.שׂ.י/ה]	you will send us away *piel ms* (10.3) ... תְּשַׁלְּחֵנוּ [שׁ.ל.ח]
you will do, make *fs* (5.3) .... תַּעֲשִׂי [ע.שׂ.י/ה]	you will throw *hifil ms* (5.2) .... תַּשְׁלִיךְ [שׁ.ל.כ]
they will do, make *f* (4.5) .... תַּעֲשֶׂינָה [ע.שׂ.י/ה]	you will throw me *hifil mpl* (5.2) ...... תַּשְׁלִיכֻנִי [שׁ.ל.כ]
prayer *f* (10.1) .... תְּפִלָּה, תְּפִלּוֹת, תְּפִלַּת־, תְּפִלּוֹת־	you will hear *ms* (5.3) .... תִּשְׁמַע [שׁ.מ.ע]
you will go out, exit *mpl* (5.1) .... תֵּצְאוּ [י.צ.א]	they will hear *f* (4.4) .... תִּשְׁמַעְנָה [שׁ.מ.ע]

GLOSSARY

לַחְקוֹר מִלִּים

ח.ק.ר. to search
מִלָּה *f* word, utterance

English / Hebrew   אַנְגְלִית / יְהוּדִית

Please refer to the introductory notes for the Hebrew-English portion of the glossary for an explanation of abbreviations and the sequence of related forms found within a given entry.

A

a little (of something), a few (7.3) .... מְעַט, מְעַטִּים
abandon, forsake (7.1) .... ע.ז.ב
afflict *piel* (10.2) .... ע.נ.י/ה
again, more, yet, still (4.1) .... עוֹד
Alas! Ah...! (5.2) .... אֲהָהּ
Alas! (8.1) .... הוֹי
alive (6.1) .... חַי, חַיָּה, חַיִּים, חַיּוֹת
all of them (7.2) .... כֻּלָּם
all that happens / happened *pt fpl* (6.1) .... כָּל־הַמֹּצָאוֹת [מ.צ.א]
also (5.3) .... גַּם
altar *f* (9.2) .... מִזְבֵּחַ, מִזְבְּחוֹת, מִזְבַּח־, מִזְבְּחוֹת־
Amittai, *masculine name* (6.1) .... אֲמִתַּי
Ammon *pn loc* (map of Israel) .... עַמּוֹן
and (2.3) .... וְ..., וּ..., וַ..., וָ..., וֶ...
And bless! *piel imv ms* (10.2) .... וּבָרֵךְ [ב.ר.כ]
and he approached (7.1) .... וַיִּגַּשׁ [נ.ג.ש]
and he built (7.1) .... וַיִּבֶן [ב.נ.י/ה]

and he came (7.1) .... וַיָּבֹא [ב.ו.א]
and he caused (someone) to fall *hifil shortened* (8.2) .. וַיַּפֵּל [נ.פ.ל]
and he declared, announced *hifil* (7.1) .... וַיַּגֵּד [נ.ג.ד]
and he drank (7.1) .... וַיֵּשְׁתְּ [ש.ת.י/ה]
and he fortified himself, took courage *hitpael* (11.3) .... וַיִּתְחַזֵּק [ח.ז.ק]
and he found (7.1) .... וַיִּמְצָא [מ.צ.א]
and he got up (7.1) .... וַיָּקָם [ק.ו.מ]
and he grabbed (7.1) .... וַיִּתְפֹּשׂ [ת.פ.ש]
and he lay down (7.1) .... וַיִּשְׁכַּב [ש.כ.ב]
and he may kill *hifil* (8.2) .... וְהֵמִית [מ.ו.ת]
and he prayed *hitpael* (11.3) .... וַיִּתְפַּלֵּל [פ.ל.ל]
and he prophesied *nifal* (7.4) .... וַיִּנָּבֵא [נ.ב.א]
and he said (7.1) .... וַיֹּאמֶר [א.מ.ר]
and he spoke *piel* (10.1) .... וַיְדַבֵּר [ד.ב.ר]
and he stationed himself *hitpael* (11.3) .... וַיִּתְיַצֵּב [י.צ.ב]
and he walked back and forth, roamed, lived *hitpael* (11.3) .... וַיִּתְהַלֵּךְ [ה.ל.כ]
and he was bound, tied *nifal* (7.3) .... וַיֵּאָסֵר [א.ס.ר]

and he was given *qal passive* (11.1)	וַיֻּתַּן
and he was lifted, carried *nifal* (7.3)	וַיִּנָּשֵׂא [נ.שׂ.א]
and he went (7.1)	וַיֵּלֶךְ [ה.ל.כ]
and he went out (7.1)	וַיֵּצֵא [י.צ.א]
and he wrote at the dictation of (10.1)	וַיִּכְתֹּב מִפִּי [כ.ת.ב]
and I will exalt *polel* (10.3)	וְרוֹמַמְתִּי [ר.ו.מ]
and I will strike, hit *hifil* (8.1)	וְהִכֵּיתִי [נ.כ.י/ה]
and it came to pass, so (6.4)	וַיְהִי
and it was spoken *pual* (11.1)	וַיְדֻבַּר [ד.ב.ר]
and it was thought, supposed *nifal* (7.4)	וַיֵּחָשֵׁב [ח.שׁ.ב]
and may he return *qal jussive* (9.4)	וְיָשֹׁב [שׁ.ו.ב]
and may I sing *or* play an instrument *piel cohort.* (10.3)	וַאֲזַמְּרָה [ז.מ.ר]
and may it cover *piel jussive 3fs* (10.3)	וּתְכַס [כ.ס.י/ה]
and she hit *hifil* (7.1)	וַתַּךְ [נ.כ.י/ה]
and she was broken *nifal* (7.3)	וַתִּשָּׁבֵר [שׁ.ב.ר]
and there was (7.1)	וַיְהִי [ה.י.י/ה]
and they consecrated themselves *hitpael* (11.3)	וַיִּתְקַדְּשׁוּ [ק.ד.שׁ]
and they swore an oath *nifal* (7.4)	וַיִּשָּׁבְעוּ [שׁ.ב.ע]
and they were cut *nifal* (7.3)	וַיִּכָּרְתוּ [כ.ר.ת]
and they were finished *pual f* (11.1)	וַתְּכֻלֶּינָה [כ.ל.י/ה]
and they worked (7.1)	וַיַּעַבְדוּ [ע.ב.ד]
and they worshipped, bowed down *hishtafel* (11.2)	וַיִּשְׁתַּחֲווּ [ח.ו.י/ה]
and we defiled ourselves *nifal* (10.2)	נִטְמֵאנוּ [ט.מ.א]
and we will praise *piel* (10.3)	וְהִלַּלְנוּ [ה.ל.ל]
and we will strike *hifil* (7.4)	וְהִכִּינוּ [נ.כ.י/ה]
and you have been compassionate *piel ms* (10.2)	וְרִחַמְתָּ [ר.ח.מ]
animal (wild) *f* (8.1)	חַיָּה, חַיּוֹת, חַיַּת־, חַיּוֹת־
animal, cattle *f* (5.1)	בְּהֵמָה, בְּהֵמוֹת, בֶּהֱמַת־, בַּהֲמוֹת־
answer (5.3)	ע.נ.י/ה
answer *m* (7.1)	מַעֲנֶה, מַעֲנוֹת, מַעֲנֵה־, מַעֲנוֹת־
anything (11.1)	מְאוּמָה
appear *nifal* (7.4)	ר.א.י/ה
appoint *qal* (6.4) *and hifil* (9.4)	פ.ק.ד
approach (7.1)	נ.ג.שׁ
Aram [Syria] *m* (map of Ancient Near East)	אֲרָם
arm *f* (4.1)	זְרוֹעַ, זְרֹעוֹת, זְרוֹעַ־, זְרֹעֵי־
army, wealth, might *m* (6.3)	חַיִל, חֲיָלִים, חֵיל־, חֵילֵי־
around (environs *fpl substantive*, 7.1)	סָבִיב, סְבִיבָה, סְבִיבִים, סְבִיבוֹת
as I was / am / will be grazing *inf c with prep* (7.5)	בִּרְעוֹתִי [ר.ע.י/ה]
as soon as [entity] is / was full *inf c, prep* (6.2)	כִּמְלֹאת [מ.ל.א]
Ashdod *pn loc* (8.2)	אַשְׁדּוֹד
Ashdodite (8.2)	אַשְׁדּוֹדִי
ashes *m* (9.3)	אֵפֶר
ask, request (2.4)	שׁ.א.ל
assembly, congregation *m* (7.5)	קָהָל, קְהָלִים, קְהַל־, קְהָלֵי־
Asshur *pn loc* (map of Ancient Near East)	אַשּׁוּר
at a distance (6.1)	מֵרָחוֹק
Shareṣer, *an Assyrian name, m* (10.1)	שַׂרְאֶצֶר

B

Babylon *pn loc* (7.4)	בָּבֶל
bad, wicked (2.3)	רַע, רָעָה, רָעִים, רָעוֹת

bag, little pack *m* (2.3)	צְרוֹר, צְרוֹרוֹת, צְרוֹר-, צְרוֹרוֹת-
be, become (4.3)	ה.י.ה
be able (2.4)	י.כ.ל
be ashamed (10.2)	ב.ו.ש
be at rest (11.2)	ש.ק.ט
be blessed *qal passive* (7.3) *and pual* (11.1)	ב.ר.כ
be born *pual* (11.1)	י.ל.ד
be broken *nifal* (7.3)	ש.ב.ר
be brought *hofal* (11.2)	ב.ו.א
be built *nifal* (7.3)	ב.נ.י/ה
be called *nifal* (7.1)	ק.ר.א
be clothed *qal passive* (8.1), *pual* (11.2)	ל.ב.ש
be commanded *pual* (11.1)	צ.ו.י/ה
be defiled *or* become defiled *qal* (10.2)	ט.מ.א
be devoured *qal passive* (11.1)	א.כ.ל
be difficult, marvelous *nifal* (10.2)	פ.ל.א
be drunk (beverage) *nifal* (11.1)	ש.ת.י/ה
be evil (5.3)	ר.ע.ע
be faithful, reliable, established *nifal* (7.4)	א.מ.נ
be feared *nifal* (10.1)	י.ר.א
be finished *pual* (11.1)	כ.ל.י/ה
be found *nifal* (7.3)	מ.צ.א
be founded *pual* (11.1)	י.ס.ד
be full *qal* (6.2), to be filled *nifal* (7.3), to fill *piel* (10.2)	מ.ל.א
be gathered *nifal and pual* (8.2, 11.1)	א.ס.פ
be given *nifal* (4.1, 7.3), *qal passive* (11.1)	נ.ת.נ
be guarded *nifal* (7.3)	ש.מ.ר
be heard *nifal* (7.3)	ש.מ.ע
be heavy, mighty (6.3)	כ.ב.ד
be high, exalted (6.4)	ר.ו.מ
be holy *qal* (11.3)	ק.ד.ש
be hot (4.2)	ח.ר.י/ה
be known *nifal* (7.3)	י.ד.ע
be led, be brought *hofal* (11.2)	י.ב.ל
be left over, to survive *nifal* (7.3)	ש.א.ר
be lifted *nifal* (7.3)	נ.ש.א
be made, be done *nifal* (7.3)	ע.ש.י/ה
be poured out *or* shed *nifal* (11.1)	ש.פ.כ
be praised *pual* (11.1)	ה.ל.ל
be put to death *hofal* (11.2)	מ.ו.ת
be overturned *nifal* (7.5)	ה.פ.כ
be recounted, reported *pual* (11.1)	ס.פ.ר
be reported *hofal* (11.3)	נ.ג.ד
be sent *nifal* (8.1)	ש.ל.ח
be sent away *pual* (11.1)	ש.ל.ח
be small, become small (5.3)	ק.ט.נ
be solid, firm, established *nifal* (7.4)	כ.ו.נ
be spoken *pual* (11.1)	ד.ב.ר
be stolen *nifal* (10.2)	ג.נ.ב
be strong *qal* (11.3)	ח.ז.ק
be struck *hofal* (11.2)	נ.כ.י/ה
be thought, be supposed *nifal* (7.4)	ח.ש.ב
be thrown *hofal* (11.2)	ש.ל.כ
be willing (6.2)	א.ב.י/ה
be written *qal passive* (11.1)	כ.ת.ב
because (7.4)	יַעַן [אֲשֶׁר]
because (10.1)	כַּאֲשֶׁר
because, that, when, indeed (2.3)	כִּי
Beer Sheba *pn loc* (map of Israel)	בְּאֵר שֶׁבַע
before *in time* (8.1)	בְּטֶרֶם
before, in front of (2.4)	לִפְנֵי
behind *or* after (2.4)	אַחַר, אַחֲרֵי

behold, here is (2.1) .... הִנֵּה
believe *hifil* (4.4) .... א.מ.נ
belly, stomach *f* (4.3) .... בֶּטֶן
belonging to the tribe of Zebulun (3.2) ...... לְמַטֵּה זְבוּלֻן
beside (2.4) .... עַל־יַד
between, among (4.2) .... בֵּין
Bethel *pn loc* (map of Israel) .... בֵּיתְאֵל
big, large, great (2.3) .... גָּדוֹל, גְּדוֹלָה, גְּדוֹלִים, גְּדוֹלוֹת
bird(s), flying insect(s) *m* (8.1) .... עוֹף, עוֹף־
bitter (3.1) .... מַר, מָרָה, מָרִים, מָרוֹת
bless *piel* (10.1) .... ב.ר.כ
blessed *pual pt* (11.1) .... מְבֹרָךְ, מְבֹרֶכֶת, מְבֹרָכִים, מְבֹרָכוֹת [ב.ר.כ]
blood *m* (11.1) .... דָּם, דָּמִים, דַּם־, דְּמֵי־
bone, inner substance, self *f* (5.2) .. עֶצֶם, עֲצָמוֹת, עֶצֶם־, עַצְמוֹת־
book, scroll *m* (2.3) .... סֵפֶר, סְפָרִים, סֵפֶר־, סִפְרֵי־
border *m* (11.1) .... גְּבוּל, גְּבוּלִים, גְּבוּל־, גְּבוּלֵי־
bread *m* (1.1) .... לֶחֶם, לֶחֶם־
break (4.5) .... ש.ב.ר
Break! *imv* (9.2) ..... שְׁבֹר, שִׁבְרִי, שִׁבְרוּ, שְׁבֹרְנָה [ש.ב.ר]
bribe *m* (7.5) .... שֹׁחַד, שֹׁחַד־
bring *hifil* (8.1) .... ב.ו.א
brother *m* (5.1) .... אָח, אַחִים, אֲחִי־, אֲחֵי־
build *qal* (7.1) .... ב.נ.י/ה
burden, oracle, pronouncement *m* (7.1) ..... מַשָּׂא, מַשָּׂאוֹת
but rather (6.4) .... כִּי אִם
but she missed, sinned (7.2) .... וַתֶּחֱטָא [ח.ט.א]
but, however, surely (3.1) .... אַךְ
buy, acquire, create (6.3) .... ק.נ.י/ה

C

call, read *qal* (5.1), meet, encounter *qal* (6.2) .... ק.ר.א
Call! Read! Encounter! *imv* (7.1, 9.1) .... קְרָא, קִרְאִי, קִרְאוּ, קְרֶאןָ [ק.ר.א]
capture *qal*; be captured, trapped *nifal* (7.1) .... ל.כ.ד
Carchemish *pn loc* (map of Ancient Near East) .... כַּרְכְּמִישׁ
cattle *m* (10.2) .... אֲלָפִים
cattle, herd *m* (9.2) .... בָּקָר, בְּקָרִים, בְּקַר־, בִּקְרֵי־
cause to come near, offer *hifil* (8.1) .... ק.ר.ב
cause to fall *hifil* (8.1) .... נ.פ.ל
cause to go out *hifil* (8.1) .... י.צ.א
cause to go up *hifil* (8.1) .... ע.ל.י/ה
cause to hear *hifil* (8.1) .... ש.מ.ע
cause to inhabit *hifil* (8.1) .... י.ש.ב
cause to inherit *hifil* (8.1) .... י.ר.ש
cause to return, bring back *hifil* (8.1) .... ש.ו.ב
cave *f* (7.3) .... מְעָרָה, מְעָרוֹת, מְעָרַת־, מְעָרוֹת־
chair, seat *m* (2.1) .... כִּסֵּא, כִּסְאוֹת, כִּסֵּא־, כִּסְאוֹת־
chest, ark *m* (7.3) .... אָרוֹן, אֲרוֹן־
chief, captain *m* (3.2) .... רַב, רַבִּים, רַב־, רַבֵּי־
child, boy *m* (7.5) .... יֶלֶד, יְלָדִים, יֶלֶד־, יַלְדֵי־
city *f* (2.1) .... עִיר, עָרִים, עִיר־, עָרֵי־
clan, family *f* (7.5) .... מִשְׁפָּחָה, מִשְׁפָּחוֹת, מִשְׁפַּחַת־, מִשְׁפְּחוֹת־
Clothe (someone)! *hifil imv* (9.2) .... הַלְבֵּשׁ, הַלְבִּישִׁי, הַלְבִּישׁוּ, הַלְבֵּשְׁנָה [ל.ב.ש]
clothe *hifil* (9.2) .... ל.ב.ש
come to an end, waste away *qal* (8.1) .... כ.ל.י/ה
come, enter *qal* (3.3) .... ב.ו.א
command *piel* (3.4, 10.2) .... צ.ו.י/ה

ENGLISH GLOSSARY / אַנְגְּלִית

commander, leader, prince *m* (7.1) .... שַׂר, שָׂרִים, שַׂר־, שָׂרֵי־

commandment *f* (5.2) .... מִצְוָה, מִצְוֹת, מִצְוַת־, מִצְוֹת־

compassion, mercy *mpl* (10.1) .... רַחֲמִים, רַחֲמֵי־

compassionate (10.3) .... רַחוּם

consecrate oneself *hitpael* (11.3) .... ק.ד.ש

container, sack, utensil, vessel *m* (2.3) .. כְּלִי, כֵּלִים, כְּלִי־, כְּלֵי־

contend *qal* (11.3) .... ר.י.ב

cord, rope *m* (7.3) .... עֲבֹת, עֲבֹתִים / עֲבֹתֹת, עֲבֹתֵי־ / עַבְתֹת־

correct *nifal* (2.3); he was established, set up *nifal* (7.3) .... נָכוֹן [כ.ו.נ]

counsel, advice *f* (8.1) .... עֵצָה, עֵצוֹת, עֲצַת־, עֲצוֹת־

count *qal* (11.1) .... ס.פ.ר

covenant *f* (8.1) .... בְּרִית, בְּרִית־

Cover! Atone! *piel imv ms* (10.2) .... כַּפֵּר [כ.פ.ר]

cover, atone *piel*, be covered, atoned for *pual* (10.2) .... כ.פ.ר

cover, hide *piel* (10.1), be covered *pual* (11.1) .... כ.ס.י/ה

cross over (3.2) .... ע.ב.ר

crown *f* (8.1) .... עֲטָרָה, עֲטָרוֹת, עֲטֶרֶת־, עַטְרֹת־

cry (4.3) .... ב.כ.י/ה

cup *f* (1.1) .... כּוֹס, כֹּסוֹת, כּוֹס־, כֹּסוֹת־

cut (4.3) .... כ.ר.ת

Cyprus, the land of *pn loc* (map of ANE) .... אֶרֶץ כִּתִּים

D

Dagon *deity* (8.2) .... דָּגוֹן

Damascus *pn loc* (map of Ancient Near East) .... דַּמֶּשֶׂק

darkness *m* (4.4) .... חֹשֶׁךְ

daughter *f* (6.1) .... בַּת, בָּנוֹת, בַּת־, בְּנוֹת־

day *m* (5.1) .... יוֹם, יָמִים, יוֹם־, יְמֵי־

Dead [Salt] Sea *m* (map of Israel) .... יָם הַמֶּלַח

death *m* (8.1) .... מָוֶת, מוֹתִים, מוֹת־, מוֹתֵי־

deceit *f* (8.1) .... מִרְמָה, מִרְמוֹת, מִרְמַת־, מִרְמֹת־

declare, announce *hifil* (7.1) .... נ.ג.ד

declares the LORD (8.1) .... נְאֻם יהוה

defile oneself *nifal* (10.2) .... ט.מ.א

defile something *piel* (10.2) .... ט.מ.א

definite direct object marker (2.1) .... אֵת, אֶת־

delay *piel* (10.2) .... א.ח.ר

deliver, snatch *hifil* (8.1) .... נ.צ.ל

descend, go down (5.2) .... י.ר.ד

descendants, seed *m* (9.5) .... זֶרַע, זְרָעִים, זֶרַע־ [זְרַע־], זַרְעֵי־

desire, delight in, prefer, be willing *verbal adj* (1.3) ... חָפֵץ, חֲפֵצָה, חֲפֵצִים, חֲפֵצוֹת

destroy *hifil* (9.3) .... א.ב.ד

Destroy! *hifil imv* (9.3) .... הַאֲבֵד, הַאֲבִידִי, הַאֲבִידוּ, הַאֲבֵדְנָה [א.ב.ד]

die *qal* (4.3) .... מ.ו.ת

different, foreign (9.5) .... אַחֵר, אַחֶרֶת, אֲחֵרִים, אֲחֵרוֹת

do [some activity] again *qal* and *hifil* (7.2) .... י.ס.פ

Do not go out! *mpl* (7.4) .... אַל־תֵּצְאוּ [י.צ.א]

Do not...! (4.3) .... אַל־

do, make (3.4) .... ע.שׂ.י/ה

Don't be afraid! *ms, fs, mpl* (4.3, 5.1) ... אַל־תִּירָא, תִּירְאִי, תִּירְאוּ [י.ר.א]

door *f* (2.4) .... דֶּלֶת, דְּלָתוֹת, דֶּלֶת־, דַּלְתוֹת־

draw near (4.5) .... ק.ר.ב

Draw near! *imv* (9.2)	קְרַב, קִרְבִי, קִרְבוּ, קְרַבְנָה [ק.ר.ב]
drink *qal* (3.1)	ש.ת.י/ה
dry, be (2.3)	י.ב.ש
dry (2.3)	יָבֵשׁ, יְבֵשָׁה, יְבֵשִׁים, יְבֵשׁוֹת
dry land *f* (3.3)	יַבָּשָׁה
dwell, inhabit (8.1)	ש.כ.נ

E

ear *f* (4.2)	אֹזֶן, אָזְנַיִם, אֹזֶן־, אָזְנֵי־
east, front, primeval time *m* (map of ANE)	קֶדֶם
eat (3.1)	א.כ.ל
Edom *m* (map of Israel)	אֱדוֹם
Egypt *f* (8.1)	מִצְרַיִם
empty (7.3)	רֵיק, רֵקָה, רֵקִים, רֵקוֹת
enter (2.4)	ב.ו.א
Enter! Come! *imv* (2.4)	בּוֹא, בּוֹאִי, בּוֹאוּ, בּוֹאנָה [ב.ו.א]
enemy *m* (3.3)	אוֹיֵב, אוֹיְבִים, אוֹיֵב־, אוֹיְבֵי־
entrance, doorway, opening *m* (7.5)	פֶּתַח, פְּתָחִים, פֶּתַח־, פִּתְחֵי־
Ephraim *m* (6.1)	אֶפְרַיִם
establish *hifil* (8.1)	ק.ו.מ
establish *qal* (11.1)	י.ס.ד
Euphrates River, the *pn loc* (map of ANE)	נְהַר־פְּרָת
every, each, all, the whole (5.1)	כֹּל, כָּל־
evil, misery *f* (7.1)	רָעָה, רָעוֹת, רָעַת־, רָעוֹת־
evil, wicked (4.3)	רָשָׁע, רְשָׁעָה, רְשָׁעִים, רְשָׁעוֹת
except for (7.3)	בִּלְתִּי
eye, spring *f* (4.2)	עַיִן, עֵינַיִם, עֵין־, עֵינֵי־

F

face(s) *m* (9.5)	פָּנִים, פְּנֵי־
faces (bowed) to the ground (11.2)	אַפַּיִם אַרְצָה
fall (4.3)	נ.פ.ל
Fall! *imv* (9.2)	נְפֹל, נִפְלִי, נִפְלוּ, נְפֹלְנָה [נ.פ.ל]
falsehood *m* (3.1)	שֶׁקֶר, שְׁקָרִים, שֶׁקֶר־, שִׁקְרֵי־
father *m* (6.1)	אָב, אָבוֹת, אֲבִי־ [אַב], אֲבוֹת־
fear, be afraid (5.2)	י.ר.א
fear, dread *f* (6.2)	יִרְאָה, יִרְאַת־
feared *nifal pt* (10.1)	נוֹרָא, נוֹרָאָה, נוֹרָאִים, נוֹרָאוֹת [י.ר.א]
field *f* (8.1)	שָׂדֶה, שָׂדוֹת, שְׂדֵה־, שְׂדוֹת־
fight *nifal* (7.4)	ל.ח.מ
fill *piel* (10.2)	מ.ל.א
finally, at last (4.4)	בָּאַחֲרוֹן, בָּאַחֲרֹנָה
find (3.1)	מ.צ.א
finish, complete *piel* (10.3)	כ.ל.י/ה
fire *f* (9.2)	אֵשׁ
first, former, foremost (7.5)	רִאשׁוֹן, רִאשׁוֹנָה, רִאשׁוֹנִים, רִאשֹׁנוֹת
firstly, at first (5.2)	בָּרִאשׁוֹנָה
fish *m* (3.3)	דָּג, דָּגִים, דַּג־, דְּגֵי־
flock(s), small cattle and sheep *f* (7.5)	צֹאן, צֹאנִים, צֹאן־, צֹאנֵי־
fool *m* (3.3)	כְּסִיל, כְּסִילִים
foot *f* (4.2)	רֶגֶל, רַגְלַיִם, רֶגֶל־, רַגְלֵי־
forever (4.3)	לְעוֹלָם
forget (5.3)	ש.כ.ח
forgive (5.3)	ס.ל.ח
former, eastern, ancient ones *collective* (11.2)	קַדְמֹנִי
fortify oneself *hitpael* (11.3)	ח.ז.ק

ENGLISH GLOSSARY אַנְגְּלִית

fourthly (5.2)	בָּרְבִיעִית
from me (4.3)	מִמֶּנִּי
from under (2.4)	מִתַּחַת
from upon (2.4)	מֵעַל
from where…? (6.4)	מֵאַיִן…?
from, מֵ before gutturals and ר (2.4)	מִן
future, perpetuity m (10.3)	עַד

G

Gaddiel name m (3.2)	גַּדִּיאֵל
garment m (7.5)	בֶּגֶד, בְּגָדִים, בֶּגֶד־, בִּגְדֵי־
gate m (8.1)	שַׁעַר, שְׁעָרִים, שַׁעַר־, שַׁעֲרֵי־
Gather (assemble selves)! qal imv (9.1)	קְבַץ, קִבְצִי, קִבְצוּ, קְבַצְנָה [ק.ב.צ]
gather (what has been scattered) piel (10.3)	ק.ב.צ
Gather (what has been scattered)! piel imv (10.3)	קַבֵּץ, קַבְּצִי, קַבְּצוּ, קַבֵּצְנָה [ק.ב.צ]
gather qal (7.2)	א.ס.פ
gather, assemble selves qal (9.1)	ק.ב.צ
Gath-Hepher pn loc (6.1)	גַּת הַחֵפֶר
Gaza pn loc (map of Israel)	עַזָּה
generation m (10.2)	דּוֹר, דֹּרוֹת, דּוֹר־, דֹּרֹת־
get up (1.3)	ק.ו.מ
Get up! (1.3)	קוּם, קוּמִי, קוּמוּ, קֹמְנָה [ק.ו.מ]
gift f (11.1)	מִנְחָה, מְנָחוֹת, מִנְחַת־, מִנְחוֹת־
give (2.4)	נ.ת.נ
give birth, beget qal (6.4)	י.ל.ד
Give ms, fs to me! imv (1.1)	תֶּן לִי, תְּנִי לִי [נ.ת.נ]
glory, heaviness m (11.1)	כָּבוֹד, כְּבוֹד־
Go in peace! imv ms, fs (1.2)	לֵךְ / לְכִי לְשָׁלוֹם [ה.ל.כ]
go out (5.1)	י.צ.א
Go out! imv (3.1)	צֵא, צְאִי, צְאוּ, צֶאנָה [י.צ.א]
Go to…! imv ms, fs (1.3)	לֵךְ אֶל…! לְכִי אֶל…! [ה.ל.כ]
go up, ascend (5.3)	ע.ל.י/ה
go, walk qal (3.2)	ה.ל.כ
God m (2.3)	אֱלֹהִים, אֱלֹהֵי־
god(s) or God m (2.3, 8.1)	אֵל, אֱלֹהִים, אֵל־, אֱלֹהֵי־
gold m (6.3)	זָהָב, זְהַב־
good (2.3)	טוֹב, טוֹבָה, טוֹבִים, טוֹבוֹת
grab (7.1)	ת.פ.שׂ
grace, favor m (5.1)	חֵן
gracious (10.2)	חַנּוּן
grave m (4.3)	קֶבֶר, קְבָרִים, קֶבֶר־, קִבְרֵי־
graze (7.5)	ר.ע.י/ה
growing stormier pt ms, pt ms (3.3)	הוֹלֵךְ וְסֹעֵר [ה.ל.כ, ס.ע.ר]
guard qal (1.2)	ש.מ.ר
guilty (7.5)	אָשֵׁם, אֲשֵׁמָה, אֲשֵׁמִים, אֲשֵׁמוֹת

H

hand f (3.1)	יָד, יָדַיִם (יָדוֹת), יַד־, יְדֵי־
hard (6.4)	קָשֶׁה, קָשָׁה, קָשִׁים, קָשׁוֹת
hate (8.1)	שׂ.נ.א
he / it will / would be known nifal (7.4)	יִוָּדַע [י.ד.ע]
he / it would be poured out nifal (11.1)	יִשָּׁפֵךְ [שׁ.פ.כ]
he abandoned (7.1)	עָזַב [ע.ז.ב]
he blessed piel (10.1)	בֵּרַךְ [ב.ר.כ]
he commanded piel (10.1)	צִוָּה [צ.ו.י/ה]
he finished, completed piel (10.3)	כִּלָּה [כ.ל.י/ה]
he gave (6.1)	נָתַן [נ.ת.נ]
he hid himself, was hidden nifal (7.3)	נִסְתַּר [ס.ת.ר]

he is dead *or* has died (6.1)	מֵת [מ.ו.ת]
he looked for, sought *piel* (1.3)	בִּקֵּשׁ [ב.ק.שׁ]
he opened (eyes, 6.1)	פָּקַח [פ.ק.ח]
he pursued (6.2)	רָדַף [ר.ד.פ]
he rescued (8.1)	הוֹשִׁיעַ [י.שׁ.ע]
he saw (6.1)	רָאָה [ר.א.י/ה]
he searched, sought *piel* (10.1)	בִּקֵּשׁ [ב.ק.שׁ]
he sent (6.2)	שָׁלַח [שׁ.ל.ח]
he set free, sent away *piel* (10.1)	שִׁלַּח [שׁ.ל.ח]
he showed, revealed *hifil* (8.1)	הֶרְאָה [ר.א.י/ה]
he spoke *piel* (10.1)	דִּבֶּר [ד.ב.ר]
he spoke *piel* (10.1)	דִּבֶּר [ד.ב.ר]
he stole (7.5)	גָּנַב [ג.נ.ב]
he survived, was left over *nifal* (7.3)	נִשְׁאַר [שׁ.א.ר]
he taught, trained *piel* (10.1)	לִמֵּד [ל.מ.ד]
he took (6.1)	לָקַח [ל.ק.ח]
he uncovered, revealed *piel* (10.1)	גִּלָּה [ג.ל.י/ה]
he was (5.1)	הָיָה [ה.י.י/ה]
he was (5.1)	הָיָה [ה.י.י/ה]
he was bound, imprisoned *nifal* (7.3)	נֶאֱסַר [א.ס.ר]
he was broken *nifal* (7.3)	נִשְׁבַּר [שׁ.ב.ר]
he was built *nifal* (7.3)	נִבְנָה [ב.נ.י/ה]
he was caught *nifal* (7.3)	נִלְקַח [ל.ק.ח]
he was commanded *pual* (11.1)	צֻוָּה [צ.ו.י/ה]
he was compassionate *piel* (8.2)	רִחַם [ר.ח.מ]
he was covered *nifal* (7.3)	נִכְסָה [כ.ס.י/ה]
he was cut *nifal* (7.3)	נִכְרַת [כ.ר.ת]
he was done, made *nifal* (7.3)	נַעֲשָׂה [ע.שׂ.י/ה]
he was eaten *nifal* (7.3)	נֶאֱכַל [א.כ.ל]
he was filled *nifal* (7.3)	נִמְלָא [מ.ל.א]
he was found *nifal* (7.3)	נִמְצָא [מ.צ.א]
he was given, put, or placed *nifal* (7.3)	נִתַּן [נ.ת.נ]
he was guarded, guarded himself *nifal* (7.3)	נִשְׁמַר [שׁ.מ.ר]
he was heard *nifal* (7.3)	נִשְׁמַע [שׁ.מ.ע]
he was killed *hofal* (7.3)	הוּמַת [מ.ו.ת]
he was known *nifal* (7.3)	נוֹדַע [י.ד.ע]
he was lifted, taken away *nifal* (7.3)	נִשָּׂא [נ.שׂ.א]
he was poured out *nifal* (7.3)	נִשְׁפַּךְ [שׁ.פ.כ]
he was trapped *nifal* (7.3)	נִלְכַּד [ל.כ.ד]
he will be called *nifal* (7.1)	יִקָּרֵא [ק.ר.א]
he will be hot (4.2)	יֶחֱרֶה [ח.ר.י/ה]
he will bring back or answer *hifil* (11.3)	יָשִׁיב [י.שׁ.ב]
he will come to an end, reach completion (8.1)	יִכְלֶה [כ.ל.י/ה]
he will come, he will enter (4.3)	יָבוֹא [ב.ו.א]
he will cut (4.3)	יִכְרֹת [כ.ר.ת]
he will descend (4.3)	יֵרֵד [י.ר.ד]
he will die (4.3)	יָמוּת [מ.ו.ת]
he will do, make (4.3)	יַעֲשֶׂה [ע.שׂ.י/ה]
he will fall (4.3)	יִפֹּל [נ.פ.ל]
he will forsake *qal indic.*, may he forsake *qal juss.* (9.4)	יַעֲזֹב [ע.ז.ב]
he will guard (4.3)	יִשְׁמֹר [שׁ.מ.ר]
he will have or show mercy *piel* (5.3)	יְרַחֵם [ר.ח.מ]
he will hit *hifil* (4.5)	יַכֶּה [נ.כ.י/ה]
he will lie down (4.3)	יִשְׁכַּב [שׁ.כ.ב]
he will live (4.3)	יִחְיֶה [ח.י.י/ה]
he will rescue us *hifil* (8.2)	יוֹשִׁיעֵנוּ [י.שׁ.ע]
he will rule (4.3)	יִמְלֹךְ [מ.ל.כ]
he will sit, dwell (4.3)	יֵשֵׁב [י.שׁ.ב]
he will speak *piel* (4.4)	יְדַבֵּר [ד.ב.ר]
he will stand (4.3)	יַעֲמֹד [ע.מ.ד]
he will think (4.3)	יַחְשֹׁב [ח.שׁ.ב]

ENGLISH GLOSSARY — אַנְגְּלִית

he will work (4.3)	יַעֲבֹד [ע.ב.ד]
he, it, that (one) *m* (2.1)	הוּא
head *m* (3.3)	רֹאשׁ, רָאשִׁים, רֹאשׁ-, רָאשֵׁי-
Hear! Listen! *imv* (5.2)	שְׁמַע, שִׁמְעִי, שִׁמְעוּ, שְׁמַעְנָה [שׁ.מ.ע]
hear, listen (3.2)	שׁ.מ.ע
heart, mind *m* (4.4)	לֵב ǀ לֵבָב, לִבּוֹת, לֶב-, לְבוֹת-
heat *m* (7.1)	חֹם, חָם-
heavy, be (2.3, 6.3)	כ.ב.ד
heavy, rich, mighty, oppressive (2.3)	כָּבֵד, כְּבֵדָה, כְּבֵדִים, כְּבֵדוֹת
Hebrew person (8.1)	עִבְרִי, עִבְרִיָּה, עִבְרִים, עִבְרִית
height, elevated place *m* (8.1)	מָרוֹם, מְרוֹמִים, מְרוֹם-, מְרוֹמֵי-
help (4.3)	ע.ז.ר
Help me! *imv ms* (4.3)	עָזְרֵנִי [ע.ז.ר]
her, it *object form* (3.4, also אוֹתָהּ)	אֹתָהּ
hide self, be hidden *nifal* (7.1)	ס.ת.ר
hiding place *m* (7.3)	סֵתֶר, סְתָרִים, סֵתֶר-, סִתְרֵי-
high place (cultic mound) *f* (9.2)	בָּמָה, בָּמוֹת, בָּמַת-, בָּמֳתֵי-
him, it *object form* (3.4, also אוֹתוֹ)	אֹתוֹ
his being found *nif inf c* (9.4)	הִמָּצְאוֹ [מ.צ.א]
his command, he commanded *piel inf c* (10.1)	צַוֹּתוֹ [צ.ו./ה]
his ears *f* (4.4)	אָזְנָיו
his eyes *f* (4.2)	עֵינָיו
his feet *f* (4.4)	רַגְלָיו
his mouth *f* (4.2)	פִּיו
his nose *m* (4.2)	אַפּוֹ
holiness, sanctuary, sacred object *m* (8.1)	קֹדֶשׁ, קָדָשִׁים, קֹדֶשׁ-, קָדְשֵׁי-
hope *qal and piel* (10.2)	ק.ו.י/ה
house *m* (4.3)	בַּיִת, בָּתִּים, בֵּית-, בָּתֵּי-
How are you *ms, fs*? (1.1)	הֲשָׁלוֹם לְךָ [לָךְ]?
How would one say in Judean... "[word]"? (2.1)	אֵיךְ יֹאמְרוּ בִּיהוּדִית "[דָּבָר]"?
How...? (4.3)	אֵיךְ...?
Hulda *feminine name* (6.1)	חֻלְדָּה
hungry (3.1)	רָעֵב, רְעֵבָה, רְעֵבִים, רְעֵבוֹת
hut *f* (7.1)	סֻכָּה, סֻכּוֹת, סֻכַּת-, סֻכּוֹת-

I

I (1.3, 3.1)	אֲנִי *or* אָנֹכִי
I am able (2.4)	אוּכַל [י.כ.ל]
I am ashamed (10.2)	בֹּשְׁתִּי [ב.ו.שׁ]
I am fine (1.1)	שָׁלוֹם לִי
I am in distress (1.1)	צַר לִי
I am not, I do not (1.3)	אֵינֶנִּי
I am sorry (lit., please forgive, 3.1)	סְלַח-נָא, סִלְחִי-נָא [ס.ל.ח]
I answered, replied (6.1)	עָנִיתִי [ע.נ.י/ה]
I asked, requested (6.2)	שָׁאַלְתִּי [שׁ.א.ל]
I came, entered (6.1)	בָּאתִי [ב.ו.א]
I (can) understand (1.3)	אָבִין [ב.י.נ]
I caused to inhabit *hifil* (8.1)	הוֹשַׁבְתִּי [י.שׁ.ב]
I caused to inherit *hifil* (8.1)	הוֹרַשְׁתִּי [י.ר.שׁ]
I caused you *ms* to go out *hifil* (8.1)	הוֹצֵאתִיךָ [י.צ.א]
I caused you *ms* to know (8.1)	הוֹדַעְתִּיךָ [י.ד.ע]
I caused (someone) to hear, I announced *hifil* (8.1)	הִשְׁמַעְתִּי [שׁ.מ.ע]
I crossed over, trespassed (6.1)	עָבַרְתִּי [ע.ב.ר]
I do not have (1.1)	אֵין לִי

I do / will / would believe *hifil* (4.4)	אַאֲמִין [א.מ.נ]
I don't want *m, f* (1.3)	אֵינֶנִּי חָפֵץ, אֵינֶנִּי חֲפֵצָה
I found (6.1)	מָצָאתִי [מ.צ.א]
I have (1.1)	יֵשׁ לִי
I heard (6.1)	שָׁמַעְתִּי [שׁ.מ.ע]
I looked for, searched, sought (6.4)	בִּקַּשְׁתִּי [ב.ק.שׁ]
I most certainly will die (5.2)	מוֹת אָמוּת [מ.ו.ת]
I most certainly will turn back, return, repent (5.3)	שׁוֹב אָשׁוּב [שׁ.ו.ב]
I must *followed by inf c* (2.3)	עָלַי ל...
I remembered (6.1)	זָכַרְתִּי [ז.כ.ר]
I saw (6.1)	רָאִיתִי [ר.א.י/ה]
I spoke *piel* (6.2)	דִּבַּרְתִּי [ד.ב.ר]
I struck, hit *hifil* (8.1)	הִכֵּיתִי [נ.כ.י/ה]
I thought, supposed (6.3)	חָשַׁבְתִּי [ח.שׁ.ב]
I took (6.1)	לָקַחְתִּי [ל.ק.ח]
I walked about *piel* (10.2)	הִלַּכְתִּי [ה.ל.כ]
I was sent *nifal* (8.1)	נִשְׁלַחְתִּי [שׁ.ל.ח]
I went, traveled *qal* (6.1)	הָלַכְתִּי [ה.ל.כ]
I will (am resolved to) seek *cohort* (9.4)	אֶדְרְשָׁה [ד.ר.שׁ]
I will (am resolved to) turn *cohort* (9.4)	אָשׁוּבָה [שׁ.ו.ב]
I will be (4.3)	אֶהְיֶה [ה.י.י/ה]
I will cause to hear *hifil* (8.1)	אַשְׁמִיעַ [שׁ.מ.ע]
I will descend, go down (5.2)	אֵרֵד [י.ר.ד]
I will eat (5.2)	אֹכַל [א.כ.ל]
I will fear, be afraid (5.2)	אִירָא [י.ר.א]
I will find (5.2)	אֶמְצָא [מ.צ.א]
I will forgive (5.3)	אֶסְלַח [ס.ל.ח]
I will give (5.2)	אֶתֵּן [נ.ת.נ]
I will go (5.2)	אֵלֵךְ [ה.ל.כ]
I will go out, leave (3.2)	אֵצֵא [י.צ.א]
I will go up, ascend (5.3)	אֶעֱלֶה [ע.ל.י/ה]
I will lift, carry (5.2)	אֶשָּׂא [נ.שׂ.א]
I will put (5.3)	אָשִׂים [שׂ.ו/י.מ]
I will repay *piel* (10.1)	אֲשַׁלֵּם [שׁ.ל.מ]
I will sacrifice (5.3)	אֶזְבַּח [ז.ב.ח]
I will sacrifice abundantly, repeatedly *piel* (10.2)	אֲזַבֵּחַ [ז.ב.ח]
I will say (5.3)	אֹמַר [א.מ.ר]
I will speak (9.1)	אֲדַבֵּר [ד.ב.ר]
I will surely strike *hifil* (5.3)	הַכֵּה אַכֶּה [נ.כ.י/ה]
I will throw (5.2)	אַשְׁלִיךְ [שׁ.ל.כ]
I would like to inquire *or* request of you *ms and fs* (4.2)	אֶשְׁאֲלָה לְךָ: [שׁ.א.ל]
idol *m* (9.3)	פֶּסֶל, פְּסִילִים, פֶּסֶל־, פְּסִילֵי־
if (4.2)	אִם
if *irreal condition* (7.3)	לוּלֵא *or* לוּ
in, with, by means of (2.4)	בְּ
in the middle of, among (2.4)	בְּתוֹךְ
indeed (11.2)	הֵן
property, inheritance *f* (8.1)	נַחֲלָה, נְחָלוֹת, נַחֲלַת־, נַחֲלֹת־
iniquity *m* (3.2)	עָוֹן, עֲוֹנוֹת, עֲוֹן־, עֲוֹנוֹת־
innocent (11.1)	נָקִי, נְקִיָּה, נְקִיִּם, נְקִיּוֹת
investigate (7.4)	ד.ר.שׁ
Investigate! Seek! *imv* (9.2)	דְּרֹשׁ, דִּרְשִׁי, דִּרְשׁוּ, דְּרֹשְׁנָה [ד.ר.שׁ]
Is / will / did not...? (4.1)	הֲלֹא, הֲלוֹא...?
Israel *m* (5.1)	יִשְׂרָאֵל
it was shed *nifal m* (11.1)	נִשְׁפַּךְ [שׁ.פ.כ]
it was taken *qal passive m* (11.1)	לֻקַּח [ל.ק.ח]
it will be revealed *nifal m* (7.5)	יִגָּלֶה [ג.ל.י/ה]

ENGLISH GLOSSARY — אַנְגְּלִית

J

Jabbok River, the *pn loc* (map of Israel) .... הַיַּבֹּק
Jericho *pn loc* (map of Israel) .... יְרִיחוֹ
Jerusalem *pn loc* (6.1) ...... יְרוּשָׁלַם (*also spelled* יְרוּשָׁלַיִם)
Jonah *m* (2.2) .... יוֹנָה
Joppa *pn loc* (6.1) .... יָפוֹ
Jordan River, the *pn loc* (map of Israel) .... הַיַּרְדֵּן
Judah *pn loc* (map of Israel) .... יְהוּדָה
judgment, judicial decision *m* (8.1) .... מִשְׁפָּט, מִשְׁפָּטִים, מִשְׁפַּט־, מִשְׁפְּטֵי־

K

kill, put to death *hifil* (8.1) .... מ.ו.ת
kindness, steadfast love *m* (7.1) .... חֶסֶד, חֲסָדִים, חֶסֶד־, חַסְדֵי־
king *m* (2.1) .... מֶלֶךְ, מְלָכִים, מֶלֶךְ־, מַלְכֵי־
King's Highway, the *m or f* (map of Israel) ...... דֶּרֶךְ הַמֶּלֶךְ
knee *f* (4.3) .... בִּרְכַּי־, בִּרְכַּיִם, בֶּרֶךְ, בֶּרֶךְ־
know *qal* (5.3) .... י.ד.ע
Know! *imv* (9.2) .... דַּע, דְּעִי, דְּעוּ, דַּעְנָה [י.ד.ע]

L

Lachish *pn loc* (map of Israel) .... לָכִישׁ
lamp *m* (4.4) .... נֵר, נֵרוֹת, נֵר־, נֵרוֹת־
land, earth *f* (3.2) .... אֶרֶץ, אֲרָצוֹת, אֶרֶץ־, אַרְצוֹת־
law, instruction *f* (5.1) .... תּוֹרָה, תּוֹרוֹת, תּוֹרַת־, תּוֹרוֹת־
learn *qal* (10.1) .... ל.מ.ד
Lebanon *pn loc* (map of Ancient Near East) .... הַלְּבָנוֹן
lest (4.1) .... פֶּן

Let them be summoned! *nifal jussive mpl* (7.4) .... יִקָּרְאוּ [ק.ר.א]
Let's call! *cohort.* (9.4) .... נִקְרָא [ק.ר.א]
Let's come, enter! *cohort.* (9.4) .... נָבוֹאָה [ב.ו.א]
Let's go! *cohort.* (7.5) .... נֵלְכָה [ה.ל.כ]
Let's repent, turn back! *cohort.* (8.2) .... נָשׁוּבָה [ש.ו.ב]
Let's seek! *cohort.* (9.4) .... נִדְרְשָׁה [ד.ר.שׁ]
lie down (3.1) .... שׁ.כ.ב
Lie down! *imv* (3.1) .... שְׁכַב, שִׁכְבִי, שִׁכְבוּ, שְׁכַבְנָה [שׁ.כ.ב]
life *m* (4.3) .... חַי, חַיִּים, חַי־ [חֵי], חַיֵּי־
Lift! *imv* (9.2) .... שָׂא, שְׂאִי, שְׂאוּ, שֶׂאנָה [נ.שׂ.א]
lift, carry (5.2) .... נ.שׂ.א
light, brightness *f* (4.4) .... אוֹר, אוֹרִים
like *or* as (2.4) .... כְּ..., כְּמוֹ
lion *m* (7.5) .... אֲרִי, אֲרָיוֹת, אֲרִי־, אַרְיוֹת־
lip *f* (5.2) .... שָׂפָה, שְׂפָתַיִם, שְׂפַת־, שִׂפְתֵי־
listen (2.4) .... שׁ.מ.ע
listen to the sound of (3.2) .... שׁ.מ.ע לְקוֹל
live (4.3) .... ח.י/י.ה
look for, seek *piel* (1.3) .... ב.ק.שׁ
Look out! Guard yourself! *nifal* (4.1) .... הִשָּׁמֵר, הִשָּׁמְרִי, הִשָּׁמְרוּ, הִשָּׁמַרְנָה [שׁ.מ.ר]
look out, beware, be guarded, *or* guard oneself *nifal* (4.1) .... שׁ.מ.ר
Look! *imv* (4.2, 6.1) .... רְאִי [ר.א.ה/י]
Lord *divine name* (1.2) .... יהוה[1]
Lord GOD (8.1) .... אֲדֹנָי יהוה
LORD God of hosts (8.1) .... יהוה אֱלֹהֵי צְבָאוֹת
lord *m* (10.1) .... אָדוֹן, אֲדוֹנִים, אֲדוֹן־, אֲדֹנֵי־

---

[1] Sometimes vocalized יְהֹוָה.

love (3.3) .... א.ה.ב

love f (10.3) .... אַהֲבָה, אַהֲבַת־

Love! imv (9.3) .. [א.ה.ב] אֱהַב, אֶהֱבִי, אֶהֱבוּ, אֱהַבְנָה

M

make holy, consecrate piel (11.3) .... ק.ד.ש

make known, cause to know hifil (8.1) .... י.ד.ע

make strong piel (11.3) .... ח.ז.ק

man, humankind, Adam m (6.1) .... [אָדָם־] אָדָם, אֲדָם־

man, person m (1.1) .... אִישׁ, אֲנָשִׁים, אִישׁ־, אַנְשֵׁי־

May he appoint hifil jussive (9.4) .... [פ.ק.ד] יַפְקֵד

May he protect you ms, fs (1.2) .... יִשְׁמָרְךָ, יִשְׁמְרֵךְ

May the LORD bless you ms, fs (1.1) .... יְבָרֶכְךָ / יְבָרְכֵךְ
יהוה [ב.ר.כ]

May the LORD protect you ms, fs (1.2) .. יִשְׁמָרְךָ / יִשְׁמְרֵךְ
יהוה [ש.מ.ר]

me object form (3.3, also אוֹתִי) .... אֹתִי

meat, flesh m (5.2) .... בָּשָׂר, בְּשָׂרִים, בְּשַׂר־

Mediterranean Sea m (maps) .... הַיָּם [הַגָּדוֹל]

meet, encounter qal (6.2) .... ²ק.ר.א

Megiddo pn loc (map of Israel) .... מְגִדּוֹ

Memphis pn loc (map of Ancient Near East) .... מֹף

men, people m (4.1, see אִישׁ) .... אֲנָשִׁים

Mesopotamia m (map of Ancient Near East) ... אֲרַם נַהֲרַיִם

messenger m (9.5) .... מַלְאָךְ, מַלְאָכִים, מַלְאַךְ־, מַלְאֲכֵי־

messenger, one who announces hif pt ms (8.1) .... מַגִּיד,
מַגֶּדֶת, מַגִּידִים, מַגִּידוֹת [נ.ג.ד]

---

² In forms where the spelling of the homonymous ק.ר.א overlaps, both meanings may be offered (to call and to meet).

miraculous acts nifal fpl pt. (10.2) .... נִפְלָאוֹת, נִפְלָאוֹת־
[פ.ל.א]

Moab pn loc (map of Israel) .... מוֹאָב

month m (8.1) .... חֹדֶשׁ, חֳדָשִׁים, חֹדֶשׁ־, חָדְשֵׁי־

morning, daybreak, dawn m (5.1) .... בֹּקֶר

mother f (6.1) .... אֵם, אִמּוֹת, אֵם־, אִמּוֹת־

Mt. Carmel pn loc (map of Israel) .... הַר־הַכַּרְמֶל

Mt. Hermon pn loc (map of Ancient Near East) .. הַר־חֶרְמוֹן

Mt. Sinai pn loc (map of Ancient Near East) .... הַר־סִינַי

mountain m (4.2) .... הַר, הָרִים, הַר־, הָרֵי־³

mouth m (4.2) .... פֶּה, פִּיּוֹת, פִּי־, פִּיּוֹת־

multiply or make numerous hifil (8.1) .... ר.ב.י/ה

my belly, stomach f (4.3) .... בִּטְנִי

my bread m (3.1) .... לַחְמִי

my enemy, my enemies (3.3) .... אֹיְבִי, אֹיְבַי

my foot f (4.4) .... רַגְלִי

my law, instruction (5.1) .... תּוֹרָתִי

my mouth m (4.3) .... פִּי

my name m (1.1) .... שְׁמִי

my soul, myself, me f (3.3) .... נַפְשִׁי

N

name m (1.1) .... שֵׁם, שֵׁמוֹת, שֵׁם־ [שֵׁם־], שְׁמוֹת־

narrow adj, or distress substantive (1.1) .... צַר, צָרִים,
צַר־, צָרֵי־

nation, people m (11.1) .... גּוֹי, גּוֹיִם, גּוֹי־, גּוֹיֵי־

near (9.4) .... קָרוֹב

neighbor, friend m (5.3) .... רֵעַ, רֵעִים, רֵעַ, רֵעֵי־

new (5.2) .... חָדָשׁ, חֲדָשָׁה, חֲדָשִׁים, חֲדָשׁוֹת

---

³ Alternative plural construct הַרְרֵי־.

ENGLISH GLOSSARY — אַנְגְּלִית — 553

night *m* (6.2)	לַיְלָה, לֵילוֹת, לֵיל־, לֵילֽ־לֵילוֹת
Nile, the *m* (map of Ancient Near East)	הַיְאֹר
Nineveh *pn loc* (1.3)	נִינְוֵה
north *f* (map of Ancient Near East)	צָפוֹן
nose, anger *m* (4.2)	אַף, אַפַּיִם
not (1.1)	לֹא
not I, apart from me (11.1)	בִּלְעָדַי
now (3.2)	עַתָּה
numerous, great, much, many *adj* (3.2)	רַב, רַבָּה, רַבִּים, רַבּוֹת
number *m* (3.1)	מִסְפָּר, מִסְפָּרִים, מִסְפַּר־, מִסְפְּרֵי־

O

obey the Lord (3.2)	ש.מ.ע בְּקוֹל יהוה
occupation, business *f* (3.2)	מְלָאכָה, מְלָאכוֹת, מְלֶאכֶת־, מְלַאכוֹת־
Of what use to me is…? (3.2)	לָמָּה זֶּה לִי…?
oil, scented oil *m* (4.4)	שֶׁמֶן, שְׁמָנִים, שֶׁמֶן־, שְׁמָנֵי־
old (6.4)	זָקֵן, זְקֵנָה, זְקֵנִים, זְקֵנוֹת
on account of (5.3)	בַּעֲבוּר
on the next day (8.1)	מִמָּחֳרָת
on this account, therefore (4.3)	עַל־כֵּן
on what account of (3.3)	עַל־מֶה
on, upon (2.4)	עַל
One day… (6.1)	וַיְהִי הַיּוֹם…
one is *or* has been overturned *nifal pt* (7.5)	נֶהְפָּךְ, נֶהְפֶּכֶת, נֶהְפָּכִים, נֶהְפָּכוֹת [ה.פ.כ]
one who asks, requests *pt* (2.4)	שֹׁאֵל, שֹׁאֶלֶת, שֹׁאֲלִים, שֹׁאֲלוֹת [ש.א.ל]
one who commands *piel pt* (3.4)	מְצַוֶּה, מְצַוָּה, מְצַוִּים, מְצַוּוֹת [צ.ו.י/ה]
one who crosses over *pt* (3.2)	עֹבֵר, עֹבְרָה, עֹבְרִים, עֹבְרוֹת [ע.ב.ר]
one who descends, one who goes down *pt* (3.1)	יֹרֵד, יֹרְדָה / יֹרֶדֶת, יֹרְדִים, יֹרְדוֹת [י.ר.ד]
one who does, makes *pt* (3.2)	עֹשֶׂה, עֹשָׂה, עֹשִׂים, עֹשׂוֹת [ע.שׂ.י/ה]
one who dwells, inhabits *pt* (8.1)	שֹׁכֵן, שֹׁכֶנֶת, שֹׁכְנִים, שֹׁכְנוֹת [ש.כ.נ]
one who eats *pt* (3.1)	אֹכֵל, אֹכְלָה, אֹכְלִים, אֹכְלוֹת [א.כ.ל]
one who guards, keeps *pt* (3.2)	שֹׁמֵר, שֹׁמְרָה, שֹׁמְרִים, שֹׁמְרוֹת [ש.מ.ר]
one who hates *pt* (8.1)	שֹׂנֵא, שֹׂנֵאת, שֹׂנְאִים, שֹׂנְאוֹת [שׂ.נ.א]
one who hears, listens *pt* (3.2)	שֹׁמֵעַ, שֹׁמַעַת, שֹׁמְעִים, שֹׁמְעוֹת [ש.מ.ע]
one who hopes *qal pt* (4.4)	קֹוֶה, קֹוָה, קֹוִים, קֹווֹת [ק.ו.י/ה]
one who is bereaved *pt* (7.5)	שֹׁכֵל, שֹׁכְלִים, שֹׁכֶלֶת, שֹׁכְלוֹת [ש.כ.ל]
one who is blessed *qal passive pt* (7.3)	בָּרוּךְ, בְּרוּכָה, בְּרוּכִים, בְּרוּכוֹת [ב.ר.כ]
one who is clothed in *pual pt, ms* (11.2)	מְלֻבָּשׁ [ל.ב.שׁ]
one who is clothed in *qal passive pt* (8.1)	לָבוּשׁ, לְבוּשָׁה, לְבוּשִׁים, לְבוּשׁוֹת [ל.ב.שׁ]
one who is covered *pual pt* (11.1)	מְכֻסֶּה, מְכֻסָּה, מְכֻסִּים, מְכֻסּוֹת [כ.ס.י/ה]
one who is drinking *pt* (3.1)	שֹׁתֶה, שֹׁתָה, שֹׁתִים, שֹׁתוֹת [ש.ת.י/ה]
one who is dying *pt* (4.3)	מֵת, מֵתִים מֵתָה, מֵתוֹת [מ.ו.ת]

one who is faithful, reliable, established *nifal pt* (7.4)	נֶאֱמָן, נֶאֱמֶנֶת, נֶאֱמָנִים, נֶאֱמָנוֹת [א.מ.נ]
one who is high, exalted *pt* (6.4)	רָם, רָמָה, רָמִים, רָמוֹת [ר.ו.מ]
one who is solid, firm *nifal pt* (7.4)	נָכוֹן, נְכוֹנָה, נְכוֹנִים, נְכוֹנוֹת [כ.ו.נ]
one who knows *pt* (6.1)	יֹדֵעַ, יֹדַעַת, יֹדְעִים, יֹדְעוֹת [י.ד.ע]
one who lifts, one who carries *pt* (5.3)	נֹשֵׂא, נֹשְׂאָה, נֹשְׂאִים, נֹשְׂאוֹת [נ.שׂ.א]
one who looks for, seeks *piel pt* (1.3)	מְבַקֵּשׁ, מְבַקֶּשֶׁת, מְבַקְּשִׁים, מְבַקְּשׁוֹת [ב.ק.שׁ]
one who loves *pt* (3.3)	אֹהֵב, אֹהֶבֶת, אֹהֲבִים, אֹהֲבוֹת [א.ה.ב]
one who opens *pt* (4.3)	פֹּתֵחַ, פֹּתַחַת, פֹּתְחִים, פֹּתְחוֹת [פ.ת.ח]
one who oppresses *pt* (7.1)	יוֹנֶה, יוֹנָה, יוֹנִים, יוֹנוֹת [י.נ.י/ה]
one who puts, places, or sets *pt* (3.4)	שָׂם, שָׂמָה, שָׂמִים, שָׂמוֹת [שׂ.י.ו/מ]
one who recounts, narrator *piel pt ms* (6.4)	מְסַפֵּר [ס.פ.ר]
one who rescues *hif pt ms* (5.1)	מוֹשִׁיעַ [י.שׁ.ע]
one who says *pt* (4.4)	אֹמֵר, אֹמֶרֶת, אֹמְרִים, אֹמְרוֹת [א.מ.ר]
one who sees *pt* (4.1)	רֹאֶה, רֹאָה, רֹאִים, רֹאוֹת [ר.א.י/ה]
one who sits, dwells *pt* (3.3)	יֹשֵׁב, יֹשֶׁבֶת, יֹשְׁבִים, יֹשְׁבוֹת [י.שׁ.ב]
one who speaks *pt* (3.2)	מְדַבֵּר, מְדַבְּרָה, מְדַבְּרִים, מְדַבְּרוֹת [ד.ב.ר]
one who stands *pt* (3.2)	עֹמֵד, עֹמְדָה, עֹמְדִים, עֹמְדוֹת [ע.מ.ד]
one who strikes, smites *hif pt* (7.1)	מַכֶּה, מַכָּה, מַכִּים, מַכּוֹת [נ.כ.י/ה]
one who swallows *pt* (4.3)	בֹּלֵעַ, בֹּלַעַת, בֹּלְעִים, בֹּלְעוֹת [ב.ל.ע]
one who takes refuge *pt* (10.3)	חֹסֶה, חֹסָה, חֹסִים, חֹסוֹת [ח.ס.י/ה]
one who throws *hifil pt* (3.3)	מַשְׁלִיךְ, מַשְׁלִיכָה, מַשְׁלִיכִים, מַשְׁלִיכוֹת [שׁ.ל.כ]
one who turns something away *hifil pt* (3.2)	מֵסִיר, מְסִירָה, מְסִירִים, מְסִירוֹת [ס.ו.ר]
one who walks *pt* (3.2)	הֹלֵךְ, הֹלְכָה, הֹלְכִים, הֹלְכוֹת [ה.ל.כ]
one who weeps, cries *pt* (4.3)	בֹּכֶה, בּוֹכִיָּה / בֹּכָה, בֹּכִים, בֹּכוֹת [ב.כ.י/ה]
one, single, same *m* (5.2)	אֶחָד, אַחַת, אֲחָדִים
ones who surround *pt mpl* (6.1)	סֹבְבִים [ס.ב.ב]
only (4.3)	רַק
open (4.3)	פ.ת.ח
open (eyes, 6.1)	פ.ק.ח
oppress (7.1)	י.נ.י/ה
oppressed, afflicted (5.3)	עָנִי, עֲנִיָּה, עֲנִיִּים, עֲנִיּוֹת
oracle, pronouncement *m* (8.1)	מַשָּׂא, מַשָּׂא־
our God *m* (3.2)	אֱלֹהֵינוּ
outcry, scream from despair *f* (5.3)	צְעָקָה, צַעֲקַת־
outside (open fields / streets *pl*) *m* (7.1)	חוּץ, חוּצוֹת, חוּץ־, חוּצוֹת־

P

particle before definite direct object, untranslatable (3.1) ... אֶת־

peace, well-being *as greeting*, *m* (1.1) .... שָׁלוֹם, שְׁלוֹמִים, שְׁלוֹם־, שְׁלוֹמֵי־

people *m* (3.2) .... עָם, עַמִּים, עַם־, עַמֵּי־

perhaps (4.4) .... אוּלַי

perish *qal* (6.3) .... א.ב.ד

personal servant *piel pt m* (9.1) .... מְשָׁרֵת [ש.ר.ת]

Philistia *pn loc* (map of Israel) .... פְּלֶשֶׁת

Philistine person (8.2) .... פְּלִשְׁתִּי

place, location *m* (6.1) .... מָקוֹם, מְקֹמוֹת, מְקוֹם־, מְקֹמוֹת־

plague *m* (*perhaps bubonic*, 8.2) .... דֶּבֶר

plague, affliction *m* (8.1) .... נֶגַע, נְגָעִים, נֶגַע־, נִגְעֵי־

please do not (*plus jussive*)… (10.2) .... אַל־נָא...

please *or* oh! (*as a sigh*) (10.1) .... אָנָה *or* אָנָּא

please, so (9.4) .... נָא

poor, needy (9.3) .... אֶבְיוֹן, ־־, אֶבְיוֹנִים, ־־

pour out *or* shed *qal* (11.1) .... ש.פ.כ

praise *piel* (10.3) .... ה.ל.ל

pray *hitpael* (11.3) .... פ.ל.ל

prayer *m* (10.1) .... תְּפִלָּה, תְּפִלּוֹת, תְּפִלַּת־, תְּפִלּוֹת־

priest *m* (7.4) .... כֹּהֵן, כֹּהֵן־, כֹּהֲנִים, כֹּהֲנֵי־

prophesy *nifal* (7.1) .... נ.ב.א

prophet *m* (1.3) .... נָבִיא, נְבִיאִים, נְבִיא־, נְבִיאֵי־

prophetess *f* (2.4) .... נְבִיאָה, נְבִיאוֹת, נְבִיאַת־, נְבִיאוֹת־

proverb *m* (11.2) .... מָשָׁל, מְשָׁלִים, מְשַׁל־, מִשְׁלֵי־

purple (material) *m* (8.1) .... אַרְגָּמָן

pursue (6.2) .... ר.ד.פ

Put! Place! Set! (2.4) .... שִׂים, שִׂמִי, שִׂמוּ, שִׂימֶינָה [ש./ו.י.מ]

put, place (2.4) .... ש./ו.י.מ

Q

queen *f* (9.1) .... מַלְכָּה, מַלְכוֹת, מַלְכַּת־, מַלְכוֹת־

question mark, interrogative particle (1.1) .... הֲ... / הַ...

R

raise high *piel* (10.1) .... נ.ש.א

really (1.1) .... בֶּאֱמֶת

recount *piel* (6.1) .... ס.פ.ר

Red [Reed] Sea, the *m* (map of Ancient Near East) ... יַם־סוּף

rejoicing, joyful *pt* (6.1) .... שָׂמֵחַ, שְׂמֵחָה, שְׂמֵחִים, שְׂמֵחוֹת [ש.מ.ח]

remember (5.1) .... ז.כ.ר

Remove! *hifil imv* (9.2) .... הָסֵר, הָסִירִי, הָסִירוּ, הָסֵרְנָה [ס.ו.ר]

Repeat, please! *imv ms, fs* (1.3) .... שְׁנֵה־נָא, שְׁנִי־נָא, שְׁנוּ־נָא, שְׁנֶינָה־נָא [ש.נ.י/ה]

Rescue me! Help me! *ms* (4.3) .... הוֹשִׁיעֵנִי [י.ש.ע]

rescue, help *hifil* (4.3) .... י.ש.ע

rest (7.1) .... נ.ו.ח

return (5.1) .... ש.ו.ב

reveal, uncover *piel* (10.1) .... ג.ל.י/ה

righteous, true to one's community, innocent (legally and morally) (10.2) .... צַדִּיק, צַדִּיקִים

righteousness *f* (11.2) . צְדָקָה, צְדָקוֹת, צִדְקַת־, צִדְקוֹת־

river *or* stream *m* (map of Ancient Near East) .... נָהָל

road, way *m or f* (4.4) .... דֶּרֶךְ, דְּרָכִים, דֶּרֶךְ־, דַּרְכֵי־

rock, cliff *m* (10.3)	צוּר, צֻרִים, צוּר־, צוּרֵי־
rule (4.3)	מ.ל.כ.

S

sack, sackcloth *m* (9.2)	שַׂק, שַׂקִּים, שַׂק־, שַׂקֵּי־
sacrifice abundantly, repeatedly *piel* (10.2)	ז.ב.ח.
sacrifice *qal* (5.1)	ז.ב.ח.
sacrifice, ritual feast *m* (5.1)	זֶבַח, זְבָחִים, זֶבַח־, זִבְחֵי־
sailor *m* (3.2)	חֹבֵל
Samaria *pn loc* (map of Israel)	שֹׁמְרוֹן
save, deliver *piel* (10.3)	פ.ל.ט.
Save, deliver! *piel imv* (10.3)	פַּלֵּט, פַּלְטִי, פַּלְּטוּ, פַּלֵּטְנָה [פ.ל.ט.]
say (5.3)	א.מ.ר.
Say! *imv* (9.1)	אֱמֹר, אִמְרִי, אִמְרוּ, אֱמֹרְנָה [א.מ.ר.]
sea captain (*lit.*, captain of the sailor[s] *m*, 3.2)	רַב הַחֹבֵל, רַבֵּי־הַחֹבֵל
sea, west *m* (3.1)	יָם, יַם־ [יָם־], יַמִּים
Sea of Chinnereth [Galilee], the *m* (map of Israel)	יָם־כִּנֶּרֶת
secondly (5.2)	בַּשֵּׁנִית
see, look (4.2)	ר.א.י/ה.
send *qal* (8.1)	ש.ל.ח.
servant, slave, worker *m* (4.1)	עֶבֶד, עֲבָדִים, עֶבֶד־, עַבְדֵי־
set free, send away *piel* (10.1)	ש.ל.ח.
seven *m, f* (7.3)	שִׁבְעָה, שֶׁבַע
shadow *m* (11.3)	צֵל
shatter *piel* (10.2)	ש.ב.ר.
she came, entered (6.2)	בָּאָה [ב.ו.א.]
she descended (6.2)	יָרְדָה [י.ר.ד.]
she hit, struck (7.1)	הִכְּתָה [נ.כ.י/ה.]
she lifted up (6.2)	נָשְׂאָה [נ.שׂ.א.]
she pursued (6.2)	רָדְפָה [ר.ד.פ.]
she threw *hifil* (6.2)	הִשְׁלִיכָה [ש.ל.כ.]
she took (6.2)	לָקְחָה [ל.ק.ח.]
she walked about *piel* (10.1)	הִלְּכָה [ה.ל.כ.]
she went out (6.2)	יָצְאָה [י.צ.א.]
she went up (6.2)	עָלְתָה [ע.ל.י/ה.]
she will break (4.5)	תִּשְׁבֹּר [ש.ב.ר.]
she will do, make (4.5)	תַּעֲשֶׂה [ע.שׂ.י/ה.]
she will draw near (4.5)	תִּקְרַב [ק.ר.ב.]
she will hit (4.5)	תַּכֶּה [נ.כ.י/ה.]
she, it, that one *f* (2.1)	הִיא
shekel, *unit of money, weight, m* (7.5)	שֶׁקֶל, שְׁקָלִים, שֶׁקֶל־, שִׁקְלֵי־
Sheol, netherworld *f* (3.2)	שְׁאוֹל
ship *f* (2.1)	אֳנִיָּה, אֳנִיּוֹת, אֳנִיַּת־, אֳנִיּוֹת־
shore, the *f* (5.2)	שְׂפַת־הַיָּם
show, reveal *hifil* (8.1)	ר.א.י/ה.
Sidon *pn loc* (map of Ancient Near East)	צִידוֹן
silver, money *m* (2.1)	כֶּסֶף, כְּסָפִים, כֶּסֶף־, כַּסְפֵּי־
sin, miss (7.4)	ח.ט.א.
sin, sin-offering *f* (7.1)	חַטָּאת, חַטָּאוֹת, חַטַּאת־, חַטֹּאות־
sing, play (an instrument) *piel* (10.3)	ז.מ.ר.
Sit! Dwell! *imv* (1.3)	שֵׁב, שְׁבִי, שְׁבוּ, שֵׁבְנָה [י.שׁ.ב.]
sit, dwell (4.3)	י.שׁ.ב.
sky, heavens *m* (8.1)	שָׁמַיִם, שְׁמֵי־
sleeping *adj* (3.2)	יָשֵׁן, יְשֵׁנָה, יְשֵׁנִים, יְשֵׁנוֹת
small, young (2.3)	קָטֹן / קָטָן, קְטַנָּה, קְטַנִּים, קְטַנּוֹת
smoke, incense *f* (10.3)	קְטֹרֶת, קְטֹרֶת־
so he answered (7.2)	וַיַּעַן [ע.נ.י/ה.]

ENGLISH GLOSSARY אַנְגְּלִית

so it was at rest *f* (11.2)	וַתִּשְׁקֹט [ש.ק.ט]
so it was recounted *pual* (11.1)	וַיְסֻפַּר [ס.פ.ר]
so that (3.1)	לְמַעַן
so they appeared *nifal* (7.4)	וַיֵּרָאוּ [ר.א.י/ה]
so, thus (11.1)	כֵּן
soft (3.1)	רַךְ, רַכָּה, רַכִּים, רַכּוֹת
son *m* (6.1)	בֵּן, בָּנִים, בֶּן־, בְּנֵי־
soul, person, life force, throat *f* (3.3)	נֶפֶשׁ, נְפָשׁוֹת, נֶפֶשׁ־, נַפְשׁוֹת־
sound, voice *m* (3.2)	קוֹל, קוֹלוֹת, קוֹל־, קוֹלוֹת־
south-country, south *m* (map of Israel)	נֶגֶב
speak *piel* (2.4)	ד.ב.ר
Speak! *piel imv* (9.2)	דַּבֵּר, דַּבְּרִי, דַּבְּרוּ, דַּבֵּרְנָה [ד.ב.ר]
spirit, wind *f* (3.2)	רוּחַ, רוּחוֹת, רוּחַ־, רוּחוֹת־
stand (4.2)	ע.מ.ד
Stand! *imv* (9.1)	עֲמֹד, עִמְדִי, עִמְדוּ, עֲמֹדְנָה [ע.מ.ד]
station oneself *hitpael* (11.3)	י.צ.ב
steal *qal* (7.5)	ג.נ.ב
stiff-necked, stubborn (6.4)	קְשֵׁה־עֹרֶף
stone *f* (1.1)	אֶבֶן, אֲבָנִים, אֶבֶן־, אַבְנֵי־
strength *m* (8.2)	כֹּחַ, כֹּחַ־
stretch out (something) *qal* (9.2)	נ.ט.י/ה
Stretch out! *imv* (9.2)	נְטֵה, נְטִי, נְטוּ, נְטֶינָה [נ.ט.י/ה]
strike *hifil* (5.3)	נ.כ.י/ה
strong, hard, tough (2.3)	חָזָק, חֲזָקָה, חֲזָקִים, חֲזָקוֹת
sun *f* (7.1)	שֶׁמֶשׁ
supplication, request *m* (10.3)	תַּחֲנוּן, תַּחֲנוּנִים, תַּחֲנוּן־, תַּחֲנוּנֵי־
surround (6.1)	ס.ב.ב
swallow (4.3)	ב.ל.ע
swear an oath *nifal* (7.3)	ש.ב.ע
sweet (3.1)	מָתוֹק, מְתוּקָה, מְתוּקִים, מְתוּקוֹת
sword *f* (6.3)	חֶרֶב, חֲרָבוֹת, חֶרֶב־, חַרְבוֹת־

T

table *m* (2.1)	שֻׁלְחָן, שֻׁלְחָנוֹת, שֻׁלְחַן־, שֻׁלְחֲנוֹת־
tablet, board *m* (11.1)	לוּחַ, לוּחוֹת, לוּחַ־, לוּחוֹת־
take (5.1)	ל.ק.ח
take refuge (10.3)	ח.ס.י/ה
Tanis *pn loc* (map of Ancient Near East)	צֹעַן
Tarshish *pn loc* (1.3)	תַּרְשִׁישׁ
taste (9.5)	ט.ע.ם
teach, train *piel* (10.1)	ל.מ.ד
Tell! Recount! *piel imv ms, fs* (6.1)	סַפֵּר, סַפְּרִי [ס.פ.ר]
Tell! Speak! *piel imv* (9.2)	דַּבֵּר, דַּבְּרִי, דַּבְּרוּ, דַּבֵּרְנָה [ד.ב.ר]
tent *m* (6.1)	אֹהֶל, אֹהָלִים, אֹהֶל־, אָהֳלֵי־
thanks, gratitude *m* (5.1)	תּוֹדָה
that which is written *qal passive pt* (11.1)	כָּתוּב, כְּתוּבָה, כְּתוּבִים, כְּתוּבוֹת
the (2.1)	הַ..., הָ..., הֶ...
Thebes [No] *pn loc* (map of Ancient Near East)	נֹא
their *mpl* soul, themselves (4.1)	נַפְשָׁם
them *object form, fpl* (3.4)	אֹתָן
them *object form, mpl* (3.4, *also* אוֹתָם)	אֹתָם
then, at that time (5.3)	אָז
then he did [an activity] again *hifil* (7.2)	וַיּוֹסֶף [י.ס.פ]
then he put (7.2)	וַיָּשֶׂם [ש.ו/י.מ]
then he took (7.2)	וַיִּקַּח [ל.ק.ח]
then he turned (9.4)	וַיִּפֶן [פ.נ.י/ה]
then she did [an activity] again (7.2)	וַתּוֹסֶף [י.ס.פ]
then they gathered together *nifal* (8.2)	וַיֵּאָסְפוּ [א.ס.פ]
then we struck *hifil* (8.2)	וַנַּךְ [נ.כ.י/ה]

there (5.2)	שָׁם
there is / are (1.1)	יֵשׁ, יֶשׁ־
there is not, there are not *constr* (1.1)	אֵין[4]
therefore (8.1)	לָכֵן
these *m and f* (3.1)	אֵלֶּה
they (beverages) were drunk *nifal* (11.1)	נִשְׁתּוּ [שׁ.ת.י/ה]
they are mighty (6.3)	כָּבְדוּ [כ.ב.ד]
they called, met, encountered (6.2)	קָרְאוּ [ק.ר.א]
they feared (6.2)	יָרְאוּ [י.ר.א]
they hoped *piel* (10.1)	קִוּוּ [ק.ו.י/ה]
they lifted up (6.2)	נָשְׂאוּ [נ.שׂ.א]
they lifted up (6.2)	נָשְׂאוּ [נ.שׂ.א]
they may be established *or* regarded as *nifal* (10.3)	יִכּוֹנוּ [כ.ו.נ]
they returned (6.4)	שָׁבוּ [שׁ.ו.ב]
they threw me *hifil* (6.2)	הִשְׁלִיכוּנִי [שׁ.ל.כ]
they were brought *hofal* (11.2)	הוּבְאוּ [ב.ו.א]
they were devoured *qal passive* (11.1)	אֻכְּלוּ [א.כ.ל]
they were sent away *pual* (11.1)	שֻׁלְּחוּ [שׁ.ל.ח]
they were stolen *nifal* (10.2)	נִגְנְבוּ [ג.נ.ב]
they were thrown *hofal* (11.2)	הָשְׁלְכוּ [שׁ.ל.כ]
they were willing (6.2)	אָבוּ [א.ב.י/ה]
they will be captured *nifal* (7.4)	וְנִלְכְּדוּ [ל.כ.ד]
they will cut *m* (4.1)	יִכְרְתוּ [כ.ר.ת]
they will do *m* (4.1)	יַעֲשׂוּ [ע.שׂ.י/ה]
they will do, make *f* (4.5)	תַּעֲשֶׂינָה [ע.שׂ.י/ה]
they will fall *m* (4.1)	יִפְּלוּ [נ.פ.ל]
they will find *m* (4.1)	יִמְצְאוּ [מ.צ.א]
they will go, walk *f* (4.4)	תֵּלַכְנָה [ה.ל.כ]
they will guard *m* (4.1)	יִשְׁמְרוּ [שׁ.מ.ר]
they will hear *f* (4.4)	תִּשְׁמַעְנָה [שׁ.מ.ע]
they will hear *m* (4.1)	יִשְׁמְעוּ [שׁ.מ.ע]
they will lie down *m* (4.1)	יִשְׁכְּבוּ [שׁ.כ.ב]
they will rule *m* (4.1)	יִמְלְכוּ [מ.ל.כ]
they will see *f* (4.4)	תִּרְאֶינָה [ר.א.י/ה]
they will taste *mpl* (9.5)	יִטְעֲמוּ [ט.ע.מ]
they, those *f* (3.4)	הֵנָּה
they, those *m, alternate forms, same meaning* (3.1)	הֵם, הֵמָּה
think, say in one's heart (4.3, 6.3)	א.מ.ר בְּלֵב, בִּלְבָב
think, suppose, be on the verge of *qal* (7.4)	ח.שׁ.ב
third (7.5)	שְׁלִישִׁי, שְׁלִישִׁית
thirdly (5.2)	בַּשְּׁלִשִׁית
this *m, f* (3.2)	זֶה, זֹאת
thought, intent, plan *f* (9.4)	מַחֲשָׁבָה, מַחֲשָׁבוֹת, מַחֲשֶׁבֶת־, מַחְשְׁבֹת־
three (4.1)	שְׁלֹשָׁה, שָׁלֹשׁ
three days *mpl* (4.3)	שְׁלֹשֶׁת יָמִים
throw *hifil* (5.2)	שׁ.ל.כ
Throw! *imv mpl* (3.3)	הַשְׁלִיכוּ [שׁ.ל.כ]
thus, in this manner (7.2)	כֹּה
Tigris River *pn loc* (map of Ancient Near East)	חִדֶּקֶל
time, occurrence, step, instance *f* (7.2)	פַּעַם, פְּעָמִים, פַּעַם־, פַּעֲמֵי־
time, point in time, occasion *f* (7.2)	עֵת, עִתִּים, עֵת־, [עֵת], עִתֵּי־
to / for me (1.1)	לִי
to / for you *ms, fs* (1.1)	לְךָ, לָךְ
to afflict *piel inf c, prep* (10.2)	לְעַנּוֹת [ע.נ.י/ה]
to announce *hifil inf c, prep* (8.1)	לְהַגִּיד [נ.ג.ד]
to answer, reply *inf c, prep* (7.1)	לַעֲנוֹת [ע.נ.י/ה]

---

[4] The absolute form is אַיִן.

ENGLISH GLOSSARY — אַנְגְּלִית

to be broken up *nifal inf c, prep* (6.2) .... לְהִשָּׁבֵר [ש.ב.ר]
to be hot *inf c, prep* (4.2) .... לַחֲרוֹת [ח.ר.י/ה]
to be reported *hofal inf c* (11.3)....................... הֻגַּד [נ.ג.ד]
to call, read *inf c, prep* (1.2).................... לִקְרֹא [ק.ר.א]
to contend *qal inf absol, prep* (11.3)............... לָרִיב [ר.י.ב]
to cover, atone for *piel inf c, prep* (10.1) .... לְכַפֵּר [כ.פ.ר]
to cross over *inf c, prep* (3.2) .... לַעֲבֹר [ע.ב.ר]
to do, make *inf c, prep* (3.4)................ לַעֲשׂוֹת [ע.שׂ.י/ה]
to draw near *inf c, prep* (5.1).................... לִקְרֹב [ק.ר.ב]
to drink *inf c, prep* (3.1)....................... לִשְׁתּוֹת [ש.ת.י/ה]
to eat *inf c, prep* (3.1) .... לֶאֱכֹל [א.כ.ל]
to enter, come, go *inf c, prep* (3.3)................ לָבוֹא [ב.ו.א]
to fight *nifal inf absol* (7.4)........... הִלָּחֵם *or* נִלְחֹם [ל.ח.מ]
to fight *nifal inf c* (8.2) .... הִלָּחֵם [ל.ח.מ]
to find *inf c, prep* (3.1) .... לִמְצֹא [מ.צ.א]
to gather *inf c* (7.2).. אֱסֹף [א.ס.פ]
to give *inf c, prep* (2.4) .... לָתֵת [נ.ת.נ]
to go *inf c, prep* (1.3) .... לָלֶכֶת [ה.ל.כ]
to go out *inf c, prep* (5.3) .... לָצֵאת [י.צ.א]
to help us *inf c, prep* (7.3) .... לְעָזְרֵנוּ [ע.ז.ר]
to investigate *inf c* (7.4) .... דְּרֹשׁ [ד.ר.שׁ]
to keep, guard *inf c, prep* (4.2).................. לִשְׁמֹר [ש.מ.ר]
to lie down *inf c, prep* (3.1) .... לִשְׁכַּב [ש.כ.ב]
to listen *inf c, prep* (2.4)..................... לִשְׁמֹעַ [ש.מ.ע]
to love *inf c, prep* (4.2) .... לֶאֱהֹב [א.ה.ב]
to perish *inf c, prep* (6.3)........................ לַאֲבֹד [א.ב.ד]
to prophesy *nifal inf c, prep* (7.1) .... לְהִנָּבֵא [נ.ב.א]
to pursue *inf absol* (7.4) .... רָדוֹף [ר.ד.פ]
to put, to place *inf c, prep* ל (3.1) .... לָשׂוּם [שׂ.ו/י.מ]
to recount *piel inf c, prep* (10.2) .... לְסַפֵּר [ס.פ.ר]
to rest *inf c, prep* (7.1)............................ לָנוּחַ [נ.ו.ח]

to return [something] *hifil inf c, prep* (7.4)................ לְהָשִׁיב [ש.ו.ב]
to rule *inf c, prep* (3.1)............................. לִמְלֹךְ [מ.ל.כ]
to sacrifice abundantly, repeatedly *piel inf absol* (10.2)....... זַבֵּחַ [ז.ב.ח]
to sacrifice *qal inf c, prep* (5.1) .... לִזְבֹּחַ [ז.ב.ח]
to say *inf c, prep* (4.1) .... לֵאמֹר [א.מ.ר]
to see *inf c, prep* (4.2) .... לִרְאוֹת [ר.א.י/ה]
to seek *piel inf c, prep* (3.1)....................... לְבַקֵּשׁ [ב.ק.שׁ]
to send away *piel inf absol* (10.3)............... שַׁלֵּחַ [ש.ל.ח]
to speak *piel inf c, prep* (2.4)..................... לְדַבֵּר [ד.ב.ר]
to stand *inf c, prep* (4.2) .... לַעֲמֹד [ע.מ.ד]
to swallow *inf c, prep* (4.3)..................... לִבְלֹעַ [ב.ל.ע]
to throw *hifil inf c, prep* (3.3) .... לְהַשְׁלִיךְ [ש.ל.כ]
to turn (or return) self toward, to repent to *inf c, prep* (3.3) .... לָשׁוּב אֶל [ש.ו.ב]
to us (4.5) .... אֵלֵינוּ
To where? Whither? (2.3) .... אָנָה...?
to, for (1.1) .... לְ...
to, toward (2.4) .... אֶל
today *m* (5.1) .... הַיּוֹם
tomorrow, next day, in the future *m and adverb* (4.3)..מָחָר
tongue, language *m* (2.1) .. לָשׁוֹן, לְשֹׁנוֹת לְשׁוֹן־, לְשֹׁנוֹת־
toward Tarshish (6.1) .... תַּרְשִׁישָׁה
toward, as far as (2.4) .... עַד
transgression *m* (10.1) ..... פֶּשַׁע, פְּשָׁעִים, פֶּשַׁע־, פִּשְׁעֵי־
tree, wood *m* (4.2) .... עֵץ, עֵצִים, עֵץ־, עֲצֵי־
truth *f* (5.1) .... אֱמֶת
turn (9.4) .... פ.נ.י/ה
Turn back! Return! *imv* (9.2).. שׁוּב, שׁוּבִי, שׁוּבוּ, שֹׁבְנָה [ש.ו.ב]
turn something away from *hifil* (3.2)........................ ס.ו.ר

turn something away, remove *hifil* (9.2)	ס.ו.ר
Turn! *imv m, f* (4.3)	סוּר, סוּרִי
two *dual* (7.5)	שְׁנַיִם, שְׁתַּיִם, שְׁנֵי־, שְׁתֵּי־
Tyre *pn loc* (map of Ancient Near East)	צֹר

U

under, instead of (2.4)	תַּחַת
understand (1.3)	ב.י.נ
upon me	עָלַי
Ur of the Chaldeans *m* (map of ANE)	אוּר כַּשְׂדִּים
us *object form, mpl* (3.4, *also* אוֹתָנוּ)	אֹתָנוּ

V

very *or* much (2.2)	מְאֹד
violence *m* (10.2)	חָמָס, חֲמָסִים, חֲמַס־, חַמְסֵי־
visit, inspect, inflict, appoint *qal* (6.4)	פ.ק.ד
vow *m* (10.2)	נֶדֶר, נֵדֶר, נְדָרִים, נִדְרֵי־

W

walk about *piel* (10.1)	ה.ל.כ
walk back and forth, roam *hitpael* (11.3)	ה.ל.כ
war, battle *f* (6.3)	מִלְחָמָה, מִלְחָמוֹת, מִלְחֶמֶת־, מִלְחֲמוֹת־
water *mpl* (2.1)	מַיִם, מֵי־
watery depths *f* (4.3)	תְּהוֹם, תְּהֹמוֹת, תְּהוֹם־, תְּהֹמוֹת־
wave, surf, breaker *m* (5.1)	מִשְׁבָּר, מִשְׁבַּר־, מִשְׁבָּרִים, מִשְׁבְּרֵי־
Way of the Sea, the *m or f* (map of Israel, note)	דֶּרֶךְ הַיָּם

we are not, we do not; he is not, he does not (3.2)	אֵינֶנּוּ
we *c* (3.2)	אֲנַחְנוּ
we came (6.4)	בָּאנוּ [ב.ו.א]
we defiled *piel* (10.2)	טִמֵּאנוּ [ט.מ.א]
we filled *piel* (10.2)	מִלֵּאנוּ [מ.ל.א]
we must...(...be sure [to]..., 3.3), upon us	עָלֵינוּ
we shattered *piel* (10.2)	שִׁבַּרְנוּ [ש.ב.ר]
we spoke *piel* (6.4)	דִּבַּרְנוּ [ד.ב.ר]
we (will) swear *nifal* (7.3)	נִשָּׁבַע [ש.ב.ע]
we understand *hifil* (3.3)	נָבִין [ב.י.נ]
we visited, inspected, inflicted, appointed (6.4)	פָּקַדְנוּ [פ.ק.ד]
we waited, hoped *piel* (10.2)	קִוִּינוּ [ק.ו.ו/י/ה]
we went out (6.4)	יָצָאנוּ [י.צ.א]
we will call, read, *or* encounter (5.1)	נִקְרָא [ק.ר.א]
we will cause (something) to go out *hifil* (8.2)	נוֹצִיא [י.צ.א]
we will cause (something) to go up *hifil* (8.2)	נַעֲלֶה [ע.ל.י/ה]
we will cause (something) to return *hifil* (8.2)	נָשִׁיב [ש.ו.ב]
we will cover *piel* (10.1)	נְכַסֶּה [כ.ס.י/ה]
we will find *qal* (5.1)	נִמְצָא [מ.צ.א]
we will fulfill, repay *piel* (10.2)	נְשַׁלֵּם [ש.ל.מ]
we will lift, we will carry *qal* (5.1)	נִשָּׂא [נ.ש.א]
we will remember (5.1)	נִזְכֹּר [ז.כ.ר]
we will set apart, consecrate *piel* (10.2)	נְקַדֵּשׁ [ק.ד.ש]
we will take (5.1)	נִקַּח [ל.ק.ח]
we would fight (7.3)	נִלָּחַמְנוּ [ל.ח.מ]
wear *qal* (9.3)	ל.ב.ש
Wear! Put on! *imv* (9.3)	לְבַשׁ, לִבְשִׁי, לִבְשׁוּ, לְבַשְׁנָה [ל.ב.ש]

Weep for…! *imv* (9.3)	בְּכֵה, בְּכִי, בְּכוּ, בְּכֶינָה [ב.כ.י/ה] לְ...
well *f* (7.1)	בְּאֵר, בְּאֵרֹת, בְּאֵר־, בְּאֵרֹת־
What? (1.1)	מַה, מַה־, מָה, מֶה
What are you doing here? (6.1)	מַה־לְּךָ פֹה?
What is this? (1.1)	מַה־זֶּה?
What is your *ms/fs* concern? (4.4)	מַה־לָּךְ?
What is your *fpl* concern? (7.3)	מַה־לָּכֶנָה:
What is your *ms* name? (1.1)	מַה־שְּׁמֶךָ?
when (entity) is / was crossing over *inf c, prep* (6.2)	בַּעֲבֹר [ע.ב.ר]
when (it) descended / descends / will descend *inf c* (6.4)	בְּרֶדֶת [י.ר.ד]
when it is / was reported *hofal inf c, prep* (11.3)	בְּהֻגַּד [נ.ג.ד]
when they threw you *pl hifil inf c* (6.3)	בְּהַשְׁלִיכְכֶם [ש.ל.כ]
when we return (5.1)	בְּשׁוּבֵנוּ [ש.ו.ב]
Where is…? (2.1)	אַיֵּה…?
which, that, who (*not interrogative*), since (2.4)	אֲשֶׁר
while being *inf c, prep* (4.4)	בִּהְיוֹת [ה.י.י/ה]
while he is *inf c, prep, 3ms sfx* (9.4)	בִּהְיוֹתוֹ [ה.י.י/ה]
while he was speaking *piel inf c, prep, 3ms suffix* (8.2)	בְּדַבְּרוֹ [ד.ב.ר]
Who knows? (5.3)	מִי יוֹדֵעַ? [י.ד.ע]
Who? (3.2)	מִי…?
Whose? To whom? (2.1)	לְמִי…?
Why? (2.3)	לָמָה…?
wickedness, disaster *m* (9.4)	אָוֶן, אוֹנִים, אוֹן־, אוֹנֵי־
widow *f* (7.3)	אַלְמָנָה, אַלְמָנֹת־, אַלְמָנוֹת, אַלְמְנוֹת־
wilderness *m* (3.2)	מִדְבָּר, מִדְבַּר־
wine *m* (7.1)	יַיִן, יֵין־
with (2.4)	אֵת, אֶת־
with [together] (2.4)	עִם
Woe is me (6.1)	אוֹי לִי
woe, alas (8.2)	אוֹי
woman, wife *f* (1.1)	אִשָּׁה, נָשִׁים, אֵשֶׁת־, נְשֵׁי־
word, thing *m* (4.1)	דָּבָר, דְּבָרִים, דְּבַר־, דִּבְרֵי־
work, worship (4.3)	ע.ב.ד
work (*of labor or of worship*) *f* (11.1)	עֲבוֹדָה, עֲבֹדַת־
work, deed *m* (8.1)	מַעֲשֶׂה, מַעֲשִׂים, מַעֲשֵׂה־, מַעֲשֵׂי־
world, eternity *m* (4.3)	עוֹלָם
worship, bow down *hishtafel* (11.2)	ח.ו.י/ה
write (10.1)	כ.ת.ב

Y

year *f* (6.3)	שָׁנָה, שָׁנִים / שָׁנוֹת, שְׁנַת־, שְׁנֵי־ / שְׁנוֹת־
yesterday (6.1)	אֶתְמוֹל
you *fpl* (3.3)	אַתֵּנָה, אַתֵּן
you *fs* (1.3)	אַתְּ
you *mpl* (3.3)	אַתֶּם
you *ms* (1.3)	אַתָּה
you *object form, fpl* (3.4)	אֶתְכֶן
you *object form, fs* (3.4, *also* אוֹתָךְ)	אֹתָךְ
you *object form, mpl* (3.4)	אֶתְכֶם
you *object form, ms* (3.4, *also* אוֹתְךָ)	אֹתְךָ
you are able *fpl* (3.4)	תּוּכַלְנָה [י.כ.ל]
you are able *fs* (3.4)	תּוּכְלִי [י.כ.ל]
you are able *mpl* (3.4)	תּוּכְלוּ [י.כ.ל]
you are able *ms* (3.4)	תּוּכַל [י.כ.ל]
you are not, you do not *ms* (3.2)	אֵינְךָ
you bought, acquired, created *fs* (6.3)	קָנִית [ק.נ.י/ה]

you caused (someone) to hear, you announced *hifil ms* (8.1)	הִשְׁמַעְתָּ [שׁ.מ.ע]
you crossed over *mpl* (6.3)	עֲבַרְתֶּם [ע.ב.ר]
you descended *fpl* (6.4)	יְרַדְתֶּן [י.ר.ד]
you do not have *ms* (1.1)	אֵין לְךָ
you do / will / would believe *hifil ms, fs* (4.4)	תַּאֲמִין, תַּאֲמִינִי [א.מ.נ]
you established *hifil ms* (8.1)	הֲקִימוֹתָ [ק.ו.מ]
you gathered (7.2)	אָסַפְתָּ [א.ס.פ]
you gave birth to *fpl* (6.4)	יְלַדְתֶּן [י.ל.ד]
you gave *fs* (6.3)	נָתַתְּ [נ.ת.נ]
you have multiplied *hifil ms* (8.1)	הִרְבִּיתָ [ר.ב.י/ה]
you heard *mpl* (6.3)	שְׁמַעְתֶּם [שׁ.מ.ע]
you must *fs*... (...be sure [to]..., 1.3)	עָלַיִךְ ל...
you must *mpl*... (...be sure [to]..., 3.3)	עֲלֵיכֶם ל...
you must *ms*... (...be sure [to]..., 1.3)	עָלֶיךָ ל...
you hid yourself, were hidden *nifal ms* (7.1)	נִסְתַּרְתָּ [ס.ת.ר]
you hoped *piel ms* (10.1)	קִוִּיתָ [ק.ו.י/ה]
you oppressed *ms* (7.1)	עִנִּיתָ [י.נ.י/ה]
you removed *hifil ms* (8.1)	הֲסִירוֹתָ [ס.ו.ר]
you showed compassion *piel* (10.1)	רִחַמְתָּ [ר.ח.מ]
you thought, supposed *ms* (6.3)	חָשַׁבְתָּ [ח.שׁ.ב]
you visited, inspected, inflicted, appointed *fpl* (6.4)	פְּקַדְתֶּן [פ.ק.ד]
you walked *fs* (6.3)	הָלַכְתְּ [ה.ל.כ]
you went *fpl* (6.4)	הֲלַכְתֶּן [ה.ל.כ]
you went *ms* (6.3)	הָלַכְתָּ [ה.ל.כ]
you were afraid *ms* (6.3)	יָרֵאתָ [י.ר.א]
you were trapped *ms nifal* (7.1)	נִלְכַּדְתָּ [ל.כ.ד]
you will answer *ms* (5.3)	תַּעֲנֶה [ע.נ.י/ה]
you will believe *hifil fpl* (5.1)	תַּאֲמֵנָה [א.מ.נ]
you will cry *ms* (4.3)	תִּבְכֶּה [ב.כ.י/ה]
you will die *ms* (5.2)	תָּמוּת [מ.ו.ת]
you will do, make *fs* (5.3)	תַּעֲשִׂי [ע.שׂ.י/ה]
you will do, make *mpl* (5.1)	תַּעֲשׂוּ [ע.שׂ.י/ה]
you will eat *ms* (5.2)	תֹּאכַל [א.כ.ל]
you will fear *mpl* (5.1)	תִּירְאוּ [י.ר.א]
you will forget *ms* (5.3)	תִּשְׁכַּח [שׁ.כ.ח]
you will go out, exit *mpl* (5.1)	תֵּצְאוּ [י.צ.א]
you will go up *ms* (5.3)	תַּעֲלֶה [ע.ל.י/ה]
you will go, walk *fpl* (5.1)	תֵּלַכְנָה [ה.ל.כ]
you will go, walk *mpl* (5.1)	תֵּלְכוּ [ה.ל.כ]
you will go, walk *ms* (5.2)	תֵּלֵךְ [ה.ל.כ]
you will hear *ms* (5.3)	תִּשְׁמַע [שׁ.מ.ע]
you will lift, carry *mpl* (5.1)	תִּשְׂאוּ [נ.שׂ.א]
you will lift, carry *ms* (5.2)	תִּשָּׂא [נ.שׂ.א]
you will remember *mpl* (5.1)	תִּזְכְּרוּ [ז.כ.ר]
you will remember *ms* (5.3)	תִּזְכֹּר [ז.כ.ר]
you will say *ms* (5.2)	תֹּאמַר [א.מ.ר]
you will send us away *piel ms* (10.3)	תְּשַׁלְּחֵנוּ [שׁ.ל.ח]
you will sit, dwell *fs* (5.3)	תֵּשְׁבִי [י.שׁ.ב]
you will speak *piel ms* (5.3)	תְּדַבֵּר [ד.ב.ר]
you will take *mpl* (4.1)	תִּקְחוּ [ל.ק.ח]
you will throw *hifil ms* (5.2)	תַּשְׁלִיךְ [שׁ.ל.כ]
you will throw me *hifil mpl* (5.2)	תַּשְׁלִיכוּנִי [שׁ.ל.כ]
you will return *fs* (5.3)	תָּשׁוּבִי [שׁ.ו.ב]
you will return *ms* (5.3)	תָּשׁוּב [שׁ.ו.ב]
your *fs* name (1.1)	שְׁמֵךְ
your *ms* God (3.2)	אֱלֹהֶיךָ
your *ms* head (4.1)	רֹאשְׁךָ
your *ms* name (1.1)	שִׁמְךָ
your *ms* request (4.4)	שְׁאֵלָתְךָ
your arm *ms, fs* (4.1)	זְרֹעֲךָ, זְרוֹעֵךְ

MAPS

Ancient Near East 564

Israel 565

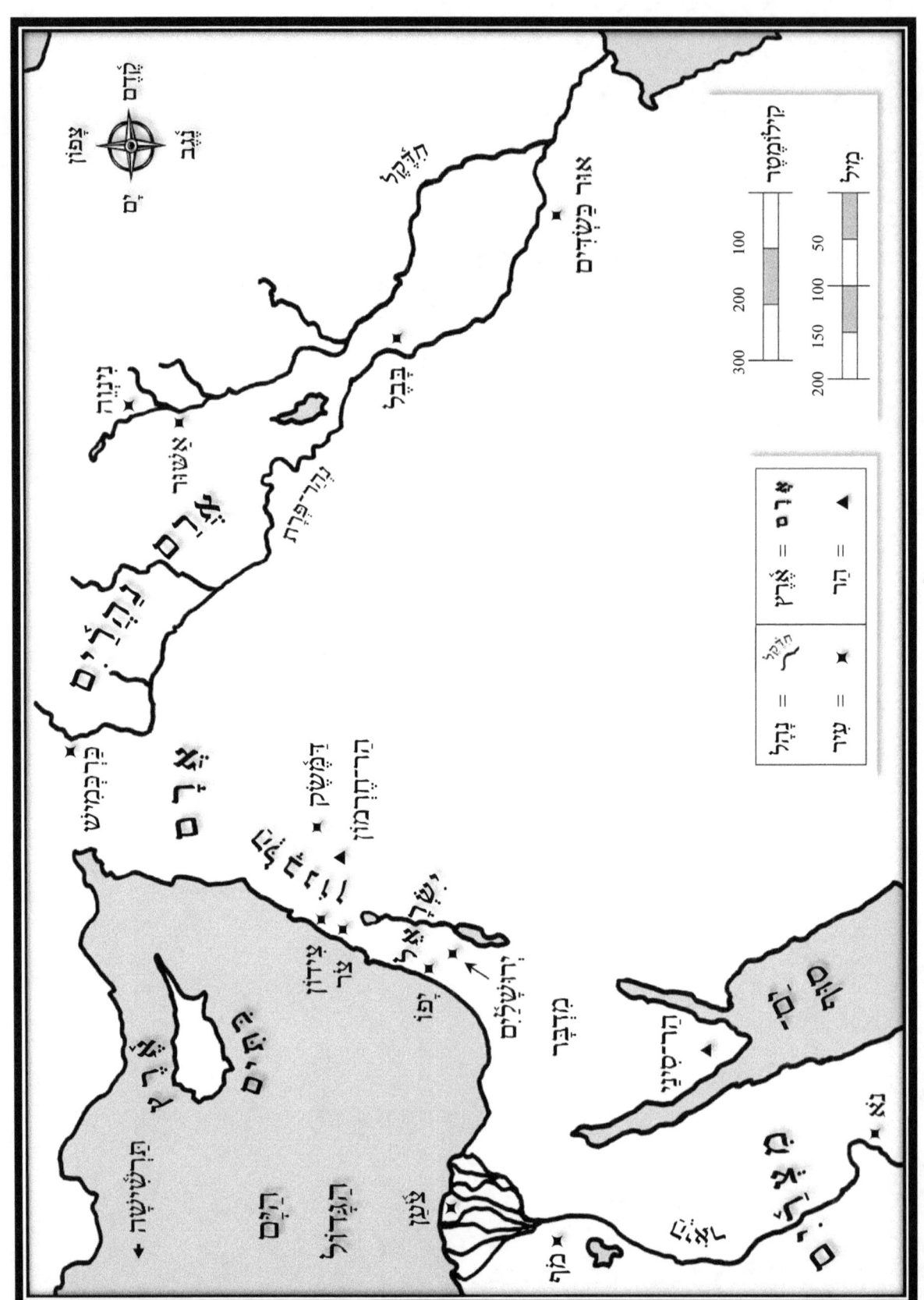

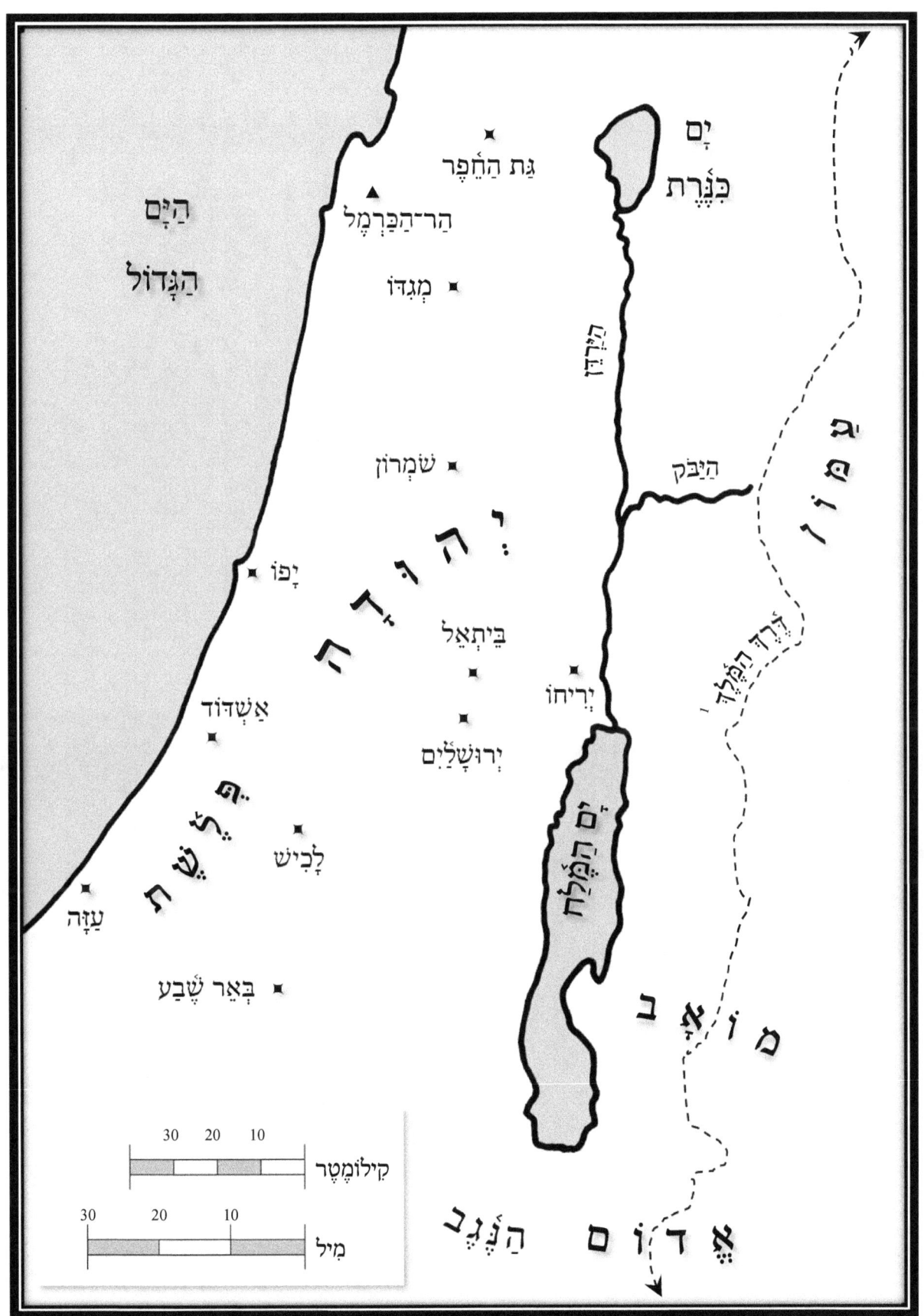

[1] For דֶּרֶךְ הַיָּם, please see §1.3.ד.

www.ingramcontent.com/pod-product-compliance
Lightning Source LLC
Chambersburg PA
CBHW081412230426

43668CB00016B/2214